THE STUDY OF SOCIETY
A Unified Approach

The Study of Society

A UNIFIED APPROACH

Alfred Kuhn

PROFESSOR OF ECONOMICS
UNIVERSITY OF CINCINNATI

1963
Richard D. Irwin, Inc., and The Dorsey Press, Inc.
HOMEWOOD, ILLINOIS

First Printing, August, 1963

301
K95s

47,459
July, 1964

Library of Congress Catalog Card No. 63–16897

PRINTED IN THE UNITED STATES OF AMERICA

To Nina,

And to Dave, Jeff, and Hank, in the hope that their generation may mold its preferences more wisely and perceive its opportunities more clearly than its predecessors.

PREFACE

ALTHOUGH A groundswell desire for a truly integrated analysis of the social sciences has been gathering momentum for many years, no book thus far seems to have brought a clearly satisfactory analysis. Some success has been achieved in bringing a multidisciplinary approach to bear on particular problems. But in most broader-based approaches, political science, sociology, and economics have continued to appear mainly as separate disciplines in books which have little unity beyond the oneness of the binding that holds the pages together.

This book attempts to provide the tightly integrated approach so long overdue. Instead of attempting to "relate" these three core analytical disciplines in a new way, while leaving each more or less intact, it pulls all three disciplines apart, throws their components into a single pile, and then attempts to reconstruct them into a new, single discipline. (The book describes only the new structure, not the process of reaching it.) The change is evident as soon as it is noted that the key analytical concepts in the new structure are *transactions* and *organizations*, each with an extremely broad definition, along with the major supporting concepts of *transformations*, *decisions*, and *communications*.

The reconstruction requires many redefinitions. In the process, the definition of every term that has been borrowed from economics, sociology, and political science has been made or selected with awareness of, and (I hope) consistency with, every other term. In short, the main subject matter of the three disciplines is dealt with through a single set of interlocking and mutually consistent concepts, in what might be referred to as a "unitary nomological set." For example, the book contains no section on economics, as such. Instead, "Robinson Crusoe" economics and the theory of the firm appear as key items in analyzing decisions; the market process is seen as one of several techniques of achieving consensus valuations in a society; while economic stability is viewed as one of many "public goods" which cannot be "transacted" through markets in any normal sense of the word. Much analysis developed separately in sociology, political science, and economics has gone into the analysis of transactions and organizations—and so on.

To achieve a wide unity it has been necessary to go outside of economics, sociology, and political science. Most notably, five chapters are devoted to psychology, as an indispensable base for the study of both decision making and interpersonal behavior, as well as of personality, culture, and communications. Some analytical tools developed in communications theory, information theory, psycho-linguistics, systems research, cybernetics, behavioral science, decision theory, and organization theory have also proved indispensable. Whenever concepts from these fields have been used, they too have been selected, defined, or redefined to make them consistent with one another and with the subsequent concepts used in the social analysis. That is, the main set of unitary, interlocking terminology and concepts extends to include important ingredients of those various fields as well as of the social sciences.

For example, human behavior is viewed as the product of a controlled —i.e., cybernetic—system. Therefore the study of psychology is couched in the framework of a cybernetic system, in which the concept-perception subsystem is the detector, the motive subsystem is the selector, and the motor and behavioral subsystem is the effector, with feedback to the detector system. The motive system is seen as dealing with preference functions and the concept system with opportunity functions. The same frame of reference is later carried over from psychology into communication and decision processes. These and other broad analytical concepts are similarly carried through the whole volume. In preparation for this type of approach, Chapter 3 is an introduction to Science, Models, and Systems, which views science largely as the search for concepts with high information content.

To the best of my knowledge, this wide set of interlocking concepts is *internally consistent*, at least in broad contours. Minor inconsistencies will undoubtedly show up upon detailed examination by specialists, and I remain braced for the possible discovery of disastrous major inconsistencies. Whether this set of concepts is *useful* is a different matter, to be found when specialists of various stripes attempt to apply it to their own fields. My own biased view at the moment is that the framework is highly useful in providing new insights into numerous areas which otherwise seem murky. In any event, it *is* an attempt to integrate boldly on a wide scale.

Even if this attempt is unsuccessful, it may nevertheless provide guidance for other attempts. I feel that we must try the experiment over and over and over until it succeeds. Unless the major concepts and types of analysis for dealing with social phenomena can be both standardized and drastically reduced in number, we may be swamped by the sheer mass of information accumulating at geometrically rising rates. This book attempts to digest and reformulate existing information into a simpler structure, not to provide new information. Among other things it reflects a modest hope that we can thereby cut down the cultural lag between the findings of researchers and the ability of the college student or educated layman to encompass them.

It is obviously impossible for anyone to become a qualified specialist in each field used in this volume. I have nevertheless had to try to choose what aspects of each field are most significant for a unified approach. Further, I have often had to redefine concepts *within* fields, or select from among existing definitions, in such a way as to provide the utmost unity *among* fields. In consequence, to perform the present experiment I at times have had to dive boldly head first into some muddy pools of knowledge where the experts still gingerly dip their toes. Whether I thereby help to penetrate these pools more quickly, or break my neck, remains to be seen. Among other things, I had no choice but to take an explicit position on some broad philosophical questions. Here I have taken the option of adopting the general position of the so-called "scientific philosophy," perhaps as modified by some philosophical propositions which seem implicit in information theory.

To preview some other risks, I have found myself stating what I hope are reasonably precise definitions of such varied concepts as society, power, organization, information, message, decision, justice, freedom, authority, sovereignty, and legitimacy. Whether these will be found acceptable and useful to others, only time will tell. In cases of doubt I have rather uniformly selected a definition which is sharp, but which may later have to be discarded as unworkable, over one whose vagueness prevents a real test of its analytical usefulness. In the same spirit, much of the writing takes the form of affirmative statements about things. Some of these do not pause to include all the qualifications the specialist might make. The purpose here is mainly heuristic; I am trying to draw a sketch which is only a first approximation, but which is clear within these limits. If all the qualifications were to be included in the first approximation model, neither the book nor the model would ever get finished.

The question might be asked why a single individual should attempt to cover material so wide in scope. Why not a committee or research group? The first answer is that communications within a single skull are much more rapid and accurate than communications between skulls. The seemingly limitless number of cross comparisons and mutual modifications of definitions which were required before the whole set became reasonably coordinated might have stretched over a lifetime of conferences and letter writing if done by a group. By contrast, the one-man method took about three and a half years. The second answer is that no editor or research leader could exert the necessary discipline. As Kaplan put it at the end of a collective venture:

> The editor, no matter how clear his original aims, nor how firm his intent to keep the work on its planned course, finds inevitably that a book written by thirty persons in twenty-four chapters, develops a course of its own and a meaning and significance that are almost independent of the original direction.[1]

In the course of analyzing some of the more intimate transactions which make up the web of life, I have had to grapple with Boulding's query whether there may not be limits in human decency about how far we ought to go in the scientific analysis of human relationships.[2] I have gone ahead nevertheless, first because I think that most of the forces revealed by the analysis are known intuitively to many persons in any event, and second because many have already been explicitly dissected in literary works and in sociological and psychological case studies, though without the present broader analytical base. There is also the background assumption, of course, that new analysis will be useful in the long run, even if disruptive or embarrassing in the short.

In general, I have struggled to keep the book free of either my own or society's value judgments. I am aware of several that have nevertheless crept into the discussion of some social issues in latter chapters, and I can only plead the difficulty of avoiding them completely in such areas. Although many illustrations are taken from contemporary America, it is hoped that most of the analysis is essentially universal; many illustrations are also taken from primitive and semicivilized societies at various ages and places of man.

The book is intended most directly as a textbook to integrate the social sciences at the undergraduate junior or senior level, or for beginning graduate students. Although some of the areas drawn upon (such as cybernetics and communications theory) are highly mathematical in some aspects, the present volume is entirely nonmathematical. On the whole I would feel that the analytical level of the material is no more difficult than that of a reasonably good introductory course in economics. However, full comprehension of the broader import of the book requires more background than is possessed by the typical college freshman or sophomore, except perhaps in colleges with carefully selected students, or in honors programs. At the same time, if such concepts as supply and demand, social structures, and the separation of powers can successfully be taught to first- and second-year college students, then so can many or most of the concepts in this book, if the teaching is properly paced.

Because the core of the social analysis is organized around organizations and transactions, it should be particularly useful as a capstone course in

---

[1] Bert Kaplan, "Editor's Epilogue: A Final Word," in *Studying Personality Cross-Culturally* (Evanston: Row, Peterson & Co., 1961), p. 659.

[2] Kenneth E. Boulding, *The Skills of the Economist* (Cleveland: Howard Allen, Inc., 1958), p. 138.

colleges of business administration. It might also do well as a senior course in social science for students in engineering or other technical schools. I have taught the course just once myself, from duplicated copies of the manuscript, with registration open to senior undergraduate majors in any social science, psychology, or philosophy, as well as to graduate students, and the arrangement seems workable. Next year I plan to admit selected junior students in the same categories. I would hope that the book would also be found widely interesting to adults for whom no such approach was available when they went to college.

The question about who should teach the course is neither readily obvious nor overly difficult. The process may be self-selective, if the teaching is done by those whom it interests. A specialist in any one of the three basic social science disciplines who feels an urge to investigate the others (and psychology) should be able to handle the course. In an age when philosophers and anthropologists are helping to teach psychiatrists; psychologists are studying labor-management relations; and economists, psychologists, and mathematicians are teaching decision making, the problem should not be too severe. It is my hope that the present wide interest in such broadly based fields as behavioral science and systems research may make it academically respectable and profitable for a person to become a specialist in teaching a course of this sort—in marked contrast to the experience with many earlier "integrated" courses.

To teach the whole book would seem to require two semesters. If the instructor would himself become familiar with the prior chapters he might make a one-semester course of the materials starting with transactions (Chapter 17), or possibly decisions (Chapter 14), and continuing through the chapter on government staff (Chapter 36). A one-quarter course covering the irreducible core of the book might be made of the chapters on transactions and organizations, perhaps preceded by those on decisions. In any shortened form, the set of definitions in the latter part of Chapter 14 would seem indispensable.

The comments of persons who read parts of the manuscript at various stages of development have been invaluable, and I am most grateful for their time, patience, and astute observations. Professors William F. Whyte of Cornell University and Walter Hirsch of Purdue read the whole manuscript. In addition the following professors read limited sections as follows: Donald Taylor of Yale on psychology, Robert Payne of the University of Cincinnati on communications, John Mee of Indiana University on decisions, and Dieter Dux of the University of Cincinnati the chapters on the whole society. Also professors at the University of Cincinnati, Walter P. Egle read the chapters on planned societies, Robert H. Wessel and Glenn E. Burress those on market systems and their limitations, William Jeffrey some sections on government and some aspects of law, and Richard Emerson some preliminary analysis on bargaining power. In their role as graduate students in the course, Alvaro Cayzedo, Claude

Gruen, Carroll Krause, Robert Riley, and John Toppen provided important analytical criticisms. As a graduate assistant, Harold Bryant helped to fill in many details of fact. Far fewer weaknesses remain as a result of these efforts; the remaining ones are my own.

Beyond these are the many persons whose names appear only in footnotes. I have discovered a disconcerting number of times in rereading my early sources that things I thought to be original when I wrote them had been cogently stated (and underscored by me) in the works of others. I have footnoted all such instances that I have found, and offer sincere apologies to any others whose ideas I unwittingly have stolen. Special thanks are due to the Charles Phelps Taft Memorial Fund of the University of Cincinnati, and to the University's grant of sabbatical leave, which together provided me a whole unencumbered year in which to acquire background, and to lay out the general plan of the book. Nina Kuhn typed the manuscript, and was indispensable in ways that are understood only in families that write books.

As one author has put it, a book is never finished, only abandoned. There are many more things I would like to do before this one goes to print. But any change may have chain reactions throughout the volume, and unless I arbitrarily stop somewhere, no end is in sight. I hope the value of the analysis as a whole will compensate for its particular remaining weaknesses.

ALFRED KUHN

The University of Cincinnati
January, 1963

TABLE OF CONTENTS

A. THE PARTS

I. On Science and Human Beings

II. Communications

III. Culture and Personality

IV. Decisions

V. Transactions

VI. Organizations

VII. The Whole Society as an Organization

VIII. The Private Production of Private Goods

culture. The Fixed Markup. External Costs. The Perplexed Consumer and Advertising. Some Miscellaneous Differences Between Theory and Practice. SUMMARY ON THE MARKET SYSTEM.

IX. The Public Production of Public Goods

X. The Public Production of Private Goods

INDEXES

A. The Parts

I. ON SCIENCE AND HUMAN BEINGS

Chapter 1

ON RELATIONSHIPS
AND PREDICTIONS

THE UNIVERSE has been estimated to consist of approximately 10^{79} corpuscles—that is, one with 79 zeros after it.[1] A single human being is made up of about 10^{25} atoms. Measured by atomic content a human is roughly as much bigger than an atom as the universe is bigger than the human, and the human thus stands near the middle of the range between the smallest and the largest things we know. Actually, a skyscraper is closer to the middle position, but compared to atoms and the universe a man and a skyscraper are about the same size.

In an automobile battery lead and copper interact in sulphuric acid to produce an electric current. This current will start the car, light the highway, convert radio waves into music, or make you jump if you happen to touch it.

A small amount of energy applied to a valve or switch can control the flow of a much larger amount of energy. If this larger energy is then used to control a larger valve or switch, which is used to control a third, and so on, a very small amount of energy can be used to control a very large amount.

Every time there is a substantial rain some soil is washed away, never to return. In this sense the face of the earth "remembers" every rain.

In 1930 two psychologists named Wever and Bray were studying how the ear of a cat detects sound and transfers it to the brain. While someone talked to the cat the two men "wire-tapped" the nerves which carry the electrical nerve current from the ear to the cat's brain. They then amplified the nerve current and played it through a loud speaker in another room. The sound which emerged was not only intelligible speech, but was of sufficiently high fidelity for listeners to identify who was speaking.[2]

---

[1] Harlow Shapley, from a lecture at the University of Cincinnati, November, 1957, and by letter of May 9, 1963 to the author, based on computations by Sir Arthur S. Eddington. "Corpuscles" are indicated by Professor Shapley to refer to "protons, electrons, and neutrons counted twice."

[2] Frank A. Geldard, *The Human Senses* (New York: John Wiley & Sons, Inc., 1953), p. 139. Subsequent to the original report of this experiment some doubt has

The most democratic government cannot follow all the wishes of all its people, nor can the most dictatorial government deny them all.

One can predict with high certainty that a ball thrown into the air will promptly fall again. He can also predict with high confidence that a healthy baby selected at random at the age of two weeks will be willing to drink milk from a nipple. But no one will venture an accurate prediction when or where a tiny dust particle picked up by the wind from a mountain top will fall. Nor will he predict whether the baby will enjoy warm beer by the age of sixteen—though knowledge that he lives in Chicago, London, or Tahiti will help.

These seven items seem ridiculously unrelated. In a sense they are. But whether two or more things are related depends on the person and the purpose. An important theme of this book is that many seemingly unrelated things follow similar or identical rules of behavior, and that knowledge of one therefore provides understanding of another. An important consequence of such similarities is that the more of them we can discover the fewer general principles we need learn in order to understand a given number of events. For example, if nerve currents and battery currents behave identically, then we need know only one set of rules to understand both.

We might hope that human knowledge has undergone a long cycle in this respect. Among the learned Greeks of the sixth century B.C. a single individual could comprehend all scientific knowledge then known. Even as late as 150 years ago it did not mark one as insane to hope to do the same. Since that time physics, chemistry, biology, psychology, and the social sciences—to mention only a few main branches of knowledge—have grown apace. At the same time each has been divided and subdivided into narrower and narrower fields of specialty. As a result a man of today often seems quite accomplished if he masters one division of a subdivision of a field, with perhaps a working knowledge of several related subdivisions and a general idea of what the whole field is about.

Recent decades have brought increasing frustration as it is found that no one or two specialties are capable of dealing satisfactorily with any one problem. The problem of smog in some urban areas, for example, involves many kinds of contributing factors. A complete understanding of the problem involves knowledge of climate, the molecular behavior of gases, the chemistry of the automobile engine whose exhaust helps create smog, the number of automobiles, the geographic layout of the city, including the location of its homes, work places, and highway arteries, the availability of alternate means of transportation, the speed of traffic and the

---

been raised whether the thing tapped by Wever and Bray was the nerve currents, as such, or certain cochlear manifestations in the ear itself. It seems clear that they did *not* pick up the spoken sounds themselves, however, but some transmutation of those sounds by the ear of the cat.

timing of traffic lights, the incomes of the population, the chemistry and biology of the lungs and blood stream, problems of microbe and virus growth under the chemical, light, and temperature conditions produced by smog—among many other problems. A problem of this sort can be dealt with only by a combination of specialists, and the "interdisciplinary" approach to problems in recent years has been rampant.

To group specialists from various disciplines around a single problem is probably a technique which the human race will have to use from here on out. Simultaneously, however, a movement is under way to combine, synthesize, and simplify some of the related fields of knowledge so that there will be fewer specialties, or at least a greater amount of common knowledge and technique which will permit a person to move more easily among different specialties, and make greater use of their special contributions. This movement is going on in many places, the Society of General Systems Research and the Center for Advanced Study in the Behavioral Sciences being among the more conspicuous examples. The present volume is an attempt to synthesize into one set of analytical relationships the presently separate fields of economics, sociology, and political science. To the extent that it succeeds it should enable a person to deal with events in any of those three fields with the same set of concepts, though it will not, of course, make anyone an expert in any one of the fields.

It is not our purpose to show the precise relationships among the seven assorted items with which the chapter opened. Each does, however, point in a preliminary way to some important problems to be dealt with later. For beings on this tiny planet even to dare to *guess* (and it is only a very rough guess) at the number of corpuscles in the whole universe is a most remarkable achievement. It requires the ability to build instruments which observe and record things larger, smaller, and of different nature from any that humans themselves will ever see, hear, feel, smell, or taste. It has required the patient counting and cataloging of millions of stars, and of atoms. It has required imagining hypothesis after hypothesis, testing each against known observations, and seeking new observations. It has involved studying the mind itself, and the process of thinking on which all scientific knowledge depends—to mention only a few of the essential ingredients. Much of the same kind of knowledge, imagination, and instrumentation which led to estimating the number of protons in the universe is now being applied to the study of living things and their behavior, including man and society. This does not mean that we are on the verge of solving all the problems of mankind. No such thing seems possible, as subsequent pages will make abundantly clear. It does mean, however, that our knowledge of human behavior is rapidly becoming more explicit and more scientifically testable than it has been in the past, and that more approaches to human problems can be made through verifiable principles and fewer through rule of thumb and "playing by ear." Such knowledge is cumulative, just as in the physical sciences, where the more we already know the better prepared we are to investigate other areas which are not yet known.

We feel confident in assuming that the rules shown in the behavior of protons, electrons, heat, light, levers, gravity, and all the other paraphernalia of the physical sciences are also followed strictly in the body and brain of man, in the laboratory, in the automobile battery, and in the spiral nebula of Andromeda. There are also reliable similarities among different humans, as for example that the nerves which actuate the muscles of the lip work the same for a coolie negotiating rice to his mouth with chopsticks, the President of the United States addressing the Congress, a shoemaker using his mouth as a tack box, or a college student experimenting in the interpersonal transfer of lipstick.

To say that man is composed of physical constituents, and to add that they follow identical rules in man as in nonliving substance suggests a deeply philosophical question: whether human beings consist *only* of physical components following physical laws, and whether their behavior can be accounted for *entirely* by those laws and components. We can, of course, give the superficial answer that *any* relationship of components is more than the sum of its parts. An atom is clearly more than the protons, electrons, and other particles of which it consists; a book is more than the paper, ink, thread, and glue from which it is manufactured; and General Motors Corporation is something more than the buildings, equipment, people, and even intangible assets listed in its records.

To go beyond the superficial, however, it is fortunate for a scientific study of humans that this question does not have to be answered. Let us suppose for the sake of argument that psychologists and neurologists some day do produce what looks like a complete explanation of the human senses and nervous system in terms of chemistry and physics, so that we have complete theories to relate the output of behavior to the input of sensory stimuli. Even so, we are still left with at least four possible different attitudes toward this fact. One is to conclude that there is nothing spiritual in man or the universe, but only matter and energy following fixed laws. A second is to conclude that only a God of infinite intelligence could have conceived of putting together so many bits of matter and energy in such an infinitely complex and sensitively balanced arrangement as the human being, and that our scientific understanding permits us to better marvel at His ways and works. A third reaction is to observe that, however well nervous systems in general may be explained, it can never be proved that *some* people do not experience visions, revelations, "grace," or other forces which enter the human being through channels not evident to psychologists or other scientific observers. And fourth, a scientific approach to human behavior need not be concerned whether certain responses are "spiritual" or "natural," the scientist's concern being solely whether they are uniform. To repeat, it is fortunate that we can examine *particular* aspects of human behavior scientifically without having to know whether *all* the answers lie in science alone. It remains true, however, that whenever a scientist performs an experiment he assumes that there *is* a scientific answer to the *particular problem he is studying.* Otherwise he would not conduct the experiment.

To return to the "unrelated" items at the beginning of the chapter, the similarity of nerve cells and a battery has already been suggested. Both generate an electric current by chemical action inside the cell. In both systems a stimulus originating at one point is conducted electrically to distant points in the system, where it produces a response. There are, of course, many differences between the electrical system of an automobile and the nervous system of a human being, but an understanding of the one has been an indispensable background for studying and understanding the other.

The principle of successive valves or switches appears in many situations, both animate and inanimate. An employee in a hydroelectric plant uses a very small amount of his own energy to push a button on a control panel. A somewhat larger amount of energy in the form of an electric current then flows into a relay, which operates a substantially larger switch. Through this second switch then flows a more powerful current which operates an electric motor. Through a series of gears the motor then opens a large valve allowing a very large amount of energy in the form of falling water to flow into the generators. In this case, the slight energy of a finger push is able through only three successive switches or valves to control the energy flow of thousands of tons of falling water.

The radio or phonograph amplifier also uses successive valves. We say loosely that such devices "amplify" an electric current. Strictly speaking, the feeble current fed into an amplifier from the air, phonograph needle, or microphone is not itself amplified. Instead it is fed into a radio tube, which is a valve, and is so named in England. Inside the tube the pulsations of this weak signal control the flow of a much stronger current, which stronger current then shows all the fluctuations (or modulations) of the weak one which controls it. The now pulsating, or modulated, stronger current is next fed into a second valve (tube), where it controls the flow of a third, and still stronger current. After three, four, or five successive stages of valves the modulated current reaches a strength perhaps several thousand times that of the original signal current, and is powerful enough to operate a loudspeaker. (The next stage is usually a request to turn the volume down!)

Many human functions operate through "successive valves." For example, a person may read the news of the day. Photon energy in the form of light reflected from the printed page is extremely small—perhaps as little as 10^{-16} foot pounds, or about $1/100,000,000,000,000,00^{th}$ of the energy required to lift this book from waist to shoulder level. The optic nerve on which this light energy falls acts as a valve, and releases a nerve current of considerably greater strength, which in turn actuates the nerves of the brain which interprets and possibly stores the information. If the message seems to call for action, the nerves of the brain act as valves which release much greater muscular energy, and the reader of the news will then write a letter, tear his hair, or gallop off on his horse firing shots into the night.

If the man also happens to be a key figure in politics or business, he in turn may act as a valve through which the news influences the direction of energy release by many other persons, organizations, or even the nation.

Holding companies (which are corporations which purchase and hold stock in other corporations without necessarily producing anything themselves) have sometimes been built up as "successive valves." Half the voting stock of the holding company controls it absolutely, and it usually takes much less. The total assets of the company are then used to purchase half the voting stock in a second holding company double the size of the first. This second company then purchases control of a company almost twice *its* size, and so on. Each level of holding company thus constitutes a "valve" by which a given amount of investment controls a larger investment which is double or more its own size. By the simultaneous use of four or five successive holding companies and some assorted other techniques it has sometimes been possible for a person to gain absolute control of a total investment a thousand or more times his own.

In many ways the study of human behavior and of society is a study of "valves." Valves are one type of control mechanism, the study of which characterizes the main stream of current thinking in the human sciences.

The term "memory" originally referred to the storing of information in the brain. The word is now widely used also to designate the information storage function of electronic computing machines. In a much broader sense any change which takes place in any person or thing as the result of some event constitutes a "memory" of that event so long as that change remains. In this sense a gully is the memory of rain, a scar is the memory of an injury, a tilted tree is the memory of a storm, and a fossil rock is the memory of past geologic ages. One might quibble whether the word "memory" ought to be applied to these things. But there is no denying that the gully, the scar, the tilt, and the fossils constitute a storage of information about past events, and that this information can be understood by anyone who has learned the proper codes. Similarly, the memory of an important man is not merely the thoughts and feelings he leaves behind, but the changes in the form of a government, the strength of a business, or the habits of thinking that persist after him.

That no democracy can follow all the wishes of all its people and no dictatorship can deny them all is rather obvious. The point to be made in a preliminary way is that any leader is dependent on the people below him in his organization, while the people below are simultaneously dependent on the leaders above. While different personalities and organizational structures can throw the balance of dependency one way or another, there is much mutuality of dependence in both the most democratic and the most dictatorial organizations. Much of our understanding of social functioning can be gained from learning the location and nature of these dependencies.

The seventh and last item of miscellany involves predictability. Predictability is often considered the prime objective and final accomplishment of scientific knowledge. When we predict that a baseball thrown into the air will promptly fall again we have no doubt about the reliability of the prediction. The reason is simple: we believe that *one* of the forces acting on the ball is overwhelmingly stronger than any other force. This force is the downward pull of gravity, which is far stronger than any probable updrafts of air, or the upward gravitational pull of the moon or sun. We need only imagine dropping a fluffy feather from a roof top on a windy day to sense that the accuracy of prediction drops precipitously when two or more different forces act on the same situation, and none is unquestionably stronger than the others.

In the realm of psychology and the social sciences we now understand many of the forces which mold human behavior. Many of these bits of understanding, *taken one at a time*, are quite as precise as many of the laws of chemistry and physics, as we shall see later. The thing that seems to make the social sciences so "unscientific" is that a large number of such forces are in action simultaneously in almost every individual event, and we have no way of knowing in advance which one, or even which few, will dominate. One of the commonest of errors on this score is to assume that uncertainty of this sort is the peculiar property of the *social* scientists. It is not. To illustrate, suppose that we tell a physicist that at precisely noon on March 13, 1980 we will release a feather from a plane flying due east over the Statue of Liberty at ten thousand feet and 600 miles per hour. Not a scientist on earth would risk a dime, much less his reputation, predicting when and where (within a hundred yards) the feather would land. Nor could any physicist after the most thorough study tell you where any particular atom in a piece of steel will be one second after he completes his study—or how fast it will be traveling.

An unseasoned physicist may dismiss the problem of the falling feather or the location of a particular atom as unimportant—not worthy of the attention of a true scientist. The mature and understanding one, however, will more probably acknowledge that the reason the physical sciences have such an apparently admirable record of predictability is that they have confined their attention mainly to the relatively simple phenomena where accurate predictability is feasible, while conspicuously ignoring the complex situations where predictive accuracy is low, on the grounds that they are problems of engineering, not science.

This is an important point and deserves further illustration. The physicist can state that any body in a state of motion will continue in the same direction and at the same speed indefinitely, unless it is acted on by some other force—and insist that the statement is always and everywhere true. If the psychologist is so inclined, he can state that a human being in a state of hunger will seek food, unless acted on by some other force—and insist that this statement is universally valid. Predictive accuracy falls markedly for both types of scientist when they face more complex problems. From detailed drawings and specifications a trained physical scientist can tell whether he would *expect* a rocket of a particular design and guidance system to reach the moon. But then ask him the likelihood that any *particular* rocket built to these specifications will *actually reach* the moon. Science will recede rapidly and he will consult his equivalent of the racing form, basing his prediction on the percentages of successes and failures that have actually occurred thus far. And yet the most complex rocket is of kindergarten simplicity compared to the human being.

It is customary to say that the physical sciences are precise and predictable, whereas the human sciences are vague and unpredictable. It is more meaningful to say that situations subject to one or a few dominant forces are more amenable to understanding and accurate prediction than situations subject to many forces with none dominant. The social sciences are less predictable than the elemental physical sciences precisely because there are so many forces in operation at any one time.

Having said these things, we must nevertheless observe several additional factors which give the physical sciences greater accuracy and predictability. First, many of their concepts are more precisely definable than those in the social sciences, the lever, atom, mass, or erg being much more sharply defined than society, personality, ego, social pressure, or government. Second, even if more precise definitions can be formulated for social concepts (and the chapters which follow try to move in that direction), few can be measured precisely, or expressed in numerical units. For example, although later chapters attempt to provide a clearly defined notion of social *power*, it is not now possible to establish and count units of power, so as to be able to say that Jim has 20 while John has 60. Nor, for the foreseeable future, does it seem likely that such quantifiable measures will be developed.[3]

Third, many experiments in the physical sciences can be repeated as often as desired, under the same conditions or under controlled changes in conditions. It is also possible to perform repeatable experiments with limited groups of persons under controlled conditions, as is done in the study of "small groups." But much of our knowledge of social phenomena comes from observing the actual behavior of whole economies, societies, nations, or cultures, and the interactions of their parts. Experiments of this sort are

---

[3] Because of the numerous experiments in sociology, economics, political science, human geography, social psychology, and related areas, whose results are stated in quantitative terms, some social scientist may dispute this statement. Although numerous details of social sciences can be dealt with on quantitative terms, and some highly successfully, we do not have quantifiable units for measuring such basic notions as society, influence, status, culture, cooperation, social structure, or social cohesion. By contrast, most basic concepts in the physical sciences can be defined in quantitative terms.

not reproducible at will, nor can they be controlled by the experimenter for his scientific purposes.

Fourth, in many respects the physical scientist can isolate the variables he studies by laboratory techniques. He can keep the pressure constant while he studies the relation between the temperature and volume of a gas, or roll the same ball down different inclined planes as he studies the relation between slope and acceleration. By contrast, the social scientist must examine the relation between two variables in individuals or societies as they actually are, and he cannot make all other variables stand still while he makes his study. Certain experimental controls can be exerted, particularly statistical ones, but these are a far cry from actually holding other variables unchanged throughout the experiment.

Fifth, once a social scientist studies a society or any part of it, and makes his report available to the people studied, the report itself may change the society. Merely to be asked questions about one's behavior— merely to know that it is being observed—may change the behavior. Although some tiny physical particles cannot be observed without being changed, for the most part the physicist can go about his work, confident that the things he studies will not change because he has studied them.

It does remain possible, however, that these factors giving greater precision to the physical sciences are themselves traceable back to the smaller number of variables. The inability to define precisely or to measure quantitatively such concepts as society, personality, or social pressure may be a direct consequence of the many component ingredients within each, and the same may be true of the inability to duplicate social experiments exactly. And although some social relations may change merely because they are observed or reported on, many social relationships are not thus affected.

Perhaps we can get the clearest idea of the relationship if we compare the social sciences to the physical science of meteorology. We can observe the weather, observe similarities from day to day or year to year, and formulate certain rules about the interactions of temperatures, pressures, humidities, and velocities. But we cannot reproduce a given type of storm at will in order to study it. No two storms or calms are precisely alike, and hence precise statements of relations are difficult to observe and generalize. Prediction of sorts is possible. But we cannot predict within 2 per cent such things as: At 6:00 P.M. next Thursday the temperature at Navy Pier, Chicago, will be 67.2 degrees, and the sun will be shining on the pier, following rainfall of 0.2 inches on the pier starting at 2:57 and ending at 4:42. Nor does it seem likely that we can look forward to such prediction on the basis of any kind of knowledge now available or foreseeable. As we increase the flow of information about weather forces, as by weather stations, observation satellites, radar, and balloons, we will be able to make more accurate predictions about the broad contours of weather, perhaps for months in advance. This is a far cry, however, from predicting precise conditions at precise times and places for more than very short periods into the future. The kind of problems faced by the physical science of meteorology are intermediate between the extremes, having measurable and definable units of their main concepts (precipitation, temperature, etc.) as in the physical sciences, but facing a large number of variables at a time, as in the social sciences.

Meanwhile the point of the miscellaneous items listed earlier is simply this. Having once been in close relation, and having then split into areas of intense specialization, scientists of various stripes are once more suspecting that they have much more in common, and more to learn from each other, than many have realized. It is in reflection of this general spirit—never dead in some souls and growing apace since World War II—that this volume is written.

Perhaps some day it will be possible to summarize all scientific knowledge in a few simple principles, without regard to whether they deal with matter or energy, the living or nonliving, plants or animals, mice or men. Anyone perturbed or elated by the thought had better not base any practical plans on it, however, as the prospect is extremely remote. Meanwhile we can note with some satisfaction the wide scope of Einstein's unified field theory in the physical realm. The social and psychological sciences are not ready for such treatment as yet, though it is perhaps not too early to experiment with concepts which seem to have general applicability to psychology, political science, sociology, and economics. The remainder of this volume is devoted primarily to such an undertaking.

Chapter 2

HUMAN INPUT IS BASIC

THE SURVIVAL of a human system, or of any other living creature, depends upon a delicate balance between its input and output. The relationship is obvious in terms of energy and substance, for any persistent unbalance in one direction will produce either endless growth or shriveling away. But we will leave matters of physique to the doctors, biologists, and dieticians, our concern in this book being with behavior. Here the input is information and the output is behavior, and a correspondence must be maintained if the organism is to survive. If the incoming information is that the surrounding atmosphere is smoke laden and about 175 degrees in temperature, then unless some output of behavior is brought into fairly close correspondence to the input of information, the whole input-output relation will shortly terminate.

The admonition "Adapt or perish" applies to the individual as well as to the species, the adaptation by the individual being that of his behavioral output to his informational input. One often hears the recommendation that we should adapt the environment to us instead of adapting to it. The advice has emotional appeal, but is meaningless. Beyond the fact that in many cases we have little choice, much of the argument disappears if we try to define its terms. If I observe a ripe apple on a tree and step out of my way to pick it, have I adapted my behavior to the environmental fact of the apple, or have I adapted the apple to my wishes by picking it? Any human act which uses natural materials is simultaneously an adaptation *to* and an adaptation *of* the environment. The recommendation also side-steps the issue in that any modification we make of the earth or its materials, from lean-to's to skyscrapers, thenceforth becomes a part of the environment to which our behavior must adapt. For this reason "adaptive behavior" is generally regarded as synonymous with "intelligent behavior," the greater the intelligence (other things equal) the greater the degree and speed of adaptation.

The first step of adaptation is to become familiar with one's environment—be it man-made or natural. All information about our environment comes ultimately through our senses.[1] Without them we could only lie as if unconscious, or move aimlessly in response to inner urges, like the newborn babe or the proverbial headless chicken. If we could move at all, without senses we would not stop at the edge of a cliff, and we would lie down on knives and knobs as if they were foam and feathers. We could not tell steaks from stones, or tangerines from termites. We could not even swallow food that fell into our mouths, for we would not know that it was there.

Our senses, then, are basic. The quality of information they provide has much to do with the way we respond to our natural environment, and our senses are the medium through which we communicate with other people. Both the state of our knowledge and the organization of our society would be much different if our senses were greatly different—as, for example, if we could see microbes with the naked eye, if we could all communicate reliably by mental telepathy, or if we had no sense of hearing. Hence, our study of behavior will start with the senses.

SENSORY INPUT EQUALS INFORMATION RECEIVED

Our senses are the medium through which we receive communication. For those not familiar with the elements of communications systems, the following introduction may seem somewhat unreal, though it should be easily understandable. Its usefulness will become evident as the details of sensing are filled in.

A communications system requires five basic elements: (1) a source, (2) a coding process, (3) a medium of transmission, (4) a receptor or detector, and (5) a decoding process. Complex systems may repeat all or parts of the process several times over, but they contain no new elements.

These elements are all found in a simple conversation. The *source* is clearly the speaker, but we are apt to overlook the remaining elements, because the common sense idea that *words* or *ideas* flow from speaker to listener is misleadingly oversimplified. More accurately, by manipulating his vocal apparatus the speaker sets up molecular vibrations in the air. These vibrations, or sound waves, are the *coded form* into which the speaker has put his message, and the air is the *medium of transmission*. The ear of the listener is the *receptor*, and the listener's extraction of meaning from the buzzings in his ear is the *decoding*. Our technical age is so loaded with mechanical codings—such as radio waves in the air, grooves in records, magnetized spots on sound or video tapes, electrical impulses in telephone wires, grains of silver in photographic prints, and so on—that we are apt to overlook such everyday code forms as printed words, the sounds of speech, and pictures. A code familiar enough to be called a language does not thereby cease to be a code.

It may come as a surprise that communications to humans from nature

---

[1] This point will be discussed more fully in later chapters on science and concept formation.

contain the same five elements, even when the source is not a conscious being. For example, a large branch breaking from a tree emits a series of creaks, snaps, and groans. While the breaking is in progress, various layers of wood rub against each other or snap off suddenly under tension, each movement in the wood creating its own particular pattern of sound. In this communications system the wood is the *source* and the sound waves are the *coded representation* of the breaking action. The medium, receptor, and decoding mechanism are again the air, ear, and brain. Anyone able to interpret (that is, decode) these sounds receives no less a communication from the tree than if it uttered the words, "I just dropped a branch." Without further examples it can be stated that all communication involves these five elements, regardless of whether any or all parts of the communication system are animate or mechanical, and regardless of what sense is appealed to (sight, hearing, touch, etc.).

The everyday language for describing sensory processes was developed long before a systematic theory of communications existed, and does not incorporate the fuller understanding embodied in that theory. In particular, normal usage makes no distinction between *detecting* and *decoding*, lumping them into a single package. To illustrate, you are in your living room some evening before dinner playing with your neighbor's five year old. At 5:45 you hear a metallic squeak followed by a rattling thud, and you say, "Jimmy, your father's home." Common parlance would say that you *heard* a car door slam. But more strictly the only thing you *heard*— that is, sensed or detected—was sound waves. Your previous experience with these sounds enabled you to decode them, that is, to identify them as the coded representation of Jimmy's father's car door being slammed. Detecting and decoding are two distinct steps, and our common tendency to lump them together produces many misconceptions. Some examples will appear later.

In human beings the detecting mechanisms are the sense organs and the attached nerves, and detecting may be referred to as *sensing*. Decoding is done by the brain, and will be considered synonymous with *interpreting*. *Perceiving* is a convenient term for sensing plus interpreting. It is not suggested that you abandon "I heard a car door slam" in favor of "I sensed a sound, which I interpret to represent the slamming of a car door." You need not even go so far as, "I perceived the slamming of a car door." It is only urged that for analytical purposes you be aware that sensing and interpreting are two operations, not one. Sensing is primarily a problem in physics and neurology while interpreting is one of logic and psychology.[2]

---

[2] Except for the relatively few philosophers and psychologists who use the information and communication model (and I am not sure that any have adopted it fully), the failure to distinguish the detecting and interpreting stages of perception has resulted in much looseness of analysis, especially with respect to the approach to "sense data." I would think of G. A. Paul's article "Is There a Problem about Sense Data?" in A. G. N. Flew (ed.), *Logic and Language* (London: Blackwell, 1955), as a notable case in point. I believe that the information model, as here used,

To deal with the physics first, each type of sensory organ is sensitive to some particular form of energy. The ears are sensitive to the energy of sound, the eyes to the energy of light, the nerves of the skin to the energy of pressure or heat, and the nerves of taste and smell to the molecular energy of chemical action. Since all knowledge of our environment comes initially through our senses, and our senses respond only to receipts of energy, all knowledge of the environment is derived from the energies which reach us.

This energy is referred to as signals, a *signal* being defined as any energy or energy change of a type and intensity to which a receptor is sensitive. This definition is broad enough to cover any kind of communications system, mechanical, electronic, or other, and can be modified for humans as any energy or energy change of a type and intensity to which a sensory nerve is sensitive. *Perception* can now be rephrased as the detection and decoding of incoming signals.

Most signals arise outside the body, as when light waves strike the eye, sound waves enter the ear, or an object presses against the skin. Some signals arise inside the body, as when hunger contractions of the stomach or the pressure of a distended bladder impinge on neighboring nerves. The definition of a signal includes a *change* of energy, since the increase, decrease, or movement of a signal may provide information quite as well as its continued presence. That the energy must be of the proper type merely means, for example, that radar waves cannot be signals to humans since we have no nerves which are sensitive to radar. We can get information from radar only if its signals are recoded by an electronic device (some sort of meter, for example) into light waves, sound waves, or some other signals for which we do have detectors. Sound and light go through the ears and eyes, which collect and focus the signals before the signals fire the nerves themselves. The signals for the other senses act directly on the sensory nerves, without the assistance or intervention of a sense "organ."

The minimum amount of energy to which a sensory nerve or organ will respond is the *threshold* of that sense. Upon receipt of this threshold amount of energy a sensory nerve *fires*. In firing (also known as *discharging*) the nerve generates and releases a small electrical charge into the nerves to which it is connected, all such charges going directly or indirectly into the brain. The sound of a heartbeat a mile away is not a signal, love poets to the contrary notwithstanding, because the level of sound energy is not intense enough to fire a sensory nerve. A cannon blast at six inches would not be a signal if it were so intense as to destroy the nerve. With this background we can now define *sensing* as the firing of sensory

---

sharpens the problem considerably by separating the detecting and decoding stages—the sensation and the interpretation. We will discuss later the situations in which signals are detected but are only partially or inaccurately decoded, or are not decoded at all.

nerves by signals. The person involved need not be awake, or even conscious, for sensory stimuli are often the cause of waking from sleep or unconsciousness, and must be sensed first.

All information thus arrives in the form of signals. How accurate the final state of the information will be depends on the fidelity with which each of the elements of the communications system operates. High fidelity communication will exist only if (1) the signals are an accurately coded representation of the source, (2) the medium transmits the signals with little distortion, (3) our sense organs are good detectors, and (4) our brain accurately decodes the nerve currents received from the sense organ. A coded message can also be accurately transmitted despite distortions or noise at some steps in the communications system if there is adequate redundancy in the message—a matter for later discussion. The remainder of the present chapter deals with the first three of these steps, the operations of the brain being reserved for later treatment.

SIGNALS, FROM SOURCE TO DETECTOR

We have already seen that everyday language confuses the issue of sensing, in that we say "I see a cat" instead of "I see light, which I interpret to represent a cat." It also incorporates another misconception, in that it reverses the direction of action. In the above sentence "I" is the subject, "see" is a transitive verb, and "cat" is the direct object. The whole sense of our grammatical structure implies that action goes from subject to object, and that "I" am doing something to the cat. The physical reality is the reverse, and would be more accurately described by some such statement as: "The cat signals me." "Seeing" is not something we do to things, but something they do to us—and the same is true of hearing, feeling, tasting, and smelling. Again, there is no need to change our speech so long as we do not mistake the linguistic relation for the physical one.

Custom speaks of five senses: sight, hearing, taste, smell, and touch. This classification is reasonably satisfactory for the first four (if we keep in mind that most "tastes" are really odors), but so-called touch is better referred to as the skin and related senses. This latter group is really a hodgepodge, with such diverse components as pressure, pain, temperature, balance, and hunger senses—to mention only a few. Sight and hearing provide information at a distance, while taste and the skin senses operate only on contact. Smell shows both traits. It is essentially a contact sense when it operates as an adjunct to taste, or in such instances as "I smell gas." But it is essentially a distance sense in such cases as "I smell a skunk."

The distance senses are far more important to the interactions among human beings than the contact senses, and deserve our first and more detailed attention. As already hinted, the first operation in communication is that the source must somehow modify the transmission medium so that the medium contains information about the source. If a rabbit hops across the snow, the rabbit (source) produces modifications (footprints) in the snow (medium), which footprints are the coded representation in the medium of the rabbit and his hopping. Anyone able to detect the tracks, and also familiar with the code, will then have received information about the rabbit. Tire prints, shadows, crushed grass, gullies, fossils, star light, smoke, and numberless other items are coded representations of some source in some medium, awaiting only detection and decoding to bring forth information about the source.

Of the three distance senses, smell is probably the simplest communications system. The source releases some of its molecules into the air, which is the medium. The modification of the medium is, of course, the resulting change in the chemical content of the air, the new chemical being the coded representation of the source which is wafted in due course to the detecting nose.

Hearing and sight show an important distinction. With rare exceptions, sound signals are generated by the source of information, whereas most light signals are generated elsewhere and are merely reflected by the source. A dog generates the sound of barking, and a branch generates the sounds of breaking, the ensuing vibrations of the air then containing information about the dog and the branch. Except to amuse vacationers in canyons or to make commercials seem impressive on TV, reflections of sound (echoes) merely confuse the signals.

Although we are sometimes interested in light as providing information about the place where it was generated, as when we observe the sun, stars, a lamp, lightning, fire, or phosphorescent materials, our interest usually lies in the object which reflects it. Light direct from the sun contains almost no information except about the sun. But once it is reflected from (say) a building, it contains far more information about the building than about the sun. Because light does not stand still while we examine it, we are apt to remain unaware that the building leaves its impression on the reflected light quite as definitely as the rabbit leaves its impression in the snow. In both cases the impression (change, modification, modulation) which the source makes on the medium constitutes the information about the source.

The term *modulation* is already used in communications to describe the modification of a medium to carry a signal—that is, to contain information from the source. To simplify subsequent discussion, we will hereinafter use modulation to include any modification of one thing by another, in which the modification contains information about the object or event which caused the modification, even when the modification is not a step in a recognized communications system.

Considering the way the term *information* is used here and by information theorists, in its broadest sense information is implicitly defined as synonymous with modulation. That implicit definition will be explicitly accepted here, and, for reasons beyond the scope of the present discussion, seems to have much to commend it. Except to get the discussion under way, we will have little occasion to use the term in this widest sense. However, the modulations of the medium in a communications system clearly fall within the definition, and are widely construed as information in communications theory. In line with the same logic, information acquired by human beings takes the form of modulations of the brain, and unless the brain is modulated in consequence of sensory or other experiences (the term "experience" to be defined later), the human being gets no information. To tie this with the more customary terminology, we may define *knowledge* as information possessed by human beings. Information theory discusses the amount of information in a transmission channel without regard to its accuracy or inaccuracy in a wider sense, and the term will similarly be used here. Subsequent pages will refer frequently to information, but seldom to knowledge.

To return to more explicit things, when a rabbit makes prints in the snow the source is the active factor as it impresses information on the medium. When light strikes a building and is reflected in modulated form, the medium is the active factor in the process of being impressed with information. So long as the medium is modulated to contain information about the source it does not matter which is the active and which the passive factor. If we wish to place a fingerprint on a piece of glass, for example, it makes no difference whether we move the finger to the glass or the glass to the finger. The information process is often reciprocal. After a tire has been driven through mud, the mud contains information about the tire and the tire carries information about the mud. Much of what is learned by the young child and the trained scientist, not to mention everyone between, comes after we have learned to decipher the forms into which the information around us had been coded.

The above description is relevant not merely to light and sound, but to all media of communication, be they natural, mechanical, or warmly human. When a message passes from teacher to pupil to parent, or from source to reporter to newspaper to reader, the end product sometimes contains more information about the transmission channel than about the source. The problem is rather like trying to look at something below the surface of water, when we are not sure whether we are seeing the object, the surface of the water, or the reflection of some object above it. As communications theory describes it, this is very "noisy" transmission. One of the fascinating aspects of some recently developed fields of study (such as communications theory and cybernetics) is that such highly dissimilar things as light rays and newspaper reporters can be dealt with in similar terms, each being an element in a communications system. Fleeting glimpses of this sort suggest that knowledge may some day be much more unified than it now is, and that communications theory may furnish an important step on the way.

HOW GOOD ARE OUR SIGNALS?

How much information we can get through our senses depends first on how much is in the signals, and second on how much of that quantity we are able to extract. "Extract" at this point refers only to detecting, the decoding operation being a matter for the following chapter.

Perhaps we should mention first some things we can *not* detect, and therefore can learn about only through instruments or deductions. We have no mechanism sensitive to magnetism. We also have no sensitivity to a static electrical charge in our bodies unless it is large enough to make our hair stand on end. We can, of course, feel even a small electron flow, as when a static charge jumps to a doorknob, or we get an electric shock.[3] We are unable to sense the identity of molecules and atoms; we have no specific organs sensitive to gravity, as such, though our pressure, muscle, and kinesthetic senses together can sense weight, and the inner ear utilizes the pull of gravity to give us a sense of balance.

Nature displays a tremendous range of radiation, to most of which we are insensitive. The whole spectrum of radiation is diagrammed in Figure 2-1, and ranges from the gamma rays which are only about one ten-trillionth of an inch in length (10^{-14} meters, shown to the left) to radio and AC waves which run up to thousands of miles in length (10^8 meters, shown to the right).

Figure 2-1
THE SPECTRUM OF RADIATION

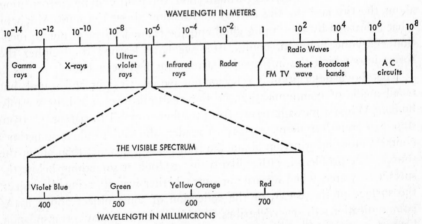

The top part of the diagram is the total electromagnetic spectrum. The bottom part is an enlargement of the visible portion of the spectrum, which lies beween the ultraviolet and the infrared. Reproduced from A. Chapanis, W.A. Garner, and C. T. Morgan, *Applied Experimental Psychology* (New York: John Wiley & Sons, 1949), by permission of the publishers.

---

[3] The startling effect of an electric shock lies in the fact that, since our nerves operate by electric current, the shock simultaneously stimulates all the senses in the area—pain, tickle, heat, cold, itch, and whatnot—plus all adjacent muscular responses. This is more than most of us are prepared to deal with, the withdrawal from even a light shock being prompt.

The term "radiation" here refers only to the electromagnetic spectrum. It does not include the broader meaning, in which we might say that sound waves "radiate" from a source, or rings of waves "radiate" from a pebble dropped into a pond.

Our eyes are the only sense organ directly sensitive to radiation, as such, and they can detect only the narrow band of wave lengths from violet through red light, shown on an enlarged scale below the main diagram. These wave lengths are known as the visible spectrum, extending from about three-eights to three-fourths of a micron in length, a micron being one millionth of a meter. Knowledge of all other wave lengths can be obtained only through instruments which recode the information into signals to which our eyes or ears are sensitive.

The nerves of the skin respond to heat, and the skin can be made hot by radiation, as when one lies in the sun. But these nerves would report heat in the same way if the skin were heated by contact with hot air or a hot object, even if no radiation were present. By contrast, even if radiation were present, these nerves could not detect it if the heat it generates were dissipated as fast as it arrived, as by a cool breeze. On the other hand, the eyes detect radiation whether it generates heat or not. This is the meaning of the statement that only the eyes are directly sensitive to radiation *as such*.

As signaling media, light and sound present an interesting contrast. Since sound waves are generated by their source, they come into existence only with activity. Sound therefore normally implies action, and the more intense the action the more intense usually will be the sound. Strong noise in nature customarily suggests danger. Absence of sound does not imply safety, of course, as a lion or the edge of a cliff can be very quiet. Even amid man-made clatter it is usually wise at least to identify a loud sound rather than ignore it.

By contrast most light signals are reflections whose strength gives no clue whatever to the intensity or the importance of the thing that reflects them. At night the avalanche goes unseen while the peaceful snow may be blinding by day.

Light will cross the universe, whereas only a very loud sound will travel more than a mile or two. We therefore have to depend on light signals alone (or on instruments) for information about anything not reasonably close. Sound turns corners, while light does not, so sound (and odors) must be depended on for signals from behind things.

These factors are all obvious, but nevertheless make an interesting combination. *Any* sound indicates action, which (since sound does not travel far) must be fairly close. Since it turns corners, sound can be detected no matter where the ear is aimed. Finally, unlike light, sound does not disappear from our natural environment for hours at a time—sound has no night. All of which means that sound is an excellent warning system.

Sound, then, alerts us to a happening, and may give a good clue to its general nature. But sound is very poor on detail. Except for some modest information contained in the timing and quality of echoes, sound carries no information about still objects—nothing about their size, shape, distance, texture, color, or constituent materials. Many sounds are brief and unrepeated, allowing no chance to examine them leisurely if we happened to miss their significance at first. (Speech presents different problems, to be dealt with later.) These limitations do not grow from inadequate hearing mechanisms, but from the inherent incapacity of sound signals to carry detailed information about such things as shape, size, or position. Sound is not a very precise indicator of direction, and can be highly misleading on this score if the signal echoes or turns corners.

By contrast, light signals are rather poor as warning, running continuously by day and stopping almost entirely at night. We see nothing behind us or behind other things. The eye is extremely sensitive, however, to any motion within the field of vision, and will normally focus on it immediately. Once focused, the eye will fill in many of the gaps left by sound. Light is extremely "fine grained." Being considerably less than a millionth of an inch in length, light waves can enter and reflect from—and therefore provide information about—the tiniest details of surfaces or structures. During daylight and under good artificial light, the medium is more than adequately abundant, millions of light rays, striking every area the size of a pinhead every second. Light travels in a straight line through clear air, thereby providing precise indications of direction and sharp outlines of shapes. Being continuous, for all practical purposes light allows us to examine a lighted object for any length of time, and in as much detail as we like.

Unlike Superman, who can see through things even more solid than his sense of duty, we cannot see through things—except glass, clear air, and an insignificant number of other substances. All of which raises the question of whether we would be better off if our eyes were sensitive to the whole spectrum of radiation. The chances are that we would not, and we might well be worse off. If we had actual X-ray sensitivity (rather than the fictional Superman version) we would see the insides and outsides of objects simultaneously, making a real hash of them. Even if we avoided this difficulty with separate sets of eyes, we would immediately face the more serious difficulty that X-ray signals simply are not abundant enough at the earth's surface to see with. If we had to depend on naturally supplied X-rays and gamma rays, all we would ever see would be scattered, momentary pin-pricks of light—never a whole scene at one time. A landscape would look like the sky on a clear dark night with a perpetually changing set of stars—beautiful, perhaps, but not very informative. Finally, X-rays are very tiny, and hence are rapidly diffracted and diffused when they strike the molecules of the air, just as ordinary, visible light is broken up by tiny water particles in the air. As a result, if we tried to see anything more than a few feet away by X-rays, all we would see would be a dense fog. Even things a few inches from our eyes would be blurred by this diffraction.

Nature also provides some long radio waves, which astronomers have been using in recent years to get information about distant parts of the universe. But judging from the size of their instruments, our eyes would have to be about a hundred feet in diameter to collect enough energy of this kind to see with. There is the further problem that waves a hundred feet or more in length cannot be reflected by a rose or even an automobile, and hence cannot be modulated to carry information about small things. All in all, our eyes are apparently well adapted to provide the maximum information about our environment that radiation is capable of supplying. Perhaps in these days of man-induced radiation, an important addition might include direct sensitivity to the harmful radiation of atomic fallout. This might be most useful if it took the form of pain sensitivity, rather than mere visibility, so that it would bring a direct and immediate avoidance response.

On the whole, with respect to the information we can get through our eyes and ears, the limitations are set much more by the nature of the signals than by any inadequacies of the eyes and ears as detectors. The eye is almost unbelievably sensitive, being able to respond to as little as one light quantum every few seconds.[4] The energy represented by this much light is about five one-hundred-billionths of an erg, an erg being about one thousandth of the energy required to jiggle a pin. As a result of this stimulus the nerve discharges an electric current having an energy content of about 42 ergs. The nerve thus acts as a relay, or valve, which sends to the brain about a trillion times as much energy as it receives.

The nerves of the ear are also extremely sensitive, being able to respond when the eardrum vibrates over a distance less than the wave length of light, or when the basilar membrane moves a distance less than 1 per cent of the diameter of a hydrogen molecule.[5] The ear's range is from about 20 cycles per second (about half an octave below the bottom note of the piano) to 16,000 or 20,000 cycles per second (about two octaves above the top note of the piano). Sounds of higher frequencies certainly occur, both in nature and in civilized life. But they are seldom unaccompanied by frequencies well inside the audible range. In consequence few events which are signalized by sounds are likely to be inaudible.

The remaining senses are complex, and difficult to describe, but a few observations seem in order. The senses of taste and smell are highly sensitive to some substances. In the case of the foul smelling chemical mercaptan, used to make household gas smellable, the nose is able to detect one

[4] Warren S. McCulloch, "Why the Mind Is in the Head," Lloyd A. Jeffress (ed.), *Cerebral Mechanisms in Behavior* (The Hixon Symposium, New York: John Wiley & Sons, 1951), p. 45.

[5] Frank A. Geldard, *The Human Senses* (New York: John Wiley & Sons, 1953), p. 115.

part in 50 trillion,[6] and the taste buds are sensitive to a solution containing three parts in 10 million of quinine sulphate. Among common substances, we cannot taste a sugar solution of much less than 1 per cent, or salt of less than 0.2 per cent. At the other extreme are the many odorless and tasteless substances, for which we have no sensitivity at all.

The phrase "sense of touch" is commonly used to cover all remaining senses, which might be referred to as the skin and related senses. Investigators are not at all sure how many independent senses of "feel" we have, but the list seems to include such items as contact, pressure, deep pressure, prick pain, quick pain, deep pain, warmth, cold, heat, muscular pressure, articular pressure, tendinous strain, ampullar sensation or dizziness, vestibular sensation or sense of translation, appetite, hunger, thirst, nausea, sex, cardiac sensation, and pulmonary sensation.[7] At some time or other, psychologists have also considered itch, tickle, vibration, suffocation, satiety, and repletion as independent sensations. Despite this battery of sensations, some areas of the body are almost completely insensitive to any stimulus whatsoever, the mucous lining of the cheeks, the back of the mouth, the "solid" organs of the abdomen, and the alimentary canal from the stomach to the gall bladder being cases in point. All in all, however, we are too well equipped to remain unaware of very many events on or in any part of the body.

Many sensations require the interpretation of two or more different kinds of stimuli. Wetness, for example, is reported to be sensed as a cold pressure uniformly distributed, oiliness as a uniform weak pressure plus warmth, hardness as an even cold pressure with a good boundary, and softness as an uneven warm pressure with a poor boundary.[8]

It is important to an understanding of motivation that the more obvious "biological urges" are by no means easy to locate in the system. It is true that hunger pains are directly related to stomach contractions. But the relations between hunger pains and eating, or between hunger pains and an empty stomach, are rather obscure. Stomach contractions stop with the first few mouthfuls, yet eating continues. Animals whose esophaguses have been attached by surgery directly to the intestines show a normal hunger drive, even though they have no stomach and no contractions. Stomach contractions in a hungry dog will stop upon transfusion of blood from a well-fed dog, and contractions will start in a full stomach upon transfusion from a starved fellow. In addition, the desire to eat may be stronger after 12 hours without food than after 4 days. In brief, there is no simple relation between eating and the biological need for food—and much the same applies to the other so-called biological urges.

In closing this bird's eye view of human informational input it should be kept in mind that we have thus far dealt only with signals and their

---

6 *Ibid.*, p. 280.
7 *Ibid.*, p. 158.
8 *Ibid.*, p. 190.

detection by sense organs. The behavior of the nerves of sensation in the eye, ear, and elsewhere in the body is inborn; the technique of sensation does not need to be learned—though the motor controls which guide the senses toward some signals and away from others are learned. Though the detected signals contain information, that information can be extracted from the signals and utilized only after the signals are decoded. However simple and automatic they may seem to adults, the interpretations which constitute decoding involve complex mental processes and a great deal of learning. Later chapters will describe the physical equipment and processes by which we do our interpreting, and thus acquire information about our environment.

Chapter 3

SCIENCE, MODELS,
AND SYSTEMS

CHARLES WHITTLESEY once observed that one cannot understand banking until he first understands money, and that he cannot understand money until he first understands banking.[1] This did not stop Whittlesey from writing a book on money and banking.

It might similarly be said that the nature of scientific thinking, especially concerning models, cannot be understood until one first understands concepts and concept formation, but that concept formation cannot be understood until one first understands models. Like Whittlesey, I mention this, but am not deterred.

In this chapter we are going to deal with some broad aspects of human information processes, with particular reference to scientific thinking. Perhaps the first thing we need to understand about scientific thinking is that it involves no distinct or unique mental processes. It is simply a more efficient way of doing the same basic kinds of thinking all of us do all our lives, such as observing, remembering, comparing, generalizing, and discriminating. Reserving mental processes themselves for later chapters, we will here examine some aspects of information, and interrelations of information, which are important to our learning processes and to science. Although the term "science" applies both to the methods of acquiring and handling information and to the body of information thus acquired, our present attention will be confined to the information processes, which are the same for all sciences, rather than the content, which differs from science to science.

THINGS, VERSUS INFORMATION
ABOUT THINGS

The debate about the relations between things and ideas—between the so-called "real" world of materials and events and the ideas about the world which exist in men's heads—has a long and thorny history, going

---

[1] Charles R. Whittlesey, *Principles and Practices of Money and Banking* (New York: Macmillan & Co., 1949), p. 3.

back in clear form at least to Plato in the fifth century B.C. A position on that dispute is inescapable, implicitly or explicitly, in many of the chapters which follow, and the one incorporated into this book may as well be made clear at the outset. Whatever the nature of the "real" world outside men's minds, we know nothing about that world (i.e., there is nothing in our minds about it) until we receive information about it. All such information comes to us initially through our senses,[2] and we think and behave about the "real" world solely on the basis of this information. Our behavior toward wasps is not determined by the *fact* that they sting, but our *information* to this effect. Until we know that they sting, the fact has no effect on our thought and action. If we have faulty information about some other insect, and believe it stings when it does not, our thought and action toward it will be based on this faulty information, not the "facts." We will not debate which is more "real," the outside world or the ideas in our heads. Wherever it is relevant, however, this book operates on the premise that human behavior is based on our *information* about things, not the *nature* of things.

It is relevant, of course, to inquire whether and to what extent our information accurately reflects the real world. If our information is accurate, then our actions *are* based on the real world. This is a large problem, and aspects of it are discussed in subsequent chapters on Concepts and Communication. Meanwhile we will observe briefly what occurs if we act on faulty information.[3] We may define *knowledge* as information possessed by human beings, and perhaps by other animals, which information in the present model takes the form of modulations of the brain. A child who acts without knowledge that wasps sting may have an unpleasant brush with "reality," and thereby acquire new information. It should be clear, however, that his revised behavior is not based upon "reality," as such, but upon his new information. If the child did not observe the wasp, but thinks that he backed into a rose thorn or a pin, his behavior with respect to wasps will remain unchanged.

Behavior is based on information, and information comes through our senses. But if we had to engage in behavior at each and every moment

---

[2] As noted in Chapter 1, we are not ruling out the possibility of nonsensory inputs of information, such as divine revelation or extrasensory perception. But we are confining our present attention to what obviously makes up the vast bulk of our information—that learned through the sensory nerves. As will become clearer from the later chapters on Concepts and Communication, even extrasensory processes or divine revelation, if and to the extent they operate, code their information in the repertoire of concepts already familiar to the recipient, which concepts are achieved initially through his senses, many from his culture.

[3] What constitutes "faulty" information can be stated only in the light of its consistency with subsequent experience, or the experiences of other persons, and "consistency" may be the closest approximation we can ever make to the meaning of "truth" about empirical or "synthetic" propositions. Whatever the ultimate solution, if any, of this philosophical problem, all of us have a common sense notion of the distinction between the real world outside us and the ideas in our heads about that world. That distinction is adequate for the present purpose, and is often referred to as "naive realism."

solely on the basis of information available through our senses at that moment, our behavior would be a sorry mess indeed. Probably none but the simplest organisms could long survive under such circumstances. A problem of learning in general, and science in particular, is to combine and store information received at different times and places so that we can have more information at any one moment than is being received at that moment. The details of how the brain is able to do this are found in later chapters, which we can summarize here by saying that the brain connects various inputs of sensory information into groups, which we call concepts.

The "Amplification" of Information

Concepts as Stored Information. We observed in Chapter 1 that sounds and other kinds of energy can be amplified. The process of amplification requires (1) the quantity of something that is to be amplified, and (2) a reservoir which can be tapped to provide a larger quantity of the first item. Instead of being used directly, the first item is used to operate a valve or switch, by means of which the much larger flow from the reservoir can be controlled.

In somewhat analogous fashion, the human being is able to accumulate reservoirs of information over a period of time. At any one moment it is possible to have more information about an event one is witnessing than is currently received, because the small amount of current information operates a switch, so to speak, which releases much larger amounts of information from the accumulated reservoir. Current receipts are thus "amplified." This process differs from amplification in the strict sense, however. True amplification produces a larger· or stronger version of the same thing, whereas the amplification of information in the present sense produces a version which is qualitatively different as well as quantitatively larger. (The meaning of quantitative differences in information will be examined in later chapters.)

We need not dispute whether concepts are the sole form in which information can be stored. They are a major form, and suffice to illustrate the process. We shall also define *cues* as any pieces of information, currently received or available, which enable us to tap the larger amounts of information stored in our concepts.

Concepts are the stored information that things in our environment exist in certain patterns, but not others. Omitting imagination and other more complex mental phenomena, and confining attention for the moment to the more obvious physical features of our environment, it can be said that we form concepts corresponding to things which are associated in our environment, but do not form concepts of things which are not associated. Rocks are associated with a location in or on the ground, not floating on water or air. Eyes appear in animals, not in plants or inanimate things. Leaves appear on plants, not yardsticks or noses, and water flows down, not up. Information about the kinds of things which are or are not associated with rocks, eyes, leaves, and water is stored in our heads in the form of concepts of these things.

It is easiest to see how this information can be tapped by cues when things stand in the relation of part and whole, in which relationship a given concept consists of certain parts, but not others. The concept of human being consists of such parts as arms, legs, and head, but not such parts as sand, stars, or mountains. The concept of rock contains such elements as hardness and heaviness, but not liquidity or growth. While we are forming concepts of wholes as consisting of certain parts, we also form concepts of parts as belonging to certain wholes. Eyes or legs never occur by themselves, or as parts of stones or cash boxes, but only as parts of animals. Leaves appear only as parts of plants, and clouds only as parts of the sky. Concepts about the relation between certain parts and a whole are inductive generalizations, which can be used as follows.

Cues as Releases of Stored Information. Once we have stored information in the form of concepts, it can be released, or tapped, by cues. To take an oversimplified example, suppose that we have formed concepts in which all animals possess eyes and legs, and that no living things except animals possess them. Assuming that these concepts are in accord with reality, if we then observe a normal, functioning eye, this observation is a cue which taps the information already stored in our concepts, and permits us to deduce the further information that an animal is present. If anyone talks about a normal, functioning eye, this permits us to deduce that an animal is part of the situation he is discussing. Similarly, the cue that an animal is present permits us to infer the presence of eyes. And further, since in our concepts eyes occur only in animals, which have mouths of some sort, the presence of eyes is a cue from which we can deduce the presence of a mouth—again, assuming normal animals. Anyone who has observed his own thought processes is aware that this kind of information tapping is going on constantly in his head. Obviously, we cannot tap the information stored in concepts until we have first formed the concepts. To tie together the language of earlier and later chapters, we can say either (1) that we cannot perceive things until we have already formed concepts[4] of them, or (2) that we cannot decode a group

---

[4] Philosophers and psychologists do not widely acknowledge the essential identity of inductive generalization and concept formation, nor of deduction and the use of cues, the latter apparently involving the same psychological processes as perception. I have argued these similarities in an article, "Toward a Uniform Language of Information and Knowledge," in *Synthese*, Vol. XIII No. 2 (June, 1961), pp. 127–53, and think I can defend it in depth. A related view appears in Feigl, when he says, "Knowledge, both on the level of common sense and on that of science, is now being regarded as a network of concepts and propositions tied only in a few places to the data of immediate experience, and for the rest a matter of 'free construction,'" though Feigl does not specifically equate induction and concept formation. The quotation is from Herbert Feigl, "Some Major Issues and Developments in the Philosophy of Science of Logical Empiricism," in Herbert Feigl and Michael Scriven (eds.), *The Foundations of Science and the Concepts of Psychology and*

of incoming signals unless we have already formed the code. In the present model our concepts are the coded form taken by the information we have previously acquired.

When the generalized relationships are not invariable, less information can be derived from cues, or the information will be less certain. If only animals have eyes, then the presence of an eye establishes the presence of an animal. But if not all animals have legs, then the presence of an animal does not necessarily establish the presence of legs—only a probability.

Concepts of Events. In addition to forming concepts of objects, which might be called concepts of static things, human beings also form concepts of events, or dynamic things.[5] The concept of rain, for example, includes the components, or subconcepts, of water, drop size, clouds, and falling. We have the concept not merely of eraser, but of the act of erasing. We also have concepts of such events as the hitting of a nail with a hammer, the erosion of a field by rain, and the making of footprints in the snow by a rabbit. In the language of the previous chapter, the position of the nail in the wood, the gullies in the field, and the tracks in the snow are all modulations which contain information about the hammer blow, rain, and rabbit hopping which caused them.

Although the information is there, the problem is to extract it. To do so requires the same kind of inductive and deductive processes described above. If we conceptualize snow as something a rabbit cannot hop on without leaving tracks, and we then observe the cue that here is a stretch of snow with no tracks, we can deduce the additional information that no rabbit has been here. If we also conceptualize snow as something which will not have little holes in it unless pressure is applied, and we then observe little holes, we can deduce that pressure has been applied. If we further conceptualize this region as containing nothing capable of making this particular pattern of holes except rabbits, we can deduce the further information that rabbits have been on the scene.

Whether the phenomenon be static (an object) or dynamic (an event) makes no difference to the information processes. Once we have formed a concept of a certain phenomenon which consists of the conjunction or association of certain components, along with the inductive conclusion that certain relations between part and the whole concept are *always* found, or are found *only* in this phenomenon, it is then possible to acquire information about the whole from the part, about the part from the whole, or about one part from another part through the whole.[6] These

---

Psychoanalysis (Minneapolis: University of Minnesota Press, 1956), p. 16. Along similar lines, Wilfrid Sellars is quoted to the effect that "concepts involve laws and are inconceivable without them." *Ibid.*, p. 18. Further sources will be cited later in chapters on concept formation.

[5] The distinction between objects and events will be drawn more precisely in Chapter 7.

[6] Philosophers customarily distinguish two kinds of invariant association, that of the attributes of a given object and that of cause and effect. I have argued in the

processes are used constantly by all human beings, and perhaps by some lower animals as well. In science they are used more regularly, systematically, and efficiently than elsewhere, though highly systematic thinking is by no means confined to scientists, or even to civilized man.

SCIENCE: OBSERVATIONS AND CLASSIFICATIONS

An empirical science is a body of information. It includes concepts and interrelations among concepts through which it is possible to derive information by deduction from other information. It does not differ in nature from the kinds of generalizations which all of us hold and use about such things as rabbit tracks and human eyes and legs, but a science covers a broader scope. A formal science includes concepts not formed by nonscientists, and often includes concepts of things which can be detected by instruments, but not by the senses. Inflation, filibusters, and social structure are concepts developed by social scientists from information which *can* be acquired through the human senses, while atoms, electrical conductivity, and viruses are concepts based on information which can be acquired only through instruments. We will later note the relationship between these concepts and a scientific device known as a "model," to be discussed below.

Observation Stage

The first step in developing a science is observation and recording. In biology, for example, the scientist observes the size, shape, color, location, growth patterns, and a host of other traits of various plants and animals. These are at first described in ordinary language, recorded, and reported so that the observations of one scientist will be available to others. At this stage the process is mostly hit or miss, with little sense of what is important and what is not. The reports and discussions at this stage of a science are mostly simple descriptions and comparisons of the things observed, perhaps accompanied by some relatively wild guesses as to what the subject is all about.

Classification Stage

The second stage is to construct a classification system, in which the things observed in the first stage can be sorted according to their similarities and differences, and the classifications can be given names. At this stage the science also begins to have a specialized language of its

---

Synthese article cited above that the notion of cause and effect is redundant (though in somewhat different language from the present), all information processes of the brain being incorporated in the dual processes of (1) concept formation and (2) acquiring in the particular instance, through perception, more information than is currently provided. The latter process is there referred to as that of making identifications from cues, cues being the information currently received and the identification being the additional information deduced from it.

own. Astronomers divide heavenly bodies into stars, planets, satellites, asteroids, and meteorites. Biologists classify things as plant and animal, and then subdivide the animals into mammals, reptiles, birds, fish, and so forth. Economists classify things as goods, utility, wealth, income, and capital —and so on for all the other sciences.

The development of a classification system is the same as the formation of a series of interrelated concepts of the things under investigation. Instead of using such concepts as two-, four-, and six-legged animals; of edible and inedible animals; domestic or wild animals; and similar everyday classifications, the scientist regroups animals into such headings as mammals, arthropods, insects, and reptiles, based on such fundamental traits as method of reproduction, or system of internal organs.

During the history of a science several different systems of classification may be offered. After trying them, scientists normally settle on a single system, at which point we might think of the science as stable, or mature. Although changes may continue to be made, these can usually be accommodated as supplements to the existing classification system, or as a larger system into which the original is absorbed. For example, the development of Keynesian economics dealing with the whole nation does not invalidate the economics of supply and demand, but supplements it. Einsteinian physics does not eliminate Newtonian physics, but fits the latter into a larger framework. Sometimes, however, a new conceptualization does require the total discard of the older one, as when the Ptolemaic concept of astronomy, with the earth the center of the universe, had to be abandoned for the Copernican concept, in which the earth revolves around the sun.

After various classification systems are tried, that one is considered best which contains the largest amount of information for the purpose of the scientists. It is the most efficient system for handling the kinds of information the scientists want, or more precisely, the system which permits the largest amounts of information to be deduced from a given amount of other information. For example, the biologist is distressed if someone refers to whales and porpoises as fish, insisting adamantly that they are mammals, not fish. We will accept his assertion that they *are* mammals under his system of classification, and go beyond to inquire why biologists prefer a classification system which thus categorizes them. They could, after all, put all water-dwelling animals in one group and all land-dwelling ones in another, with appropriate but nonoverlapping subdivisions of each. In such a system the whale and porpoise could never fall into the same category with any land animals, as they now do.

We will now try to see why a system which classifies whales and porpoises as mammals, which are overwhelmingly land animals, provides more information than a system which classifies them as water animals. Under the existing system, if we possess a specimen of a thing called a fish, we know without looking further that we will find a particular kind of circulatory, nervous, excretory, and other systems, and that we will also find gills for the breathing of water. Suppose instead that the term "fish" were broadened to include whales and porpoises, because they look like fish and live in the water. Then even if we knew that we had a fish in front of us, this fact would not tell us whether the specimen has lungs or gills, or what kind of other internal systems it would show. Another well known conspicuous example is the classification of bats as mammals instead of birds.

At this point the person naive in these matters may object: "But whales and porpoises *are* mammals! This is not simply a matter of convenience for biologists." This feeling reflects the same confusion about systems of classification which children show in connection with names. As Vigotsky[7] reports, if children are asked whether we could switch names so that a cow would be called ink, and ink cow, they reply, "No, because ink is to write with, and cows give milk." Just as the average child thinks that the names of things reflect their immutable nature, and cannot be switched without violating nature, so does the average adult think our classifications of things reflect their immutable nature. Both are wrong. As we shall see in the chapter on concepts, things are not categorized as chairs, mountains, trees, and rivers because things *are* that way, or because these are the things that *exist*. They are categorized for human convenience, or because of certain psychological and historical processes by which we originally became familiar with them.

It is true that biologists have other reasons for preferring the system they now use, notably that it ties in well with the apparent evolutionary development of many species. This fact leads us to another aspect of information content. If two classification systems are equally good within a given area of knowledge, but one can also be used in a second area while the other cannot, the system which can be used in two areas contains, or conveys, more information.

For example, suppose that for all purposes except evolution biologists could create just as satisfactory a classification system with whales and porpoises grouped under water-dwelling animals as they now have created with whales and porpoises grouped under mammals. Suppose that they then discovered strong evidence that these two species had evolved from land-dwelling animals similar to the mammals. Within the field of knowledge of evolution, biologists would then have to use a different classification grouping from that used for nonevolutionary knowledge. Such a dual classification system would seriously reduce their information. As it now stands, information gleaned from the structure and behavior of animals often provides a clue to their evolutionary connection, while evidence about a common evolutionary background often suggests

---

[7] L. S. Vigotsky, "Thought and Speech," *Psychiatry*, 1939, #2, p. 36, from Jerome Bruner, Jacqueline Goodnow, and George Austin, *A Study of Thinking* (New York: John Wiley & Sons, Inc., 1956), p. 279.

previously undiscovered similarities of structure or function. Assuming that two or more classification systems are equally satisfactory *within* a field, that system which is also satisfactory in a second field will carry the greater information—if the two fields are, in fact, related.

The information content of a classification system can be stated only with reference to a particular purpose. The fisherman who is interested in light- versus dark-meated fish, or in deep-feeding versus shallow-feeding ones will have little use for the biologist's classifications, and will find more information in his own system.

In summary, the problem of classifying the data of a science is that of finding the grouping which provides the most information with least effort. It is only in recent years that we have been inclined to express the problem in this way, but it seems to reflect what scientists have done.

SCIENCE: FUNCTIONAL RELATIONS AND CAUSES

When we classify objects, our task is relatively simple. We can often examine them for as long as we like, put two side by side, take photographs, make measurements, and otherwise take great care in noting similarities and differences. Further, although there are many kinds of objects in existence, the kinds are by no means limitless, and most remain similar from year to year and century to century.

By contrast, events can take almost any turn, and many never happen the same way twice. The dropped jug may break in two or in hundreds of pieces, or not break, and the thrown rock may bounce up, down, back, or sideways from a boulder. The child may be killed or only bruised when he falls, and the circus lion may promptly obey or suddenly turn on his trainer. Although certain relationships in events are highly reliable, such as those of mass, distance, and velocity between the sun and planets, or those of soil fertility and rate of plant growth, many of these relations are not so easy to observe as the relations among parts of objects.

Much of what is known as the "scientific method" consists of the techniques of distinguishing regular and reliable aspects of events from the irregular and unreliable ones—the same process involved in concept formation as described by psychologists. Various breeds of scientists observe the dependable aspects of relations between such things as mass and acceleration, the length and force of levers, pituitary secretions and rates of growth, bacteria and disease, stimulus and response, drugs and irritability, crime and divorce, or income level and voting habits. In each attempt to find whether two things are reliably related, it is necessary to eliminate the influence of all factors except the two in question. "Sound experimental method" consists of the techniques for doing precisely that. We need not go into the details of experimental method here, which includes such things as laboratory controls, random samples, control and experimental groups, and the rules of statistical inference.

Experimental techniques can determine whether a *functional relationship* exists between two variables, a variable being anything which can exist in two or more different states, such as large or small, hot or cold, present or absent, with leaves or without leaves. If we find that trees regularly have leaves during the warm part of the year and are without leaves during the cold part, we have established a functional relation between two variables, temperature and leafiness. A variable is *discrete* if we distinguish only two (or a limited number) of alternate states, such as with leaves and without leaves, above and below 60 degrees. It is *continuous* if we can distinguish any number of possible intermediate states, as when we describe a temperature along an unbroken scale of degrees or fractions of degrees, rather than simply as hot or cold. Here there is no theoretical limit to the number of alternate states, although the number is limited in practice by the sensitivity of our measuring instruments.

Experimentation can establish the presence, absence, or degree of a functional relationship, but does not itself indicate the direction of cause, if any. Scientific techniques can discern a relationship between the amount of rainfall and the depth of a river. But only common sense or other information can determine whether a deep river causes more rainfall, or more rainfall causes the river to be deeper. Assuming that a relationship is found, statistical techniques do not themselves tell whether crime causes divorce, divorce causes crime, or whether both are the common effect of some third factor. It may be possible to measure lead or lag, in which case we usually assume that the factor which occurs first is the cause of the other.

We also distinguish between the hypothesis, theory, and law. The *hypothesis* is a tentative proposal that two things are functionally or causally related, a *theory* is a hypothesis which has been partially tested and still remains tenable, while a *law* is the statement of a relationship which always occurs, to the best of our knowledge. The distinctions between hypothesis, theory, and law are generally well known, and need not be pursued further here.

Just as with the associations of the parts of an object, as soon as a functional relation is found to be reliable, then information about one variable provides information about the other. If no other significant influences are present, then information that it has rained provides information about the height of the river, and conversely, information about the height of the river provides information about the rainfall. Hence, we can say that knowledge of functional relations, like the establishment of good classification systems, is a technique for increasing the amount of information which can be extracted from other information.[8]

---

[8] For reasons implicit in the preceding discussion, but the fuller exploration of which is beyond the scope of this volume, it can be argued that the discernment of functional relationships is an extension of classification systems from objects to

Action-at-a-Distance

In closing this discussion of events, we may note that all scientific investigation along these lines uses a working premise that action-at-a-distance never occurs. This means that a cause cannot produce an effect unless some force acts between the cause and effect. The engine cannot turn the wheels unless connected by a drive shaft. You can hear sounds only if sound waves travel to your ear, and you can see the sun only if waves or particles travel the intervening distance. If one thing is affected by another, then something must move between or connect the two.

SCIENCE AND MODELS

Two additional techniques are now widely used in science—models and systems. Although actual use of both is quite old, the conscious and deliberately controlled use of both is relatively new. The conscious use of models can perhaps be traced back to Willard Gibbs in the physical sciences, to about 1875, while the development of systems analysis has occurred mainly during and since World War II. As the terms are generally used, the model is a particular type of system. We will discuss the model first, and then show its relation to the remaining varieties of systems in the following section.

To understand the model we must draw upon some aspects of concepts to be discussed more fully in Chapter 7. In the same sense that a voice entering a telephone, or a picture entering a TV camera, must be recoded into electrical impulses, and then be reconstructed into patterns of sound and light in the receiver, so must all information received by the brain be coded into electrical impulses in our sensory nerves, and then be reconstructed into a pattern in our brains. The corresponding "picture" in our brain does not, of course, consist of light waves or sound waves bouncing around there, but of patterns of nerve connections. The pictures we reconstruct inside our heads of the things outside are the concepts of those things, which may or may not be accurate reconstructions.

About the ordinary things with which we are intimately familiar, our concepts are presumably fairly accurate—such as our concepts of hammer, chair, mountain, water, uncle, or cat. For other things our direct, sensory information is vague, sporadic, and sparse—as with the nature of lightning, the solar system, or viruses. Yet the brain does form concepts of these things, and these concepts as they appear among primitive peoples without scientific instruments and accumulated observations strike civilized man as naive.

Virtually all fields of science now use models, which are formalized and explicitly defined concepts. Depending on the problem at hand these

---

events, both being acts of developing efficient concepts. The necessity of using more elaborate techniques for events reflects their greater variety, the larger numbers of variables and the greater difficulty of noting and recording the details of events, probably attributable mainly to their evanescence.

may be physical scale models, schematic or diagrammatic, mathematical, analogous, or conceptual models. If we wish to construct a model of the atom, a physical model might consist of balls of different sizes held together with wire or rods; a schematic model might be a sketch of the same kind of thing; a mathematical model might consist of a group of symbols in an equation, with coefficients to represent distances, velocities, and forces; an analogous model might be indicated by saying that an atom is "something like" the solar system; and a conceptual model is expressed if we say, "Let us suppose that the atom consists of such and such."

The essence of the scientific building and use of models is as follows, using the conceptual model of the atom as an illustration. Without initially debating whether the assumptions are valid, we assume that an atom consists of certain components, with certain specified properties. This set of assumptions is an analytical model of the atom. It is also a hypothesis of how an atom is constructed—though it should be noted that scientists in some fields construct and investigate models without caring whether they approximate the real world, particularly in mathematics and economics. Having made our model, we then investigate how an atom would behave if it were exactly like our model.

Since we know all about our model (having constructed it to our own specifications) we can predict what it will do under specified conditions. If the consequences of certain behavior of the model coincide with the observed consequences of certain behavior of the atom which cannot be directly observed, we then tentatively accept the model as a description of the real atom. If the model also leads us to expect certain things which have not yet been encountered, and we then find those things when we look for them in real atoms, our confidence in our model is increased. If the model leads us to expect things which do not in fact occur, we then discard or modify the model.

In the social sciences, as well as in others, models are often constructed as deliberate oversimplifications of complex situations, either to reduce the complexity to a level which the mind can grasp, or to make a first, rough approximation to the actual state of affairs. Economists are foremost among the social scientists in using models, but their use in other areas is growing rapidly. An important part of economic analysis utilizes a model consisting of assumptions of pure economic man (who has no desire but to maximize his income), a perfectly competitive market, and complete information by all concerned. The analysis then consists of exploring deductively how an economic system would behave if made up of such components. Although the model obviously does not correspond to reality, it does perform both of the functions mentioned above. It provides a rough first approximation of actual behavior, actual economic systems in the long run behaving much more like the model than is often recognized. It also enables the student of economics to grasp its fundamentals in a way he could not do if he had to deal with all its complexity from the outset, after which he can gradually add the complexities which bring his picture of economics closer to reality.

One of the dangers of using models is that the user may forget that his model is not reality, and start making unrealistic prescriptions for treating the troubles of the real world on the assumption that it is like the model. Another is to forget the original purpose of the model, and the investigator who finds that the real world and his model do not correspond sometimes urges that the world be revised to fit the model. If we want our heads to contain accurate pictures of the world outside, all of us must be prepared to revise our concepts of things as we acquire new information, and scientists must be prepared to revise their models. Both processes are the same, in mental terms, the main difference between the models of the scientist and the concepts of the rest of us being that the scientist uses models under more conscious control, and deals with subject matter more remote from everyday experience.

There may or may not be any correspondence between a model and reality. If we deliberately create a model to represent reality, then the model is a hypothesis about reality from the outset. In other cases a model may exist for years without pretending to represent anything real. However, as soon as it is proposed that the model corresponds to some segment of reality, then the model becomes a hypothesis about reality. It is also possible to make hypotheses that certain propositions can be reached by deduction from the model, and deductions from models are an important phase of scientific investigation. If the model is assumed to represent the real world, then the deductions from the model would also apply to the real world. For instance, if we create a model of economic man as a creature intent on maximizing his returns, we can deduce from the model that in a choice between two sources of identical products he will choose the one with the lower price. If we also establish that John Doe is in fact an economic man (that is, that there is a correspondence between reality and the model) then we can predict that John Doe will in fact select the lower-priced source. If John Doe does not correspond to the model, and is not a pure economic man, we cannot reliably predict his behavior from the model, since he might buy from the source with the most beautiful clerks.

SCIENCE AND SYSTEMS

Along with the model, the system is a relatively new technique of scientific analysis. In its broadest sense a *system* is any set of interrelated components. Wires, tubes, capacitors, resistors, and speakers are components of a sound amplifier system. Locomotives, tracks, cars, switches, and signals are parts of a railroad system. Missiles, launching pads, tracking devices, computers, and control devices are components of a missile system. Parties, constitutions, elections, campaigns, nominations, and control of office are parts of a democratic political system—and so on.

We can classify systems as *analytical* and *real*. An *analytical system* is the same as a model, as already described, and is used for the purpose of understanding, describing, analyzing, or planning. As noted, it may or may not be intended to correspond to anything in the real world. A *real system* can be either man-made or natural. Political, communications, transportation, and missile systems are man-made, while the solar system, a river system, or the circulatory system of the dog are natural.

Either real or analytical systems can appear in hierarchies. An atom is a subsystem in a molecule. The molecule is a subsystem within a living cell, which is a subsystem of the heart, which is a subsystem of the circulatory system, which is a subsystem of the human system. Biologists frequently study ecological systems, which are the dependent relationships among a set of plants and animals. For example, the way in which bees pollinate the flowers that provide their food, and the way in which the waste products, dead bodies, or live bodies of some plants or animals become the food of others are typical of the interrelations within an ecological system.

We can have an analytical system, or model, to help us to understand either a man-made or a natural system. Models of atoms made of balls and rods are scale analytical models made to help us to visualize the real atom. The economist's model of the economy is a device for helping him to analyze the real, natural economy. This analytical system exists simultaneously with the real economic system, with its firms, customers, workers, and enterprisers. In natural systems, or man-made systems which have grown bit by bit over the years, the real system exists first, and the analyst may thereafter try to make an analytical model to understand it better. To illustrate the latter, a large railroad system may have grown piece by piece over a hundred-year period, after which the managers of the railroad may make an analytical model in order better to comprehend the complex reality. By contrast, many present-day missile systems are created first as analytical systems on paper or in the brain, in their entirety. Only later is the real system created, to correspond to the model. Thus, in man-made systems the analytical system, or model, may come into existence either before or after the real system.

A substantial body of literature has accumulated thus far on systems analysis, dealing with such varied topics as inventory systems in business, communications systems in the military, guidance systems in the migration of birds, optical systems in microscopes, and the system of relationships among the id, ego, and superego in the human personality.

Simple Action Systems, or Nonfeedback Systems

A system was defined above as a set of interrelated or interacting components. We must now distinguish between simple action systems and feedback systems. We will define a simple action as one in which the action or causation, no matter how complex, proceeds in one direction only. The washing of gullies in a field is a system whose components are rain, run-off, and erosion. The action moves in one direction only. The amount of rain has important effects on the erosion, but the erosion has no effect on the rainfall. The light reflected from a landscape acts upon a photographic film in a camera, but the taking of the picture has no feedback action which in any way affects the landscape. If the system involves only two components, A acting on B, it is an instance of a simple cause-effect relation. The relationship becomes more worthy of the name "system" when the length or width of the chain enlarges. For example, A may affect both B and X, whereupon B acts upon C, which acts upon D, while X acts upon Y, which acts upon Z. No matter how large the number of components, or how long the chain of action, we will refer to it as a simple action system so long as the actions proceed in one direction only.

Feedback Systems

A feedback system stands in marked contrast to a simple action system. No matter how complicated the "simple" action system, and no matter how long the chain of steps, every single one of the actions in it, taken by itself, can be diagnosed as a simple cause-effect relation. A feedback system, on the other hand, involves a quite different set of relations, namely a *mutual* cause-effect relation. In the simplest case, A acts on B, while B simultaneously acts on A. The change in A then has a new effect on B, which acts back on A, and so on. In longer chains A may act on B, which acts on C, which then acts back on A, the reaction on A going again through B and C and back again. There is no limit to the number of steps in the chain before the reaction gets back to A, the underlying problem remaining the same. As in simple action systems, the chain may be branched, A acting on both B and X, one or both of which directly or indirectly may react on A. If several different kinds of interactions are occurring simultaneously (as if B should also act on X, while Y is acting on C, C on Z, and Z on A), it may be useful for understanding the relation to diagnose the whole system as a related group of subsystems. Each subsystem can be diagnosed separately, after which the subsystems can be conceptually reassembled into a total system. Any action back upon A from a point beyond it in the chain of action may be called *feedback*. The term "feedback" has sharpest meaning in connection with controlled systems, to be discussed below. In an uncontrolled system in which A affects B while B also affects A, the feedback is mutual, and it seems preferable to use the term "mutual interaction."

For even the simplest feedback system, ordinary analysis of cause and effect is inadequate, and a distinct type of analysis is needed to supplement the causal relations in such a system. We will call this the analysis of feedback systems.[9] Feedback systems can be divided in turn into uncontrolled and controlled systems. The latter are also known as *cybernetic*, or *servo*-systems.

Uncontrolled Feedback Systems

An uncontrolled system can be illustrated by an open tank, into which water flows from above, and out of which it flows through a pipe at the bottom. Assuming a constant input at the top, and an outlet pipe capable of discharging that input if some pressure is exerted, we find the following feedback relation. Starting with an empty tank, when the water rises just high enough in the tank to cover the outlet, the water will not flow out as fast as it flows in, since there is very little pressure behind it. The level of water will therefore rise. As it rises the rate of output will also increase, since the pressure at the outlet is directly proportional to the height of the water. The water level will continue to rise until it creates pressure at the outlet just sufficient to discharge the water as fast as it comes in. Assuming no change in any other forces, the height of the water will remain stable at this equilibrium level. This set of relations is a feedback system, because the rate of discharge is a cause of the height of water in the tank, while the height of the water is simultaneously a cause of the rate of discharge.

A feedback system can reach an equilibrium under certain conditions. First, the input and output capacity must be within a certain range. If a tank with a one-inch outlet receives Niagara Falls as input, it will be full at all times, since the input-output ratio is beyond the range in which an equilibrium is possible. In the opposite direction, if a normal kitchen sink receives only the slow drip from a leaky faucet as input, the sink will be empty at all times, as this input-output ratio is also beyond the range which permits an equilibrium. Second, a stable equilibrium is possible only if the causal relation is *direct* in one direction, and *inverse* in the other. In the tank, for example, the rate of discharge varies *directly* with the height of the water, but the height of the water varies *inversely* with the rate of discharge. In a thermostatically controlled heating system, the temperature of the room varies directly with the amount of fire in the

---

[9] If the term "system" were not already so strongly intrenched in describing sets which do not necessarily include feedback, it might be desirable to refer to unilateral action as causal analysis, and bilateral action as system analysis. The term "system" would then encompass only those things which are now known as feedback systems, though with the broader sense of mutuality described just above. We cannot apply the term "cybernetic" to all feedback analysis, since mutual interaction also occurs in feedback systems which have no governor and no goal, as will be seen below. Instead of having *causal analysis* and *system analysis* as the two basic types of the science of events (the apparently preferable arrangement), unless we can either dethrone the term "system" from part of its present use, or give it this additional, special meaning, we must apparently content ourselves with naming the two approaches "causal analysis" and "feedback system analysis." The latter terminology is used here.

furnace (the more the furnace burns, the higher is the temperature in the house), while the amount of fire varies inversely with the temperature (the hotter the room, the less will the furnace operate). In an economic system both supply and demand are related to price. An equilibrium price of potato chips is possible, because the supply varies *directly* with price (the higher the price the more will be offered for sale), while demand varies *inversely* (the higher the price the less will be purchased). An equilibrium position is also possible with two continuous variables, both of which are direct or both inverse if they show a different degree of slope, so that the lines cross when graphed. The equilibrium will be unstable, however, and we will confine attention to the stable equilibriums of opposing slopes.

In any feedback system, if the relation is direct in both directions, the system will "explode" if the variables get started in an upward direction, or shrink to zero if they get started downward. For example, if we can somehow imagine that in the tank a faster discharge would cause the level of water to rise, which would cause a still faster discharge, which would cause a still higher level, and so on, the tank would in due time overflow. This would end the original system, as there no longer would be any relation between water height and rate of discharge. A burning house is an "explosive" system: the greater the fire the higher the temperature, and the higher the temperature the greater the ensuing fire. To return to the tank, if the water level starts down, it would get lower and lower if both relations are direct, until the tank were empty, and it would stay empty. If the relationship were inverse in both directions, the system would also either expand or contract till it either overflowed its capacity or emptied itself. This relation is universal. If the relations are both direct or both inverse the system cannot reach stable equilibrium, nor, except by accident, can it continue to exist in its original form. Although the tangible ingredients of the system, such as the tank or economy, may not go out of existence, the *elements* of the system (which will be explained below), cease to exist.

Cybernetic Systems, or Controlled Feedback Systems

In an uncontrolled system like the tank and the economic system, the equilibrium is not *controlled*. If the inflow of water is increased, the equilibrium level of the water will rise. If the outlet hole is enlarged, the equilibrium level will fall. Nothing in the system functions to keep the water at a constant level in the face of changes of other variables. If the demand for potato chips rises, or the supply falls, the price will rise. In a free market system no control is exerted to keep the price at any particular level, and the actual level is that which brings an equilibrium of supply and demand. The equilibrium could conceivably occur at ten cents a pound, or at ten dollars.

By contrast, a controlled system is one in which at least one of the variables is kept at a constant level. That is, the system produces a *particular* level of equilibrium, not just *an* equilibrium. The thermostatic control in a house and the system of floats and valves in the household toilet tank are examples of mechanisms designed to maintain temperature or water at some fixed level. Named for a Greek word meaning "steersmanship," these are called *cybernetic* systems, a cybernetic system being a steered, controlled, or governed system. Norbert Wiener, the founder of the science of cybernetics, defined the field as "the science of control and communication, in the animal and the machine,"[10] while Ashby defines its domain as the study of "all possible machines."[11] The term "machine" is construed broadly to include any animate or inanimate system. Some of the advanced levels of cybernetics are highly complex and mathematical, but the essentials are not.

Most of our study of human beings and of society deals with selective, or adaptive, behavior. This does not involve simple responses to some force, but responses selected to improve the chances of reaching some goal. Hence, the cybernetic system is the primary tool for analyzing goal-directed behavior.

We have seen that action-at-a-distance is rejected as impossible, while we accept the notion that some connection between a force and its effect is the minimum condition for cause-effect relations. In the same sense we can say that the cybernetic system is the minimum additional condition for controlled, adaptive, or selective behavior. By extension, it is also a prerequisite for learning.

Figure 3-1 illustrates a simple cybernetic system for controlling the water level in a tank at a given height. Here the water flows in at the right. The inflow is not controlled, but the outflow is controllable by a valve in the discharge pipe. Through three connected rods, this valve is controlled in turn by a float on top of the water. (We will ignore for the present the part of the lever and rod drawn in broken lines which lead to a valve in the input pipe, assuming for the moment that it is not present.) Whenever the level of water is low, the block in the outlet valve will drop all the way to the bottom of the outflow pipe, stopping all discharge. Any water entering the tank under those conditions will remain there. If water continues to enter, the float will eventually rise, opening the discharge valve. Once the water has reached the prescribed level it will remain there, with only small variation. If no water flows in, none will flow out; but when water is flowing in, it will be allowed to flow out. The level at which this balance will occur will depend upon the lengths of the float arm, the valve arm, and the control lever, and the

---

[10] Norbert Wiener, *Cybernetics* (New York: John Wiley & Sons, Inc., 1961), subtitle.

[11] W. Ross Ashby, *An Introduction to Cybernetics* (New York: John Wiley & Sons, Inc., 1958), p. 2.

Figure 3-1

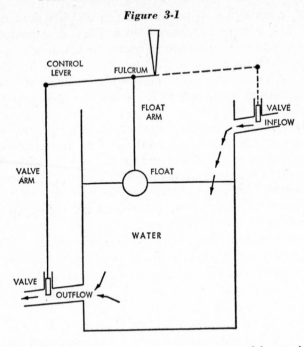

point at which the float arm is attached to the control lever. A change in any one of these items would change the equilibrium height of the water.

As in the earlier illustration, the rate of discharge varies directly with the water level, while the water level varies inversely with the rate of discharge, this oppositeness of relationship being essential to a stable system. But, unlike the earlier illustration, this one contains a *governor*, in the form of the float, lever, and valve arrangement, which maintains the equilibrium at a *particular* level. A governor can accomplish this result by changing the value of some variable in the system in such a way as to offset, or compensate for, a change in some other variable which otherwise would push from its equilibrium position the variable which is to be kept at some desired level. Without reference to whether human desires are reflected in any way, or whether the system came into existence by design or accident, the particular level at which the equilibrium will be maintained by the system is called the *goal* of the system.

A cybernetic system involves at least three variables. First is the one not controlled, which may change for reasons outside the system. This is the input in Figure 3-1. Second is the variable to be kept at a constant level, which is the water level in Figure 3-1. Third is the variable which is acted on so as to offset any changes in the first variable, this compensating change being the means of keeping the second variable at the desired level.

In Figure 3-1, the system could be rearranged to put any of the three elements in any of the three positions. If the outflow, rather than the inflow, were beyond the control of the system, then a different lever (shown in broken lines) could control the inflow so as to maintain the water level constant. By more complicated mechanics it would also be possible within limits to keep either the inflow or the outflow constant, but our main attention centers on keeping some value in the "middle" of the system constant by controlling the output to compensate for changing inputs, or vice versa.

Components. The minimum components of a cybernetic system are (1) a *detector*, or sensor, which is sensitive to the state of the variable to be controlled; (2) a *selector*, or governor, which is capable of selecting among two or more possible responses, on the basis of (a) the information sensed by the detector and (b) the "preference" of the governor; and (3) an *effector*, which is capable of producing some change in the state of affairs sensed by the detector. These three functions can be diagrammed in a triangular relationship.

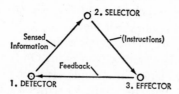

In Figure 3-1, the float is the *detector* which senses the height of the water. The fact that the float arm is fastened to the control lever to the left of the fulcrum determines the direction of the response, and therefore constitutes the *governor*, or *selector*. To anthropomorphize, when the float arm is connected to the left of the fulcrum, the governor "prefers" to open the valve and let more water flow out when the water level rises above the "goal" level. If the float arm were connected to the control lever on the right hand side of the fulcrum, it would produce the opposite effect on the control lever, reflecting an opposite "preference." The outlet valve is the *effector*, which speeds or slows the discharge of water and keeps the water in the tank at the prescribed level.

In the diagrams of most cybernetic systems the arrows indicate a communication between the parts. The communication may take the form of language, electrical impulses, mechanical connections, chemical changes, or other forces. The term is used here in the broadest possible sense, meaning that some force must act between the sensor and the governor so that the latter will be modified by—i.e., contain information about—the former. In Figure 3-1 the float arm communicates information about the water level from the float to the control lever, and the valve arm communicates the selected "instruction" to the valve to open or close. The result of the behavior of the valve is fed back to the float by the height of the water, to complete the triangular circuit. The float then once again senses the water level, communicates it to the control lever, and so on.

A widely familiar mechanical cybernetic system is the thermostatic control of the temperature in a house. Assuming that it is cold outdoors, if we start with furnace off, the temperature will in due time drop below the level for which the thermostat is set, because of the outflow of heat from the house. A detector in the thermostat box will sense this condition. On the basis of this detection, the thermostat will select between the on and off positions of a switch, at this point turning it on. The switch will turn on the furnace, which is the effector. Thereupon the temperature will rise in the house till the detector senses that it is higher than the prescribed level, the selector will turn the switch off, and the furnace will stop producing heat. The cycle can be repeated indefinitely.

Similar results can also be achieved by different arrangements. For example, if we are trying to control the temperature of a small box instead of a house, rather than control the fire we might control the distance between the box and the fire, moving the box closer when the fire is low, and farther away when it is high.

The three components of the cybernetic system should be thought of as functions, or operations, rather than parts. One, two, or even all three operations may be combined in a single element. The thermostat in an automobile cooling system, for example, senses a change in temperature by expanding or contracting. This same expansion or contraction is simultaneously both the selecting and effecting mechanism. Under most circumstances, and in nearly all involving human beings, the detector, selector, and effector are distinct, and communication between them is a separate element. For most human behavior, the perception system is the detector, the motive system the selector, and the muscles the effectors, with communication between them through the nervous system. In organizations the three functions are usually performed by different persons or groups.

Any cybernetic system so arranged as to maintain any one particular state, such as that of Figure 3-1, or the household thermostat, is called a *homeostatic* system. The human body contains many homeostatic systems, including those which maintain body temperature, blood count, blood sugar, bile, oxygen content, stomach acid, and hormones, either at constant levels, or at levels appropriate to the particular condition of the body. It is also possible to produce a homeostatic rate of change. For a certain period, at least, by attaching a clock mechanism to a household thermostat the system could be made to maintain the room at a temperature which rises or falls by one degree per day. We have been searching for decades for a homeostatic governor, either automatic or consciously controlled, which would eliminate the booms and depressions of our economic system in favor of a steady level of activity. More recently we have been seeking to discover and utilize, if feasible, the kind of governor which would provide a homeostatic rate of growth of the economy, at perhaps 4 to 6 per cent a year.

Oscillation

We have talked thus far as if a cybernetic system could maintain some variable, such as water level or temperature, at some value, with no change whatsoever. This is not precisely the case. The value of the controlled variable must *change* somewhat before the sensor can detect the change, and start compensating actions. The movement between the low point and the high point is called *oscillation*, which may arise from either insensitivity or delay.

Suppose a thermostat is insensitive, being unable to detect a change until the room temperature is 5 degrees above or below the setting. If set for 70 degrees, such a thermostat would not turn the furnace on until the temperature dropped to 65, or turn it off until the temperature rose to 75. This system would oscillate between 65 and 75. If the thermostat were sensitive to 1 degree deviation, the oscillations would be confined to the range of 69 to 71 degrees.

As to delays, suppose there is a lapse between the time the furnace is turned on and the time the heat gets into the room, and that the temperature falls another 5 degrees during this interval. Suppose also that once the furnace is hot it continues to feed heat into the room after it is turned off, and that the temperature rises another five degrees during that interval. Even if the thermostat were perfectly sensitive, this lag would allow an oscillation of 10 degrees. If the system shows both insensitivity and lag, the total oscillation will normally be the sum of the two separate ones. For example, if the thermostat shows 5 degrees of insensitivity and the heat distribution system a 5 degree lag, the temperature in the room would oscillate between 60 and 80 degrees. Business cycles are oscillations of the economic system which show both insensitivity and lag.

A *damper*, or *damping effect*, is any force or process which restrains or reduces the scope of the oscillation, and need not be discussed further here. Insensitivity or delay in *any* element of the system could produce oscillation. Since no detector is infinitely sensitive, and no governor or effector can operate without some time lapse, some oscillation seems unavoidable in any cybernetic system, unless (1) the system exists in a perfectly stable environment, in which case no control system is necessary, or (2) the changes in the controlled variable can be predicted, and compensating action can be instituted before the change occurs. The first situation would be illustrated by the house located in a climate which was always 70 degrees, and the second if the control system were geared to the rate of heat loss through the walls so that heat would be fed into the room at the same rate it was being lost. This would be similar to a modification of the system in Figure 3-1 so that the inflow would be controlled from the outflow, instead of from the height of the water.

SOME GENERAL CHARACTERISTICS OF SYSTEMS

Examples of physical systems have been cited above, because their physical ingredients are more sharply definable than other types, and, hence, most clearly convey the idea of a system. Within recent years the analysis of systems has moved to the point where their general characteristics can be described without regard to whether the components are physical, biological, psychological, or social. This fact makes the physical examples useful, even though this book is concerned with matters of psychology and social science. System analysis shows much evidence of being an extremely useful way of examining a very wide variety of problems. Hence, the characteristics of systems deserve attention.

Systems and Subsystems

We have already seen that many things can be thought of as a hierarchy of systems, from the tiniest things we know to the whole of the universe. The earth and the moon are a system. This is a subsystem of the solar system, which is a subsystem within our galaxy, and so on. The same kind of relation also occurs in social and biological systems.

For any one system, the larger system to which it belongs is its *environment*, and the smaller systems within it are its *components*. Any system must contain at least two interacting components, or it is not a system, the interaction of the parts being a distinctive part of the system. A table knife is not a system, for example. Its only components which interact are its molecules, but their interaction is in no way distinctive, being the same as if the same piece of metal were a spoon or part of a camera.

A given system may be a component of two different systems. A human being can simultaneously be a component in a social system and in a "natural" system, the latter including his inputs and outputs of air and food. The nerves which control the heart are simultaneously parts of the nervous and circulatory systems, while the rear wheels of an automobile belong to both a propulsion and a braking system. Each of the larger systems to which a given system belongs is part of its environment, and it may respond to two or more simultaneously. For purposes of analysis, any interaction of the parts of a system may be referred to as the "behavior" of that system, and all "behavior" in the universe can be thought of as interactions of parts of systems among themselves, or of systems with their environment or subsystems.

Boundaries of Systems

The *boundaries* of a system are not inherent characteristics of things, but of the kind of problem facing the person who is studying or dealing with the system. We can clarify the meaning of boundaries by describing how we define a system. Defining a system is the process of listing its

components as contrasted to the elements of components of its environment, the boundary being the distinction between what is inside and what
is outside the system. The boundaries may be physical limits, in the sense
that the cell wall is the limit of a living cell. Or they may be behavioral or
functional limits, in the sense that a given radio communications system at
a given moment includes all persons who are listening in, and excludes
those who are not. A supply and demand system for parsnips includes all
persons currently interested in buying or selling parsnips, and excludes
all others.

We can illustrate the statement that boundaries depend on the problem at hand, not on the "nature of things," as follows. If we are interested in the internal relations of parts within a human muscle cell, the
cell wall is the boundary of the cell system, and the blood flowing around
it is part of the cell's environment. But if we are interested in the whole
nutrition system, the muscle cell, the blood, and the digestive tract all
fall inside the system, while the brain, bones, and ears fall outside it. If
we are interested in the automobile as a propulsion mechanism, the motor,
gears, and wheels fall within the system, while the highway and gasoline
station lie outside. If we are interested in the whole physical system of
automobile transportation, the automobile, highway, and gasoline stations
are components, while the railroads and state taxes are outside the system.
If, however, our attention is focused on the economics of total transportation, then the railroads and the state taxes (including those *for* roads
and *on* railroads) are part of the system. If any given study is to be fruitful, the boundaries of the system must be appropriate to the problem.

Any effect of the environment on a given system is an *input* to the
system, and any effect of the system on its environment is an *output*. The
effect of one component on another component within the system is a
functional relation (or interaction) within the system. Inputs and outputs are functional relations between the system and its environment,
which is another way of saying that they are functional relations within
some larger system in which both the smaller system and its environment
are components. In the thermostatically controlled room, the relations
among room temperature, thermostat, and furnace all are functional relations within the system. Flows of heat in or out through the wall constitute inputs or outputs, respectively between the system and its environment.[12] The furnace meanwhile is a subsystem of the heating system
with many internal relations of its own. It also has environmental relations which can be ignored in the room-control system, such as inputs
of fuel and outputs of smoke.

---

[12] However, if the outside wall of the room is only a few feet from another
building, and we are interested in the temperature of the air between buildings,
then this outside air, and the air in the room, are both elements of a larger system,
which also includes the temperature inside the other building. Here again we find
the mutual interaction which characterizes a system, the temperature in that space-
way affecting the operating time of the furnace, while the operation of the furnace
also affects the temperature in that space.

In controlled, or cybernetic, systems, the setting of the governor is done by the larger system which is the environment of the cybernetic system. The thermostat is not set at 70 degrees by the thermostat system itself, but by the human beings whose feelings of warmth or coolness are the governor of the larger system to which the heating system belongs. The governor of the temperature-regulating system in the human body is not set for 98.6 degrees by that system itself, but by the evolutionary system of which it is a part. As we shall see later, the sense of right and wrong which in part governs the behavior system of the individual is not established by the individual, but mainly by the cultural system to which he belongs. In the language to be introduced below, the setting of the governor of a cybernetic system is a parameter of that system, determined by its environment.

IS THIS A SYSTEM?

If the feedback system is to take its place beside cause-effect relations as a tool of rigorous scientific analysis, the system itself must be carefully defined and described. The requirements of systems have been well summarized by Hagen.[13] First, the analytical system is defined by defining its elements and their interrelationships. This step has already been discussed above, by noting that the components within the system must be listed, and be distinguished from the components of the environment. The process of separating these two things defines the boundaries of the system.

A second point is highly important, but widely overlooked. The elements, or components, of a system are *not* the *entities* in the system, but qualities or states of those entities. In the thermostatic system, it is not the air in the room, but its temperature, which is the element in the system. It is not the thermostat, but the position of its switch. It is not the furnace, but its state of being on or off. Similarly, the environment is not the outside air, but the temperature of the outside air, along with the properties of the wall which determine how fast heat will move between system and environment. In order to introduce the notion of a system, the preceding discussion was simplified by referring to the thermostat, air, and furnace as elements. Having done that, we must now note that the elements of systems are states or conditions of things, not the things themselves. In systems involving persons, it is not the *person* who is an element, but his state of hunger, his desire for companionship, his state of information, or some other trait or quality relevant to the system.

Third, an element in a system must be capable of taking two or more alternative states of values, and these differences must be discriminable. That is, it *must be a variable*, not a constant, and its changes in state must be observable and measurable. The person must be capable of being hungry or not hungry (or some intermediate state), the thermostat must

---

[13] Everett E. Hagen, "Analytical Models in the Study of Social Systems," *The American Journal of Sociology* (September, 1961), pp. 144–51.

be on or off, the air must be hot or cold, and it must be possible to discern which state prevails. The functional relationships to be studied are not the relations between the air and the thermostat, but between the temperature of the air and the on-or-off position of the thermostat. The functional relationship can then be described as follows. The two possible states of the air are *above* 70 degrees and *below* 70 degrees, and the two possible states of the thermostat are *on* or *off*. The *on* position of the thermostat is then functionally related to the *below* state of the air, while the *off* position of the thermostat is functionally associated with the *above* state of the air. In a system involving a human being and eating, it is not the person and the food we are interested in, but the hungry or not-hungry state of the person (one variable) and his eating or not eating (the second variable).

Fourth, for some types of study a system should be "closed," by which we mean that it should be isolated during the study from changes in its environment. If we are studying the relation between breathing and oxygen content of the blood, and wish to understand the mutual interactions between the two variables, we should keep the rate of exertion constant through the period of study, as well as the oxygen content of the air being breathed. Assuming the subject is not burning up oxygen faster than his lungs can supply it, we will discover that for a given rate of exertion and a given oxygen content of the air, a given rate of breathing will keep blood oxygen constant. The percentage of oxygen in the air and the rate of exertion are outside the system under immediate study, which includes only blood oxygen and breathing rate.

Any state or magnitude determined wholly outside the system, and which remains unchanged during the period of study is called a *parameter*. The outside temperature is a parameter for the study of the thermostat system, and air oxygen and exertion rate are parameters for the study of the system of breathing and blood content. For a given set of parameters, it could then be observed how fast the breathing rate would be, or how many minutes per hour the furnace would be turned on in order to maintain blood oxygen or room temperature at a given level.

Fifth, once the set of equilibrium conditions for one set of parameters has been determined, the system can be "opened," by which we mean that a change in parameters might be observed or allowed. If the original study of the thermostat system was made when the outside temperature was 50 degrees, the same study might be made again with an outside temperature of 30. If the first study of breathing rate was made under relaxation, a second study might be made under moderate exercise.

If a system is allowed to reach an equilibrium under one set of parameters, if the system then undergoes a change in parameters and is allowed to reach an equilibrium under the new parameters, and if the change in parameters is compared with the change in equilibrium states, such a study is called *comparative statics*. If a continuous series of different parameters is compared with the corresponding series of equilibrium positions, such a study is said to deal with a *moving equilibrium*.

Sixth, the study of a system in a state of disequilibrium, and the successive steps it goes through in the process of reaching equilibrium, is known as *dynamics*. For example, if a person goes from a state of rest to a state of moderate exertion, his breathing rate will not jump instantaneously to a new, higher rate. It will not rise at all at first, as the muscles work for a while on the existing "inventory" of oxygen in the blood. Because of the faster rate of oxygen usage, the oxygen level of the blood will fall, whereupon the breathing control center will step up the rate of breathing. For a while the increased rate of breathing will not only have to take care of the higher rate of oxygen consumption, but will also have to make up for the accumulated deficit. Once this deficit has been made up, the breathing can slow somewhat to the level needed to maintain the higher consumption rate—the so-called "second wind." Whereas a study of comparative statics provides information mainly about the relation between a system and its environment, a study of dynamics reveals the nature of the internal operations of the system, and the functional relationships of the various elements in the system.[14]

Seventh, and finally, any value or magnitude which does not change is not an element, or component. This is another way of saying that the elements of the system consist solely of variables. If the arteries expand or contract so as to transport a larger or smaller volume of blood at a given level of blood pressure, the diameter of the arteries (not the arteries themselves) is a variable in the circulatory system, and hence is one of its elements. If the diameter of the arteries remains unchanged, no matter what happens to other elements, it is a constant, and therefore cannot be considered an element. This does not mean, of course, that the size of the arteries is immaterial, since it is obviously highly important. It means that the arteries serve as parameters, or environmental limitations, not as active elements. Further, if anything connected with the system changes, but the change does not affect any element, the thing which changes is also not part of the system. For example, if the arteries should change color as the oxygen content of the blood rises, but the change of color in no way affects the performance of the circulatory system, the change of color is not an element in the system. In short, an item must not only be a variable, but it must both *affect* and *be affected by* other variables if it is to be an element.

Learning in Systems

The meaning of learning in the ordinary sense is clear. Just as many other terms have been accorded parallel usage in animate and inanimate

---

14 The present usage of these terms follows Hagen, *ibid.*, pp. 147–48. As he notes, within the social sciences, the term "comparative statics" is used solely in economics, while in psychology the term "dynamics" has two distinct and confusing uses, both of which seem so well established as not to be lightly unseated.

applications, the term "learning" can also be extended to cover inanimate systems. If, as a result of a given input, some element in the system is changed in such a way that, when the same input is received again, either the output or the equilibrium position, or both, is different from its value the first time that input was received, learning has occurred. In psychology, *learning* is said to exist when, as the result of experience, a given stimulus (input) elicits a different response (output) than it did before. If we think of the "response" as including the extraction of information from a given stimulus input, or think of a change of information state as a new "equilibrium," the above definition clearly includes learning in the ordinary sense.

In Figure 3-1, if the float arm could be pushed along the control lever, some occasional spurts of inflow might push it to the left. With the float arm attached to the control lever a greater distance from the fulcrum, the equilibrium level would now be different than before, and we could say that the system has "learned" from the sudden spurts of input.

A human system in which learning occurs can include more than one person. The detector might be an observer in the reconnaissance plane of an army. The information he detects about the enemy is transmitted to the general. The general is the selector, determining what action should be taken in light of his goals and the incoming information. The response he selects is transmitted to the troops, who are the effectors. The cybernetic cycle is complete when the detectors transmit a feedback of information to the selector about the new state of affairs after the effectors have acted.

Learning and nonlearning systems show an extremely important difference in ability to adapt and survive. The homeostatic nonlearning system can achieve and maintain a given goal through a certain range of environmental change. But beyond that range either it is engulfed by its input, or has insufficient input to function. In either event it ceases to function as a system, which is the equivalent of death or coma. A learning system, by contrast, is capable of changing its goals as it acquires new information about its environment. Although not all such learning increases the ability of the *particular* system to survive, systems which can learn have a much higher average survival potential in the face of a changing or complex environment than those which cannot. As we shall see in subsequent chapters, the human being is by far the most versatile adaptive system we know, and is able to adapt both its behavior and its goals over an extremely wide range of environment.

CONCLUDING OBSERVATIONS

This chapter is intended in part to say some new things, but in greater part to express some old ideas in new language. "New" does not mean that these things have not previously been said, but that this particular way of approaching them is only a decade or so old. The language of this approach is deliberately designed to be universal, in the sense that we need not change vocabulary or method of analysis when we move from one field of study to another, even if the fields are as different as astronomy, anthropology, zoology, and computer technology.

If the reader is upset at finding mechanistic language applied to human beings, or humanistic language applied to the inanimate, let him recall that we are dealing here only with analytical tools—with ways of thinking about problems—which show promise of increasing our understanding. The human being is not one whit less human because we examine his tissues with a microscope, analyze his skeleton as a set of levers, or discover that his nerves operate electrically and that his eye is a lens. The purpose of the language, like the whole of this book, is to try to reduce the number of concepts needed to understand the world around us, including human behavior. Whether this approach will ultimately be found to be useful, only time will tell. But it does seem worth a trial.

In recent years, systems research has grown hugely. Among other things, the present chapter has attempted to single out the unique feature of the system as a technique of scientific analysis. This seems to be the *mutual* cause-effect relation, which requires an approach beyond and distinct from traditional causal analysis. It is the core of the analysis of equilibrium, adaptive systems having survival value, including the human brain. As we shall see, we can sometimes acquire new understanding of long familiar things merely by viewing them as a system, and asking the questions appropriate to system analysis.

If this chapter has seemed somewhat formidable to some readers, they need not despair. Although a full sense of what it describes will considerably deepen the understanding of some of the chapters which follow, the major sense of those chapters can be grasped without the present one. Even if the present chapter is not followed in detail, a reading of it should help to give some of the *feel* of the present-day approach to things.

Chapter 4

HUMAN INFORMATION
PROCESSES

HUMAN BEINGS receive information in the form of signals. But they are not mere machines for receiving and storing information. They engage in adaptive behavior. By this we mean that on the basis of information received about the world around them, they select behavior which is in some measure adapted to their environment and to their own wishes. In layman's language, they adapt because life is pleasanter or lasts longer than if they don't. There are many possible responses to any situation, and adaptive behavior consists of choosing the relatively satisfactory responses in preference to the relatively unsatisfactory ones.

Now adaptation is not mere conformance—not the mere molding of behavior to environment. It is rather a matter of discovering what is possible, and then of selecting the *preferred* behavior from among the *possible* alternatives. Those things which are possible will be referred to as *opportunities*. The group of opportunities available in a particular situation can be described as an *opportunity set*, or an *opportunity system*. Those opportunities which the individual has information about, or is aware of, are his *perceived opportunity set*, which he learns about through his *information system*, *information processes*, or *information inputs*. Decisions about these matters are known as *factual judgments*, or *scientific judgments*.

But information alone does not determine behavior, since behavior consists of pursuing some opportunities and neglecting others. In addition to his information mechanisms, the human being also consists in part of a switching mechanism which selects between the opportunities to be pursued and those to be neglected. This switching mechanism can be referred to as *motives*, or as a *motive system*. It can also be referred to as *preferences*, or as a *preference system*, or a set of likes and dislikes. The former term is used primarily in connection with the psychological aspects of behavior and the latter with the conscious decision aspects, but there is no hard and fast dividing line between the two sets of terms. Decisions about these matters are also known as *value judgments*.[1] The whole problem involved here will be discussed in later chapters on decision.

Behavior thus does not depend on either information or motives taken alone, but on the interaction of the two. Hence, an understanding of human behavior requires attention to both. These items provide the elements of a cybernetic system, in which (1) the detector is the concept and perception system which discerns what opportunities are available, (2) the selector, or governor, is the motive system which reflects preferences, and (3) the effectors are the muscles and the motor nerves which control them. Our next problem is to examine the nature and relationships of these components of the human behavioral system.

THE NATURE OF THE PROBLEM

As you are walking down the street, suppose you spot a twenty dollar bill flapping lazily on the sidewalk. With or without knowing any psychology, I can predict rather reliably that you will pick it up. In psychological lingo, I can say that you received the stimulus of perceiving the bill, and gave the response of picking it up. In the language of an information processing system, I might say that you received an informational input in the form of light signals reflected from the bill, processed that information, and gave the behavioral output of picking up the twenty. Although we will use both kinds of statements, and perhaps others at some later points, we will examine human learning and behavior primarily as an information processing system—the model which seems most useful for the overall purposes of the present volume.

The problem can be outlined by examining further the act of picking up the twenty dollar bill. True, you received the stimulus of seeing the bill and gave the response of picking it up. But at approximately the same moment that you did this, you also saw pavement, people, shop windows, traffic lights, and sky. Further, you simultaneously heard people talking, horns blowing, and brakes screeching, while you also smelled exhaust, felt sweaty, ached in the feet, and thirsted in the throat. Of all the many stimuli reaching your brain at that moment, why did you attend to this one? Further, how did you know what it was—since you obviously were

---

[1] In some of the psychological literature the terminology is used as follows. The motive, or preference, side of the fence uses such terms as drive, motivation, conation, emotion, and libido—all of which are *activating* agents. On the other side are concepts, habit strengths, associative tendencies, ego, and cognitive maps, which, when taken in conjunction with external stimuli, are *guiding* agents which determine the direction of behavior. Some persons object that this distinction is not tenable, since some forces, such as shock, affect both aspects simultaneously. This kind of argument is a short cut to chaos for all science. It is equivalent to suggesting that physicists should not distinguish between the magnitude of a force and its direction, since no force can exist without both magnitude and direction. It is precisely the ability of scientists to isolate conceptually those things which are not isolable in fact which makes science possible. For a short discussion of this problem, see Judson S. Brown, *The Motivation of Behavior* (New York: McGraw-Hill Book Co., Inc., 1961), pp. 57–60.

not born with the ability to recognize a twenty dollar bill? And finally, why did you pick it up instead of kicking it down the sewer or ignoring it?

To outline the main directions of our search for answers, we can note first that some kind of *selective process* operated on your information input. Of all the visual, tactile, aural, and other stimuli impinging on your nervous system at that moment, your system selected the light waves reflected from that twenty as the information input on which to focus, as information about other things receded into the background. Next, these visual signals were decoded. That is, they were interpreted as representing a twenty dollar bill, not a leaf, a spot of paint, a French horn, or an oil well. This decoding is also a selective process.

Having selected a particular information input, you next selected a response. You could have screamed and fled, lighted a match, gone home and planted sesame seeds in your ear, or urged your congressman to vote against aid to Viet Nam. Among a near infinitude of possible behavioral outputs, you selected that of picking up the money.

The perception of the twenty dollar bill can be described as a stimulus, and picking it up is the ensuing response. The study of stimulus-response (SR) psychology has made indispensible contributions to our understanding of learning and behavior, whether the SR relations have been studied in rats, pigeons, monkeys, or human beings. But much more is required than simple SR if we are to understand the whole range of human behavior. In a previous chapter we noted that in most situations we possess far more information than we are currently receiving. This is possible because the small amount of information currently received is added to, or taken in conjunction with, information previously received. In the present example, if we had not had previous experience with money, in which we learned both to identify and to want it, we might have paid no attention to that little green spot on the pavement. In short, a stimulus is not merely a batch of sensory signals, but the outcome of an information processing operation in which those signals are only a part.

The whole of this information process is very complex, and we know some things about it, but not others. In the information model through which we will attempt to describe human behavior, we will distinguish two major steps of information input. First, an individual must develop the system in which he will code his information, the code, or coding system, also being describable as a classification system, or categorizing system. The process of doing this will be considered identical with what pychologists refer to as *concept learning*. For reasons to be seen later, we will construe the notion of concept learning, or conceptualization, broadly enough to include the learning and use of language and other symbols. We will also tentatively identify this process with what the logicians and philosophers refer to as induction.

Second, once we possess a set of concepts we can identify particular receipts of information as representing particular things in our environment, the process we call *perception*. To illustrate the relation of concept learning and perception, we cannot identify a batch of green light rays entering our eyes as representing a twenty dollar bill until we have learned what paper money *is*—that is, until we have learned the *concept* of paper money. Nor could we have identified it as a leaf or a spot of paint (if that is what it had been) until we first had formed the concepts of leaf or paint. To follow the terms defined in Chapters 2 and 3, we can *sense* signals without learning, but we cannot *interpret* their meaning until we possess a concept of the thing they represent. In information language, we can *detect* signals by sense organs alone (without learning), but we cannot *decode* them until we have first learned the code. However, once we have learned a set of concepts, or code, we can receive information about our environment when we have detected *and* decoded (information language), or we can perceive when we have sensed *and* interpreted (psychological language).

Since the detection of signals requires no learning, our main interest in perception lies in the second step, that of classifying or interpreting. Is that spot of green on the pavement money, paint, vegetation, or something else? We make this act of classification (categorizing, or identifying) on the basis of certain cues which we have already learned to be associated in certain ways with certain concepts. We will also tentatively suggest that this process is the same as that of deduction, which we will tentatively define as the process of making identifications from cues.[2]

When we are interested in perception as a general process of acquiring information, it can be referred to simply as perception. When we are interested in a *particular* perception, particularly in the context of trying to relate a behavioral response to it, we can refer to the perception as the

---

[2] I have argued elsewhere in favor of identifying inductive processes with concept formation and code formation, and of identifying deductive processes with perception and making identifications from cues. See "Toward a Uniform Language of Information and Knowledge," *Synthese,* Vol. XIII, No. 2 (June, 1961). Attneave utilizes both steps under the process of perception alone. He suggests that in the learning stage (which I would classify as part of the stage of concept formation) a perceiver locates the points which transmit the most information, after which in the performance stage he utilizes these cues as means of identifying the stimulus. See F. Attneave, *Applications of Information Theory to Psychology* (New York: Henry Holt & Co., 1959). Charles M. Solley and Gardner Murphy do not use this approach even modestly in their *Development of the Perceptual World* (New York: Basic Books, 1960), the term "concept" appearing neither in their index nor their glossary, and their process of perceiving not seeming explicitly (on the basis of a quick survey of the book) to depend on prior concept formation. Nor does William Dember, in his *The Psychology of Perception* (New York: Henry Holt & Co., 1960), make perceptions dependent on prior concepts. Because the information model, with its code formation and code utilization, *does* seem tentatively to correspond to concept formation and perception in psychology, and with induction and deduction in logic, it seems potentially a powerful tool of analysis, and hence is used here.

identification of a stimulus. We should never lose sight of the fact, however, that in our model a stimulus cannot be responded to until it is identified—that is, perceived. For probably the great majority of stimuli received by persons beyond infancy, the stimulus cannot be perceived unless a concept of the stimulus has previously been formed. Reflexes are, of course, excepted, and so, conceivably, may be a limited list of more complex stimulus identifications and related responses somewhat similar to those involved in instinctive behavior in other animals, depth perception being a possible case in point.[3] The statement above involves a potential circularity. It indicates that perceptions generally cannot take place without prior concepts, but it might also be alleged with equal force that concepts cannot be formed without prior perceptions. We will deal with this problem in later chapters on concepts. Responses, and the learning of responses, will also be examined later.

To summarize thus far, the purpose of the next several chapters will be to examine the human being *as a behavorial system*. We will not attempt to quantify the component variables in this system, but merely try to identify them, and to note the major relationships among them.

In this system the inputs are information and the outputs behavior. If we wished to stretch the terminology of stimulus-response relationships, we might say that the inputs are stimuli and the outputs responses. Whichever terminology is used, however, we must be aware that in all but the simplest cases a stimulus is not the "thing" or situation which faces us, but an interpretation of the input of information from that thing, in the light of all our previous learning and experiences. In its totality this input-output relation involves not merely those principles dealt with by traditional SR psychology, but also concept learning, perception, motivation, and performance patterns, perhaps including Gestalt and Freudian psychology. Since the extent to which all of these steps may eventually be reduceable to common rules or principles is as yet unknown, it is necessary at present to deal with them in at least partially independent terms.

In the present model, the inputs of information from the senses are viewed as being handled in an information system consisting of two interacting subsystems—concepts and perceptions. Concepts are the stored information accumulated over a period of time.[4] Perceptions are the information about particular things currently happening, this information being derived by combining sensations currently received with the information stored in the concepts previously formed. Perceptions are the

---

[3] See Eleanor J. Gibson and Richard D. Walk, "The Visual Cliff," *Scientific American*, April, 1960, pp. 64 ff.

[4] So far as we now know, synaptic connections provide the physiological mechanism both for *connecting*, or relating, information and for *storing*, or remembering, it. Since concepts presumably take the form of neuron networks, the neuron connections which form this network can thus be viewed as constituting both the *patterns* and the *memory* of information.

decodings of signals currently detected, which decoding assumes that the code has already been learned.

The outputs of the system are behavior. These outputs are not random, but are *selected* from among the various responses which perceptions indicate to be possible. Selection in a system implies a *controlled system*, which in turn implies a governor. The governor which selects responses from among the perceived opportunities is a *motive*, or combination of motives.

The purpose of this chapter and the several which follow is to trace the main outlines of the processes by which outputs of behavior are related to, or proceed from, the inputs of information. We will first examine the nervous system, the primary instrument in which learning takes place, along with the so-called laws of learning. Motives, the selectors of output, will be examined next, followed by concepts and perceptions, the selectors of informational input.

THE HUMAN NERVOUS SYSTEM

The actual nervous system is incredibly complex, but consists of three main sections. The first handles the inputs of information, the third handles the outputs of behavior, and the middle "switching" section handles the connections between the other two. It is often likened to a telephone exchange, with its incoming lines, outgoing lines, and the switching mechanisms which connect the two. The analogy is useful for a rough introduction to the nervous system, but should not be carried further. Among other differences, in a telephone exchange messages go in and out over the same wires, whereas in the nervous system the incoming and outgoing "wires" are separate and distinct sets. Further, there is no meaningful similarity between the techniques of making connections in nerves and telephone systems. The two systems are similar only in that both have inputs and outputs, which are connected through a central switching mechanism.

The nervous system consists of nerves, or *neurons*, each a long, thin single biological cell. The input or *sensory nerves* come from the sense receptors, and discharge into central nerves. The outgoing *motor nerves* go to and control the muscles. *Central nerves*, which make up the brain, lie between the sensory and motor nerves, performing a pure connecting function. We also possess a whole system of autonomic nerves controlling biological functions of the body, which need not concern us further. Sensory nerves are stimulated by signals at the sense detectors, and discharge a small electric current into the central nerves. Central nerves are stimulated by the sensory nerves which feed into them, by thinking or dreaming, and (to an extent not significant to our present purposes) by random forces. Motor nerves are stimulated by the central nerves (in the form of "instructions"), and occasionally by reflexive connections with motor nerves.

Inherited or Built-in Connections

Perhaps the most important distinction for our purposes is that between built-in, inborn nerve connections of sensory and motor nerves, and noninherited, learned connections. Aside from the autonomic system, built-in connections are of two sorts. The simplest are two-neuron arcs, in which a sensory nerve feeds directly into a motor nerve, producing an immediate, specific, and unlearned reflexive response, such as the knee jerk, sneezing, coughing, withdrawal from pain, and blinking.[5] There are also some glandular reflexes, such as those for saliva or tears, which need not concern us.

The second, and much more complex, built-in connection is the instinct. *Instincts* involve not a fairly simple response to a particular stimulus, like the reflex, but a series of responses to a series of stimuli. The highly specific nest-building habits of birds; the hive-building, honey-seeking and swarming behavior of bees; the dam-building activity of beavers; and the migrations of salmon are instances of the complex, but specific, unlearned, and unmodifiable behavior which we call an instinct. Thus defined, it seems safe to say that human beings have no instincts. To examine the most elementary survival mechanism, eating, the human baby's inborn response is sucking, a simple reflex. Beyond that, as any parent can sadly report, even the simple act of putting food into the mouth is not a neatly inherited art, but a slowly and painstakingly learned one. The physical manifestations of emotions, such as the startle reaction or the smile, are essentially reflexive, even though they are more complex than the knee jerk or coughing. Unlike the instinct in the lower animals, these emotional manifestations do not involve specific responses to external, unlearned stimuli.

It might on first thought seem advantageous to have our patterns of behavior ready-made, without having to learn them. The trouble with a built-in mating dance or a built-in technique of house building is that it is the *only* technique the organism is capable of. If it does not produce the desired outcome, or if the necessary materials are not available, the animal has no alternatives. At the cost of losing an inborn ability to construct his house, the human gains the ability to make his house of any material available. The bird is born with the ability to build a house, but any possible improvement he may learn during his lifetime dies with him. The human is born without that ability, but the lack is more than offset by the ability to learn from his ancestors. In the early stone age, the advantage in favor of man might not have seemed so convincing. But since the invention of printing and the development of modern science there seems little ground for dispute—although if the insects keep de-

---

[5] More recent information would indicate that even the reflex is somewhat more complicated than the simple two-neuron arc, and probably involves some feedback. In this connection see George Miller, Eugene Galanter, and Karl Pribram, *Plans and the Structure of Behavior* (New York, Henry Holt & Co., 1960), pp. 25 and 29 f.

veloping resistance to poisons as fast as our laboratories can turn out new ones, our victory in the struggle for control may not be so certain.

THE CENTRAL NERVOUS SYSTEM

Mediated Connections

If all our neural connections were hereditary, man could neither learn nor forget behavioral responses. He might also be able to perform specific tasks with dispatch and efficiency, in the sense that the social organization in the ant hill or bee hive reaches a surprisingly high level. But surprising as activities of lower animals sometimes seem, they are surprising only compared with the widespread assumption that they are "stupid." The actions remain rudimentary compared to the capacities of man. It is fascinating, for example, to note the apparently complex system by which a bee can report back to his fellows about the direction and distance in which he has found food, or the way in which a hive of bees can "debate" for several days about the selection of the best spot for a new hive, and then "vote" on the choice.[6] But a human being can study bees, and report his findings to his fellow men in great detail; whereas if we try to imagine a reversal of these roles, we sense the vast gulf between the capacity of the bees and that of the human being to engage in widely varied behavior.

This capacity depends on the human brain, or more particularly on the cerebral cortex, which consists solely of central, connecting nerves. Since the cortex stands *between* the sensory and motor nerves, behavior which depends upon connections in the central nerves is often called *mediated* behavior. With little exception, we will confine our attention to mediated behavior, and to that portion of the brain where mediation takes place.

Unbelievably minute and complex in detail, fairly simple in basic outline, the main parts of the nervous system are shown in Figure 4-1, which is a highly simplified, schematic diagram.

The sensory nerves at the left make a point-to-point connection between the sense organ and the outer section (a) of the central sensory area (known as the central projection area). That is, each receptor cell in the eye, ear, or skin is connected directly to a specific point in the central sensory area of the brain. In consequence, if a particular point in the optical tract of the brain were destroyed, the corresponding point in the eye would go blind, a parallel situation applying for each of the other senses. And if a particular point in the optical section of one's brain is artificially stimulated with an electrical current, he will "see" a spot of light at the corresponding point in the eye. The optic nerves (like the others) can also be stimulated in part by pressure—which is why we "see stars"

---

[6] See, for example, J. B. S. Haldane, "Communication in Biology," in London University Communication Research Centre *Studies in Communication* (London: Martin Secker & Warburg, 1955), pp. 36 ff.

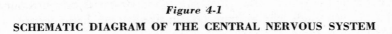

Figure 4-1
SCHEMATIC DIAGRAM OF THE CENTRAL NERVOUS SYSTEM

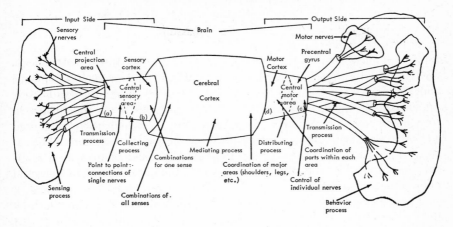

when the head is severely jolted, or "see" blobs of light when pressure is exerted on the eye.

On the right, the outer section of the motor area (known as precentral gyrus) shows a similar point-to-point connection to the muscles. Any particular muscle can therefore be made to move by electrically stimulating its connecting nerve in the brain, or it can be paralyzed by destroying that nerve. Psychologists and neurologists have plotted the outer parts of the central sensory and central motor areas in minute detail, so that we now know virtually millimeter by millimeter which parts of the body connect to what points in the brain—for both sensory and motor nerves.

Section (b) represents the inner portion of the central sensory area which coordinates incoming sensory signals of each type. Each signal from the eye, for example, corresponds to only a single dot in the whole field of vision. Until these dots are reconstructed into a pattern approximating that which confronted the eyes, the only "pattern" available to the brain would be something like a scrambled mosaic or (a highly parallel case) the "snow" in a badly adjusted television set. The visual section of the cortex creates a coordinated picture out of the incoming spots. Signals from tactile nerves are similarly coordinated here. By combining signals from various parts of the skin it is possible to tell the shape, texture, hardness, and so forth of an object in a way which no single nerve or uncoordinated group could do. The other senses are similarly coordinated here into a single, total "picture" for each sense.

The next step is to combine and compare the incoming "pictures" from *all* the senses. This is apparently done in the sections of the cerebral cortex which adjoin the sensory cortex. We can identify many things by one sense alone, but combinations of senses are sometimes needed. If we want to know whether a Christmas handbag is pigskin or plastic, we may need the combined effects of sight, feel, smell, and temperature sense. Combinations of senses are highly important in first becoming acquainted with new things, particularly in childhood.

The function of the motor section can be seen if we return to the twenty dollar bill on the sidewalk. Let us assume that we have perceived it, and "instructed" the motor nerves to pick it up. Now the novice may think that picking up a twenty is a simple operation. But a little experimentation will show that the picking-up motion requires the simultaneous coordination of the eyes, neck, back, thighs, calves, arches, toes, shoulders, upper arm, forearm, wrist, hand, and fingers, each of which consists in turn of several different sets of muscles, some of which must be tensed and others relaxed—not to mention that the senses of balance and of time sequence must also come into play. The "simple" picking-up motion probably requires the simultaneous and sequential coordination of several million motor nerves.

The process on the outgoing side reverses that on the incoming. The total instruction "Pick it up" goes to the section of the cerebral cortex adjacent to the motor area. Here all of the *major* motor areas are coordinated, as separate orders to the back, shoulders, arms, and so forth. These are then subdivided in the motor cortex, where (for example) the instructions for the arm are broken down into orders to upper arm, lower arm, fingers, and so forth, which orders are further subdivided in the precentral gyrus.

To summarize, on the sensory side thousands or millions of discrete signals are combined in successive steps until in the cerebral cortex they become a single, total message. After a course of action is selected in the cortex a total order goes out. This total order is then divided successively until it reaches thousands or millions of selected muscle fibers, coordinating all toward effectuating the decision. The whole set of relationships closely parallels that of organizations of many human beings, to be seen in subsequent chapters.

THE NATURE AND BOUNDARIES OF THE SYSTEM

The human brain can be described as an electronic recording machine, with built-in sub-assemblies having both permanent and circulating memories, the functioning of which is modulated by a biochemical multi-directional or broadcasting process (i.e., the emotions) via a thalamocortical clearing center. The organism contains approximately 9 billion nerve units, each requiring 0.07 volts for firing, the total requiring some two watts of power for operation.[7]

The Dorkovich statement is essentially correct, in that our present state of knowledge provides no ground to disagree. We might also say

---

[7] Victor Dorkovich, in Appendix of Norbert Wiener, *et al.*, *Cybernetics and Society* (New York: Executive Techniques, Inc., 1951), p. 39.

that an automobile can be described as a self-propelled, four-wheeled organism whose motive power normally resides in an internal combustion engine. However "correct" either statement may be, it leaves many details to be filled in, and neither gives much hint as to how to correct a malfunction. Some persons may be perturbed when living material is called a machine, or nonliving an organism. But as we shall see in connection with communication, this is a question of words, and the problems of the brain are the same whether we call it a machine or an organism.

In any event, it is "all but hopeless at this time to trace or even to infer what actually happens in the brain during learning."[8] More explicitly, we simply do not know what is different in the brain after learning than before. There are a few things, however, we do know with reasonable confidence. First, all nerves operate basically by electrical current, and by attaching a galvanometer to a nerve we can tell if a signal is on its way through. Second, all nerves discharge on an all-or-none basis, there being no intermediate state. Third, learning takes place at the synapses, apparently by some process which reduces resistance to the nerve current. Fourth, the arrangement of the neurons in the cortex is extremely complex, so that each nerve is connected directly or indirectly with every other. Fifth, no particular idea, concept, or perception is located in any particular part of the cortex, and, if it is reasonable to speak of the physical location of an idea at all, each occurs simultaneously in numerous parts of the brain. The chief evidence for this is the fact that injury to or removal of substantial parts of the brain do not impair any one kind of mental ability, or any one kind of concepts, more than others. We are speaking now of information content; certain sections do have definable effects on emotions and desires.

The boundaries of the system we are now analyzing are those of the nervous system itself. Although various other parts of the body do undergo some changes in consequence of behavior, virtually all *learning* significant to the present volume takes place in the nervous system. The environment of this system thus includes everything outside the nervous system itself. This is an important point, and should clearly be noted. It means that the behavioral system we are studying at this point is not the whole person, but the nervous system. A hunger pang caused by contractions of the stomach walls is a stimulus from outside the nervous system just as much as is the pain of a rope being tightened around the ankle. Sensations from other parts of the body, including those associated with the emotions, also are external stimuli in the present model. Whether the governors of our motive system lie inside the nervous system, or some-

---

[8] Anatol Rapoport, "A Critique of Frederick Mosteller & Robert R. Bush's Stochastic Models of Learning," *Behavioral Science*, Vol. 1, No. 1 (January, 1956), pp. 59–60. See also Warren S. McColloch, "Why the Mind Is in the Head," in Lloyd A. Jeffres (ed.), *Cerebral Mechanisms in Behavior* (New York: John Wiley & Sons, 1951), p. 55.

where in the body but outside the nervous system, is a matter for the chapter on primary reinforcers.

To define the boundaries of the behavioral system at the limits of the nervous system does not imply that other things are unimportant, particularly glandular secretions, which have tremendous effects on behavior. However, the general effects of these nonneural body processes do not differ greatly between man and other animals. The model reflects our central concern with typically human behavior, which depends upon the nervous system, not the stomach or glands. Nonneural factors are important to individual differences, and hence will be given attention in connection with personality.

THE PSYCHOLOGY OF SR

Although the general idea that a stimulus can produce a response must be very old, not until the late nineteenth century was a systematic study undertaken of the learning of particular responses to particular stimuli. Untold thousands of experiments have been conducted since, with monkeys, rats, mice, dogs, cats, pigs, sheep, pigeons, ducks, porpoises, earthworms, fish, and even single-celled animals—not to mention humans. Small animals are more amenable to testing, not the least of the reasons being that some human subjects object to electrodes in their brains, or to being kept hungry for three days to motivate them to run a maze. Then too, rat mazes are cheaper than human size, and rats do not talk back, or try to outwit the experimenter. There is no reasonable doubt, however, that neurons are much the same in mice and men, and follow the same basic neural rules. In psychology as in medicine, conclusions obtained from rats and monkeys do not necessarily apply to humans. But they can be extremely useful in formulating hypotheses and giving them preliminary tests.

We shall define a *stimulus* as any energy or change of energy which sets off activity in the nervous system.[9] Sensory signals, including those from the organs and skin, constitute the most obvious types of stimuli, but are by no means the only ones. In all the higher animals, and certainly in humans, memory, the spontaneous firing of cortical neurons, and the response to a previous stimulus all constitute stimuli. Under experimental conditions an electrical potential applied directly to some part of the nervous system also constitutes a stimulus.

A *response* is any activity of the nervous system set off by a stimulus. If any motor nerves are activated by a stimulus, then, of course, muscular activity will ensue, and if some other afferent nerves are activated,

---

[9] This definition follows closely the tenor of that of Frank H. George and Joseph H. Handlon in "A Language for Perceptual Analysis," *Psychological Review*, No. 64 (1959), p. 14. Their definition is, "Any change of energy which impinges on the nervous system such that it brings about activity of that system. The source of the energy change may be either external or internal to the organism."

glandular or emotional reactions may follow. But it should be made clear that the *response* is defined here as neural activity, whether overt activity follows or not. A contestant watching his opponent arc through the air in a diving competition may merely think, "How distressingly graceful!" the thought being the sole response to the visual stimulus. Though this may, of course, stimulate other thoughts, such as a firm resolution to out-grace the opponent.

Needless to say, the fact that a stimulus may arise from inside the brain itself, and that a response may consist of nothing more than the cerebral discharge of an idle thought, places a tremendous limitation on the ability of psychologists to observe the whole of the SR reaction. It is precisely this ability of the brain to undergo SR activity entirely within itself which provides humans with their tremendous mental capacity.

To illustrate, let S represent any stimulus which arises from sensory nerves, and let s represent any stimulus arising inside the brain. Similarly, let R stand for any motor response, while r stands for any response of the brain cells alone. The four possible combinations of these items may be illustrated as follows. (1) My wife asks me to buy some paint tomorrow (external stimulus S), and I write "paint" into my pocket diary (external response R), the symbol being SR. (2) My wife asks me to buy paint (S) and I make a mental "note" of it (neural response r), the total being Sr. (3) While sitting at my desk I recall that we need some paint (neural stimulus s) and jot it down in my diary (R), giving the symbol sR. (4) I recall that we need paint (s) and make a mental note to buy some tomor-row (r), symbolized as sr.[10]

For convenience we will refer to an *experience* as any stimulus and the ensuing response, whether the combination takes the form SR, Sr, sR, or sr. In the third and fourth types, sR and sr, a recollection served as stimu-lus. Under other conditions a recollection can also be a response (r), as when hearing the words "Thanksgiving dinner" reminds us of "Grandma's house." Thus, a recollection can consist of the s, the r, or both in an ex-perience. For accuracy, experiences involving external stimulus and re-sponse should be symbolized as SsrR, since all sensory stimuli must first become cortical stimuli and then cortical responses before they can pro-duce motor responses—reflexes excepted. Even this is highly simplified, most experiences taking a form such as Ss-r-s-r-s-R, or something more complicated.

Conditioning: Bringing Neural Connections into Correspondence with Environmental Connections

We are concerned with the nervous system as a mechanism of adaptive behavior, this being behavior which corresponds in some way to the en-vironment. As the first step in this process the nervous system must ac-

---

[10] My wife insists that in trying to get children and absentminded husbands to do certain jobs there is a fifth category—a simple S standing alone.

quire information about the environment, which means that information from the environment must somehow modulate the brain in correspondence with the environment. The basic process is that phenomena (objects or events) which are related in the environment must also become related in the brain. Simultaneously, things unrelated in the environment must remain unrelated in the brain. Although there are numerous complications, the basic action of the brain which produces this result is known as *conditioning*.

The simplest type of conditioning is the conditioned reflex, also known as "classical" conditioning. This is illustrated by Pavlov's dogs. When a bell was rung regularly just before food was presented, in due time saliva would flow when the dogs heard the bell. More typically, a conditioned response is only a partial response. For example, a dog given an electrical shock just after a buzzer is sounded will withdraw its leg and yelp when the shock is felt. After conditioning, the dog will withdraw its leg to the sound of the buzzer, but will not omit the yelp.[11] Characteristically the conditioned response resembles, but does not fully duplicate, the unconditioned, inborn response.

An important fact of the conditioned salivation reflex is that it involves no motives. Life is no pleasanter, nor are the chances of survival increased, if the dog salivates to the sound of a bell. No selective process is present, the animal learning the conditioned response to whatever stimulus happens to be present. The avoidance reflex, however, does involve selection in one sense. The dog *does* find life pleasanter after he learns to lift his leg upon hearing a buzzer—if in his environment buzzer sounds are followed by electric shock. However, the initial unconditioned stimulus and response (the shock and the leg withdrawal) are not learned, the only learned item being the conditioning of the unlearned response to a new stimulus.

By contrast, in full selective behavior we start without any unlearned SR connection. This is known as *instrumental* conditioning by some psychologists, since the learned behavior is an instrument toward achieving a reward, and as "operant" conditioning by others. In experiments in selective conditioning, it is not prearranged that the animal be doing anything in particular. He may be running, sniffing, looking for food, or doing setting-up exercises. But the experiment is so arranged that some particular act is followed by a reward—usually food, drink, a mate, or release from discomfort. Each time the specified act is performed the reward follows; otherwise no reward is given. In a typical experiment, pigeons are placed in a container, where they may bend, stretch, flap, or preen feathers as they choose. But every time a pigeon's head rises above a certain level, he receives food. Almost imperceptibly at first, but

---

[11] Ernest R. Hilgard and Donald G. Marquis, *Conditioning and Learning* (New York: Appleton Century, 1940), pp. 37–39.

with mounting regularity, erstwhile stooping pigeons will be observed to walk with their proud heads high—at least when hungry. Thousands of experiments of this general sort have been performed with many different animals, leading to the inescapable conclusion that in a given situation any activity (response) which leads to a reward is strengthened. Whereas in the conditioned reflex the brain formed connections to correspond to the connectedness of two events in the environment, in this kind of conditioning the brain forms a connection which ties together a particular rewarding event in the environment and a particular response by the subject. As we shall see in the next chapter, this kind of connection is highly important to the development of motives.

An extension of this kind of experiment adds a prior stimulus. For example, a guinea pig is placed in a stall, and from time to time a buzzer is sounded. If the guinea pig happens to turn its head to the right just after the buzzer sounds, it is allowed to nibble briefly on a carrot. If it does not turn its head to the right following the buzz, no reward is received. In due course the guinea pig regularly turns its head to the right on hearing the buzzer. The buzzer is now a conditioned stimulus, and the turn of the head a conditioned instrumental response.

In both instrumental conditioning and conditioned reflexes, *higher order conditioning* is also possible. In the above illustration, the sound of the buzzer might be associated by conditioning with a flashing light, after which the flashing light would bring the response of turning the head, even though the light had never before been directly associated with a reward.

Although experiments with humans are often complicated by such factors as the subject's possible desire to outwit the experimenter, embarrassment which blocks normal learning, conscious attempts to assist or withhold reflex actions, and the like, when all is said and done

> The facts of conditioning are indisputable . . . the data show a regularity and a lawfulness; and they can be reproduced by anyone who chooses to fulfill the conditions. . . . The case of instrumental conditioning is more complex; but learning again seems to be a slow wearing down of paths, the cumulative strengthening of the final instrumental act, the gradual attachment of a chain of subordinate instrumental acts to this final one.[12]

Conditioning occurs not only in pigeons, humans, and other animals possessing brains, but also in protozoans, worms, and snails. Although the speed and capacity for learning differ widely from the lower to the higher species, and although some kinds of responses are far more difficult to condition than others (some kinds not being possible), the basic nature of conditioning is a fundamental process of learning. As a result of repeated experience, a stimulus which originally brought one response may be conditioned to bring a different response, or a response which originally

[12] Lawrence E. Cole, *Human Behavior* (Yonkers, N.Y.: World Book, 1953), p. 305.

followed one kind of stimulus (including random behavior) may be conditioned to follow a different (or definite) stimulus. In all these instances *neural associations are formed in the brain which correspond to associations of events outside the brain.* We might variously describe this result by saying that the neural connections have been modulated by sensory perceptions, that the brain connections constitute a coded impression of events repeatedly connected in an individual's experience, that the brain has adapted to the individual's environment, that there is a positive correlation between brain connections and event connections, or simply that the individual has learned about his environment. The method of stating it is not important, so long as conditioning is understood as a mechanism by which brain connections come to be related to event connections.

The Laws of Learning

Now human behavior, even human learning, is a far more complicated thing than the simple conditioning described above. But at the same time learning cannot be understood without understanding the conditioning process, and our next task is to examine the "regularity and lawfulness" according to which conditioning operates.

Thus far, mention has been made only of the process of *making* connections in the brain—of associating things not previously tied together in the brain—the process known as *reinforcement*, or strengthening of a connection. But if neural connections are to correspond to the connections of outer events, then when previously connected outer events cease being connected, the brain must also abandon *its* corresponding connections. When a conditioned response to a particular stimulus ceases to be reinforced, it will decline in strength or frequency, and eventually disappear. This decline or disappearance is known as *extinction*. Since we do not know how the neural connections take place in reinforcement, we know even less what happens during extinction. The evidence is rather clear, however, that extinction is *not* mere forgetting, or erasing of the previous connections. Extinction is at least in part an active process, such as establishing new connections through which the conditioned stimulus will discharge (including neural discharge without any motor response), or of inhibiting the previous conditioned response. Hence, it is stated that in extinction the *response* declines or disappears; the neural connection apparently remains largely intact.[13]

One form of response to some external stimulus is that of simply paying attention to it. If this response is unrewarding, it will be extinguished like any other response. Thereafter the event in our environment which previously commanded the response of attention will no longer do so, the ex-

---

[13] As it will be used here, "to reinforce" means "to strengthen." In parallel, "to extinguish" will mean "to weaken"—not "to wipe out entirely," which is the more customary meaning.

tinction of the response of *attending* being the new response of *ignoring*. Learning to ignore a stimulus is known as *adaptation*, and is illustrated by the factory worker who ceases to respond to the noise around him. We should note that in adaptation there is no lessening of signals actually received, however, since the sensory nerves continue to detect the sounds and feed them into the cortex. Only the responses are extinguished.

The *laws of learning* are statements of factors which influence the strength or speed of reinforcement or extinction. The *strength* of learning shows in several different ways. One is in the amount of the response, the response of Pavlov's dogs being stronger if more saliva is secreted. A second evidence is a reduction in the time required to perform the response. When the rat is fully conditioned to a maze, pauses and hesitations cease, and the maze is traversed in a smooth running, fast performance. A third evidence of strength is reduction of errors. False starts, wrong turns, and unnecessary movements decline and then disappear. Finally, strengthening reduces latency, which is the interval between receiving the conditioned stimulus and beginning the response. When the bell is first rung, no saliva flows until the food reaches the dog's mouth. As trials proceed, saliva starts farther and farther in advance of the food, until eventually it appears promptly after the bell, at which time latency has dropped to its physiological minimum. The strength of a conditioned response is thus indicated by its being large, fast, error-free, and immediate—or such combination as is appropriate to the particular situation. (There is no point, for example, in talking about the *strength* of the response of choosing the white over the black box, since in such a case only the promptness and regularity of the response are relevant.) The correlation among these various aspects of "strength" is not reliably high, which suggests that "strength" of a response is really a multiple, not a single phenomenon.

All conditioned responses presuppose some response which does *not* require conditioning, to which the conditioned response can be attached. In classical conditioning of the Pavlovian type the unconditioned response is a reflex—a built-in response which is attached by conditioning to a new stimulus. Instrumental conditioning does not depend on a built-in response, but on an urge of some sort, in which case the urge performs the function comparable to that of the reflex in classical conditioning. The whole wording could also be reversed, and we might say that conditioning can take place only where there is an urge of some sort, the urge in classical conditioning consisting of the simple tendency to perform the reflex response. Stated still differently, there must exist some kind of response which would occur *without* the presence of the conditioned stimulus, such as salivation or eating, and to this unconditioned response some new stimulus (a buzzer), some new response (holding the head high), or both (turning the head to the right on the sound of a buzzer) can be attached. There must be a pre-existing SR pattern to which the new stimulus, response, or both, can be conditioned.

The first principle, or law, of learning, called the principle of *intensity*, states that conditioning can take place only in the presence of some pre-existing tendency (reflexive or motivated) to respond, and the strength and speed of learning depends mainly upon the strength of that pre-existing tendency.[14] Under some circumstances and to some degree the learning may reflect the strength of the conditioning stimulus (as a louder bell or a brighter picture), but the relationship is not dependable and can be omitted without serious loss. A variety of reservations surround the operation of this principle, particularly involving problems of measuring the strength of the pre-existing tendency, and provide somewhat less confidence in this principle than in the other two which follow.

The second principle is that of *recency*. If several different items (stimuli or responses) occur in sequence before the pre-existing response occurs, the last item in the sequence—that is, the one occurring most recently before the pre-existing response—will be the most promptly and most strongly conditioned. Several kinds of examples may be given. A rat running a maze containing three successive right-or-wrong turns, A, B, and C, will first learn the final turn, C, then B, and then A. The final turn, C, is performed most recently before the food is reached, and is learned first and most strongly. The less recent turns B and A fall in line behind. As another example, the following sequence may be presented to a dog. First, a bell is sounded, after an interval a light is flashed, and after another interval dry food is placed in the dog's mouth. After the whole sequence is repeated a number of times, the dog will learn to salivate in response to the light *or* the bell. But he will learn to respond *sooner* and *more strongly* to the light, the stimulus which more recently precedes the unconditioned salivation. If the rat must press a bar *and then* choose a round door over a square one before food is presented, the choice of the proper door will be conditioned sooner and more strongly than pressing the bar, again emphasizing the greater recency of that response.

Recency also applies when only a single stimulus or response is being conditioned, rather than a sequence. The shorter the interval between the new response and the old response to which it is being conditioned, the stronger and faster the conditioning.

Last, but by no means least, is the principle of *frequency*, or *repetition*. Other things equal, in simple conditioning the first few trials show a weak response. As trials are repeated the conditioned response strength-

---

14 Hilgard and Marquis state that classical conditioning depends on the strength of the unconditioned response, and instrumental conditioning on the strength of the reward. But the strength of a reward can be measured only in terms of the strength of response it produces. The footnoted statement seems to avoid any possible circularity of this sort. The term "pre-existing tendency" seems a satisfactory way of accommodating both the reflexive and "rewarded" responses, and also of avoiding commitment as to whether or not the "pre-existing tendency" is itself learned—i.e., whether it is a primary or secondary reinforcer.

ens, up to a total of about 15 or 20 instances. Thereafter the conditioned response may be further strengthened, but at a declining rate.

Time intervals can also be conditioned. If a bell is rung, and 30 seconds later an electric shock is sent through a dog's foot, the dog will learn to lift its leg somewhat short of 30 seconds after hearing the bell.

How well an organism learns something from a given amount of effort depends in part on the spacing of the repetitions. In most laboratory animals the strongest conditioning from a given number of repetitions occurs when the trials are spaced, at, say, three or four per day. Faster repetitions will, of course, speed the amount of learning that takes place within a given amount of time. No fixed rules are available on this score, the most effective amounts of spacing apparently depending on the kind of thing being learned, on the individual, and on other factors. Despite large individual differences in the speed and intensity of learning, the basic principles are never reversed.

Time sequence is highly important. If a new response is to be conditioned to a pre-existing response, the new response must appear *before* the pre-existing one. This relation is equally important whether the pre-existing response is reflexive or rewarded. Bells which ring *after* the dog has salivated from actual receipt of food, or turns of the head made *after* the carrot has been nibbled produce little or no conditioning, though they occasionally produce some. In simple conditioning the reward must *follow* the performance to be learned, or the learning will be highly inefficient.

Extinction. In contrast to reinforcement, *extinction* is the process by which the response *ceases* to follow the stimulus to which it was previously conditioned. The conditions which bring about extinction are simple in essence, namely nonreinforcement. If the dog has been conditioned to salivate to the sound of a bell, and the bell is then rung repeatedly without being followed by food, the bell will in due time cease to bring forth the salivation. If the pigeon raises his head in the experimental cage and no food is forthcoming, the head-raising gradually dies down to random levels, and so on with any conditioned response. The progress of extinction is similar to that of reinforcement, but in reverse. That is, a period of fairly rapid decline ends with a slow fadeout. The explanation is that extinction is not "unlearning," but new learning of a different response.

If a conditioned response is partially extinguished, and a period of rest is then allowed (of, say, a day or so), experimental animals show a partial and sometimes full recovery of the conditioned response. However, additional exposures without reinforcement will eventually bring full extinction. It generally takes about the same number of trials to eliminate a conditioned response as to create it in the first place.

Evidence that "complete" extinction does not "wipe the slate clean" is found in the fact that an extinguished response can be reconditioned more easily than one not previously conditioned. If the process is repeated, after about seven to ten extinctions and reconditionings only one or two reinforcements may be required to bring the conditioned response back to its full strength.[15]

Instrumental conditioning has been discussed thus far only for positive rewards. The principles of learning apply equally to responses of avoiding punishments, with one important exception. If a dog receives a shock through the floor after a buzzer is sounded, the dog will lift its leg on hearing the buzzer. The exceptional condition grows out of the fact that the reward in this case is avoidance of shock. Once learned, an avoidance response may be difficult to extinguish, for by lifting its leg the dog eliminates the possibility of discovering whether the shock is still being administered.[16] The reward for lifting the leg is *not* being shocked, and this reward continues, even when no current is present. A sure way to bring extinction would be to hold the leg forceably on the floor after the buzzer sounded. A slower and less certain extinction may get started on its own if the withdrawal response for some reason is not made. To generalize, avoidance responses may be difficult to correct because there is no feedback of information when the situation changes, a matter having obvious implications to personality problems of fears and withdrawals.

In summary, conditioning is a process by which things related in experience come to be related in the brain. The relationships can be purely informational, reflecting nothing more than the fact that two things have repeatedly occurred together (or in sequence) in the person's experience. They can also be motivated, in that rewarding responses are reinforced, while unrewarding or punished experiences are extinguished. These aspects will be elaborated later, our present concern being merely that the laws of learning as found in conditioning are important statements about the conditions under which connections within the human brain are made, not made, or broken, in reflection of relationships which exist, do not exist, or cease to exist in man's experience. Some other rules will be seen later in connection with motivation, concept formation, and perception. But

---

[15] Cole, *op. cit.*, p. 281. In many aspects of more complex behavior persons show clear evidence of learning a particular SR relation on a single exposure, with evident disregard of the principle of frequency. If such behavior takes place with respect to things about which the person is intimately familiar, a single instance—even a single verbal instruction—may be enough to bring a response as full and efficient as if it had long been conditioned. In simple SR terms, the instruction to "Pass me the apricots" could not be performed efficiently the first time apricots appeared on the table. Instead, the response would first be performed clumsily, and then by 15 or 20 repetitions be built up to a level of efficiency. But if the response of "passing" other things has already been conditioned and extinguished many times, as have also the references to "apricots" and "me," then a single verbal stimulus may be sufficient to produce a response of full strength and efficiency the very first time a particular stimulus situation occurs. We do not know that SR relations can be extended to explain phenomena of this sort, but, given the obvious importance of conditioning, the possibility that it might explain other more complex phenomena of this sort seems worth exploring.

[16] *Ibid.*, p. 291.

those found in connection with the conditioning in the study of stimulus-response psychology are important to wide areas of human behavior, and could conceivably be relevant to some aspects of motivation, conceptualization, and perception as well. Within that important area in which conditioning operates, frequency, recency, and intensity are major rules by which associations in experience are reflected in associations in the brain.

The laws of learning, however, are far more than mere statements of the rules of conditioning. Since the concepts which contain our information about the world outside us are in important respects formed according to these same laws (see Chapter 7), the laws of learning mold or modify our information about the world. By analogy, the nature of the picture taken by a camera depends on such things as the quality of the lens, the type of film, and the kind of processing it receives. A picture taken with a Zeiss Tessar lens will differ markedly from one taken with a pinhole lens or the bottom of a beer bottle. One taken on color film will differ from one on black and white, and strong, contrasty developing will produce a different picture than will soft developing.

In a significant way the laws of learning are the "lens" through which information about the world gets into our brains, and if the laws of learning were markedly different we almost certainly would have a different view of the world. Since these laws are also related to those of forgetting, they also do much to determine the sharpness and intensity of our mental pictures at any moment in time. Although the effects of these laws are diluted as information becomes collective and is written down, the information of any one person at any one moment is nevertheless strongly determined by these psychological "lenses."

Chapter 5

MOTIVES: THE LEARNING OF PREFERENCES

In the present model, the behavioral system has concepts and motives as its detecting stage, motives as its governing stage, and muscular responses as its effector stage. Previous chapters have dealt with the whole system, and this and the next three chapters will examine the major components in more detail. Since we have no interest in the effector stage, as such, attention will be confined to detection and selection. Each will be viewed as a subsystem within the larger system. The detector subsystem may be said to involve concepts, perceptions, information, opportunities, or judgments about facts or science, depending on the emphasis. The selector subsystem can be said to involve motives, preferences, rewards and punishments, or value judgments, again depending on the emphasis. The present chapter will examine the subsystem by which motives are learned, and the next will deal with unlearned motives. Chapter 7 will analyze the concept subsystem, after which Chapter 8 will discuss some important relationships between the motive and concept systems.

To move to the question of motives, although we have already noted that rewarded responses are reinforced and unrewarded ones extinguished —a relation generally known as the Law of Effect—we did not examine *what* is rewarding, or *how* a reward can reinforce a response. This is the problem to which we now move.

Incidentally, these chapters on psychology will handle general problems of motives and concepts without specific reference to whether the processes are conscious or unconscious. Fully conscious response selection will be dealt with later, under the heading of decision making.

Learning as a Cybernetic System

Animal learning exemplifies selective, or adaptive, behavior. Hence, it must contain the minimum conditions of a cybernetic system. Looking first at the ingredients, or contents, rather than the mechanisms, let us examine a simple act of selective behavior.

Assume that a laboratory rat has already learned that food lies behind a white door, but not behind a black one. As a cybernetic system, this situation is comparable to a household thermostat already set for a certain temperature. The rat's stomach nerves detect emptiness, and so inform the brain. On the basis of this information the brain selects an eating response, instructions of which are transmitted to and effectuated by the appropriate muscles. Performance of this response brings a change in the condition which provided the original stimulus, as the stomach changes from empty to full. The detector next reports this change of state to the brain as feedback information, and the brain then selects a different response, the cessation of eating.[1]

In this particular illustration, the rat has *selected* behavior, giving different responses (eating and not eating) to two different stimuli, empty stomach and full stomach. Within the scope of this already conditioned response, however, the rat did not *learn*. By that we mean that the relation between the stimulus and the response did not undergo any change by virtue of this experience. This kind of action is comparable to that of the preset thermostat: when stomach content falls below a certain level the rat eats, and when it rises above a certain level the rat stops. This relation can continue indefinitely. Although this particular SR relation in the rat was learned to begin with, similar abilities to distinguish food sources are inborn in some animals.

The major concern of this chapter is not that of learning overt *responses* (a matter discussed in the previous chapter), but of learning *preferences*. In simple learning, a new SR relationship is established, while the reward-punishment preference scale presumably remains unchanged. In this chapter we are concerned with changes in the preference scale itself, which means a change in the cybernetic governor. To illustrate with a very simple preset alternating change in the "preference" of the governor, a household thermostat can be attached to a clock, which will hold the governor at 70 degrees during the day and 60 at night. The selector itself changes under the control of some larger, or higher, system, which constitutes its environment. Since motives are the governors of our system of learning responses, we are now concerned with a change in governors.

Now it is true that lower animals can also learn new preferences. But the variety of such learning is not large, and the much greater facility of human beings in this respect virtually places them in a distinct category. This second level of learning makes it possible to engage in adaptive behavior to a degree utterly impossible under simple adaptation of responses. In the framework of the previous language, with this facility the human being not only selects what he prefers from the list of what is possible, he also learns (in a general way) to prefer what is possible. This fact

---

[1] In line with the observation in Chapter 3 about the necessity of two opposite relationships for stable systems, it may be noted that that condition is fulfilled here: eating varies directly with hunger, but hunger varies inversely with eating.

almost undoubtedly has enabled man to live satisfactorily in a wider variety of environments than almost any other of the more complex animals. Unquestionably, it also allows a degree of adaptation which is inconceivable under response adaptation alone.

To suggest a *change* in motive implies that some prior state of motives existed before the change. Because we feel surer about the ways in which motives change than we do about where they start, we will discuss the changes first, reserving for the next chapter the topic of "original" motives.

Motives in Common Sense Terms

This problem of what motives *are* can be approached at two levels. One is concerned with the brain structures or mechanisms which determine motives, a matter for the next chapter. The other deals with the content of motives, which we will examine first in the common sense terms: What kinds of things do people want?

At the common sense level, much of the answer is simple. Like other animals, we have physiological needs and urges. These include the urges for food, shelter, sex, physical comfort, exercise, and rest. As the body goes through various cycles and changing environments, one or another of these urges rises to the fore, and the activities which lead to satisfaction of the urge are reinforced, while others are extinguished. It is also easy to list a group of widely found nonphysiological desires. Depending on which psychologist or sociologist is making the list, these will include such "urges" as those for security, superiority, praise, response of other persons, acceptance by the group, humor, new experience, and repetition of the familiar (nostalgia). Still speaking in common sense terms, these things lead to pleasing emotions, or states of emotional well being. These "positive" emotional states constitute rewards, and are reinforcing. Their opposites are such "negative" emotional states as insecurity, fear, anger, grief, frustration, boredom, and the like, which tend to extinguish the behavior which leads to them.

The purpose of the above list is merely to suggest the kinds of things in everyday life which are generally rewarding and unrewarding. The list is unimportant in itself, and has no scientific standing. What is important is that somewhere in the organism is a thing which is usually called an *affective state*, or a state of well- or ill-being. It is a state of feeling or emotion, not of knowledge, though one can have knowledge about his affective state. The important thing is that these states can be described as having a *valence*, positive or negative. A positive valence is an emotional or affective state which is described as good, pleasant, desirable, or other such words, while a negative one is described as bad, unpleasant, undesirable, and so on. Continuing in layman's terms, feedbacks which show positive valences are reinforcing, while negative feedbacks are extinguishing of the behavior which led to them. That is, they are selectors of behavior.

With respect to the above layman's list, it should be noted that the valences of particular emotional states are not the same for all persons, nor are they necessarily constant for the same person. On some occasions, and to some persons, emotional states which are normally negative can become rewarding, as when someone seems to "enjoy" sorrow, inferiority, or pain—and the reverse sometimes goes for the normally positive ones. The reversal of the customary valences toward such feelings, if strong and long continued, is considered one form of emotional illness.

SECONDARY REINFORCERS

Motives Can Be Learned (Like Other Responses)

Most people believe that human beings have a number of built-in, hereditary drives or urges, such as those mentioned above. For the moment we will not dispute that proposition, but will simply label any such hereditary urges as *primary reinforcers,* without quibbling about what they may consist of. Psychologists nowadays are very wary about labeling any particular urge as a primary reinforcer. But they are quite sure that behavior *is* selected, and that the selectors themselves undergo change. While recognizing the difficulty of making foolproof definitions of these things, we will refer to any inborn motive, or behavior selector, as a primary reinforcer, and to any learned or acquired selector as a secondary reinforcer. As will be seen later, a secondary reinforcer must presumably be derived from a primary one.

Stated differently, a *secondary reinforcer* is anything which by virtue of being associated with desired things, itself becomes sufficiently desired so as to reinforce other behavior which will help achieve it. More technically, a *secondary reinforcer* is any stimulus or response which, by virtue of itself being reinforced, or of being conditioned to a reinforced response, itself becomes a reinforcer of other responses. More simply, it is anything which a person has learned to want (in contrast to having an inborn desire for it), and which will act as a reward for other behavior. Some types and examples follow.

The most obvious type of secondary reinforcer is the instrumental—one that serves as a means of accomplishing something else. We want food. A kitchen and its equipment are instruments which help us to have food, so we want a kitchen and equipment. The kitchen is a secondary reinforcer, since the acquisition (or prospective acquisition) of a kitchen or its equipment is rewarding, and reinforces other activities which lead toward the acquisition. If an interest in music and poetry is perceived as instrumental to holding a young lady's attention, the young man may develop a desire for concert tickets and books, which desire may prove the reward which will reinforce other activity, such as working, borrowing, or stealing.

These instrumental reinforcers can be distinguished from intrinsic ones.[2] An instrumental secondary reinforcer can become intrinsic if, with use and familiarity, it becomes rewarding in itself. The interest in music and poetry might continue to be the grand passion of the young man, even after he has ditched his first love for a second who detests the stuff. And the woman might come to like her kitchen for its own sake, even though she has no expectation of using it. The case is simply that of wanting the means until it becomes an end in itself, and will thereafter reinforce other actions to achieve it. Along similar lines (although to illustrate a different point), Allport distinguishes between a boy's original interest in politics as instrumental to satisfying a father-identification, which interest later becomes intrinsic as the boy matures.[3]

In other instances things can come to be wanted because they have been associated with rewarding events. One can come to want to hang out a flag on the Fourth of July if flags were always out on the happy Fourths of childhood. He may want awnings over his windows if awnings were associated with the clubhouse where he won the tennis championship. A rat which has heard the click of a bar as it releases food may learn other responses merely to get the reward of the click.[4]

In layman's language, we can say that the flag or awnings are "wanted" or "liked" because they "remind" one of the earlier rewards. And the development of an "intrinsic" interest in music and poetry can reflect some new objective to which this interest is instrumental, in which case it might be said that it remains instrumental, not intrinsic, but with a new orientation. These distinctions may be valid, but they do not really matter. The important thing is that things which were originally merely instrumental come to be wanted in their own right. When we examine the possible mechanisms of secondary reinforcement below, it will be seen that these things probably *are* rewarding in themselves.[5]

Generally speaking, the rules for the development of secondary reinforcers (which may also be referred to as secondary motives) follow those for other learning. With respect to instrumental reinforcers, the more frequent the reinforcement of the secondary motive (frequency), the

[2] James Olds, *The Growth and Structure of Motives* (Glencoe: The Free Press, 1956), p. 28.

[3] Gordon W. Allport, "The Trend in Motivational Theory," in Chalmers L. Stacey and Manfred F. DeMartino (eds.), *Understanding Human Motivation* (Cleveland: Howard Allen, Inc., 1950), pp. 62–63.

[4] Norman L. Munn, *The Evolution and Growth of Human Behavior* (Boston: Houghton Mifflin, 1955), p. 224.

[5] The psychological literature does not seem to have developed any sharply defined line between instrumental and intrinsic secondary motives. We can nevertheless make a distinction on the following basis. Let us assume that C is a means to getting B, which is a means of getting A, which is wanted. If the person wants C only when he wants A, then B has instrumental reward value only. But if he wants C as a means of getting B, even when he does not want A, then B has intrinsic reward value. A further possible distinction on a neurological basis will be made below.

greater its proximity in time to its reinforcement (recency), and the more successful it is in bringing about the desired result (intensity), the stronger and more permanent does the secondary motive become.[6] The factors governing the learning of intrinsic secondary motives are more difficult to discern, but apparently behave in much the same way.

If we think of "wanting" as a response, then the conditioning of secondary reinforcers seems parallel in important respects to the higher order conditioning of other responses. We can let A represent a primary reinforcer—an original "want" response. By conditioning B to A, through instrumentality or mere association, a person will learn to give the response of "wanting" to the stimulus B. Once that response is firmly attached to B, then by independent associations from which A is absent, the response of "wanting" can be attached by higher order conditioning to C. Hence, the response of "wanting" has been transferred from A to C through two steps of conditioning, even though A and C may never themselves have occurred in conjunction. For reasons to be seen below, for purposes of understanding the learning of secondary reinforcement, it is very useful to think of "wanting" as a response.

Behavioral responses can be extinguished as well as reinforced, and the same is true of secondary motivation. The experimental evidence on precisely how they are extinguished is meager thus far, but does not seem to argue that the rules are essentially different from those of extinguishing overt responses. That is, if a secondary reinforcer (B) is presented repeatedly without the reward (A) which originally reinforced *it*, then B will gradually lose its own ability to reinforce C.

The process of extinguishing secondary motives has tremendous repercussions on human behavior, both individual and social. One aspect of this phenomenon concerns the relation of the extinction and the original reinforcement. If a motive has been learned by regular and reliable reinforcement, it is learned quickly, and becomes a strong reinforcing motive. But it can also be extinguished quickly. To use a human parallel to some animal experiments, suppose you put ten quarters in a slot machine and get ten successive wins. To play the machine will then be highly rewarding. It will be learned quickly and will strongly reinforce other activities instrumental to playing the machine, such as walking to the casino or waiting in line at the machine. Suppose you now lose on every one of the next ten tries. The motivating power of the machine will decline rapidly, and perhaps disappear.

By contrast, if the successes at first are only occasional, the reinforcing value of the machine will never rise to so great a height. At the same time, however, the reward value will be far less subject to extinction. For example, if you have ten straight wins, your desire to play will rise very high.

6 These are not the precise factors listed by Olds (*op. cit.*, pp. 35 and 76–78), but they seem to be very closely related.

But if you then have ten straight losses, your inclination to go further will drop precipitously. On the other hand, if you had two wins out of the first ten tries, your desire to play will be less strong. But ten straight losses will then not reduce your desire as low as if you had had all wins to begin with.[7]

It would seem probable that this particular type of action would account for the persistence of many "habitual" and superstitious practices and beliefs. Something may work once or twice out of the first dozen times it is tried, but never thereafter. But the "belief" in it—though not strong—will persist. By contrast, if it had worked *all* of the first dozen times, but never again, the belief would probably disappear early on the grounds that the subsequent situation is "not the same." Gambling is another strong illustration of the same psychological trait, which, as we will see later, is also important in dealing with uncertainty under decision making.

Chains of Motives

The desire for A can reinforce the response B, which can reinforce C. This is the simple pattern of secondary motives. But the human brain can hold incredibly long chains of connections. C can take on an intrinsic reward value, whereupon it can reinforce D, which can reinforce E, and so on through the alphabet and back. It is difficult to acquire experimental evidence on things of this sort. Animals of the level of the rat are handy to experiment with, and their motives are uncomplicated. But their brains cannot make connections beyond the secondary, or perhaps tertiary, level. Human brains can form long chains. But they are difficult to analyze rigorously, because different chains in the same person get mixed up. We therefore cannot say with authority that *all* desires for all things derive by secondary, tertiary, and more remote reinforcement from a limited list of primary reinforcers. But we are faced with two alternatives.

First, we can assume that it is theoretically possible for this to be the

---

[7] This illustration is stated as if the experimental results with animals can be applied directly to human beings. This procedure is not strictly valid, since the response of the human being will be influenced by certain information, correct or incorrect, about statistical probabilities, and by such things as moral judgments about gambling, the pressures of time or other persons in his immediate social environment, and many other factors. It does seem likely that the human being would also show the same response if no other factors influenced the situation except the laws of learning as applied to this particular problem. There are many independent observations of human behavior which seem to show that *on the average* this kind of response can be anticipated. There is, however, a distinct difference between subjective and objective probabilities, which will be noted in a later chapter on decision making. There is also a statistical validity to this behavior. Ten straight wins followed by ten straight losses constitute statistical "proof" that the machine has changed between the two series—that the machine of the second series of ten trials was "not the same machine" as that on which the first series was run. On the other hand, it is statistically reasonable to conclude that the machine which produced no wins out of ten is still "the same machine" as the one which earlier produced two wins out of ten.

case, even though we cannot trace the actual developments. On the other hand, we can hypothesize that some additional "higher" process(es) explain some of the more complex and subtle human rewards, such as enjoyment of the arts, working for the good of humanity, or learning self-discipline and self-denial. The present approach unequivocally follows the former route, in conformance with Lloyd Morgan's canon. In 1894 this principle was laid down by one of the founders of modern animal psychology, and "has commended itself to nearly all the hard-headed students of animal behavior who have labored since that date."[8] The principle states, "In no case may we interpret an action as the outcome of the exercise of a higher psychical faculty, if it can be interpreted as the outcome of the exercise of one which stands lower in the psychological scale."[9] This choice is also consistent with the "rule of parsimony," which is virtually universally accepted among scientists: namely, that when two or more possible explanations of the same phenomenon exist, the conceptually simpler is preferred.

This set of relationships in a chain of motives can be well-described in terms of "successive valves" introduced in Chapter 1. Some inborn motive acts on a "master valve," which serves as Motive A in the series. We can now think of two alternative responses (kinds of behavior) which affect A, which we will call B_1 and B_2. B_1 helps to satisfy Motive A, and is reinforced, while B_2 does not, and is extinguished. The flow of energy which A is capable of releasing can now be directed, at least in part, toward B_1, while none of that energy will be released in the direction of B_2. Motive A thus can be seen as a valve or switch which controls the release of energy into B_1 but not B_2. The flow of energy which flows through B_1 now has the capacity to actuate the flow of energy as between C_1 and C_2, and so on. If we think of A as some motive closely related to survival, it is thus possible through a succession of switching operations for that motive to control a vast array of motives and their ensuing actions so as to contribute directly and indirectly to survival. As we shall see, even if we start with only one or a few basic motives, the possible complexities and interrelations are many, and so are the opportunities for error—"error" in this instance meaning that some apparently antisurvival motive gets hooked into the system, such as a desire to engage in auto racing. We do not mean by this that the racing driver *wants* to reduce his chances of survival, but that in some chain of secondary motives he has learned to like racing, which has an antisurvival aspect to it.

The usefulness of this arrangement to human performance can easily be seen if we imagine any accomplishment which requires a long sequence of related acts. For example, if a basic desire is to marry and raise a family,

---

[8] Robert S. Woodworth, *Psychology* (New York: Henry Holt, 1929), p. 131.
[9] *Ibid.*, from C. L. Morgan, *An Introduction to Comparative Psychology* (1894), p. 53.

this reinforces the desire for a house and contents, which reinforces the desire for money, which reinforces the desire for a job, which reinforces the desire for professional training, which reinforces the desire for a college education, which reinforces the desire for books, and so on. We are now dealing with so-called conscious decisions. Returning once again to Lloyd Morgan's canon, we thus far have no conclusive grounds for assuming that conscious desires and decisions follow different rules than do unconsciously conditioned ones. The apparent difference is that instead of running through SR trials with sensory stimuli and muscular responses, we run through sr trials with mental stimuli and mental responses. For example, instead of having to run through a series of actual trials in order to have the work response rewarded with income, we acquire information about these things (a matter for Chapter 7). Thereafter all we need do is to run through the *thought* of working and find it rewarded with the *thought* of income, whereupon the thought of working is reinforced. (The thought of working also has some extinguishing consequences—a matter for the section just below.) Continuing on the basis of mental rewards, the thought of working can now become a secondary reinforcer merely on the basis of having thought about its consequences, whereupon it can reinforce either the thought of the fact of other actions which are contributory and instrumental to getting and holding a satisfactory job.[10] In short, if we introduce into our model the notion that *thoughts* of things can be satisfying or dissatisfying, then the ability of the brain to perform higher order conditioning of motives makes it possible to explain how a human being can be motivated to perform a step far removed in a chain of events from the accomplishment of a final goal.[11]

Generalized Reinforcers

Suppose we want food. Somewhere in the chain of events that leads to the acquisition of food we find that we want money. We also want shelter, and find that money is also instrumental in acquiring it. Our wants include travel, entertaining, books, gasoline, and a host of other things. At some stage in the attempt to satisfy each of these wants we find money a useful instrument. In consequence, the desire for money is reinforced separately and independently as secondary to many other wants. Because it is instru-

---

[10] This particular way of approaching the subject has perhaps been made most explicit by Charles E. Osgood in "Behavior Theory and Social Science," *Behavioral Science*, Vol. 1, No. 1, pp. 167 ff. Osgood discusses the grave limitations of explaining behavior in terms of the overt SR observances. Referring to the internal, purely neurological sr activities as "symbolic," he then says: ". . . in pointing out these insufficiencies of the SR model I am not claiming that its basic principles are thereby invalid—to the contrary, in dealing with the symbolic processes, at least, the same general principles will be assumed to operate." Osgood's statement does not refer specifically to the reinforcement and extinction of motives, but no clear reason appears why they should behave differently than do other responses.

[11] We will return to this problem in a different context in connection with future-oriented behavior, in Chapter 8.

mental to so many wants, the desire for money is reinforced frequently. Many of the desires which can be satisfied with money are very intense— hence, the desire for money is supported by the intensity factor. Since we live in a money economy, and it is seldom long between occasions when we want money, the desire will normally have been reinforced recently. Money is seldom found to be disadvantageous; hence, it is unlikely to be negatively reinforced. Given the almost certain occurrence of frequency, recency, intensity, and absence of negative "rewards," the desire for money in the normal adult in a money society can hardly escape being strongly reinforced. Anything instrumental to a wide variety of different desires, and reinforced from many directions, is said to have received generalized reinforcement.

There are many means of acquiring money. Since the desire for money is itself so highly reinforced, it is able in turn to reinforce a wide variety of activities which help to acquire it. We say that anything thus instrumental to many other different motives can be called a *generalized reinforcer.*

In our society, money is perhaps the strongest generalized secondary reinforcer which is obviously not inborn. Some other motives are quite as obviously generalized, but some authorities consider them inborn rather than secondary. Without debating whether they are primary or secondary, we will merely note their role as generalized and powerful reinforcers. One is the desire for approval. From an early age every person learns there are many things he cannot provide for himself, and that other persons must cooperate if he is to have them. If he is accepted and approved by others, they will do these things for him. If he is rejected they will not. Hence, approval is an essential instrumentality to a tremendous variety of wants. Further, it is learned at an earlier age than the desire for money, and in connection with a larger variety of circumstances. It also prevails in societies which do not use money. For similar reasons, love is also a powerful generalized reinforcer, learned early in life. Work is another general instrumentality. Despite some aversions to it, if it leads to rewards often and strongly enough, it, too, may become a generalized reinforcer. So can saving, hoarding, or acquisitiveness.

Some generalized reinforcers may be so highly rewarding in so many circumstances, and be acquired so early in life, that they acquire extremely high intrinsic value. They may remain through life with all the appearances of an inborn motive. If widely found, such secondary motives may be mistakenly thought of as an inborn "human nature." They help hold a society together, since the reward value of such things as money and acceptance can be used reliably to control behavior toward socially prescribed goals.

It is often felt that the desire for power is an important generalized reinforcer. This proposition is accepted here, with the following modification. As the term will be defined later, power is not something distinct from money, position, social approval, or other similar things. To illustrate from the physical sciences, power is not different from electricity, pressure, heat, falling water, and so on. Rather, all of those things are particular instances of power, power being the generalized concept of the ability to do work. Similarly, power in human analysis will mean the generalized ability to satisfy wants—money, status, knowledge, acceptance, persuasiveness, skill, and so forth being particular forms of power. Power is the generalized concept of instrumentality. In that sense, everyone has a desire for power if he wishes to accomplish anything at all. But this gives no clue to the *particular kind* of power he wants, any more than the desire for power to run a ship tells in itself whether steam, diesel, or atomic power is desired.

Generalized reinforcers almost inevitably reinforce each other to some degree. Suppose that a person has acquired a generalized desire for acceptance. He will probably discover that money sometimes assists in being accepted. The desire for money is therefore reinforced by the desire for acceptance. Under different circumstances he may find that being accepted assists in acquiring money, in which case the desire for acceptance is reinforced by the desire for money. More broadly, *any* instrumentality may conceivably help to acquire some other instrumentality.

For these reasons there is no fixed sequence in which a particular set of secondary and tertiary reinforcers appear. They may come in the order *A B C*, *C B A*, or any other. In addition, *A* and *B* may mutually support *C*, or *C* may simultaneously support *A* and *B*, and so on. The same item may appear at several different points in a longer chain, such as *A B C B A C*. We often speak of persons as having "mixed motives" in doing something. Considering the tremendous interrelation of motives, it is doubtful if an adult can have any motive which is *not* mixed. The usual problem is not whether motives are mixed, but which one is dominant, and whether the dominant one is different from the one stated. All of which leads to a fuller discussion of such mixtures.

CONFLICTING MOTIVES

Nature of the Problem

Up to this point we have examined the development of responses and motives in what might be called a line, or directional approach. We have looked at the single stimulus, and observed whether a particular response was or was not conditioned to it. Or we examined a particular stimulus or response to determine whether it behaved as a reinforcer or extinguisher.

In many real life situations, however, we do not face a single stimulus, to which we either respond or do not respond. Instead we face pairs, scores, and hundreds of simultaneous stimuli. In the classroom, the student meets not only the sound of the professor's voice, but his scribbling on the blackboard, the expression on his face, his walking across the platform, and the removal and replacement of his glasses. There is also the student to the left smoothing her hair, the one to the right tapping his pencil, the breeze through the leaves outside, and the sound of a mower beyond—not to mention the fixtures and furniture in the room and the many associations any of these things call to mind. Of all these competing stimuli, which will be observed and which will not? Which will hold the attention at any given moment? Which will be attended to long and strongly enough to produce learning? Will the attention to a lecturer who asks repeated questions be the same as to one who never asks questions? These are pertinent questions, which merely begin to indicate the degree of complexity involved.

This may be referred to as a "field" approach, as contrasted to the SR approach, and is far more complex.[12] To begin with, in SR psychology it is necessary to know in many experiments only the valence of the stimulus: whether it is plus or minus, reinforcing or extinguishing. Further, it is necessary in most experiments to deal with only one stimulus at a time. By contrast, with the field approach it is necessary to deal simultaneously with *all* of the stimuli in the field. To venture a prediction about the behavioral outcome in such a situation, it is necessary to know not only the valence of each stimulus, but its approximate strength as well. For example, the relative loudness of the professor's voice and the mower would be one factor determining which would receive the greater attention. Other factors which influence attention are called *attention cues*. These include not only the quality of the stimulus, but also certain habits and response factors in the individual. The mower will tend to command more attention than otherwise if the student himself must do some mowing after class. The professor's voice will tend to command more attention than otherwise if the subject of the lecture will be covered in an examination immediately thereafter.[13]

The SR and field approaches are not in conflict. In part they supplement each other, and in part they are just different. Through a basically SR approach, for example, we can discern the steps by which a particular person developed a liking for photography, basketball, and gardening, and a dislike for hockey, opera, and boating. Knowledge of the previous "line" development of the separate preferences would enable us to predict with

---

[12] The reference to this kind of problem as a "field" approach uses the word "field" in the sense employed by Kurt Lewin in works such as those to be cited below. The term "field" is also used in a quite different sense by some psychologists, such as Köhler, to offer an alternate or supplement to synaptic connections as an explanation of the behavior of the brain. In this sense the "field" is a polarization, magnetic alignment, chemical sensitivity, or other kind of change which may affect the whole brain or substantial portions of it at a time, with different kinds of "alignments" reflecting different kinds of information, states of readiness, or feelings. The field approach in this second sense does not now seem to command a sufficient following, or explain brain behavior sufficiently well, to justify further discussion.

[13] A similar problem has been dealt with by Maslow in connection with the relative strength of primary motives when two or more are simultaneously present, and will be discussed briefly in the next chapter.

some reliability that in a given choice he would prefer photography to opera, or basketball to hockey. But it might allow only a highly unreliable prediction whether he would choose basketball over photography, or whether he would choose either over eating or swimming. Although at the present stage of knowledge we can hardly even suggest the direction in which the answers to this kind of question lie, we nevertheless can make somewhat more explicit several major points at which uncertainty is focused.[14]

Ambiguity of Stimulus

A condition almost certain to create conflict and uncertainty occurs when one is not sure which of two (or more) things the stimulus actually *is*, when the alternate possible interpretations call for oppositely valued responses, or produce an expectation of oppositely valued feedbacks. To illustrate with a laboratory experiment, a rat or dog can be conditioned to expect food to a metronome beat of 120 a minute. It can also be independently conditioned to expect electric shock if the beat is 80. If the animal is then presented with a beat of 100, what does it do? The answer is what any layman might expect—it acts worried, tense, and neurotic, and may not give either response.

Human beings face similar problems of ambiguous stimuli. Is that lone headlight a motorcycle or a one-eyed automobile? Is that stranger really friendly, or is he softening me up for something? Did my congressman amend the bill I supported in order to emasculate it, or to improve its chance of passing? In these cases our response may be uncertain, not because we do not know what we want, but because our identification of the situation we are responding to is not clear. The problem of identifying stimuli will be discussed in a later chapter.

Bivalent Feedback

A second major case of uncertain response occurs when a particular response will create both desired and undesired consequences, as when a boatride after the dance would be great fun, but would incur parental wrath and restrictions. A variation occurs when one must choose between two alternatives, both of which are rewarding, as between the dance and the boatride, if both are scheduled at the same time. Or both alternatives may be punishing, as when one must choose between jumping from the third-story window and running down the burning stairs.

---

[14] The reader who is seriously interested in the field approach to psychology should certainly consult the various writings of Kurt Lewin. Of particular interest are his articles "Defining the 'Field at a Given Time'" and "Field Theory and Learning," which are Chapters III and IV of a collection of his papers, *Field Theory in Social Science* (New York: Harper, 1951).

Further pursuit of the distinction between the SR and field approaches might lead to an inquiry whether the distinction parallels that between time and space relations (or temporal and formal relations) as drawn by Leslie A. White in Chapter 1 of his *The Science of Culture* (New York: Grove Press, Inc., 1949).

Handling Conflict

The Law of Effect tells us that one will select a rewarding response and avoid a punishing one. But it gives no direct clue as to what will happen when a given response is both rewarding and punishing, or when we face two alternatives, both of which are rewarding or both punishing. This is the essential problem of the field approach, and predictions are difficult to make. We can, of course, say that the organism will select the *most* rewarding or the *least* punishing line of action. This is eminently sensible, but does little to identify *which* alternative that is.

We seem here to be forced back to the proposition advanced in Chapter 1 about large numbers of variables as contrasted to small numbers—the airplane dropping a heavy streamlined object as contrasted to dropping a piece of paper. SR psychology usually deals with a small number of variables, and we can often achieve predictable results in simple situations. Field psychology deals with many variables, and does not show such predictability. We can narrow the problem, however, when an obviously dominant force exists in a complex field. If we see a barefoot boy bouncing across the grass, we can predict reliably that his pace will slow abruptly when he reaches the sharp-stoned driveway. Even though the boy faces many stimuli—the sounds of birds, the smell of flowers, the wind in his face, and thoughts of a package in the mailbox—we know that in the driveway the pain in his feet will be dominant over competing stimuli, and control the response. In such a situation it seems sensible to conclude that intensity, which is one of the factors in SR learning, is also a factor which affects dominance in a field situation.

So is frequency, or the extent or depth to which a habitual response has been developed. If a situation contains three competing stimuli, one of which has a strongly conditioned response while the other two have no conditioned responses attached to them or only weakly attached ones, the first (other things equal) will probably prevail. If a student is strongly conditioned to listen to lectures, while he is thoroughly conditioned to ignore the sound of mowers, his response of listening to the lecture will tend to dominate. By contrast, a child who has been rewarded with candy every time he identifies the sound of some piece of machinery, but who has no conditioned responses to classroom lectures, would respond to the two competing sounds by rushing to the window and shouting "mower."

Recency may also have an effect. If the lecture is on history, the person who has just taken a master's exam in history may find it easy to follow the lecture, while one who has just returned from a biology field trip may find his ears tuned to the crickets and tree frogs.

The relative strength of motives also plays a part. The student who came to learn will probably attend to the lecture, while one who came for other reasons may attend to the girl smoothing her hair.

Thus, although SR psychology can by no means deal fully with problems of competing motives and ambiguous stimuli, it is not necessarily totally useless. To conduct rigorous experiments in this area, however, entails grave difficulties, such as measuring the intensity of motives as well as their direction. Even in relatively simple situations involving lower animals, these measurements are uncertain, and they are not linear. We cannot say that a 20-hour deprivation of water is twice as strong a thirst drive as a 10-hour deprivation, or that a sex drive which will entice a rat across a 20-volt grid is twice as strong as one which just brings him across a 10-volt one. Nor are the measures always internally consistent, as when a four-day hunger drive may not produce as much eating as a two-day drive. In experiments with human beings we are even less able to measure motive strength, and the measurements may be circular. We can say that the person will respond with that choice toward which he is most strongly motivated, but the only measure of his motive strength is to observe his response.[15]

Having noted some of the problems of the field approach, we will not pursue it further. As indicated, we will return to it in a different form in Chapter 14, on decision making.

---

[15] Despite the generally pessimistic things said here about analyzing the more complex situations of multiple or ambiguous stimuli or valences, the reader interested in an attempt to systematize the approach to these problems might consult Frank A. Logan, David L. Olmsted, and others, *Behavior Theory and Social Science* (New Haven: Yale University Press, 1955), Chap. 6, "Free Behavior."

Chapter 6

MOTIVES: THE SOURCE
OF PREFERENCES

THE PROBLEM OF PRIMARY REINFORCEMENT

IN DISCUSSING secondary reinforcers, we have seen how some existing motive, by a process of conditioned association, can pass its "motive power" on to other behavior. An existing motive thus acts as a valve which can release motive power into other behavior—which can in turn reinforce still other behavior, and so on. This whole structure, however, presumes some pre-existing motive which was *not* learned. The problem is like that of a row of dominoes. We can explain the fall of any one in the row by the push of the one before it. But to explain the fall of the first one we must look for some independent, and different, force. This "first push," whatever it may be, is a primary reinforcer, or an inherited motive. The purpose of this chapter is to inquire what these primary reinforcers are, and what mechanism allows them to operate. The first push is the main governor in the cybernetic system of learning and behavior.

Before exploring details it seems useful to inquire into the presumed origin of the system. It is almost universally accepted in scientific circles that the human species has developed by a process of evolution. The cybernetic control of evolutionary development is natural selection, through the "selector" criterion of survival. Biologically, any structure or function of the body which possessed survival value tended to be preserved in the species, since those individuals who possessed this item were more likely than others to mature and reproduce. Those without it were more likely to die before bearing children. Hence, survival traits survive in the race, while nonsurvival traits disappear.

The neurological and motivational systems of human beings must be presumed to have taken their present shape by the same selective process. Unlike many lower animals, which inherit specific and detailed *behavior* systems, human beings inherit mainly a behavior *selecting* system. If such a system is to select some behavior "in" and others "out," there must exist some criterion, or cybernetic governor, which reinforces some types of behavior and extinguishes others. Since the motive system of man must itself be presumed to have been selected by evolution, and the cybernetic control of evolution is survival, then the motive system of man must in turn be presumed to be geared for survival. More explicitly, the survival of an individual to the age of procreation depends not only on his biological traits, but also on his behavior. Any individual whose motive system reinforces such behavior as eating stones or inhaling water is unlikely to survive to become a parent. The evolutionary process must similarly eliminate behavior which is inimical to survival.

These statements are intended in a scientific, not a moral or ethical, spirit. They do not imply that survival is a "highest goal" of mankind, or even that it is desirable. The statement that the behavior-selecting system must have a survival orientation, or the human race would have perished, is parallel in spirit to a statement that the human race must at all times have had water available, or it would have perished. A human being is, after all, a highly developed form of self-preserving system, capable of maintaining itself in the face of highly divergent environments.

As Ashby puts it, after diagnosing a long train of successively complex systems:

> The development of life on earth must thus *not* be seen as something remarkable. On the contrary, it was inevitable. It was inevitable in the sense that if a system as large as the surface of the earth, basically polystable, is kept gently simmering dynamically for five thousand million years, then nothing short of a miracle could keep the system away from those states in which the variables are aggregated into intensely self-preserving forms.[1]

The present volume is intended solely as a science of human society, not an ethic. All we are saying here is that a survival criterion is a *necessary* condition for the present existence of the human race; this is a scientific, not an ethical statement. Whether the existence of the race is desirable is a matter we will leave for discussion elsewhere—though I confess a strong personal bias in its favor. To use the language of system analysis, human beings prefer survival because their cybernetic governors are set for survival, in the same sense that the thermostat in the house "prefers" a temperature of 70 degrees because it is set that way.

Before we enter the next stage of the problem it may be well to note the limitations on the state of our knowledge. As one psychologist put it: "We are a science still groping for the identification of our own basic variables."[2] He added later that the difficulties "even in the initial mapping of what we have called 'value-properties,' are such as to require the efforts of the most imaginative investigators our field can produce for many

---

[1] W. Ross Ashby, *Design for a Brain* (New York: John Wiley & Sons, 1960), p. 233.

[2] Sigmund Koch, "Behavior as 'Intrinsically' Regulated: Work Notes Towards a Pre-theory of Phenomena Called 'Motivational'," in Marshall R. Jones (ed.), *Nebraska Symposium of Motivation, 1956* (Lincoln: University of Nebraska Press, 1956), p. 42.

years."[3] Despite the still somewhat undeveloped state of the science, we will try to make some formulations of the problem which will meet our present needs, the material immediately below leaning more heavily on Olds than on others.[4]

The Mechanism of Primary Reinforcers

To say that the behavior-selecting mechanism presumably has a survival orientation does not mean that any particular act must be directly related to survival. An important difference between human beings and lower animals is the ability to go counter to immediate survival needs in the short run, in ways which greatly increase long-run ability to survive. We should also note that evolution works through traits which favor survival *on the average*, not in every individual case. For example, it seems possible that the desire to form concepts is an inherited urge. It is easy to see the survival value of curiosity, which is essentially the same as the desire to form concepts, since the curious person is likely to learn things which will give him an advantage over his less curious competitors. Despite this *average* advantage, curiosity will occasionally induce people into dangerous situations which will shorten life.

Olds[5] makes an important distinction between *needs* and *motives*. A *need* is something the absence of which, if persistent, will terminate the life or health of the organism. Some of the most obvious needs are those for food, water, excretion, rest, and protection from injury and disease. A *motive*, on the other hand, is a response selector. Although the two are partly related, they are not the same thing. By analogy, an automobile engine "needs" a certain ratio of air and gasoline if it is to function. This "need," however, is not the same thing as the carburetor, which controls the air-gas ratio. The "need" of the human body to remain at 98.6 degrees is not the same thing as the mechanisms which maintain that temperature. Merely to know that the body will not function well at different temperatures tells us nothing about the temperature control mechanisms. Similarly, to know that the body needs food gives no clue to the mechanisms by which food-getting behavior is reinforced. Further, although for fairly obvious reasons psychologists were inclined for many years to equate motivation with need reduction (eating reduces the need for food; therefore we are motivated to eat and rewarded by eating) this simple relation is no longer accepted.[6] For example, we often speak of the "body wisdom"

---

[3] *Ibid.,* p. 82.

[4] James Olds, "Physiological Mechanisms of Reward," in *ibid.,* 1955, pp. 74 ff.

[5] *Ibid.,* pp. 74–77.

[6] *Ibid.,* p. 76; Koch, *op. cit.,* p. 76; Gordon W. Allport, "The Trend in Motivational Theory," in Chalmers L. Stacey and Manfred F. DeMartino (eds.), *Understanding Human Behavior* (Cleveland: Howard Allen, Inc., 1958), pp. 55, 64; Paul T. Young, "The Role of Hedonic Processes in Behavior," in *Nebraska Symposium on Motivation: 1955,* p. 211; B. F. Skinner, *Science and Human Behavior* (New York: Macmillan, 1953), p. 82.

which leads the organism to eat the kinds of food it needs, even though there is no conscious desire for it. Numerous experiments indicate that eating habits do tend to *form* in conformance with body needs, but that these habits persist when the need no longer exists.[7] Rats with a vitamin deficiency learn a preference for food containing vitamins. But the same preference continues after the vitamins are transferred to a different food.[8] Rats will also work to achieve the sweet taste of saccharine even though it meets no body need, and they will accept sweet-tasting foods when they are not even hungry.[9] There is no one-to-one relation between our needs and our motives, and the relation sometimes seems remote indeed. The actual mechanism seems to be as follows.

To judge by (1) what is logically necessary in our model, and (2) what actually seems to be present in the brain, our behavioral control system contains two distinct elements. One controls the *amount* of energy release (much or little) and the other controls its *direction* (approach or withdraw, back or forward, plus or minus). These are roughly parallel to the accelerator and the forward-reverse shift of an automobile.[10]

This distinction and some of its ramifications are outlined in Figure 6-1. We will look first at some stimulus which is valued positively by the organism—say, food. If the animal is stimulated slightly by "reward associates," such as the smell of food or the rattle of a plate, the animal must be stimulated to action if the hint is to be converted into reality. But once the food is eaten and the need filled, action should be inhibited. With positive reinforcers, the hint or suggestion should initiate action, and the actual accomplishment or full stimulation should inhibit further action (so far as this particular stimulus is concerned).

For negatively valued stimuli, such as pain or hunger, action is called for when the stimulus is strong or actually under way, the actions being such things as flight, fight, or search. But mild stimulation or the stimulation of "punishment associates" should normally lead to inaction or caution. (Actual identification of a stimulus as dangerous should be construed as a strong stimulus.) Thus, positively valued stimuli must call forth action when weak and inaction when strong, whereas negatively valued stimuli must call forth inaction when weak and action when strong. As Olds observes, a single control mechanism cannot do this. There need be only one power source, or drive center (the engine). But the center which controls the amount of activity released in response to rewarding stimuli (forward gear) must be distinct from that which controls the amount of

---

[7] Young, *op. cit.*, p. 227.

[8] *Ibid.*, p. 230.

[9] *Ibid.*, p. 211.

[10] This distinction is by no means confined to Olds' approach. See, for example, D. O. Hebb, *A Textbook of Psychology* (Philadelphia: W. B. Saunders, 1958), pp. 156 ff, whose distinction is closely parallel, and Donald W. Taylor, "Toward an Information Processing Theory of Motivation," *Nebraska Symposium on Motivation: 1960* (reprint), p. 11.

energy released by punishing stimuli (reverse gear), since the two show opposite relations between the amount of stimulus and the amount of appropriate response. This much of the analysis does not pretend to be the whole story, but it covers an essential aspect of the beginning.

Figure 6-1

VALENCE OF STIMULUS

		REWARDING (REINFORCING)	PUNISHING (EXTINGUISHING)
DEGREE OF STIMULATION	SLIGHT OR SUGGESTED	ACTION (APPROACH)	INACTION (CAUTION)
	STRONG OR ACCOMPLISHED	INACTION (SATIATION OR REPLETION	ACTION (FLIGHT OR AGGRESSION)

Source: Diagrammed by the author to illustrate the argument of James Olds in "Physiological Mechanisms of Reward," *Nebraska Symposium on Motivation, 1955.*

The brain seems to possess these ingredients. As to the accelerator, if we follow Olds' usage, *drive* will refer to "anything which produces an increase in the general activity of the organism."[11] The reticular formation of the brain seems to perform this function, as do some other areas.[12] When stimulated, these areas prepare both the brain and muscle systems for action, and facilitate response. Stimulation of the reticular area will also wake a sleeping animal.

As to the forward-reverse controls, some parts of the brain are clearly rewarding when stimulated. The limbic system is particularly so. When rats are fitted with electrodes so that they can stimulate this section by pressing a bar, they will spend about half their time in self-stimulation. One part of the limbic system, the septal area, is even more rewarding, inducing self-stimulation about 75 per cent of the time.[13] The behavior goes in cycles of steady stimulation, satiation, and cessation of stimulation, followed by a return to regular stimulation.

Less clearly, other parts of the brain are punishing when stimulated.[14] Rats will not self-stimulate these areas, and will go out of their way to avoid stimulation. Both the rewarding and punishing sections show evidence of connection to the reticular, or "drive," area. Such a connection, direct or indirect, is necessary for the type of control system outlined by Olds. This is the stage at which weak or strong stimulation of the reward center would lead to action or inaction, respectively, from the activating center, as diagrammed in Figure 6-1. The reverse relationships would

[11] Olds, *op. cit.*, p. 74.
[12] D. O. Hebb, *The Organization of Behavior* (New York: John Wiley & Sons, Inc., 1949), p. 219.
[13] Olds, *op. cit.*, pp. 90–94.
[14] *Ibid.*, p. 77.

prevail for punishing stimuli. Some other sections of the brain show neither reward nor punishment responses.[15]

If we tentatively accept the hypothesis that primary reinforcement consists of the stimulation of certain reward sections of the brain, two stages of the problem still remain. First, inborn connections to these reward sections must exist, so that certain experiences will be rewarding the first time they occur, without learning. Otherwise they are not inborn, and cannot be *primary* reinforcers. Second, a technique must exist whereby new experiences can be conditioned to the initially reinforcing ones so that the new ones in turn will acquire the ability to stimulate the reward centers.

To restate it, in this hypothesis primary reinforcement works on essentially the same principle as a reflex, and secondary reinforcement works like a conditioned reflex. For both reflexes and primary reinforcement, the stimulation of some sensory nerves feeds by inborn connection into certain other nerves. In the reflex the "other nerves" are motor nerves, which bring a muscular response. In the primary reinforcer the "other nerves" are a reward center in the cortex, which bring a "pleasure" response. This is the point at which the analysis is greatly sharpened if we think of "wanting" as a neural response, rather than as some passive state of preference.

To illustrate, let us suppose that the sensory nerves which detect the arrival of food in an empty stomach have inborn connections to a reward section of the brain. If so, the arrival of food in the stomach will be pleasurable to the infant the first time it occurs, without learning. If activity in this set of nerves is accompanied or shortly preceded by activity in the sensory nerves of the mouth, then conditioning will occur, after which stimulation of the nerves of the mouth will constitute a conditioned stimulus which will activate the reward section of the brain. As a result of conditioning, the primary reward value of food in the stomach thus produces a secondary reward value for food, or perhaps a nipple, in the mouth. By successive stages of conditioning, other conditions accompanying or just preceding eating would also produce the pleasure response and become desired in their own right. In the infant these might include the feeling of softness and warmth, or such acts as sucking or reaching for food.

In parallel, some inborn connections must presumably exist through which sensations of conditions not conducive to survival (such as pain) feed into the punishment sections of the brain, to which secondary extinguishers can be conditioned. The fact that reward sections are more readily apparent in the brain than the punishing sections may suggest that

---

[15] This general hypothesis by Olds is by no means firmly established. But David McClelland described it as one of the most intriguing and stimulating shots in the arm that the psychology of motivation has had for a long time, and A. H. Maslow called it a major breakthrough on the neurophysiological front. See their respective comments immediately following Olds' article.

the negative controls of behavior operate more largely through nonreinforcement of rewards than through reinforcement of punishments. It
could also, of course, merely reflect greater success of experimenters in
locating reward sections.

Several other aspects of the system remain to be examined. The hypothalamus seems to hold the main clue to the possibility of built-in connections like those described above. This is the section of the brain which
controls the inborn responses of the autonomic nervous system. It also "is
in close connection with all the incoming sensory streams from the receptors."[16] In particular, the sensory nerves from the skin and internal organs
have relays in the thalamus (which adjoins the hypothalamus and has
many connections with it) from which point the sensory fibers form
synapses with nerves radiating into the cerebrum.[17] If some of these go
directly into the pleasure or pain areas—a matter apparently not yet determined—the control system is logically complete.

In addition, the hypothalamus contains the neural networks which control the inborn physical manifestations of the emotions, such as dilations
of the pupil, tensing of muscles, curling of the lip, discharge of sugar or
adrenalin into the blood, and other external and biological manifestations
of pleasure, pain, anger, fear, and other emotions. Considering the extremely close relations of both emotions and sensations with the rewarding
or punishing nature of various experiences, the important role of the hypothalamus in sensations and emotions suggests that it is probably a key coordinating factor in motivation.

The role of the emotions themselves in this complex is not clear, though
it appears that they have two different aspects. One is the overt emotional
response to certain situations, such as facial expressions, body postures,
laughing or crying, and hormone secretions. As indicated by "sham rage"
in the cat, it is possible by electrical stimulation of the hypothalamus to
arouse all the overt physical manifestations of an emotion, including dila-
tion of the pupils, arching of the back, baring of claws and teeth, and
hissing. It is not certain whether the cat has the "feelings" appropriate
to this response. It is expected that he does not, however, since he returns
to normal calm almost instantly after the electrical stimulus ceases.[18] It is
apparently necessary that the inputs which stimulate the hypothalamus also
discharge simultaneously into other parts of the brain if the "feelings" of
the emotion are also to be present. If Olds' hypothesis is correct, then
presumably the cortical discharge associated with some emotions are intrinsically rewarding and others intrinsically punishing. An alternate explanation would be that the physical manifestations of the emotions are

---

[16] Lawrence E. Cole, *Human Behavior* (Yonkers: World Book, 1953), p. 318, and
Frank A. Geldard, *The Human Senses* (New York: John Wiley & Sons, Inc., 1953),
pp. 11, 27, 175.

[17] Geldard, *op. cit.*, p. 175.

[18] Cole, *op. cit.*

sensed in those parts of the body where they have somatic effects, and that these sensations are then fed back to the reward or punishment centers by inborn connection. In either event, the feedback mechanism is available to complete the control circuit.[19]

Olds has noted the opposite effects on degree of action as between strong and weak stimulation of the punishment and reward centers. There is a possibility that the amygdala may control the degree of response, at least for some types of behavior. Its removal brings loss of ability to make "motivationally relevant distinctions." An animal thus treated will eat anything eatable, or sexually approach anything capable of providing sexual stimulation.[20] An animal's intake of food can be similarly affected by stimulation or removal of the ventromedial hypothalamus. If this, or the amygdala, is removed, the animal does not know when to stop eating.[21]

One other factor must be added. Not only the *type* of response is important, but the direction of change. For example, although pain is a punishing stimulus, a *reduction* of pain must behave like a rewarding one. The literature cited above apparently does not suggest a model to explain this phase of the problem.

Most experiments with cortical excisions have been conducted on animals. Although the physical location of some specific control functions differs among species, the basic nature of the mechanisms seems similar among the species, including man. Removal of or injury to sections of the human brain brings behavioral changes comparable to those in other animals.

At this point the layman may complain impatiently: "Any fool knows that a person will learn to avoid fire, because it is painful, and seek food because it stops hunger pangs, so why all the fuss about reward and punishment centers?" The answer is twofold. First, important errors have been made in the past by psychologists and social scientists, and are still made by laymen, in assuming that there exists some clear, inborn, unchangeable, universal "human nature" which we can ignore only at our peril. The weight of current evidence, whether from psychology, comparative anthropology, or elsewhere, is overwhelmingly to the contrary. Whatever may be the urges all men share by birth, they are flexible in

---

[19] There does not seem to be any need to go further into theories of emotion for our present purpose. An excellent summary is that of Magda Arnold, "The Status of Emotion in Contemporary Psychology," in A. A. Roback (ed.), *Present Day Psychology* (New York: Philosophical Library, 1955), chap. vii. Ross Stagner, *Psychology of Personality* (New York: McGraw-Hill Book Co., Inc., 1961), p. 93, notes that, by contrast to feelings, emotions seem to be more the products of learning than of heredity, adding that "When we examine an emotion critically, we usually find that it can be analyzed into a feeling or feelings, plus certain expectancies about the object of the emotion." Acceptance of that general position means that the role of the emotions is implicitly covered in the present discussion of primary and secondary reinforcement, and does not require separate treatment.

[20] Olds, *op. cit.*, p. 117.

[21] *Ibid.*, pp. 118–19.

the extreme, and can be accommodated to any social structure compatible with biological survival. Second, the fact that pain is painful or pleasure pleasurable does not explain *how* it affects behavior. For example, if we are to learn responses which avoid pain, information about pain must get into the cortex, where it must extinguish behavior which accompanies it, even though reinforcement is the usual result of temporally related stimulations. To say "Something hurts; therefore we avoid it," is common sense, but does not tell us *how* this happens. As Young observes, whether or not Olds has found it, we *must* assume some physiological basis for the primary reinforcers. "Affective processes exist objectively within the tissues of the organism."[22]

HOW MANY PRIMARY REINFORCERS, AND WHAT ARE THEY?

From the preceding discussion it can be seen that it is theoretically possible that all motives could be derived from a single positive and a single negative primary motive, and conceivably from a single positive one. For theoretical purposes it makes no difference *what* that motive is, so long as there is at least one with an inborn connection to the brain. However, there is no apparent upper limit to the number. The satisfaction of any bodily need (as defined by Olds, and often referred to as "drive reduction" by others) could conceivably provide a primary reinforcer—though we have seen the relatively poor correlation between motives and physiological needs. If so, then food, water, air, comfort, relaxation and sleep, freedom from pain and irritation, sex, elimination of wastes, and numerous others might be primary reinforcers. In common sense terms it seems difficult *not* to accept many of these as primary, along with such things as the widespread acceptance of sweetness and avoidance of bitterness—even though these likes and dislikes can be modified through learning.

We should distinguish, however, between reinforcers in the sense we have been using the term, and body needs which are normally met by reflexive or autonomic action. To illustrate first with a fully inherited control, the body has a "need" to maintain a given level of blood oxygen. Part of the mechanism for meeting this need is under the control of the

---

[22] Paul T. Young, *op. cit.*, p. 203. See also W. T. Powers, R. K. Clark, and R. I. McFarland, "A General Feedback Theory of Human Behavior: Part I," in *General Systems*, vol. V, 1960. The authors there conclude that "the 'reference-signals' must be genetically determined, not determined by experience . . ." (p. 69), the 'reference signals' in their system being the same as the governors in the present system. Ross Stagner, *op. cit.*, pp. 88–93, uses a model generally similar to the present one, but without including Olds' point that the pleasure and pain responses must be oppositely connected with the center controlling the amount of response. Stagner includes the role of "visceral feedback" through the thalamus, his diagram (p. 91) being particularly useful for this purpose. He identifies four "feelings" rather than two: pleasant, unpleasant, excitement, and depression. But he identifies pleasant and unpleasant with valences, and excitement and depression with activity levels (p. 92), and is therefore in agreement with Olds on this point.

autonomic nervous system. But it never influences our motives. Breathing is also a "need," and in part it can be consciously controlled. But it plays very little part in our motive system. Although deprivation of these things has obvious destructive physiological consequences, we should be cautious not to assume that these needs influence motives until the connection can be shown.

The logic of evolutionary survival would also allow a variety of non-physiological inborn desires, such as freedom from restraint. This is illustrated by the tendency of babies and lower animals to resist confinement of arms or legs. It is questionable that the resistance is inborn and universal, however, in light of the ready acceptance of papoose sacks by babies of several cultures. Inborn desires for love, acceptance, companionship, superiority, improvement and exercises of skills, sensory stimulation, and others might all be argued to have survival value, and, hence, to be candidates for a list of primary reinforcers. However, attempts to pin down their inherited nature meet repeated frustration. For example, the widespread occurrence of status seeking among chickens, pigeons, cats, seals, and many other animals seems to suggest that this urge is universal and inborn. On the other hand, certain experimental situations will reliably induce inferior-superior status relations in animals who did not previously show them, suggesting that status behavior is learned, not inherited.

It is sometimes mistakenly believed that if a certain motive is inborn, man is helpless in its grip. This could hardly be the case, since one inborn tendency often conflicts with another, as when a man with an injured lip can meet his inborn tendency to eat only by overcoming his inborn tendency to avoid pain. Even inborn tendencies in the form of reflexes can be brought under the control of learned motives, as when a person trains himself not to blink when his eye is touched. Certain activities can even acquire a learned reversal of valence if the reversal is rewarding in some context. To illustrate, in some societies even pain acquires reward value if the ability to endure pain brings status.

Maslow[23] has tried to compile what he calls a "hierarchy" of needs, which we presumably possess on an inherited, "instinctoid" basis. In decreasing order of strength these are (1) physiological needs essential to the biological continuation of the system, (2) safety needs, as freedom from pain, discomfort, and threatening circumstances, (3) love and belongingness needs, including sex, love, desire for children, and desire for acceptance, (4) esteem needs, such as prestige, fame, and recognition, and (5) the need for self-actualization, as in self-expression, self-fulfillment, and sense of growing or "becoming" something. On a tentative basis he also adds (6) the desire to know and understand, and (7) esthetic needs. Maslow proposes that any one need will take precedence over those below

---

[23] A. H. Maslow, *Motivation and Personality* (New York: Harper & Bros, 1954).

it in the list, and that the lower ones tend to be fulfilled only after the higher ones have been relatively satiated.

The list and the approach it represents are fascinating but experimentally on weak ground. As to the difficulties, inherited motives cannot easily be separated from learned ones, and there is strong evidence that even such "basic" urges as for food and sex can be greatly strengthened or weakened by training and experience. Further, under appropriate circumstances the meeting of one need can be instrumental to another, almost any one being capable of bringing prestige. Further, in many instances one motive can in part "compensate" for lack of fulfillment of another. Finally, to test the relative strength of any two urges experimentally requires that the subject be put in a state of equal deprivation of both. But how long a period without sex constitutes equal deprivation to 24 hours without food? How much lack of recognition is equal to how much lack of self-actualization or freedom from threat, and in what units are the deprivation and ensuing satisfaction to be measured? In addition to these weaknesses, this approach also does not provide the essential link of showing how the "need" is reflected in the nervous system in a form which can control behavior. For such reasons Maslow does not seem to offer a particularly fruitful approach.

In conclusion, several points about motivation are important to the study of society in later chapters. First, although in our model there must be at least one primary motive, we are not at all sure whether human beings possess one or a dozen such motives, or what they are. Hence, we would be on treacherous ground to build either social policy or a science of society on the assumption that social structure or function must reflect some basic, universal "human nature." In fact, as we shall see later, it seems that the thing often thought of as "human nature" is more a product of culture than culture is of human nature—and most psychologists and social scientists avoid using the term "human nature."

Second, the relation of primary to secondary motives can be described as that of system to subsystem, as follows. The governor of the major motivational system is the primary reinforcer, or set of reinforcers. The effector of this major system is the process of developing secondary reinforcers, by conditioning, from the primary one(s). While being the effector stage of the major motive system, these secondary reinforcers are simultaneously the governors of the subsystems of responses which make up day-to-day behavior. The detector of the main system apparently cannot be precisely identified at this stage of knowledge, but may be a process of comparing satisfaction actually received from a given response with that expected. The meaning of such a comparison will be clearer after we discuss the interactions of concepts and motives in Chapter 8. The relation of the main motive system and its subsystem is diagrammed on page 102.

Through additional similar steps, sub-subsystems of behavior can arise

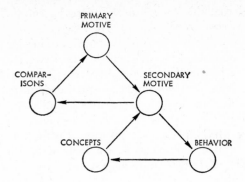

within the subsystem, and so on. Although statements of this sort are difficult to test empirically, presumably the greater the number of steps by which a given motive is removed from the primary one, the less will be its similarity to the original. The ability of the human brain to engage in almost indefinitely long sequences of higher-order conditioning of motives, and thus to create behavioral subsystems whose governors are far removed from the controlling criteria of the overall system, makes of the human being a creature whose behavior is extremely complex and difficult to predict. When particular behavior is subject to the control of two or more subsystems with conflicting governors (a matter described earlier as the "field" approach), predictability drops to even lower levels. As if this were not complicated enough, a person may perceive a given stimulus in a multitude of different ways, each having a different appropriate response. But this is a matter of concepts and perception, to which we now turn.

Chapter 7

CONCEPTS: THE LEARNING OF OPPORTUNITIES

NATURE OF THE PROBLEM

WE HAVE no reason to believe that the emotions and primary reinforcers of human beings differ significantly from those of apes, dogs, or rats. Nor does there seem to be any important difference in the rules by which conditioning takes place—either of responses or of secondary motives. But when we move to the question of *what* human beings are capable of learning, and *what* secondary reinforcers they are able to acquire, the difference is stupendous. At present this difference is hypothesized to be related to brain size, the average human being having a brain size roughly two and a half to three times that of the large gorilla. The relationship is not continuous—that is, the ability to learn is not directly proportional to brain size. Instead, there seems to be a critical threshold at about 900 to 1,000 cc. of brain capacity, below which a brain is not capable of typically human learning, and above which it is. Once it exceeds this critical threshold it makes no apparent difference whether the cubic content is 1,000 cc. or 1,600.[1] This critical threshold is something like that of the freezing point of water. At 32 degrees the consistency of water changes from liquid to solid, or the reverse, but its temperature can change great distances beyond without further change in consistency.

For many years the superiority of man's mental capacity over that of lower animals was believed to lie in the ability to handle abstractions, while more recently it has been felt that the crucial difference is found in the ability to engage in symbolic behavior, particularly in the use of language and other symbols in communication.[2] As we shall see in connection with communication and culture, symbols are so closely related to abstractions that it seems doubtful whether this distinction reflects a real difference; both statements will therefore be retained for the present. Perhaps the most useful way of distinguishing between man and lower

---

[1] See Mischa Titiev, *The Science of Man* (New York: Henry Holt & Co., 1954), pp. 159–60.
[2] *Ibid.*

animals is to say that man is capable of forming and using concepts of immensely higher information content.

Certainly linguistic communication depends on concepts, language itself consisting of a group of signs which stand for concepts—as we shall see in a later chapter. Human culture may be said to depend on the unique ability of human beings to give outward expression of concepts.[3] Differences in personality from person to person depend in highly important ways on the differences in the ways different persons conceptualize things. In addition, the process of making decisions consists of making selections among alternate opportunities, the opportunities (insofar as they are relevant to the decision maker) consisting of a set of conceptualizations. The central role of concepts in these important human activities indicates the crucial part they play in human behavior. Concepts are the things we think with, perceive with, communicate with, and build a society with. Hence, the study of concepts is basic to an understanding of human behavior and society.

INFORMATION ABOUT OPPORTUNITIES: CONCEPTS PLUS PERCEPTIONS

In the present approach, behavior reflects the selection of preferred alternatives from among the possible ones. The past two chapters have dealt with the learning of preferences; this chapter will deal with the other half of the behavior model—learning about opportunities. To do this we will explore in more detail the items introduced early in Chapter 4, particularly the nature and necessity of both concepts and perceptions if we are to know about the situations around us.

Among other things, the hillside behind my house contains young scrub elm and walnut trees. Because walnuts provide valuable wood and are relatively attractive, while scrub elm is neither, I have already formed a preference *for* walnut and *against* scrub elm. On occasional forays with ax and machete I therefore want to cut the elms and leave the walnuts, perhaps in the hope that my great-grandchildren will profit from the latter. As I approach any young tree I must make a decision to cut it or let it stand. With my preference already formed, the only remaining task is to identify whether it is elm or walnut—assuming that I have already identified that it is not a fence post, poison ivy, or a neighbor. Before giving a response, I must know what opportunity faces me, which, within the context of this situation, is the same thing as *identifying the stimulus*, or perceiving.

Before I can make this identification, two distinct things must happen. First, I must have formed two concepts, one of elm tree and one of walnut, so that there resides in my brain information about the characteristics

---

[3] See Chapter 12, and Leslie A. White, *The Science of Culture* (New York: Grove Press, 1949), Chap. 2, "The Symbol: the Origin and Basis of Human Behavior."

of both. Second, information about this *particular* tree must get to my brain. There it must be compared with those concepts of walnut and elm, from which comparison the identification can be made. The identification may be verbalized, or it may be signalized by my cutting or not cutting the tree.

The learning of a concept either includes or consists of learning *cues*. The twigs of elms are fine and grayish, those of walnuts are stubby and brown. Walnut branches also are smooth until they are thicker than a thumb. Elm leaves are single and rough surfaced, while walnut leaves are multiple and smooth. Walnut leaves have a characteristic pungent odor if crushed, while elms do not. We might now say that the concepts of walnut and elm trees consist of the basic concept of tree (presumably formed first), plus cues which distinguish these trees from others. We will define a *cue* as any information which assists in making an identification, and *sufficient cues* as that amount of information which enables us to make an identification with a degree of confidence satisfactory for the purpose at hand.

We have stated earlier that the process of learning a concept, which we now have defined to include the learning of cues, is another name for learning codes, or code formation.[4] We have also indicated that perception is the process of decoding a particular receipt of information in the light of the code previously formed. We can now add that it is not possible (in this model) to acquire information about the current state of our environment without both steps. I can examine trees by touch, sight, smell, or any other way I choose. But unless I already possess the concepts of elm and walnut trees, including the cues, I cannot tell which is which. I can also possess perfectly formed concepts of these trees, but unless I receive sensory cues from a particular tree, I cannot tell which it is.

The act of perceiving is an act of classifying or categorizing some particular thing on the basis of cues as being or not being a member of some particular concept. An act of classifying is an act of inference.

Categorizing an event as a member of a class and thereby giving it identity involves, as we have said, an act of inference. Whether one is deciding what the blob was that appeared for a few milliseconds in a tachistoscope or what

---

[4] Note the wording of Bruner, Goodnow, and Austin, *A Study of Thinking* (New York, John Wiley & Sons, 1956), p. 7, where they say in discussing the formation and learning of categories: "The study of equivalence becomes, essentially, a study of coding and recoding processes employed by organisms who have past histories and present requirements to be met." A concept is defined in the same volume (p. 275) as "a way of grouping an array of objects or events in terms of those characteristics that distinguish this array from other objects or events in the universe."

Ranan B. Banerji in "An Information Processing Program for Object Recognition," *General Systems*, Vol. V, 1960, p. 118, puts it: "We shall call a subset of the Universe a *concept* if (1) it is the value of a property of the Universe, (2) it is a union of concepts, (3) it is an intersection of concepts." This statement emphasizes not only characteristics or properties, but also a point to be used below, namely, that a concept can consist of relationships or conjunctions of other concepts.

species of bird it is that we have our binoculars trained on or what Pueblo period this potsherd belongs to, the basic task is not only to make an inference but to make the "right" inference. Is the blob a face, the bird a scissor-tailed flycatcher, the potsherd from Pueblo II?[5]

The authors add, "Let it be clear that we are not asking philosopical questions"—though I would insist that their questions have philosophical importance. "We want to know, simply, how people make sure (or make sur*er*) that they have placed an event in its proper identity."[6]

To say that identifying is inference does not mean that it necessarily involves conscious logic, but merely that inference is implicit in the process. The implicit inference can be verbalized: "Only walnut trees have leaves with a particular pungent odor. The leaves of this tree have that odor. Therefore this is a walnut tree." The experienced botanist identifies a walnut instantly from this odor, just as you and I identify a house from the cue of a doorway glimpsed through the trees, or "perceive" a man on the porch from the cue of a face peering through the window. Whether the performance is slow and conscious or swift and unconscious, to perceive any object in the environment requires deductive inference in essentially syllogistic form. The major premise consists of information stored in the concept, principally of the relation of cues to the concept. The minor premise consists of the information currently sensed. If the minor premise is a sufficient cue, from the two premises together it is possible to deduce that an instance of the concept currently exists in the environment. If either the concept or the current information is faulty, the resulting perception will be incorrect or uncertain.

The inference which takes in perception is the stage at which the information currently received is "amplified" by controlling the release of prior information stored in the form of concepts, as described in Chapter 3. When we see a face on the porch we assume that a whole man is present. A current input which sets off a perception rarely includes as much information as the concept itself. All the information included in the concept but not present in the cues constitutes an inference made in the act of perceiving. This is the contribution of previously accumulated information to information currently received. The smallness of the information in a cue compared to full information about it, as well as the tiny amount of information in a cue which may permit positive identification, is beautifully illustrated by Wittkower in the difference between a child's drawing of a man and a drawing by daVinci, the one a merest hint and the other with full detail.[7]

By contrast to perception, concept formation is an inductive process.

---

[5] Bruner, *et al., op. cit.,* p. 17.

[6] *Ibid.*

[7] R. Wittkower, "Interpretation of Visual Symbols in the Arts," in *Studies in Communication* (London: Martin Secker & Warburg, 1955); see Plate I, opposite p. 112, and the discussion on pp. 109–10.

The major premise in the above example was the inductive generalization: "Only walnut trees have leaves with this particular pungent odor." Generalizations of this sort can be formed only by examining and comparing many specimens of things—or, of course, by being told the generalizations by others who have themselves made the comparison. How we do these things will be examined below. As with the deductions of perception, the inductions of concept formation may be performed consciously or unconsciously. But they must be performed.

Two additional phenomena observed by psychologists require mention in connection with perception: illusions and hallucinations. Expressed in the language of the present model, an *illusion* is a situation in which signals are detected by the organism, but are improperly decoded. The sensation is normal, but the interpretation is in error. By contrast, in the *hallucination* decoding takes place in the absence of detected signals; interpretation occurs without sensation. Illusions can occur to any normal individual, principally when cues appear in some unaccustomed situation. Hallucinations, however, are a definite abnormality, in which imagined events are not distinguished from real ones. Having identified these things in the language of the present model, we have no need to discuss them further.

THE LEARNING AND USE OF CONCEPTS

Some Areas of Ignorance

Before we discuss further formation and use of concepts, we will note some important unknowns. First, we are almost totally unable to explain consciousness, although every reader knows what we mean by the term. Miller *et al.* suggest it is akin to the processing unit in an electronic computer, as contrasted to the transmission and storage units.[8] This makes sense, but does not really help much. Second, although every mentally normal individual knows the difference between a factual statement (George Washington was the first president of the United States) and a fictional one (George Washington never told a lie), we do not have even a hazy guess as to how the brain keeps these things separate and avoids making real responses to unreal situations. (The number of radio and TV fans who send real contributions to real studios to help fictional husbands of fictional wives recover from fictional diseases in fictional hospitals, however, is mildly upsetting.) Along related lines, the ordinary individual often has a clear idea whether a particular perception is certain or dubious, but we have almost no idea how the brain keeps track of the difference. Finally, although we can observe operational steps in conceptual and perceptual processes and note that they are inductive and deductive, we know extremely little about what goes on neurologically in these processes, or how the individual learns to do them. To narrow the igno-

---

[8] George A. Miller, Eugene Galanter, and Karl H. Pribram, *Plans and the Structure of Behavior* (New York: Henry Holt & Co., 1960), p. 198.

rance slightly, we might say that either (1) concept learning and perception involve different processes from those found in SR learning, or (2) the SR laws operate in these areas through complex configurations not yet known.

More hopefully, it seems safe at least to suspect that concept formation involves the tying together of cortical neurons into networks, and that perceptions involve the discharge of these networks more or less as units upon appropriate sensory stimulation. The evidence in this area is complex, and need not be examined here.[9]

The Beginnings of Concept Formation

A neat problem has been lurking in the background of the foregoing discussion. A person cannot perceive things unless he first has a concept of them. But how can he acquire the information with which to form concepts except through perceptions? If we take the previous discussion literally, then either a person is born with concepts already installed, or he is foredoomed to perceive nothing. We are certain that neither is the case, and must deal with the dilemma.

We are relatively sure that the newborn infant does *not* know the following things and that his later information about them is learned. He does not know words or even that they exist. Nor does he know the *things* which adults refer to as I, you, person, water, sky, distance, or food. He has no idea of himself or that his hands and feet are part of him. He has no idea of the differences between living, nonliving, and dead, and when he begins to learn, he usually identifies life with motion. When the city child begins to learn about water, he does not know that it is not manufactured in the wall behind the faucet, that it is the same basic substance as snow and steam, or that a body of water cannot be walked on. He does not know that there is such a thing as the earth, much less that it

---

[9] The interested reader, however, might examine such sources as D. O. Hebb, *The Organization of Behavior* (New York: John Wiley & Sons, 1949), various articles in Lloyd A. Jeffres (ed.), *Cerebral Mechanisms in Behavior* (Wiley, 1951), or Ernest Hilgard and Donald Marquis, *Conditioning and Learning* (New York: Appleton Century, 1940). The neurological process by which the brain recognizes (decodes, or categorizes) incoming signals is one of the major, unsolved mysteries of psychology. On the basis of not-yet-published findings of experiments conducted while at the University of Cincinnati, Alfred Kristofferson has hypothesized that sensory inputs modulate a scanning wave, something like the *alpha* rhythm, and in this form are carried through the various neuron circuits of the brain. "Recognition" occurs when the regularity of the wave is broken up by some kind of correspondence between the modulation of the scanning wave and some characteristics of the particular concept network. According to the hypothesis, the breaking up of the scanning wave allows the network to discharge into, or have access to, an operating center of the brain. I interpret this action as parallel to the operation of a radio receiver, with one important difference. Whereas the detector stage of a radio receiver is tuned to detect a particular carrier wave, regardless of its modulations, the neuron network is "tuned" to detect a particular set of modulations imposed upon an otherwise unvarying carrier wave.

is round, and when he learns that lights can be turned on and off with a switch, he is apt to assume that so can the sun.[10]

On the other hand the infant does "have" (i.e., receive) sensations. Although some sense organs are not fully developed at birth, his optic nerves respond to light, the nerves of his ear to sound, and the normal quota of nerves of pain, pressure, smell, cold, and so forth are fully operative. We can now rephrase the infant's abilities and inabilities and simultaneously start to deal with the dilemma. The infant possesses a reasonably full mechanism for *detecting* information. But until he forms concepts he has no means of *decoding* it. With some reluctance to speak in terms of awareness at this age, we can nevertheless make an important point by saying that the infant is aware of having sensations, but he has no idea about the nature of the things outside himself which set off those sensations. As Sellars puts it, "We *have* sensations but *perceive* things."[11]

Now it is possible that the infant might inherit a few concepts, and that these might perform the same kind of function in concept formation that primary reinforcers perform in motivations, where a host of learned preferences can be derived from a single inherited one. Certainly many concepts are born into lower animals, who recognize and respond to food, enemies, or nest materials on the first exposure. For example, with absolutely no previous experience, the graylag gosling will retreat in flight when a hawk-shaped silhouette moves across its pen.[12] There is now substantial evidence suggesting that human infants inherit the conceptual apparatus necessary for depth perception, and that, if not available immediately at birth, it develops by maturation at an early age.

Although inherited depth perception (if it really exists) might provide an important tool for learning some other concepts, it seems woefully inadequate for the total job, and suggests that we look in another direction. An answer seems readily available. Although the infant cannot *perceive* from sensations alone, there is no reason to assume that he cannot *form concepts* from them. The way out of the dilemma is to assume that the infant forms pure sensory concepts, first at an extremely elemental level, then at a more complex level by combining the elemental concepts. With these concepts, some perceptions can take place. These then form the building blocks for still more complex concepts, and so on. To illustrate, the infant may repeatedly hear the door of his nursery close. Sheer repetition builds up a simple sensory concept of that sound. When he hears it again, he "recognizes" the sound as familiar. But he has no idea what a door is, much less the closing of one, or that the sound emanates from it.

---

[10] These illustrations are taken from John Gabriel Navarra, *The Development of Scientific Concepts in a Young Child* (New York: Teachers College, Columbia University, 1955), *passim.*

[11] Roy Wood Sellars, "Sensations as Guides to Perceiving," *Mind*, Vol. LXVIII, No. 269 (January, 1959), p. 15.

[12] Bruner *et al., op cit.,* p. 13.

Whereas *you* perceive a door closing if you hear that sound, the baby only hears the sound. To verbalize what at that stage is unverbalizable, the baby does not think, "I hear a door," but "That's the same sound I heard before." It is only later when the child has the combined experiences of seeing the door close, hearing it close, walking through it open, closing it and not being able to walk through, all many times over, that he finally forms a reasonably clear concept of doors, their opening and closing, and their sound. Or take the following patterns of sounds of feet on steps. You and I would recognize who was going down the steps, as indicated:

The infant would learn to recognize the patterns of sound, but would have no idea that the sounds represented footsteps, much less whose. Because these early concepts are subverbal, and not easily described in words, we will use a roundabout path to get to the topic, by examining the learning of motor concepts. First, however, we will digress by examining the size of the job to be done.

The Magnitude of Concept Learning

The growing child learns his sensory concepts so early, and his more complex concepts so gradually, that he has no real notion of what goes on in his information apparatus. Although many persons from Plato and Aristotle onward have shown deep insight into the problem of learning from sense data, the incredible complexity of the process, and the real depth of our pristine ignorance have not been fully recognized till recent decades. New insights have been gleaned from experiences of human beings and other animals raised to maturity without sight, who have then had full vision restored.

Several cases are on record of persons who were blind from birth until a congenital cataract was surgically removed from the adult. No lack of intelligence was involved, as some of these persons while blind were graduated from college with good records. Observations of behavior after surgery were made in some cases by trained psychologists, not impressionable relatives. In these cases, the full *detection* apparatus of sight is available immediately upon removal of the bandages, except for the quickly learned skills of focusing and bioptic coordinating.

On learning that a previously blind person has suddenly received full use of his eyes, our impulse is to say: "Oh, how wonderful! Now he can see everything!" The actual fact is that the light which enters his eyes has no more meaning to him than a page of Japanese writing has to you if you have never studied Japanese, as indicated in Figure 7-1. He knows

Figure 7-1

生産計画者の当面する経済問題は，ある目的を達成するために，種々の稀少資源（たとえば人，機械，材料）を割り当てることにある．この問題は多くの場合，ある所与の生産高，または選好対象の生産高を得るためには，相互依存関係をもっているいくつかの生産活動を計画することを必要とする．多くの生産工程は一連の同時連続作業からなり，その投入量は定まっているか，または選好性があり，その生産能力には制限がある．

ある製品の生産を例にあげれば，ポンチ盤作業のつぎにはポンチ抜きした部品の組立作業が行なわれる．それと同時に他の部品の製造が行なわれ，つぎに最終組立と包装が行なわれる．もしもある１種類だけの製品を一定の需要量に見合うだけ作るのならば，主要な問題はロットの大きさ，資材の在庫量，設備配置，製造方法等を決めればよいのである．しかしながら生産計画を立てる人が，しばしば当面する問題は，工場施設の利用に際して，経済的な面からいずれを選択するかをみつけることである．

たとえば，ある場合には必要な製品を現有の製造能力でまかなえるかもしれないが，生産管理者としては，各種製品の見込み需要量に見合うように，利用できる設備能力の時間の割当をもっとも利益があがるように決定しなければならない．需要量が時期的な変動をきたし，しかもその変動する量が不確定な場合には，問題を拡張しなければならない．たとえば種々な寸法の部品を作っているフライス作業班の組長が当面する問題を考えてみよう．所要量の日程計画で，いつ，どの寸法のものが，いくつ必要かを決めるのである．組長は製造能力と効率にちがいのある，種々の機械を利用できる．彼は，たとえば，最小の費用といったような目的を達成するために，これらの機械に所要生産量を割り当てなければならない．これは計画を立案する問題であり，図解式または数学的手法で解明されうるであろう．

前章では，図式手法（ガント・チャート）を扱った．この第II部では，計画立案に際して必要な解析の数学的手法を述べる．

Assuming that you have not studied Japanese, how much information do you get from this page? There is much there for those who know the code.

If you had been blindfolded from birth until now, and suddenly removed the blind, the sight of a landscape or a room would have no more meaning to you than the characters on this page. The patterns of light, shadow, and color which enter your eyes from the things around you are also a language—a sort of one-way language—which you cannot understand without learning. In fact, learning to read the "language of light" by those newly seeing is at least as difficult as learning Japanese by those who have seen from birth, and probably more so. Whereas Japanese characters are all spread out flat on a page, all the objects which constitute the "characters" you see around you must be identifiable when viewed from the top, bottom, sides, or corners. Besides, they look much different in sunlight and cloudiness, or when lighted from different angles, and they occur in a far greater variety of juxtapositions than occur in language.

So congratulate yourself that before you were three you had learned to read a language more complex than Japanese!

that information is entering his eyes, which will be available when he learns to decode it, just as you know that Japanese writing contains information for those who know the code. And that is about all—although we have already mentioned the possibility of inherited depth perception.

Some of these persons could read and write braille fluently, converse readily, and easily identify many complex shapes by touch. Even with training, however, weeks after the restoration of sight they typically could not identify by sight such simple shapes as triangles, squares, and circles, though they could immediately do so by feel. Their only perceptions of "shape" at the outset were horizontality and verticality.[13]

Learning to distinguish shapes by vision is slow and painstaking for these persons. Their eyes must seek out the corners of a triangle before they can be sure it is not a circle. After many months they must count the corners before they can tell a square from a triangle. If they examine a shape, such as a triangle, under one color of light until they identify it, and the color of light is then changed, they will lose the identity and have to start over. On the other hand, even subtle color distinctions are sensed immediately, and color names are remembered well.[14]

Compared to the circle or triangle the human face is a complex and subtle shape. Two years after cataract removal an exceptionally intelligent person "had learned to recognize only four or five faces and in daily conference with two persons for a month did not learn to recognize them by vision."[15] It takes time and careful examination to learn to discriminate faces, and the plight of these persons is a more complete version of that of the homegrown American to whom "all Chinese look alike."

Experiments with visually normal monkeys, pigeons, and rats confirm these findings. When they are reared to maturity in total darkness and then put into the light, their behavior indicates that they receive little or no information through their eyes, and must learn through the same slow process as the newly born. In fact, they may learn more slowly, because of the long disuse of the visual cortex. Regardless of the speed of learning, the nature of the process and the necessity of learning visual concepts before any animal can receive visual perceptions (again perhaps excepting depth perception) are clear. Our evidence about the other

---

[13] Hebb, *op. cit.*, p. 81. It seems possible that the perception of straight lines and simple curves is built into the visual mechanism, but in a mechanical way rather than as an inherited concept. See John R. Platt, "How We See Straight Lines," *Scientific American* (June, 1960), pp. 121 ff.

[14] It is apparently not yet known whether different colors are sensed through different sets of nerves, or through different combinations of nerves. Colors apparently are, however, distinguished by some inborn mechanism at the detection stage. There is apparently no such mechanism for distinguishing shapes at the detection stage; the distinction can in that case be made only at the cerebral, decoding stage, and only after a concept of the shape has previously been formed. See *ibid.*, pp. 28, 50, 80 for both general and specific information on congenital cataract, and Colin Cherry, *On Human Communication* (New York: John Wiley & Sons, 1957), p. 261, for a similar discussion of the general problem.

[15] Hebb, *op cit.*, p. 114.

senses is less direct, but the physics and physiology of the other senses suggest that the problem is essentially the same there—though odors probably have the same kind of sensory directness and simplicity which colors show at the visual scale.

To get some idea of the magnitude of this learning task we may note both the fantastic volume of information received by our senses and the almost incredible capacity of the brain to sort, store, and find it. Each eye has approximately 100 million photo receptors. Each is capable of firing or not firing as much as a thousand times per second. Since not firing (black) is just as much a part of a visual picture as the light, this means that the eye is capable of sending the brain 100 billion bits of information per second.[16] Even when the eye operates at only 0.1 per cent of this capacity, it still provides the brain a respectable 100 million bits per second. Judging by the number of nerves in the olfactory bulb, the nose is capable of transmitting to the brain no less than 16 million distinct combinations of odors.[17] While you are listening to a symphony concert your brain is receiving between several million and a billion bits per second. It has been estimated that the total number of nerves actuated in a lifetime is approximately 10^{20}—a number which would require about 100 billion years to count at the rate of one a second.[18]

How the brain can handle such huge inputs of information can be vaguely appreciated by an attempt to sense its stupendous capacity. We have already noted that nerve networks apparently are the device for storing information in the head. The cerebral cortex contains approximately 10 billion nerve cells, among which it is possible to form somewhere in the neighborhood of 10^{10^9} different circuits. This number is fantastically incomprehensible, having about 8 billion digits—compared to the number estimated to represent all the protons in the whole universe, which has only about 79 digits. As one of our greatest mathematicians, intimately familiar with electronic computers, stated in referring to some other aspects of the brain, "We have absolutely no experience with systems of this degree of complexity."[19]

---

16 These figures are from Warren S. McCulloch, "Why the Mind Is in the Head," in Lloyd A. Jeffres (ed.), *op. cit.* pp. 44–45. The meaning of a "bit" of information will be dealt with in later chapters on communication.

17 R. M. Hainer, A. G. Emslie, and Ada Jacobson, "An Information Theory of Olfaction," *Annals of the New York Academy of Science (1954)*, pp. 158–74, from abstract in *Behavioral Science*, Vol. 1, No. 2, p. 247.

18 John von Neumann, "The General and Logical Theory of Automata," in Jeffres, *op. cit.*, p. 18.

19 The quotation and estimate of the number of cells in the cortex (which is sometimes put at only 9 billion) are from von Neumann, *op. cit.*, p. 13. The estimate of the number of possible circuits is my own, made by using Stirling's formula in connection with the following assumptions. These neurons are so intricately tied together that every cell is connected directly or indirectly with every other cell. It also seems possible that for any particular circuit any nerve can either precede or follow any other, either directly or with other nerves intervening. Recirculating loops of cells are also apparently used, and the same neuron may be used several

Despite this huge capacity, it takes time for the brain to organize itself to make sense of the billion or so bits of information it receives per second from our eyes under normal light. We will not bother with the highly tentative theories of how it does so, but merely note that normal visual perception is a far more difficult technical accomplishment than that of being a piano virtuoso or a trapeze artist. The difficulty of the skill is not recognized because everybody acquires it at an early age.

If this seems surprising, we may note that by the time a person is five years old he has had approximately 25,000 hours of practice in using his eyes, and by the time he is twenty he has piled up another 90,000 hours or so—to which he keeps adding about 16 hours per day. This much practice ought to keep any skill in reasonably good shape! The same kind of observation applies to the other senses only in lesser degree, because other senses are not used as continuously as the eyes.

The Learning of Motor Concepts

We will now start an indirect way of describing the development of concepts—indirect because the nonverbal nature of elemental concepts makes them difficult to talk about. The basic process, however (as it presumably operates), can be described by analogy with motor operations.

The new infant cannot walk, pick things up (as contrasted to holding on to something placed in its hand), or even reach out to touch your nose. It can perform numerous random flexing and stretching movements, but at first these are not controlled toward any goals. In due time the baby learns to extend its arm a given distance and touch your nose, by coordinating certain eye and muscle movements. We will refer to the group of neuron connections whose simultaneous and sequential operation in a particular pattern produce this kind of movement as a *simple motor concept*. Probably as a separate operation the baby will learn another simple motor concept, in which the muscles of the wrist and fingers are coordinated to grasp and pick up an object.

Once each operation has been learned by itself, the two can be put together. Neurologically, once a neuron network has been built for each motor concept, the two can be tied together into a larger and more complex network, to produce the coordinated acts of reaching *and* picking up. Even if each separate operation was smooth, the coordination of the two will at first be clumsy, but will eventually merge into a single smooth performance.

Later the child will learn the motor concept of walking, and another of squatting. These two can then be combined into a more complex one of

---

times in the same circuit, just as a vacuum tube is often used at several successive stages in the same radio circuit. If we assume for our first approximation that those combinations of cells which are physically impossible are numerically offset by multiple uses of cells and loops of cells within a given circuit, this estimate is then made on the basis of the number of permutations of 10 billion cells taken any number at a time.

walking-to-a-given-spot-and-then-squatting. The child now has two larger motor concepts, each a combination of two subconcepts. When it combines these two larger concepts into a still larger one, the child will then be able to walk to where a toy lies on the floor, squat, reach, and grasp it. With adequate practice the whole operation becomes a single coordinated movement. The child no longer performs four separate operations. He actuates only a *single* motor concept, which now includes the whole sequence. The sequence becomes still smoother when the child later abandons the squatting posture for bending over.

Depending on the method of instruction, the adult may go through similar stages when he learns a new sport. He learns as separate steps how to put the left hand on the club, how to put the right hand on it, how to lift the club for the swing, where to look while swinging, how to move the elbow as the club comes down, how to move the wrist, and how to follow through—not to mention the actions of shoulders, knees, ankles, feet, and hips. With practice the separate motions join into subgroups of two's and three's, and then the subgroups join into larger groups, until some happy day they all come forth as a single, smoothly coordinated performance. The golfer now possesses a single motor concept for the whole sequence. The "smoothing" process, incidentally, not only ties separate parts into a larger whole, but also eliminates motions which were appropriate to the separate steps, but which are not needed for the total movement.

The successive formation of more inclusive and complex motor concepts is inferred from overt behavior. Although the development of nonmotor or information concepts is less easy to observe, we have sufficient observations of natural concept learning by school chidren, of concept learners under experimental conditions, of lower animals, and of introspection to leave a strong impression that nonmotor concepts follow the same general steps as motor ones. Starting from modest concepts of simple sensations, these combine, recombine, and drop irrelevant parts, until a given concept can be very complex, very far from its original sensory base, and contain large amounts of information. This observation applies primarily to concept formation rather than concept attainment, as these terms will be defined below.

The Learning of Information Concepts

The learning of concepts can proceed in either of two directions. In the one, which we will call concept *formation,* we start with an assortment of objects or events—say, plants. On the basis of observed similarities and differences, we divide them into different groups, or categories, such as flowers, weeds, bushes, vines, and trees—to use everyday designations and keep the illustration simple. (Concepts can exist without names, as in the case of the simple sensory concepts referred to above, but in writing a book it is easier to use concepts *with* names.) The categories do not exist in our minds as separate concepts until we observe the similarities and differences, and distinguish between the groups. In concept formation, we start with specimens and create concepts which separate the specimens into groups appropriate to our purpose.[20]

By contrast, in concept *attainment* (or *acquisition*) we start with a concept already formed, normally by someone else, and the task of the learner is to discover what traits or cues will enable him to determine whether particular specimens are or are not representatives of the concept (or members of the category.) When the concepts cited above have been attained, the learner will be able to look at a particular plant and tell whether it is a flower, weed, bush, vine, or tree.[21]

Concept formation on his own is indispensable to the child until he reaches the age of speech, after which he mainly attains the concepts formed by others. Concept formation is also the only source of concepts for a whole people, or culture, as they gradually learn about and conceptualize their environment. Concept attainment, by contrast, is the process by which each individual learns the set of concepts already formed in his culture. The simplest way to attain a concept, of course, is to be given a definition—that is, a list of the cues which permit identification. When the definition is unsatisfactory, either because we are not old enough to use it or because it does not provide a clear picture, concepts are attained by the more tedious process of examining and comparing exemplars with nonexemplars of the concept until we have discerned the list of cues which make the distinction. As each specimen is examined, some criterion must be present which informs us whether that specimen does or does not belong to the category. If someone is teaching us, he will indicate which specimens are included or excluded. On the other hand, if we must depend on experience to tell us which items are and which are not members of the category, say, of edible mushrooms, we can find out whether a particular specimen is edible by feeding it to someone and observing the result.

Concept Formation. Most of the literature on concepts deals with concept attainment—which fact leaves the ensuing discussion of concept formation on tenuous ground. It seems probable, however, that the laws

---

[20] This approach is thoroughly approved by some philosophers, and is in line with the main body of present-day analysis of linguistics. As noted in Bruner *et al.*, *op. cit.*, p. 7, one of the difficulties of science has been to shake the dogma of naive realism, and to recognize that the categories of things in nature are invented, not discovered, and that the value of any such invention is its usefulness in permitting us efficiently to acquire and process information. As was seen in Chapter 3, some conceptual systems, or ways of classifying things, contain more information than others, and hence are more efficient. Jean Piaget likens the learning of identity (through categorizations) to the conservation of energy in physics—as reported in *ibid.*, p. 3, from an unpublished lecture by Piaget.

[21] This distinction between concept formation and concept attainment is taken from *ibid.*, pp. 21–22. Earl Hunt does not make this distinction in his *Concept Learning: An Information Processing Problem* (New York: John Wiley & Sons, 1962), pp. 6 f, preferring to deal merely with "concept learning." For reasons which should be clear from the ensuing discussion, I feel the distinction is important.

of learning as discovered in SR psychology are relevant here, at least in part. To start with frequency, if the shapes $\triangle$ and $\bigcirc$ appear frequently in our field of vision, the brain will form networks which correspond to the coded representation of the things we call triangles and circles. Since rats, pigeons, and ducks can learn to perceive triangles and circles (implying they have learned the concepts) these concepts can presumably be learned by human children long before they learn the words. On the other hand, if such shapes as $\not\supseteq$ and $\diagdown$ are sensed only rarely, the factor of frequency is not present, and no concept networks will be formed. Among a group of people, the frequently found shapes conceptualized by most persons will be given names, while the infrequent ones will not. The same thing will occur with nonvisual stimuli, such as patterns of sound, odors, feelings of texture, degrees of warmth, particular types of pain, and so forth. To revert to earlier language, the brain comes to contain information about the environment by forming neural connections in correspondence to things frequently associated in our environment, and not forming neural connections for things not regularly associated.

The factor of recency also applies. When two sensations occur in quick succession, as lightning and thunder, the brain associates them more quickly and strongly than those long separated or irregularly related, as sunshine and rate of plant growth. On the whole, concepts of objects are probably formed more readily than of events, since objects can be studied at leisure, and show more stability from specimen to specimen.

Although the discussion above has all been conducted in terms of concepts of concrete objects, it is assumed that the same general principles also apply to concepts of events, including such things as gerrymandering, class structure, juvenile delinquency, or patriotism. Complexity of the concept and uncertainty or nonstandardization of the cues among different persons do not change the psychological or logical status of these things. The discussion has focused on concrete objects mainly because concepts of these things can be built by one person from sensory cues alone, and can also be perceived without assistance. Information about concepts such as gerrymandering or class structure can be acquired only through verbal communication, which adds a complication we are not prepared to deal with at this point.

Intensity, which is related to strength of response, can be involved in concept learning in the form of motivation. The learning of concepts (either formation or attainment) requires judgments whether two stimuli are the same or different, which judgments are referred to by psychologists as generalization and discrimination. There is some evidence that we tend to treat two things as the same until we are motivated to discriminate.

To illustrate, suppose an animal is conditioned to go for food on a metronome beat of 120 per minute, what will he do if he hears a beat of

80? Normally he will give the same response as to the beat of 120, though less strongly at first. This act the psychologist describes as generalizing the stimulus of 120 to include 80. In the language of logic, the animal's response indicates that the beat of 80 falls into the same category as the beat of 120, and in information language a single code item includes both beats. The two beats are exemplars of the same concept, and are perceived as the same thing.

If we then shock the animal following each 80 beat, while continuing to give food at 120, the animal will soon *discriminate*, forming two categories, codings, or concepts of rates of metronome beat instead of one. If the animal did not previously confuse metronomes with bells, his situation is somewhat like that of the person who never had any difficulty distinguishing trees from shrubs, and has just learned to tell elms from walnuts. And just as the animal may never distinguish between 80 and 120 beats until he is motivated, so will many human beings never learn the difference between elms and walnuts unless motivated. The speed of discrimination learning is closely related to strength of motivation, for which reason the factor of intensity may be said to affect such learning. Other intensity factors, such as loudness or brightness of the stimulus and the intensity of the reward or punishment, will also affect the strength of learning.

The SR factors of learning seem useful in explaining why the brain will form certain concepts corresponding to certain groupings of things in experience. We have seen other aspects of concept formation, however, particularly the fact that the same set of phenomena can sometimes be grouped in different ways,[22] and the concept former must choose one over the other. There is no known way, at least thus far, by which we can explain this choice in terms of the rules of conditioning. Nor does any other explanation seem particularly satisfactory, and we will have to leave this as an open question. There are hints the process may be related to the conservation of energy, and some of the discussion below about concept attainment may be pertinent.

Before going on to that subject, however, we can illustrate a problem raised earlier in the chapter by carrying the illustration of discrimination one step further. Assuming that the animal has been strongly conditioned to give a food-seeking and shock-avoiding response to beats of 120 and 80, respectively, what will happen if the experimenter then sets the metronome for 105? We have previously seen that the animal will display tension and uncertainty, but we are now looking at a different facet of the problem. His responses are already learned—to seek food or avoid shock. His problem is not to select the response, but to identify the stimulus. Is the 105 beat a member of the same category of things as the 120 beat, or the 80 beat? Or is it some new category to which the response of tension and frustration will be given until a new and more satisfactory

---

[22] See the discussion of the problem of classifications in science in Chapter 3.

one can be found? It is not the *sounds* alone which constitute the stimulus, but the outcome of *classifying* the sounds. A stimulus is not a stimulus until it is identified.

Concept Attainment.   In contrast to concept formation, psychologists have given much attention in recent years to concept attainment. Here the laws of SR learning seem to fail utterly—at least at the level at which the problem has thus far been studied. In controlled studies of this phenomenon the experimenter typically provides the subject with two groups of samples. All items of one group are members of the concept and all members of the other are not. By examining and comparing the two sets, the subject must develop a definition of the concept. In Figure 7-2, for example, the subject might be told: "Items 1 to 6 are Urgles, and items 7 to 12 are not Urgles. What is an Urgle?" After comparing the exemplars with the nonexemplars, the subject will presumably come to the conclusion that an Urgle is three figures within a square, the figures consisting of any combination of squares, circles, or triangles, without regard to size or relative location.

Figure 7-2

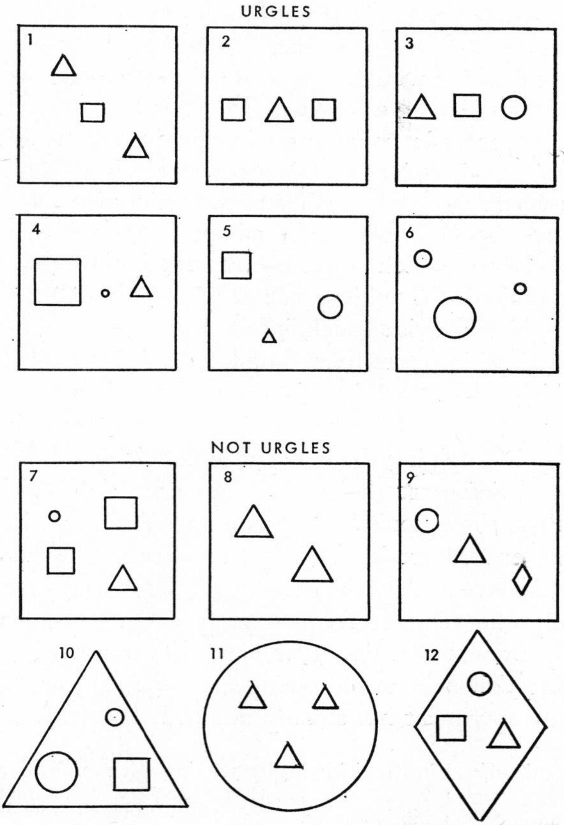

These experiments follow diverse paths. All items may be displayed to the subject simultaneously, or they may be shown only one at a time. The subject may be allowed limited or unlimited time, he may be shown only a limited number of items, and he may or may not be allowed to re-examine items upon request. Many conclusions have been reached thus far about how people proceed.[23] Rather than give the findings themselves, their general nature can be described by saying that, whereas some simple concept formation seems to follow the rules of SR conditioning, or the "line" relation described in Chapters 4 and 5, concept attainment (along with the selection aspect of concept formation) shows more similarity to the "field" relation described in the latter part of Chapter 5. It involves not a mere strengthening or weakening of connections, but a selection based on some kind of preference. There is selection not only of a result, but also of the process, or strategy, by which a result is achieved.

This kind of selection implies a preference, which implies a motive. It now seems probable that both concept formation and concept attainment are rewarding experiences, accompanied by what is referred to as the "Aha" or "Eureka" feeling. If the motive is inborn, it would seem doubtful that the mechanism of primary reinforcement hypothesized in the previous chapter would explain it. If not inborn, the motive to learn concepts would be an early acquired generalized secondary reinforcer, since almost all subsequent rewards would depend on the successful learning of concepts.

Motivation appears in concept attainment in a more explicit way as well. The subject who tries to attain a concept behaves as if the information to be derived from each specimen he examines is a thing of value. He also prefers specimens or sequences of specimens which provide much information to those which provide little. If his time or the number of specimens is limited, the subject will take greater risks. He will attend to instances which provide much information if successful, but little if they are not. Experimenters have found some fairly well defined sets of strategies which subjects tend to follow under particular sets of circumstances. Some are the most logical, in the sense that they show the greatest probability of attaining the concept under the conditions allowed by the experiment. Some are designed to minimize the strain on memory, while still others show doubtful logic on any observable basis.

At the moment the students of this field are not prepared to explain why subjects behave as they do, or where or how they learn their strategies. Certainly the rules of frequency, recency, and intensity are not conspicuously present. On the other hand, if we are to venture a guess, we might note that anyone old enough to be a subject for this sort of psychological experiment has already attained thousands of concepts. In

---

[23] Many are described in detail in Chapters 3 through 7 of Bruner *et al.*, *op. cit.*, and in numerous articles in recent years. Earl Hunt, *op. cit.*, summarizes the field and provides an excellent bibliography.

the course of doing so, some strategies have been found successful, and have been reinforced, while others have been extinguished. The notion that the process of attaining concepts is itself learned is supported by the fact that many subjects improve their efficiency at attaining concepts during successive experiments. Viewed in this light, if the less-than-human animal can develop a motor concept which controls relatively long sequences of muscular response toward a previously selected goal, it seems tenable to suppose that the human animal can develop a parallel type of information processing concept, or concept attainment concept, which will control relatively long sequences of cortical responses toward the goal of attaining a concept. There is no reason to assume that these concept attainment concepts would be conscious, though they might be in some cases.

SR psychology accounts nicely for associations on a simultaneous basis, but is weak in explaining how the fact of neuron connections can bring about a series of responses in an ordered sequence, a problem sharply outlined by Ashley.[24] There is the further problem that once started a certain pattern of behavior tends to run its course to completion. Not only does it seem not to need motivation at intervening points, but completion of the behavior cycle seems to be independently motivated. Once released, such a sequence is resistant to interference or change. The self-performing aspect of serial behavior is treated in detail by Miller, Galanter, and Pribram,[25] with much attention to what they call *plans* and *intentions*. Plans in their terminology might be another way of expressing an information concept parallel to that of the complex motor concept, while intentions might be such a concept with a motive attached—as will be discussed in the next chapter. The whole problem of serially ordered behavior has been relatively neglected. If it could be approached successfully through the motor concept, we have the advantage that we could return to the rats and cats for experimenting. With respect to concept attainment, this still leaves open the problem of conflicting strategies, and the similarity to the "field" approach in the sense stated above. Given the close relation between the field approach and decision making, Hunt's statement should be noted that both the acquisition and the use of concepts are both decision-making situations, in which the learner must choose between hypotheses.[26] Taken as a whole, this area of psychology needs much more work.

Concept Learning in Scientists and Children

To move to a different area of concept learning, the scientist working at the forefront of his subject faces problems of concept formation and of perception. He has little or no problem of concept attainment, since

---

[24] K. S. Ashley, "The Problem of Serial Order in Behavior," in Jeffres (ed.), *op. cit.*, pp. 112 ff.

[25] *Op. cit.*

[26] Hunt, *op. cit.*, p. 160.

he is developing new concepts, not trying to learn those already developed by others. Concept formation by the scientist is now generally known as model building, as described in Chapter 3, and is essentially the same thing as creating new theory. Starting from a group of items previously viewed as discrete, but which the scientist suspects to be related, he tries to form a concept, or model, which will incorporate all of the items as parts of the same concept. For example, the model of the atom, with its protons, electrons, and other particles is a concept which includes (i.e., "explains") such erstwhile discrete phenomena as chemical valence, electrical conductivity, atomic weights, and the release of various particles upon bombardment. The model of an economic system similarly relates within a single concept such otherwise unrelated phenomena as prices, quantities of goods, individual incomes, supplies of factors of production, national income, and inflation.

It is possible to construct models which have no relation to reality. So long as no one tries to pretend that they represent reality, these may provide interesting exercises, and sometimes turn out later to be useful. As noted in Chapter 3, as soon as one suggests that his model corresponds to reality, however, it becomes an hypothesis or a theory, subject to testing and to acceptance, rejection, or modification.

We have already seen that concept formation or model building (which we now also refer to as theorizing or hypothesizing) is an inductive process. Once we have formed a concept, we use it to perceive with, via cues. For example, having formed the concept of a human being as consisting of certain necessary parts, we need see only the face in order to perceive (by deductive inference) that there is a whole man on the porch. By "whole" we mean at least a whole torso, neck and head, since we know that a human can live and function without limbs. Having inferred a whole man from the face, suppose we were to go to the porch and discover a creature normal in shape and function from the top of the head to the bottom of the chest cavity, but that is all. Now although neither you nor I is prepared to accept this as a real possibility, let us accept it for the sake of making the point. Our observation of the actuality is now inconsistent with the perceptual inference that a whole human being was present. If we examine the specimen carefully and accept his reality, we now have no choice but to modify our concept of human beings. We may note that it requires only a single verified instance of a human being with only half a torso to force us to revise our concept—i.e., to "disprove" it. We can also, of course, establish a new concept.

Scientists similarly "perceive" with their models. Given cues sufficient to establish the presence of an instance of their model, they infer the presence of the rest of the model. If other observations force them to conclude that the whole model is not present, or that some part of actuality differs from that perceptually inferred from the model, the scientist must do the same thing we do when we walk onto the porch and discover the "man" is not as perceived—revise the model. Again, it requires only a single firmly established instance in which the model leads to faulty perception to invalidate the model or disprove the theory. We are assuming, of course, a model or hypothesis which proposes an invariable relationship. A "probabilistic" model is not invalidated by a single exception.

Once models have been tested frequently, and accepted as not leading to faulty inferences, the scientist thereafter confidently perceives with them. The physicist observes certain cues in the form of tracks in the cloud chamber or readings on an instrument or both, and says, "We've just knocked two electrons off the outer ring of a carbon atom." In a known competitive industry the economist observes a rise in price while the supply remains constant, and "perceives" that the demand has risen. The scientist also describes his experiments largely in the language of his model.

Without the formality of scientific language or logical thinking—in fact without language or conscious thought at all—it seems that the young child must go through essentially similar processes when he assembles the flood of unorganized information from his senses into coherent pictures of "what's there" in the world outside his nervous system. We recognize the difficulties faced by astronomers over the centuries as they have fitted together thousands of pieces of information about sizes, angles, colors, and movements of heavenly bodies. From these, after trying and rejecting numerous combinations, they have eventually come up with a reasonably coherent picture of the universe. Physicists have similarly put molecules, atoms, protons, neutrons, positrons, electrons, and other particles together into a coherent picture by piecing together thousands of discrete bits of information. We marvel at the scientists' ingenuity in creating such pictures from the kinds of indirect evidence they deal with, very little of which is directly accessible to the human senses.

But when we think of how direct and concrete it seems to see a tree, feel a pin prick, hear the baby cry, or smell a skunk, we tend to think we are doing something far simpler than the scientist. At this point we should recall that all information about the outside world is in our brain, not our eyes, fingers, ears, or nose. The tree, the pin, the crying, and the odor do not get to the brain, only electrical impulses. The task of sorting these out, creating from them tentative pictures of what the outside world is like, and revising or changing the pictures as new information requires—all this is essentially a process of constructing a model, testing the model by perceiving with it, and retaining or revising the model, just as it is done by scientists. It is perhaps reasonable to believe that insofar as we deal with basic relationships, rather than with such things as equipment and personnel, the formal procedures of science are an application to areas of new knowledge of the same basic mental processes used by all of us from the moment of birth. Only when we learn to talk do we shift our learning heavily from forming and testing our own concepts to attaining those already developed by others. Much formal education consists of concept attainment, while in "thinking for oneself" one forms his own concepts.

The two are also alike in an important respect stated earlier. When the ordinary individual or the scientist engages in behavior related to the "real" world, his behavior is based on his model. We do not respond to reality; we respond to our information about reality. The model in our heads may or may not reflect reality closely. But it governs our behavior, for that model is our best picture of what reality *is*. If we do not base our behavior on that, then what do we base it on? We may, of course, sometimes acknowledge that our picture is uncertain, and hedge our bets, especially for the more complex physical and social phenomena where we know that other people's pictures do not correspond to our own.

We can now sense the tremendous importance of concepts to behavior. They are our pictures of the world, including ourselves. We cannot perceive without them, or think without them. For reasons we will see in later chapters, we cannot communicate, build houses or tools, or create or maintain a social organization without them. Without concepts formed in advance of behavior we could not plan and execute any but simple animal-like patterns of behavior. There is even reason to believe we could not remember much except in the coded form of concepts.[27] All in all, the ability to form, attain, and use complex concepts is the distinguishing feature of man, and, hence, lies at the core of the analysis of human behavior.

THE RANGE AND CONTENT OF CONCEPTS

Although some hints were dropped of grander things, the discussion thus far has been confined largely to concepts of physical objects. The unique abilities of human beings depend on concepts of other things, to which we now move.

We not only *have* sensations, but we conceptualize them. The foot hurts, but that is not all. After we have had the experience several times we also have a concept of pain, and of feeling pain. If we did not, we would be unable to talk about it, to feel sympathetic responses when others are in pain, or even perhaps to remember it. These concepts probably heighten any sensation, whether of pleasure or pain. Any stimulation which occurs after the concept is formed sets off not only the unlearned reaction of the sensory nerves, but also the cortical network of the concept, along with all associated feelings. This is presumably one reason why a pain seems less intense if our attention is distracted.

The same observation applies to the other senses. In addition to seeing, hearing, smelling, and so forth, as such, we also develop concepts about the process of seeing, hearing, and smelling. The evidence again is that we

---

[27] See George A. Miller, "The Magic Number Seven Plus or Minus Two," *Psychological Review*, No. 63, pp. 81 ff., where he discusses the use of symbols in increasing the storage capacity of the brain.

can talk about these things, which we could not do without concepts of them.

In perception we generally make identifications directly, as indicated when we say "I see a unicorn" or "I hear a cuckoo." But we can also attend to and form a concept of the sensory stimulus itself, as reflected in "I see spots of blue" or "I hear a high-pitched tone."

In addition to objects and sensations, we conceptualize and perceive *events*. In everyday terms, tree, bird, water, and sun are objects or things, while a tree falling, a bird dying, water freezing, or the sun setting are events. We will make a more precise distinction than this by considering objects or things as a static view of a phenomenon and an event as a dynamic view, corresponding roughly to a snapshot and a motion picture respectively. At any given moment in time a given pattern of things exists —the tree stands, the sun is 10 degrees above the horizon, and so forth. But over a period of time, all patterns change at some rate of speed—the tree falls, the sun sets, the bird dies, the pyramids crumble, and the universe expands. An object or thing is the static view of a pattern at a given instant; an event is the dynamic view of a change in pattern.

In ordinary usage, a particular arrangement of things which changes relatively slowly is considered a thing—like Grant's Tomb. But ordinary usage is not clear about things which retain a given pattern for only a limited time. For example, is each of the following an object or an event? An ocean wave? A pattern of sand left by one wave and obliterated by the next? A poodle-shaped cloud? The funnel of a tornado? The beam of a searchlight? In a static-dynamic approach, by contrast, the distinction is sharp. If we focus on the static pattern of the wave at any given moment, or on the continuity of pattern as it moves across the water, we can view it as a thing—even though the water which makes up the wave is constantly changing. On the other hand, if we focus on the change occurring within the wave we can view it as an event. The absolute duration is irrelevant. A static pattern can be conceived as an object even if it lasts only a fraction of a second—like the pattern of air compressions made by a bullet leaving a rifle barrel, or the track left by a subatomic particle in a cloud chamber. A change in pattern can be conceived as an event, even if it takes billions of years, like the geological formation of the earth. Although the terms are rather poorly applicable to many abstractions, the concept of a thing is essentially that of a relationship in space and an event a relationship in time. If he is so inclined, the zealous devotee of systems analysis may think of the object as a closed system at a stable equilibrium and the event as a system, either open or closed, in process of dynamic change.

Events are more complex phenomena to conceptualize, since they require static concepts of the initial state, the end state, and perhaps of intermediate states, whereas the object requires only a single static concept. However, since the brain can form many concepts, and since the formation of many static concepts also requires multiple steps (as we will see shortly), the only basic difference between the learning of static and dynamic concepts is that between the learning of space relationships and time relationships. Although we have less of an idea how the brain handles the latter, as we have seen earlier, we know that relatively simple animals do handle matters of time sequence in their motor behavior, so that time sequence, as such, is not a problem unique to higher learning.

Human behavior is itself an important kind of event about which we form concepts. To form concepts about the behavior of others is basically no different from forming concepts of the falling tree or the thunderstorm, except that human behavior is usually more complex. We are apt to overlook, however, that we conceptualize our own behavior. The information unit we are studying is the nervous system. For me this means that *my overt behavior* is an event *outside my nervous system* just as much as is your behavior. I do, of course, have information from inside my head about what I intend to do, or think I am doing. But to know what I am *actually* doing I must depend on information from my sensory nerves— somesthetic and kinesthetic as well as those of sight, hearing, and so forth. That we perceive our own behavior as an external phenomenon at the same time we execute it provides important feedback with which to correct and refine the concepts with which to guide future behavior.

Abstraction, and the Making of Concepts from Concepts

The really crucial problem of human behavior, apparently, is that of forming complex concepts, which in turn require *abstraction*. Abstracting utilizes higher order conditioning as applied to concept formation, in which successive levels of concepts are further removed from the original sensory base. We will first illustrate the abstraction of relationships, using music as an example. A pure musical tone is a succession of simple sensory signals. We can sense it, and we can also form a concept of it. A chord is a simultaneous relationship of two or more tones. We can sense it directly, of course, but the *concept* of a chord to one who studies the physics of sound or the theory of music is that of a simultaneous *relationship* of two or more tones. A harmonic sequence is the sequential relationship of two or more chords—i.e., a relationship of relationships. In a different direction, a melody is a sequential relationship of two or more tones, while the harmonization of a melody is the relationship of harmonic sequence (a relationship of relationships) to a melody (a relationship of tones). Any particular musical instrument has a particular tone quality, which is a relationship among its fundamental tone and its overtones. To achieve the "tone color" which comes from orchestrating a chord, a composer creates a relationship of tone qualities (which are relationships of fundamentals and overtones) in a chord (which is a relationship of pitch levels). He uses these simultaneously with melodic lines and harmonic sequences—the whole being a relationship of relationships of relationships, and so forth, which we will not attempt to verbalize. Fortunately, one can enjoy Bach or bop without forming all these concepts—though not without "relating."

As a different sort of illustration, the economist observes an exchange, say, of ten oranges for two coconuts. Firts, the numbers used to count the items are abstractions, being relations of magnitudes. He then says that the coconut has a value of five oranges, value being the relationship of the number of coconuts and oranges in the exchange. He may next say that the price of a coconut is 25 cents, this being a relationship between the value of the coconut and the value of money. The economist may next state that the price of coconuts is 50 per cent higher than in 1955, a relationship of two prices over time, after which he may add that the index of all prices in March, 1962, was 105 on a 1957–59 base, which is a particular kind of relationship of price relationships. If we retrace these steps, we will find that a price index is a relationship of relationships of relationships of relationships of relationships.

International politics is a relationship of nations, which are complex relationships of people. Acceleration is a relationship of velocities, which are relationships of time and distance, each of which is in turn the expression of a relationship. On every side we observe the ability of the human brain to conceptualize relationships. Once conceptualized, a relationship is treated as an *entity*, whereupon the brain notes relationships between that entity and other entities, and conceptualizes that relationship as *another* entity, and so on.

In similar fashion, we make entities out of qualities or attributes of things. When a substance behaves in a certain way, we say that it is tough, and then abstract toughness as the quality of that kind of behavior, and we do the same with hardness, sweetness, versatility, intelligence, stubbornness, fairness, and so on. The word form may be that of a noun, but the essential idea is that of adjective or adverb. Having made these things into entities, we form concepts of the qualities of qualities, such as stubborn fairness or versatile intelligence. We also conceptualize change or action itself, as indicated by such words as growth, transition, performance, movement, transportation, transaction, and accomplishment; as well as spacial and temporal relationships indicated by such words as under, beside, after, or since. Having conceptualized all these things, we then conceptualize all kinds of permutations and combinations of them, such as relationships of qualities, qualities of qualities, qualities of relationships, qualities of actions, relationships of actions, changes of relationships, changes of qualities, changes of qualities of relationships, and so on and on.

Each such concept is formed by tying together all or part of two or more prior concepts, usually parts, in the sense that the concept of hardness can be formed by combining part of the concept of stone with part of the concept of steel, and the concept of growth can be made by combining part of the concept of child behavior with part of that of plant behavior.

Here, as in the case of motives, we are perhaps observing a fundamental trait of the human, as contrasted to the lower animal: namely the ability to carry on higher order conditioning indefinitely without diminution of strength. A motive ten stages removed from a primary reinforcer can apparently take on as much strength as the original, and a concept abstracted ten stages from its sensory base can control behavior just as effectively as things directly perceived. Patriotic nationalism, for example, is presumably many stages removed from either primary reinforcement or sensory perceptions, yet to some persons it can become a dominant controller of behavior. By contrast, the rat is apparently capable of only second or third order conditioning of either motives or concepts. This, conceivably, could be the critical factor in brain size: up to a given size only limited order conditioning is possible, and beyond that size unlimited chains of conditioning are possible without loss of strength.

With this background we will distinguish between logical abstraction and psychological abstraction. In either sense to abstract is to conceptualize some trait or quality of a group of phenomena separate from the concept of the phenomena themselves. For example, from a red sunset, a red book, and a red rose we can abstract the notion of redness, and form a separate concept of it. This is *logical abstraction*. As the term is defined here, *psychological abstraction* is essentially the same, but applies only to instances in which the quality abstracted is not directly detectable by sensory nerves alone. Although redness is a logical abstraction, it is not a psychological one, since it is detectable by unaided sensory nerves. It can also be detected by far simpler animals than are capable of logical abstraction. Other colors are not psychological abstractions, nor are warmth, coldness, loudness, sweetness, and other sensations. On the other hand, such things as toughness, roughness, wetness, and triangularity *are* psychological abstractions. We have no nerves sensitive to these things *as such*, and they can be perceived, but not sensed. Each requires the combining of several different kinds of sensations in the brain to form a new concept. These are the kinds of sensory concepts the child presumably forms at an early age, and from which he builds abstract concepts far from the sensory base.

It is the ability to abstract things psychologically[28] we are mainly interested in, though as soon as we pass beyond the first or second level the logical and psychological probably coincide. In the example above, the concept of a price index is five levels of abstraction removed from its

---

[28] The notion of mental ability is traditionally related closely to the ability to make abstractions, which ability is here identified with the higher order conditioning of information concepts. It might be interesting to toy with the idea of viewing intelligence as facility in high order conditioning in connection with concept attainment, and imagination as high order conditioning in connection with concept formation.

sensory base in the perception of oranges and coconuts, and may be considered even farther removed if we wish to include the steps necessary to learn to count the items exchanged. We can also describe the same sequence from the top down by saying that there are five steps in the *chain of reduction* from the concept of price index to its sensory base.

Abstraction and Language

We can speculate that the ability to form long chains of associated concepts is closely related to our ability to communicate by language. A sentence is a sequence of signs, each of which refers to some concept. (To be strictly accurate, a sentence contains some signs having no conceptual referent, whose function is to indicate the relations among the other signs—a matter for a later chapter.) The person hearing the sentence uses these signs as cues for "perceiving" a sequence of concepts he already knows, and for assembling them into a new arrangement indicated by the sentence. How the brain is able to make such new combinations at the speed one hears speech—without the repetition required by normal conditioning—is one of the great unknowns of present day psychology. Whatever it is, it is probably related to our ability to form a clear mental picture of some landscape or other scene from only a short viewing.

The ability to speak might be said to bear the same kind of relation to hearing and understanding language as the performing of motor concepts bears to the forming of those motor concepts. This, too, we are currently unable to explain.

The Brain Will Accept Any Concept

As a final aspect of the formation and use of concepts, the human brain shows no apparent innate preferences for any particular ways of conceptualizing things, which is the price of versatility and a consequence of the absence of inborn concepts. It will accept equally the notion that lightning is an electrical discharge or the gods belching fire; that the earth is round or flat or square; that rain is condensation of water vapor in the air or an Olympian shaggy dog shaking himself after bathing. We accept the notion that some things float and others sink, but if that is the way things were, we would equally accept that all float or all sink, or that bricks and books float in the air but nothing else does. We learn that a hole is something that both light and solid objects will pass through, but later accept the window as a hole for light but not for objects. We have long known about screens, which will allow the passage of air but not objects, but in recent years have accepted the previously preposterous notion of an air curtain which will pass objects but not drafts of air. We used to learn that any solid object which goes up must come down, but children growing up in the space age accept a different notion just as easily. We learn that things grow, shrink, die, burn, or decay, but do not turn into other things, as from frogs to princes. Yet children accept any kind of transformation as possible until they learn differently, and all of us accept the change from maggots to flies and caterpillars to butterflies. We can form all sorts of concepts of what happens to people after death, in heaven, happy hunting grounds, or Sheol. Concepts about life after death are particularly persistent because of the absence of reliable feedback against which to check them.

These observations are pertinent to persons who believe that understanding of the universe will come to us if we but contemplate deeply. If contemplation means forming new concepts by combining those already in our heads, then contemplation is extremely important. But whole chains of concepts developed without the check of observation can move far from reality. This is why science insists on a constant interaction between theory and empirical research, the concept formation and perception of science.

CONCLUSION

It is by no means certain that concept formation and attainment entail any *fundamental* problems not found in motor concepts. Motor concepts involve the problem of serial order. Complex motor concepts involve the formation of higher order concepts, generally known as molar, by combining, recombining, and re-recombining lower order atomic concepts, while simultaneously sloughing off parts of the atomic concepts which are irrelevant to the molar one. Motor concepts certainly involve conditioning of the SR type as these concepts are formed. But they also involve selection. The organism tries various combinations and sequences of atomic responses, accepting some and rejecting others before smoothly coordinated molar performance is achieved. The organism "prefers" efficient to inefficient motor performance, and reinforces the one while it extinguishes the other. With respect to the simple and moderately complex molar responses of the sort virtually all of us use regularly (like picking up a twenty dollar bill), most of us probably approximate the most efficient possible combination—though the relative roles of experience and imitation here may be somewhat uncertain. As motor responses become still more complex and more specialized, the less efficient combinations of atomic responses seem less likely to be eliminated by experience and performance alone—as any industrial methods engineer can attest. Responses which are overtly large are not necessarily neurologically large or complex; we sometimes start with the large but conceptually simple response, the later complexity taking the form of filling in and smoothing the details.

With appropriate substitution of words, every statement about the formation of motor concepts in the preceding paragraph is also apparently true of the formation of information concepts—assuming that each reference to motor performance implies a motor concept, and that efficient processing of information is construed as the information equivalent of efficient motor performance. The place of the methods engineer can be taken by the teacher, and the increased complexity which takes the form of filling in detail can be illustrated by the fact that the teacher may sometimes ask the graduate student the same question he asks the freshman, but expect quite different amounts of detail in the answers.

In short, if we view the brain as an information-processing mechanism, no fundamental principles or types of operations are involved in processing concepts which are not also involved in processing muscular responses. By whatever techniques it develops a "program" for controlling complex series of motor responses, it can presumably also develop a "program" for controlling complex series of steps in handling information, including programs for strategies in attaining concepts.[29] This, of course, does not tell us how the brain does it, though perhaps it does help to clarify the kind of thing to look for. Nor does it even hint at how the brain compares current inputs with existing concepts, and then makes a selection, which comparison and selection constitute the process of perception. These remain large unknowns.

It does seem fair to say, however, that the technique of viewing the brain as an information processing machine—the use of the information model—does assist greatly in sharpening our picture both of what we know and what we do not know about the operation of the brain. To return to our larger problem, it helps us to understand how we become aware of the alternative behavioral and environmental opportunities from among which, on the basis of preferences formed within the same brain, we select our behavioral responses.

---

[29] See Miller, Galanter, & Pribram, *op. cit.*, pp. 184 and 197 ff., for the conceptualization of these things as "programs."

Chapter 8

SOME INTERRELATIONS OF CONCEPTS AND MOTIVES

THE MOTIVATION TO FORM CONCEPTS

WE HAVE already noted that both the formation and attainment of concepts seem to be independently motivated, and provide definite satisfaction when the tasks are completed. Inability to form or attain satisfactory concepts gives rise to frustration, and conflicting concepts motivate activity which will remove the conflict.[1] We are in no position at the moment to suggest whether the motivation is primary or secondary.

If primary, then according to the model in Chapter 7, there would have to exist some inborn connection between the learning of a concept and the reward sections of the brain. This is conceivable, but is much more difficult to imagine than inborn connections from the stomach, skin, or muscles. If not inborn, concept formation would nevertheless start to receive reinforcement almost from birth, and certainly from the point where complete helplessness of the infant is ended. The baby will be helpless to achieve rewards and avoid punishments unless he can form the neural networks which are the physical basis of concepts. It may even be that at the very early stages of development, the process of identifying the stimulus by discriminating it from other stimuli is part and parcel of the same process of distinguishing responses from one another. Concept formation might then be construed as rewarding, because it is indistinguishable from the rewarding response. It may be that only later does the brain further distinguish between identifying the stimulus and selecting the response, since the act of categorizing a stimulus is itself an act of selection. If so, then the satisfaction from forming a concept or making an identification could logically be the consequence of secondary reinforcement. For present purposes, and in the absence of further informa-

---

[1] See Leon Festinger, "The Motivating Effect of Cognitive Dissonance," in Gardner Lindzey (ed.), *Assessment of Human Motives* (New York: Rinehart & Co., 1958), pp. 65–86.

tion, there is no profit in pursuing that topic further. People *do* get satisfaction from forming concepts and making identifications, which is another way of saying that concept formation *is* motivated.

THE CONCEPTUALIZATION OF FEELINGS AND MOTIVES

It was noted earlier that we not only *have* sensations, but that we form concepts of them. The same is evidently true of motives and feelings. We say such things as "I feel wonderful," "I am frustrated," or "I can hardly wait for vacation." As with sensations, we can *have* feelings and motives without conceptualizing them, and they can influence our responses. But unless they are conceptualized, we cannot report them.

Once we have conceptualized motives and feelings, we can also think about them. A motive can then become a part of our conceptual or cognitive process as well as our affective ones, as we go through such thought sequences as "If I want that car, I will have to earn more," or "If I don't learn to control my temper I will get myself in trouble." Although desire and anger are themselves feelings or motives, once they are conceptualized the brain can handle them like concepts of the external environment. The ensuing thought process is no different than if the concepts involved were external, as in the statement, "If the Phillies want to win the pennant, they will have to improve their hitting." As was noted earlier, if we define our environment for behavioral purposes as everything outside the nervous system, then many feelings are part of the environment, since they reside at least in part in chemical and physical states of the body, not in the nerves. Our concept of a feeling then takes on the same logical character as our concept of a house or of government, just as does the concept of our own behavior, as described in the preceding chapter. This does not mean, of course, that the effect of the emotion is then confined to the cognitive sphere, since the emotion is still there, and affects behavior by feeding stimuli into the affective structures of the brain.

SECONDARY MOTIVES ARE ATTACHED TO CONCEPTS

A primary reinforcer need not be conceptualized to be reinforcing. We can achieve satisfaction from assuaging hunger, since the condition of hunger is within the human system, and so is the state of satisfaction. But before some external can become an object of desire as a secondary reinforcer, it must be conceptualized. We cannot want *bread*, as contrasted to cardboard or stones, unless we have a concept of bread, and can identify bread as the substance which has led to previous satisfaction. We cannot have desires indicated by such phrases as "I want to go to college," "I must marry Nelly or I'll die," "We ought to have more efficiency," or "I'll give my life in the fight against tyranny," unless we first have formed concepts of college, Nelly, marriage, efficiency, fighting, and tyranny. This relationship, incidentally, helps to clarify one aspect of primary motivation. Unless we inherit concepts of things outside ourselves, which seems most doubtful, we cannot inherit the desire for those things. It is not only the *want* that is learned, but also the *thing*. Any secondary reinforcement must be preceded or accompanied by concept formation of the secondary reinforcer, and our secondary motives are oriented around these concepts. If we say "I want a horse," the psychological phenomenon we are describing is that the *concept* of having a horse is a secondary reinforcer. The discharge of the *neural network* of the concept is the reinforcer, not the external object. One manifestation of this is that after we have come to want something, we receive satisfaction just from thinking about it.[2]

MOTIVES ABOUT MOTIVES AND CONCEPTS

The plot now thickens. Our secondary motives are oriented around concepts. But included in our concepts are those about motives themselves, including the conceptualizations of wanting and of not wanting. In this connection, we can want to want something, we can want not to want, we can not want to want, and we can not want not to want. Some of these wants about wants can be highly instrumental. Our society approves honesty, education, and freedom. It also approves *desire* for these things. Since approval is a strong secondary reinforcer, individuals can *want* to want these things, even if they never succeed in actually wanting them. (For years my wife has wanted to want beer, but has never succeeded in wanting it.) The reverse, of course, applies to disapproved desires, as for personal power, overindulgence, or masochism.

Society further approves and disapproves certain concepts. In the Middle Ages, one opened himself to severe punishment if he conceived the earth as not the center of the universe, or the king as not divinely ordained. In present day America an adult will face social disapproval if he conceptualizes babies as being brought by storks, or capitalism as evolving inevitably into socialism. In consequence, other things equal, one will *want* to conceptualize things in the ways approved by society, and will want *not* to conceptualize them in disapproved ways.

Although wanting to want certain things, and wanting to form certain conceptualizations may at first glance seem rather remote kinds of influences, they are in fact potent instruments of social control.

ASPIRATIONS—THE EXPANSION
AND CONTRACTION OF GOALS

The capacity of the human system to reinforce or extinguish motives far removed from the primary reinforcers enables human beings to avoid

---

[2] If I interpret correctly, this section is squarely in accord with Parsons, when he says, ". . . personality is a system of differentiated motivational flows or currents *organized* about the structure of an internalized object system, or system of systems." See Talcott Parsons and Robert F. Bales, *Family, Socialization and Interaction Process* (Glencoe, Ill.: The Free Press, 1955), p. 139.

both death from frustration and aggravated idleness in the face of opportunities. Not only do our actions adapt to the world around us, but so do our wants. Our goals and aspirations expand or contract in proportion as we are successful or unsuccessful in satisfying our prior goals. The discussions above lay the base for this phenomenon.

Our goals are not the external things we say we want. They are the fact that a certain concept is reinforcing. Now all of us daydream, in which process all kinds of desires are fulfilled—some of a sort society allows us to mention and some not. But we are normally not confused between these daydreams and our memories of reality. If some desire is to produce action, rather than mere daydreaming, the thinking about the proposed action must lead to thoughts of actually achieving the goal. More precisely, if we have some goal (i.e., if the concept of some thing is a secondary reinforcer), and if certain instrumental actions are conceived as bringing it about, then if the goal and the instrumental action are thought about together, the concept of the instrumental action will itself become a reinforcer by being conditioned to the concept of the goal.

But suppose that subsequent information leads to a revised conclusion that the proposed behavior will not achieve the goal. If some alternate behavior is conceived as instrumental to the same goal, the original action will be extinguished and the new one reinforced, and we go on as before. But suppose that a survey of the field does not reveal *any* line of action which will produce the desired result. *No* instrumental behavior will now be reinforced by the erstwhile goal—not because the goal is no longer desired, but because no action is conceived as fulfilling it. The goal therefore motivates (or controls) no current behavior—leading to the widely observed generalization that a person must view a goal as realizable or it will have no motive power. An unrealizable goal becomes inactive.

Because we conceptualize motives, or the having of goal objects, as well as the goal objects themselves, another thing happens. If the goal seems realizable at some future time, though not now, the goal may be "deactivated," but not extinguished, coming back to life if it again seems realizable. But if the goal seems permanently unattainable something different happens, as can be seen by a review of the steps. First, when reasonably immediate accomplishment seems possible, thoughts of the instrumental steps are rewarding. Second, if the goal is seen as temporarily not accomplishable, thoughts of the instrumental steps are extinguished, but thoughts of retaining the goal itself continue to be rewarding. But third, if the goal is seen as permanently impossible, then even the thought of continuing to hold it as a goal is no longer rewarding, and the desire for the goal is itself extinguished. At each step we say that the aspiration has accommodated itself to the perceived opportunities. If we actually pursue the instrumental steps and fail, the goal may be extinguished—but not necessarily. The goal may instead be reinforced if the failure is seen as providing clearer information about how to succeed. The goal may also be reinforced if subsequent success is now seen as demonstrating one's ability to doubting scoffers, or even to one's self. Thus can success after failure provide greater reward than success on the first trial. This fact may more than offset the extinguishing effects of initial failure.

Success is reinforcing, not only of the efforts directed toward a particular goal, but also of the concept of having goals and working toward them. Success further rewards the concept of one's self as competent, and reinforces the desire to achieve competence. Viewed from the level of completed accomplishment, goals which formerly seemed impossible may now seem possible. Hence, success reinforces both higher specific goals and a stronger concept of one's own power to reach them.[3]

Future Orientation and the Neurological Present

The discussion of goals takes us into the realm of future oriented behavior, which often leads to a question of the following sort: "How can you hope to explain human behavior as a scientific effect of past causes when it is obvious to even the simple minded that much behavior is related to the *future*, not the past?" Without commenting on the scientific status of things obvious to the simple minded, we will try to make more explicit some answers which are implicit in much of the preceding discussion.

Suppose we approach a person in the midst of the tedious, messy, smelly job of painting his living room, and ask, "What keeps you going so long?" (This description of painting was submitted to a paint manufacturer as possible advertising copy, but was rejected.) He answers, "I just keep thinking how nice it will look when it's finished." The answer is difficult to validate experimentally, but is also difficult to deny on common sense grounds, and contains a key point. The *concept* of the finished living room is in his head *now*. A substantial *satisfaction* is attached to that concept *now*. If the man were not now receiving satisfaction from the thought of the finished job, his painting behavior would be unrewarding *now*, and he would stop.

But how can this mental picture be as rewarding as the real thing? Perhaps it can't. But that is irrelevant, since the mental picture is reward-

---

[3] An article of interest in connection with the relation of concepts and motives, and particularly the expansion and contraction of goals, is that of Ulric Neisser, "The Imitation of Man by Machine," *Science*, Vol. 139, No. 3551, January 18, 1963, pp. 193–97. An important trait of the computer is that it has only the single-minded goal introduced by its operator, whereas the human being has multiple goals in almost everything he does, and these goals are subject to repeated or continuous change throughout the course of learning or performing any set of behavior. As Neisser describes it for the human, "Needs and emotions do not merely set the stage for cognitive activities and then retire. They continue to operate through the course of development. . . . To think like a man, a computer program would need to be similarly endowed with powerful internal states." (p. 196) Another important difference is that the entire memory of the machine is wiped clean after each problem is solved, so that it deals with each new problem with only that information provided for it, or accumulated by it, in connection with that particular problem.

ing enough to keep the man at work. In any event—and this should be carefully noted—when the completed work is viewed with satisfaction, the only thing that will get into the brain even then is the mental picture. That mental picture will be based on then-current sensations, whereas the present one is based on a mental recombination of past experiences. That is, the question of how a person can visualize how a thing will look in the future is not a question of the future as such, but a question of how he can form concepts of things he has never experienced. The answer lies in higher order conditioning, which is the technique by which the brain associates the concepts of things which were never associated in experience. The part of the problem to which we can give a less satisfactory answer is that of performing an organized sequence of behavior directed toward a goal. This is partially discussed in Chapter 7 in connection with serial order behavior. Human beings, along with lower animals, can learn coordinated sets of responses, the mental correlates of which are called motor concepts. If we now assume that human beings are able to put motor concepts together in their heads in the same fashion they put informational concepts together, we then have the basis for performing sequences of behavior never performed overtly before. If the above analysis is correct, the lovely things we imagine in our daydreaming must provide an important segment of our total motivational set. And so do the horrible things which sometimes happen in our daymares.

We will examine another example to see how a sequence of simple conditioning can produce a behavioral response we would describe as involving foresight. My study is at the top of an enclosed stairway, at the bottom of which is a door, and the TV set is just beyond. The door is normally open, but should be closed if the TV is on and I am working in the study. The following learning sequence occurred.

My son would turn on the TV, whereupon I would shout a request that he close the door. Because it carried better, I shortly substituted whistling for shouting, and the son soon became conditioned to close the door on hearing the whistle. To speak of mental pictures, at this stage the sound of the whistle brought to his mind the picture of closing the door, which picture was then carried into action.

In due time (an incredibly long one in my opinion) a second step of conditioning set in. Because the turning on of the TV was regularly followed by the whistle, he became conditioned to expect the whistle when he turned on the set. But the whistle was already a conditioned stimulus for closing the door, so that now, by second order conditioning of TV-to-whistle-to-door-closing, he would think of closing the door immediately upon turning on the TV, and close it.

A third step is now partly, but not reliably, established. Now merely to *think* of turning on the TV brings the conditioned responses of expecting the whistle and closing the door, and he sometimes closes the door first. Thus, simple third order conditioning produces behavior which we describe as involving foresight and future orientation. Whatever its external time orientation, each step was the result of a past cause, and the whole sequence now occurs in the neurological present. We are not prepared to argue that all foresight arises in this fashion. Nor are we prepared to insist that any does not. It is not clear whether or not the formulation of the "plans" and "intentions" of Miller, Galanter, and Pribram, as discussed in Chapter 7, can be reformulated in the same context. Certainly their execution cannot.

SOME OTHER INTERRELATIONS
OF MOTIVES AND CONCEPTS

Motives expand or contract with the generalization or discrimination of the concept to which they are attached. Let us say that you have a yen for sports cars, including a fondness for the Thunderbird. Subsequently, however, you attend a sports car rally and discover that the Thunderbird is simply not *in* among true lovers of sports cars. By narrowing your concept of sports cars via discriminating it more narrowly from nonsports cars, you now no longer desire what was formerly desired. Or perhaps you have spent a season in an Italian villa and have come to like tile floors because of their appearance and ease of maintenance. Later you learn that some of these same traits are shared by terrazzo and vinyl, whereupon the scope of your liking for tile may expand with the concept to include terrazzo and vinyl. In these instances there is no reinforcement or extinction of secondary motives, as such, but rather growth or contraction of the concept to which the motive is attached.

Another aspect of these interrelations is that, having the ability to conceptualize motives and feelings, we can also conceptualize them as parts of some external thing. "We had a wonderful time in Paris." If so, then the concept of a wonderful time may become part of the concept of Paris, so that thoughts of the city include thoughts of a good time. One may conclude that "Utrillo's paintings excite me," whereupon excitement becomes part of the concept of Utrillo paintings. At this point in history the greatness of the Mona Lisa perhaps lies not so much in the painting as in the fact that greatness is by now a part of everyone's concept of the painting. If feelings of depression are stimulated by several accounts of the Iron Curtain, depression becomes part of the concept "Iron Curtain." We do the same with persons, including as part of the concept of the person some of the feelings he engenders. As a result, many concepts contain a value or motive component along with their information component. This might also be described by saying that many concepts contain information about affective states as well as about the outside world, and we find it pleasant or unpleasant merely to think about them.

Because we perceive through the use of concepts, a complicating consequence is that the valences attached to concepts often influence our perceptions. If something is particularly unpleasant, we may say "I'd rather not see it" or "Please don't discuss it." If the thought of atomic war is too horrible, we may pay more attention to suggestions that it can be avoided than to the opposite. Similarly we tend to spend time with persons who think well of us, and avoid those who do not. The former enhance our picture of ourselves, and are rewarding, while the latter do the opposite. We tend to concentrate on the good points of the candidate we support, and on the bad points of his opponent. The actor tends to reread his good reviews, and bury the bad ones. Sometimes one cannot see the faults in self or friends, or the virtues of enemies. The fact that we attach valences to certain concepts thus changes the likelihood that we will perceive instances of them. This situation is often self-aggravating, in that a valence about something biases subsequent information, which further strengthens the original bias. Our concept of what *is* tends to be pushed in the direction of what we would like it to be. An important feature of the human information system is that the valences attached to our concepts are an astigmatism in the lens through which we perceive them.

The way in which perceptions are modified by desires is illustrated by experiments which show that when and to the degree that one is in doubt about the proper interpretation (decoding) of a set of stimulus signals, his interpretation tends to conform to that of the persons around him, and that the strength of the tendency to conform is related to the value of conformity in the group. This phenomenon has been found experimentally in the perception of physical events, such as the distance a point of light is moved in an otherwise darkened room. The influence of others on one's perceptions of social phenomena, such as the consequences of a court decision on civil rights, is so marked as hardly to need comment. As Hare puts it, "generally, the greater the ambiguity of the object, the greater will be the influence of other group members in determining the judgment of the subject."[4]

Among other wants, in many cases we want desired things to be easy to acquire. A bias which makes things seem more nearly as we would like them will presumably also make wanted things seem easier to achieve than they actually are. Several results follow. First, positive motivations are stronger than they otherwise would be, and we are more willing to work toward delayed goals, since the reward value of the goal is enhanced relative to our shrunken view of the costs of achieving it. Second, a circular interaction sets in, for if the goal seems easier to achieve, it then also becomes more rewarding. We have probably all observed a relatively quiescent desire suddenly blossom when some change of circumstance has made a previously unattainable goal seem possible. The goal suddenly becomes more urgent, and the hurdles in its path much

---

[4] A. Paul Hare, *Handbook of Small Group Research* (New York: The Free Press of Glencoe, 1962), p. 31. Hare's discussion is based on the works of M. Sherif and others.

smaller. The whole of this logic applies in reverse to unwanted things.

The upshot of these relations would seem to be a greater concentration of effort than would otherwise be the case, as we overstate one goal and understate another. Both enthusiastic attachments to and stubborn avoidances of goals can result.

To move to a slightly different problem, we have seen that concepts are necessary to identify any but the simplest sensory stimuli. This same observation also applies to feedback stimuli. Before any response can be reinforced or extinguished, the feedback must be classified as rewarding or not. Suppose a housewife sells Christmas cards some November in the expectation of earning $100, but actually earns only $60. Will the $60 act as a reward, and reinforce the desire to sell cards? Or, compared to the goal, will it be an "unreward" and extinguish it? This is a problem not encountered in comparing lollypops versus spankings for children, or food versus shock for rats, and what is rewarding or punishing for the woman will depend on how she perceives the feedback. If a friend says, "Oh, you were lucky; I only made $25" the $60 may act as a reward, while if the friend says, "It's not worth all that effort for a piddling $60" it may serve as an extinguisher. In short, valences are attached to feedback stimuli as well as to initial ones, and the valence of the feedback stimulus cannot be determined until the feedback itself has been categorized and evaluated. In layman's language, a situation must be viewed in its context. In present language, a subconcept must be dealt with as part of the concept of the whole situation.

Despite the constant interaction between motives and concepts in fact, it is important to keep the ideas themselves distinct. One of the prerequisites of high level adaptive behavior—presumably indispensable for objective scholarship—is the ability to conceptualize and identify things with a minimum of influence from values and motives.

Figure 8-1 is a convenient means of distinguishing the two things

Figure 8-1
SOME SIMPLE RELATIONSHIPS OF CONCEPTS AND MOTIVES

MOTIVE SCALE
(Values, or preferences)

		REWARDS (Reinforcers)	UNREWARDS OR PUNISHMENTS (Extinguishers)
CONCEPT SCALE (Information, perceived opportunities)	SAME (Generalization)	A- Desire for A is reinforced B- Desire for B is reinforced	A- Desire for A is extinguished B- Desire for B is extinguished
	DIFFERENT (Discrimination)	A- Desire for A continues reinforced B- Desire for A is not generalized to B	A- Desire for A remains extinguished B- Extinction of A is not generalized to B

and illustrating some relationships between them. The horizontal scale represents motives, the left side reward or reinforcement, and the right side unreward (or punishment) or extinction. It can also be referred to as a value or preference scale.

On the vertical scale the top half represents a judgment that two things are the "same." This can also be described by saying that *B* is perceived as belonging to the same category of things as *A*, or that *A* is generalized to include *B*. The bottom half represents a situation in which two things are judged to be "different." Here *B* is perceived as not belonging to the same category as *A*, *B* being discriminated from *A*. The vertical scale can also be thought of as dealing with information, with perceived opportunities, or with judgments of science or fact.

In the upper left box, *A* is rewarding, and hence reinforced. Since *B* is perceived to be the same as *A*, *B* is also reinforced. In the upper right *A* is unrewarding, and *B* is judged the same as *A*. Hence, the desire for *B* is extinguished along with that for *A*.

In the lower left *A* is rewarding, and hence reinforced. But *B* is perceived as different from *A*, and therefore remains unreinforced unless it is independently rewarded. Finally, in the lower right *A* is unrewarding and extinguished. But since *B* is perceived as different from *A*, the extinction of *A* will not extend to *B*. The chart is a general statement that reinforcement and extinction cannot occur on the basis of motives until and unless the thing to be reinforced or extinguished has been categorized on the basis of concepts. If we add to this the strong suspicion that concept formation and attainment may not occur unless motivated, we see the importance of keeping each in mind while attempting to study the other.

SOME MISCELLANEOUS NOTES, INCLUDING FREUD

We are now approaching the end of the discussion of psychology. But no mention has been made thus far of the unconscious, hypnotism, psychoanalysis, hypertension, repression, Gestaltism, or the Freudian school. These omissions are not intended to mean that no value is seen in these things, but rather (1) that these things are not needed within the scope of the present discussion, or (2) that their content has already been expressed in a different way.

Hypnotism

Hypnotism falls in the first group. It is extremely useful for diagnosing and treating certain mental conditions, and for learning more about the psychological nature of the human being. But the method of treating specific mental disorders is of no more concern to a broad discussion of human behavior than are the techniques of medicine. To the extent that the understanding of psychology in general has been furthered by hypnosis, its findings have already contributed to the discussions above.

Perhaps the most important finding via hypnosis which is not yet mentioned is that of regression. Under hypnosis, senility, or certain kinds of shock, persons often behave as if their learning is built in layers, any one layer being able to dip into and utilize the layers below it, but not above. Under some circumstances a person may act as if some of the top layers have been stripped off, and he must rely solely on the lower ones. When deeply hypnotized, a person may be told "You are now six years old." During the hypnosis he then returns to his own characteristics at the age of six. His speech (including a lisp if he had one), his muscular actions, and his whole mode of thought and motivation are those of himself at six. He is not "acting," since he performs all kinds of motions which he could not duplicate if awake. He will not understand words he did not know at six, and he may remember long-forgotten details of things he had known at six. During old age and under shock, persons may similarly regress in whole, or in part, to patterns of an earlier age. No explanation of this phenomenon is yet known. We are sure that information is *not* stacked in layers in the brain, that reference being pure analogy.

Gestalt Psychology

Although Gestalt psychology has received declining attention in recent years, and probably never generated as much interest in the United States as in Europe, the absence of earlier mention does not imply that the field has made no contribution. Instead of dealing with Gestaltism as such, we will say several things about the present approach in the light of Gestalt interpretations. Previous chapters suggest that all "larger" concepts are built from "smaller" ones. This suggestion was deliberate. However, although the overt discussion was largely nonneurological, it was based on an implicit neurological model. In that model some initial networks are formed. As concept formation proceeds, some neural networks are tied together into new networks. For simplicity we refer to the latter as "larger." However, although it seems simpler to suppose that *more* neurons are involved in these joint ventures, this is not necessarily so, and our ignorance in this realm is reasonably profound.

If this relationship were translated literally into the formation of concepts about the outside world, it would imply that we always start with concepts of parts of things, which we piece together into larger things, always moving from the atomic to the molar. The Gestaltist emphasizes the opposite approach—starting with the crude, large concept, perception, or response, which is then gradually refined to include the details.

As indicated briefly in the previous chapter, in the present model it is supposed that the *neuron networks* move from small to large (if that is the appropriate terminology) by combining, recombining, and re-recombining. This neural pattern is assumed to be equally valid whether the external objects represented by these networks move from small to large, parts to whole, or the reverse. The child may learn first about individual instruments and then later about the combined form of an orchestra. Or he may learn first about an orchestra, after which he breaks it apart. The child may first learn about doors, floors, windows, and stairs, and only later form the concept of house, or he may reverse the order. The same may be said about almost any concept, the sequence in a particular child depending on the sequence of his own experiences. Whether the second stage is a combination or a differentiation, it involves a neurological and conceptual structure which grows from and depends upon the first stage. Nothing in the present model contradicts the notion that the young child senses things first in big blobs, from which it gradually discerns more precise patterns, or that many of its motor responses also develop from the gross to the refined. And there is certainly no objection to thinking of that part of a stimulus situation to which a person attends as the "figure" and the parts not attended to as the "ground"—a central part of the Gestalt approach. Certainly, too, the present model insists that a stimulus is not a *thing* in the environment, but a perception, which depends on what the subject attends to and how he conceptualizes it. The present model is conceived to include the viable features of Gestaltism, not to ignore them.

Perhaps the most significant contribution of Gestalt psychology is the finding that things are perceived as wholes, not as collections of parts. In perception the brain will fill in missing parts of things, ignore certain kinds of deviations, create illusions, and do all manner of other things not specified by the signals entering the senses at any given moment. This central core of Gestaltism is in no way at odds with the present approach, and the notion of The Gestalt seems to coincide nicely with the pre-existing concept which earlier chapters have insisted is indispensable for perception.

The Freudian School

Freudian vocabulary is notably absent from the preceding chapters, with no mention of such terms as the unconscious, id, ego, superego, libido, wish-fulfillment, repression, guilt, instincts, or psychosexual stages. The reasons are twofold.

First, although Freud performed heroic service in calling attention to the various forces at work in human beings, and in insisting that conscious controls are but a limited part of our system, few psychologists or psychiatrists now accept the original Freudian formulation literally. Many do, however, accept the broader Freudian implication that experiences of early childhood may have a compelling influence on the adult personality. The present model does not gainsay the latter conclusion, which is in part accepted in later chapters on personality and culture. And lest an "information model" seem to emphasize conscious behavior to the neglect of unconscious—an unconscionably un-Freudian approach —let the earlier disclaimers be repeated. Nothing about the information model presupposes that the behavior it describes is conscious. Certainly much of the learning of concepts and secondary reinforcers can happen at the unconscious level, and so can the ensuing behavior. The present model in itself thus neither affirms nor contradicts the Freudian insistence that the major controls of behavior are unconscious, and the later chapter on culture would tend to affirm it.

Second, Freud did not accompany his components of the personality with an explanation of their neurological mechanisms. The present model reverses the emphasis, in a fashion more compatible with the spirit of recent decades. It assumes that no behavior is possible unless some mechanisms are present to effectuate it—be they nerves, glands, muscles, or other accoutrements. The behavior is seen as the performance of the mechanism —in the same sense that an electric current is the product of a generating mechanism, or a mathematical computation is the functioning of an electronic computing mechanism. Where we cannot identify the physical mechanism, we try to describe a phenomenon in terms of such relatively elemental operations as conditioning, secondary motivation, concept formation, perception, and the like. Many Freudian concepts can apparently be analyzed in this model which seems to me to "contain more information."

Part of the difference between the two systems is purely terminological. An "oral need" or a "sex drive" seems to mean about the same thing as to say that oral stimulation and sex are reinforcers. Either terminology implies that a person will engage in behavior perceived as leading to oral stimulation or sex. However, the Freudian language—and we will here deal with the general flavor of the subsequent Freudian school rather than with Freud's own formulations—has an aura of inbornness, which is currently highly suspect. Further, "reinforcer" implies a mechanism which can be experimented with, whereas "need" does not. As Kelly observes, the Freudian theory "was designed in such a manner that it tended to defy both logical examination and experimental validation."[5]

Important differences, however, are conceptual. Assuming that both the Freudian and the present model deal with the same total picture (which is doubtful), the two models have cut that picture into jigsaw pieces of different sizes and shapes, so that pieces from the two sets are not interchangeable. To borrow a phrase from linguistics, the two systems have "sliced up reality" differently. With some trepidation we will nevertheless attempt a brief cross-referencing.

In the present model, inner behavior is sliced into two major divisions, preferences and opportunities. Preferences are partly inborn (primary reinforcers) but mostly learned (secondary reinforcers), and are tied to

[5] George A. Kelly, "Man's Construction of His Alternatives," in Lindzey, *op. cit.*, p. 34.

an energy control. We thus have mechanisms for controlling both the amount and the direction of energy release. Opportunities are learned through the information processes of concept learning and perception, our present emphasis being on concepts, since we can perceive only those things for which we have concepts. Above the most elemental level, reinforcing power is also tied to concepts, not things. Finally, as a necessary part of the system, the brain is capable on a purely internal basis of connecting, disconnecting, and reforming concepts, and attaching or detaching motive power to them.

Expressed in the above terms, the Freudian elements of the personality seem to come out as follows. The *Id* includes both the basic energy source and such assumedly primary reinforcers as the desire for food, sexual stimulation, physical comfort, and the release of emotions. If there were no other components of the personality, and nothing to stop him, the individual would spend his energies in sensual gratification. (To match Freud's own later position some modifications would have to be made to accommodate a death wish, or instinct.)

In Freudian terms, the *Ego* is the guiding component which steers the individual toward pleasurable and away from unpleasurable things, through perceptions and contact with reality. It is not enough to want pleasure. One must also know where and how to get it. According to Freud the Ego has no energy of its own, but can utilize some from the Id. In the present system something which steers the individual toward pleasure and away from displeasure could be described as the conception and perception system (providing the information) in which many of the concepts have valences attached (providing the guidance toward pleasure). The two systems basically agree that the energy source is separate from the information system. They differ in that Freud combines the energy and pleasure aspects in a single unit, the Id, whereas in the present system the energy is a separate unit controlled by the *joint* action of the information and motive systems.

Freud's *Superego* is a monitor or conscience which, when some deliciously despicable thought crosses our mind, says, "Now, now, you know that's wrong!" It is character and will power. It is not merely fear of punishment, which could be provided as part of the information corralled by the Ego, but an inner feeling which inhibits "wrong" behavior, even when we cannot possibly be caught or punished. Freud recognized that the Superego at least in part reflects the standards of our culture. In present terminology certain behavior—whether of performance or inhibition—is perceived as sufficiently rewarding in certain contexts to acquire a strong intrinsic reward value. Whether the initial reward value arises from social approval, from a sense of longer run instrumentality (this would be fun, but may get me into trouble later), or from some other source or combination of sources does not matter. Once that behavior achieves intrinsic reward value, it will in itself control other behavior in its direction. And besides, experience may suggest that disapproved behavior probably *will* be found out, in which case the instrumental value of "right" behavior also remains.

Such things described by Freud as repressions and unconscious drives are very real, and the present system would be weak if it could not accommodate them. If we recall that the brain can make and break connections internally, some of the so-called unconscious motivation seems easily explainable. For example, we have seen that when some overt response is punishing it is extinguished. But if *thinking* about that response leads by association to *thinking* about punishment, then *thinking* about the response will also tend to be extinguished.[6] The extinction of "thinking about something" would seem to approximate the Freudian "repressions." In similar fashion, if society disapproves not merely *doing* something, but also the desire to do it, then the thought of *wanting* to perform the act may also be extinguished, resulting in a Freudian suppressed desire. Since the act of *wanting* can also be conceptualized and acquire a valence, if wanting is not completely extinguished, when it occurs the thought of the punishment will accompany it, producing a Freudian guilt feeling.

To follow another step, under some circumstances the thought of actually *performing* some act may be rewarding, such as (to follow the Freudian spirit) some taboo sex relationship. But because the act is taboo, the thought of *wanting* to perform it is punishing. If so, then the thought of performing the act would be reinforced, while the thought of *wanting* to perform it would simultaneously be extinguished. The result is a condition of wanting but denying the want, another kind of suppression. Freud put much emphasis on the role of suppressed desires. This, too, is in accord with the present model. The chapters on motivation noted that any kind of "need," such as breathing, which is easily and automatically satisfied, has almost no influence on motives. When the ability to breathe freely is denied, however, the need becomes a strong reinforcer, as when one is under water or in a tightly closed small space. In the present model a desire need not be suppressed to reinforce behavior. But it must be unsatisfied, at least in part and until it acquires intrinsic reward value.

To shift to neurological aspects, when an overt response is extinguished the neural connections do not disappear. They become inactive while new connections are set up in a different direction. Under appropriate stimulation the original connections can be reactivated, to produce the original response. If internalized connections follow the same rules, the cortex retains connections for *thoughts* which have been extinguished. The reactivation of such connections under appropriate stimulation could be manifested as presumably suppressed desires again rearing their ugly

---

[6] For a discussion of the assumption that internalized behavior of this sort follows the same rules as the external, see Charles E. Osgood, "Behavior Theory and Social Science," *Behavioral Science*, Vol. 1, No. 1, pp. 167 ff.

heads. Further, considering the general free ranging associations which occur in dreams, it is not unlikely that these extinguished thoughts should be reactivated during sleep. We can also observe that internal conflicts may be more likely to cause mental disturbance than external ones. External conflicts are normally of limited duration, as some change in circumstance will usually either eliminate the conflict or force a choice. By contrast, conflicts at the conceptual level can be rehashed a hundred times a day, and go on indefinitely.

We have talked thus far as if the brain operates on a sort of reverse Gresham's law, under which good, pleasant thoughts drive out bad, unpleasant ones. This kind of mental behavior is evident in much daydreaming, and we can explain it merely by internalizing the normal rules of reinforcement and extinction. It is abundantly clear, however, that human beings can spend much time haunted by unpleasant thoughts, such as those which produce fear, apprehension, guilt feelings, or tension, and that they can sometimes have great difficulty driving these thoughts out in favor of pleasant ones. The normal rules of conditioning do not account for such mental behavior, and we must look elsewhere for an explanation.

It can be deduced that for evolutionary survival the organism must possess some mechanism which will give higher priority to the avoidance of dangers which immediately threaten survival than to the achievement of pleasures, all of which can be delayed for hours or days without producing death or permanent injury. Without at this point attempting to specify neurological mechanisms, we can hypothesize that perceptions which produce emotions of fear will take precedence in the attention center(s) of the brain over those which produce emotions of pleasure, as is clearly the case when we are actually confronted with danger. But it is also clear that in the normal individual who is not currently perceiving either dangerous or pleasurable situations, *thoughts* of fear and danger do not persistently take precedence over those with positive valences.

Although we are not presently prepared to specify the mechanisms (and I am not sure that the problem has previously been stated precisely this way), we are apparently forced (in the present model) to hypothesize some arrangement, presumably operating through the emotion centers, which gives priority among *perceptions* to those of threatening things, but among *recollections* and imaginings to those of pleasant things. The complex learning system of human beings, and perhaps of some other animals, nevertheless makes it possible for the actual result at any given moment to reverse the inborn priority. We thus can worry, even when there is nothing immediately present in our environment to worry about.

It is not the purpose of this section to try to equate particular Freudian ideas with particular neurological or behaviorist phenomena, but merely to indicate that some undeniable aspects of behavior described by Freud can also be described within the present system—which is essential to the defense of the system.

In closing this discussion of psychology, it must be recalled that much of our knowledge of what goes on in the brain is still fragmentary. Many hypothesized details are filled in by inferring what it seems *must* be there if the observed external behavior is to be explained. Other types of information about behavior, on the other hand, have been verified by massive experimentation. Still others, particularly that on the internal aspects of thinking and motives, are assisted by introspection.[7]

The Freudian school is recognized to have made a tremendous contribution to the development of some aspects of psychology, as have also the behaviorists and the Gestaltists. Although picturesque, it is perhaps no longer fruitful to debate whether every individual goes through an oral, anal, and phallic stage, whether we have a life wish and a death wish, or whether man is still "half-tamed, half-civilized, with love and hate contending within his breast for mastery"[8]—as it is virtually impossible to design experiments to test such statements. The model used in the past few chapters is essentially an information model, which seems to provide a niche in which to place most of the significant psychological findings, and simultaneously to be couched in terms which are subject to experimentation. It is probably closer to behaviorism in its recent garb than to any other one psychological school, though it deviates significantly at points. As with all other phases of the present volume, where alternate models were available within a given field of study, that one was chosen which seemed to be most applicable in other fields as well.

---

[7] It might be noted at this point that Allport strongly insists that the healthy individual has excellent conscious awareness of his motives, and that "direct and projective performances in healthy people are all of a piece." (Gordon W. Allport, "The Trend in Motivational Theory," in Chalmers L. Stacey and Manfred F. DeMartino (eds.), *Understanding Human Behavior* (Cleveland: Howard Allen, Inc., 1958), p. 63.) In the same vein, he states that "Psychodynamics is not necessarily a hidden dynamics," (p. 60) and that the "patient should be assumed insightful until he is proved otherwise." (p. 61.) He does not feel that Freud was in error in looking for "hidden" motives, however, since "Freud was a specialist in precisely those motives that cannot be taken at their face value." Insisting on my own mental health, I have used introspection at some spots where objectively measurable data are not available, particularly where the performance introspectively observed seems to follow the same rules developed in connection with overt behavior.

[8] Lawrence E. Cole, *Human Behavior* (Yonkers: World Book, 1953), p. 704.

II. COMMUNICATIONS

Chapter 9

COMMUNICATION:
INFORMATION,
SEMIOTICS, SEMANTICS

WHY STUDY COMMUNICATION?

COMMUNICATION is at the heart of civilization. Man's brain has the neurological capacity to form the complex concepts which distinguish civilized man from the beast. But one man's experience is small, and unless he has access to the collected pool of experiences of countless thousands before him, his behavior will be only a little different from the apes. In fact, if apes are raised in the company of human beings, their behavior will be more "civilized" in some ways than that of human beings raised in the company of apes. In some experiments where human and chimpanzee babies were raised together, the chimps excelled the humans in some respects, learning more complicated things more rapidly. The reversal came when the human child was able to learn language and the chimp was not (except to follow a few simple commands). Thereupon the child entered on the road to becoming a fully possessed human being, while the chimp, without language, continued at an intellectual level approximating the three-year-old.

A child raised to the age of six without language, having no contact with other humans except a deaf mother, showed the behavior of a six-month old and the intelligence of about nineteen months. She showed all the signs of being feebleminded and almost completely uneducable. Under intensive training, however, concentrated largely on the use of language, she had reached normal levels by the age of eight and a half.[1] Without language she could learn to sit, dress, eat, and sleep in reasonable human fashion—as the chimp is able to do—but little more. *With* language,

---

[1] This case is described by Kingsley Davis, "Final Note on a Case of Extreme Isolation," in Harold E. Briggs (ed.), *Language . . . Man . . . Society, Readings in Communication* (New York: Rinehart & Co., 1949), pp. 24–27, reprinted from the *American Journal of Sociology* (January, 1940), pp. 554–565.

the whole gamut of civilized behavior is available to her. In short, without language, the individual is able to progress to about the intelligence level of the three-year-old, and that is all.

The problem is not only that language enables us to learn from the experience of others. It is not only that we can describe our experiences to others, thereby confirming our own observations by finding if things seem the same to others—although this is an extremely important part of learning. In addition, a language itself contains a tremendous amount of information, and merely to learn it acquaints us with much accumulated knowledge. To learn a language is to learn the meaning of its words, and one cannot learn the meaning of such words as ship, eclipse, lever, jury, Arctic, noun, price, or organization without learning important things about his environment.

In Chapter 7 it was said that our thinking is done with concepts. Further, our thinking is greatly simplified by using words, the verbal symbols of concepts. The reader can readily check this for himself. If you start to think about this problem, you will probably find going through your mind are words such as, "Now let me think; do I really use words while I am thinking or don't I?" The process is not entirely verbal, but it is doubtful if we could form many of our more complex concepts without using words to think with.

If the proper study of man is mankind, that study must include language, which makes the key difference between man and the other animals.

SCOPE AND NATURE OF THE PROBLEM OF COMMUNICATION

In its broadest sense, communication means a transfer of information, *transfer* meaning a change of location. Unlike physical objects, information can be transferred without necessarily ceasing to be where it was, or the teacher would be in a pitiable state indeed.

Perhaps *information* must be listed among the indefinables. Like space, time, distance, force, probability, and some other fundamental notions, it may perhaps be given synonyms and illustrations but not definitions.[2]

----

[2] Communications theorists seem generally to accept Hartley's definition of information as the successive selection of signs from a given list. See Colin Cherry, *On Human Communication* (New York: John Wiley & Sons, 1957), pp. 43, 48, and *passim*. As will be seen below, this approach will be accepted here for the *quantitative measure* of information, or information capacity in some particular channel or medium. But to define a unit of measure does not define information itself, any more than to define an inch provides a definition of length. Information has also been defined as the reduction in doubt. (Cherry, p. 180.) But doubt is the absence of information, and is meaningless until information itself has been defined. Kecskemeti defines information as "knowledge communicated by way of transmitting symbols, as distinct from knowledge acquired at first hand." (Paul Kecskemeti, *Meaning, Communication, and Value* [Chicago: University of Chicago Press, 1952],

At the same time we have already noted in Chapter 2 that "information" seems to be defined implicitly in information theory as synonymous with "modulation." We will tentatively accept that definition, and briefly review here some uses of the word mentioned earlier. Perhaps the best general statement is to say that whenever *B* is modulated by *A*, then *B* contains information about *A*. When a rabbit hops in the snow, the snow is modulated by the rabbit, and contains information about it, or when light is reflected from the face of a building the light rays are modulated by contact with the building, and contain information about it. The carrier wave of a radio broadcast or of a telephone line is modulated by a voice, and thereafter contains information. Photographic film is modulated by light, a field is modulated by a plow, stairs are modulated by the feet which climb them, paper is modulated by the printer's ink, and so on. The medium in each case thereafter contains information about the source which modulated it. In Chapters 3 and 7 we stated that the brain contains information about the outside world in the form of the modulations impressed on it through the senses.

In Chapter 2 we saw that a communications system (which may be thought of as the relationship in which information is transferred from *A* to *B*) consists of a source, coding, a medium, detection, and interpretation or decoding. To shorten the statement, we will say that the source, *A*, modulates the medium, which subsequently modulates the receiver, *B*. The first modulation constitutes coding (or encoding), while the second constitutes detection and decoding. In a high fidelity system, there is just as much information at any one of the five steps as at any other, and the receiver cannot acquire information which was dropped or missed at any preceding step—although, if there is a redundancy (a matter for further discussion below) the receiver may not lose any part of the "message," as that term will be defined below.

The total scope of information transmission is almost limitless—if one cares to use its language to express things. We can say, for example, that the hormones carry information through the human system, "telling" one part of the body what is going on elsewhere. The genes contain information (the blueprint, so to speak) about the structure and functioning

---

p. 12.) This gives us the synonym, knowledge, a gain of dubious value, while the remainder of the definition constricts information to a considerably narrower field than information theory usefully suggests. Churchman uses a limited-purpose definition of "recorded experience which is useful for decision-making," (C. West Churchman, *Prediction and Optimal Decision: Philosophical Issues of a Science of Values* [New York: Prentice-Hall, 1961], p. 100) while noting that this decision does not correspond to that of information theory, as in R. L. Ackoff, "Towards a Behavioral Theory of Communication," *Management Science*, No. 4, 1958, pp. 218–34. I have not yet checked the latter, but Ackoff later (*General Systems*, Vol. 5, p. 4) notes Rappoport's urging that we need a model of the cognitive aspects of communications theory, but he provides no further definition of cognition.

of the matured plant or animal. The fossil contains information about how things were a million years ago—and so on.

Having noted these possible ramifications of information theory, we will confine our attention here to deliberate communications of direct concern to human beings. These can involve animals, machines, and human beings themselves. There can, for example, be communication between two animals (as between sheep dog and sheep), between two machines (as between an automatic pilot and the plane it controls), and between two human beings. There can also be communication between machine and animal (as between an automatic heart and a dog under experimental operation), between man and machine (as in the use of a computer), or between human being and animal (as between boy and dog). There are many other forms of interanimal communications, but we are concerned here only with those which are more or less consciously arranged or used by man for his own ends. Having mentioned these possibilities, we will now narrow our interest still further to communication between human beings—though many of the principles are the same for any communication, whether A or B are human, animal, or machine. We will also pay no direct attention to the processes of encoding or decoding, as such, but assume that the communicators know how to do these things.

Although all communications systems, animate or inanimate, have the same basic steps in common, communication between human beings is unique in one highly important respect. Human beings, and no other animals to a significant degree, communicate with learned, arbitrary signs or symbols—the things we call language. "Learned" means not inborn, and "arbitrary" means that there is no necessary similarity between the sign and the thing it refers to. Some words do have onomatopoeic resemblances to their referents, like "hiss" and "plop." But these are relatively rare, and there is nothing about such words as "dog" or "river" to give the slightest hint of their meaning. The meaning of "sign" will be discussed in detail below, and the distinction between symbolic and nonsymbolic behavior will be examined in full scope in the chapter on culture. Signs are the core of the problem of language, and man is either the only animal that uses language, or he has such a tremendous superiority in this skill that no other animal is even remotely close. In studying language and signs, we are studying not only a medium of communication, but the thing which permits man to form the varied and complex concepts which make civilization possible.

SEMIOTICS

Semiotics is the name given to the study, or science, of signs. It is the heart of the study of human communication. The idea can be succinctly expressed: "A issues x as a sign of y, and B receives x as a sign of y," in which process y is communicated from A to B.[3] We may recall that it is not thoughts or ideas which move from one person to another, but signals in the form of light, sound, or other energy. These signals must have certain forms, patterns, or groupings if they are to carry information. These forms, patterns, or groupings of signals will be referred to as signs, to which we now turn our attention.[4]

In Chapter 5 we defined a *sufficient cue* as that amount of information which will enable us to identify a concept. We also indicated that any stimulus which serves to identify a concept is a sufficient cue. The cue can be some portion of the concept itself, as when we identify a house from a glimpse of the doorway. Or it could be some sign, like the word "house,"

or a conventionalized picture ⌂, which, through association, will permit the receiver to identify that concept. We will therefore define a *sign* as a collection of signals which constitute a sufficient cue for purposes of communication.[5]

In the vast bulk of communication of civilized man, the signs are already in existence and mutually understood prior to any particular communication—in the sense that I am now writing words in the assumption that the reader is already familiar with them. By appropriate arrangement of cues it is possible to create signs which the receiver will probably understand (decode) without prior agreement. To leave an envelope with a person's name on it on the floor just inside his door would be interpreted by most persons as a sign to pick up the note and read it, even if they had never experienced this precise situation before. A large picture

---

[3] See A. J. Ayer, "What Is Communication?" in *Studies In Communication* (London: Martin Secker & Warburg, 1955), p. 24. Morris says, "The most effective characterization of a sign is the following: S is a sign of D to the degree that I takes account of D in virtue of the presence of S," where S is the sign, D the designatum and I the interpreter. Charles W. Morris, "Foundations of the Theory of Signs," *International Encyclopedia of Unified Science*, Vol. 1, No. 2, University of Chicago, 1938, p. 4.

[4] The term "semiotics" is generally used in a narrower meaning than it is here accorded. In its traditional meaning it might, for example, exclude such aspects of structural linguistics as morphological variations in words, inflections, intonations, systematic modes of pattern formation, or discriminable meanings wholly independent of vocabulary. In the present usage, a sign is *anything* which does the work of conveying information, whether it is a clearly recognized vocabulary item, a syntactical device, a frequency probability of sound transitions, or any kind of relationship or grouping of sounds, shapes, tempos, pitches, colors, or any other medium. In short, in the present meaning, *any* discriminable event can be a sign, and hence is encompassed under semiotics.

[5] This definition follows that of Cherry (*op. cit.*, p. 7) rather closely, Cherry's definition being "any physical event used in communication." As the term *signal* is defined here (Chapter 2), signals are physical events. Like Cherry's, the present definition is tied to communication. In the present definition the words "sufficient cue" make explicit what is clearly implicit in Cherry's later discussion—namely, that the signals permit an identification to be made, which is another way of saying that signals enable the receiver to decode the sign. The term *symbol* will not be used here in any technical sense in connection with communication—again following Cherry. It will be reserved instead for rather extensive use in connection with culture, in Chapter 12, to refer to any outward manifestation of information concepts, along lines developed by anthropologists.

of a milkshake in front of a store suggests the availability of milkshakes inside, and even crudely drawn pictures may convey a message clearly with no prearrangement about their meaning.

There are many forms of improvised signs of this sort, and probably all of us use them at times. Having mentioned them, we will confine attention to signs understood in advance. These are by no means confined to words or pictures. Putting one's shoes outside a hotel room is a sign they are to be polished, or raising the hand is a sign attention is desired. Gestures, behavior patterns, art forms, diagrams, and rituals also are signs. When we say they are mutually understood in advance, we do not mean that the two parties have got together and agreed, but merely that both have previously learned them.

A *referent* is that concept or other sign for which a particular sign constitutes a sufficient cue. To deal first with a concept referent, it is the idea to which the sign refers, or, in layman's language, the *meaning* of the sign. If someone not familiar with a motorcycle asks what the word means, he can be shown a motorcycle or a picture. Or he can be given a description couched in words for concepts he already understands, such as wheels, motor, bicycle, automobile, and so forth. The person must first form the concept, and then attach the word to it, whereupon he knows the meaning of the word. If he merely memorizes a dictionary definition, the word continues to have no meaning until he has formed the concept. The meaning is never any clearer than the concept.[6]

A *code* is a list or system of signs and their referents, along with the necessary rules for encoding and decoding, the list constituting the vocabulary, and the rules, the syntax.[7] Codes are of two types, which

---

[6] The "general" semanticists have widely considered the referent to be the *thing*—object or event—in the real world to which the sign refers. That approach seems much less useful, and much more confusing, than to take the concept as the referent. The former approach seems to imply that "things are things." Under the present approach it is considered problematic whether there is something in the real world which corresponds to our concepts. This approach seems to be consistent with the so-called "scientific philosophy" and with the more recent findings of psycholinguistics and the psychology of concept formation. Nor is there any reason to believe that communication about unicorns is any less accurate *as communication* than communication about cows, just because the unicorn is a mythical beast.

More specifically, when the referent is defined as a concept rather than some "real" thing, it is possible to speak of accurate communication between two persons who possess closely similar concepts, whether or not the communication refers to any thing in the real world. We might even suggest that some of the most error-free communication occurs in the languages of logic and mathematics, where there are no *real* referents at all. Further, the system of signs in any culture parallels its system of concepts, not the structure of things in its environment—as a comparison of the languages of two drastically different cultures in the Whorfian manner will promptly reveal.

[7] Along lines indicated in an earlier footnote about the present scope assigned to the term "semiotics," the term "code" will also here be intended to include *all* signs which may actually convey information, whether they are listed in the "code book" or not. Intonations in spoken language, for example, are signs within the present meaning, even though they do not appear in the dictionaries or grammar books.

may be called direct, or *semantic*, *codes* and indirect, or *transmission codes*. In a *semantic code* the referent of each sign is a concept. This concept can be large and complex. If the armed forces have three plans of strategy, *A*, *B*, and *C*, the three letters are the signs, and each referent is a whole set of plans, which could run to thousands of pages. Our main interest in semantic codes will be ordinary language, in which the words or parts of words are the signs, and the concepts which constitute their meanings are the referents. The vocabulary can be illustrated roughly by the list of the words in a dictionary, and the syntax is the grammar. These referent concepts differ considerably among themselves in complexity; the concept of "pin" is much simpler than the concepts referred to by "revolution" or "psychoanalysis."

A *transmission code* is a system of signs whose referents are other signs. Morse code, semaphore, and other things known as codes to the layman are included here. With the help of a code book, a communication can be transposed from its semantic form to its transmission form, or the reverse, without knowledge of its meaning. Transmission codes need not concern us here.

Semantic signs are not confined to words. Such things as a nod, pat, or gesture also have semantic meaning. Smoke signals, hand signals of the deaf-and-blind can have direct concept referents, even if they are thought of primarily as indirect means of transmitting words. Word signs can be transmitted in either spoken or written form. The ability to produce the sounds of speech is learned early in life by trial and error and imitation, usually shortly after one learns to understand the speech of others, and we need not discuss it further.[8]

Visual languages may consist of either semantic or transmission codes, which means they may code concepts directly or indirectly. To illustrate a direct, semantic code, in the flag signals widely used at sea before radio, a single flag can represent an idea, like "storm" or "please stand by." This method is very efficient so long as the number of possible messages is small. The indirect method, or transmission code, uses one flag for each letter of the alphabet. This is relatively inefficient for any one message. But there is no limit to the number of different messages which can be sent with the same limited set of signs.

Anyone reading this book is familiar with alphabet coding of words into

---

[8] An interesting analysis of the development of speech from more primitive forms of communication among animals is found in Charles F. Hockett, "The Origin of Speech," *Scientific American* (September, 1960), pp. 99 ff. Of particular note is Hockett's emphasis on the importance of total feedback—the fact that the speaker hears his whole message through his own ears just as the receiver hears it, a point also made earlier in a social context by George H. Mead, *Mind, Self, and Society* (Chicago: University of Chicago Press, 1934), pp. 69–70. This is in contrast to such communicative signs as the mating dance of the stickleback or the informational dance of the bees, in which the source never observes his own signals in the same form they are observed by the receiver. Similar total feedback also occurs in writing.

written form. This is an indirect, or transmission, code for the concept code of spoken language. By contrast, the "picture" languages of Japanese, Chinese, and ancient Egyptian are direct codings, each symbol having a semantic meaning, arranged in the following way.

Initially, each character was a simplified picture of the idea represented. As time passed, the desire for efficiency led to greater simplification, in which a relatively complex shape might be suggested by a simple curve, angle, or loop. Two or more such idea pictures could then be combined into a more complex concept, which in turn might be simplified pictorially. For example, if a small circle represents the sun, and a small convex angle a mountain, sun-over-the-mountain 人 might then mean "morning," which in due time could be simplified to 人. "Up" might be signified by an upward pointing arrow. By combining morning with up, we get "to arise." This could then be shown as 人, which simplifies to 人. More complex concepts are formed by more complex combinations of signs, mostly conventionalized, as above.

In "picture writing" there is no direct relation between the visual and the aural language; the picture provides no clue to the sound of the corresponding spoken word. To illustrate with western languages, the picture "word" △ might be pronounced "house," "maison," or "casa." Similarly, the conceptual content of a sign ろ on the highway is readily evident, but the sign provides no clue whether the aural equivalent is pronounced "winding road" or "camino sinuoso." The written language might have the same basic set of words as the corresponding spoken language, but the written forms represent the meanings directly, not indirectly through the aural form. We might also say that the same vocabulary of words is represented by two separate sets of signs, one aural and the other visual. This is in contrast to alphabet writing, where the referents of the written signs are the *sounds* of the spoken language, not their meanings. That is, the referents of the written signs are another set of signs, not a vocabulary.

The "progressive" method of teaching reading in the United States in recent decades is a direct method, in which the child learns to attach meaning directly to a pattern of letters, rather than to decode the letters first into sounds, and then into meanings. All rapid reading, of course, is direct. Whether the direct method is the best way to *start* to learn to read is a matter we will not debate here.

In alphabet systems it is theoretically possible to have a direct one-to-one correspondence between the spoken and visual signs. This would occur if each letter of the alphabet had one and only one pronunciation, and each spoken sound could be spelled in one and only one way. Then anyone who could pronounce a word correctly could spell it, and vice versa. Spanish and Finnish approximate this situation, though with some irregularities. English is particularly loose. It is difficult to maintain strict correspondence, since spoken words undergo evolutionary changes in pronunciation. We thus face a choice of two evils, the one a discrepancy between the written and spoken form, and the other a constant revision of spelling. In addition, many languages have many dialects. If sounds were to correspond to spelling in each, then each would have its own spelling. For such reasons strict correspondence between written and spoken forms seems unlikely.

In the ensuing analysis we will deal with semantic language codes. Once we have expressed a spoken word in letters, that particular combination of letters is then a sign for the word. We will deal with words, as such, without regard to whether they are written or spoken—except where the form raises special questions.[9]

Information versus "To Inform"

In Chapter 7 we noted that certain concepts of action or behavior are linguistically coded as nouns, and that this fact sometimes creates confusion. Now the noun *information* is extremely useful. It is also useful, however, to focus on the verb, *to inform*. The general idea of informing someone is that he knows more after he receives the communication than before—that his state of information has been changed. Now we can get into some extremely sticky problems if we start making the concept of "informing" depend on the receiver's knowing more than before, particularly when a given message can throw doubt on what previously seemed clear.

We will therefore focus on the information *process*, and will examine the circumstances in which new information *can* be conveyed, whether or not the information is actually new. "I bought you a boa at the pet shop today" is a message even if it is an absentminded repetition of the same statement made an hour before.

The minimum information content which can constitute a message is three items, two of substance (with semantic referents) and one of relation between them. These three items can appear in several forms. We will deal first with an affirmative statement which is not a command, ex-

---

[9] It should also be noted that Cherry (*op. cit.*, p. 7) applies the term "code" solely to what are here called transmission codes. This is in accordance with everyday usage, which does not treat language itself as a code. In the present formulation, the main purpose for construing language as a code is to maintain consistency with the terminology of communications systems. Human communication starts with a concept in one brain and attempts to recreate that concept in another brain. The first step is to express neural networks in words. It seems entirely appropriate to describe this step as *encoding* thoughts into words, which words are then further encoded into sounds. Reversing the sequence, the receiver *decodes* the sounds into words, and then further decodes the words into concepts. There is no feasible way to define the terms *encode* and *decode* to omit these steps of spoken communication without creating a special language for interhuman communication distinct from that of other communication. That in turn would eliminate much of the important unity which information theory can contribute to diverse fields, even if that unity is not (as Cherry notes) as tremendous as some of its early disciples preached. But we can hardly call the putting of thoughts into language "encoding" if we refuse to call language a code.

clamation, or the answer to a question. We will assume also that we are dealing solely with words, as in writing, with no gestures, intonations, or other auxiliary signs.

In such an affirmative statement, a single word cannot convey a message. Suppose I speak the word "chair" to you. If you already possess the concept, and recognize "chair" as the sign for it, then the sign alone contains no new information. On the other hand, if you do not yet know the concept (or the sign, or both) then you will not receive any information from the sign, since you do not know its referent. In short, when a single sign is used in a declarative statement not answering a question, either the receiver already knows the referent of the sign or the sign has no meaning. In either case he gets no message.

Suppose we issue two signs, "chair" and "book." We have now taken a type of communication with zero message content and doubled it. The result remains zero. But as soon as we add a third item to establish a relation between the other two, we can have a message. These might be such relations as "chair bent book," or "book hit chair."

Suppose, however, that I issue the two signs "book torn," do not these two signs alone convey a message? The answer is yes, but three signs are present, not two. "Torn" is the past participle of "to tear," and the words are "book torn," not "book tear." The third sign consists of the form of one of the words. A sign of relation is also found in the word order, since "book torn" is not the same as "torn book." These indicators of relation will be discussed further under syntactics. Meanwhile we will rest with the assertion that a message must contain at least three signs, two of content and one of relation.[10] There is no upper limit to the number of signs in a message, and the whole of a book can be considered a message. Most of our attention will be directed to relatively short messages of the sort which are called sentences by grammarians and propositions by philosophers.

This same relationship seems to apply to the languages of mathematics and logical calculus as well. Nothing is conveyed by the mathematician if he simply states x, nor if he states both x and y. But if he states x and y *and* some relation between them, he has then indicated a different concept. Examples would include such things as $x \cdot y$, $x + y$, x/y, $x(y)$, $x = y$, or any of a variety of other relationships.

Similarly, in the logical calculus no meaning is conveyed if we merely state A, or B, or both together, unless some relationship is indicated. These logical relationships may take such forms as A implies B, A implies non-B, A or B but not both, A or B or both, both A and B, and so on. (If these statements make little sense to the reader, he should either study logic or ignore the examples.)

To move now to statements which answer questions, the three items

---

[10] This, I take it, is the essential meaning of the assertion of Charles Pierce that signs are never used in isolation, but that every sign requires another "to interpret it," as reported in Cherry, *op. cit.*, p. 264.

are as follows. Since we are attempting to deal with the minimum conditions for a message, we will examine the smallest possible answer, such as a simple yes or no. The question to be answered constitutes one of the two substantive items, and must, of course, be understood in advance by both the source and the receiver. The item of relationship must also be understood: namely, that the sign given by the source is the answer to the question. In answering a question it is thus possible for information apparently to be conveyed by a single sign, such as yes or no, up or down, war or peace. The appearance is deceiving, however, the single sign being merely the completion of a communication, at least two signs of which had previously been transmitted.

In order for any one sign to have meaning, it must be selected from a list of two or more possible alternative signs. This condition is true for any sign in any location or circumstance. It is most obvious for a single sign which answers a question, as follows.

Ashby's example concerns the woman who asks the warden to give her imprisoned husband a cup of coffee. The warden believes that a possible attempt at escape is afoot, and that the wife is trying to inform the prisoner that it has or has not been arranged. He therefore suspects that something about the coffee may be the coded yes or no. Could it be the presence or absence of sugar? The warden will put sugar in it, and tell the prisoner that the cook put sugar in all the coffee. Could the message lie in sending coffee instead of tea? The warden will send coffee and tell the prisoner there was no tea. In each case the warden destroys the prisoner's ability to extract information from the sign by making it appear that only one sign was possible, and that the one selected was not selected from among two or more. A sign cannot convey information if it is the only one which can issue under the circumstances.[11] As Lewis Carroll put it:

It is a very inconvenient habit of kittens (Alice had once made the remark) that, whatever you say to them, they *always* purr. "If they would only purr for 'yes,' and mew for 'no' or any rule of that sort," she had said, "so that one could keep up a conversation! But how *can* you talk with a person if they *always* say the same thing?"[12]

Ashby also cites the following example. Suppose two soldiers are captured by enemy countries A and B. Their respective wives both subse-

---

[11] This illustration, very slightly modified, and the following one, are from W. Ross Ashby, *An Introduction to Cybernetics* (New York: John Wiley & Sons, 1958), pp. 123–24. The question might be raised whether the sign "yes" or "no" has substantive content. The answer is clearly affirmative. For we are now dealing not with the conceptual content of the word itself, but with the kind of code described earlier in which a sign may stand for a whole program of action, or the whole body of information in some document. Thus the yes or no which answers a question has some specific semantic content, such as Program A or Program B. "Yes" and "no" are not signs with relatively fixed referents, like chair and book, but are "floating" signs whose referent changes every time the question changes.

[12] Lewis Carroll, *Through the Looking Glass*, as quoted in Cherry, *op. cit.*, p. 167.

quently receive messages, "I am well." But Country A allows the soldier to chose from among three messages: "I am well," "I am slightly ill," and "I am seriously ill;" while Country B is known to allow only one message: "I am well." The first wife has received significant information about her husband's health, while the second has received none, since there is only one possible sign. Even from Country B another set of alternatives does exist: message and no message. These are two signs with the respective referents: "definitely alive," and "possibly dead." In this instance, the fact of receiving a message is itself a sign from among two or more alternatives, and hence can convey information.

A command, or imperative, is similar to the answer to a question. The single word "Stop!" or "Quiet!" certainly conveys information. Whereas in the answer to a question, the question has already been communicated between the parties, in the command some situation exists which is mutually recognized, as is the relation of the command to the situation. This relationship can be illustrated by an example where the situation is *not* clear. Suppose I am sitting at the table loudly munching celery, making scuff marks on the wall by swinging my foot, and writing on the table cloth with ink, when my wife says "Stop!" This command is not clear, because there is no previous understanding about which activity the command applies to, and it would obviously be beyond the bounds of reason to stop all three.

The exclamation involves somewhat different logic. A strict exclamation is not a communication, but simply an act reflecting some state of the person emitting it. If you hit your thumb with a hammer you may wave it, swear, or say "Ouch!" None of these acts is a deliberate communication involving signs, and if by observing them I become aware that you are in pain, this is an act of perception on my part, not basically different from concluding from its yelp that a dog has been hurt, or from a cracking sound that a branch has fallen. This basic proposition is not changed if some of the sounds you issue happen to be words which in other contexts are used for deliberate communication.

We have observed that if you come up to me and say "Soufflé" no message is transmitted, and cannot be until you add another sign in some relation. If you say "ouch" in a perfectly flat voice and with no sign of emotion, you still have said nothing. But if you say "ouch" as you wave your thumb, you have now produced one linguistic sign indicating pain and a gestural sign indicating thumb. This means that a single message may utilize two or more media of communication, no complete message appearing in any one. Gestures, intonations, a factual context known to both parties, and other elements may provide one sign while a word provides another. If I say "Banana and spinach soup" and your face then shows disgust, you have communicated. But your sign has meaning only in the same sense that a yes or no has meaning in answer to a question. The same gruesome contortion of your face would have no meaning without that background. Here the sign of relation is the sequence, the meaning being quite different if you show disgust first and I then say "Banana and spinach soup."

The sign of relation between your waving your thumb and saying "Ouch!" is of a sort we are not prepared to pin down. The mere fact that the two signs are not in the same medium may itself be a sign of relation. Or it may be that a sign of relation can be omitted in these circumstances. We are dealing here with borderline cases between communicated messages, which require all three signs, and perceptions by one person of another's state, the latter not requiring any signs at all—though, of course, it requires signals. An obvious borderline situation exists if a person deliberately communicates by acting a part which the other person perceives. Further analysis is required before we can decide whether such actions can fruitfully be analyzed in the same model as language, particularly when we are no longer using the arbitrary signs which constitute the core of language.

We will not here attempt to diagnose a message as a system. For anyone inclined to do so, we can note that some basic ingredients exist—two or more components in a relation, in an environment of a communications context, with subsystems of phonemes and morphemes.

Two more terms should be introduced. Philosophers, information theorists, and others distinguish between *object language* and *meta-language*. Object language is that of ordinary use, in which the subject of our discussions is the real world. Meta-language, on the other hand, is language about language, which is what much of this chapter consists of. A number of so-called paradoxes result from confusing the two. In "This sentence is false," for example, the quoted words are meta-language, since the words "This sentence" refer to language, not the real world. The confusion arises because the sentence, which is in meta-language, is treated as if it were in object language.

We will also distinguish between *historical languages* and *"constructed" languages*, the latter also being known as *language systems* or *sign systems*.[13]

Historical languages are those customarily referred to as languages, such as English, French, Japanese, or Congolese. Historical languages develop by evolution in use. Words are added, dropped, combined, or changed as the people who use the language see fit, and so are the rules of grammar. Words are borrowed from other languages, with or without changes of spelling, pronunciation, or meaning. The same word (i.e., the same combination of sounds or letters) may have anywhere from one to several dozen meanings, which change with the times and the context.

A constructed language, on the other hand, is consciously created as a coordinated system of signs by some authority for a special purpose. Each

---

[13] See Cherry, *op. cit.*, p. 7.

sign has only one meaning, and the rules of the relationships are strict. Changes are made only upon due consideration of their possible effect on the whole system, and only when there is prior assurance that ambiguity will not result. Mathematics and logic are two such language systems.[14] *Loglan* is a hybrid, having a syntactical system which is wholly "constructed" but a vocabulary whose words are constructed in form but historical in origin. It was formed from the most common component sounds or letters in the languages representing the major fraction of the world's population.[15] The following discussion of language will deal with historical language. But it will carry on the discussion largely as if the language contained only simple, logical, and consistent rules, and a clear, unequivocal vocabulary. After this simplified version is discussed, we will add some of the complications of actual historical language.

SEMANTICS

The science of semiotics is divided into three main branches.[16] *Semantics* is the study of the relation of signs to their referents. *Syntactics* covers the relation of signs to other signs—that is, of signs to each other. *Pragmatics* deals with the relation between signs and their users, particularly such questions as whether the signs can convey the desired information, whether the participants know the code, or how much the communication will cost. We will deal first with semantics—although some aspects of both semantics and syntactics have already been mentioned above.

The Vocabulary

The heart of a language is its vocabulary, by which we mean roughly (but only roughly) the list of words in a dictionary, and their referents, the stated meanings. For the moment we will omit words whose function is syntactic or relational only. To deal with the function of language, it is necessary to review several points.

---

[14] Logic can probably be regarded as pure syntactics, its nonsyntactic signs having no semantic content. Mathematics is also pure syntactics when it deals with variables of unspecified magnitude, such as the customary x and y. With awareness of the thinness of the ice under foot, I prefer to walk toward the shore which classifies numbers as "real," or semantic. As noted in Chapter 7, untold hundreds of concepts about the real world express relationships of things at rather abstract levels. "Bravery" is a kind of relationship between a type of behavior and a type of situation, and "louder" is a type of relationship between two sounds. I see no point in suggesting that "bravery" and "louder" do not refer to the real world simply because they refer to relationships, not "things."

Similarly, "two" is the relationship between * and **, between *** and *** ***, or between $ and $$, and I see no reason to rule this relationship unreal simply because it is more general than the relationships implied by "bravery" or "louder." If we rule numbers unreal because they represent only relationships, we run the serious risk that by following this path we will be forced to rule *all* concepts unreal, an outcome of doubtful merit.

[15] James Cooke Brown, "Loglan," *Scientific American* (June, 1960), pp. 53 ff.
[16] This division is taken from Charles W. Morris, *op. cit.*, p. 77.

First is the scope of the term *"concept."* As used here (and as seems essential for an understanding of language) the term is extremely broad, and we may think for the moment of a notion we may call "all possible concepts." We can have a concept of a point of light, or of the whole universe. We can have a concept of tree (any and all trees) or of the particular tree in the front yard; of human beings, as well as of any particular human being, or group. "Going shopping" is a concept, and so is "I went shopping on August 20 and bought trousers and a jacket." Some concepts are shared by millions, like book or highway, while others are possessed by one person alone. In short, any identifiable notion in anybody's head is a concept to that person. Should anyone care to, he could combine his concepts of the Bible, an ear of corn, and the Statue of Liberty into a new concept, perhaps calling it Bicorstat.

If there is any reason to do so, any concept ever held by anyone can be given a sign—that is, be named. Thereafter that sign can be used by any source to call that concept to mind in any receiver who knows the concept and its sign. For obvious reasons, we give names only to concepts which are widely held and repeatedly used, while refraining from giving names to too many things lest the vocabulary become too large. Generally speaking, we do not give names to events which happen only once, unless they are important enough to receive repeated attention, like the American Revolution, the Inquisition, the Renaissance, the Reformation, or the Exodus. Some are named simply by the place where they occurred, as in the case of Yorktown or Teheran, their place in some sequence, as the Eighty-fifth Congress, or by some other convenient sign.

Events which happen only once to one individual or limited group are rarely named unless they are of unusual importance, such as the Hejira, the Crucifixion, the Discovery of America.

The naming of physical objects follows a similar pattern. We name anything which we have occasion to refer to often, and leave other things unnamed. We have generic names for human beings, as well as such group names as Caucasians, Westerners, Americans, or Methodists. But since each individual must also be referred to many times, each person also has his own name. By contrast we have the generic name for trees, as well as such group names as pines or the Black Forest. But we do not give names to individual trees unless they are outstanding for some reason, such as the Charter Oak, the Geoffrey Pine, or the General Sherman Sequoia. Whenever it proves useful, however, we give a name to every discernible specimen of some object, as the astronomers have catalogued and named (by number) all of the conspicuous stars in the sky, and thousands of not-so-conspicuous ones. If we had any reason to do so, we could similarly give a name to every tree, every leaf, and every blade of grass. But we do not bother, since we can get along satisfactorily merely by pointing to *that* tree or *this* blade of grass as the occasion arises.

We also give names to types of events which must be referred to frequently, while avoiding names for less frequent events. The concept of a group of contestants competing to see which can run a given distance in the shortest time is called racing, or a race. The act of traveling some distance to and from work is called commuting. Hence, a person can communicate efficiently the idea that he travels back and forth to work regularly over some distance merely by the two words, "I commute." If we liked, we could define "tasket" to mean the act of returning home from work, and "tisket" as the act of a black cat's crossing the road. Then instead of saying, "As I was coming home from work today I saw a black cat crossing the road," we could say, "I saw a tisket during tasket today." We possess the simple verb, "to plow." This verb implies not only an act of a certain sort, but also implies an actor, an instrument, and the soil. But we do not have any single word which with similar efficiency refers to the act of relining brakes or turning off the radio, since these terms have not yet been used widely enough to justify words.

Now all of this is of tremendous importance, both philosophical and practical. The fact that any given object, act, quality, or relationship has a name indicates very little about the nature of the world. But it indicates a great deal about the convenience and processes of human communication and experience. Our code of words is not so much an indication of what *is*, as an indication of what impresses us, and what we wish to communicate. We will return to this problem later in connection with culture, meanwhile pursuing its importance to communication.

Before proceeding, however, we will note that the vocabulary of named concepts is not confined to those for which we have discrete words, names for concepts including units both smaller and larger than words. Often the sign for a concept consists of only part of a word. If someone argues *hotly*, the semantic referent is indicated by *hot* alone, the *-ly* being solely a syntactic sign which shows the relation of *hot* to other words in the sentence. The unit which carries the meaning is called a *root*. It can be a *free* form (stand alone), like hot, child, or pen. Or it can be a *bound* form, which is used only as part of a word, such as morpho-, psycho-, opti-, tele-, or -ology. Roots, rather than words, are the smallest building blocks of semantic content with which a language is constructed. Some agglutinative languages, such as Eskimo, Hungarian, Turkish, Finnish, and Bantu make heavy use of combining forms of this sort, and are sometimes loosely described as not using sentences. The difference is purely superficial, for whether roots are used in free or bound form they are nevertheless put together in groups having definite syntactical relations in order to convey messages.

In other instances we have collections of two or more words which are regularly used together, and which behave as a single word. Such phrases as never-to-be-forgotten, the other side of the tracks, whichever is the greater, football game, will-o'-the-wisp, tough nut to crack, upper crust, top drawer, lift oneself by his own boot straps, and hundreds of other clichés all are concepts which could just as easily be expressed by a single word. Having noted that the semantic units of actual language consist of words, parts of words, or combinations of words, for simplicity we will discuss language as if all its semantic signs consist solely of words.

The smallest unit which has meaning is known as a *morpheme*. If it has semantic content, it is called a *root*, as indicated above. A morpheme may merely indicate some change in meaning or use of the root, as when we add *s* or *ed* to "hook" in order to produce "hooks" and "hooked." The *s* and *ed* are morphemes, in that they produce a change in meaning. Some morphemes are purely syntactical, as the word "to" in "to go" or the *-ly* in "hotly." Either roots or nonroots can appear as either free or bound forms, depending on usage. Since a morpheme is the smallest unit with meaning, if it is divided it has no meaning, merely sound, as the *-ook* in "hook" or the *ma-* in "man." A unit of sound is known as a *phoneme*. Variations of a given morpheme having different sounds but the same root meaning are called *allomorphs*, such as "sing" and "sung," "heat" and "hot," or "annual" and "biennial."

Conveying Information by Speech

It is an accepted rule of definition that the definition may not incorporate the word being defined, in either the same or a variant form. We may not, for example, say that length is "how long something is," since "long" and "leng-" are allomorphs of the same morpheme. This practice implies that the concept for every word in the dictionary is capable of being described by some combination of other words. If, for example, we define a *dwelling* as a building designed for human beings to live in, this means that we could, if necessary, dispense with the word *dwelling*, and substitute its definition whenever we wanted to refer to that concept. In similar fashion, we could express the meaning of any one word by using a group of other words, the combination of which has approximately the same meaning. The approximation may be close in some instances, and poor in others.

This relation points up the basic nature of speech. There is an almost limitless number of concepts which human beings can form, and which they may wish to express to others. But only a limited number is used often enough to justify receiving a name. Even though every concept *could* theoretically be named, the vast majority are not. The use of *language in communication* is therefore seen as the process of combining the signs for concepts which have names in such a way as to represent concepts which do not have names.

We can now see the nature of language in relation to its psychological base. Simple sensory concepts are formed from the relationship of two or more sensations, and by combining these sensory concepts we form the more complex concepts of things in our environment, as well as of things solely imagined. A concept is thus a combination of two or more things in some relation. Similarly, if by language we wish to convey some new concept, which new concept consists of a relation of two or more existing concepts, we must use signs for two or more concepts, along with a sign which indicates what kind of relation they are to take. Language is a reflection at the external level of the mental processes by which we form concepts at the internal level.

To illustrate simple visual patterns first, we have the word "square" for the concept □, and "triangle" for the concept △. But we have no word for the concept ◁□. However, we can describe the ◁□ as "a square to which is attached an equilateral triangle, one of whose sides coincides with the left side of the square." The words in quotes form a group or set of signs so selected and arranged that they jointly represent ◁□.

Let us take the sentence, "John's fiancee, Gerta, went downtown last Thursday and bought a new hat with the money he gave her for the down payment on a house." If we liked, we could coin the word *forswoozle*, and say that its meaning is that a fiancee goes to town on a Thursday and buys a new hat with the money given her by her intended husband for making a down payment on a house. We might then say "Gerta forswoozled John last week." To distinguish this occurrence on different days of the week, it might be forswozle if it happens on Monday, forswuezle on Tuesday, and so on. Casual gossip then might include such tidbits as "Jane forswizled Jim," or "Alice forswuzled Ellis" (except in states with Sunday closing).

We could also set up the term, *The Forswizle*, which refers to the one particular instance in which Helen forswizled Hector on Friday the 13th of October, 1961, in Oshkosh. Taking *The Forswizle* as one sign representing one concept, we can now return to the earlier statement that a message must contain no less than two signs with semantic content and one of relation. Suppose we are chatting at a student-faculty tea, and I say "The Forswizle." If you are a meek student, you may just stand with an expectant look. If you are more forthright, you will say either "What's that?" or "What about it?" If you do not already know the referent, this one sign has no meaning. If you do already know it, the sign alone again can convey no new information. Whether we have ever analyzed it or not, all of us are thoroughly aware of this relationship, and avoid stating simple names of things, to which the obvious response is either "What's that?" or "So what?"

In the other direction, if we retain the generic term, the word "forswizle" alone still conveys no message, but "Jane forswizled" or "June forswuezled" does. This word, incidentally, illustrates why a sign should be defined as having a *concept* as a referent, rather than some real event in the real world. As defined, the concept *forswoozle* is very clear, and no confusion is likely to arise between people who use the term, even if no actual case of forswoozling has ever occurred. The broader aspects of this problem will be returned to later under the heading of *pragmatics*.

We opened this chapter by noting that communication is at the heart of civilization, and is a fundamental item which reflects the superiority of man's brain over that of other animals. Having observed the nature of messages as combinations of signs which represent combinations of existing concepts into new concepts, we can now note that to extract meaning from a spoken or written message means to form new concepts by combining old ones at a speed represented by the rate of speaking or reading. To the best of our knowledge, no other animal is able to combine old concepts into new ones at this rate. This, too, is a manifestation of man's mental capacity.

Chapter 10

COMMUNICATION: SYNTACTICS, BITS, PRAGMATICS

SYNTACTICS

SYNTACTICS, or just plain syntax, is the relation of signs to signs. We have seen in Chapter 7 that our more complex concepts consist of a combination of subconcepts. When we try to express these in language, the set of signs which represent the more complex concepts consists of a combination of the signs of the subconcepts, along with some indication of the kind of relationship which must exist between the subconcepts to form the larger one. That is, in the process of indicating the relation of sign to sign syntax necessarily indicates the relation of concept to concept.

Once again, we can resort to visual concepts. Let us start with three short lines, which represent subconcepts. These can be put together in the relation ⊥, which we may call an I-shape. Or they can be put together in the relation △ (a triangle), H (an H), or A (an A). We cannot know the nature of the larger concept unless we know the relationship in which the three subconcepts are combined. In this instance the "statement" of the relationship is made by the act of drawing. We can, however, state the same relationship verbally, as follows. The "I" shape can be expressed: "Place one of the lines vertically and the other two horizontally, so that the top of the vertical line connects with the mid-point of one of the horizontals and the bottom connects with the mid-point of the other." Once we possess the concept, however, the term "I-shaped" expresses the whole relationship.

The same principle is involved when we combine the signs for concepts which do not have shapes, or whose relationships are not spatial. Let us take the three concepts designated by the signs "Jack," "lion," and "to eat." The particular larger concept which will emerge from relating these three subconcepts depends on the nature of the relationship. Four possible relations are: "The lion eats Jack," "Jack eats the lion," "Jack and the lion eat," and "Jack and the lion are eaten."[1]

We are now in the thick of verbal syntax, traditionally referred to as grammar, but now as *language structure*. "Jack eats lion" is a crucially different concept from "Lion eats Jack." Linguistically, however, the only difference is the order of the words. *Word order* (or *sign sequence*) is an important syntactic device in all verbal communications.[2] The distinction is just as clear when we use only two substantive signs, the difference between "Jack eats" and "Eats Jack" is just as crucial, even though the lion is omitted. To return to the earlier statement that the message must contain no less than three signs, two of substance and one of relation, in "Jack eats" the two signs of substance are "Jack" and "eats," while the sign of relation is the word sequence. Reversing the sequence to "eats Jack" produces a different concept.

A second syntactical device is word form, including affixes and inflections. When we compare "You eat" and "eat you," word order alone determines whether "you" is the subject or the object of "eat." But if we take the two words "eat" and "I," we now have one word which takes a different form in the subject and object relation, and we need not depend on word order to tell whether "I" is subject or object. Nor need we depend on word order if the two signs are "eat" and "me." The distinguishing feature might be in the verb rather than the noun. Contrast "It eats you," "It eat you," "You eats it," and "You eat it." Each of these four samples shows two different relation signs, one of word order and one of word form. In the first and last items the two relation signs agree, and the meaning is clear. In the second and third items, however, the relation indicated by the word order conflicts with that indicated by the verb form, and we must look for other information before we can tell which is intended. If we find that the writer is poorly schooled, and we suspect that word order is more strongly sensed than word form, then we would conclude that the words in the second and third samples are subject, verb, and object, respectively, and that the verb forms are syntactical errors. On the other hand, if the source is found to be a recognized poet of meticulous care, we know that such persons take great liberties with word order but do not make errors in word form. Hence, we would conclude that the second and third items have the meaning indicated by object, verb, and subject, in that order. The meaning is then clear, even if we exude mutterings about poets.

---

[1] In the sentence form, no new semantic ideas have been added. We still retain only Jack, the lion, and to eat, the insertion of articles and a conjunction, as well as the changes in verb form, merely indicating different types of relationships among the three base concepts.

[2] The word "verbal" is frequently used as distinct from "written." Unless indicated to the contrary, "verbal" will be used here only in its broader, original sense, meaning "in words," as contrasted to gestures, pictures, or other types of signs.

The declensions of nouns and adjectives and the conjugations of verbs are examples of inflection, which provides varying *word forms* whose function is to indicate the relationship among the root meanings. The greater the variety of word forms in a language, the greater is the flexibility of word order which can be tolerated without confusion. Where the words themselves take only a single form ("Jack eats lion" and "Lion eats Jack"), word order must be rigidly adhered to. Much of our language incorporates great redundancy, in that we use word form, word order, and possible other syntactic signs simultaneously when a single one would theoretically do.

Just as things and the concepts of them can take many different relationships, so must a language which transmits information be capable of expressing these relationships. These consists of such relationships as time, place or space, direction of action, probability, implication, conjunction, disjunction, and degree, indicated respectively by such words as "after," "under," "toward" (as well as subject-object relation in a sentence), "perhaps," "refers to," "also," "however," and "very." Any one of these relations can be indicated by a sign consisting of word order, word form, a separate word, punctuation, or the intonation of speech. To detail just one set of relations, the major time relations (or temporal sequence) can be indicated by three basic times, with three subdivisions of each.

If we let "before" represent past time, "now" present time, and "after" future time, the three major times could be stated as *before, now,* and *after,* as indicated in Column 1. But we also have occasion to refer to things which happened *before* some past time, *at* some past time, or *after* some past time but before the present. Similar situations occur in connection with the major present and future times. Something which occurred before a stated past time can be referred to as "before before," and so forth, as in Column 2. Column 3 shows the way each of these times would be expressed for the verb "to go," and Column 4 indicates the tense name for each time.

1	*2*	*3*	*4*
	Before before	Had gone	Past perfect
Before	Now before	Was going	Past progressive
	After before	Was to go	?
	Before now	Went, have gone	Simple past, perfect
Now	Now now	Goes, is going	Present, pres prog.
	After now	Will go	Simple future
	Before after	Will have gone	Future perfect
After	Now after	Will be going	Future progressive
	After after	Will then go	?

These nine periods are indicated in most languages by different verb forms, including compounds, although the English language does not have recognized tense names for "after-before" and "after-after." Other signs could be used for the same purpose. For example, if we use *b, n,* and *a* to stand for "before," "now," and "after," respectively, then "had gone" could be written as bb-go, and "will have gone" as ba-go. Suffixes or other devices, of course, could also be used. Time relations can also be indicated by words, such as "subsequently," "later," and "to precede."

In historical languages the means of conveying all these relationships are diverse. A time or space relation can be indicated by a noun, verb, adjective, adverb, preposition, conjunction, prefix, suffix, or allomorph, and most of the other relations can also be expressed in a variety of ways. An artificially constructed language, such as Loglan (short for "logical language") can express all possible relational (operational) functions in 112 "little words," all but a few of which have only one or two letters.[3] If a little two-letter word means "before" when used as a preposition, it also indicates the past tense when inserted in front of a verb, and "pastness" in any other connection.

The traditional method of studying grammar and sentence structure has missed some important points by focusing on *meaning* rather than form. To illustrate, the concept "understand" has the same essential meaning throughout all its morphemic variations. It can appear as a verb, as in "I think I understand you." It can be a noun in "I have achieved an understanding," and adjective in "He is an understanding person," or an adverb in "She deals understandingly with the problem." Other morphemes show similar variations, as in *final, finally, finale,* and *to finalize* (the latter with apologies). The importance of structure or syntax can be illustrated if we compare a "sentence" consisting of meaningless "words" in proper syntactical relation with another "sentence" of meaningful words in improper relation.

Let us say: "The rombit ilvin sambly plarked a suntering axticon." A short analysis leaves little doubt that *ilvin* and *axticon* are nouns, being subject and object respectively, and being modified respectively by the adjectives *rombit* and *suntering*. *Plarked* is the verb (transitive), modified by the adverb *sambly*. The only "real" words in the sentence are "the" and "a," neither of which has any fixed semantic content. Now one could, of course, "interpret" this sentence differently, although the stated "meaning" seems the most probable. Almost any person well versed in English could give that analysis even though no word in the sentence has meaning.[4] The sentence certainly conveys the feeling that something is happening, of the sort "The avid hunter quickly shot a fleeing antelope," or "The happy winner early took a commanding lead." Given correct syntax, the combination has obvious "jointness." It is a system, capable of doing something even if there is nothing at the moment to be done, like a railroad network, complete with tracks, switches, and stations, but with empty trains. Warfel makes the point that "a language is not its work or

---

[3] James Cooke Brown, "Loglan," *Scientific American* (June, 1960), pp. 53 ff.

[4] Cherry insists that a sentence is not completely devoid of meaning so long as *some* semantic or syntactic elements of the language are present: Colin Cherry, *On Human Communication* (New York: John Wiley & Sons, 1957), p. 13.

its messages," but a communication system which is capable of performing communication work.[5]

By contrast let us take: "Earthly a mechanizes migratory to spaghetti none the which." Every item in this group is a normal English word. But the group is not a sentence. It has no "jointness," like a bunch of loaded trains scattered all over the country, but without tracks. It does not suggest that the combination of words has any meaning over and above the meanings of the parts, whereas the first group does.

The first group is roughly equivalent to the mathematical expression: $y = a + bx$. Here we have two syntactic signs in the plus and equals signs. But the "semantic" signs, a, b, x, and y are simply signs, having no more meaning than "rombit," "ilvin," or "plarked." We can produce a complete and meaningful mathematical sentence, however, if we identify y as the price of wheat, x as the number of bushels offered in the market in a given year, a as \$2.58 and b as $-.0000006$. The equation then takes the form: $y = \$2.58 + (-.0000006)\ x$—a meaningful statement. On the other hand, if we take the signs which provide the full semantic content of this mathematical sentence and rearrange them in improper syntactical relations we have virtually nothing—as: $00x00y8 - + 5\$. = 6)\ (200.$

We can illustrate the same problem in the language of logic. Let us take the example, "*A* implies *B*; *B* implies *C*; therefore *A* implies *C*." This combination of signs constitutes the form of a logical sentence, but without semantic content. We can give it semantic content if we say that *A* stands for rain, *B* for water, and *C* for wetness, giving us: "Rain implies water; water implies wetness; therefore rain implies wetness." By contrast, all of the same semantic content provides no meaning in improper syntactic relation, as: "Implies wetness rain water water wetness implies therefore rain implies." (Perhaps the illustration implies Gertrude Stein—a matter we will not discuss further.)

It is probably pointless to argue whether the form is more important than the content, for much the same reason that it is pointless to argue whether plans for a house are more important than its materials. Perhaps in mathematics and logic there is more profit in studying the forms, while in all other fields more is to be gained by focusing on content. In any event, it would seem doubtful that a systematic language such as Loglan will advance knowledge by facilitating thinking, as suggested by Brown.[6] New ideas, like those of Copernicus, Newton, Locke, or Rousseau do not arise from language, but from internal communications *within* the brain. Although the brain uses words to an important degree, truly new ideas involve new concepts for which there are no existing words, or at least to which existing words do not apply. The communication within a single

---

 [5] Harry R. Warfel, "Code and Vocabulary," *The CEA Critic* (October, 1961), p. 5.
 [6] *Loc. cit.*

brain is so much more efficient than any communication which can be reduced to words, that words do not seem to be the bottleneck in developing new knowledge. It was easy enough to coin the phrase "circulation of the blood" once Harvey had the idea; the words, after all, had been around for centuries.[7] Viewed as a system, any existing language on earth is apparently capable of expressing almost any idea its users have in mind if they will provide the semantic vocabulary. Although a systematically constructed language such as Loglan would probably not *advance* thinking, inadequate vocabulary almost certainly inhibits both thinking and communication—as we shall see in connection with culture.

SYNTACTICS AND THE TRANSMISSION OF SIGNS (SOME NOTES ON COMMUNICATIONS THEORY)

We communicate by means of signs. The amount of information which could be conveyed depends upon (1) the number of signs transmitted and (2) the amount of information per sign.

To start with the second item, in human communication the referent of a sign is a concept, and a concept takes the physical form of a neural network (or rather, a network of interconnecting networks) within a human brain. There is at present no way by which we can quantitatively measure the amount of information a particular sign means to a particular person. A single sign can refer to a concept as simple as that of a nail, or as complex as that of the Roman Empire or the Gold Rush, and it is doubtful if we ever shall be able to measure the amount of information in such concepts. Since the amount of information per message depends on both the number of signs and the amount of information per sign, and we cannot measure the latter, we seem forced to conclude that the information content of a message cannot be measured.[8]

On the other hand, it is possible to count the number of signs transmitted. It is also possible to compute the number of signs which a given transmission medium can carry. To use a simple example, if with a given margin, style of type, and page size it is possible to average 500 words (signs) per page, then it is possible to transmit 50,000 signs in a 100-page book. If an operator can transmit 20 words per minute in Morse code, then 20 words per minute is the information rate of this telegraph system,

[7] With respect to the greatly superior communication within to that between persons, see Karl Deutsch, "Autonomy and Boundaries according to Communications Theory," in Roy R. Grinker (ed.) *Toward a Unified Theory of Human Behavior* (New York: Basic Books, Inc., 1956), especially pp. 293–94.

[8] Russell Ackoff, "Systems, Organizations, and Interdisciplinary Research," *General Systems*, Vol. V, 1960, p. 4, notes that "in dealing with communication among linked individuals we have tended to use the information theory on 'bits' developed for the communication engineering. Such a formulation is useful for determining channel capacity . . . but is not maximally useful for studying decision making in groups. Here one needs a model of the cognitive aspects of communication theory . . ." (As Ackoff notes, this idea is taken from Haire in a discussion of ideas by Rapoport.)

measured in number of signs. If the operator records his tappings on tape at 20 words per minute, after which the tape is played over the wire at 50 times the recording speed, the information rate of the system rises to 1,000 words per minute.

Information is transmitted by a tremendous variety of media. Most obvious are spoken and printed words. Information also goes by Morse and other codes in the form of dot-dash. It is impressed in grooves in records, converted into radio and TV waves, and recorded on magnetic tape. Bats and porpoises transmit high frequency sound waves and get back information about their environment from the modulated reflected waves. Migratory birds seem to get their bearings from the stars. Of particular interest in recent decades are electronic computers, into which are fed seemingly endless quantities of information for sorting and computing. For technical reasons connected with computers, telephonic communication, and others, it has been found extremely useful to have some clear measure of *information capacity*. How much information can this machine handle? How much information can that telephone line be made to carry?

To handle questions of this sort we must have some standard measuring unit of information. This unit is called the *bit*, which is short for *binary digit*. A bit is one act of selecting between two alternatives—as between on or off, yes or no, 0 or 1, top or bottom, and so on. Most computers handle information in the form of binary numbers. These are expressed as 0 or 1, and are handled by the machine as flow or no-flow (on or off) of a circuit.

We have already seen that there must be at least two alternative signs before any one sign can convey information. The bit is the smallest amount of information possible—a single selection between two alternatives.

The nature of the problem is seen in the game of Twenty Questions. Here the identity of some person is guessed after asking twenty questions, each of which is answered by a simple yes or no. In the language of information theory, the guesser is allowed twenty bits of information. Twenty bits is highly inadequate to make a positive identification from among possible thousands of persons, but may be enough to permit a shrewd guess.

The problem in communication is concerned with the number of bits required for *positive* identification from among a preselected list already known to both the source and the receiver. To start with a simple situation, the receiver of a message wants to know whether the answer to a question is *A* or *B*. *A* and *B* may be signs for previously understood messages. Or they can stand for letters with which a message is to be spelled. If the question is framed, "Is it *A*?" then an answer of yes positively identifies *A*, while a no positively identifies *B*. One bit selects between two alternatives without doubt.

Suppose there are four alternatives, *A*, *B*, *C*, and *D*, arranged in a column:

$$A$$
$$B$$
$$\overline{}$$
$$C$$
$$D$$

Let us suppose that the letter to be indicated is *C*, and we ask, "Is it in the top half?" The answer is no, which eliminates *A* and *B*, but leaves doubt as between *C* and *D*. With reference to the bottom half already selected we ask again, "Is it in the top half?" The answer is yes, which identifies *C* and eliminates *D*. Since it requires two successive yes or no answers positively to select one item from among four, we say that to select one sign among four requires two bits of information. It similarly requires three bits to select one sign from among eight, four from among sixteen, and so on.

Let us now look at the same thing from the reverse direction. If it requires one bit of information to select between *A* and *B*, then we will say that to be able to select between *A* and *B* is to contain or possess one bit of information. In the game of Twenty Questions, if I ask "Is this person real?" (in contrast to fictional), the answer cuts the range of doubt in half. I possess one yes-or-no answer, or one bit. Had there been only two alternatives to the whole question, the full answer would "contain" only one bit. Had there been four alternatives, when I knew the correct one I would "contain" two bits of information, since two bits are required to make a positive identification from among four items. If I know the correct sign from among eight, I would "contain" three bits, and so on.

As a different illustration, suppose that in front of me are eight letters, *A* through *H*, with a light over each. A distant sender has a switch for each letter, by which he can light the corresponding letter on my list. The sender presses his *G* button and my *G* light goes on. How many bits of information have been transmitted? The answer is three, since it requires three bits to select one signal from among eight. If our lists contained sixteen letters, the selection of one sign would represent four bits, and so on. If from among sixteen signs the system could make 100 such four bit selections per minute, the system would be handling 400 bits per minute, or have an information rate of 400 bits per minute.

The number of bits in any message (or within any given period of time) is thus the number of signs in the message (or within the stated period) multiplied by the number of bits per sign. The number of bits per sign is $\log_2 \cdot N$, where *N* is the number of signs in the list (vocabulary or code) from which the signs are selected. As we have seen the number of bits per sign (or $\log_2 \cdot N$) is 1 when there are 2 alternative signs in the list, since 2 raised to the first power (or 2^1) is equal to 2. The number of bits per sign (or $\log_2 \cdot N$) is 2 when there are 4 signs in the list, since 2 to the second power (or 2^2) equals 4. The number of bits per sign is 3 when there are 8 signs in the list, since 2 to the third power (or 2^3) equals 8, and so on. In each case the number of bits per sign is the same as the power to which 2 must be raised in order to equal the number of signs in the list. If we let n represent the number of signs in the message (or in a given period of time) the number of bits in the whole message (or time period) thus becomes $n \cdot \log_2 \cdot N$. This is the *information rate* measured in bits.[9]

The full mathematical expression of information rate is far more complex. Without going into the details, the two major things which must be added are (1) that the number of signs in a given list is not always an even power of 2, and (2) that the signs in the list are not equally likely to occur. To illustrate both points from the English alphabet, since there are 26 letters in the list, the number of bits per sign selected is not a whole number. As to the second point, the letters e and z are not equally likely to occur. The lower the probability of any one sign, the greater is its information content. That is, a letter z does much more to help identify a word than does an e. To illustrate further, suppose that e would appear as often as all other letters put together. This is the same as saying that the letters in messages can be classified into two groups, e and *not-e*. To identify an e therefore requires only one bit; hence, an e would be said to contain only one bit. In actuality e appears about 60 times as often as z.[10]

What Use Has All This?

But where do bits get us in understanding human and social behavior? The answer is partly accomplishment and partly potential.

We can start by noting that any information capable of being transmitted can be reduced to a binary code. By the use of only two signs, dot and dash, the Morse Code can transmit any information expressible in any alphabetic language. The alphabet can also be coded into binary numbers, so that electronic data processers can handle verbal as well as numerical information. We have already seen that the neurons in the human nervous system operate solely through two alternative states, discharge or non-discharge. We might thus say that all learning, thinking, or other information processing done by the human brain is handled by means of a binary system, or bits. (Memory is a different matter, consisting of switching connections to form networks.) The fact that any communication can be reduced to binary digits means that it is possible to measure the sign-designating information content of *any* message (or the information capacity of *any* channel of communication) in bits, whether or not the particular message or channel actually uses binary techniques. We thus have a universally applicable standard measure of the quantity of information, expressed in signs, which can be used without regard to the nature of the message, medium, or channel.

The most direct use of mathematical communications theory lies in telecommunications, electronic data processing, and computing, the first being the area in which it was originally developed by Shannon and

---

[9] Colin Cherry, *op. cit.*, pp. 170, 173.
[10] *Ibid.*, p. 36.

Weaver.[11] With their formulas it is possible to compute how much information can be carried over a wire, or over a radio band of a given frequency and amplitude—a matter of great importance in reducing transmission costs. The efficient use of electronic data handling would similarly be greatly handicapped without this approach.

To move toward the human and social uses of communications and information theory, we can start at the biological level. We have already seen that the human sensory system has the ability to detect and send to the brain information at the rate of millions of bits per second. By contrast to our tremendous capacity to handle large numbers of bits in sensory form, we find a most modest ability to handle information in sign form. A skilled pianist can read musical notes at the rate of about 22 bits per second, about 25 can be reached in silent reading, and an extemporaneous but organized lecturer can deliver about 18.[12] If we assume that in thinking we can process information at roughly the same rate as in reading or organized speaking, then it would seem that the human system can process information in the form of networks, concepts, or signs (depending on which aspect we are thinking of) at only about 1/100,000th of the rate at which we can handle it as sensory signals. We may refer again to Miller's conclusion that the brain can handle only about seven pieces of "symbolic" information at a time.[13]

Norbert Wiener has argued in terms of information content that very little human learning could be inherited. He calculated that the total amount of information in our chromosomes is sufficient to specify the connections of only about 10,000 neurons. The connections of the other 99.9999 per cent could not be determined by heredity, since the controlling, or information-containing, mechanism of heredity cannot hold that much information.[14] In many other areas it is meaningful to inquire whether certain events can be controlled from certain sources on the basis of the amount of information capacity between the two, as, for example, when we will later deal with the information capacity of political elections. And although human beings use signs with indefinitely large information content, there are numerous problems where the number of signs is important in itself.

Information theory has been of much use in studying linguistics. Both speech and writing can be analyzed so as to compare the amount of in-

---

[11] Claude Shannon and Warren Weaver, *The Mathematical Theory of Communication* (Urbana: University of Illinois Press, 1949).

[12] Richard L. Meier, "Communications and Social Change," *Behavioral Science*, Vol. 1, No. 1 (January, 1956), p. 53, and Cherry, *op. cit.*, p. 284. Meier's article provides an excellent survey of the origin and early development of cybernetics and communications theory, even though it is perhaps overoptimistic about the potentialities of these fields.

[13] George A. Miller, "The Magic Number Seven, Plus or Minus Two," *Psychological Review*, No. 63, pp. 81 ff.

[14] Warren S. McCulloch, "Why the Mind is in the Head," in Lloyd A. Jeffres (ed.), *Cerebral Mechanisms in Behavior* (New York: John Wiley & Sons, 1951), p. 55.

formation actually transmitted as compared to the quantity which could be carried with the same instruments of voice or pen. These analyses have made use of the concepts of *redundancy* and *noise*. *Redundancy* is described as the amount of information which could be carried as compared to the amount actually carried by a given number of signals. Normal written English text, for example, is estimated to be approximately five-sixths redundant. According to estimates, it actually carries only about one bit per character, but could theoretically carry about six bits.[15] *Noise* is the presence of signals which detract from the ability to identify signs, as in the case of static on a radio, a background conversation during a lecture, or attention to a speaker's necktie instead of his words. Analyses of noise and redundancy have been essential to the development of machine translation of language, and of machines which will recode printed material into braille, as well as for programming computers to solve problems in logic.

In human organizations the development of techniques for the mass handling of information is tremendous. Decisions can be made in many areas with far more information than was dreamed possible a decade ago. More complex organizations may become feasible with the ability to coordinate larger groups of parts and subparts. It may shortly be possible to compute both the cost and value per bit of certain kinds of information, so as to be able to make more objective decisions about whether or not to compile the information. Further, as more people become familiar with information theory, we should achieve a wider understanding of the nature, uses, and limitations of information and of language. We have already increased our understanding of the brain, the nervous system, perception and pattern recognition, and even the nature of thinking with the assistance of quantitative measures of information.

Several related areas of knowledge help support each other. Developments in the field of linguistics, for instance, have contributed to an understanding of information, as well as the reverse, while developments in logic and mathematics have helped both.

PRAGMATICS

As contrasted to the study of the relation of signs to signs (syntactics) and signs to referents (semantics), pragmatics deals with the relation between signs and users. The interaction works in both directions, users having effects on signs and vice versa.

If the referent of a sign is understood to be some object or event in the external world, then semantics can be studied with relatively little attention to the particular persons who use the signs, since the referent is independent of the user. But if the referent is understood to be a concept (the present approach), then it may make a great difference who uses a sign, since the referent may not be the same in the minds of any two users. In

---

[15] A. H. Rubenstein and Chadwick J. Haberstroh, *Some Theories of Organization* (Homewood, Ill.: The Dorsey Press, Inc., 1960), p. 232.

that event the relation between the sign and its referent is intimately tied to the relation between the sign and its user, at which point semantics and pragmatics merge. Under the present approach we will therefore find several problems under the heading of pragmatics which are often discussed under semantics. They do not therefore cease to be semantic problems, however, in the broader sense of the word.

Purposes of Communication

People have many different purposes for communicating, including amusement. Ackoff[16] suggests three major groupings of purposes: to inform, to instruct, and to motivate.

We will here divide the purposes into only two, to inform and to motivate. This usage carries into the field of communication the basic dichotomy on which much of this book is built—the distinction between preference functions and opportunity functions, between motives and concepts. Communication will thus be seen as having two possible major functions, the one to alter a receiver's concepts, which we will construe as the information function, the other to change his preferences or feelings, which we will construe as the motivation function. This seems a reasonable reduction of Ackoff's threefold distinction. The problem of communication *as communication* is basically the same for informing and instructing, involving the transmission of clear conceptualizations, while these differ significantly from that of motivating or forming preferences. To make the analysis as sharp as possible we will say that the first purpose is to inform, regardless of the effect on the receiver's preferences, and that the purpose of the second is to affect preferences without regard to the effect on information.

Most actual communications have both mixed purposes and interacting effects. When the parent explains life, love, education, religion, government, or a thousand lesser things, he seeks to create both understanding and valences in the child. When the child describes what he has been doing for the past hour, or wants to do for the next, the description will seek to influence the parent's attitude as well as his information. Sometimes we can influence motives by changing the concept—from Franklin Roosevelt as savior of private capitalism to Franklin Roosevelt as its destroyer, or vice versa. We have already seen that an attitude can be part of the concept, as when a good time is part of the concept of Paris. Hence, to change in attitude is a partial change of concept. Despite these mixtures and overlappings in fact, the ensuing discussion will try to isolate those aspects of communication unique to informing from those unique to motivating—the effective from the affective. Communication designed to amuse can be considered as affective. Some conversations are more nearly verbalized daydreaming than communication. We cannot examine all the combinations and degrees of such things, but will assume that the combi-

---

16 Russell Ackoff, *op. cit.*, p. 6.

nations can be understood best if we first understand the pure forms. For purposes of the next section, references to *concepts* are intended to exclude affective components of the concepts.

Pure Information Objective. We will deal first with communication whose sole purpose is to transmit information accurately from one person to another, but without regard to whether the concepts to be transmitted are real or fictional, true or false. The problem is to discern the conditions for conveying accurately that information which the source wishes to convey. In brief, what are the semantic conditions for high fidelity communication?

First let us review what happens in accurate communication. A concept exists within the brain of the source, and the objective is to bring that same concept into existence in the brain of the receiver, who does not already possess it. The concept may be widely known and have a name, or it may be unique to the source. In the first case, the source desires to teach an already recognized concept (such as the meaning of "filibuster") to someone who does not yet know it. In the second, he wants to inform the receiver of some concept which is not widely known, such as that the source would like a scotch and soda. In either case, it is necessary to describe the concept to be communicated, in terms of signs for other concepts.

If such communication is to be successful, three conditions must be met. First, the source must avoid signs not in the repertoire of the receiver. Second, each sign must have the same referent in the receiver's list as in the sender's. Third, both must accept the same syntactic rules. If these three conditions prevail, the communication will be accurate (barring technical errors in coding, transmission, detection, or decoding—all matters we need not go into here).

We will deal briefly with syntax, then move to the other items. In the narrow sense, correct syntax means simply that grammatical construction be clear. In a more extended sense, it means a well constructed total message, with the major parts clearly separated, along with transitional sentences or paragraphs which show the relationships among them. The whole organization of a communication (such as an academic paper) is a part of syntax, which indicates the relation of concepts. Although the usual rules of syntax, as formulated by linguists and grammarians, do not extend to relationships beyond the confines of the sentence, these larger aspects are all syntactical, in the fullest meaning of the word.

As to the problem of having the source use only signs which are available in the repertoire of the receiver, this may or may not create much difficulty. Assuming that the signs are words in an alphabetized language, there should be no difficulty in identifying the words, or of finding them in a dictionary. The main problem is that of the receiver's not knowing the referent of the sign, or of having a referent which does not correspond closely to that of the sender. This is the core of the semantic problem in communication.

If the sender codes his message in Morse and the receiver decodes it as International Code, the receiver will quickly discern that he has a garbled message. The problem in language is that receivers often interpret a message in a different code from that used by the sender, but are not aware that they are doing so.

We can introduce this problem by saying that it is virtually certain that no message couched in language will be decoded with precisely the same referents used by the sender. The referents are concepts in the minds of the sender and receiver respectively, and no concept is precisely the same in the minds of any two people. As noted in Chapter 7, the "same" concept (i.e., the concept designated by the same sign) may be formed by very different sets of experiences in different persons. Hence, the "image" brought to mind by a particular word is found experimentally to vary greatly from person to person.[17] Yet each person's "image" is the "meaning" of the word to him. The practical question, therefore, is not whether the referents are identical—which they never are—but whether they are sufficiently similar to accomplish the purpose of the communication.

Suppose someone says, "I just got a new dining room table." The speaker may have in mind a massive four-by-eight foot oak table he has just inherited, while the hearer may visualize a two-by-four tubular aluminum construction with a plastic top. If the purpose of the speaker is to provide some picture of how his dining room now looks, this discrepancy in images produces a highly faulty communication. But if the speaker is known to have been without any table for months, and he wishes to convey only that he no longer eats from his lap, the discrepancy does not distort the message. Similarly, "I am eating at Bob's tonight" is an accurate message if its sole purpose is to inform my wife that our son will not be home for dinner. But it is inadequate if its purpose is to let her know where to pick him up after the meal. For that purpose she must be further informed whether Bob Brown, Bob Green, or Bob White is the host. To illustrate further, suppose I am to pick up a friend at the third house from the corner. The assumption is that the term "third house" has the same referent to both of us. But suppose the end building is a double house, with two front doors, while the next two are singles. Is the third house the third *building* of a house-like nature, or the third *dwelling unit?* Whether the communication will be faulty (assuming that my friend and I have different concepts) will again depend on the purpose at hand. If I am to ring the bell, the discrepancy is significant. If the friend is to wait at the curb, it is not.

Taken on the whole, numbers are about as free from differences in referential content as any concepts in general use, particularly when applied to discrete units, such as automobiles. But even with numbers, confusion may result in connection with continuous variables unless tolerances

---

[17] Jerome Bruner, Jacqueline Goodnow, and George Austin, *A Study of Thinking* (New York: John Wiley & Sons, 1956), p. 274.

are also specified. A foreman may say, "Bring me a six-inch length of quarter-inch brass rod," having in mind a piece of about five to seven inches, to be used as a temporary crank for his casement window. On the other hand, the worker who gets the rod may spend half an hour making the piece accurate to a thousandth of an inch, thinking it is intended as a replacement part in a machine. The worker who asks, "What do you want it for?" is not necessarily being nosy, but may simply be trying to clarify the communication.

When we move from relatively concrete ideas to high level abstractions, the likelihood of accurate communication drops precipitously. A "fair" distribution of income to one person means that everyone gets equal shares, while to another it means that everyone gets what he can earn. To one person "left wing ideology" includes the federal income tax and municipal control of smoke pollution, while to another anything less than full socialization is "far right." To one person "government control of the economy" means monetary and fiscal policies designed to avoid depressions and stimulate growth, while to another it means telling businessmen how to run their operations. A man may ask, "Do you believe in God?" and be answered "Yes." But the man who asks may conceive God as a man with a white beard sitting on a cloud, while the man who answers may conceive God as natural force. Further, to the questioner "believe" may imply unquestioning certainty, while to the answerer it may mean anything less than full rejection.

The list of examples could be endless, but the central point is clear. No two persons have identical concepts of anything, which means that the sender and receiver have different referents for the signs used in the message. Hence, there can be no such thing as "perfectly accurate" communication by words, and our concern is whether the referent concepts are similar enough to accomplish the purpose at hand. In thousands of messages in daily life they are sufficiently accurate. No confusion arises from a sentence like "Bring me that pound of arsenic from my bottom bureau drawer." In thousands of others dealing with poorly defined concepts the accuracy of communication is minimal, as with "Bureaucracy buries the government in red tape." The accuracy of communication can be improved only to the extent that the senders and receivers share common concepts of the referents.[18]

Pragmatic problems of two sorts arise in this connection. One is whether

---

[18] Important pioneering work in this area of social interaction in communication was done by George H. Mead, *Mind, Self, and Society* (Chicago: University of Chicago Press, 1934), especially Part II, "Mind," and Part IV, "Society." Mead emphasizes that the meaning of a symbol lies in the response given by the recipient (pp. 75–76). The present approach is not in conflict with this, but would merely specify that the response is the meaning of the sign *to the receiver*. Mead focuses on the sign and its meaning *in a society*, a way of viewing the problem which we will get into in a subsequent chapter on Culture. Our focus at the moment is on the agreement or discrepancy of meaning between a particular sender and a particular receiver.

the source couches his message in terms known to his particular audience. The teacher cannot be understood by his introductory students if he uses the language of his professional journals, and the specialist in any field cannot use technical language in talking to the general public, even though the message might be clear to other specialists. The solution to this problem is easy in principle, though it may be difficult in fact. It consists of wording messages in the vocabulary of the audience to whom they are directed. The second problem is that of messages which have no clear, uniform meaning to any audience, because the referents are not clearly or uniformly defined. "Win the cold war," "Strengthen the voice of conservatism," and "disembody the concept of the absolute" will have widely varying interpretations among the members of any audience, since it is unlikely that any two persons will have the same conception of what these words signify. The solution here is to use words with sharper meanings, which usually means to be more explicit. "Do you believe in limited government?" is essentially meaningless, since anyone except the advocate of complete totalitarian dictatorship would have to answer no. But a more explicit question may have reasonably clear meaning, such as, "Do you believe that the federal or state governments should regulate TV broadcasting?" In this second problem clearer thinking is often called for before the language can be clarified. Messages can also be unclear for technical reasons, such as faulty syntax, poor pronunciation, and inadequate explanation, which we need not discuss further. We will return to this problem in a different context below, under the heading of "Syntax Without Semantic Content."

Pure Motivation Objective

If the objective of communication is to motivate, some problems are the same as and some are different from those of informing. For instance, we must still select signs as the instruments of communication. But the objective of communication may or may not be to build some concept in the mind of the receiver, and that concept may or may not be the same as one in the mind of the sender.

We might think of communication whose objective is motivation as "propaganda" rather than "information." The scope of motivational communication is too wide, and the unpleasant connotations of "propaganda" too deep to recommend this usage. As Haldane has pointed out,[19] a very substantial portion of all communication is not intended to inform but to affect feelings or mood. Many things said to the child, to friends, or to rivals are designed to create feelings, not concepts.

This shift in objective brings a shift in the semantic content of communication, but not in the basic elements. We must recall that we are dealing with verbal communication, and that words are learned, not inherited like

---

[19] J. B. S. Haldane, "Communication in Biology," in *Studies in Communication* (London: Martin Secker & Warburg, 1955).

reflexes. In saying "You were magnificent," or "You are a filthy swine," our sole goal may be to create a feeling. But even with this noninformational objective, the receiver must identify the stimulus. This process occurs in the cortex, not the bowels, and can take place only if the receiver has previously formed the concepts of "magnificent" or "filthy swine," and properly decodes the current message.

Affective reactions thus come in addition to, not instead of, cognitive ones. The affective ones apparently involve two steps. First, we must recognize that a value judgment, or valence, is attached to the words "magnificent" and "swine." But this, too, can remain at the cerebral level. If we are informed that the Duchess of Wentworth called the Duke of Burleigh a swine, and if we have no notion of who either of these estimable personages is, our adrenalin does not flow nor our blood pressure rise. But if the words are directed at *us*, or at someone or something we care about, this is a different matter. To pursue this distinction further, if someone says "X is a swine," before I can become elated or annoyed (rather than merely informed) I must have (1) conceptual knowledge of the valence attached to "swine" and (2) a conditioned emotional relation to X. The emotional relation may grow from personal relations with X, from the fact that he is a friend of a friend, from his holding similar political views, or from numerous other sources. I might also have some emotional feelings toward the word "swine," but unless these feelings are unusually strong, my response will be determined mainly by my feelings about X.

A common technique for communicating motivation is to issue words to which a valence is already attached in conjunction with words to which we desire to attach the same valence. Advertising does this regularly, as when fun, pleasure, health, youth, popularity, comfort, and other words with positive valence are issued repeatedly in connection with the advertised product. Pain, discomfort, loneliness and other negative valence ideas may simultaneously be associated with its absence.

In politics the positive-valence words issued in connection with a policy one wants to promote are freedom, liberty, democracy, long-established, progressive, far-sighted, statesman-like, intelligent, efficient, sound, and so on. If one wants to kill a policy he will attach to it such words as ill-conceived, arbitrary, dictatorial, shortsighted, reactionary, radical, opportunistic, or wasteful. The long-experienced advertiser, politician, or other molder of public attitudes issues words of the appropriate sort almost automatically in connection with favored or disfavored items, quite regardless of their relevance to the topic at hand. This is not to suggest that this practice is confined to these molders of opinion. To some extent it is practiced by all of us in our daily speech, often unconsciously, as we go about hanging little tags of goodness and badness on things. The listener's defense against this practice is to learn to replace these value-laden words with a *blank* just as automatically as the speaker issues them, until and unless he can establish for himself that the adjectives are justified. "This progressive, far-sighted, well-conceived policy" then becomes "This blank, blank, blank policy," the final word being the only one with semantic content which should be accepted until the hearer has independent reason to do so.

Messages designed to motivate *can* be strictly factual, as in stating the rewards which are contingent on some specified behavior. For example, "If you do X I will give you Y." This is an offer of a transaction, as the term will be defined later. The message could also be a prediction based on cause and effect relations, as in: "If you do X then Y will probably follow." If Y has either a positive or negative valence to the receiver (and if he believes the message) he will then be motivated to do or avoid doing X—the result presumably desired by the source.

FEEDBACK AND MEDIA

A different sort of problem is that of determining whether and to what extent communication has been successful. Did the message get through? The question is equally appropriate whether the purpose of the communication is to inform or to motivate. The measure of success lies in the feedback. If the message calls for overt action, and the action is performed, the communication is presumably successful, though it is always possible that some other stimulus set off the action. If the action is not forthcoming, we may need further investigation to find whether the failure lies in the communication or the performance. Sometimes the social consequences of not responding to a received message are more unpleasant than those of not receiving it, in which case the receiver may pretend it has not arrived. Feedback may be very informal, such as a nod or a smile. Or it may be more formal, as by having the receiver repeat the message. If the feedback is a reasonable response to a question, one can assume that the question got through. A teacher's examinations measure and motivate students; in part they also measure the success of the teacher's own communication. In these various respects communicative behavior follows the same pattern as all other adaptive behavior. Its success can be determined only by the receipt and evaluation of feedback.

Another important aspect of pragmatics is the selection of an effective medium of transmission. Shall we code the message in sounds, written letters, pictures, role playing, or what? This question is highly important to successful communication. But it is beyond the scope of the present analysis, and requires detailed knowledge of the kind of content, the capacities of various media, and such characteristics of the receiver as his previous experience, attention span, level of intelligence, receptivity to aural as compared to visual or other stimuli, and the like. Communications to the general public must choose as among newspapers, radio, television, billboards, personal speeches, mailings, or telephone. These, too, are technical problems well beyond the scope of the present study.

In closing I would like to voice a strong suspicion that some allegedly profound philosophical questions reflect nothing more than a failure to understand the nature of language. We might take a longstanding argument, on which philosophers disagree, as to "whether there are abstract objects."[20] This may be illustrated by asking, "Do *miles* exist?"

Now nobody but a philosopher tries to answer questions of this sort, and if you ask such a question of the nonphilosopher he will return a fishy stare and move away. All but philosophers recognize that this question violates the unwritten syntax of our (historical) language, and must be disallowed as meaningless. If the question is in the philosophers' own language (rather than historical language), they need but define how they intend to use the words "abstraction" and "exist" and they will answer their question, which in fact will cease to exist. In particular, the word "exist" was presumably created by man for purposes of communication, not handed down from on high. The question is not whether abstractions exist, but whether philosophers will have a better analytical system if they do or do not apply the word "exist" to abstractions.

I have consistently followed this recommended practice throughout this book. I have never raised the question about what words mean. I have examined existing usages and definitions. Where they seemed useful, I have retained them. Where they seemed to impede rather than facilitate analysis, I have either avoided or redefined them. Needless to say, this practice can be applied to only a few terms within any one discourse, and presumably to key ones, or communication itself will be impeded.

---

[20] Willard Van Orman Quine, *Word and Object* (New York: John Wiley & Sons, 1960), p. 233.

Chapter 11

COMMUNICATION: HISTORICAL LANGUAGE, NONLINGUISTIC COMMUNICATION

HISTORICAL LANGUAGE

THE PREVIOUS discussion went forward as if language consisted of a relatively precise set of words and rules, even if some people occasionally violated these rules in actual use. This is hardly the case. We have already noted that mathematics and formal logic are special languages created for special purposes. Although both continue to add to the implications of their main syntactic rules, both are basically syntactical systems without semantic content. Loglan has also been cited as a possible all-purpose language. Its syntax is complete, and could presumably go on forever without alteration. Its content words, however, are compilations of those already in existence throughout the world, and are necessarily subject to change. This latter problem will be amplified later.

But the language of ordinary speech consists of a highly illogical set of signs, and a syntax which is extremely flexible. We will start with the most regular aspects, taking our illustrations from English. Most of the syntactical signs are clearly understood, and provide little trouble. Confusion over such words as *and, moreover, nevertheless, by contrast, instead of, in, from,* and so forth, is rare with persons familiar with a language.

The major difficulties of historical language are two—so far as the semantic problem of sign and referent is concerned. The first is the multiple use of the same sign. Perusal of a dictionary often shows the same "word" (i.e., the same combination of letters) to have ten to twenty different meanings. Even in an abridged dictionary the verb "to rise" shows thirty. Many are closely related, although "to rise in revolt" has a quite different meaning from "to rise to a standing position." "Hock" refers to a joint in the hind leg, a Rhine wine, and a condition of being in debt. One can make a hitch in a rope, do a hitch in the navy, or have a hitch in the proceedings. Though one can imagine certain historical relationships, "hard" has rather unrelated meanings in a hard stone, hard heart, hard job, hard master, hard water, hard liquor, and hard of hearing. Ringing a bell is different from ringing a bull—and the list could continue indefinitely.

In each case where the same word (identical in both spelling and sound) has two or more different referents, then some additional sign(s) must appear in the sentence to distinguish which is intended. These other signs are usually referred to as context. "I am going to ring that bell" identifies which "ring" is intended by the word "bell." Sometimes it is necessary to go beyond the sentence to find the extra sign(s). For example, "I am going to ring that bell with flower pots" could mean that I am going to put a circle of flower pots around the bell, or that I am going to cause it to ring by throwing flower pots at it. Such uncertainties, which require additional signs for clarification, could be eliminated by confining the word "ring" to circles, and instituting "pling" for sounding the bell. In practice, there is little point in doing this, since the context usually provides the necessary cues.

More importantly, however, it is not possible to create a language for dealing with the real world in which each word has one and only one meaning. Here we return to the problem discussed early in connection with concepts. No two objects or events are identical in every respect. Hence, "same" does not mean identical, but that the differences are unimportant for the purpose at hand. For example, is rising from a chair the "same thing" as rising from a bed or from a kneeling position? Is rising from a kneeling position with the left foot first the same thing as rising with the right foot first? If the occasion warranted, we could coin a different word for each of these different actions. But it does not seem to be important, so we use the same word, and add other signs to note the differences when they matter. Multiple uses of a word keep down the size of the vocabulary, and in some respects we really have no choice.

We also have words which sound the same but are spelled differently (bored and board), and those which are spelled the same but are pronounced differently ("primer" as a first reader and a first coat of paint, or "lead" as a metal and as giving guidance). As with the problem above, whenever such words are used, the receiver must look for additional signs to distinguish which alternative is intended.

Spoken Language

Spoken language uses a wide variety of signs which are not transcribed when the speech is put into writing. Being variations in sound which are not parts, or segments of words, they are now widely referred to by students of linguistics as "supra-segmental phonemes."

The first is *pitch*. This has the same meaning to the linguist as to the musician and the physicist, and refers to the frequency, or number of vibrations per second, which to the layman is the highness or lowness of the tone. The second is *stress*. This is what the musician calls volume or loudness, and the physicist calls amplitude. The third is *juncture*, and refers to timing. It involves slightly what the musician calls tempo, but mainly rhythm—the relative duration of sounds and of the pauses between them. The physicist also calls such relationships rhythm when he has occasion to use them. Juncture is sometimes expanded to cover the relative probabilities of sound sequences, the flow from one to the next, and the interacting effects thereof.[1] *Intonation* is the name given to the whole of the problem of sounds in pitch, stress, and/or juncture.

To illustrate the importance of stress, Cherry[2] cites the sentence, "Do you think that one will do?" suggesting that it be pronounced successively with the stress on different words.

In some languages the same "word" has different meanings at different pitch levels. In Mixteco, for instance, one set of phonemes means "mountain" if pronounced at high pitch, but "brush" at medium pitch.[3] In English, "Oh!" in response to some statement is an expression of surprise if spoken with a rising intonation, and of "Really? I didn't know that" if spoken with a declining intonation. On the basis of my own observation I would suggest that a rise of about a whole tone is a routine acknowledgment that a statement has been heard. A rise of about a fifth indicates some surprise, an octave definite surprise, and a tenth or more surprise approaching incredulity, the latter tending to drop again at the end.

Juncture, in the form of speed of pronunciation also affects meaning. This is formalized among the Guarani Indians, where the past tense is indicated by adding *-yma* to a verb, greater distance into the past being indicated by slower pronunciation of the suffix.[4] Indicating greater magnitude of the concept by greater duration of the sound is also used informally in English. An old man is not so old as an o-o-o-old one, nor is a deep lake so deep as a de-e-e-ep one. Juncture includes the duration of pauses as well as sounds. The most important use of pauses is to separate sentences and major parts. In addition, a pause just before a word tends to emphasize it, and pauses can have the effect of spoken quotation marks. "He took his niece to New York for a weekend" changes considerably if we insert a pause before and after "niece."

Many other examples could be cited. The point is that intonation provides spoken language with signs not available to written language. It is therefore theoretically possible in speaking to convey information with fewer word signs than in writing. This possible greater efficiency is often lost, however, since we are not as careful about economy in speaking as in writing.

The above statements about intonation apply whether or not the

---

[1] Colin Cherry, *On Human Communication* (New York: John Wiley & Sons, 1957), p. 98.

[2] *Ibid.*, p. 120.

[3] Roger Brown, "Language and Categories," in Jerome Bruner, Jacqueline Austin, and George Austin, *A Study of Thinking* (New York: John Wiley & Sons, 1956), p. 253.

[4] *Ibid.*, p. 280.

speaker can be seen. If he can be seen, still other signs come into play, such as gestures and facial expressions. The words can say "I don't think we should ever see each other again," while the eyes and face say "Please don't ever leave me for a minute." Lifted eyebrows can say "I am doubtful" just as well as words, and a shrug can clearly say "It doesn't matter." Some of the signs can be combined with the items in the environment. "I water my plants every day" has a different meaning when the speaker is standing in his rose garden than when he is looking at two geraniums on his window sill.

For many kinds of communication, speech has a great advantage, being able to convey, by intonation, gestures, facial expressions, and environmental context, thoughts which can be expressed only roundaboutly, if at all, in writing—not to mention, of course, the much greater speed of speaking than of writing. The advantage is particularly great where feelings and emotions are to be communicated. By contrast, in communicating high level abstractions, these additional signs available to speech add little or nothing that cannot be communicated in writing. Further, if the abstractions are not thoroughly familiar to the receiver, it might be much better if he can take his own pace, as in reading, with the opportunity to go back at will. For these reasons, written language is usually better for abstract messages. A common audience comment after hearing an abstruse academic paper is, "It sounds Okay, but I want to see it in print."

NONLINGUISTIC CODES

Language is by no means the only set of signs we use for communication, even if we construe language to include the intonations, gestures, and context which accompany it. From among other possible sets of signs, we will discuss the graphic arts, music, ritual, and prices.

Graphic Communication

Spatial and functional relationships are usually communicated better by pictures than words. An architect's drawing of a house, or the schematic design of an amplifier circuit readily conveys what would be extremely difficult in words. So does a map of the world, a photograph of Notre Dame cathedral, or a materials-flow chart of a factory.

Visual representations can be used for the same communications purposes as can language, having the purpose of conveying pure information, pure motive or feeling, or some combination of the two. At one end of the spectrum we might think of a mechanical drawing whose purpose is solely to inform, while at the other end we might find a painting or sculpture whose purpose is solely to arouse some mood or feeling. The former attempts to arouse concepts in the receiver, and the latter to arouse affective states. Between the extremes we can, of course, also find mixtures, such as the architect's drawing which creates a mood as well as informs, and the artist's painting of an Indian village which informs as well as conveys a feeling. As with language, information is transmitted visually by issuing signs to which concepts are conditioned; and affective states are transmitted (or aroused) by issuing signs to which valences are conditioned.

The distinction made earlier between sensory and abstract concepts seems to apply here as well. If the artist arranges colors, lines, and forms in relationships which are found in actual sensory experience—if he draws a house or a man so that it "looks like" a house or a man—his painting is "realistic" or "concrete." If he assembles his components in relationships not previously experienced in external reality, the painting is abstract.[5]

The artist, however, has far greater flexibility than the normal user of words. Whereas there are usually only a few verbal cues for any given concept, there are almost limitless selections or combinations of parts of ingredients which can be used as visual cues. For example, a human finger, nose, or eye is readily identifiable. Since in normal experience these things never occur in isolation, a drawing of any such part implies a whole human being. The artist can confirm this inference by adding a line or two which approximates the contour of some other part of the body. Houses, trees, ships, mountains, and other visual objects can similarly be suggested by partial cues, and one of an artist's first tasks is to decide which cues, and how complete a set of cues, he is going to provide. He may put them together in normal fashion, for simple identification, or in some abnormal fashion to imply some kind of force or situation which would cause the abnormal relationship.

Artists often use signs from various areas of knowledge as cues for conveying a message, and the ancient and medieval artists were strong examples. From Greek mythology, Neptune and the trident might be used as signs for the sea, Cupid for love, Diana for the hunt, and so on. Religious art is replete with madonnas, angels, seraphim and a host of other cues from the literature of the church. Numerous recent paintings take their cues from psychoanalysis, attempting to depict the id, the superego, and other internal entities or conflicts of personality—though the artists do this on their own, Freud having provided no visual images of these entities.

Art in such forms as paintings or drawings and sculpture may have numerous objectives. One may paint to while the time away, to get his name in the paper, to make money, to vent frustration, to annoy his parents, to use up some old canvas, to cover some rough wall plaster, or to see if he can confound the critics. Two widely stated goals of painting are self-expression and communication. We will examine these briefly,

---

[5] Once again we should recall what we are doing in the present discussion. We are not trying to state "fundamental truths" about art and other graphic communication. Rather, having created a model for the analysis of human behavior we are now trying to describe graphic communication in the language of that model. The analysis should tell us something about the usefulness of the model as well as possibly telling us something about graphic communication.

though to ignore the other motives does not imply that they are insignificant.

To deal first with self-expression, if I feel exuberant, I may express this feeling by shouting and dancing, doing cartwheels, zigzagging down the highway at 90 miles an hour, throwing a party—or smearing paint on canvas. There are similarly many acts I might engage in to express depression, quiet humor, or other moods—again including painting. I might also decide to make a painting which will express jubilation, then work on it for months, even at moments when I am not jubilant. For purposes of pure self-expression I can put down anything I like, and say "This is *my* expression of jubilation." Whether to someone else it looks like the Black Hole of Calcutta, Montparnasse, or a pile of chicken feet is a matter of indifference. It expresses *me* and *my* feeling. To take a linguistic parallel, I sometimes type out ideas to help me remember or think about them. Whether anyone else can make sense of it does not matter, since the expression is solely for me.

But if my goal is to communicate, another dimension is added. I cannot now use signs just because they please me. Whether I write words or paint pictures, I must use signs which are identifiable by those with whom I wish to communicate, and which have the same referent to both of us. I cannot as an author write "Tuxr wnitplu viznox ut buntib stob borxl" and then complain that you, dear reader, are a stupid, insensitive dolt if you do not get my message. Communication requires a common set of signs and referents between sender and receiver, and in this case there is neither. Nor can I put some blobs, sworls, splots, and smears on a canvas in a combination of shapes and colors not previously known to you, and then properly complain if you see no meaning. In the one case, you might say, "There is a *t*, a *u*, an *x* and an *r*, but I don't have the vaguest idea what they mean." You might similarly say, "There is a blue blob, a sweeping sworl, a splendid splot, and a smashing smear, but dashed if I have the haziest notion what that chap is driving at." Whatever the merit of either as self-expression, neither is a communication. If communication was intended, the fault in both cases lies with the source, not the receiver, since he has failed to provide the minimum elements of a communication.

A particular "release" may have communications objectives other than to "say something" to the immediate recipients. I might, for example, put out my "nonsense" sentence as an experiment in linguistics. On seeing it you might say: "That 'Tuxr wnitplu viznox ut' doesn't seem to get anywhere, but from that 'buntib stob borxl' I gather he must be going down for the third time." If other readers had similar reactions, I might conclude that certain letter combinations, word lengths, sounds, or other traits of this "sentence" do serve as signs, and make further use of them. On the other hand, if the interpretations were random, I would conclude that the nonsense sentence has no meaning and abandon its elements for communicative purposes.

Similarly, if the blobs, sworls, splots, and smears bring no consensus as to their meaning, the artist should conclude that the painting does not communicate, and that its elements have little or no value as communicative signs. In that event they should either be abandoned, if the artist's purpose is communication, or be taught to the viewers. If a consensus does arise, then the painter could learn something about the signs he uses, after which he might communicate more clearly. That some contemporary artists seem little concerned about viewers' interpretations seems to imply that they are not interested in the communicative aspects of their paintings. It is therefore perhaps understandable that a frequently observed comment on modern paintings is the cocked head, the knitted brow, and the shrugged shoulder.

Certain elements in abstract designs can, of course, convey feelings, by virtue of similarity to things in the real world. That is, they can be improvised signs, the visual equivalent of onomatopoeic words. A design which is essentially triangular, with its base horizontal and the peak not too high, suggests strength and stability, since any solid figure thus constructed would not crush or topple easily. Large masses suggest strength, since objects of this sort are hard to break. By contrast, a triangle with its apex downward suggests instability, and a long slender one frailty. Many combinations of sizes, shapes, and colors have counterparts in real experience, and meaning can therefore be suggested by them, even if they are not "realistic." To the extent these experiences are common to all, like the triangle and the heavy shapes, the interpretations will tend to be uniform, even if the viewers do not consciously discern its basis. To the extent these experiences are unique, so too is the meaning of a painting. Realistic paintings contain signs known to all, and have some meaning to all, whether or not it happens to be the one the painter had in mind.

Even in abstract painting, the self-expression aspect need not be confined to the affective realm, but may also involve the conceptual. Much the same motive which leads the scientist to seek new concepts infects the artist as well—and we have already seen that forming new concepts seems to be independently and sometimes strongly motivated. In the artist the results are experiments in new and different ways of putting visual elements together. The new combinations may sometimes be carefully planned, the artist reasoning that a particular group of elements whose separate effects are known should produce a calculable effect in combination. Or the experiments may be done on a pure let's-try-it-and-see basis. Creative scientists similarly use both planned and unplanned approaches, trying new combinations and models in their heads, on paper, and in the laboratory.

Viewers of art may approach new types of paintings in the same spirit. Even if the viewers have not themselves had the fun of forming new concepts, they can at least experience the result. In a sense the earlier distinction between concept formation and concept attainment may be relevant here. The creative artist or scientist *forms* new concepts. By means appropriate to his own field he then sets them forth to others, who then seek to *attain* them. The motives both to form and to attain new concepts are widely found.

At this point art and science seem to part company, however. A new experiment or model by the scientist is judged against fairly rigid criteria —does it bring us closer to reality (i.e., produce more accurate predictions), and does it raise the information content of our concept systems? Precisely what the criteria are for judging the value of new concepts in art is not easily answered. That they are closer to reality or have higher information content than previous art forms seems difficult to sustain.

The nature and function of art and artists is a problem with a long and tortuous history, and it is not our purpose to suggest an answer. In the light of the model developed in previous chapters it does seem appropriate, however, to delineate the conditions which must be met if a piece of art is to function as communication.

Music

In one sense music, particularly instrumental music, is more abstract than visual art. All but the most abstract painters use some shapes and patterns consciously and directly borrowed from real things. By contrast, the tone qualities of few musical instruments duplicate, or are intended to duplicate, sounds found in nonmusical experience. Nor does the overall structure of a rondo or a sonata imitate any natural sequence. In that sense, music is created to a significant extent from arbitrary signs, like spoken language, not from analogous ones like realistic and semirealistic painting. At the same time, however, music also uses ingredients which have more direct access to human feelings than does painting.

We may note first that music has a time span. This makes possible a sequence of different moods, each undiluted at a given moment, which can carry us from calm to storm and back again.

Second, some musical elements seem closely related to basic human experiences. As to rhythm, we can look first at a simple repetition of an impulse over time, or pulsation. This is a symbolic duplication of the heart beat. A simple two beat (as in 2/4 time) at the rate of about 60 double counts per minute suggests brisk walking, and a marching band normally plays at about this speed. This is also about the speed of the heart. A faster beat suggests running or a faster heart beat, both of which are associated with excitement—whether from anticipation, competition, excess energy, or fear. Slower beats suggest leisurely walking, or the walking of older persons, while very slow beats suggest the slow pace of weariness or grief, or quiet relaxation. A triple beat, or waltz time, does not occur in normal walking or running, and hence must suggest some other ambit. A triple beat approximates skipping, or some other locomotion where the body is projected into the air for one beat, followed by two steps on the ground. The sequence is float-step-step-float-step-step-. . . . This kind of gait occurs with carefree exuberance, but never with danger, age, or sadness. All other beats are combinations of twos and threes, the four-beat being a double two, the six-beat a double three or triple two, the five-beat a three plus a two, and so on.[6] Syncopation is clearly "out of step." This would seem to imply more than one person, and possible conflict, since the beats are definitely "not together." A very heavy beat suggests many people walking, or a heavy person, while a light beat suggests few or one, or a very light person. Rhythm may thus be more "primitive" than painting, in that it has direct connection with emotional states. Many of its "improvised cues" may not require the conceptualizations on which visual art depends.

Tone quality also has rather direct emotional connections. In man, and in part in the lower animals, sounds made during emotions of love, tenderness, and peace are relatively quiet, legato, regular, and smooth. ("Smooth" tones mainly consist of the fundamental tone and consonant overtones.) Those made in fear or anger, however, are loud, staccato, irregular, and rough. ("Rough" tones contain many overtones and dissonances, with relatively little fundamental, as well as pitches not in a musical scale at all.) While we must certainly avoid any thought that music is "nothing more than" a simple extension of sounds from man's natural habitat, there also is no point in neglecting some obvious similarities. In Western culture many simple melodic lines follow the same general contours as the cadence of the voice in a simple sentence, and the drop of the voice at the end of many sentences has a parallel in the drop of conventional harmonies from the fifth to the tonic at the end of a musical sentence.

Other kinds of connections would presumably enter. A sound with the general pitch and quality of an oboe would virtually never be made in nature by a large or ponderous object, nor could a tuba-like sound be made by a small one. The oboe suggests frailty, since only a frail object could emit sounds of that quality. Onomatopoeic relations of similar sorts occur in language itself. When English-speaking persons with no knowledge of Chinese are told that *ch'ing* and *ch'ung* stand for heavy and light, and are asked to identify which is which, 91 per cent correctly match *ch'ing* with light and *ch'ung* with heavy.[7] Similarly a *plink* is made by a smaller object than a *plunk*, *sharp* is a sharper word than *blunt*, and *bright* is a brighter word than *dull*.

All of these observations must be taken in the light of the facts that most words have no observable onomatopoeic significance at all. In addition, many peoples, particularly orientals, have musical sounds whose "meaning" is clearly at odds with the above suggestions about notes in the musical scale. Whether these represent the particular musical instruments which happen to have been discovered early, or were used or liked

---

[6] This discussion of beat and rhythm roughly parallels Leonard Bernstein's television discussion of March 13, 1960.

[7] Roger Brown, *op. cit.*

by important historic personages, is apparently not known. The "natural" and the "historical" or "cultural" connections are equally learned, and one set can be learned as easily as the other. On the other hand, it is difficult to imagine that *any* peoples could be given a feeling of repose by music with a gradually loudening and accelerating beat, and with sharp staccatos or syncopations, or that they could be moved to a sense of impending doom by a Strauss waltz.

In these senses, music is a language with significant and, in a broad way, fairly consistent signs which are mutually understood between composer, performer, and listener. This does not mean that at any one moment the listener can tell what mood the composer intended since many compositions are intended to be merely interesting, ingenious, or different—i.e., new concepts.

Many kinds of compositions have a definite syntax. Popular songs show perhaps the most rigid syntax. Their choruses with rare exception have eight bars of main melody, a repetition of those eight bars, eight bars of secondary melody, and an ending which repeats the first eight bars. The secondary melody is in a different key from the main one, typically a fourth or a fifth higher. Perhaps the rigidity of the syntax continues because of the many such compositions musicians must learn, and the much greater ease with which the listener can follow. Certainly the rigid, stereotyped syntax of such music partly explains why acceptably coordinated music can be produced without scores by an unrehearsed jam session of persons who have never played together before. Certain older forms of classical music, such as the rondo of Mozart's time, were also highly rigid, and could similarly be improvised by musicians familiar with the pattern. Certain harmonic sequences are also extremely common in musical literature, as even the casual listener will recognize them if he hears the "syntactical" sequence of chords, I, IV, I, V, I, in either major or minor.

"All Possible Combinations"

In both pictorial art and music, artists and composers gradually exhaust the reasonably original combinations which can be produced within any particular set of signs and syntax. Some imaginative artist or composer then founds a new "school" or "movement," which consists of a set of new concepts and relations—a new set of signs (and perhaps their referents) and syntax. As we have seen, this is roughly parallel to the way in which creative scientists develop new conceptualizations with new relations among them.

It is interesting to note that a similar development has been occurring simultaneously within art, music, and science. This can be best described by a short historical sketch. In the past, each field has experienced new discoveries, or "schools." Each tended at first to be ignored, ridiculed, and doubted; then tried; and finally exploited—though rejections as well as acceptances have occurred. After reasonably full exploitation, each school would then give way to a new one, and the cycle would be repeated.

This has now happened often enough for the cycle itself to become familiar, with the following result. Workers in all three fields seem to be working with a new concept, which we may call "all possible combinations," instead of looking at existing forms and asking, "What changes can we make to produce something new, interesting, and useful?" Musicians now see the possibility of a near infinitude of possible combinations of pitches, chords, chord sequences, tone qualities, rhythms, and tempos. With electronic organs and other sound generators it is now theoretically possible to manufacture any desired pitch, volume, chord, or tone quality. By manipulating tapes, any given sound pattern can be raised or lowered in pitch or volume to any desired level, and be shortened or extended to any desired duration. A note in a bird call which lasts only a half second can be dropped two octaves and extended to last for a half hour, if desired. Thus it was possible to produce the Symphony of Birds, a reasonably conventional composition in form and melody, but with unusual tonal qualities. No source of sound was used except bird calls. Along similar lines Ferrante and Teicher have manipulated sounds created by pianos into sounds generally unlike any ever heard before, as illustrated in their record, *Soundproof*.[8] Robert Craft has conducted compositions with a small group in which each member plays at a different tempo, one perhaps retarding while another is accelerating, and so on.[9] Modern composers write "melodies" in which successive notes may be four octaves or more apart—a procedure clearly violating earlier syntactical rules, which required that melodies be singable. Different instruments or sections of the orchestra may be scored to play in two different keys simultaneously, discarding another earlier rule of musical syntax. With results that may or may not be good, musicians now experiment in "all possible" tones, pitches, tempos, and combinations thereof.

The same thinking is now being applied in the sciences. We have seen that cybernetics is defined by Ashby as the theory of all possible machines. "Systems research" deals with the common elements in systems ranging from the atom and microbe to the solar system and the universe, including the relationship between an auto driver and the highway, or the President and the Congress en route. Behavioral science, action systems, and other fields are growing all around us, in which the investigator attempts to think in terms of "all possible" things within his realm. In some ways the preceding chapters take the form they do because the discussion of concept formation and communication has been couched in an analytical context of "all possible concepts."

Graphic artists show the same approach to paint. Put it on with a brush, or perhaps a palette knife. Smear it on with the fingers, blow it on

8 Westminster #6014.
9 *New Directions in Music 1*, Columbia, ML 5275.

with an air brush, drop it on, throw it on, splatter it on, run it on, or smear the paint on a nude and push her around the canvas. Pour on the paint and then roll up the canvas, agitate the wet canvas in a washing machine, run the lawn mover over it, drop old bread crumbs on it, or perhaps throw on a live fish or a snake. Controls are sometimes exerted by the artist. At other times the process is strictly on a "Let's see what happens" basis. Viewed as communication, it would seem doubtful that the result of an uncontrolled experiment will convey much more information than that the artist is an experimenter.

Rituals

Rituals are a highly important technique by which society imparts to its members certain concepts and values. Some other aspects of rituals will be discussed in the chapter on Culture; at this point we will note an important communicative function. Many things in daily life are simple and concrete—chairs, pencils, stoves, zebras, and coconuts. Few persons have difficulty learning these concepts or appropriate responses to them. But to build an orderly society requires its members to form some highly abstract concepts about relationships of persons, to recognize instances of them, and to develop appropriate responses. These are not easy to learn, and the parent cannot point out things for the child and say, "This is a kinship system. Over there is God, and just beyond is a system of governmental checks and balances. Examine these things, and after you are familiar with them I will show you how to use them."

Rituals and ceremonies may not provide a clear idea of what these things are. But they do provide an explicit referent for some of the terms, and a definite set of attitudes and feelings to accompany it. Whereas "God" may be a very hazy notion, the church, the incantations, the frenzied dancing or the splendid quiet, the prayers, the hymns, the images, the baptism, the slaying of a sacrificial animal, or the ordered movements of the holy man are all very real, and the attitudes and feelings engendered by them become associated with "God." "God" thus acquires semantic content. Those who are able go on to form more abstract concepts of God, as their religion or searching suggests. But the sensory and emotional base remains, and so do the associated valences.

Rituals about basic social organizations perform a similar function. In place of, in addition to, or as a base for the more intangible concepts of kinship, government, or country, these rituals provide flags, totems, pledges of allegiance, dances or marches, body movements such as swaying or saluting, fires or fireworks, and regular repetition of key words or phrases. In the United States the stars and stripes are a visual symbol, the eagle is a totem, and Uncle Sam is a personification of government. Patriotic speeches and editorials provide the incantations, in which liberty, freedom, sovereignty, separation of powers, rugged individualism, pioneer spirit, and others are the reliable verbal symbols. The flags, salutes, marches, anthems, and phrases are semantic referents for "country" and "patriotism." Again, those who are able go beyond the rituals to the more abstract concepts, for unless at least the leaders deal with the realities beyond the symbols, the system cannot function. A perpetual problem, augmented during stressful times, is that persons who think mainly at the ritual level tend to suspect the sincerity or loyalty of those who, understanding the abstractions, feel no personal need for the rituals.

Whether rituals contribute to understanding the abstract concepts probably depends more on corollary activities than on the rituals themselves. For example, sermons and discussion groups may explain and interpret the ritualized concepts, in which case the rituals and discussions may reinforce each other. Ritual without such corollary activity will probably not produce concepts beyond the ritual level.

Rituals also tend to provide strong feelings of unity and solidarity, as an almost inevitable outcome of their relatively rigid rules. A man attending a church service may disbelieve the creed, reject the sermon, and consider the ceremony primitive. But the code of ritual keeps him silent. A man attending a patriotic ceremony may know that his government is corrupt, its coffers bankrupt, its constitution outmoded, and its foreign policy immoral. But he will not interrupt the ritual of praise. There is solidarity in ritual because dissent is taboo.

As between information and motivation, ritual is presumably far more effective in communicating the latter. Many rituals probably impede the flow of information. But whereas the abstract concepts behind the rituals will vary greatly from person to person, the associated feelings and motives may be highly similar. Ritual thus communicates attitudes deemed essential to society, but which are otherwise difficult to communicate.

Prices

We will mention one final sample of nonlinguistic communication, though its main ramifications come later. The prices at which things sell communicate information and motivation simultaneously. If a man knows both the price of his labor and the price of a motor boat, he then knows how much labor he must give to acquire the boat. If he knows the price of clothing, the price of his present house, and the price of a bigger one, he can readily compute how much clothing he would have to do without to afford the bigger house. Similar comparisons can be made among a multitude of things, even including the price of government. By comparing the prices of various things with the intensity of his wants, one is motivated to buy or sell, to use or not to use particular things. Among things which carry price tags, the relationships among those prices, and between the prices and desires, provide a vast network for communicating both information and motivation. Although this communication and motivating system is used most widely in capitalist nations, prices are by no means insignificant in similar ways in socialist or communist ones. Fuller ramifications of communication by prices will be examined in a later chapter.

III. CULTURE
AND PERSONALITY

Chapter 12

CULTURE

CULTURE AS A SYSTEM

CULTURE IS both a body of content and a set of relationships, in much the same sense that language is a set of semantic content and a set of syntactic relations. Both the content and the relationships depend on the ability of human beings to communicate, and to engage in related behavior which uses the same level of psychological competence which distinguishes man from all other animals.

The relationships act as a system. Culture as a system is universal, the same at all times and places of man. Culture as a set of content is never precisely the same in any two places, or at any two times in the same place, although in certain primitive and isolated societies the content may not change perceptibly for centuries.

Culture as a system is extremely simple. Perhaps best described as the human environment of humans, the system aspect of culture is the set of relationships that makes it possible for human beings to create a society, to pass the accumulated learning of the species from generation to generation, and to continue to make the accumulations of learning which compose the crucial distinction between human beings and the most advanced of the lower animals. By "learning" in this connection we mean the whole set of concepts and motives learned by man. The concepts include not only the informational ones, or "knowledge" in the narrower sense, but also those concepts which are reflected in artifacts, sociofacts, and performance skills, to be discussed below. The system aspect of culture is diagrammed in Figure 12-1.

The relationship between the individual and the culture is a chicken-egg situation. We will break into the cycle the way each of us sees it—as an individual entering an already established culture. As each child grows and matures he learns many things about the world around him. Many of these, such as the ability to distinguish shapes, colors, sounds, smells, touches, temperatures, pressures, and numerous objects, he may be able to learn from his own sensory experience before he can talk. These he could conceivably learn if he were alone on earth, and the apes and other animals also learn these things.

But in contrast to the ape, most of a man's learning is acquired from those around him. In Chapter 9 on communication we observed that to learn a language means to learn the accumulated concepts and attached valences developed by our ancestors. Partly through language, and partly

Figure 12-1
THE SYSTEM OF CULTURE

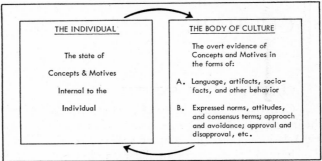

through observation and participation, the individual also learns about the social structures, patterns of behavior, artifacts, and attitudes of those around him. The total collection of the things people do, say, believe, and make (to be described in more detail below) are the *content*, or body, of a culture.

No one individual learns the totality of the content of a culture. Further, different individuals are exposed to different segments of it, and they show individual differences in their learning of and response to the portion they are exposed to—an aspect of behavior we will examine in the next chapter, as personality. In parallel, neither are any two individuals exposed to precisely the same sample of the natural environment, nor do they respond the same way to it. Nevertheless, the body of the culture *is* the human environment into which the human being is born, and from which he learns about interpersonal behavior. The things he learns from those around him become part of his neural and somatic system. They largely determine what kind of overt response he will give to a particular stimulus, and whether it will produce in him joy, sorrow, fear, or anger. Despite individual differences, for the moment we need only observe that the general patterns of behavior—of likes and dislikes, and the way one understands and responds toward the world—are highly similar among all Eskimos, but widely different as between the Eskimos and the Australian Bushmen.

Once these patterns are acquired by the individual, his overt behavior reflects the same set of patterns. He says hello and goodbye like those around him. He wears the same kinds of clothes, eats the same foods, speaks the same language, and generally approves and disapproves the same things. This is the first half of the system: the surrounding culture molds each individual approximately into its own image, as indicated by the lower arrow in Figure 12-1.

The second half of the system is the influence of the individual on the culture, indicated by the upper arrow. This is simple in the extreme. Each person's behavior *is* part of the culture which is everyone else's environment. This half of the relation is particularly conspicuous in the case of parents. They are the major part of the human environment of the child, who learns the set of concepts and values reflected by his parents. Not all such things are received from parents. The six-year-olds teach the five-year-olds, who a year later teach the then five-year-olds, and so on. Although any *particular* thing may be learned from a parent, sibling, cousin, aunt, friend, or stranger, directly or indirectly, the important thing is that the great bulk of information of any one person is acquired from other human beings around him, and that he in his turn becomes one of the human beings from whom others learn.

This is the mutual interaction of the existing body of culture on the individual, and of the individual upon the body of culture which we call the *system* of culture, as diagrammed in Figure 12-1. This is the universal aspect of culture, the self-perpetuating vehicle for carrying human learning from generation to generation in endless succession. Even though its content may change, the nature of the system never changes. This transmission from generation to generation takes place through communicational, transactional, and organizational relationships, as the latter two terms will be defined in later chapters.

When viewed in terms of the characteristics of systems outlined in Chapter 3, the cultural system is clearly an uncontrolled, not a cybernetic, system. No governor is present which issues orders to bring the culture back to a particular position if a detector senses a deviation. Viewed in large perspective it is not even an equilibrium system. The content of the culture varies directly with the concepts and motives of the people, which concepts and motives vary directly with the content of the culture. A culture system thus has no *a priori* "preference" for one position rather than another. Depending on the circumstances it can range anywhere along the spectrum of total possibilities, and can "explode" (expand beyond the limits of feasible operation as a single system) or shrivel away.

On the other hand, any operative culture system contains subsystems which establish and maintain certain norms, or consensus values about many things. These subsystems do have an equilibrating action which tends to maintain whatever particular level the system happens to have attained. The main subsystem is essentially that of deviation and conformity, in which the pressure to conformity varies directly with the deviation, and the deviation varies inversely with the pressure to conformity. The nature and sources of consensuses and the means of enforcing them are important aspects of culture. But an understanding of them depends on analysis we have not yet done. The discussion of this phase of the problem will therefore have to wait till later chapters, especially 19.

The Prerequisites of a System of Culture

If culture is the unique thing which sets off man from the other animals, what crucial factor makes culture possible in man but not in other animals? If we start with culture as a system, or process, this system depends on the unique feature that human beings are able to engage in deliberate, controlled communication by means of arbitrary or conventionalized signs, primarily in the form of language. We have seen that bees and some other animals communicate information to other members of the species. But such behavior is apparently an inborn response to some experience of one member, which he would perform whether or not his signals were observed by others. Certain vocalizations of pleasure, pain, or anger also serve as signals among some animals other than man. But these, too, are apparently simple responses to a stimulus, not sounds deliberately uttered to convey an idea. Such communication is like that mentioned earlier, where the breaking of a branch or an exclamation is communicated to any hearer who understands the code. Even if we accept claims that some animals do emit certain signs for communicative purposes—as that a dog may sit up to "beg" for food, or scratch his master's leg when he wants to go out—these signs are extremely limited in scope and content.[1] While the dog may convey the idea "I am hungry," he cannot distinguish it from "*You* are hungry," or "I *was* hungry." Nor does he have signs for such simple things as food (as distinguished from hunger), ground, air, tree, or table. He can point to things, but the sign is the same whether the referent is "tree" or "food," having the same significance as the words "this" or "here." This sign can only call for attention, and the dog is helpless to answer, "What about it?"

No animal except the human being can describe where he has been, what he has done, or the neighboring tribe's conditions for peace. Only the human can tell his offspring what makes the lightning and thunder, or what makes the daisies grow—even if the explanation is a bad one. Only the human being has signs for wife, mother, daughter, sister, niece, or aunt. Although the ape can learn by imitation certain manual operations requiring dexterity, such as simple weaving or threading a needle, one ape cannot *tell* another how to do it. No ape or other animal can tell his son that apples and cheese go well together, that bragging annoys others, or that it is considered immoral to marry one's sister.

Communication is basic to the system of culture, since only by communication can each generation learn the concepts developed by its forebears, and learn which behavior is approved or disapproved.

But why is the human being able to communicate while the ape is not? If there is a physiological answer, it apparently lies in brain capacity. As we have seen earlier, a brain capacity of about 900 to 1,000 cc. apparently

---

[1] There is now a strong suspicion that porpoises, which are perhaps the most intelligent mammals other than man, have a language, which linguistics experts are trying to decipher. Even this is not anticipated to include signs for things other than relatively simple overt behavior and objects.

represents a threshold level. Below it the brain is able to form sensory and motor concepts, even fairly complex ones, and to form concepts of spatial and temporal relationships. But below that threshold the brain is unable to go beyond second or third order conditioning, or to combine in the brain concepts which were not combined in experience. That is, the largest nonhuman brain cannot perform abstraction beyond the first or second level. We do not know what level of abstraction *is* required for communication by signs, but it clearly is not possessed by the most intelligent of other animals. That communication by signs necessarily involves the ability to make abstractions is clear from the earlier discussion of communication. A message consists of the signs for two or more concepts in some relation. Unless the receiver of the message is able mentally to combine the concepts represented by the signs, he cannot get the meaning of the message.[2] As noted earlier, the Kellogg family raised a chimpanzee baby, Gua, along with their own from infancy, treating both identically, in the midst of an ordinary human family life. Gua learned all things the Kellogg child learned, sometimes better, until the child began to learn language. Gua showed no ability to learn to speak or deliberately to use communicative signs in any way. From that point the child developed into a human being, while Gua remained an ape.[3]

Psychologically speaking, the essence of speech is the overt reproduction of a pattern which exists internally in the brain. But speech is not the only manifestation of this process. To clarify the next point, we may note that many animals can reproduce externally the patterns of inherited concepts. The pattern of the beaver dam, the beehive, or the bird's nest illustrates such external reproduction of a concept residing somewhere in the nervous system. Man's uniqueness in this area lies in his ability to reproduce a *learned* pattern from memory. The pattern he reproduces may be a tool, a house, a headband, or a social structure. This ability is not distinct from that of conscious communication. Both consist of reproducing a learned pattern in some medium outside oneself, whether the medium be stone, wood, other people, or air waves. Neurologically, presumably the ability to speak is identical with the ability to build a house according to a learned pattern.

The ape does not lack any of the physical equipment used by man for these purposes. His vocal chords and muscles are capable of producing all the sounds of human speech, and apes actually make most of them. His arms and fingers are capable of performing the most dextrous skills

---

[2] We again withhold judgment on the porpoise, whose brain capacity averages 1,886 grams, as compared to man's 1,300—though a large optical and auditory tract constitute a substantial part of it. See A. F. McBride and D. O. Hebb, "Behavior of the Captive Bottle-Nose Dolphin, Tursiops Truncatus," *Journal of Comparative and Physiological Psychology*, Vol. 41, 1948, p. 111. The article notes (pp. 120, 122) that we have as yet no direct evidence of the porpoise's intelligence.

[3] Mischa Titiev, *The Science of Man* (New York: Henry Holt & Co., 1956), pp. 179–81. This experiment is widely reported elsewhere, and with the same conclusions.

known to man, and the ape has the advantage of more versatile feet. It is not the lack of physical equipment but of mental equipment that keeps the ape where he is.

While the apes cannot use language at all, in the sense of deliberate issuance of arbitrary signs for communication (though they can learn to receive simple communications via signs), they can to a limited degree create external patterns of objects according to learned patterns. When faced with some problem, for example, the ape can form a concept in which he, a tool, and some object he wants are related, and then proceed to execute behavior which brings these three things into a relation that first existed in his brain. But he is apparently capable of holding the mental concept only so long as the objects are actually in front of him. The ape can also imitate a human being or another ape in making these relationships. But whether he imitates them or figures them out for himself, he does not remember them from one situation to the next. Although the ape can *invent* tools, he possesses no carry-over, and he must invent the tool all over again the next time he needs it. Man's unique ability is that of being able to *remember* the conceptual relationship among the parts, and to *reproduce it from memory*, whether or not the ingredients of the combination are currently present in his environment.

We will define this ability to reproduce in some external medium, from memory, the pattern of a learned concept, the *ability to symbol*. The external pattern thus reproduced is the *symbol* of the concept. Signs and artifacts are widely recognized by anthropologists as such symbols, or outward manifestations of internal concepts. To sharpen the analysis, a pure sign is a symbol used solely for communication, in the manner discussed in earlier chapters. In parallel, a pure artifact could be some tool, building, bowl, or piece of clothing having solely utilitarian functions. In actuality, many mixtures occur. Artifacts often contain, or function as, signs, in either their basic shape or their decoration, as in the historical information conveyed in the decorations on some early Greek vases and buildings, or the status symbolized in the ruffed collars of Elizabethan England. Signs often take physical form, particularly in mottoes which decorate the entrances to buildings, or the totem poles of the Alaskan Indians.

If the ability to symbol is the psychological faculty of reproducing a learned concept in some external medium, this ability is not confined to language and the making of artifacts. A social structure, in the large or in some detail, is a *sociofact*. In precisely the same way that men transported to distant shores will proceed to reproduce the same kinds of artifacts already known to them, if the materials are available, so will they reproduce the same or similar sociofacts. Social structures, methods of selecting leaders and making decisions, rituals, techniques of exchange, and other interpersonal relations will be reconstructed from the memories of previous experience. Skills will be performed as before, and will be taught to sons by the same methods they were taught to the fathers. All such replications are instances of and dependent on the ability to symbol, as defined above. This is the unique ability which distinguishes man from all other animals.[4]

Important as it is in itself, the ability to symbol has its greatest importance in making it possible for culture to accumulate. Everything learned by the ape, or any other animal, dies with him. Without language he cannot tell others what he knows. If he creates some improved artifact, his fellows are not able to reproduce it after he dies, and he could not necessarily create it a second time himself unless the original conditions were repeated. Learned (or other acquired) characteristics cannot be inherited biologically. For all animals but man this means that *no* learning can be passed from one generation to the next. But through his ability to symbol, man can reproduce his concepts externally, in such form that new information acquired by one person *can* be passed on to other persons and to succeeding generations. Man can reproduce what he learned by accident or thought, and others can copy it. Whether or not it actually adds anything of consequence, each generation of man *potentially* starts where its ancestors left off. In short, it is not the inability of lower animals to *learn* that prevents the system of culture from operating among them; it is their inability to accumulate and communicate what they learn.

Although the apes do not have the mental capacity to develop a culture, they do possess several other traits which are probably necessary, but not sufficient, conditions for culture. These probably explain why human beings developed from ape-like, rather than from canine, feline, reptilian, bovine, or other stock. (1) The opposable thumb and relatively long fingers enable man to manipulate things, both to examine and to transform them. (2) The ability to walk on two appendages leaves the other two free for manipulating things. (3) Man's vocal chords can produce a wide variety of controllable sounds for communicative purposes. (4) The slow rate at which babies mature allows a long time for exploration and learning. (5) In contrast to all other animals, which engage in

---

[4] Anthropologists, and notably White, use the verb "to symbol" to include only communication by language and the making of artifacts (Leslie A. White, *The Science of Culture* [New York: Grove Press, Inc., 1949], chap. II). Once these abilities are reduced to their psychological base, it seems inescapable that the creation of sociofacts from memory exemplifies the identical type of ability, and must logically be accepted as a parallel act of symboling. To the extent that certain behavioral skills are incorporated in information concepts rather than solely in motor concepts, they, too, should apparently be included. For example, a person may have a clear information concept of the technique of spearing a fish or performing a rain dance, and be able to instruct another to do it, even though he cannot himself perform the act. While leaving the way open for the possible inclusion of additional items, we are therefore defining the ability to symbol to include communication by language, the making of artifacts and sociofacts, and the conceptualization of skills. The concentration by some anthropologists on tools made to a fixed pattern as the distinguishing feature of man presumably reflects the fact that the tools are the only remaining evidence of symboling among long extinct peoples, and hence the only evidence for classifying them as man rather than beast.

sexual relations only during limited cyclical periods when the female is in heat, the anthropoids and man are subject to a more or less continuous sex urge. This has led to permanent relationships between male and female, unlike the temporary relationships during mating season characteristic of other animals. While our major interest in this fact appears in a later chapter on the family, it does provide for close and continuous relationships between persons, under which culture and language can develop.

Culture and Society

Before we move from culture as a system to culture as a body of content, we will note that any particular body of culture belongs to a *society*, which is any group of people having a common body and system of culture.

The boundaries of any society cannot be precisely defined, because there is no precise dividing line between "same" and "different" cultures. "Same" and "different" are not characteristics of *things*, but of the classification system, the observer, and the purpose at hand, and any two things in the universe can be classified as "same" or "different," depending on the circumstances. With respect to languages, for instance (a highly important portion of culture), German, Danish, and Swedish can be classified as "different" if we are comparing spelling of particular words, vocabulary, and some aspects of grammar among those three languages. But these three languages may be considered the "same" if we are dividing them as one group from Latin, Spanish, French, Portuguese, and Italian as another group. On a still different occasion we might classify all eight of these languages as the "same" if we are distinguishing between the writing of vocabulary languages and sign languages, or between Indo-European and Ural-Altaic languages. For this reason, we can say that two groups have the same, or common, culture, only with respect to some particular problem. We might say, for example, that all persons on earth possess a common culture, in the sense that all have language and make tools according to a learned pattern, in contrast to all the lower animals, which do not.

It is relatively easy to define the boundaries of a society for a people who have been isolated for centuries, as in the culture of an island small enough so that all its inhabitants interact among each other, but far enough from others to make communication difficult. Only a relatively primitive culture can retain this condition, since transportation brings advanced societies into contact. Many islands of the South Seas show this situation. So do the Eskimos and Laplanders, whose contacts remain limited by virtue of climatic isolation. Even within the same continent, however, it is possible to have little enough interaction for cultures to remain distinct. The culture of the Hopi Indians is quite distinct from that of the Iroquois, and the Aztecs and Incas showed very little interconnection.

Within a large cosmopolitan area, such as Europe or the United States, cultural lines can be drawn on varied bases. We can, for example, refer to Western society, as distinct from Eastern. The culture of each includes certain broad attitudes toward the origins and purpose of life, toward work, toward animals, and toward other human beings. Within the West there are distinguishing features which mark off the attitudes and beliefs of the French, the German, the British, and the American cultures—among others. Each of these can be considered a society, with its own subculture within the general heading of Western culture. But American society is not a unitary thing. The Southern mountain white, the share-cropper, the plantation owner, the semiskilled Northern factory worker, the New York business tycoon, the New England fisherman, and the Iowa corn and hog farmer all belong to societies whose habits, beliefs, language, and life patterns differ widely from one another. Each has its own subculture within the American culture. Each can be divided and subdivided in turn, almost without end. The mountain whites on one ridge differ from those on the adjoining ridge, and the skilled culturologist might tell them apart by certain attitudes or pronunciations. Even in the relatively homogeneous small town, the inhabitants of the east end differ in some ways from those of the west end, and the precise set of attitudes in one family differs from that of its next door neighbors. As will be suggested later (Chapter 26), it seems possible that the unit recently much analyzed under the heading of the "small group" can meaningfully be viewed as a small subsociety with its own miniature and partial subculture. We cannot subdivide culture further, for to do so would bring us to differences among individuals, and these are matters of personality, not culture. On the basis of whatever traits we choose to distinguish cultures, a given society and its culture are, by definition, coextensive. The society is the group of people who have a common culture, and a culture is the set of external manifestations of the common motives and concepts of a society. If two widely separated and noncommunicating groups of people were to show identical *bodies* of culture, we would nevertheless not consider them as parts of the same society, since they are not part of the same cultural *system*. Interaction within the group is thus an indispensable attribute of a society.

Culture as Input and Output of a Society

So long as we keep in mind that learning is a phenomenon of the nervous system, and hence something that can happen only within the individual, it is nevertheless useful to reconstruct Figure 12-1 to show *society* rather than *the individual* in the lefthand box. In this sense, a culture is the product, or net result, of a living society. It is the output of the society, the symbolization of the concepts and motives held by its people. Simultaneously, however, the culture created by the society is the environment in which its people live—the human environment which delineates the opportunities and molds the preferences of its members. In this sense the body of culture is the input of the society, and the set of parameters to which its members adapt. It is this distinctive feature, in which the body of culture is simultaneously both the output and input of the society, which gives the typical society its stable, self-perpetuating nature. The society and its culture remain a closed system so long as the cultural output and input are essentially identical. The system is open, and subject to a change in its equilibrium, when for some reason a discrepancy arises between the output and input phases. We will return to this problem later, as cultural change.

In any culture, but particularly in that of a complex, cosmopolitan society, any one individual participates in numerous subcultures. He can therefore also be said to belong to numerous subsocieties. One can simultaneously be a member of a neighborhood, the Lutheran Church, the Masons, the American Legion, the Chamber of Commerce, a civic theater, and the American Management Association, while one also spends his summers alternately in Mexico and Canada. Each of these bits of subculture reflects a different set of concepts and values. To return for the moment to the relation between the individual and the culture, each of these subcultures is modified slightly, as the result of the output activities of the individual, and his influence may be slight or great. More importantly, the totality of the subcultures to which an individual exposes himself constitutes the *particular cultural input to him.*

In the primitive society, virtually all members may be exposed to an essentially identical set of subcultures, and hence have the same basic cultural input. The more complex and diverse the society, however, and the greater the freedom of the individual to select the subsocieties he will join, the greater is the likelihood that no two persons will have precisely the same total cultural input. This fact would tend to produce a wider variety of personalities in the complex culture. It is offset, however, to the extent that the widespread participation of all kinds of people in all kinds of subsocieties tends to bring the cultural content of these subsocieties toward greater uniformity among themselves. It is reasonably certain, for example, that the individual above, who is a Mason, Lutheran, and so forth, will not come out of his multisubcultural experience with the Hindu belief that cows are sacred, or the Latin American feeling that it is indecent to conclude a business deal in less than three days. Each society he belongs to is a subculture of Western, American culture, not a distinct major culture of its own.

THE CONTENT OF CULTURE: CONCEPTS

We have described the human nervous system as capable of learning two main kinds of things, concepts and motives. Since the body of culture consists solely of learned things, its content can similarly be said to consist of a set of concepts and a set of motives or values. And just as concepts and motives are much interrelated in the individual, so are they intertwined in the culture.[5]

Language

All known human societies have a well-developed language. As noted in Chapter 9, as each new generation learns the language it necessarily learns the concepts which are the referents of its semantic signs. In the relatively simple society with spoken language only, each individual may learn virtually the whole vocabulary, which means that he learns most important concepts of the culture. In the advanced society, the individual learns the concepts common to the whole culture, but not those of all the specialized technical subcultures, or localized general cultures. Advanced societies depend on written language, in which form information can be stored permanently and in huge quantities. Written information can be studied at leisure, and is free from the distortions and other limitations of human memory.

Language is much more than the set of signs and referents for communication. The concepts which are its referents are also what we think and perceive with. When either you or a primitive man sees the shadow

---

[5] Although this classification is not "officially" used by anthropologists, it can easily be reconciled with existing classifications. White divides "the components of culture into four categories: ideological, sociological, sentimental or attitudinal, and technological." (Leslie A. White, *The Evolution of Culture* [New York: McGraw-Hill Co., Inc., 1959], p. 6.) As he describes them, the ideological fall easily and clearly within the present category of conceptual, including a "belief that the world is round or flat, that owls bring bad luck, that when tempering material is added to clay better pottery can be made, that man has a soul, or that all men are mortal"—White's own illustrations. The technological component can also be classified as conceptual with no difficulty, technology involving a people's concepts of tools, materials, processes, and methods. That some of these concepts involve the gods or the supernatural, and are faulty by modern standards, does not make them any the less concepts. The sentiments or attitudes, which White also describes as the subjective aspect of culture, clearly fall into the category of values, or valences attached to things. White's sociological component is part conceptual and part value. A rule that cross cousins may marry but parallel cousins may not, for example, involves the concepts of cross cousins, parallel cousins, and marriage, and a value attached to each.

Honigmann states that "Culture refers to the activities, thoughts and feelings, and artifacts which man acquires as a member of society." (John J. Honigmann, *The World of Man* [New York: Harper Bros., 1959], p. 12, from Edward B. Tylor.) The activities certainly reflect concepts of doing things, and artifacts as the outward expression of concepts have already been discussed. "Thoughts" presumably refers to concepts, since concepts are apparently what we think with, while feelings are clearly values about things. The approaches of some other anthropologists have also been examined, and can similarly be reclassified as concepts and values. White himself leans in this direction when he says that ". . . every culture trait, or element, has both subjective and objective aspects; indeed the one implies and requires the other. An ax is indeed an object, with its locus outside the organism. But, as a culture trait, it is meaningless without an idea, a *conception* of its nature and use. It is inseparable, too, from an *attitude* or *sentiment*, with regard to its use." (White, *op. cit.*, p. 15. Emphasis added.) The present classification thus seems to be consistent with the psychological model of the present volume, without doing violence to conceptual schemes currently accepted by important anthropologists.

of a tree, you can both *perceive* the tree and the sun in a particular relation, even though the tree and the sun are themselves out of the line of
sight. But if both of you see a curved shadow across the moon, *you* may
perceive the sun, earth, and moon in the relation known as an eclipse,
while the primitive may perceive the moon hiding her face from the sin
of man. The difference lies not in the sensory signals, which are the same
for both, but in the decoding of those signals according to a different
system of concept referents for the word for "eclipse." If you feel a slight
sting in your hand as you touch a doorknob after walking across a wool
rug on a dry day, or see your hair rising to meet a comb, you "perceive"
a static electrical charge. The primitive perceives only a sting in the
finger or the rising of hair, since he has no concept of static electricity. In
short, you cannot perceive what goes on in the world around you except
through the lens of the set of concepts you have inherited from your
culture.

Nor can you tell your children what you have seen except through
the language of your culture, which language corresponds to the set of
concepts through which you perceive. With small exception, your child
cannot perceive what you cannot, unless he moves in a different culture,
as by studying in fields you do not know, or by living through a period
in which the culture itself has changed. This is the lesson long sensed and
partially expressed by the astute, which has been sharply confirmed only
in the past two decades or so by such studies as comparative linguistics,
psychology, neurology, and information theory.

Three major reservations soften, but do not invalidate, this generalization. First, every individual is able to examine many objects in great detail, and to have hundreds or thousands of experiences with them. A stool,
ax, tree, house, baby, or water—each is something about which his own
personal experience provides such detailed information that he can form
his own concepts. The only thing provided by the culture is the name,
and, in the case of artifacts, the pattern and the technique of making them.
But whenever the individual can personally observe only a small part of
some phenomenon, or can observe it so infrequently that he has little
opportunity to study it closely, the concept based on his own observation
is necessarily inadequate. For concepts of such things as thunder, weather,
astronomy, disease, growth, death, and the origins of the world, he must
depend on the concepts of his culture. Nevertheless, to the extent that the
individual has experiences with phenomena not common to his culture,
he can develop concepts about them. Unless these experiences are detailed and repeated, however, his concepts may remain fuzzy, and not
clearly expressible. Sometimes the concepts differ among cultures because
the natural environment itself is different. "Trees" and "ocean," for instance, have quite different meanings to the Samoan and to the Laplander.

Second, language is a technique for communicating concepts without
names by combining the signs for concepts *with* names. This implies that
the language *can* express concepts not embodied in its vocabulary. For

example, it is possible in English and other "advanced" languages to describe any concept that anthropologists have discovered in primitive languages. This fact seems to contradict the assertion that one's concepts and perceptions are confined mainly to those embodied in the language, and indicates that the concepts which can be expressed *by* a language are not confined to those *in* the language. This reservation is not as great as it might at first seem. Although advanced languages with large vocabularies may be able to express concepts of primitive languages, the reverse is not necessarily true. The Zulu would be almost completely unable to return from an education in the United States and tell his people, "I majored in economic theory," or "The number of filibusters has been hypothesized to vary directly with the degree of interparty disequilibrium at the polls." This does not mean that the man in the street in the United States would get much meaning from these sentences. But the ideas *can* be expressed succinctly in English, whereas it is doubtful that anything more than the haziest notion of them could be expressed in Zulu, even through a half-hour discourse.

It would similarly seem that the anthropologist who expresses concepts of the primitive society in his own language is not bound by the latter. But all we are saying is that the person who takes the trouble to learn the concepts of other cultures is no longer confined to his own, and this is true for both the Oxford professor who studies Zulu and the son of the Zulu chieftain who studies at Oxford. Even the anthropologist who wishes to communicate frequently about concepts of other cultures is likely either to borrow the words of that culture or to coin new ones, witness the presence in English of such words as taboo, berdache, Manitou, igloo, cross cousins, bride price, medicine man, and totem. When we say that a person's thinking, perception, and communication are bounded by his culture, we are referring in the strictest sense only to the person who learns only his own culture.

The third reservation is that concepts *do* change, both by the addition of new concepts and by the alteration of old ones. Many of these changes are thought of as scientific developments or discoveries. In due course, ideas which were once in the forefront of scientific knowledge become the common property of all—such as the roundness of the earth, the circulation of the blood, or the inferiority complex. Whether one is impressed more by the phenomenal advances of man since his early days, or by the almost incredible slowness with which new ideas accrue, is a matter of individual taste. The important thing is that additions and reformulations do take place, and that it is precisely the ability of culture to *accumulate* that makes man distinct from all other animals.

A fascinating question arises from all this. Up to the present time, our thoughts have been slave to our culture, particularly its language, although many men of the arts, sciences, and letters have always been less bound than the general population. Knowledge of anything has nearly always made us better able to control and use it to our advantage. To repeat the language of an earlier chapter, we now recognize that concepts are not right or wrong, but merely more or less useful. This is another way of saying that some concepts contain more information than others, in the sense indicated earlier that the Copernican system of astronomy contains more information about more things than does the Ptolemaic, and that classifying whales and porpoises as mammals contains more biological information than classifying them as fish. The question now arises whether our understanding of our dependence on conceptualizations will significantly increase our ability to formulate better ones. In one sense it should: a forthright acknowledgment that the criteria of a new concept are usefulness and information content, not "correctness," should open the way for greater willingness to experiment with new formulations. Since the present volume is written in the "new spirit," it should provide some test as to whether this approach is more fruitful.

No revolutionary transformation may result, however, from this relatively new insight. Each of the thousands of scientific discoveries to date does provide a reconceptualization. Whether a new conceptualization is originally formulated in the "new" or the "old" spirit, its usefulness must still be tested by experience and experiment. This testing deals mainly with internal and external consistency, and proceeds along established lines known as the scientific method. In short, this approach may bring a greater willingness to *try* new concepts, and may produce a frightful mess if every Ph.D. candidate tries to get into the act. But there is no reason at this point to expect that it will facilitate the testing of new concepts.

New concepts with revolutionary effects have been introduced from time to time, some involving information concepts, some artifacts, and some sociofacts. Each changed the world in important and permanent ways, as in the discoveries of fire-making, the wheel, writing, trigonometry, monarchy, printing, Copernican astronomy, civil liberties, or atomic structure. Their effects are revolutionary because they do not stand alone. The revolutionary information concept is the basis for reconceptualizing whole areas of previous concepts, and the revolutionary artifact or sociofact makes a whole series of interconnected behavior possible which previously was out of the question.

To an important degree the set of concepts in any culture is self-validating. Because people cannot clearly perceive things which do not conform to existing concepts, they receive little feedback of other information with which to evaluate the usefulness of existing concepts. One reason culture is so stable is that it contains this built-in mechanism of self-preservation.

Another aspect of language should be mentioned, though it is too complex for full discussion here. A message puts together signs for several concepts in a new relation. Since the syntax of a language is the set of rules for relating signs, in some part it also provides the rules for relating concepts. Further, much of our thinking is done with words, often in sentence form. To a degree currently subject to much dispute, the syntax may therefore modify, control, and/or reflect the logic of the people who use it. It is also possible that certain notions of causation and of deductive inference are reflected in or modified by lexical syntax.

Because the concepts held by a society are expressed in its language, the language itself may seem to be a key factor in the level of understanding. Much emphasis has been put on this factor by such authorities as Edward A. Sapir and Benjamin Lee Whorf, particularly the latter. Now it is certainly true that the absence of an important word in a language, or the presence of one whose referent is confusing or unmanageable, may inhibit thinking. The time sense of the Hopi, for example, may be vague because their language contains only three tenses: past, present, and generalized.[6] And it seems almost unquestionable that language is the main vehicle of the culture for perpetuating the existing set of concepts. The language may make it less likely that persons in a society will observe, think about, or formulate new concepts. But as between the two, it seems that the degree of understanding in a given society is limited by the state of development of its concepts, rather than by its language. It is also possible that the widespread tendency to give noun form to words whose referents are actions does much to muddy thinking—even among the reasonably sophisticated and intellectual. The use of the word "mind" when we are speaking of the functioning of the brain, or our customary references to "beauty" or "ugliness" instead of to pleasurable or unpleasurable responses are instances of this sort we have already mentioned.

Science, magic, and religion are related to and partially expressed in language, and much that is said here about language applies to them. They also contain other ingredients, however, and the main discussion of them will therefore be deferred till later in the chapter.

Nonlinguistic Concepts

As the process of expressing an internal concept in an external medium, symboling is not confined to language. As we are using the term, it includes artifacts, sociofacts, conceptualized skills, and possible other expressions of concepts.

To start with skills, although a given individual may initially learn how to make pottery by imitation, and use motor skills almost exclusively, in due time most persons will conceptualize the skill. They will do this when called on to teach it to someone else, if not earlier. At this point they will have to think that "first you mix the clay to a smooth, workable consistency, then you put it on the wheel," and so forth. Weaving, basket making, and other crafts are things that people not only *do*, but are capable of conceptualizing and explaining. In short, people can form an information concept of a motor concept.

To make an artifact is not only a skill, conceptualized or imitative; it is also an overt manifestation of a concept in the head of its maker. As the

---

[6] Honigmann, *op. cit.*, p. 549.

work progresses the craftsman continuously receives feedbacks of information by observing his product. These are compared with the concept in his head, and transformations are made in the product until it conforms, within practical limits, to the concept. Animals other than man can similarly produce artifacts to match a pre-existing concept, such as the nest of the bird or beaver or the hive of the bee. But their artifacts reproduce biologically inherited concepts, not learned ones. The motor concepts which constitute the skill of lower animals are also apparently inherited.

In connection with communication, we observed the widespread tendency of human beings to express themselves in art forms. As a reflection of this tendency, we find extensive and elaborate decoration on many artifacts. The general style of decoration reflects the culture of the artisan, be it Navajo, Inca, Ming, Alsatian, or Pennsylvania Dutch. But unless it is done for some ceremonial purpose which prescribes a rigid, invariable pattern, the decoration is likely to show individual variations which reflect the imagination and preferences of the craftsman.

Advanced complex societies show wider variations in both the basic patterns and the decorations of their artifacts, because of the wider variety of available materials and techniques, as well as the more diverse skills and subcultural groups. Whereas the primitive society may have all dwellings built to a single basic style, the advanced one may have several dozen basic styles, with hundreds of distinctive variations, while larger and more complex commercial and industrial buildings are designed as discrete units for particular purposes.

Sociofacts are the remaining major item of content of the culture. In a given society the family consists of parents and children, while in another it includes uncles, aunts, cousins, and grandparents. The husband may pay a price for his bride or receive a dowry; the wife may leave her family to join the husband's, or the reverse. A man may be expected to marry his brother's widow, and the child may have to go through puberty rites at the age of fourteen. Social decisions may be made by vote, a council of elders, a parliament, a single king or chief. Only men may be expected to work in the fields, only women, or both. The division of labor between the sexes is usually rationalized, on such grounds as that women do not have the strength and bravery for hunting, or that men lack the patience for weaving. One society may have clearly defined hereditary classes while another has much social mobility between classes. These are the sociofacts which make up an important part of the body of a culture, and in which the seemingly limitless differences do much to distinguish one society from another.

THE CONTENT OF CULTURE:
MOTIVES AND VALUES

The second half of man's learning process is that positive or negative valences are attached to many of his concepts. We have motives to do or not to do certain things, to approach or avoid them. We have likes and dislikes. Some things are rewarding, or reinforcing, and others are punishing, or extinguishing. All these are different ways of saying the same thing, which can also be expressed by saying that man has motives, or values. The nature and operation of primary and secondary reinforcers were outlined in Chapters 5 and 6, and need not be reviewed here. Nor need the precise meaning of value, which will be defined in Chapter 14.

The point of this section is that man acquires not only most of his conceptualizations from his fellow men, but also most of his motives and senses of right and wrong. These are the second major aspect of culture. Since we are speaking of learned values only, the culture, as such, is concerned only with secondary motives.

Perhaps most compelling, at a very early age we acquire a powerful generalized secondary reinforcer in the approval of others. Thereafter we tend to approve what those around us approve, and to disapprove what they disapprove. Otherwise we lose their approval of *us*. The second main mechanism is that valences are already attached to many of the concepts we learn. The Godless Russians, the thieving east-enders, and the self-reliant pioneers are phrases which introduce us to particular groups of people—and are hardly neutral in feeling. Signs of disgust or horror accompany the mention of certain habits of dress, combinations of colors, types of haircut, accents, religious belief, or food, while signs of admiration, pleasure, and approval accompany others. Even though one has had no personal experience with them, one can learn deeply to fear mice or snakes, or yearn for filet mignon or a cashmere coat.

As with concepts, values differ among subcultures as well as major cultures. Even if he never examines the matters himself, the person who frequents the Chamber of Commerce will probably approve of laws restricting labor unions and disapprove of steeply progressive income taxes. The person who frequents union meetings will probably show the reverse set of values. Unless they are exposed to other subcultures by contact or reading, their respective children will hold the same sets of values.

The culture also defines in-groups and out-groups. The in-group(s) are those people who hold or are believed to hold the same basic sets of values as the main culture. The in-group to which one belongs is universally considered superior to all other groups, in manners, morals, wisdom, strength (at least inner strength), and kindliness. The rules of courtesy, kindness, law-abidingness, and general good behavior apply to the in-group. Out-groups, however, are conceived as displaying contrary traits, and hence as not deserving of courtesy or kindness. The Brotherhood of Man, as taught by some of the world's major religions, extends the in-group concept to include the whole human race.

Once these classifications and the attached valuations have been formed, they are remarkably immune to change, because of certain attached habits of biased feedback. If any member of the in-group is brave, strong, or intelligent, he is held up as a noble representative of the group. If any member is cowardly, weak, or stupid, the error is interpreted as his alone, which he somehow developed despite the good influences around him. Reverse interpretations are applied to out-groups. Despicable specimens are construed to be representative of the out-group, and admirable ones exceptions. The narrower one's personal experience, the greater is his tendency to make these distinctions. They may break down as the observant person becomes more familiar with different peoples and ages of man, though some individuals maintain their stereotypes despite a remarkable breadth of experience.

The culture defines the attitudes toward family size—whether the large family is to be desired or avoided. As will be seen below, factors outside the system may help determine whether the culture itself will favor large or small families. The culture strongly influences individual behavior at any moment in history. The culture will specify whether great freedom for children (permissiveness) or strong early discipline is the desired pattern, and whether love or fear of father is the appropriate attitude. The culture will determine whether old people are to be revered as wise counsellors, or deemed an intolerable drain on the food supply, to be driven out so the more vigorous can live. The culture may teach that vigor, self-assertiveness, and excellence in sports are the prime virtues of manhood; or it may deem self-assertion presumptuous, and grant approval to the quiet, cooperative, and helpful.[7] One culture may teach that hard work, self-denial, and asceticism are the highest virtues, while another may decry such values, teaching that the maximum enjoyment of each passing moment is the highest goal. Personal acquisitiveness is applauded in one culture and scorned in another. Whether life should be tense or relaxed, present-oriented or future-oriented, gentle or bellicose, are all matters that cannot be scientifically determined—though bellicose attitudes, acceptance of discipline, and the desire for physical toughness and bravery may show objective superiority if two societies engage in contests of military strength. They are values which, for the most part, each person adopts from the society around him, and passes on to his children. For reasons to be seen in more detail in the next chapter, some persons will resist the norms of the culture, but most will accept them and conform.

A study of anthropology is perhaps the only way to get a really satisfactory sense of the diversity among peoples, and we will try to provide a taste by quoting from a noted anthropologist.[8]

Let us consider a few areas of behavior. Take food habits for example. Man is one but his tastes vary enormously. A food loathed by one people may be a delicacy to another. Many Chinese cannot bear the thought of eating cheese,

---

[7] In this connection, one might observe the contrast between the Arapesh and the Mundugumor societies, as described in Margaret Mead's *Sex and Temperament* (New York: William Morrow & Co., 1935); also available in paper—Mentor Books.

[8] Leslie A. White, *The Science of Culture* (New York: Farrar, Straus & Company, Inc., copyright 1949 by Leslie A. White), pp. 152–55. Quoted by permission, with footnotes of the original omitted.

whereas most Europeans are very fond of it, and the choicest cheeses are often those with an odor of putrefaction or ordure. Neither do the Chinese like milk—even Grade A. Some tribes will not eat chicken or eggs. Others will eat eggs but prefer rotten eggs to fresh ones. The choicest porterhouse steak has no charms for the Hindu, nor baked ham or pork chops for the Jew. We have an aversion for worms and insects as food but many peoples eat them as delicacies. The Navajos will not eat fish. We will not eat dogs. The eating of human flesh is regarded with extreme revulsion by some peoples; to others it is the feast supreme. It would be hard indeed to name an edible substance that is regarded everywhere as food. The aversions and loathings likewise vary. What then can we attribute to "human nature?" Virtually nothing. What a people likes or loathes is not determined by the innate attractions and repulsions of the human organism. On the contrary the preferences and aversions are produced within the human organism by a culture acting upon it from the outside. Why cultures vary in this respect is another matter; we shall turn to it later on.

Is it human nature to kiss a loved one? If it were, then the practice would be universal. But it is not. There are peoples who do not kiss at all. Some rub noses. Others merely sniff the back of the neck of children. And in some societies a parent or elder relative will spit in the face of a child; saliva is here regarded as a magical substance and this act is therefore a sort of blessing. Among some peoples adult males kiss each other. I once witnessed greetings between men in one of the isolated valleys of the Caucasus mountains. They kissed each other fervently, pushing aside a thick growth of whiskers to reach the lips. Other peoples regard kissing among adult males as unmanly. Where does human nature enter this picture? It does not enter at all. The attitude toward kissing as well as its practice is not determined by innate desires of the human organism. If this were so, kissing behavior would be uniform throughout the world as the organism is uniform. But this is not the case. Behavior varies because cultures differ. You will do, or taboo, what your culture calls for.

Human behavior varies widely at other points. Sexual jealousy is so powerful and so poignant in some societies that to doubt that it is a simple and direct expression of human nature might seem almost absurd. It is "just natural" for a lover to be jealous of a rival. If a man kills the "seducer" of his wife, a jury of his peers may let him go scot free; it was only natural that he should do this, they observe. Yet, we find societies, like the Eskimo, where wives are loaned to guests as a part of hospitality. And Dr. Margaret Mead reports that the Samoans simply cannot understand jealousy among lovers, and find our sentiments in this respect incredible or preposterous.

In some groups premarital sexual intercourse is not only permitted to girls but the practice forms an integral part of the routine of courtship. Out of these intimacies come an acquaintance, a sympathy, and an understanding that make for an enduring marriage. In other groups, brides may be subjected to chastity tests and killed if they fail to pass them. The unmarried mother is stigmatized in some societies, taken for granted in others. Attitude toward homosexuality varies likewise; in some groups it is a mark of shame and degradation, in others it is recognized and accepted. Some societies recognize and give status to a third, or intermediate, sex—the *berdache*, transvestite—in addition to man and woman. A man must avoid his mother-in-law assiduously in some societies; he must not speak to her or allow himself in her presence. In other tribes, a man must have no social intercourse with his sister. Some peoples regard polygamy with aversion, even horror. To marry one's deceased wife's unmarried sister is a crime in some societies, a sacred obligation in others.

In none of these instances can we explain custom or institution in terms of the innate desires, sentiments, and aversions of the people concerned. It is not one set of sentiments and desires that produces monogamy here, another set polygamy there. It is the other way around; it is the institution that determines the sentiments and behavior. If you are born into a polygamous culture you will think, feel and behave polygamously. If, however, you are born into a Puritan New England culture you will look upon polygamy with marked disapproval.

White then adds a note on conscience. Conscience is popularly regarded as an inner voice, inborn or vouchsafed from On High, which tells us the difference between right and wrong. The study of culture suggests a different view. "Right and wrong are matters of sociocultural genesis; they are originated by social systems, not by individual biological organisms." "Actually, . . . this still small voice of conscience is but the voice of the tribe or group speaking . . . from within.[9] That some persons with cross-cultural experience, outlaws from a culture, or persons with highly atypical experiences may not accept the norm of their group (perhaps even forming a society of one) does not deny the broad validity of this observation.

MAGIC, SCIENCE, AND RELIGION

Along with other aspects of a culture, science and religion are important, and, in primitive cultures, so is magic. Every known society, however primitive or advanced, contains some kind of religion, philosophy, and notion of the supernatural.[10] (We are, of course, speaking of major cultures, and not of a subculture consisting solely of atheists.) These are large topics. Only a brief discussion is possible here, which will be confined mainly to fitting these topics into the present conceptual scheme.

Despite some impressions to the contrary, it would seem that even the most savage and primitive societies we know have some information of the sort we could classify as scientific.[11] They know the relation between absence of rain and the wilting of plants, between the planting of seeds and the subsequent appearance of young shoots, or between overeating and feeling sick. Some have a fairly elaborate science of boat building, and are accurately aware of the relations between such factors as width, outriggers, and stability.[12] Such knowledge is part of the conceptual part of the content of culture.

In Malinowski's view, magic and religion are sharply separated, and we will follow that distinction here. Magic is essentially the extension of

[9] *Ibid.*, pp. 156, 157.

[10] Ruth Benedict, "Religion," Chapter XIV in Franz Boas and Others, *General Anthropology* (New York: D. C. Heath & Co., 1938), p. 628.

[11] Bronislaw Malinowski, *Magic, Science and Religion* (Glencoe, Ill.: The Free Press, 1948), p. 1. Malinowski was much influenced by James G. Frazer's monumental, *The Golden Bough* (London, MacMillan & Co. Ltd., 1911).

[12] *Ibid.*, pp. 11, 12, 16.

"science" into the realm where cause-effect relations are not clearly observable or testable. It is easy enough to observe the connection between heavy rain and swollen streams, and to conceive rain as the cause of floods. It is also relatively easy to establish a similar "scientific" relation between dark clouds and rain. But in the absence of weather balloons, radar, and the detailed comparison of humidities, temperatures, and the related densities and velocities of air, it is not easy for the primitive to form concepts of what causes clouds. And while he can easily note the relation between planting the seeds and the later arrival of plants, he cannot so easily determine the causes of germination rates or fertility. Since hypotheses about cloud formation and fertility are not subject to checking by primitive man, almost any hypothesis seems tenable. It is thus possible to retain a hypothesis that rain clouds are caused by a ceremonial dance, or that fertility is related to sleeping under a tilted papaya tree at the proper phase of the moon in the proper curled-up position.

In primitive magic a clear cause-effect relation is always sensed, and magical ceremonies or actions are engaged in for clear instrumental purposes.[13] If the magic does not work, some defect is present, such as the wrong tilt to the papaya tree, the wrong phase of the moon, or the wrong curl to the sleeping position. Or some counter-magic may have been instituted somewhere. To the primitive, magic cannot fail if everything is done right, just as to modern man the motor cannot fail to run if the plugs, valves, ignition, and so on are all just right. Nor (and this is perhaps a closer modern analogy to magic) can the television set fail to work if everything is properly adjusted. As Malinowski views magic, we can include it with science in the present framework under the heading of the conceptual content of culture. The primitive is not confused as between the things we refer to as his science and his magic.[14] If the magic works through the propitiation of gods, demons, or sprites, rather than through totally impersonal supernatural forces, these beings will or must respond as desired if the proper ceremony is performed. Magic is thus conceived as a precise science to its believers, even if they do not know or cannot control all its variables.

By contrast, religion is not an instrumental act, but is its own reward or justification. Religious ceremonies are a body of self-contained acts, which are themselves the fulfillment of their purpose, and are not directed toward any subsequent event.[15] They are expressive of sentiments, values, and attitudes. Some themselves create an inner set of sensations, whether of reverence, ecstasy, sensualism, stupor, hypnotic trance, or exhaustion. Some religious ceremonies are designed to transmute, soften, or enhance emotions or feelings already present for other reasons, such as death, marriage, coming of age, or the recognition of human impotence. Per-

---

13 *Ibid.*, p. 21.

14 *Ibid.*, pp. 11–12.

15 *Ibid.*, pp. 21, 68.

haps because death of a loved one brings the most intense feelings in its mixture of grief, love, horror, loneliness, helplessness, and awareness of one's own brief tenure, religion is grasped most strongly at this point. In these and other ways, religion is a key ingredient of the motivational and value content of culture.

Although in their major aspects science and magic fall in the conceptual area of culture, and religion within the motivational, these things, like most others, are not pure specimens. Science and magic also have their motivational aspects, whether in the urge to know, the thrill of discovery, or the awe of magical rites. Religion also has its conceptual aspects in the nature of God or gods, the structure of the church, or the nature and sources of religious authority. Many religions include a cosmology or ethnology to explain the origins and history of the world or the group. These are partly conceptual. But they also typically attribute a purpose to the world, to the human race, or to the group, and thus include important value or motivational components. Many religions also prescribe a set of ethics and morals. Although they are analytically distinct, in the study of culture as in all other aspects of human behavior, motives are attached to concepts, and we conceptualize and rationalize our motives.

When primitive man fills the world with gods, demons, spirits, gnomes, or disembodied will he is often thought by more "enlightened" men to show great flights of fancy. On the contrary, for his level of information he is engaging in precisely the same kind of psychological behavior all of us display. In the absence of clear reason to discriminate, he generalizes the concepts he knows to include or "explain" those he cannot closely observe. Given the widespread observations of motivated behavior in himself, his friends, and the animals all about him, he generalizes this concept to explain all kinds of "behaving" things, such as the wind, rain, waterfall, thunder, winter and summer, the rising and setting sun, and the growth of plants. The beings which inhabit these things must, of course, be appropriately modified so that they can live in the fire, water, or earth, and endure forever.

Psychologically and neurologically, there is no reason to assume that concepts about things religious differ from those about things scientific. Spirits and gods are no less conceptualizations of incoming information than are phlogiston, ether, atoms, or gravity. As White observes, "Spirits or gods are conceptual expressions of significant attributes of the world that man lives in."[16]

When forces are conceptualized as personified demons or gods, however, they tend to bring different behavior from that which accompanies impersonalized concepts. First, they may bring such responses as fear, love, awe, and loyalty, which are not appropriate to obviously inanimate

---

[16] Leslie A. White, *The Evolution of Culture* (New York: McGraw Hill Book Co., Inc., 1959), p. 358.

things. Second, personalized entities may be pleased or angry, and man must therefore be careful not to offend them. Since the feedback of their moods is not widely observable, there can arise a group of specialists, the priests, who are experts in discerning these things, and who can therefore prescribe what pleases or displeases the gods. Third, the gods and demons would presumably be offended if man did not believe in them, and would punish man for disbelief. There thus exists a strong bias toward continuing to accept such conceptualizations, even in the face of evidence which would otherwise cause rejection. Even when the concepts of gods become highly refined, the odds are strongly in favor of belief, as can be seen from a payoff matrix of the situation.[17] Assume that the gods will reward and punish if they exist, but will, of course, do nothing if they do not. The payoffs of belief and disbeliefs are then as follows, assuming the extreme reward and punishment of eternal salvation or

	Belief	Disbelief
Right	Eternal Salvation	Nothing
Wrong	Nothing	Eternal Damnation

damnation. If you believe and are right, you gain eternal salvation, whereas if you believe and are wrong, you lose nothing (so far as your relation with the gods is concerned). If you disbelieve and are right, you gain nothing (from the gods), but if you disbelieve and are wrong, you face eternal damnation. Given this payoff, even the highly rational, and certainly the intuitive person, will be disposed in favor of belief. The payoff here illustrated deals solely with the relation to the gods. If the priests or church in charge of a particular religion also prescribe behavior, attitudes, and social structures, and if accepting the beliefs is inescapably tied to accepting these other things, the payoff matrix must be modified to include these important, and highly realistic, ingredients. The main point seems valid, however, that a personalized concept has greater survival value in the face of conflicting concepts than an impersonal one.

Fourth, personalized and nonpersonalized concepts have been institutionalized differently. Originally both the priests and the magicians had access to occult knowledge not available except to the initiated, and both dealt in some degree with personalized forces in the world. In due time the magicians gave way to the scientists, who dealt with impersonal forces, while the priests remained the sole group dealing with personalized ones. Because science is open to all, guided by reason and corrected by observation,[18] and because it was therefore able to challenge directly the area formerly held by the magicians, the scientists and magicians have been relatively unable to hold a monopoly on their authority.

---

[17] See Chapter 16 for further discussion of the payoff matrix.
[18] Malinowski, *op. cit.*, p. 3.

Through much of human history the priests have claimed a monopoly on communication with the gods, both in speaking to and receiving feedback from them. Since the nonpriest has no such communication, he has little opportunity to check what the priest says against his own observations. As between the two, it is therefore easier for the priests than the scientists to maintain a tight monopoly. Viewed in perspective, the Renaissance in a sense asserted each man's freedom to be his own scientist, after which the Protestant Reformation asserted his freedom to be his own priest. Perhaps the subsequent political revolutions which sought to establish democracy were attempts to assert each man's freedom to be his own king. In the long view, despite cyclical variations, there has been a persistent and, in total, a very large shift from personified and supernatural to nonpersonified and "natural" conceptualizations of things—a steady decline in the area of specialization of the priests and an increase in that of the scientists.[19]

CULTURAL CHANGE: CULTURE AS A SYSTEM, AGAIN

Some cultures remain without noticeable change for centuries, while other cultures, or the same cultures at other times, change at breakneck pace. Why? We can deal with this question by returning to the system of culture.

The system described at the beginning of the chapter contains two variables: (1) the concepts and values in the individual nervous system, and (2) the behavior, artifacts, norms, and so forth which overtly manifest those concepts and values. Anything except these two ingredients falls outside the system, in the environment.

According to the general notions of systems, a system closed to its environment will reach an equilibrium. It will retain that equilibrium (or return to it after slight dislocations) unless (1) a change impinges on the system from its environment (i.e., the system undergoes a change in parameters), or (2) some internal change occurs in one or more of the variables, as by growth, decay, or some systematic change in the functional relationship. A culture can therefore remain static (1) if it is closed, or if its environment does not change, and (2) if no internal changes occur in the system. A cultural system in turn can remain closed if (1) it has no contact with other cultures and (2) there is no change in its physical environment, or in the culture's relation to that environment. A change in physical environment could include a change in climate, an increase in the fish population, a devastating forest fire, or the movement of a glacier. A change in the relation of the culture to its environment could include a rise in the population relative to natural resources, or the depletion of resources by the people. The conditions for a static culture are therefore absence of contact with other cultures, unchanging physical environment, no exhaustion of natural resources, and

---

[19] Titiev, *op. cit.*, pp. 408–9.

no significant change of population relative to those resources—along with the absence of internal change.

Even a closed culture, however, can undergo an evolutionary internal change, through discovery, invention, and certain psychological processes. Discoveries and inventions tend to be cumulative, so that a closed system can change progressively over time—the essence of human culture. As to psychological processes, much information in primitive societies (and only primitive ones are closed) is stored in memories and is transmitted by word of mouth. Changes arise over the years through faulty memory and communication. Further, since there are no written records, it is extremely difficult to *know* whether change occurs or not. Detailed memorization of chants, stories, and rituals do make it possible, however, for some aspects of the culture to remain remarkably constant.

By contrast, change will be most marked in the open culture. Changes in physical environment are usually slow, and so are the cultural changes they induce. The most significant cultural changes occur when markedly different societies come into contact or merge.

The merger, *fusion*, or assimilation of societies has occurred many times, as when the "barbarians" from the north merged with the inhabitants of the Greek peninsula, the Norman invaders were assimilated into English society, dozens of nationality groups were merged in the United States, and the Chinese absorbed numerous groups of invaders over the centuries. Other occasions have witnessed the *diffusion* of cultural traits without mergers of populations, as when the Phoenicians brought back ideas from their far-roving merchant ships, and Japan has been Westernized during the past century. Smaller scale contacts often bring changes in parts of a culture, as when the natives around a military base or industrial installation make shoes from discarded truck tires and other artifacts from oil drums. When an advanced culture meets a primitive one it seldom borrows much of the latter's science. But it may make use of its art forms, games, foods, or even some drugs.

The difference between fusion and diffusion can be shown diagrammatically in the system of culture. We can start with a Society A and its Body of Culture A, as in Figure 12-2-a. At the moment of *fusion* we can imagine Society B entering from the environment and taking its place beside A, as in Figure 12-2-b. The body of culture is still labeled A, since that of B has not yet made itself felt. By contrast, at the moment of *diffusion* (if we can imagine it as occurring suddenly) The Body of Culture B has entered the system from the environment, as in Figure 12-2-c, and has taken its place beside Culture A. Whichever occurs, because of the system interaction a single society and culture will emerge, both of which may be labelled A-B, as in Figure 12-2-d, unless some barriers to interchange keep the two subsocieties sufficiently out of contact. Figure 12-2-d does not imply that the outcomes of fusion and diffusion are identical, but merely that the end result of either will be a society *and* a culture, both of which will include the elements of both A and B. Fusion

Figure 12-2

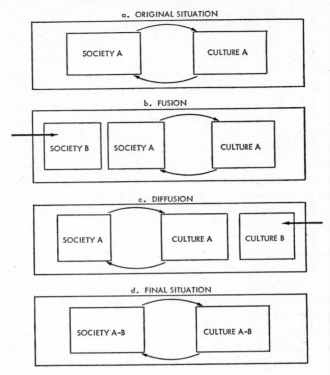

and diffusion, of course, can occur simultaneously, and more than two cultures or societies can be involved.

Advanced societies usually have continuous and systematic intercourse in ideas about art, literature, music, and science, and to this extent behave more like a single system of culture than a number of separate ones. It does not matter, however, whether two cultures were previously at the same or different levels, primitive or advanced; when two come into contact, each gains new ideas.

More important, intercultural contact generates ideas not previously present in *either* culture, and is more than mere addition. This follows from the psychological analysis which construes all complex concepts as conjunctions of two or more other concepts. When cultures meet, many persons learn two conceptualizations of the same phenomena, from which they form new concepts incorporating the most useful features of both. Throughout history, the fusion or diffusion of cultural streams has provided the occasion for great strides in art and science, and White defines a *genius* as a "human organism in which an important synthesis of cultural elements has taken place."[20]

---

[20] White, *op. cit.*, p. 226.

As to the evolutionary changes which occur within a closed system of culture, White makes an impressive argument that this evolution can be traced back to the earliest forms of life. He regards it as the successive organization of larger and larger amounts of energy under the control of the organism, in what the physicist would call negative entropy.[21] To White's emphasis on the increase in energy it would seem that we should add the increase in information, the formula for which suggests that it may be another form of negative entropy.[22] It is important not only to have energy at our disposal, but also to control the timing and direction of its release. The controls are matters of information. We also might speculate that the evolutionary process at the level of both biology and culture is essentially a reverse entropic process, and that information is one form of organized energy used as the cybernetic governor to control much larger amounts of energy in the effective stages of human behavior.

Written records of the Egyptians date to about 3000 B.C. and those of the Sumerians go even earlier, which means that for more than 5,000 years the human race has deliberately accumulated information in writing. In addition to mere accumulation, the speed of acquiring new information and reconceptualizing old is increased by periodic reappraisals of its existing state, by discerning gaps in knowledge, and by consciously searching for the means to fill them. Interdisciplinary research is a deliberate technique for fusing the streams of different scientific subcultures in the hope that new and more useful concepts will emerge. We are just opening the uses of electronic computers and data processors. It is conceivable that these machines can be programmed to generate new concepts by the millions, and to test each against certain criteria. Because computers are now being designed which can perform operations in billionths of a second, these machines may generate and test in hours or days concepts which would otherwise require decades to examine. They might also systematically generate and test *all possible* concepts within a given range of types, whereas normal mental processes must depend heavily on chance combinations of elements.

Considering that symboling, which is an information process, is widely considered the heart of culture, and that the use of energy depends on

---

[21] Leslie A. White, *The Evolution of Culture, op. cit.*, chap. 2, "Energy and Tools," and *passim*. The idea of entropy is not easy to state briefly for the layman, but for the present purpose "disorder" and "randomness" are good first approximation synonyms. A tree is a highly ordered, or nonentropic, state of matter. But when it dies and decays into a pile of uniform soil it is much more entropic. When a sheet of hot metal is placed in contact with a cold one there is an increase in entropy as the heat moves from one to the other until both are the same temperature. The randomness of entropy is in contrast to the differentiation of parts or states in an ordered system. Negative entropy is movement in the direction of increased order or differentiation, away from the random, disordered, homogeneity of the state of entropy.

[22] Colin Cherry, *On Human Communication* (New York: John Wiley & Sons, 1957), pp. 212–16.

prior information about the nature and harnessing of energy, the development of information processes should perhaps be considered *the* most important component of cultural evolution. If so, then such inventions as speech, writing, printing, and electronic data processing are the key points in the development of human culture. The ability to store and transmit large quantities of information by telephone, radio, film, or magnetic tape; the ability to reduce all information to the same elemental unit, the bit; and the ability to relate and compare information at extremely high speeds suggests that we are on the threshold of a new era in which new information can be acquired, processed, and digested at a rate inconceivable only a decade or two ago. If so, our culture henceforth may also change at an unprecedented rate, particularly if developments in the field of energy keep pace with those in information, which seems probable.

This approach parallels that mentioned in Chapter 11, where we noted a tendency of musicians to think in terms of all possible sounds. Painters, philosophers, linguists, and modern psychologists similarly think in terms of all possible colors and shapes, logics, languages, and concepts and motives, respectively. It is similarly possible to stop thinking solely of actual, historical cultures, and to think instead of all possible cultures. It is conceivable that we might select from among these the type that seems most desirable, and attempt to mold society toward it. But the evolution of a culture includes changes in motives and attitudes toward things, not only changes of concepts. This important fact, taken in conjunction with certain difficulties about the processes of making social decisions (to be examined in later chapters) makes it highly debatable whether social policy can be oriented around such an approach. The approach might nevertheless be highly useful for diagnosing and classifying the traits of various cultures.

Chapter 13

PERSONALITY

OUT OF the approximately three billion people on earth, no two are precisely alike, although "identical" twins can be remarkably similar. They differ in such obvious traits as shape, size, age, race, and sex. More important for our purposes, they also differ in behavior. If four persons from different cultures were offered a raw fish head to eat, eyes wide and glistening, one might rub his hands in glee, one might remark that he is not *that* hungry, one might beat a hasty retreat, and a fourth might fall trembling to his knees and pray. Within the same culture, some persons like their beds soft and others hard, some vote Republican and some Democratic, some never work if they can avoid it and some seem to work all the time. In these and thousands of other ways different persons react differently to similar situations.

The total set of behavior patterns which characterize a particular person will be referred to as his *personality*.[1] Appearance, age, sex, race, or other physical traits are not part of personality, as such. Appearance, however, is partly controlled by behavior, as in the case of grooming and selecting clothes. Physical traits will also affect personality, as we shall see. Although we will not explicitly include them in the definition, a person's whole set of concepts and motives is implicit in the definition, since his behavior is based upon them.

Personality is the focal point for the interaction of social forces with biological and psychological. The preceding chapters on psychology outlined some of the major processes by which man learns, these processes being inherent in his biological system, supplemented by what he learns about how to learn. But most of the typically human things man learns come from his culture. His learned behavior, which is the most important part of his personality, then acts back upon and is part of the culture, as we have seen in the preceding chapter. The closeness of this interaction led Ruth Benedict to say, "Cultures . . . are individual psy-

---

[1] Richard T. LaPiere and Paul R. Farnsworth in their *Social Psychology* (New York: McGraw-Hill Book Co., Inc., 1942), p. 147, define personality as "the sum total of the acquired behaviors of a given human being." If "acquired" is taken to include the changes in behavior induced by changes in glandular and other somatic conditions, then that definition apparently coincides with the one used here.

chology thrown large upon the screen, given gigantic proportions and a long time span."[2]

We might add in reverse that personality is culture writ small. We might also say that culture is the personality of the group, or that personality is a subculture of one person—though the statement is figurative only, "culture" and "personality" referring by definition to groups and individuals, respectively. We might also say that personality bears the same kind of relation to the individual that culture bears to the society.

In the chapters on psychology we observed the influence of psychological *processes* of learning, and in the chapter on culture we observed the influence of the culture on the *content* of learning. But at no time did we focus attention on the totality of the *combined* effects of both sets of forces in an individual. Having previously noted that behavior is the outcome of the interaction of concepts and motives, in personality we are interested in the *particular* effect of a *particular* set of concepts and motives in a *particular* person.

A gentle reminder: personality is not an entity, residing somewhere in the head or chest. In the sense used here, personality is not something one person has while another does not, and our habit of making nouns out of words which are essentially verbs is sometimes confusing. Personality is *behaving*, with particular emphasis on differences in behavior. To make an entity of it in the popular sense is something like giving the name "respiration" to fast breathing but no name to slow breathing, and then saying of the person who breathes rapidly that he "has respiration." Just as slow breathers also "have respiration," so do all persons have personality, which bears the same kind of relationship to the person as mind bears to brain, or operating bears to an automobile engine.

It has been said that in some respects each man's behavior is like that of *all* other men; in some respects it is like that of *some* others, and in still other respects it is like that of *no* others. The problem of personality is that of discovering why *one* particular person's set of behavior patterns is what it is, including both the similarities and differences between persons.

It has also been said that personality is indescribable. Terms such as warm, gay, phlegmatic, irrepressible, hidebound, and so on, as well as more poetic phrases such as "like a pure mountain stream," "ox-like," "like fire and rain, summer and winter, war and peace, all rolled into one," all give impressionistic pictures of personalities. But such characterizations provide only the vaguest information, if any, as to whether the subject is honest, well educated, tolerant of other races, interested in music, or even basically sane.

The reason why personality is indescribable is quickly seen if we refer back to the problem of language. We can describe things accurately

---

[2] Ruth Benedict, "Configurations of Culture in North America," *American Anthropologist*, No. 34, 1932, p. 24.

only with words with reasonably unequivocal meanings. To illustrate, let us assume that we can somehow reduce all human traits (such as intelligence, energy level, appetite, sense of humor, athletic ability, esthetic appreciation, etc.) to a bare dozen, and then assume that there are only ten possible different levels or degrees of each trait. Certainly this would represent a tremendously oversimplified picture of the myriad characteristics which make up the human personality. Yet ten different degrees of each of a dozen traits can be arranged in enough different combinations to make a trillion (10^{12}) different personality types. Even two different degrees (high or low) of each of twelve different personality traits would make over 4,000 (2^{12}) distinct personality types. Obviously we do not have, and have no intention of inventing 4,000 separate names for different types of personality, much less the trillion required to describe a relatively simplified classification system. Personality remains indescribable because we do not have a systematic scheme for classifying and naming personalities, and possibly never will. The usual technique for the layman is to refer to characters of history, literature, or common experience, thus designating a particular personality as Quixotic, Pickwickian, Job-like, Durocheresque, or "like Phil Philips down at the shop."

We also describe personality by traits. Allport and Odbert counted 17,953 trait names in English.[3] Although many are synonyms and short term states rather than permanent traits, the large number nevertheless illustrates the wide variety of aspects of personality.

THE STATE OF THE SCIENCE

There has been much argument whether there is, or ought to be, a science of personality. The question is thus far unanswered. Much of the crux of the argument is revealed in Brand's discussion of the definition of personality,[4] and revolves mainly around the question of whether an understanding of psychology automatically provides an understanding of personality. The problem is common to many fields of knowledge, as follows.

The operation of an internal combustion engine does not involve any principles not encompassed within the sciences of chemistry and physics. Yet the automobile engine does involve a *particular kind of relationship* of physical and chemical forces which do not arise within the sciences of chemistry and physics *as such*. It is also true that the reason why a particular red oak grows tall and straight while another is stunted and gnarled can be explained in biological terms. Yet the explanation of such individual differences requires that we organize biological knowledge, and relate it to other kinds of knowledge, in a particular sort of way.

---

[3] Gordon W. Allport and H. S. Odbert, "Trait Names: a Psychological Study," *Psychological Monographs,* Vol. 47, No. 211, 1936.

[4] Howard Brand (ed.), *The Study of Personality* (New York: John Wiley & Sons, 1954), pp. 1–27.

Here we would have to give attention to variations in soil conditions, moisture, wind, the density of other vegetation, and so on, the shape of an oak growing alone being different from one in a forest.

Similarly, all aspects of personality can be dealt with in psychological terms, and no one suggests that personality formation violates psychological principles—even if we do not yet know all the principles. It nevertheless remains true that to study personality requires a particular kind of grouping of psychological knowledge around a particular problem, while simultaneously relating psychological knowledge to other kinds of knowledge. On the basis of the previous discussion, it would seem inconceivable to study personality except in connection with culture. Yet it would not seem unreasonable to study *psychology* without culture— as was in fact done in Chapters 3 through 8. Whether personality constitutes a distinct science, we will not debate. We will simply note that certain kinds of generalizations arise from a study of personality, as such. While these may perhaps be properly regarded as psychological generalizations, they do not arise from any kind of study except that focused on personality.[5] In addition, the study of the *whole* individual, as the coordinated functioning of his myriad components, involves problems not encompassed by the separate study of the components. This is true of the study of individual differences in any field, but is accentuated by the fact that the individual person is a problem of much more concern than the individual oak, engine, or salt crystal.

If the study of personality is to be considered a science, it is an immature one. At the moment it has not yet accomplished the second major step of a science as described in Chapter 3, there being thus far no standard, widely accepted system of classifying personalities. Cattell has been experimenting for some years in an attempt to discover important regularities of groupings of personality traits, and he reports progress.[6] He organizes these into "surface traits," referring to such overtly observable characteristics as boldness, liveliness, egotism, curiosity, amorousness, and asceticism, with tests for measuring and distinguishing between degrees of each trait. Behind the surface traits in his system lie source traits, which he hopes will eventually provide the key to understanding the surface traits. The source traits include such items as ego strength versus proneness to neuroticism, dominance and submissiveness, and surgency versus desurgency. Using a modified Freudianism, Parsons and Bales trace personality development from the merest infant to adolescence and adulthood, providing a possible classification system for personalities based on the kinds of solutions the individual finds to crucial turning

---

[5] I am essentially accepting Brand's position here, when he says, "On purely logical grounds the general-behavior definitions of personality should be omitted because they define personality out of existence," (*Ibid.*, p. 9) though I would be more inclined to say that they define a *science* of personality out of existence.

[6] Raymond B. Cattell, *Personality and Motivation Structure and Measurement* (Yonkers: World Book Co., 1957).

points in personal development.[7] The Freudian-psychoanalytic approach also provides schemes for describing personality types, and some other systems are summarized briefly by Stagner.[8] It can hardly be said, however, that any uniform system of classifying personalities has yet been widely agreed upon by psychologists.

If and when such a classification system has been achieved, the presumed next step would be to seek the causes of various types of personality. The result of such study would be statements of the sort: "Experience sequence A leads to personality type X;" or "experience sequence B at development stage Q, when taken in conjunction with glandular balance K and family structure M produces personality type Y in 6 out of 10 cases." Whether meaningful statements of this sort will ever be possible cannot now be predicted, though in a less universal way this is the kind of thing Freud was attempting to do in relating adult personalities to supposedly crucial childhood experiences. At the moment psychologists would be delighted to be able to describe reliably the causes of any one personality trait, such as sense of humor or adaptability, or in many cases even to define these traits themselves precisely. For example, does a person who is always telling jokes but is offended by humor at his own expense have more of a sense of humor or less than one who seldom tells jokes, but can always see the humor in his own situation? Our trouble is again the huge number of variables in the human personality. Not only are there the many facets of the personality (Cattell lists twenty "surface traits"), but each in turn may have anywhere from two to a dozen or more dimensions within itself. Some persons are scrupulously honest with friends and neighbors but dishonest with corporations or foreigners, and some would not dream of misrepresentation in their personal relationships but freely write advertising copy containing gross distortions.

Nor is it possible to conduct carefully controlled experiments with whole human beings over a period of years. Even if we were willing to raise some children from birth to maturity under minutely controlled experimental conditions—which we are not—it still does not seem possible to provide different children with identical experiences in order to find if they would emit identical responses. If children were raised in complete isolation they would remain crude and ape-like, lacking all the things learned from the accumulated culture, and their behavior would tell us little about *human* personality. If two were raised together their environments would not be identical, since the human environment of A is B, and that of B is A, and A and B are themselves not identical. In any event, two persons raised without other human contact would still remain nonhuman savages. If we want them to be reasonably human, experimental subjects must develop among a variety of other persons. But

---

[7] Talcott Parsons and Robert F. Bales, *Family, Socialization and Interaction Process* (Glencoe, Ill.: The Free Press, 1955).

[8] Ross Stagner, *Psychology of Personality* (New York: McGraw-Hill Book Co., Inc., 1961), chaps. 7, 8.

if so, their environment ceases to be the carefully controlled one of the laboratory, and becomes instead the heterogeneous laboratory of real life.

Out of the relatively large and rather diffuse materials on personality, the following discussion will attempt to arrange some of the reasonably assured conclusions on a twofold basis.

We shall examine first those factors which make for similarity of personality, and then those which make for diversity, in the following framework. Imagine a dinner plate onto which we will pour a tablespoon of sugar in a fine stream from a height of about ten inches. The sugar will form a pile whose maximum height will be directly under the stream, but which will spread for some distance, at least a few grains being found in every major part of the plate. This represents the idea that in every major group of people, personalities tend to cluster around some main type, but that individuals differ from the main type in many directions, with fewer and fewer lying at points farther from the center. Without attempting to define which dimensions or how many dimensions are involved, we can observe that if all persons had identical personalities, all would be located in a tall thin pile directly over the center of the plate. By analogy we will examine personality by asking (1) what forces tend to bring all persons toward a common center point; and (2a) what forces place the centers of "piles" of persons at particular points other than the center; and (2b) what forces cause individuals to fall at points not the center of their own piles? The forces making for similarity and difference can also be thought of as centripetal and centrifugal, respectively. In statistical terminology they are forces of central tendency and forces of dispersion.

FORCES MAKING FOR SIMILAR PERSONALITIES

A statement that two personalities are similar does not mean that two similar *entities* exist. It is a shorthand way of saying that two persons behave similarly in their patterns of overall behavior. In examining forces making for similar personalities we are thus asking why people tend to behave alike.

Inheritance

First, the biological mechanisms of all human beings show great similarity. We are all born, grow physically for about twelve to twenty years, mature into the ability to procreate at about the age of twelve, become parents, go through certain other phases of the life cycle, and die. We all eat, breathe, sleep, excrete, and afford our bodies certain physical protection. These biological similarities give rise to certain common types of behavior. In these respects we also show similarities to other animals, whose life cycles show generally parallel ingredients.

Our basic psychological mechanisms are also highly similar. Although we are uncertain about what our primary reinforcers are, they are presumably the same for all peoples and ages. We all have the same set of senses, and our neural mechanisms for developing learned concepts and motives all work on the same principles.

Learned Behavior

We have seen that nearly all of a man's behavior which distinguishes him from the lower animals depends on the cultural accumulation of things learned by his ancestors and passed on to him. Within a given culture all new arrivals draw their concepts and motives from the common accumulated pool, and hence tend to be similar.

Further, all persons go through common experiences in early life. Each starts life absolutely dependent upon others. Each must learn gradually increasing independence, motor skills, concepts about the things around him, language, and a host of minor details. Very importantly, each must learn to conceptualize himself as an entity—to achieve the consciousness of self as distinct from others. Whether we learn many of these things independently; whether we go through an oral, anal, and phallic stage in the Freudian pattern; or whether our major patterns of behavior are learned by a sequence of binary fissions[9] is not answerable at the moment. Whatever the major stages are, there are certain kinds of experiences all infants apparently have in common, and certain kinds of things we all must learn.

To illustrate some almost inevitable similarities, and at the same time carry forward from Chapter 6 the discussion of the way in which a wide variety of behavior could be learned from a minimal list of primary reinforcers, let us trace the possible sequence of steps by which the infant learns the love relation. To begin with, the human being is capable of learning even before birth, the seven or eight month foetus having been made to develop a conditioned response to stimuli introduced through the abdominal wall of the mother.[10] All children possess the sucking reflex at birth, and the vast majority start using it very shortly thereafter. Since sucking is promptly and regularly associated with the satisfaction of hunger, which seems an almost inescapable primary reinformer, the act of sucking becomes an important secondary reinforcer, and will shortly be engaged in for its own sake. In less behaviorist and more Freudian language, the child is now said to have a sucking need.[11] Let us assume further that from prenatal experience, from association with early feeding, or from a possible inborn primary status, the feeling of softness and warmth is also a strong reinforcer. This "need" is found among monkeys

9 Parsons and Bales, *op. cit.*, mainly chap. II.

10 N. L. Munn, *The Evolution and Growth of Human Behavior* (Boston: Houghton Mifflin Co., 1955), p. 179.

11 It is reported that infants reared from birth on cup feeding do not develop a sucking need, which is the basis for referring to it here as a secondary reinforcer. See David C. McClelland's comments on a paper by A. H. Maslow in *Nebraska Symposium on Motivation, 1955,* p. 32.

as well as human beings, and is apparently a precondition for the more complex love response we are about to describe. Monkeys placed with a "mother" of soft cloth will return to it regularly for comfort and re-assurance, and the monkeys with such a mother behave in general like those with a real mother. But monkeys given a "mother" of wire and wood show no affection for it. They do not turn to it for security or reassurance, and show timidity and insecurity in other activities. Starting from the reinforcing quality of softness and warmth, or "comfort," we shall trace four successive stages of the development of a full love rela-tion between mother and child.

The infant's first stage is that of being loved. If the mother feels love toward the child, the child will receive comfort from her. Along lines outlined in Chapter 6, we will assume that some kind of reward center is stimulated by the receipt of these sensations. As a second step, since comfort is repeatedly received from the mother, the presence of the mother will become a conditioned stimulus which will set off at least part of the same rewarding response as does actual comfort. For this pur-pose it does not matter whether the mother is identified by appearance, voice, footsteps or other cue. Since recollections can also constitute a stimulus, at this point merely to think about the mother will be rewarding. When the mere thought of the mother brings these pleasurable responses, we will say that the child loves the mother.

In the third step the feeling of comfort is not merely experienced, but is also conceptualized. At this point the thought of the *feeling* (not merely of the mother) is rewarding, in part bringing on the feeling itself. At this point it becomes possible not merely to have the experience oneself, but to identify—that is, to imagine someone else as having the same ex-perience. Since a valence is attached to the thought of the experience, satisfaction can now be received by thinking about that experience in another person. At the end of this third stage the child can receive pleas-ure by giving pleasure to the mother. At first this association can take place most easily by the physical contacts of affection themselves, but later from other acts which bring forth signs of pleasure from the mother.

The fourth stage is awareness that the mother reciprocates the feeling, which brings us full cycle to satisfaction received by the child from being loved by the mother. But a new dimension has now been added. This is the ability to receive satisfaction from mere awareness of the *fact* of being loved, even during periods when no overt manifestations are present. At this stage the child also recognizes the relation between the internal feel-ing of loving and the overt behavior toward the loved person which accompanies it. By what is essentially a logical process, even if not con-sciously reasoned, the child recognizes that his own continued receipt of loving treatment is assured if the mother feels love toward him. Being loved is thereafter a reinforcer, and is almost certain to take on intrinsic reward value. In nonbehaviorist language, the child then possesses a full-blown love need.[12] The mother has presumably learned the whole relationship long since, and in fact or anticipation receives satisfaction from all steps from the very start.

From this base the child can learn that approval by mother brings forth the love response, while disapproval often withholds it, whereupon approval will become a reinforcer and disapproval an extinguisher. The child will subsequently find approval to be important in relations with other persons where the love relation is absent, and approval may then become a strong generalized reinforcer with wider currency than love. It is capable of passing its reinforcing value to still other things, such as praise and status. Although some individuals may miss one or more stages, it seems probable that the vast majority of the world's population undergo this same set of experiences, or something similar to it, in the early years of life. This common experience is an important force for similarity of behavior.

Each individual will also encounter a series of "leavening" forces. These reflect the fact that no individual lives alone. Others have their own desires, and in a world of scarcity some desires for some persons can be satisfied only by leaving some desires of others unfilled. An early instance is awareness that the child is not the only claimant on his mother's love, which must be shared with other children and the father. Other wanted things are also discovered to be scarce, and an adjustment must be made to the fact that other persons also want them. Still other wants can be satisfied only by joint action, and cooperation must be learned. Thus the development of the individual personality merges into the problem of interpersonal relations. These will be examined under the headings of *transactions* and *organizations*, which make up the core of the social analysis in later chapters. They involve such things as bargaining power, consensus, coalitions, authority, government, and other relationships well beyond the scope of personality as such.

In summary, given the similar biological equipment of all human beings, the complete dependence of each at the start of life, the highly probable love relation with the mother, the learning of language and of the self, and the necessity of sharing or exchanging and cooperating—these and numerous other things provide a core of basic experiences which are similar for nearly all persons, regardless of degree of education or level of culture of the parents or of the society. Hence, despite the almost infinite adaptability of the human creature, this dependable core of similar significant experiences provides a substantial unity to basic patterns of behavior and feelings among people at all times and ages of man. This similarity is great enough and dependable enough so that—so long as we carefully note that it is learned, not inherited—awareness of

---

[12] In a general (but only a general) way, this analysis leans on Chapter II of Parsons and Bales, *op. cit.* In a broader way it reflects a gradually widening scope of the development and interrelations of concepts and motives as described in Chapters 5–8 above.

it has all but made the term "human nature" once again respectable, if not among psychologists, at least among anthropologists.[13]

FORCES MAKING FOR DISSIMILAR PERSONALITIES

One of the forces tending to produce similarity of personality is culture—but with the reservation that it produces similarity *within the culture*. To return to the pile of sugar on the plate, a common culture explains why a group of people will tend to have personalities approximating the norm for that culture. But since cultures differ widely among themselves, culture is a differentiating force to the human race as a whole. Major differences in behavior patterns can be reliably predicted between two persons simply from knowing that one is a French Canadian raised in Montreal and the other a Uganda tribesman raised in a native village. The vast differences between cultures thus become the first and most obvious source of difference in personalities.

Different cultures bring differences in more than language, understanding of science, tastes in food, and related items. They also bring differences in the normal kind of attitude toward life and other people. The Orientals place high value on contemplation, the Westerners on material accomplishment. In two neighboring tribes in New Guinea, the Arapesh personality is typically relaxed, cooperative, permissive, and affectionate, while the Mundugumor is stern, self-disciplined, demanding, and competitive.[14] In terms of temperament, the Arapesh pile of sugar centers around a spot on the plate far removed from the Mundugumor pile, even though in the scattering *some* Arapesh approximate the Mundugumor norm, and vice versa. Given that culture is the most obvious determinant of the most probable position of a given personality, or the central tendency, the second phase of the problem is to find why the individual differs from the norm of his culture, providing dispersion. This is not a matter of cultural difference, but of individual difference within a culture.

---

[13] Milton Singer, "A Survey of Culture and Personality Theory and Research," in Bert Kaplan (ed.), *Studying Personality Cross-Culturally* (Evanston, Ill.: Row, Peterson & Co., 1961), pp. 17–22. Singer also notes a somewhat greater recent acceptance of the role of instinct. This does not mean acceptance that actual patterns of behavior are inherited, but rather that certain inherited biological and psychological traits virtually guarantee certain experiences, from which behavior patterns will be learned. Along tangential lines we have already noted the emphasis laid by George Miller, Eugene Galanter, and Karl Pribram, *Plans and the Structure of Behavior* (New York: Henry Holt & Co., 1960) on the apparently inherited capacity of the human nervous system to carry through complex patterns of behavior with relatively little intervening thought, once some overall goal has been conceptualized (my term) and the pattern of behavior has been released for execution. We have thus come full cycle from an original belief that much human behavior was instinctive, to a conclusion that almost none is inborn, and back to the present position. The latter can be summarized by saying that the *explicit* behavior patterns are *learned*, but that certain inherited traits and inescapable developmental cycles virtually guarantee that they *will* be learned.

[14] Margaret Mead, *Sex and Temperament in Three Primitive Societies* (New York: Mentor Books, 1950, originally published in 1935).

Individual Differences

Although all men have certain common biological traits, they are not biologically identical in detail. They differ in size and strength, weight, metabolic rate, appetite, general health, and other obvious physical characteristics, as well as in the balance of secretions of their endocrine glands. Many of these factors will produce direct differences in personality, as between those with boundless energy and those who tire quickly, those who need much food and those who need little, those who are easily excitable and those who are calm. Further, the effect of some of these differences in physical and glandular equipment tend to be cumulative as learning takes place. If the man of muscle tries to knock heads together to get things done, he succeeds, and the knocking behavior is reinforced. If the 90-pound weakling tries the same thing, his own head gets knocked instead, and knocking behavior is extinguished. Meanwhile other techniques will be at least relatively more successful, and hence be reinforced.

It is often said that the weak man "compensates" for lack of strength by developing skills in other directions. So long as the term "compensation" indicates merely that one kind of activity is extinguished and another reinforced, it is satisfactory. It should not be thought, however, that the learning system contains some sort of automatic seesaw, one end of which necessarily goes up when the other goes down. We do have a truly phenomenal set of *biological* compensating mechanisms, by which the body makes up for certain deficiencies.[15] But to the best of our knowledge these do *not* extend to include learned behavior.

Being beautiful or plain is not part of personality, as such. But the beautiful woman will be treated differently from the plain one, and hence will develop different responses. Level of intelligence is also not a personality trait as such. But the intelligent person will learn more, and more quickly, and the difference in his state of information will affect his behavior. Differences in sensory acuity will have similar differentiating effects, affecting the ability both to perceive and to enjoy sensory stimulation. Being male or female is also not part of personality in itself, but it too produces obvious differences in learned behavior. The differences in behavior patterns between male and female probably depend much more on the patterns established by the culture than on inherited factors, though differences in physical strength, and in the relation to child bearing and child care, bring high probability of differences in learned behavior.[16]

Experiences. No matter how homogeneous the culture or tightly knit the family, it is virtually impossible that any two children will have the same set of experiences from which they learn, identical twins possibly excepted.

---

[15] A good summary is provided by Lawrence E. Cole, *Human Behavior* (Yonkers: World Book Co., 1953), p. 171.
[16] Margaret Mead, *op. cit.*

Except for twins, no two children are born into the same family at the same time. Between births the parents learn some things, forget others, and possibly change in health, energy, and interests. The third child does not generate the same excitement or care as the first. As a typical parent who is also interested in photography, I number the early pictures of my first son in hundreds, the second in dozens, and the third in units. In the nuclear family, the first child has no siblings to share parental affection at first. But he must later learn to share it. The last child has less attention at first, but never experiences a later rival. Further, the younger children learn things from their older siblings which the oldest one learned for himself—though the importance of this distinction depends much on the degree of integration of the nuclear family into the larger clan or neighborhood. Often the composition of the family changes. The grandparent who spoils the first child may die before the tenth arrives, or a widowed aunt may arrive to help to raise the second child. The family income or status may rise or fall, the family may move, or do other things which affect successive children differently. All these things prevent any two children even in the same family from having the same set of experiences. Children in different families will show even greater differences.

For many years it was argued whether heredity or environment had the greater influence on personality. We will not review the dispute, having already presented our own version of the factors. In any event it seems wise to think in terms of experience rather than environment. Two children may live in an assumedly identical environment, in that they have the same house, parents, school, and so forth. But as the two are walking atop a fence one may have a nasty fall and the other not. This is not a difference in environment, in the usual sense. But it is a difference in experience, and will produce different learned responses.

From time to time each person will have *key experiences*. These select one fork where the behavioral road divides, often being small movements at first, but gradually leading to far divergent destinations. Key experiences are also something like carefully balanced boulders, which require only a slight push to start moving in any direction, but which have tremendous force once they are started.

A key experience may be highly dramatic, like a serious accident or disease, victory in a fight, or a humiliating failure. Or it might be some seemingly trivial phrase or idea which starts a train of thought in a new direction, eventually producing a reconceptalization of a whole area of thinking. It might be meeting someone who becomes a "hero," and is imitated in great detail. Perhaps the first big project a person tries goes well, producing a conviction that it pays to think big—or vice versa. In any of thousands of ways, a particular experience may start a channel in a new direction, which gradually strengthens until it is a strongly entrenched aspect of the personality.

We now come to a really crucial aspect of the forces producing different personalities. We have just stated that it is experiences, not environment, which mold learning. In an earlier chapter we defined "experience" to include purely internal stimuli and responses. That is, an "experience" can consist simply of thinking about something. This means that the forces which develop personality differences include not merely overt experiences, but also the way in which, and the number of times, a person thinks about those experiences. Further, we have seen that no two persons have identical concepts of the same thing, since the concepts arise from different sets of overt experiences, or of similar overt experiences taken in the context of different background concepts. Hence, two people will not think about things in the same way, which means that they cannot have identical internal experiences. Once again we are face to face with the tremendous number of variables which produce the human personality, and make a scientific approach so difficult—particularly when many of the variables cannot be observed by the outsider at all, and are only vaguely observed by the person himself. Like the external ones, these internal experiences may create different concepts, different motives, or both.

The Role of Role. Personality is not only behavior, but also behavior in conjunction with others. This raises complications, because in a relation of A and B, A is part of B's environment and B is part of A's. Assuming that each to some degree adapts his behavior to that of the other, the relation of two persons is thus a mutually interacting system. When two persons first meet, the mutual adaptation may be rather large, as A adapts to B, who then adapts to A's new behavior, and so on. In due time the relation "shakes down" to an equilibrium, in which each knows fairly well what to expect of the other, and behaves accordingly. This fact also tends to make for individual differences. For if A and B are not alike to begin with, then A is a different stimulus to B than B is to A.[17]

Although an individual has only one personality (even if split), he may have as many roles as the number of persons he deals with—or more. To take some obvious instances, one does not behave the same toward his spouse as toward his parents, his children, or his siblings. He does not behave the same toward his brother as to his sister, to his younger brother as to his older one, and he plays a different role with his grandparents than with his grandchildren. He may have several different roles with the

---

[17] Performing a role is a mutual interaction. It is therefore a feedback system between two persons. According to the analysis of feedback systems in Chapter 3, if an equilibrium is to be reached, the system should include one direct and one inverse relation. I have not explored how this would work out in such factors as dominance and submission. However, later chapters will analyze the interpersonal relation as a transaction, with attention focused on bargaining power. In that relation, A's bargaining power varies directly with one set of factors, while B's varies inversely with the same factors, thus providing the conditions for an equilibrium. Looking beyond the present volume, it seems possible in a preliminary way that dominance and submission could be analyzed as a type of intertransaction relationship, in some cases including a consensus relation, as those terms will be defined in later chapters.

same person, as when the father is companion and playmate to his son at one point, and teacher and disciplinarian at another. Just to complicate things, one not only has different roles with his boss than with a fellow worker, but holds a third one in reserve for when he deals with both together. If a fellow worker is likely to become boss, the role is still different. Surrounding circumstances also bring changes, and one may not use the same language to a fellow worker on Sunday in church as he uses on Monday in the shop—even if no one else is listening.

In addition to being performed, roles are also conceptualized. Like most other concepts, the individual learns roles from his culture, along with his concepts of rivers, rugs, styles of houses, techniques of agriculture, and religion, the role belonging to the class of culturally transmitted concepts whose outward manifestations are known as sociofacts. Since the general nature of the relationship between husband and wife, parent and child, employer and employee, official and citizen, medicine man and patient, priest and parishioner, and many others are prescribed by the society, there is no need for each new relationship to begin as a blank. Instead, each tends to follow the pattern already known to both parties. As a result, I feel reasonably sure that when I tell a student in class that he gave a wrong answer, he will not come forward and rap my knuckles with a ruler. If he did (and unless I had grossly abused my position as teacher) I would not be alone in defending my knuckles, but the rest of the class would participate. Beyond the immediate physical restraint, they would also use a variety of techniques to be described in Chapter 19 to enforce conformance to the socially defined role of students. (I am not without some power of my own if the student hopes to graduate.) In addition to the social controls over roles, once the individual has learned one he tends to maintain it out of habit.

Roles have been discussed thus far as if they are two-person affairs. But a person can also have a role in a group (leader, errand boy, peacemaker) and a group may have a role in some larger group. These larger configurations do not involve any essentially different principles, and they need not be discussed separately at this point.

To the extent that the society prescribes roles, it seems to provide a force for similarity of behavior. This is true as among different persons who fill the same kind of role. At the same time, differences in personality are engendered as among persons assigned to different roles. Further, in a complex society, no two persons occupy the same combination of roles. That is, if we view culture as a set of influences forming a particular personality, in a modern complex society no two persons belong to quite the same subculture. This returns us to the notion of personality as a subsociety of one person—a definitionally improper but pedagogically useful way of looking at it. Further, no culture has found techniques for enforcing its prescriptions completely. Almost any socially defined role restricts the person who occupies it, and some will break out of the mold, either without social punishment, or with willingness to accept it.

Finally, as part of the conceptualization of the self, each individual becomes aware of his ability to manipulate things, and to make them conform to his will. Being able to do or not do certain things as he decides, he develops some sort of notion of free will. To a degree which varies widely with individuals and cultures, he will then assume that, despite obvious limitations, there are nevertheless substantial areas in which he can do as he wants. Having formed a concept of freedom of this sort, he becomes somewhat less disciplinable than he otherwise might be. With growing experience he also discovers that he can in part get others to do what he wants, by appealing to the proper motives at the proper times. Going a step further, he may then also see the possibility of molding his own knowledge, skills, attitudes, and other traits toward specified goals. That is, he can plan not only specific actions, but to a certain extent he can plan and help to form certain broad traits of his own personality. He can, of course, use this ability to mold himself toward the norm of his society. But he can also use it to make himself different.

PERSONAL INTERACTIONS AS A CULTURE SYSTEM

We have discussed in Chapter 12 the mutual interaction between a society and its culture as a system, in which the society molds the culture and the culture molds the society. We have also seen that the personality is roughly the logical equivalent of the culture of one person. In important respects the analysis of the system of culture is useful for understanding the relation of the individual to other persons and organizations —an analysis partially opened above under the heading of "role." The interaction is as follows.

Every individual develops a personality, by which we mean that he tends to respond to situations in his environment in particular ways. In normal life the most important parts of his environment are other people. But while the individual is responding to those around him, they are also responding to him. He not only adapts to his environment, but he also helps to form it, in a mutually interacting miniature system of culture. These interactions are perhaps most obvious in the organization, where interpersonal relations continue for long periods, and certain mutual accommodations must be made to get the work of the organization done.

In this context it becomes obvious that some adaptation of personality is not only possible but inescapable. In the factory, for example, in some degree the worker adapts his behavior to that of the foreman, and the foreman adapts in some degree to the worker. Supervisors in many plants are given special training in how to deal with employees, and union representatives sometimes receive similar training for dealing with supervisors. Whether this is thought of as training in supervision, human relations, or applied psychology, it is designed to alter some facet of the trainee's personality, in that he is expected to respond differently to other persons after the training than before.

Nonsupervisory jobs also are affected by personality. One employee's personality may make him unsuited to be a salesman, a second may raise difficulties in the office, a third may be disruptive in a close-knit research team, and a fourth may seem ill-adapted for repetitive work, or for the highflown tasks of the structural iron worker. In such situations the worker might be discharged, or transferred to different work. He also might be given training or encouragement to perform the work satisfactorily, which is to say that he may be taught to develop some new traits of personality. There is also the possibility that the job may be modified to suit the man, or that other persons may learn to treat him differently. Each instance involves some change in the man, in his environment, or both.

There are no set rules about what should be adapted to what, since much depends on the nature of the situation. Some individual traits seem difficult to change, while others are highly flexible—as when the youth who faints at the sight of blood later becomes a successful surgeon, or the one who trembles to peer over the second floor balcony later munches casually on a sandwich as he strolls along a steel girder forty stories above the street. Jobs may be tailored to fit human capacities, as we avoid creating jobs which human beings are biologically or temperamentally not equipped to perform. We similarly try to arrange organizational structures, committee meetings, and decision processes to match the capacities of human beings, while we simultaneously train human beings to perform successfully in these situations.

All of this is a very long story. We can do little more than mention it here, and again in our later discussion of organizations. Our main point is to note that such phenomena exemplify the system of culture in miniature. The human being influences the other persons in his environment; he simultaneously learns from and adapts to his human environment. When these things happen in the small, they are subject to much conscious control. Further, the qualitative changes may be much greater and the speed of change much more rapid than when the larger aggregates of a whole society are involved. It nevertheless seems useful to think of these interactions of roles as essentially the same as the operation of the system of culture in the small.

SUMMARY

It is probably pointless to discuss whether personality is determined more by inheritance or learning. To begin with, "more" implies quantitative measure of influence, which we do not have. It is also something like arguing whether the gasoline and spark are more important than the valves and pistons in an automobile motor. If each of two things is absolutely indispensable, which is more important?

We have a long way to go before we have a really satisfactory system for classifying personalities, and a longer one before we can predict a personality accurately from knowledge of the background forces. Among other things, forces which stop one person serve as challenges which another surmounts, in which case the same general forces provide the background for almost opposite personalities. Whether all these things will ever be meaningfully unravelled we do not know. We will rest for the moment with having reviewed some forces which apparently make for similarities, and those which make for differences in personality. To the extent that different cultures produce differences in modal grouping, we return to another piece of rather large ignorance—the reasons why cultures are different to begin with, particularly those without histories.

On the whole, the pattern of the past seems likely to continue into the future. A substantial core of similarity will prevail among all people, beyond which large individual differences will remain. Increased communication and transportation will probably reduce the differences between the norms of different cultures, but probably not the dispersion of types within cultures. The latter seem to be based on irremovable differences in life experiences.

IV. DECISIONS

Chapter 14

DECISIONS: FRAMEWORK OF THE PROBLEM

DECISION AS ADAPTIVE BEHAVIOR

WHETHER THEY choose to or not, human beings must choose. The person free to spend all day on the beach cannot lie face down and face up at the same time. Even if he alternates, at any one moment he must choose.

When the laboratory rat regularly finds food below a triangle and electric shock below a circle, he adapts by reinforcing the approach to the stimulus of triangles and extinguishing the approach to circles. Such adaptation necessarily involves six elements, three of which are of immediate importance to our discussion. First, the rat must be able to distinguish triangles from circles, which we will call *identifying the stimulus*. Second, he must be able to *perform* (or refrain from performing) *the response*. And third, he must previously have a positive *valence* toward food and a negative one toward shock.

We might say that the rat *decides* whether to approach or avoid the triangle stimulus, basing his decision on previous experience. We do not normally apply the word "decision" to response selection at this level, reserving it for more complex choices faced by human beings. We will follow that usage here, but nevertheless reflect the universality of the basic ingredients by defining *decision* as the process of selecting responses under conditions where the stimulus situation, the valences, and/or the possible responses are complex.

Being defined in terms of *complex* stimuli, valences, and responses, decision implies previous adaptive learning, without which complex levels of these things cannot be developed. As indicated just above, adaptive behavior involves six distinct steps. These fall into the following two parallel groups:

THE STAGES OF ADAPTIVE BEHAVIOR

A. Performance Stage:
   1. Identify stimulus.
   2. Select response.
   3. Perform response.

  B. Adaptive or Learning Stage:
     4. Identify feedback stimulus.
     5. Evaluate feedback stimulus.
     6. Reinforce, extinguish, or modify appropriate aspects of any preceding steps.

All six steps are essential to even the simplest motivated (nonreflex) conditioning, and adaptation will fail in the absence of any one. It was not necessary to spell them out in connection with simple animal conditioning, because some of the steps are so obvious at that level. We took for granted such things as the rat's ability to identify a triangle (Step 1), to run through a door (Step 3), to have the sensation of eating (Step 4), and to evaluate eating as desirable and shock undesirable (Step 5). In complex behavior, however, these things can no longer be taken for granted, and each must be dealt with explicitly.

These stages correspond to those of a controlled system, in which stimulus identification is the detector, response selection the selector, and response performance the effector stage. We need not at this point decide the best way to diagram the relation between the performance and learning stages, which may be similar to that between the primary and secondary motive system shown in Chapter 6. It would seem logical to think of the performance stage as a subsystem within the more comprehensive adaptive, or learning, stage.

In studying decisions we enter an area of "field" psychology introduced briefly in the latter part of Chapter 5. Here we face such complications as multiple or ambiguous stimuli, and bivalent feedback stimuli which contain both rewarding and punishing elements simultaneously. These are precisely the ingredients from which decisions are made. We will therefore draw upon the spirit of the field approach to sense the nature of the problem, but will use materials from decision theory, economics, and other areas to develop procedures and rules of decisions.

The Meaning of "Complexity" in Decisions

The term *complex* in the definition of decision excludes any stimulus situation to which a reliable response has already been learned. The reason is clear. We have seen that many apparently simple acts, such as identifying a person by sight, actually require complex learning. If I can nevertheless identify a man and respond with his name on sight, the identification and selection of response are not complex in the sense involved in decision making. If a seasoned administrator can give a prompt response to an involved situation which twenty years earlier would have required an anguished week to resolve, the problem is not "complex" to him. With scarcely a thought an experienced driver may negotiate a traffic snarl which would strain the novice's attention and decision faculties. "Complexity" can be defined only with reference to the state of learning of the decision maker. It excludes already well-developed responses to situations, no matter how complex the situations may seem at other times or to other persons.[1]

Decision theory is not normally couched in a psychological framework. It is usually expressed in terms of sets of alternatives (here called opportunities), from among which the decision maker selects one alternative on the basis of utilities (here called preferences). Decision making is thus not different from human behavior as diagnosed in previous chapters, but is an extension of psychological processes into more complex situations. Although stimulus-response psychology is of little help to understanding decision processes, as such, it is important for perspective to keep in mind that no degree of complexity changes the fact that a decision *is* the selection of a response to some kind of stimulus situation.

Decision making in a narrow sense includes only the first two steps of adaptation, these being minimal to response selection. However, most of life's decisions are not one-shot affairs in totally new circumstances. They are repetitions in changed circumstances of decisions made earlier, and either the learning or factual outcomes, or both, of previous decisions are ingredients in a present decision. If I must make a decision whether to spend the evening correcting manuscript or reading new material for this book, the decision situation is an outcome of my earlier decision to write the book, and the decision itself will reflect what I have learned from previous decisions about the relative fruitfulness of reading and revising. For reasons of this sort it seems inescapable that the ingredients at steps 1 and 2 of one decision will include learning or factual outcomes of previous decisions. That is, the performance stage in any one decision is a subset within the larger set of the adaptive stage. Hence, although decision making will focus mainly on the first two steps, all six are at least implicitly included.

1. Identifying the Stimulus

Unlike the almost instantaneous identification of a triangle or a traffic light, identifying a complex stimulus is a relatively slow process. It requires the perceiver separately to perceive many details, to relate those details by logic, to separate relevant from irrelevant parts of the whole situation, and perhaps to modify some concepts along the way. Suppose that the chancellor of a university observes a student riot, after which he must decide what action to take. First, to identify a student riot from a mass of sensory stimuli in itself is an act of perception far beyond the ability of any animal except man.

---

[1] Again we observe circularity when we get to fundamentals. A decision involves a complex situation, a complex situation being one which requires a decision. In a common sense way complexity can be thought of as involving both large numbers of variables and uncertainty about at least some of them. For more technical analysis I would be inclined to define complexity with reference to a multiplicity of variables alone, and reserve uncertainty for separate consideration. Under such definitions a decision could involve complexity, uncertainty, or both.

This level of identification is inadequate for the chancellor's purpose, however, and he must further categorize the riot as (say) an exuberant outburst over a football victory, or a political protest set off by some lunatic fringe. This further identification requires much attention to assembling and evaluating cues. In similar fashion, the doctor studying a patient's symptom, the geologist examining an unfamiliar rock, the diplomat laboring over communiques from a foreign government, or the economist comparing indexes of production: each is attempting to identify a complex stimulus which faces him.

As we get into still more complex situations, not only may the situation itself be complex, but there may be a half dozen lines of action open, each of which might have a half dozen different possible consequences, each with varying degrees of probability. At a very simple level the stimulus situation is not only that the gas gauge shows nearly empty, but that the car will soon stop if something is not done about it. At a more complex level, if the chancellor finds the riot to be politically inspired, the question of disciplining or not disciplining the students has possible repercussions on the students' feelings, on future orderliness, on the students' sense of political freedom, on the state legislature, on potential donors to the university, and on the president's stature as an academic leader—to mention only a few conspicuous items. For subsequent analysis, it seems more reasonable to describe this step as "formulating the decision set" than as "identifying the stimulus." To maintain perspective, however, we should recall that even the laboratory rat faces alternative responses, even if only of moving or not moving, which in his experience leads to different consequences, such as food or shock. Though the rat's choice is simpler than the chancellor's, both must make a selection among alternate possible responses with different associated consequences. The thing that the rat or the chancellor responds to is not merely the perception of something in his immediate environment, but also the consequences which are associated with his alternative responses. Having thus elaborated the content of the stimulus (or stimulus situation), we will use the phrase "formulating the decision set" as the equivalent at the complex level of "identifying the stimulus" at the simple one. In pure form, it is a perception which permits conceptualization of the situation—a scientific judgment about available opportunities. We have, of course, seen (in Chapter 8) the frightfully promiscuous intermingling of concepts and motives, which often impedes our ability to get clear pictures of what *is*. This mingling in fact does not detract from the desirability of keeping these two things separate for analytical purposes.

2. Selecting the Response

Once the situation has been perceived, the alternative responses listed, and their probable consequences catalogued, the first step is complete. The second step is to select among the listed alternatives on the basis of motives, or value judgments. Does the rat *prefer* food to shock? If he must accept shock to get food, does he *like* food more than he *dislikes* shock? If disciplining the students will both reduce the freedom of student expression and make it harder to raise money for the university (among other possible results), which is higher in the chancellor's preference system? Not all such value decisions are as subjective as the chancellor's, as, for example, in a businessman's decision between two courses of action, one of which will bring a profit of $100,000 and another of $200,000. The essence of the second step, however, is to attach relative preferences to each of the step 1 alternatives, and then to choose the one most preferred under all the circumstances of the case. This step completes decision making in the narrower sense.

3. Performing the Response

Once the preferred alternative is chosen it is executed. The rat runs across the grid to the food or he does not. The chancellor disciplines the students, gives a speech on freedom and responsibility to the next student convocation, or performs whatever other alternative appeared at the top of his preference list. The actual performance of such responses is hardly within the scope of this volume. We may note, however, that few but the simplest decisions are made in their entirety at the outset; many details must be handled as subdecisions of implementation as the effectuation proceeds.

4. Identifying the Feedback Stimulus

Certain consequences flow from performing any response. The receipt of food below the triangle is the feedback stimulus from approaching the triangle, and shock is the feedback from approaching the circle. The sight of the nail deeper in the wood is the feedback stimulus from swinging a hammer. If one is to adapt his behavior, feedback information about the consequences of behavior is indispensable.

The problem of identifying the feedback stimulus is basically the same as that of identifying the original stimulus, involving scientific judgments about what *is*. As such, it is subject to all the earlier discussion about concept formation, perception, and stimulus identification. It requires the additional information as to whether a consequence which *follows* a response is a *result* of that response. This is a problem in scientific judgment with numerous ramifications, several of which deserve mention here.

When the feedback is prompt and clear, as when approach to the triangle is followed immediately by food, or a question is followed immediately by an answer, no problem arises. Sometimes, however, the feedback is long delayed, and its relation to the original response is highly uncertain. When parents handle their children in a certain way in the hope of making them into responsible adults, it may be ten or twenty years before the results are observable, at which point it may be uncertain whether the behavior occurs because of or despite the parents' actions.

Feedback can have a systematic bias. A driver may pass you on the highway like a madman. If you catch up to him at the next traffic light, you receive clear feedback which demonstrates that demonic driving does not save time. But if you do not see him again, you may forget the incident, while he meanwhile has forged miles ahead. Your conclusion about demonic driving may or may not be correct. But the feedback tends to be biased, in that you are more likely to observe failures than successes.

We have earlier observed information biases due to motivations. We seek out, attend to, and mentally repeat the observations which attest to our ability and success, since these are rewarding. But we tend to avoid the evidences of our failures, except when we deliberately seek them for self-correction. For example, no one really expects us to continue to associate with persons who regularly criticize us. This kind of bias makes life more pleasant, but it does produce biased feedback. Certain manners and customs add to such bias. For instance, if a person's habits produce unpleasant breath or body odor, our code of politeness inhibits his receiving adequate feedback. To repeat, a prerequisite of accurate adaptation is clear and unbiased feedback, accurately identified.

5. Evaluating Feedback (Evaluating the original decision via feedback)

If the problem at step 4 is to determine what the consequences of our previous decision are, the problem at step 5 is to determine whether we *like* those consequences. If the only available alternatives were to receive food or a shock, it is easy enough to evaluate food as good and shock as bad. But the feedback in complex situations contains numerous elements, some favorable and some unfavorable, in varying degrees and proportions.

The decision at step 2 presupposes that one course of action has been seen in prospect as more satisfactory than another. The function of evaluating feedback is to determine whether the best alternative was, in fact, selected. This evaluation then serves to improve the quality of future decisions. The evaluation consists essentially of remaking the original decision in hindsight, and its outcome often starts with the words: "If I had it to do over, knowing what I do now. . . ."

We will leave till later the question whether to seek the best possible decision, or merely a satisfactory one. If the goal is the latter, a decision is found to be satisfactory if the feedback is satisfactory, and the reverse. If the original goal was to achieve the *best* decision, however, the evaluation is more complex. For this purpose it is necessary to determine not only what *did* happen, but also what *would* have happened if a different decision had been taken.

The most accurate information about alternatives is obtained by actually trying them. We may try different highways, foods, tools, materials, or friends until we find which are most satisfactory. Other evaluations are made amid irreversible events, where one decision forever precludes the alternatives. We cannot rerun World War II to see what would have happened had we entered sooner, and marrying Jane limits our chance of marrying Helen to see how *that* match would have fared. Perhaps we cannot even *try* one marriage, since a marriage viewed as a trial differs importantly from one viewed as permanent.

The greater our ability to try alternative responses, the better can we evaluate any one. Where multiple trials are not possible, the best we can do is to learn from our own previous experiences in analogous situations, from others, and from history. In any event, the end product of the evaluation is a conclusion that the decision at step 2 was good, bad, or mediocre, in whole or in part. The evaluation at step 5 parallels that at step 2, in that it makes a value judgment among a group of alternatives, the alternatives themselves having been listed during the previous step in the process.

6. *Reinforcing, Extinguishing, or Modifying Appropriate Aspects of the Preceding Steps*

At the simple behavioral level of the rat, food is evaluated at step 5 as desirable; hence, at step 6 the responses which preceded it are reinforced. Shock is evaluated as undesirable, and the responses preceding it are extinguished. The same observations can be made for relatively simple SR behavior in human beings. In these simple situations the observed behavioral adaptations consist of an increase or decrease in the probability of the main, overt response, which constitutes step 3.

Whether modifications of other steps also occur in simple SR experiments is difficult to determine, and psychologists seem to have given rather little attention to the problem in this context, although they do experiment with generalization and discrimination of stimuli, which include modifications of stimulus identification. It is abundantly clear in complex human behavior, however, that adaptations can and do take place at any of the six steps, covering either the whole step or some part of it. A step 5 conclusion that the main decision itself was wrong (at step 2) produces a modification of subsequent decisions, and hence of subsequent responses at step 3. It may be concluded at step 5 that the proper decision was made, but that it was built on a faulty formulation of the decision set at step 1. The appropriate adaptive response at step 6 is then to improve the formulation procedures, not the response selection. It might be concluded that the decision was correct but its execution poor, an adaptation then taking place at step 3.

If the decision is concluded to be bad, but it also seems that adequate information was available at the time, then the decision process itself might be reevaluated for possible change. Finally, if the chosen alternative proves harder or easier to achieve than anticipated, the preferences themselves may change. Preferences may also change at step 1 and step 2 if perceived opportunities are found to be unexpectedly easy or difficult.

CONCLUSION AND INTRODUCTION

The simplest learning by the laboratory rat necessarily involves all six steps of adaptive behavior; the omission of any one precludes learning. These six steps make up the framework within which we can place the more complex decision processes of human beings, decisions thus being seen as our main adaptive feature. Steps 1 and 4 are scientific judgments based on perceptions and concepts, and steps 2 and 5 are value judgments based on motives. To list six steps suggests formal decisions, with people taking notes and making computations. Not necessarily. The eight-year-old saying, "That was scary. Let's do it again," as he heads back to the roller coaster is verbalizing step 5 and executing step 6, having already been through steps 1 to 4.

When we speak of preferred alternatives we place no limitations on the kinds of motives at work. One may enjoy feeding his family, sky diving, playing roulette, pulling wings from flies, or pleasing God.

In decisions we enter a level of psychological processes which cannot thus far be described in the language of conditioning, concept formation, perception, reinforcement, and extinction, even though those terms will not be completely abandoned. We will largely take psychological processes for granted from here onward, assuming that people will do that which is preferred, without inquiring further into the psychological mechanisms of preference.

Externals

So long as we speak in psychological terms we can maintain at least a sideways focus on internal states. The things we call satisfaction and dissatisfaction are inside the neurosomatic system, not outside it. In Chapter 8 we observed that motives above the level of sensory gratification or pain avoidance lie in concepts with valences attached. When we speak of decisions, and later of interpersonal behavior, we must shift from internal states to the external things with which they deal. Although we will continue to assume that the internal states—the concepts and evaluations of things—are the basis of behavior, subsequent analysis will deal with external behavior, and the external things around which it is oriented. For this stage of analysis a whole new set of terms is needed.

SOME BASIC CONCEPTS FOR THE EXTERNAL ANALYSIS OF BEHAVIOR

If any given external thing (object, event, or condition of things) is perceived as wanted, we will say that it possesses *utility*. In psychological terms, if the concept of some external thing reinforces behavior perceived as leading to its acquisition or accomplishment, that thing will be said to have utility. Whether it actually does or would produce satisfaction if achieved is immaterial to the definition. If the thing fails actually to produce satisfaction it will at some point cease to be reinforcing, at which point it will also cease to have utility. If a word of praise is desired or satisfies a want it has utility. So has a tomato if it satisfies a want for food. Utility is not a characteristic of the thing alone, or of the person alone. It is the person's response to the thing.[2] In the days when tomatoes were considered poison they had no utility as food. It might be argued that they had *potential* utility, and anyone who likes may embrace the term. But this concept has no utility for analyzing personal and social phenomena in the present model, and we will confine the term to things actually wanted. A person may exchange something he does not want for something he does, in which case the former has instrumental utility to him. Although for analytical purposes in psychology we can distinguish between instrumental and intrinsic wants, for social analysis it is unnecessary to know whether a particular person's want for any particular thing is intrinsic, instrumental, or both. Our only concern is that it is wanted—that it reinforces behavior.

Nor does the definition specify how many people want a thing, or for how long. Air to breathe has utility to everyone, everywhere, always. A piece of used chewing gum may have utility to one boy for fifteen seconds to extract a dollar bill from a storm sewer. Both have utility.

If the word is used alone it means *positive* utility. An external can also have negative utility, or *disutility*, which means that it creates dissatisfaction, or is undesirable. A storm, fire, or accident which destroys property or injures persons has disutility. So do weeds in the garden, a pain in the neck, insulting remarks, or mildew on clothes. In each case there is less satisfaction with than without them. They will extinguish behavior which brings them on, and reinforce behavior which avoids them.

Any external which has utility is called a *good*. Goods include material things from lollypops to the St. Lawrence Seaway, and nonmaterial things from a word of praise or the scratching of an itch to the operations of the United Nations or a national security system. A good can be some commodity or service, such as a steak or haircut, or a state of affairs like a sunset, a pleasing curve in a river, the prevalence of justice, or a friendly relation between two business partners.

The term "good" by itself means a positive good, a negative good being anything with disutility. Something having both positive and negative qualities, like an effective but unpleasant medicine, will be classified by the behavior it actually induces—a matter we will see later in connection with decisions. Sometimes the zero reference is not clear for distinguishing between utility and disutility. For example, a small pain presumably has disutility. But it has utility, and therefore is positive, compared to a large

---

[2] Once again we are apt to be confused by the fact that a noun form is given to a word which is essentially one of action. Utility, like beauty, is not a quality of an external. It is our response to that external, the response depending on our previous conditioning. If anyone cares to join the fray, I am prepared to argue that much the same may be said of *truth*.

pain. Whenever such cases arise, it may be said that a thing is a positive good if it increases utility, and a negative good if it decreases utility.

Anything having neither utility nor disutility is a nongood. Its existence is irrelevant to human decisions. Precisely what constitutes a nongood in any absolute sense is difficult to state. The Polar ice cap is a good, since if it were to melt most coastal cities would disappear under water. So is the sun, since without it life on earth could not continue for even a day. Having acknowledged that these things fill the definition of goods, we will confine further attention to goods we make decisions about.

"Goods" and "utility" are obviously borrowed from economics. Other social sciences and psychology frequently refer to such things as aspirations, goals, and goal objects. Economists define goods as *anything* capable of satisfying wants, and then (usually without explanation or apology) proceed to ignore all goods which are not exchangeable through markets. The present usage does *not* adopt that limitation, meaning literally *anything* which has utility. To "have a goal" means the same thing as "to want," or "to have a want." "Goal objects" could probably be substituted for "goods" in all uses, and sometimes fits better. But for overall use I prefer "goods," because it is shorter and because my background is in economics. It should clearly be noted, however, that *goods* include desired states of affairs, as well as the usual commodities and services. For him who wants it, presidency of the Society to Eradicate Eczema in Azusa is a good, and so can be the ability to get Aunt Hepzibah to take a bath in the middle of the month. The purpose of this extension of meaning is maximum unity of analysis. The general proposition of the chapters which follow is that certain aspects of behavior related to decisions and interpersonal relations are uniform with respect to wanted things, and that this uniformity is quite independent of the nature of the thing wanted. If the behavior is uniform, then the objects of the behavior should be given a single name, lest a single analysis perhaps look like a multiple one. Anyone who likes may substitute "goals" or "goal objects" for "wants" or "goods," so long as he does not change the definition.

COSTS AND THE NECESSITY OF CHOICE

A basic fact of life is that we cannot have everything we want. A more precise statement is that most goods have costs. Defined internally, *cost* is the satisfaction denied in the course of achieving other satisfaction. Defined externally, *cost* is the goods denied in the course of achieving or acquiring other goods. A mixture of the two versions is sometimes applicable, as when we say that cost is the satisfaction denied in the course of producing goods. (In customary usage, "achieving" and "acquiring" apply to differential kinds of goods. To simplify discussion, the reader should assume that hereinafter any appropriate words, such as getting, receiving, acquiring, accomplishing, producing, or achieving are to imply the consummation of goal-seeking activity, whether this be the receipt or production of a tangible good, the act of having a service performed, or the reaching or continuance of some state or condition in life.)

Goods and utility can be positive or negative, and so can the ingredients of costs. One form of cost is the denial of positive goods, called *opportunity costs*. The other is the receipt of negative goods, called *disutility costs*. Opportunity and disutility costs each have two subtypes.

As to opportunity costs, the denial of positive goods means the pleasant things which might otherwise have been acquired. Opportunity costs can arise from either or both of two sources, *incompatibility* and *scarcity*.

I cannot go from New York to San Francisco in half a day without entailing the risks attendant upon leaving the ground, since surface transportation and the necessary speed are presently incompatible. I cannot achieve the satisfaction of having my word believed whenever I speak, and also tell lies whenever I like, since regular lying and a reputation for integrity are incompatible. I cannot spend the summer prospecting for uranium in Death Valley and simultaneously enjoy cool forests and gurgling trout streams. In each case the cost of achieving one good is the denial of an incompatible one.

Incompatibility reflects the nature of things, which can sometimes be changed. A century ago, being in Chicago on Monday was incompatible with being in New York on Tuesday. But faster transportation has eliminated the incompatibility. Other incompatibilities are difficult or impossible to change, as in the cases of Death Valley and credibility. Further, to have my house white with green trim is irretrievably incompatible with having it cream with maroon trim at the same time, and no technological change seems likely to change this fact.

The second source of opportunity costs is scarcity. A trip to Europe is not incompatible *by nature* with having a new car. But if my income is not large enough, to buy one prevents me from buying the other. If I have only one hour free, I cannot both play tennis and hike to the top of a nearby mountain. There is nothing basically incompatible about the two, but my time is insufficient for both. If the club has four tennis courts, and fifty people want to play at the same hour, some persons' desires will be satisfied while others' will be denied—not because there is anything incompatible by nature in having fifty people playing simultaneously, but simply because there are not enough courts. Under the latter circumstances, the denial of the courts to some people is the cost of making them available to others—which illustrates that costs are not always borne by the same persons who achieve the satisfaction.

Unlike incompatibility costs, opportunity costs due to scarcity can be reduced or eliminated by having *more* of the thing in question—more income, more time, or more tennis courts. (Such costs can also be reduced by wanting less.) Since the cost could be reduced by having more, the ultimate source of such costs lies in the limitations on having more. These are the limited resources from which wants are satisfied. There is only so much oil, coal, and iron ore in the ground, only so much rainfall, arable land, sunshine, and so on. At any one point in history, time, human effort, skill, patience, and equipment are also limited. As to some less tangible satisfactions, there are only so many crisp October days, thrilling sunsets, and warbling birds.

Costs due to scarcity can generally be reduced if we increase our productive ability. To get more steel from a ton of ore is as good as more ore in the ground. To produce the steel with fewer man hours reduces cost by releasing manpower to produce other things. We may not be able to increase the number of beautiful fall days or spectacular sunsets. But if we increase our productivity of other goods, we may have more time to enjoy them. As we improve and increase productivity, we increase our ability to have *both* of two things.

This does not mean that scarcity costs will ultimately disappear as we get more productive. Utility is not a trait of goods alone, but a relationship between goods and human desires. Similarly, cost is not the time or iron ore used up in making steel, but the satisfactions which could have been achieved if the time and ore had been put to other use. "Other use," incidentally, includes keeping it for possible future use. If our wants expand with the output of goods (as the nature of aspirations suggests), opportunity costs due to scarcity will never disappear. For "scarce" is not the *quantity* of goods, but the quantity relative to desires.

Whereas opportunity costs are doing without what we want, *disutility* costs are having to accept what we do not want. These also take two forms. The first is direct and immediate *unpleasantness*. This might arise while some good is actually being received, as in the cases of flies on the beach, bones in the fish, or people climbing past us in the theater. These are instances of unpleasantness in consumption. Perhaps more important are unpleasantnesses in production. Creating goods may entail sweat, tears, pain, embarrassment, or frustration. Or it may require us to work in isolation, to accept inferior status, to discipline ourselves to regular hours, or to work in boxed-up places amid noise or fumes. Displeasure incurred in producing a good is part of the cost of that good.

The second form of disutility cost is *destruction* of existing goods in the course of creating others. To produce a refrigerator, raw materials are used up and factory buildings and machinery are worn out or become obsolete. In winning an election, gaining a promotion, or managing a publicity campaign, one may lose friends, impair his health, or have doubts cast on his integrity. In each instance, some valued thing has less utility after than before, and this loss of utility is part of the cost of achieving a desired result.

Risk is also a cost in this sense, in that a certain percentage of items may burn, spoil, and so on. (Risk can also have unpleasantness costs in fear and worry, as well as utility value in the enjoyment of its excitement.)

The total cost of a good is the sum of its separate costs, since no two offset each other or are double counted. For instance, the opportunity cost of working for one good consists of the other goods which could have been made with the same time, effort, and materials. But if the work is also onerous, this disutility cost is added to the opportunity cost.

Costs can be clarified further by distinguishing between free goods, which have no cost, and those referred to by economists as economic goods, which do have cost. To say that a good is free means that no other satisfaction must be sacrificed to get it. The most unequivocal example is the air we breathe. We can usually inhale and exhale to our lungs' content, without denying any other satisfaction. Breathing has no scarcity cost, since there is more air than we can conceivably breathe. There is no incompatibility cost since no other normal activity must be suspended so we can breathe. Opportunity costs of breathing do arise if we swim under water or walk through poison gas. Breathing also has no disutility cost, being neither unpleasant nor destructive. Nor does it normally leave either the breather or the atmosphere less useful, thus incurring no loss of value. Both kinds of disutility costs can, of course, arise under unusual conditions. To an injured person breathing can be painful, which is one form of disutility cost, and a diseased person can contaminate the atmosphere of a room with his breathing, which is the second form. The atmosphere is the only material good which is normally completely free, being available in unlimited quantities, when, where, and in the form we want it, without our even having to think about it.

Free nonmaterial goods are a less clearly identifiable concept. They presumably include such states of nature as temperature, sunlight, sunsets, landscapes, or pleasant breezes, which we can enjoy without denying other goods. Free nonmaterial goods also include satisfying states of human relationships, such as humor, affection, acceptance, or sympathy, if no costs are incurred in creating them.

SOME FURTHER CONCEPTS ON CHOICE

Since most satisfactions have cost, in that they cannot be achieved without denying other satisfactions, to achieve any one satisfaction then requires a choice as to which satisfaction is accepted and which denied. Wherever we are not complete slaves of environment, costs and the necessity of choice are not merely inseparable, they are virtually indistinguishable. Before we can proceed further, some additional concepts are needed, as follows.

1. *To choose* is the act of selecting one good or of initiating one course of action rather than another. If the act is later changed for some reason, the choice will be said to have changed at that point.

2. *To prefer* is to place one good or course of action higher than another in a preference rating (or preference ordering). Preference is the anticipatory mental state which precedes choice. The preferred of two items is the more strongly motivated, or the one in a choice between in-

compatible goods which would reinforce behavior instrumental to itself and extinguish behavior instrumental to the other item. One prefers Y to X if, in a choice, he would take Y rather than X, or if, in an exchange, he would give up X for Y. In an overt act the fact of choice is, by present definition, the measure of preference, and it is a contradiction to say "He preferred X but actually chose Y." It is possible, of course, to have vacillating feelings. One may prefer X at the moment of choice and actually select it, even though a moment before and a moment later he preferred Y. Preference encompasses *all* factors relevant to the choice, including the choice situation itself. The schoolboy may not select the same library book when his English teacher is watching as when he is alone. The choice actually made, however, remains the measure of preference, at the moment of choice and in light of all the circumstances. If the situation in which the choice is made modifies the longer-run preference it may be wise, as a purely practical matter, to change the surroundings. This is why some people never make an important choice in the presence of a salesman.

A *gross preference* reflects utility, and is the relative preference between two things if neither has any cost. *Net preference* is their relative position after the costs of each have been taken into account. The full meaning of gross and net preference can be seen only in an actual choice situation, and will be returned to later.

3. *Value* is the relative position of a good in a preference ordering, and the higher its position the greater is its value. The preference ordering may be that of an individual or a group, a matter we need not deal with further at this point. Preference is based on the perceived relative utility of different goods. We cannot now establish cardinal measures of utility, and it seems safe to say that we probably never will—which means that we will have to be permanently content with ordinal measures only. If under given circumstances I prefer coffee to milk, and milk to tea, I can say that coffee to me has a greater value than milk, and that tea has a smaller value than milk, and I can then place their values in first, second, and third positions. But there is no reason to believe that we shall ever be able to say that coffee has 10 utils—a *util* being a hypothetical unit of utility—milk 6 and tea 2. Value, as the position of one good among others in a preference ordering, is thus a summary statement of its utility, and for some purposes the terms value and utility are interchangeable.[3] We have already indicated that to choose *Y* over *X*, or to exchange *X* for *Y*, is a measure of higher

---

[3] As we shall see later, a certain statement of value within a group, which will be called a consensus valuation, *can* be cardinally measured, particularly when values are stated in money. "Value" nevertheless remains a position in a preference ordering, the preference ordering then being the same as a price ordering. Just as the fact of choice is the measure of preference, so are terms of actual exchange the measure of value.

There are certain circumstances where preferences may not be transitive. That is, to prefer *A* to *B* and *B* to *C* does not necessarily mean that *A* is preferred to *C*. The exploration of those cases does not seem to be necessary for the present purpose.

preference for *Y* than for *X*. Hence, to say that *Y* has more value than *X* is a shorter way of saying that *Y* occupies a higher preference position.

The terms "value system" and "preference set" are rough synonyms. We will follow general usage, however, in which a value system refers to the general feelings of a substantial group toward large issues, such as education, religion, honesty, work, and marriage, while a preference set (or system) refers to the relative preferences among less important things, such as shoes, automobiles, and political candidates, and usually refers to the preferences of an individual or small group rather than a whole society.

The items in any particular value system or preference ordering can be either positive or negative. So, therefore, can value, as when I say that hitting my thumb with a hammer has a negative value. We should nevertheless recognize that many of life's situations provide no permanent zero reference from which we can say that one thing has positive utility and another negative. Often we can say only that something is better or worse than something else. A room temperature of 85 degrees may have disutility compared to one of 75, but utility compared to temperatures of 100 or 30. Fortunately for the logic of decision making, no zero reference is necessary; all we need do is select the item higher on the preference list at the expense of a lower one. As will be seen, this and some other measures of costs and values can be measured only in the context of a particular decision. To formulate the net preference set in a particular choice situation is the same as the second step of adaptive behavior outlined above.

In parallel with gross and net preference, *gross value* is the value of a good without reference to its costs, and *net value* is its gross value minus its costs.

4. An *opportunity* is any one of two or more alternatives, positive or negative, perceived as possible to achieve in any given choice situation. "Opportunities," or "opportunity set," are the total set of such alternatives. As indicated in earlier chapters, one's perceived opportunities are his concepts of the situation which faces him. In pure form they are formulated by judgments of science or fact. Formulating the opportunity set is the first step of adaptive behavior. The meaning of a "choice situation" will be clarified later.

5. To *transform* is to bring about some change of state in the environment, or, to some degree, in one's self. A *transformation* is the act or result of transforming. Although the term will normally be confined to changes of things outside oneself, a change in one's appearance or physical state, as by a beautician or physician, can also be a transformation. For certain purposes, so can a change in one's skill or information. In connection with the earlier discussion of learning, "environment" was defined to include anything outside the nervous system. With respect to wants and want-satisfaction, a transformation similarly involves anything outside the *volitional* system. Any change except a change in the state of desire or

satisfaction itself can be a transformation. In most situations it is unnecessary to draw the distinction this fine, and attention can normally be confined to tangible commodities and overt acts. Changes in sociofacts constitute transformations as well as do changes in artifacts, including such things as a reorganization of the Supreme Court or rescheduling of a tribal rain dance.

6. *Production* is any transformation which is expected to increase utility. It can also be described as transforming a good or set of goods into other good(s) higher on a preference scale. If lumber, glue, and other already available ingredients are transformed into a chair, the component goods have been converted into a new good whose utility is greater than the total utilities of the ingredients. If a steer is transformed into steaks, roasts, leather, glue, and fertilizer, the total utility of the separated components is greater than the utility of the whole steer. Production can also be thought of as a quasi exchange, in which the ingredients of the chair have been "exchanged" for a finished chair, and the steer has been "exchanged" for its ingredients.[4] The term "production" has the same meaning when applied to the creation of sociofacts, such as the formation of a new corporation or government bureau or the reshuffling of lines of authority in the Salvation Army. If anyone finds this extension of the term "production" offensive to traditional usage, he may refer to these things as "useful transformations."

We can express the resulting relationship in either context, first by saying that a productive process will not rationally be engaged in unless the final good is expected to possess more utility than the goods (including labor) consumed, or second by saying that one will not be willing to make an exchange unless the goods he receives are expected to be more valuable to him than the ones he gives up. In production, as elsewhere, mistakes are possible. An error in production would exist if the transformed goods were less valuable than before the transformation.

As in economics, production includes transformations in place (transportation) and in time (storage). Personal services by one person to others also are production, as in the case of diagnosis by a physician, advice by a counsellor, teaching by an instructor, haircuts by a barber, or the creation of sounds by a musician. The present definition differs from that customarily used in economics in that (a) it is broader in one respect, including the creation of such nontransferable goods as friendship, respect, and government, and (b) it is narrower in another respect since it excludes exchange (the creation of possession utility).[5]

---

[4] See Kenneth E. Boulding, *The Skills of the Economist* (Cleveland: Howard Allen, Inc., 1958), p. 10.

[5] This exclusion draws a sharp distinction between transformations and transactions. Under the present definitions it is conceptually unequivocal to say: "There are two main ways to acquire a good—either to produce it for oneself, or to produce something else and exchange it for what one wants." By contrast, if production is defined to include exchange, the quoted statement becomes conceptually fuzzy.

Production enlarges or improves opportunities. After the lumber and glue have been transformed into chairs, or steers into meat and leather, we are faced with more or superior opportunities than before the transformations. For this reason, production can be viewed as the most important normal source of enlarged opportunities, at least for the whole population. Fortuitous events can increase opportunities, but on the average they are just as likely to decrease them. Individuals or groups may improve their own opportunities at the expense of others. This provides no increase in average or total opportunities, for which we must look to production.

7. *Destruction* is the opposite of production, being any transformation which reduces utility and opportunity, subject in reverse to all the above comments about production.

8. *Consumption* is the act of extracting satisfaction from a good, as in eating an orange, living in a house, listening to a concert, or receiving the protection of police. Consuming a tangible good is usually destructive —immediately, as in the case of drinking milk, or slowly, as in the case of wearing out an automobile. Some tangible goods are actually improved by use, however, as in the case of a path through the woods or the patina on a solidly built wooden chair.

9. *Exchange* is a situation in which each of two parties provides some good(s) to the other. In the strictest or most obvious exchanges the giving up of goods by one party is specifically contingent on receipt of goods from the other. The subsequent analysis below, however, includes many looser exchanges in which there is no such explicit contingency. A *party* can be either a person or an organization, the latter to be defined below. To "provide" tangible goods is to transfer ownership or control, in whole or part. To "provide" services means to effectuate some transformation desired by the other party. For example, in providing a service, the transformation performed by A for B may take the form of a change in B's person (as with a haircut or a massage), a change in A's behavior (A is to stop making nasty remarks about B), or a change in some external not in itself involving the state or behavior of either (A will cut B's grass, or veto a bill disliked by B).

10. A *transaction* is an exchange, along with the attendant bargaining or negotiations. Transactions among three or more parties are also possible. They are more complex, but involve no significant additional concepts.

11. *Organization* is any relation of persons for joint production. Organizations and transactions will receive detailed treatment later, and need not be discussed further at this point.

12. *Cooperation* is a situation in which the same good satisfies two or

---

Because transactions are given such a prominent place in the analysis of interhuman reactions, it is imperative in the present model that production and exchange be sharply separated.

more wants, in either the same or different persons. Examples will be given later in connection with decisions and transactions.

13. *Conflict* is a situation in which one satisfaction can be achieved only by denying some other satisfaction. Broadly, the existence of conflict is the same as the existence of costs, but with two differences in emphasis. First, "costs" refers to *all* the costs of a given good, whereas "conflict" usually refers to a relationship between a wanted good and some one or few of its costs. A trip to Europe can entail all four types of cost. An incompatibility cost may be missing your brother's wedding; a scarcity cost may be doing without a new car; an unpleasantness cost may be getting seasick; and a destruction cost may be wear and tear on clothes. All four are costs; any one or combination of them may be said to be in conflict with the trip.

Second, conflict is the relation between two goods in the predecision stage; cost is the same relation in the postdecision stage. Two things are in conflict if, once a decision is made, one will become a cost of the other. Once the decision is made, however, conflict ceases and costs begin. If the relation continues or is repeated, however, conflict can also continue or be repeated.

Conflict is often interpersonal, which means that to satisfy one person's desires may require the sacrifice of another person's desires. That is, one person bears some part of the cost of another's satisfaction. It is often said under such circumstances that the two *persons* are in conflict, though the conflict, strictly speaking, is between their desires. The term also frequently refers to the emotional state of an individual faced with conflicting alternatives, or to overt fighting (verbal or otherwise) to settle a decision between conflicting parties. For the most part the word will not be used in the latter meanings in this book.

14. *Resolution of conflict* is the decision which terminates the state of conflict, producing the satisfaction of some desire(s) and the denial of those which constitute its cost. If the situation resolved by the decision is unique and irreversible, that conflict is forever ended. If the situation is a continuing or reopenable one, it remains resolved so long as the decision is accepted. If a resolution is accepted overtly, but one or both parties do not accept it subjectively and bide their time till an opportunity arises to change the situation, a state of *tension* will be said to exist. A state of tension in connection with transactions is parallel in important respects to that of illegitimacy in organizations, as will be seen in Chapter 29.

With these definitions under our belt we will now say that the major ingredients in the ability of humans to satisfy wants are decisions, transformations, transactions, and organizations, with the help of communications. Except for relatively rare free goods, one can have goods only if transformations are made. He can make transformations for himself. Or he can make transformations of goods to exchange for what he wants, through transactions with others. He can also make transformations jointly with others, in organizations. In any and all of these activities he must make decisions—to transform, to transact, to join an organization or leave it, or to engage in certain transformations or transactions within it. The organization uses the same basic method as the individual to satisfy wants: transformations and transactions. The new factors in the organization are that its transformations are joint, and that it conducts transactions within as well as outside itself.

In one form or another, the remainder of this book is taken up with the analysis of decisions, transformations, transactions, and organizations, including the flows of information relevant to making decisions. Transformations have both human and nonhuman aspects. We shall examine only the former.

$\mathcal{C}hapter$ 15

DECISIONS: COMPLEXITY, AND SOME DIMENSIONS

THE COMPLEXITY OF CHOICE, AND THE NECESSITY OF SIMPLIFICATION

Infinite Interrelationships

ANY EVENT on earth can be shown to have some conceivable relationship to any other event, and the beginning of wisdom for decision makers is to recognize that they can deal with only a tiny fraction of what is possibly relevant—even with electronic computers.

Suppose I ask why I am sitting here writing this sentence. I can refer first to the immediate circumstances. I am eager to get on with the book so I can take a vacation. I have finished lunch, completed an urgent letter, have no pressing engagements, and am awake. But these things would be irrelevant if this were Wednesday instead of Sunday, in which case I would be teaching instead of writing. To this we might add that no one has dropped in for a visit or invited us out, and since I have just assigned some special chores to my son I feel that I, too, should look busy.

To open the question more widely, I would not be writing this book at all if I were a plumber or architect, and if I were teaching in a different university with a different environment I might be writing instead about union-management relations among the Seminoles. Thus, the explanation of my present writing includes the reasons why I happen to be at the University of Cincinnati, why I became a teacher, and why I went to college.

Still more broadly, I am able to write because I am still alive, which hinges on the reasons why some occasional close calls happened to turn out in my favor. To this must be added the fact that I was born, which brings in the life histories of my parents, and of their parents.

From this point, much of human history can be retraced, since if any one of my ancestors had not been born, neither would I. If my existence does not hinge on the fact that some Greek soldier met some Persian maid when Alexander the Great invaded Persia in 331 B.C., it does hinge on a host of equally precarious accidents of history. Behind these are the facts that evolution took the course it did, that the geology of the earth was conducive to life, that the earth is a certain age and distance from the sun, and so on *ad infinitum*. Since the existence or behavior of any person, animal, building, mountain, or river is similarly related to certain features of our common past, each of these is indirectly related to my existence and behavior—and such relations will also prevail in the future.

Now this discussion has deliberately been carried to ridiculous lengths to emphasize a crucial point—that we can never know *all* the consequences of any act or decision. This means in turn that we can never know whether any decision is desirable, in light of *all* its ultimate results. Most decisions must, in fact, be made with extremely limited knowledge of their total costs and values. As Ashby has put it, every problem "embodies no less than an infinite number of variables, all but a few of which must of necessity be ignored."[1]

A Simplified Model of Decisions

Methods have been developed for formalizing certain elements in decisions. These do not give answers to decisions, but they do help to clarify the decision process, and to identify some important limitations on rational decisions. Some elements seem to be common to all decisions, from shining your shoes to launching a "preventive" war, whether the decisions are minutely reasoned or strongly intuitive.[2]

In a given decision situation, any one possible behavioral alternative is designated a. The total set of possible alternatives consists of a_1, a_2, . . . a_n, the whole set being designated A. A given decision maker may not perceive all possible alternatives; the set he does perceive is A^*, the difference between A and A^* being the unperceived alternatives.

S is the total set of possible outcomes of carrying out all possible actions in set A, s being any one outcome within set S. If each action, a, had only one possible consequence, s, the decision maker would then have to choose among a set of paired relationships of the form: if a_1 then s_1; if a_2 then s_2, and so forth.

A particular line of action might, however, have more than one possible consequence, in which case S_a designates that subset of S which includes all the possible consequences of a. We then cannot say: if a then s. We can only say: if a then S_a, which means that if we choose alternative action a, the results will be one or more of the s's in S_a. Any one s is now not a definite outcome of a, but only a possible outcome with some degree of probability. The probability that a particular s will result from action

---

[1] W. Ross Ashby, *Design for a Brain* (2d ed.; New York: John Wiley & Sons, 1960), p. 15. Although Ashby is speaking of "machines," his observation is highly pertinent to the present discussion.

[2] The set of symbols used here is taken from Herbert A. Simon, "A Behavioral Model of Rational Choice," chap. 14 in a collection of Simon's papers, *Models of Man* (New York: John Wiley & Sons, 1957), p. 244. Simon refers to the decision techniques which explicitly consider every possible detail as "global," and less ambitious techniques as "limited."

a can be written: $P_a(s)$, which can be read: "the probability that if action *a* is chosen, it will lead to outcome *s*."

This much of the process deals with the first step of adaptive behavior described in the preceding chapter: the listing of possible responses to a given situation, and the probable consequences of each. The next step is to attach a value or utility to each of the possible outcomes. The decision maker would then state a value, V, for each *s* in the set S, each indicated as $V(s)$. In some cases nothing more might be needed than a simple ordering of pairs—as, for example, that $V(s_1)$ is greater than $V(s_2)$. Where possible, cardinal measures of value might be attached, as in saying that $V(s_1)$ equals $500 and $V(s_2)$ equals $400. On the basis of these valuations, the alternative with the highest valuation (with due consideration to its probability) would be chosen. This completes the second step of adaptive behavior, and completes the decision in its narrower sense as described in Chapter 14.

This is a relatively simple model, reflecting, as Simon suggests, the common ingredients of both limited and global decision processes. More complex models of decisions include additional dimensions, as well as additional detail to the dimensions already included. We will not specifically state such a model, but the greater complexity will be implicit in the ensuing discussion, which will point out both what would be needed for a completely logical decision, and why it is not possible. The above model does include alternate actions, alternate outcomes of those actions, with the outcome of each expressed as a probability rather than a certainty. It does not include some other dimensions of choice, to be investigated below. Nor does it indicate why the problem is formulated as it is, how wide the question is to be opened, or how the list of perceived actions and possible outcomes is arrived at. Nor is a goal included—e.g., is the best possible solution wanted, or merely a satisfactory one? It is not an outline of decision making, but a framework on which to hang the rest of the outline.

THE GENERAL RULE OF DECISIONS

We will first state what we will call the General Rule of Decisions, and later elaborate both its meaning and its uses. The rule is: *starting from any given point, total satisfaction will be increased if a decision is made in favor of any alternative whose value exceeds its cost, when both value and cost are measured forward from the moment the decision is effective.*[3]

---

[3] The term "increased" in this definition is satisfactory for the vast majority of decision situations. To give the decision full scope, instead of saying that satisfaction will be increased we might say that it will be higher than it otherwise would be. We can also say that strict application of the rule will maximize satisfaction—although this version of the rule is subject to important observations about maximization in succeeding pages, and in the latter part of Chapter 16.

A decision can reflect only the information possessed at the time the decision is made. This, of course, may subsequently turn out to be wrong. As a statement of effects of decisions, the rule is valid as it stands. When we are actually making

That satisfaction will be increased by a decision in favor of any alternative whose value exceeds its cost is a truism. It is axiomatic, being logically inescapable once we have defined satisfaction, value, and cost. Regardless of what position we start from, if we take some action which creates more satisfaction than it destroys (i.e., its value exceeds its costs), satisfaction will be increased. The meaning of the phrase, "forward from the moment the decision is effective" will be examined in the next chapter. Meanwhile we must examine the meaning of costs and values in a particular decision situation.

Gross and Net Costs and Values in Particular Decisions

Perhaps the human brain can compare only two values at a time. It might find X preferable to Y, and Y preferable to Z and thereby conclude that X is preferable to Z. Or it might compare X to Y and X to Z and reach the same conclusion. Whether we can compare more than two items simultaneously, rather than flit rapidly among pairs, it is definitely easier to *explain* comparisons in pairs.

In the previous chapter we distinguished between gross and net positions of preferences and values. The term "preference" or "value" without qualifying adjectives will mean the gross figure. The term "costs" will similarly refer to all costs relevant to the decision. If X is a yacht and Y a ham sandwich, to say that I prefer (gross) the yacht to the sandwich means that if offered a choice between the two at no cost, or at equal cost, I will take the yacht. A net preference for the yacht means that I prefer the yacht at the cost of a yacht to the ham sandwich at the cost of a sandwich. You might suspect that if I can afford the yacht I can probably also squeeze enough out of my budget for the ham sandwich. This leads us to the fact that some decisions require the selection of only one item out of a list of alternatives, while others allow the selection of two or more items, or perhaps two or more units of the same thing. Since the latter is in reality a succession of separate decisions, we must first understand decisions in which the selection of one alternative requires rejection of the other(s).

Suppose I can afford only one mower, and am choosing between a rotary (X) and a sickle bar (Y). To illustrate some of the less obvious problems, let us assume equal prices and performance (both contrary to fact). Some nonmoney costs of mowers are fumes and noise, effort of handling, risk of injury, motor maintenance, and maintenance of good cutting condition. For comparing net values of X and Y it does not matter whether these negative factors are added to cost or subtracted from value. Let us say that the risk of injury from the rotary is greater; that noise,

---

any particular decision, we must apply the rule to the *information* about costs and values, as best they can be assessed at the moment the decision is made. Economists will recognize the rule as a generalization from the principle that profit is maximized at the point where marginal costs and marginal revenues are equal.

fumes, and motor maintenance are about the same; and that effort of handling and maintaining good cutting condition are far greater for the sickle bar. All factors considered, in my scale of values, as weighted by the probabilities, let us assume that the rotary shows greater net value.

The obvious rational decision is to choose the alternative with the higher net value. But suppose *both* mowers have a positive net value. Under the General Rule, the value of each exceeds its cost, and the rule would seem to dictate that I buy both. This is not so, for two reasons. First, let us assume that I absolutely cannot get both (without quibbling how absolute "absolutely" is). If so, X is an opportunity cost of Y, and Y of X, the purchase of either eliminating the other. A thing which we may call the *final net value* of X in a decision is the net value of X minus the net value of Y. Since the net value of X is greater than that of Y, the *final* net value of X will be positive, and that for Y negative. The denial of Y *is* part of the cost of X, and it is the *final* net value which applies in the General Rule. Since it is mathematically impossible for both alternatives to have a final net value in excess of zero, the General Rule does not call for purchasing both mowers.

To make a more general statement, in a particular decision between X and Y, one of the costs of each is to do without the other. To do without Y in order to have X will be called the Y cost of X, and to do without X so as to have Y will be called the X cost of Y. In a decision between X and Y, we will define the net value of X as the gross value of X minus the non-Y costs of X, and the net value of Y as the gross value of Y minus the non-X costs of Y. A rational choice will select the one with the higher net value. The final net value of X is the net value of X minus the Y cost of X, and the final net value of Y is the net value of Y minus the X costs of Y.

If only one item is to be selected from among three, X, Y, and Z, then the selection of either X or Y necessarily eliminates the selection of Z. The Z cost of X thus equals the Z cost of Y, and does not influence the choice between X and Y. By extension, the same reasoning applies to any number of additional alternatives. In a paired comparison of two from among three or more alternatives, only those costs of one which are not costs of the other can be considered, for if we charged to any one alternative the total opportunity cost of *all* other alternatives, almost nothing would be found worth doing.

A second reason for buying only one mower instead of two is diminishing utility. As soon as I have acquired one mower, my most intense need is met, and the gross value of a second mower is much smaller. Hence, the net value of the sickle bar shrinks to less than zero, and I do not buy it. Further ramifications of diminishing utility will be discussed later.

The upshot of this analysis is as follows. We seem superficially to have two rules: (1) from among alternatives, select the one with the highest net value, and (2) decide in favor of *anything* whose value exceeds its cost.

We can now see that these rules are not contradictory, or even supplementary, but two different ways of stating the same thing. In deciding between two alternatives, if we charge each with the net value of the other as an opportunity cost, then one, and only one, can have a value which exceeds *all* its costs. The two rules seem different only if we omit the opportunity cost of the alternative denied—a seemingly improper procedure. Whether we approach decisions from decision theory, from marginal analysis of economics, or from other directions, we thus arrive at a single rule: choose any alternative whose value exceeds its costs, and value will be increased. The meaning of marginal analysis will be seen further below.

SOME FURTHER NOTES ON COMPLEXITY

Despite the neat model and straightforward one-sentence rules, a logical decision is a complex thing. The complexity does not lie in the rules or model, but in the details of implementation. Viewed as a logical, rational process, even apparently simple decisions have many dimensions, and sometimes almost infinitely complex interrelations. The major dimensions are quality, quantity, time, and probability, plus a different kind of dimension in the scope of the decision itself.

As to quality, any cost or value may include different types of satisfaction or dissatisfaction. Going to college shows such different types of values as the enjoyment of learning, increased earning power, the making of friends, and participation in sports. It has such different kinds of costs as money, time, self-discipline, and perhaps leaving a comfortable home or postponing marriage.[4] The quantity dimension has two subdimensions, the magnitude or intensity of satisfaction from a good, and the number of units of the good. The time dimension includes both duration and time sequence, along with some other complications to be seen. Probability is the likelihood that a particular thing will occur. To illustrate some of these dimensions, the *magnitude* of dissatisfaction from breaking an arm is greater than that of bruising it. The *duration* of satisfaction from a wise choice of a wife or profession is much greater than from a wise choice of today's lunch. The *probability* that I will actually get lunch if I stand in the cafeteria line is much higher than the probability that I will win the Irish sweepstakes if I buy a ticket. These dimensions affect both costs and values, as when I am certain that I am enjoying a party but am uncertain how I will feel the next morning. The net (or total) effect of all dimensions depends on interrelating them in some way.

The Cost-Value Chart. Figure 15-1 illustrates the problem of this interrelationship at its simplest level, using only two dimensions, magnitude and duration. Values are shown on the horizontal scale and costs on the

---

[4] In one sense each such quality is itself a dimension, which in turn has the other dimensions of quantity, time, and probability. Although that phraseology is perhaps more customary, it is also more clumsy, and adds nothing to the analysis.

vertical. Only two magnitudes of costs and values are shown, large and small, and only two durations, short and long. The preferred traits of values are that they be large and long, and of costs that they be small and short. To make the comparisons as simple as possible, we will assign an arbitrary value of +1 to any value which is small and short, +2 if it is small and long, +3 if it is large and short, and +4 if it is large and long. A cost will be assigned a value of −1 if it is small and short, −2 if small and long, −3 if large and short, and −4 if large and long.

The squares are numbered from 1 to 16, in rows from upper left to lower right. The worst possible combination is in block 1, where a large long cost of −4 provides only a small, short value of +1, for a net value of −3. The best possible combination is block 16, where a large long

Figure 15-1

COST-VALUE CHART

General Form

VALUES

		SMALL		LARGE	
		SHORT +1	LONG +2	SHORT +3	LONG +4
LARGE	LONG −4	1 −3	2 −2	3 −1	4 0
	SHORT −3	5 −2	6 −1	7 0	8 +1
SMALL	LONG −2	9 −1	10 0	11 +1	12 +2
	SHORT −1	13 0	14 +1	15 +2	16 +3

(COST, at far left vertical label)

value of +4 is achieved at a small short cost of −1, for a net value of +3. Blocks numbered 1, 2, 3, 5, 6, and 9 show a net loss, the costs exceeding the values. Blocks 8, 11, 12, 14, 15, and 16 show a net gain, the values exceeding the costs. The four blocks on the diagonal from upper right to lower left (numbers 4, 7, 10, and 13) are neutral, with a net value of zero.

It is not easy to cite examples for particular blocks, because people have different value systems, and because the terms large and small, long and short, are far from precise. Finally, the chart includes only two of the four dimensions, omitting quantity and probability. Despite these limitations, we would probably receive general agreement on several things as having long large costs and small short values, and hence as falling into the first square. These might be such things as trying to save the change-purse from a burning house, playing "chicken" with automobiles on the highway, using dangerous stunts for fraternity initiations, ruining one's reputation for petty gain, risking illegitimate pregnancy, taking dope, and the like. Society widely labels things with such highly unfavorable value-cost relationships as bad, foolish, and immoral. For the present we will assume that the costs are borne by the same person who receives the benefits, reserving different situations for later discussion.

The lower right corner represents the obviously desirable things with small short costs and large long values. Many are strongly urged by society—such as being honest, courteous, reliable, and orderly; taking stitches in time (preventive maintenance); learning simple but useful skills; or planting literal or figurative acorns whose value rises with the simple passage of time.

Some business promotion schemes fall into block 15, since they often bring large quick returns, mostly at the risk of other people's money. Expensive but successful surgery to a child might fall in block 8, while that to an aged person (by comparison) might fall in block 7. Since different persons place widely different values on things, many decisions are peculiarly personal. A marriage ending in early divorce, no children, and large alimony might fall into block 16 for the woman who measures all values in money, but in block 1 for the woman who wants a home and family, and whose religion prohibits remarriage.

The chart is not a guide to practical decision making, but an introduction to its complexity. Even though only two dimensions of costs and values are shown, and only two degrees of each, this highly simplified arrangement nevertheless shows 16 possible cost-value combinations. The strictly logical decision maker would have to determine which of the 16 most nearly represents the net value of any one alternative, and then compare it with the position of each other alternative, similarly arrived at.

The Complexity of a "Simple" Decision. As we move to more realistic levels, the complexity of logical (as contrasted to intuitive or impulsive) decisions grows at a frightening rate. To the above cost-value chart we must add the dimension of probability. And if we are to provide even modestly sensitive distinctions, each of the dimensions must be divided into at least five gradations (instead of two), perhaps as follows:

Very Large	Large	Medium	Small	Very Small
Very Long	Long	Medium	Short	Very Short
Highly Probable	Probable	Uncertain	Improbable	Highly Improbable

Let us now examine a type of decision which occurs in everyday life, showing five kinds of costs, five kinds of values, and five possible degrees, or gradations of each of the three dimensions of cost and value. A penurious student meets some of his better heeled friends on their way to an expensive restaurant, and they ask him to join them. The five kinds of value he sees in joining them might be the satisfaction of hunger, the nutritional value of food, a respite in a hectic day, an opportunity to find if expensive food really tastes better, and the off-chance of meeting a wealthy woman who often eats there, and who sometimes befriends needy students.

If the student were to make a fully rational (i.e., "global") decision, he would have to classify each of the five kinds of value into one of the five grades of magnitude, of duration, and of probability. For instance, the value of satisfying hunger might be classed as large, short, and highly probable, while the value of getting help from the wealthy woman might be very large, long, and highly improbable. Each of the remaining three types of value would have to be similarly evaluated, after which the joint effect of all five evaluations would have to be ascertained. Since there are five types of value, each having five possible magnitudes, durations, and probabilities, the resulting judgment represents a selection of one from among 625 possible combinations of value.

Let us assume that the student's joining the group also involves five different kinds of costs, such as time, money, parental disapproval, embarrassment at his shabby clothes, and indigestion from missing his special diet. Five different degrees each of magnitude, duration, and probability produce 625 possible combinations of costs, from which he must select the appropriate one.

We now face a cost-value chart (or matrix) with 625 divisions each on the value and cost scales, the whole containing 390,625 cells. The student can then determine which of these cells most nearly represents his true situation, compare it with the value of the cell similarly determined for each possible alternative activity, and choose the one with the highest net value. If he does not starve first, he *may* reach a truly logical, reasoned decision. Although the *decision* may be rational (within this simplified version of complex reality), the *decision process* obviously is not —a matter we will return to later.

THE DIMENSIONS OF DECISIONS

To say that even a simple decision of ordinary life is hopelessly complex if it is to be made "rationally" does not mean that we must give up. By examining certain details we can nevertheless learn much to increase understanding of the decision process, both as decision makers and as social analysts.

The Quality Dimension

Costs. In the preceding chapter we have seen that costs can be classified into four main groups: the opportunity costs of incompatibility and scarcity and the disutility costs of unpleasantness and destruction. Each can have many subspecies, and we have already noted five different kinds of costs for the student deciding whether to enter the restaurant. There is almost no limit to the number of kinds of costs of a given activity, which might include risk of injury, risk of poison, embarrassment, frustration, dirt, sweat, boredom, anger, fear, disgust, loss of influence, loss of sleep, itching, pain, destruction of property, risk of money, or loss of friends.

The costs may be borne by an individual or a group, the latter ranging from a collectivity of two to the whole world. In groups the degree of cost may differ from person to person, and from subgroup to subgroup.

When an individual makes a decision, all these things are evaluated and balanced within the same brain and the same preference system. If the costs are spread among a group, further tremendous complications arise. One person may enjoy a good sweat but value his time highly, while a second may hate sweat but have time to squander. What the total costs of a little sweat and much time are to a group with divergent values is essentially imponderable.[5] We will omit the complicating factor or group values for the present, returning to it in connection with social decisions in a later chapter, although the problem is present in any decision affecting more than one person.

Two or more costs may be related, rather than independent. A common relation is joint costs, in which the expenditure of one cost brings two or more separate values. If both meat and glue are made from the same animal, the cost of raising the animal is joint to meat and glue. If you can go shopping and visit a friend on the same trip, the trip is a joint cost of both results. Joint costs is another way of saying that a given cost may bring two or more distinct kinds of values, or that the relationship is co-operative.[6] Joint costs raise a complication for decisions, since we cannot know how much of a joint cost is to be charged to one value until we know how much can be charged to the other, and the allocation in most decisions is highly imponderable. If only one value is wanted (we want meat but not glue), the whole cost must be charged to that value.

Values. Like costs, values appear in bewildering variety. A given decision may bring values in income, power, security, or affection. It may bring humor, relaxation, sounder sleep, stronger friendships, prompter obedience, coolness, cooperativeness, or education. Or it may bring paintings, vacations, watches, concerts, television shows, television repair, shoe laces, loans, or a safe deposit box. To know the total value of any decision, the decision maker must know *which* of these things he will receive, and their relative importance. Values to a group raise the same kind of question as do group costs, and having mentioned them we will go on.

Also like costs, values can be interrelated. First, two values can be substitutes or compliments. To an important degree pork is a substitute for beef, which is a substitute for fish, and so on. In some uses copper is a substitute for aluminum, a well is a substitute for a spring, and irrigation is a substitute for rain. Within limits, but often wide ones, one mystery

---

[5] A pioneering work along these lines, built on previous work by welfare economists and related lines, is Kenneth J. Arrow's *Social Choice and Individual Values* (New York: John Wiley & Sons, 1951).

[6] Joint costs are related to the economic concept of joint supply. A related economic concept, composite supply, has no apparent useful counterpart for costs. Its parallel would be alternative kinds of cost expenditures for the same thing. This is part of the essence of the decision, not a supplement to it.

story is a substitute for another, a Picasso is a substitute for a Braque, a dog is a substitute for a child, travel is a substitute for formal education, status is a substitute for affection, and brains are a substitute for brawn. The general relationship is of the sort: if A and B are substitutes, then to possess A decreases the utility of B, or to possess B decreases the utility of A. In reverse, the absence of either *increases* the utility of the other.

The opposite relationship exists when two things are complements, in which case the possession of A increases the utility of B, or the possession of B increases the utility of A. In this case the absence of either good *decreases* the utility of the other. When one has an automobile or a motor boat he has a complementary desire for gasoline, and for highways or waterways. A camera brings a complementary desire for film, and perhaps for light meters, enlargers, or projectors, and a decision to run for public office brings complementary desires for speaking engagements, newspaper publicity, campaign funds, and poor opposition candidates. Complementarity arises in whole-part relationships, in the sense that automobile and gasoline are parts of transportation, and that speaking engagements are a part of the whole process of running for office.

Other wants are unrelated in any direct sense, the desire for chewing gum, gasoline, votes, education, and a family being essentially independent.

Wants (and hence the values or goods which satisfy them) can also be relative or absolute. *Relative wants* include the desire for improvement (doing better than in the past), and for superiority (being better than others). Desire for improvement is essentially competition against oneself, and can be endless. Desire for superiority is a competition against others, and can also be endless if others keep improving, or if the competition keeps moving into new areas.

Absolute wants can be completely satisfied, leaving no further want. Many biological wants are of this sort, a certain amount of food, for instance, leaving the desire completely satisfied. True, the organism recycles, but there is nevertheless a definite limit to the food one can eat in a lifetime. The desire to have the driveway paved or to get a college degree may develop complementary desires. But each is absolute in itself. Absolute desires are subject to diminishing utility (to be discussed below), whereas relative ones are not—if we assume "pure" cases of each. It is often difficult to separate the two in fact, and both could conceivably appear in the want for any one good. We may want a new car because the old one is falling apart (absolute) and also to keep up with the Joneses (relative). The absolute aspect of the want is satisfied as soon as we acquire the new car, but the relative want remains if the Joneses get a newer one.

Goods achieved through a long series of instrumental acts, like climbing Mt. Everest or being elected governor, may undergo many changes of attitude toward the costs and values en route. We will mention this complication, but will not deal with it further.

The Quantity Dimension

Quantity appears in decisions in two senses. One is the magnitude of cost or value of a unit of good, and the other is the number of units. Many goods come in indivisible units. We either run for governor, join the army, marry Joan, or sell the house—or we do not. Here we face a simple selection among alternatives, as outlined in the initial model. These are "chunky," or "all or none" decisions between incompatibles, in contrast to variable magnitude decisions, where we can choose more or less of a given thing. In the latter, choices are repeatable, or open to increase or decrease. Having eaten one cookie, should I eat a second, and having eaten a second, should I eat a third? Having swum twenty yards from shore, shall I swim another twenty, or a hundred? Having successfully planted a dozen strawberry plants, shall I plant another dozen? Having produced and sold twenty thousand sets of brass knuckles, should I produce and try to sell another set, or another thousand sets?

An obvious fact of life is that we do not apply all our resources toward any one goal. We do, or acquire, some units of this, then some units of that, followed by some units of still other things. In deciding the number of units we wish to acquire of any one thing, beyond some quantity, we represent an equilibrium system. As seen in Chapter 3, a stable equilibrium system requires one direct and one inverse variation, or the system will either explode or shrivel away. In decisions about multiple units of the same goods, the cost varies directly with the number of units and the value varies inversely.

The inverse relation between value and quantity is known as diminishing utility. Beyond some quantity, the larger the number of units of any good we acquire, the smaller will be the additional satisfaction produced by each additional unit. One hamburger satisfies greatly, a second satisfies less intense hunger, and so on, until the twentieth hamburger (at a sitting) has negative utility. To be elected president of one club may be highly elating, but being elected president of a tenth may be rather a bore.

The direct relation between cost and quantity may have either or both of two sources. One, which may or may not exist within the confines of a particular decision, is increasing cost, which is more widely known as diminishing productivity. After we have swum a hundred yards, fatigue produces fewer additional yards for a given amount of time or effort. After putting a hundred strawberry plants in the window box, we will find the second hundred less productive. The second twenty thousand brass knuckles are more costly if they overtax the capacity of the plant, which was built to produce twelve thousand. Diminishing productivity of successive units of input is the same thing as increased cost for successive units of output.

Even if increased costs per unit due to diminishing productivity do not appear within the limits of the decision (the twentieth hamburger has the same money cost as the first), increased costs will nevertheless appear sooner or later in the form of rising opportunity costs, at the level of production, consumption, or both. To illustrate first at the consumption level, suppose that hamburgers and milkshakes are both 25 cents. Starting from a given state of hunger, suppose they also have the same utility to me, as follows. The first hamburger would give me 100 utils of satisfaction, the second 90, the third 80, the fourth 70, and so on. Four successive milkshakes would provide identical amounts of satisfaction. If I spend the first quarter for a hamburger, should I then spend the next quarter for a second hamburger or for a first milkshake? If I spend it for the milkshake, I receive 100 utils. The opportunity cost is that I forego the hamburger, which would give me only 90 utils. By contrast, if I should spend the second quarter on a second hamburger, I would receive 90 utils at an opportunity cost of 100.

Let us jump farther down the scale and work back. Suppose I have enough money and appetite to consume eight items. Shall I take eight hamburgers and no milkshakes, eight milkshakes and no hamburgers, four of each, or what? As a point of reference let us start with four each. The fourth hamburger will provide 70 utils, and so will the fourth milkshake. Suppose I contemplate five hamburgers and only three milkshakes. The fifth hamburger would provide 60 utils, but require me to forego the fourth milkshake at 70 utils. A sixth hamburger would provide 50 utils, but make me forego the third milkshake at 80 utils, and so on. In this relationship the opportunity cost of a fifth hamburger is 70 utils, and the opportunity costs of the sixth, seventh, and eighth are 80, 90, and 100 respectively.[7]

The illustration is given in terms of only two goods, but applies universally. To speak of things purchasable with money, the hamburgers and milkshakes bought with a dollar have such opportunity costs as a movie ticket, part of a haircut, two pocket mysteries, or partial savings toward a vacation. Expenditures of time operate in the same way. As to other nonmoney items, if you want a small wedding, the more relatives you invite the fewer nonrelatives you can have. The more of your jokes you tell at the table, the fewer you have left for after dinner. The more of your credibility you use up on false alarms, the less will you have left when the wolf really arrives.

Rising opportunity costs also appear at the producer level. Every additional acre used to grow oranges means one less acre on which to grow lemons, and every man hour used to make marihuana means one less available to make opium.

Whether this force operates instead of or in addition to diminishing

---

[7] The problem is stated here as a sequence of decisions for purpose of the explanation. The problem of deciding the total number of each item is basically the same even if I place my total order immediately at the outset. We will disregard variations based on various sequences of actual eating—which, incidentally, help illustrate the complications of fully rational decisions in even apparently simple matters.

productivity, the costs of successive units of a given good will rise. At the same time, as we have already seen, the value of successive units will go down. If each successive unit has a higher cost and a lower value, the cost will eventually equal the value, and then exceed it if still more units are acquired. The point of equality is the equilibrium point of this system. Any additional quantity up to that point adds to satisfaction. Any additional quantity beyond that point reduces satisfaction. Following the lead of economics, we will call the additional cost of any one additional unit its *marginal cost*, and the additional value of any one additional unit its *marginal value* (or marginal utility).

This relation can be graphed, as in Figure 15-2, with a falling line of marginal value and a rising line of marginal cost. As we acquire additional units starting from the left, each unit adds to satisfaction by the distance between the two lines. At the eighth unit the lines cross.

Figure 15-2

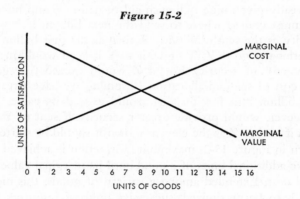

This means that cost and value are equal for the eighth unit, and that satisfaction is neither increased nor decreased by acquiring it. Beyond that number, the costs exceed the value, and satisfaction will be decreased by a ninth, or any further units.

This principle applies to the consumer deciding on hamburgers and milkshakes. It applies to a business firm deciding to produce one, ten, or ten million units; to hire one, ten, or ten thousand employees; or to purchase one, a dozen, or a hundred machines. It applies to the presidential candidate deciding how many appearances to make in a given state, to the person deciding how many friends to cultivate, or to a nation cultivating the friendship of other nations, where the cost of closer ties with one nation is greater estrangement of another.

The Principle of Equimarginality. Since part of the cost of any one opportunity is to forego alternative opportunities, it is not rational to spend any cost on one opportunity if it would bring more satisfaction in an alternate one. It is irrational to spend money on a second hamburger if it would bring more satisfaction on a first milkshake. It is irrational to spend a billion dollars on military aid to nation X if it would bring greater security if spent on economic aid, or on military or economic aid to nation Y. Nor is it rational to spend a first billion on nation Y if it would bring greater returns as the tenth billion to nation Z—all of these statements being subject to later comment about the meaning and limitations of rationality. Here we are concerned not with quantity alone or with quality alone, but with the *quantity* of a given *quality* (type or source) of satisfaction that will be sought before a switch is made to achieve *some quantity* of a *different quality* of satisfaction.

We have already seen that (1) choosing the alternative with the highest net value and (2) choosing anything whose value exceeds its cost amount to the same thing if the opportunity costs of the alternatives denied are considered. When we view the whole of our resources, or of any given resource, any additional unit of resource can be applied to acquiring either different goods or additional units of the same goods. Suppose we have already given nine billion in aid to nation Z and none to nation Y, and we must choose where to send the next billion. If it would bring more security as the tenth billion to Z than as the first billion to Y, then it should rationally go to Z. To give it to Y instead would mean that the opportunity cost of security lost at Z would exceed that gained from Y, and the cost of such an allocation (assuming we have already decided to put the billion into foreign aid) would exceed its value. If the next billion, however, would provide greater security if sent to Y as the first billion than if sent to Z as the eleventh, then it should be shifted to Y.

As shown in Figure 15-2, maximum satisfaction is achieved if we continue to take additional units of a good until its marginal value just equals its marginal cost. Extended among a variety of goods, this means that if satisfaction is to be maximized, successive units of resources must be so applied that the value they produce from one use will just equal the value in any other use. The opportunity cost of the fifth hamburger is the denial of the third milkshake, and unless the quarters are so spent that they will produce the same amount of satisfaction whether spent for another hamburger *or* another milkshake, one desire will be oversatisfied, and the other undersatisfied. This set of relationships is known as the principle of *equimarginality*, any violation of which will satisfy a smaller want at the opportunity cost of leaving a larger want unsatisfied, and thus prevent maximum satisfaction.

Chunky Decisions.   Many of life's goods do not allow us to take a little, and then a little more, in order to maximize our satisfaction. Having won a war we do not have to decide how much additional satisfaction would arise from winning a second or third over the same enemy. Having won the election or pushed the villain off the cliff, we need not contemplate the additional value of another vote or a second push. Decisions involving this all-or-none quality can be referred to as "chunky," discontinuous, or discrete. They do not allow us to spread our resources over various satisfactions, but require that we either do without something entirely, or incur a larger cost than we might be inclined to do.

To illustrate, you may have only a small desire for a car of your own —say for perhaps a hundred dollars worth per year. But the ownership of an automobile is chunky, the minimum cost normally running from three to five hundred dollars. You must either get less automobile service than you want, namely none, or spend much more than you wish. Or you may have two young ladies with whom you would like to spend about equal time. But if one will cut you off cold if you so much as speak to the other, she destroys your freedom to allocate your time and affections so as to equalize their marginal returns in alternate uses, and has forced you to deal with a chunky decision between incompatible alternatives. Or you might want to spend your spare time about equally between making photographs and playing chamber music. But if doing so leaves you too little time to become competent at either, you may get more satisfaction if you devote all your time to one and none to the other.

Decisions may be chunky for numerous reasons. Their universal effect, however, is to prevent us from getting the precise quantity of something that we want, requiring us to take either more or less than would maximize satisfaction. Chunkiness does not invalidate the principle of equimarginality, but it does prevent us from achieving the point of maximum satisfaction in fact.

Is this principle a rule of decision making, a normative prescription of what people ought to do, a description of what they actually do, or what? First, it is not a recommendation, as this book is intended as a science (however much it may fail), not an ethic. As noted earlier, the General Rule is axiomatic, following inescapably from the definition of its terms. The principle of equimarginality is directly deduceable from it, and hence is also inescapable. Neither rule suggests what *ought* to be done, but merely what *must* be done *if* maximum satisfaction is to be achieved—subject to some observations about rationality in the next chapter.

Although no one would pretend that human beings apply the rule precisely, it nevertheless does have much explanatory value for describing actual behavior. We do not buy all hamburgers and no milkshakes. We do not put all our foreign aid into one nation, nor do we divide it equally among all nations. Although the housewife could usefully spend more time in almost any one activity, she divides her time among house cleaning, laundry, cooking, sewing, decorating, and caring for children. If we ask why the housewife (or any other person) spreads time among various activities instead of concentrating it all on one, it seems impossible to answer without using language which describes behavior directed *toward* equimarginality. The point of equimarginality is presumably never precisely reached except by rare accident, but to say that a given force does not operate precisely is by no means the same as saying that it is insignificant. The General Rule, and the principle of equimarginality derived from it, seems to be not merely logically inescapable, but also a reasonably good first approximation description of what people actually do.[8]

---

[8] In similar vein, in connection with the impact of economic forces in wage determination I have argued that "we must be careful not to equate imperfection with impotence." See Alfred Kuhn, "Toward an Integration of Wage Theory," *The Southern Economic Journal* (July, 1959), p. 15. We must similarly be careful not to throw out a model or theory which provides a respectable first approximation description just because some of its overzealous supporters claim it to be a *complete* description—at least not until we have a better model, which in this case we do not have.

Chapter 16

DECISIONS: MORE DIMENSIONS, SCOPE, AND OVERVIEW

THE TIME DIMENSION

THE TIME dimension enters decisions in at least three ways. The first is simple duration. As to costs, a mortgage on the house or an amputated arm lasts a long time. And as to values, the ability to enjoy music usually lasts longer than ability as a track star, and a roof of copper lasts longer than one of thatch.

The second aspect of time is that a future value is not the same as a present one. In Western society, at least, goods in the present are usually valued more highly than goods in the future. This relationship is known as *time preference*. It is widely reflected in the fact that borrowers will pay interest to get something sooner than if they had to save for it in advance, while lenders expect interest for having to wait for use of their money. The lower present price of a future value is known as *time discount*, indicated by the fact that a promissory note for a given amount will not command as high a price in the present as it will when due at some time in the future.

For some purposes a thing may be more valuable in the future than the present. Savings to put a son through college or for retirement are more desired at the future point when those events arise than at the present. These exemplify a reverse, or negative, time preference. During inflation material goods rise in value and during deflation money increases in value. A painting or antique may rise in value merely because of passing time, while an automobile or encyclopedia may go down, even in the absence of wear and tear.

To be rational, any decision whose effects cover a span of time must consider future as well as present costs and values.

A third aspect of time is that costs and values undergo changes in relationship. Not only do real prices rise or fall, but innumerable changes during life alter the amount of satisfaction we can get for a given amount of dissatisfaction. The amount of value which can be received from a given cost will be called the value-cost ratio, or V/C. Obviously it is possible to achieve greater satisfaction under a high value-cost ratio than a low one, and hence a high ratio has high instrumental value.

Variable, Fixed, Investment, and Sunk Costs

It is often possible to do something which, without bringing any present satisfaction, will nevertheless make it easier to achieve a given amount of satisfaction in the future—that is, will increase the future V/C. Any such activity constitutes *investment*, which will be defined as any present cost over and above that incurred for the receipt of present value which is intended to bring an improvement in the future value-cost ratio. An "improvement" in V/C means that a given value will have a lower cost, that a given cost will bring larger value, or both.

By contrast, a *variable cost* is one incurred to acquire present value under the existing value-cost ratio.

If I go to the woods each summer to pick blackberries, I am incurring variable costs of time, effort, sweat, and scratches. But if I transplant some of the bushes to my back yard in the fall, the costs of so doing are an investment. These bring no berries at the time, but reduce the time and effort required to pick berries in the future. Hence, they improve the future V/C ratio. If I go to college, the costs are variable to the extent that college is satisfying in itself—a present return for a present expense. But to the extent that college costs more than I would spend for the immediate satisfaction, that additional expense is an investment toward being able to produce more goods or get more satisfaction from given costs in the future.

Investment may take the form of creating or improving tools, factories, roads, or other equipment. It may consist of improving one's knowledge and skill, as by study, practice, or self-discipline. It may also take the form of improving one's relationships with others, as by going out of one's way to develop a reputation for integrity, cooperativeness, or reliability, or to develop deeper friendships, mutual confidence, or smooth working relations with associates.

To apply the terms "cost" and "investment" to such things is not intended to cheapen them, but rather to indicate the universality of costs. It does not imply "using" friends or "coasting" on a reputation to recognize that persons with many friends and good reputations do, in fact, find it easier to accomplish many things. If so, friends and reputation provide a higher V/C ratio in achieving objectives. The friendship itself often provides much satisfaction at little cost, which is another aspect of a high V/C. Since to build an intimate friendship or an excellent reputation usually entails some costs which are not immediately rewarding, those costs fill the definition of investment. If filching my good name leaves me poor indeed, a good name is a thing of great value, often worth large investment.

Deliberate self-denial dedicated to better self-control or a better seat in heaven is also investment. As will be seen later, so is the use of power to increase future power. Obviously, to put money into a business for profit—the traditional meaning of the term—is also investment. If successful, it raises future value relative to future costs. The mere saving of money is investment. It is a cost, in that the saver must deny himself present goods. It is investment, in that the saver can acquire value in the future without incurring opportunity or disutility costs of the money at that time, those costs already having been incurred when the money was originally set aside.[1]

Fixed costs are current costs necessary to prevent deterioration of the V/C ratio. If we refer to such deterioration, which is the reverse of investment, *as disinvestment*, then *fixed costs* are those current costs necessary to prevent disinvestment. Fixed costs may also be considered as *maintenance costs* of the existing V/C ratio. In business many fixed costs consist of legal or contractual obligations, such as property taxes or rent. Prevention of such disinvestments as fire, theft, or accident often takes the form of the fixed cost of insurance premiums. Buildings require paint and repair from the ravages of time, machines must be prevented from rusting, food from spoiling, land from eroding, and flowers from being choked by weeds. Not to spend these fixed costs means that the V/C ratio will deteriorate. This relationship is equally valid whether the ratio at a given moment is the result of prior investment or a gift of nature. It is equally a fixed cost whether the expenditure is made to offset depreciation (actual deterioration of condition) or obsolescence (a decline in value due to the mere passage of time without deterioration).

Some disinvestment is caused by use, rather than mere passage of time or decay. Examples include wear and tear on machinery, roads, rugs, or clothing, or the deterioration of a reputation for impartiality occasioned by taking sides in a particular dispute. Since this kind of disinvestment does not occur unless the investment is used, it is a cost of value currently produced or received. If we currently repair or replace the deterioration as it occurs, or currently set aside money or materials to cover such repair or replacement, the immediate effect of such disinvestment is the same as a variable cost, and it may be treated as such. If not so handled, such cost remains a permanent disinvestment, unless, of course, it is restored by subsequent reinvestment.

Fixed costs are sometimes improperly thought to be unavoidable. Any cost is avoidable if one is willing to accept the subsequent deterioration of his V/C position. The deterioration may take such varied forms as bankruptcy, disintegration of one's house, loss of friends, incarceration, or death. To say that a fixed cost is unavoidable simply means that the deterioration resulting from failure to pay it is larger than one is willing to contemplate. The present definition makes no such prior assumption, and is universally applicable.

---

[1] This analysis is in agreement with the economic proposition that, *ex post*, savings and investment are necessarily equal.

Because these terms are borrowed from economics, and are widely thought to be relevant only to economic phenomena, it may be useful to elaborate somewhat their application to other areas. A reputation for professional competence improves one's V/C ratio in his work, and hence the building of such a reputation is an investment. Since the reputation will deteriorate if its holder turns in a series of poor performances, or drops too long from circulation, he must provide more or less continuous, high level performance as the fixed cost of maintaining the reputation.

Some intangible investments must be handled with the same care as explosives, without even being insurable. Like a single match in the munitions works, a single violation of his basic integrity in a conspicuous spot can blow up a man's career. Political liberty, academic freedom, and freedom of speech and press are also things of great value, won through large investment by our ancestors, and maintained by the fixed cost of eternal vigilance. For example, a single obvious and unrectified violation of academic freedom can have tremendous cost by making every professor on a campus fearful to speak his mind. Persons who understand and value freedom therefore often accept the fixed costs of time, effort, money, and sometimes serious risk to their personal positions, to prevent disinvestment in freedom, even in cases which do not directly affect them.

Most of life's investments and fixed costs are neither monetary nor momentous. We invest in a rack to make tools more accessible, and incur the fixed cost of keeping the rack in good order. We invest careworn hours in training children to pick up behind themselves—an investment which (I am told) pays great dividends if successful. Even if successful it may incur fixed costs in constant checking up lest this highly perishable habit be extinguished, and an even higher cost in the necessity of maintaining a good example. We invest time and effort in developing skill at basketball, carpentry, lecturing, or fiddle playing, only to discover that disinvestment will occur unless we pay the fixed cost of continued practice. We invest God knows what to mold a young lady's affection toward us, perhaps to discover that the fixed cost of keeping it is greater than the original investment. The movie starlet invests two brawls and a slight plane crash to build a given level of public attention, thereby incurring the fixed cost of a divorce every other year to avoid disinvestment.

Not all investments add to fixed cost, and many are made expressly for the opposite purpose. A copper roof, a paved walk, or a drip-dry shirt are investments which may reduce the maintenance costs of roof repair, shoveling back the gravel after rain, or ironing. A firmly established friendship is less touchy than one half built, and may go unscathed through incidents or neglect that would wreck the lesser one. The investment of building the second half may thus reduce the ultimate maintenance costs. And the children's habit of picking up *may* go on without further work by the parents.

A final type of cost is sunk cost. A *sunk cost* is any cost already incurred which cannot be recovered, whether variable, fixed or investment.

"Already incurred" means that the satisfaction(s) whose denial constitutes the cost have already been destroyed or denied, or have been irretrievably committed, as by contract. Costs in time and disutility are sunk
when they occur, since they cannot be recouped. Incompatibility costs are
also necessarily sunk when nonrepeated opportunities are missed. A cost
already incurred is *not* sunk to the extent it can be recovered. A business
investment is not sunk if the share can be resold without loss. An expenditure for wood to make a table is not sunk if the wood can be returned
for credit, or used for something else; it is sunk as soon as the wood is cut
up far enough to be unusable for any other purpose. An uncancellable contract to lease a buliding or hire a comedian for five years at $1,000 a
month is a fixed cost when signed; each $1,000 becomes a sunk cost when
actually paid—though if the contract is absolutely "tight" (i.e., enforceable), for all practical purposes the whole $60,000 is sunk when the con-
tract is signed.

Generally, any cost already expended is sunk unless the transaction or
transformation for which it is spent can be reversed or redirected. If you
buy a snail shell factory, the price is tentatively sunk at the moment of
purchase, whether or not you ever produce any shells. But if you could
resell the building at the price you paid, only the transaction costs would
be sunk. Sunk costs would rise or fall (perhaps shifting into profit) if the
building could be resold for less or more than you paid.

Sometimes it is not possible to tell at the moment a cost is incurred
whether some or all of it will be recoverable. Its status, however, can always be clearly identified at the moment when the *next* decision involving
it arises. Suppose five years after buying the snail shell factory you decide
you must either remodel it or sell it and buy a new one. Any amount
of money you can get for the factory at the moment of the next decision
is not sunk; all remaining cost of the building is sunk.

Types of Costs and the General Rule

We have stated the General Rule that total satisfaction will be increased
if a decision is made in favor of any alternative whose value exceeds its
cost, when both value and cost are measured from *after* the moment the
decision is effective. We have already seen the general relations between
value and cost, and their net effect on satisfaction. We now turn to the
time aspect, which states that values and costs are to be measured from the
effective point of the decision forward.[2]

---

[2] Kenneth E. Boulding, *The Skills of the Economist* (Cleveland: Howard Allen,
Inc., 1958), p. 60, makes the point that "the marginal analysis, in its generalized
form, is *not* an analysis of *behavior* but an analysis of *advantage*." (Emphasis in
original.) In line with this spirit I am construing the economic analysis of the firm
not so much as a scientific description of what businessmen do, but as an important
part of decision theory. Two aspects of marginal theory seem crucial for this
purpose. One is the doctrine that future or anticipated, not historical, costs are the
logical basis of economic decisions. The second is the economic distinction between
the market period, short run, and long run analysis. When generalized, the latter

It should be noted that the rule is not a prescription of what anyone *ought* to do, nor a statement of what they *do* do. It is a simple analytical statement which will distinguish decisions which increase satisfaction from those which decrease it.

If we imagine that you own a piece of woods in which you sometimes camp, we can illustrate all aspects of the time relations in different types of costs. From the site of the tent it takes six minutes to walk to a stream, get water, and return. If you need a bucketful for dishes, only variable costs are involved. At a cost of six minutes time and the necessary effort you can have the bucket of water at the tent, and if the value of the water is greater than this cost, you will presumably get it. If you say, "It's worth it, but I just don't feel like going right now," you are explaining that your state of mind or body is such that present effort is costly in your present preference system, and that the total cost of going for water *now* is higher than its value to you *now*.

Subjective considerations of this sort make it extremely important to understand that the *rules* are independent of the *content* of decisions. ALL COSTS AND ALL VALUES ARE IN THE FINAL ANALYSIS SUBJECTIVE, being satisfactions achieved and satisfactions denied. Units of money or of goods are often useful for counting costs and values, but the goods themselves have value only because they are desired, and have cost only because satisfactions must be denied to produce them.

To return to the camp, in due time you start down the path, bucket in hand, when your father calls, "Why don't you bring two buckets and save a trip later?" The decision must now be reoriented. To get two buckets does not require any significantly increased time, nor any additional travel distance, but only the extra effort of carrying two buckets instead of one. Unless this extra effort is considered more costly than a separate whole trip for one bucket (one bucket is easy, but two put a crick in your back), the second bucket has less cost than the first. Hence, it need be only as valuable as the *extra* effort to justify bringing it.

When your father suggests bringing two buckets, the problem may be more complex than this. You may have figured that you would be off swimming when the next bucket was needed, and someone else would get it. Perhaps to *you* the extra effort of bringing the second bucket is a pure loss—all cost and no value. There is also the possibility that your cheery willingness or grudging reluctance to carry the second bucket will have repercussions on your concept of your own personality or sense of importance. It may also affect your father's desire to do things for you in the future, or to ask other things of you. One might say that things of this sort are petty. Perhaps they are, but they are very real factors in hosts of

---

distinction becomes the present statement that values and costs are to be measured from the moment the decision is effective forward, which automatically implies that sunk costs are irrelevant. If we care to use the phrase, it also makes "sunk values" irrelevant.

decisions, and to omit them makes thin broth out of what is really a very thick soup. It is also imperative *not* to put all these complications into the first approximation model, or the model will become incomprehensibly complex. (The kinds of effects your response has on your father will be considered in later chapters under the heading of "interrelated transactions.")

If you bring two buckets when only one is needed immediately, the extra effort is an investment. For instance, at midafternoon you awake in the hammock feeling thirsty. If you had not brought the second pail, you would have had to go all the way to the stream for a drink, but as it is you need go only to the table, the latter representing a higher V/C ratio.

If you expect to spend much time at this spot in the future, you might contemplate an investment in an improved water system. After studying the terrain you conclude that it would take about 20 hours to dig a trench to divert some water to a point only one minute away, and wonder whether the five minute saving per trip would justify digging the trench. To simplify the problem we will consider only the time element, ignoring the sweat and blisters.

Since the trench would save five minutes per trip, in 240 trips you would save the equivalent of the 20 hours required to dig the trench. We then say that the investment in the trench will "pay for itself" in 240 trips, and is "sound" if you expect to make more than 240 trips thereafter. The 20 hours of digging are an investment, as defined, since they (1) are current costs over and above what is necessary to provide water in the present, and (2) increase the future V/C ratio by reducing the future cost of water from six minutes to one minute per trip.

The decision, however, is more complex. Even if time is the only cost, a concentrated chunk of 20 hours may not have the same value as 240 bits of five minutes each. Further, time in the present may be more valuable than time in the future, and militate against the investment. Conversely, if present time is *less* valuable than future time, it might be worth digging the trench, even if it is expected to save only 10 or 15 hours in the future.

The trench may also bring on fixed costs, such as maintaining it against the depredations of beavers, cave-ins, or falling leaves. If you expect it to take about an hour each year to keep the trench open, this annual fixed cost must be added to the original cost to determine whether the trench will pay for itself.

Suppose you actually dig the ditch, and use it one summer. The following spring you face the question whether to spend an hour to clean out the winter's debris. Suppose that you plan to spend very little time at the camp this year, and probably will not need water more than six times. A saving of five minutes per trip would amount to only 30 minutes, whereas it would take an hour's work on the trench to save that half hour. Should you conclude that it is not worth the fixed cost to reopen the trench? Or are you foolishly throwing away the 20 hour investment for lack of an hour's extra work?

The General Rule states that the decision should be based on a comparison of costs and values as viewed *from the effective moment of the decision forward*. Since the time originally spent on the trench can never be recovered, it is logically a matter of complete indifference whether the trench took 20 hours, 1,000 hours, or no hours to acquire in the first place. At this moment the only question is whether the future use will justify the cost of one hour to reopen it. Since this seems improbable, the logical decision is to leave it closed this year and walk the longer distance for water.

Next year, of course, is also still in the future, and if you expect to spend much time at the camp next year, this must also enter the decision. If it seems quicker to clean the trench each year than to let dirt accumulate for several years, you may clean it now even though it is not worth it for this year's use alone. The logic of this is to save *next year's* time, not the 20 hours already sunk. To repeat, at this point it is irrelevant whether the trench originally cost 20 or 1,000 hours, or was opened by a freak tornado. Only the costs and values from this moment forward are relevant.

The following year you may wonder whether to install a pipe to avoid the fixed cost of cleaning the trench. Does the investment in the trench have any bearing on this decision? According to the rule, the original cost of the trench is sunk, and irrelevant. But if the pipe can be laid in the trench, the *fact* of the trench will reduce the *future* cost of laying the pipe. This *is* relevant, even if laying the pipe is not the purpose for which the ditch was originally dug.

The application of the General Rule can now be summarized more explicitly. Before an investment is made, the total value it is expected to produce should exceed (or at least equal) the total costs of producing that value—investment costs, fixed costs, and variable costs. In the example above, the value of water at the camp must equal the 20 hours investment in trench digging time, the annual hour of fixed costs of cleanup, and the one minute variable cost per trip. Once the trench has been dug the investment is sunk. Thereafter the trench should be maintained if it is more valuable than the annual fixed cost of cleanup plus the one minute variable cost per trip. Finally, once the cleanup has been done in any year, the water should be carried on any occasion in which its value exceeds the one minute of variable cost.

These levels of decision can be thought of as a pyramid of steps. If the goal is at the top, and each step is a cost, the value of the goal must exceed the cost of all the intervening steps, or the climb should not be started. Once any step has been climbed its cost is sunk, and no longer relevant. From that point one need consider only whether the goal is more valuable than the *remaining* steps. The obvious consequence is that the closer one approaches a goal, the more compelling is the decision to spend the small costs still remaining.

If a job is partially completed and something destroys the work up to that point, how does this affect the decision to start over? Again the cost already incurred is sunk and irrelevant. If the job was originally worth its full cost, it remains worth that cost. Suppose you had spent five hours on the trench when a side caved in, leaving you as much work still to do as before you started. Although you have lost five hours, the question which faces you now is precisely the same as at the beginning: is a completed trench worth 20 hours of work viewed from this point? If no other factors have changed, the answer is still yes.

But other factors may have changed. With five hours gone your remaining time may be more valuable, and although the *number* of hours is still 20 the cost of using 20 hours may have risen. One earth slide may suggest a second, and may revise your estimate of the time required. However, unless the cave-in revises your estimate of costs or values still in the future, the effect on the decision of the five hours' work now obliterated is the same as if that time had been spent hiking or repairing the roof.

Decisions are carried out by human beings as well as being made by them, and the effectuation process often entails values not included in the goal itself. You may want to demonstrate that you can complete a project despite obstacles. If so, completing the ditch has value which justifies more cost than does the water alone. Further, the habit of completing tasks may seem worth cultivating, even if some of the tasks are not themselves worth the effort. Or you may want to demonstrate that you know when you are licked. Again recalling that all costs and values are ultimately subjective, it is no less rational to base decisions on values of this sort than on a sheer count of hours gained and lost. In any event, it is the *value* of the hours, not the number, which should be considered. Highly personal values can, of course, create difficulties if two or more persons are involved, unless both have much the same set of values. The illustration has been drawn in objectively measurable units of hours, for only thus is it possible to describe the decision process precisely.

In closing this section we may note a bias sometimes observable, at least in the United States, in the direction of giving disproportionate weight to objective criteria. In this case, this might be to give major consideration to a simple count of hours, without considering the value of hours at different times or in different sized batches. In a different area, a job applicant's scores on aptitude tests may be given more weight relative to (say) dependability than would otherwise be the case, simply because the test results are expressed in numbers and reliability is not. If one route for a highway costs more money, but destroys less scenic or historic interest than an alternative route, the money cost may be given more weight because it is objectively measurable, even though the taxpayers who foot the bill may independently approve expenditures of more than the difference to preserve scenic and historic values elsewhere. If professors are promoted for teaching ability, knowledge of their field, status in the profession, and publications, the latter often receive disproportionate weight because they can be counted. The objective and numerically expressible value seems to have a more tangible quality which often seems to be given undue consideration. There is no ready way of knowing how seriously this bias may prevent our achieving the most desired state of affairs, but we can at least be aware of it.

PROBABILITY (UNCERTAINTY)

A fourth major dimension in decision making is *probability*, which is sometimes subdivided into risk and uncertainty. *Risk* is a known probability and *uncertainty* an unknown one. One cannot know the likelihood that he will die or that his house will burn within the year (barring planned operations), but from actuarial tables he can learn whether the chances are one in ten or one in ten thousand. This is *risk*. By contrast, *uncertainty* means that one does not even know the probability.

Having noted this distinction, we add that the term "uncertainty" is also widely used in a broader sense to indicate *any* degree of lack of knowledge, whether that of probability or of uncertainty in the narrower sense. It will be used in both ways below, mainly the broader one, the meaning being clear from the context.

Areas of Uncertainty

Uncertainty can arise at any or all of the six steps of adaptive behavior. Thinking of the narrower range of decision making we will confine attention to the first two. At the first step there can be uncertainty about (1) the existing state of affairs to which one is to respond, (2) the list of possible alternative responses, and (3) the outcomes of each of the possible responses. Either the costs, the value, or both can be uncertain for any of these three things. The uncertainty may arise because the needed information is beyond the current scope of knowledge—like the temperature and humidity outside the Waldorf Astoria next Wednesday, or the price of AT&T stock six months hence. The information may be within the scope of possible knowledge, but has not been collected—like the average age of the oldest living aunts of fifteen-year-old girls. The kind of information needed for a specific decision may be too expensive for the purposes of the decision, like trying to learn the insect population of a given farm area before deciding how much insecticide to stock.

To the extent that uncertainty is lack of information about the environment, we can distinguish four environmental states under which decisions may have to be formulated. The first is a static environment. An engineer can normally plan a bridge with confidence that the geologic foundation will not change during the period with which he is concerned. The life insurance company can be confident that the death rate will not rise significantly between the time it computes its premiums and meets the claims of its policyholders. Since everything in the universe presumably undergoes *some* change, "static" does not mean literally without change, but with change which is insignificant during the relevant period.

In the second state, the environment changes significantly, but the change is independent of actions of the decision maker. Between platform writing and election day, events beyond the candidate's influence may make his platform obsolete. The snow may melt between the planning and execution of a ski meet.

In the third state, the decision maker's own actions change the environment. A candidate's speeches may arouse the voters, after which the candidate faces a new environment partly of his own making. Biologists, psychologists, social scientists, and physicists dealing with tiny particles sometimes change the specimen by examining it. Sometimes a dam may change its own geological substructure, in which case the engineer must be prepared to deal with an environmental change he himself will bring on. Each time you hit the nail, its changed position is the consequence of your own action. In this third state, the change in the environment is a feedback from the decision maker's own prior acts.

Fourth is an environment of persons (or possibly other animals) who deliberately react to influence the decision maker. The reaction may oppose his goals. Once the candidate has taken a stand, his opponents may modify *their* stand so as to undermine him, and his supporters may then shift to sustain him. In the bargaining between union and management, in international negotiations, in war, politics, and poker one party must adapt to changes deliberately created as a response to his own actions.[3]

In connection with decisions related to other persons, we must distinguish carefully between *affecting* them and merely adapting to them. To stay away from a park because it is crowded, or to use statistics on disease to evaluate medical research is adaptation, which would fall into the first or second states of environment. To enlarge an organization's staff, negotiate with the staff, or try to predict their response to a new personnel policy involves actions which *affect* other persons. These all fall into the third or fourth environmental states.

DEALING WITH UNCERTAINTY

Despite the huge volume of material written on the subject since World War II, dealing with uncertainty is still a highly uncertain process, and we can only outline a few major observations.

If we are dealing with a static environment, uncertainty can lie only in weakness in information. The actual state of affairs is fixed and definite, and the problem is to learn what that state is. We may make decisions with no shadow of doubt that the White House is in Washington, and that the sun rose before 8:00 this morning. Information about many other things is hard to come by, however. Is there oil within 5,000 feet

---

[3] Expressed in the language of systems, these four states can be described, respectively as (1) a closed system at equilibrium, (2) a system open to changes in parameters, and/or in dynamic motion, (3) a system whose outputs are in process of influencing the environment, and (4) a system being acted on by another system in its environment.

under my back yard? How many families in Indiana own between one and five hundred dollars worth of common stocks? Why does my neighbor's baby seem perpetually listless? Where is Captain Kidd's treasure? Information about static states is like knowledge of objects; it may be unknown but it is not essentially unknowable.

Knowledge of changing states is more difficult. Knowledge of the existing state of affairs (which is the total information required for dealing with static states) is only the starting point. Knowledge of the history of the situation is required, for only with knowledge of previous states, and the direction and speed of change, is it possible to predict a subsequent state. If the states at two points in time are known, a linear extrapolation can be made. Information from three or more points will usually greatly improve the predictive accuracy. If we were to judge the future position of a baseball solely from its positions one second and two seconds after a high pop fly is hit, we might predict that it would pass the moon within several months. But if we also measure its location at the end of the third second, we would predict instead that within another four seconds or so it would be back to earth. On the other hand, thousands of observations may be insufficient to predict subsequent states of complex phenomena with accuracy, like business cycles, the weather, or the next diplomatic move of the Russians. Detailed previous knowledge nevertheless often sets reliable limits on expectations. I can be almost certain that it will not snow in Cincinnati in August, and that Russia will not soon offer free elections in Poland and Hungary.

The likelihood that a present state will be succeeded by a given subsequent state is called a *transition probability*, but naming it does not increase our state of information about it. Logically we start with the present state, and then make a decision on the basis of the expected probability that the present state will be succeeded by some specified subsequent state. The usual problem in decisions is not that of understanding this relation, but of computing the transition probabilities. Under certain circumstances we must not only know the probability of a given transition, but the probability that the probability itself will change to a different probability—a kind of relation known as a stochastic chain. To deal with a changing environment is thus more complex than dealing with a static one.

Dealing with an environment which we ourselves influence may or may not be more complex than dealing with one which changes for reasons beyond our control. Dealing with water for crops is greatly simplified at the agricultural level if we irrigate or learn to control rainfall, even though increased complexity is encountered at the control level. To the extent that we can learn to eliminate business cycles, the problem of planning will be simplified for business firms. Assuming knowledge, intervention in the environment generally makes it easier to predict and deal with, not harder. At the same time, to know *how* to influence the environment may require more information than merely to adapt to its changes. For control we must know not only its transition probabilities, but the kind of effect our behavior will have on them.

Our influence on the environment is not always premeditated. Our factories and bombs may pollute the atmosphere, our poisons may kill birds and fish as well as insects, and playing around with gadgets may produce wonderful new inventions. To borrow some subsequent vocabulary, unpremeditated consequences imply that our decision set has omitted some relevant factors.

With the fourth state of the environment we move into a very different kind of ingredient, the deliberate attempts of others to influence us or things of interest to us, while we attempt to influence them or things of interest to them. This area is widely analyzed under the heading of *game theory,* and in the present volume falls mainly under *strategy and tactics in transactions.*[4] This is a highly complex area which we can do little more than mention at this point. The "game" may be as simple as tic-tac-toe, with a very limited number of possible moves and only two outcomes (win or lose), or as complex as a major war on land, sea, air, and space, with improving weapons, changing technologies, uncertain alliances, and shifting ideologies. Games under complex situations can require all the knowledge relevant to the second or third states of environment, plus that of trying to outguess the opponent, or possible alliances of opponents.

Decision Techniques for Uncertainty

Among the many complexities of dealing with uncertainty, we will mention two main techniques. The first deals with risk, and merely multiplies a given value by its objective probability. A fifty-fifty chance of getting a dollar is worth fifty cents (.5 × $100) and a one-in-twenty chance is worth five cents. If you send your young daughter to the corner grocer for a jar of olives, and there is a one-in-five chance she will break it on the way home, the jar worth a dollar at home is worth 80 cents in her hands at the store. If the price of a ticket to the ball game is $2.50, but there is a fifty-fifty chance you will meet a friend with an extra ticket, the cost of going to the game as modified by this probability is $1.25.

The usual problem here is not of how to handle a probability once it is known, but of learning the risk in the first place. This is by no means a routine operation, even in areas where objective probabilities have been carefully computed. To illustrate just one difficulty, although we speak of the death rate of a whole population with reasonable reliability, every individual is a member of some subset of the population whose death rate differs from that of the whole population. If so, is the likelihood of death of a person aged 20 the average probability of the whole population, or the average of those aged 20? If he has tuberculosis, is his

---

[4] See Chapter 17.

probability that of the whole population, of the subset with tuberculosis, of the subset aged 20, or the sub-subset of those aged 20 with tuberculosis? If *you* do not have tuberculosis, is your probability that of the whole population, or that of the subset which does not have tuberculosis? If we keep classifying and subclassifying we could end with each person a subset of one, with no accuracy at all to the probability. This is not to suggest that probabilities have no use, but to caution that probabilities can be stated only for categories of things. Although the probability for a given category may be precise and objective, deciding which category is relevant to a given decision may be a highly imprecise and subjective affair.

Numerous studies of actual risk situations, and of laboratory subjects, make clear that people do not in fact follow objective probabilities closely. They tend to favor "long shots" (being willing to pay more than a cent for a one-in-a-hundred chance of winning a dollar) and disfavor high probabilities (being unwilling to pay as much as fifty cents for a one-in-two chance). Some experiments indicate that the break-even point, where behavior about risk coincides with the actual objective risk is about .2, but results are by no means consistent. It also seems probable that humans do not show the same set of responses to negative as to positive risks.[5]

Where there are few alternatives, which mean essentially chunky decisions rather than continuous probability functions, a payoff matrix shows the alternatives more clearly. An illustration is the sentry during war who is not sure whether the man approaching him is an enemy or a returning scout. Assuming no foolproof way of identifying, the sentry must decide whether to shoot. His decision factors can be displayed as follows:

	Friend	Foe	Net Value of Response
Shoot	Safe +2 Sorry −1 (Wrong)	Safe +2⎫ Glad +1⎭ (Right)	+4
Don't shoot	Safe +2 Glad +1 (Right)	Dead −2⎫ Disaster −2⎭ (Wrong)	−1

To simplify discussion, numerical values have been attached to the utility of the alternatives.

The chart shows two alternative stimulus identifications on the horizontal scale, and two alternative responses on the vertical, the possible outcomes and their attached utilities being shown in the cells. The sentry's

---

[5] Ward Edwards, "The Theory of Decision Making," in Albert H. Rubenstein and Chadwick J. Haberstroh (eds.), *Some Theories of Organization* (Homewood, Ill.: The Dorsey Press, Inc., 1960), pp. 404, 408. This article is a useful summary of risk and uncertainty in decision making, including the psychological, mathematical, and economic approaches.

own life is valued at two points (in his value system), plus for alive (safe) and minus for dead. The life of a friend is valued at plus or minus one point.[6] A dead enemy is valued at one positive point, and a live enemy at minus two, since he might create disaster if allowed to pass behind the lines.

Both right decisions—to shoot the enemy and not to shoot the friend —show a value of +3. Obviously a right decision is better than a wrong one. But since error is possible, which mistake is less bad? Shooting a friend leaves the sentry sorry but alive, for a net value of +1. Not shooting a friend is less bad, and the matrix suggests that when in doubt, shoot.

For greater refinement, the payoff matrix can itself be modified by probabilities. On closer inspection the sentry might conclude that the chances are nine-to-one that the man is a friend. This greatly increases the expected utility of not shooting. Not shooting the friend has a utility of +3 in the original chart. Multiplied by a probability of .9 this now becomes +2.7. Not shooting the enemy had an original value of −4. When multiplied by the .1 probability that the man is in fact an enemy, this now declines to −.4. The "don't shoot" row now shows +2.7 and −.4, producing a net value for the row of +2.3. With the nine-to-one presumption that the man is a friend, the whole of the "shoot" row, whose net value is +4, is now multiplied by .1, for a new net value of +.4. Whereas with equal probability of identification the value of shooting was −4 and of not shooting −1, the nine-to-one probability shifts these values to +.4 and +2.3, strongly in favor of not shooting.

The payoff matrix, with or without probability weights, can be applied to almost any situation with discrete, rather than variable, outcomes. The number of rows or of columns can be increased to accommodate larger numbers of alternate states of the environment, or of alternate decisions. In games the columns can be used to represent alternate moves by an opponent, and again can be weighted by probabilities if available.

Numerous strategies have been defined for different situations and goals. Suppose the payoffs in a given situation are as shown in Figure 16-1.

Figure 16-1
PAYOFF MATRIX UNDER STRATEGY

		POSSIBLE COUNTER MOVES BY OPPONENT	
		X	Y
POSSIBLE DECISIONS	A	+4	+2
	B	−1	+6

---

[6] To clarify these values, "friend" means merely that the man is not an enemy, not that close personal bonds exist. In the latter case, both the values and the problem of identification would change considerably.

If achieving the largest possible payoff is a dominant motive, anything else being neither useful nor devastating, this would call for choosing alternative B. This will provide the largest possible payoff if the opponent chooses Y. The outcome of −1 if the opponent chooses X instead is still not considered too bad. This is called the *maximax* strategy.

The *minimax* strategy is perhaps more widely applicable, which seeks the "best worst" solution. Although alternative B contains the best possible outcome, it also contains the worst, at −1. Although the best outcome of choice A is less good than the best of B, the worst outcome of choice A is +2, which is three points better than the worst outcome of choice B. Under the minimax strategy, alternative A would be chosen, as providing the "best worst" outcome, or the largest minimum.

The choice of strategy depends on the situation and the goals. If Figure 16-1 represents the profits of a Soviet enterprise whose manager will be promoted if the profits are 4 or greater, but who will be exiled to Siberia if they are zero or less, he will presumably prefer the minimax strategy. It is easier to identify strategies than to provide rules about which to choose.

The usefulness of the payoff matrix depends much on the type of problem at hand. In many of life's situations only a few alternatives are possible. Here the problem is not in laying out the matrix, but in discovering the values to be put into the cells—a matter of empirical science, experience, and intuition. Once these values are known, the ordinarily intelligent person could probably make the correct decision even if he never heard of a payoff matrix. By contrast, in numerous technical problems with many variables, clearly definable goals, and measurable components, the matrix makes it possible to handle problems otherwise extremely clumsy.

THE OCCASION FOR DECISIONS

We have thus far said much about how to make decisions, but nothing about when or why to make them. To return to the original framework, a decision is the selection of a response. It is an act of adaptive behavior when the stimulus situation, the motives, and/or the possible responses are complex. The occasion for a decision arises when a change occurs at one or more stages of adaptive behavior, with the result that what was previously deemed satisfactory is now deemed unsatisfactory.

At the first stage, a change in stimulus identification may occur—either because the stimulus itself has changed, or because the concept of the stimulus has changed, resulting in a changed perception or identification of the same stimulus. Common changes in stimulus arise from cyclical or progressive changes in ourselves or environment. Day changes to night, summer to winter, children to adults, and energy to fatigue. Other changes in the stimulus situation occur when some kind of activity has run its normal course, and a goal has been completed—as when we graduate from school, finish weeding the garden, or reach the top of a mountain. The completion of any cycle or goal leaves us facing a new stimulus situation, which may call for a decision.

Noncycled events also occur which provide a new stimulus, as when the farmer's crisp crops unexplainedly go limp, the motor suddenly dies on the turnpike, a vigorous new company enters our field of competition, or the premier of an allied nation starts publicly criticizing us.

Not all changes require decisions, which were defined to exclude well established responses. We do not make decisions about habitual responses, like rising, dressing, going to work, or sleeping, unless unusual circumstances are involved. Even important events which happen only once to an individual will not require decision by him if the culture prescribes the response, as with rituals which often surround childbirth, adolescence, marriage, death, and other important occasions.

Still at step 1, the overt stimulus may not change, but a decision may be opened because of a reidentification of the stimulus—perhaps by closer perception and perhaps by reconceptualization of it. To change an identification from garter snake to small rattler, or to conclude that the rolled-up canvas in the attic trunk is a Grandma Moses instead of Junior's fourth grade art work, is a reidentification which may open a decision where none had seemed needed. To reconceptualize fence straddling from irresponsible evasion to a precondition of being elected (in some districts) may open a decision the voter had thought was settled.

Since the selection of a response at the second step of adaptive behavior constitutes the main decision itself, and we are now examining possible causes for *changing* that decision, we will move directly to the third step, the actual performance of the response. The most obvious kind of change at this step is some kind of block to the performance of the selected response. An overturned truck is found to block the highway, a nasty cold stands in the way of a planned weekend of swimming, Congress has amended the law under which we were going to get a housing loan, or the price of a new oboe has risen beyond reason.

At the fourth step, we may continue to perform the old response in the same way, but receive a change in feedback. The child discovers that the baby talk which brought adoration at two brings jeers at six. A joke which brought guffaws the first time brings only tired smiles the fifth time. And just as we may change our identification of the original stimulus, so can we change that of the feedback—as when we conclude that a student's good answers came from copying, not brains, or that today's rain is produced by today's atmospheric conditions, not by yesterday's rain dance. A changed identification of feedback also occurs when the bride's tears turn to smiles when she learns that her pound cake is not *supposed* to be light and fluffy.

At the fifth step, we may undergo a re-evaluation of the feedback stimulus. Such a re-evaluation may arise from a change in our own motive state. If the feedback from having wavy hair is that girls stroke it, the boy may evaluate this feedback differently at eighteen than at twelve. If the feedback from growing a vegetable garden is that it saves the family $50 a year, this feedback may be evaluated differently when a man earns ten thousand dollars than when he earned two. The man who moves from union member to supervisor may re-evaluate the feedback from his off-hand nasty remarks about management.

Feedback may also be evaluated differently if one becomes aware of new and superior alternatives. The evaluation of a highway may change from satisfactory to unsatisfactory the moment a parallel freeway opens. Running a statistical test on the desk calculator may suddenly seem unsatisfactory when the electronic computer appears—and the same kind of thing may occur with insecticides, friends, advisors, research processes, or shoes.

To conclude, a change at any of the first five steps of adaptive behavior may bring a conclusion at the sixth step that a modification of behavior is called for, and initiate a decision.

The opening of decisions need not depend on events which are either fortuitous or beyond the control of the decision maker. Many organizations have periodic decisions built into their routines. Some are regular audits, which ask in appropriate detail, "Are we doing as well as possible?" or "Is there a better way?" In a less obvious way, annual reports, financial statements, or budget making may reopen questions for decision. (Reports can also be written to hide the need for decisions.) In a sense the inquiring mind and the liberal education create a steady flow of information about new alternatives, and hence a succession of occasions for opening questions for decision. "Liberal" here does not mean any particular body of content, but merely broad ranging education not oriented toward immediate, explicit objectives.

THE SCOPE OF DECISIONS

We have dealt with techniques for answering questions, and with the occasions for asking them. But perhaps the most decisive thing about any decision is a prior concern: What is the question? Poor answers probably result more often from poor questions than from any other cause. Although there is no apparent prescription for asking right questions except intelligence, objectivity, and familiarity with the field, several general observations can be made about the scope of a question, or the degree to which it is opened.

Sets and Subsets

Life falls into hierarchies of sets and subsets of decisions, rarely presenting isolated decisions. One faces the set of alternatives, to go or not to go to college. Within the affirmative alternative lie a series of subsets of decisions, such as: what college does one prefer; which will accept him; should he live on campus or off; should he join a fraternity; and what program should he take? Each subset entails sub-subsets, such as which section of a course to take, and whether to study in the library, local bar, or dorm. The details do not all have to be settled before the main decision is made. But any one level of decision both subtends subsets of decisions and is itself a subset of some larger set.

Even the apparently uncomplicated choice of coffee, tea, or milk in a restaurant is part of a hierarchy. It is a subset within the decision to eat in a restaurant, which is a subset within the decision to eat or do something else, and so on. To make the choice in favor of coffee opens such sub-sets as to have cream or sugar, and how much, to have the coffee with the entree or with the dessert, to drink it hot or let it cool a bit, and to sip it or gulp it. Should we care to trace them, there are further sub-subsets at the levels of tilting the cup and the swallowing, and neurological and physiological subsets within these. Many of these behavior selections are below the level we dignify as decisions, and our purpose is not to view the choice of coffee as a decision, but to demonstrate the hierarchical relationship of behavioral acts, and hence of decisions. This is a more specific form of the earlier assertion that any event on earth can conceivably be shown to have some relation to any other event. A major problem in formulating any decision is to determine which set or sets are open for decision, and which are closed, or "given."

This leads us to the fact that complicated decisions require decisions about decision techniques, and about the formulation of the question. These questions, too, often come in hierarchies of sets and subsets, and must be answered prior to or along with the main question. Having mentioned this, we will confine attention to the main question itself.

To illustrate the problem of scope, suppose on your way to work you find an overturned truck blocking the street ahead of you. Not being too familiar with what lies off the main street you contemplate (1) driving around the truck by pulling onto the curb, (2) going around the block, or (3) choosing some item from among a set of larger and more comprehensive actions. After a brief investigation you conclude that (1) and (2) are not possible. Having been forced into alternative (3) you find a new subset of alternatives, all of which are potentially more costly in time or money, and you might: (a) wait for the truck to be removed, (b) park your car and try to get a taxi beyond the truck, (c) go back to bed, or (d) go back and take a train.

If you feel that a particular teenager has been improperly treated in juvenile court, you might send him condolences, help to appeal his case, try to get the judge removed, work for reorganization of the whole local government, blame the situation on capitalist selfishness and advocate a utopian state, or conclude that man is vile and increase your contributions to the church. If you are failing medieval history you might study harder, drop the course, challenge the professor to a duel, leave college, or conclude that anything that happened before you were born is irrelevant.

It is usual to examine first the smallest change which will accommodate the problem. This means to drive around the truck, express condolences, or study harder. If this smallest change seems unsatisfactory, wider alternatives may be considered. To open wider alternatives does not mean to choose them, however, since the wider or deeper the change the greater normally will be its cost, though the greater also may be its value.

Narrowly formulated decision sets are typically thought of as "conservative" and widely formulated ones as "radical." These terms give no clue, however, to the appropriate scope for analyzing any particular problem. It can be an equally costly error to revise a whole foreign policy if all that is needed is tougher talking, or to rely on tougher talking if a basic revision is imperative. A whole product should not be redesigned if only stronger fasteners are needed, nor should a company continue to stake its reputation on stronger fasteners if its product is basically unsound.

If at the outset the broad and narrow scope seem equally likely to be correct, the normal rational sequence is to open the narrower question first. The decision sets then open for discussion are: Where, when, and how do we talk tougher? What kind of improved fasteners will do the job? If the answers at this level do not solve the problem, the wider scope can then be opened. How do we fundamentally revise our foreign policy? What basic redesign of the product will get the company off the skids?

But if disaster may strike before both levels of answer can be tried, the bias in favor of the narrower scope disappears, and it is imperative to get the right answer at the outset. Further, if the probabilities of success are not equal at the narrower and broader levels (as when a half dozen alternatives from the subset level have already failed), the approach may be modified accordingly. It is obvious, however, that properly defining the scope of the question is often crucial to reaching a correct decision. There is no formula for determining the proper scope, and all we can do here is to note its importance.

Having opened certain sets for decision while leaving others closed, the next step is to list the alternatives available in the open set—that is, to define the content of the set. Again there is no rule for doing this except to be wise and knowledgeable in the field.

Sunk Costs, Closed Sets, and Closed Systems

Three different things discussed thus far show a clear similarity, and perhaps are the same thing viewed from different angles. First, as we move closer to any goal, all irrecoverable costs already spent are irrelevant to a decision about things still in the future. Second, if we protest the judge's decision, but do not raise the question of whether he should be replaced, the question of who should be judge remains a closed set. These two things seem logically equivalent. To say that a sunk cost is irrelevant means that it lies within a closed decision set. Not to question the judge's incumbency is logically to treat that incumbency as a sunk cost. In each case we start with a set of "givens," and it is logically indifferent whether we consider those givens as "sunk" or as lying in closed sets. "Sunk" or "closed" refers to factors which are accepted as irreversible under the circumstances of the case. The decision to jump off a cliff is sunk once the body is free in space, a decision to go to Los Angeles is sunk once the nonstop flight leaves the ground in New York, the damage of a storm is sunk once the tree has blown down, an election is sunk once the votes have been cast, and a court decision is sunk if the losing party decides not to appeal. "Under the circumstances of the case" means that one is unwilling to undertake those actions, if any, which might conceivably reverse the situation. For example, with sufficient persuasion or payment the plane flight *might* be reversed, and by bribery or violence an election or judicial decision might be overthrown. Short of divine intervention the body free in space is truly sunk, and so is the uprooted tree.

A decision can also be thought of as a cybernetic system, whose components are the costs and values of various alternatives, and the governor of which is the motive system of the decision maker. Defining the scope of the decision is the logical equivalent of defining the boundaries of the system. To treat some decision factors as closed sets is to construe them as parameters determined by the environment of the system, the system being analyzed as closed to environmental changes for the duration of the decision process.

AN OVERVIEW ON DECISIONS

Chapter 15 opened on the theme that every problem involves no less than an infinite number of variables, and that the beginning of wisdom for decision makers is to recognize that they can explicitly deal with only a tiny fraction of all that is potentially relevant. The intervening pages have tried to delineate what does or does not contribute to a rational decision. It is not to deprecate that intervening material, but merely to maintain perspective, to recall that there are no significant rules for the two most important steps of decision making—formulating the scope of the decision, and listing the alternatives to be considered within the set. We have seen that the student faces an impossibly complex problem if he is to make a "completely rational" decision about entering the restaurant with his friends, and his first task is to ignore all but two or three of the most important elements in the case.

The necessity of ignoring most elements brings us to a condition known as "bounded rationality." As Simon puts it, "The capacity of the human mind for formulating and solving complex problems is very small compared with the size of the problems whose solution is required for objectively rational behavior in the real world—or even for a reasonable approximation to such objective rationality."[7] All of this brings us to a really tacky problem.

---

[7] Herbert A. Simon, *Models of Man* (New York: John Wiley & Sons, 1957), p. 198. Bounded rationality is also discussed in James G. March and Herbert A. Simon, *Organizations* (New York: John Wiley & Sons, 1958), chap. 7, "Cognitive Limits on Rationality."

The inability of the brain to consider all factors is by no means the only limitation, or even the most important one—if we are considering inability in an absolute sense. Many items are quite within the realm of *possible* consideration. But they do not seem important enough to bother with. The decision process itself involves costs, both to acquire information and to evaluate it, and these costs may include time, money, and mental and emotional strain. Suppose we face a choice between two alternatives, which omniscience knows would provide 10 and 15 utils respectively. But the decision maker does not know the payoffs, and it would entail 7 utils of information and evaluation costs to find them out. If he makes the decision by flipping a coin he will receive no less than 10 utils, and possibly 15, whereas if he spends 7 utils to assure the superior choice, he will receive only 8 utils net of the decision costs. If the minimum net value of a random or intuitive decision is greater than the maximum net value of a "rational" decision, then even in a strictly objective sense the intuitive decision is more rational than the "rational" one.

This is no mere verbal game, but serious business. Not only in personal and family affairs, but in industry, government, charity, and education we face many decisions in which the loss from a wrong intuitive decision is less than the information and decision costs of assuring a right one. Further (and here the problem gets really tacky), we often have no way of knowing whether the information is worth its cost until after it is gathered. Electronic computers and data processors may change the location of the break-even point in such matters, but can never eliminate the fundamental problem. There will always be situations, and numerous ones, in which (1) the information required to assure correct decisions will not be worth its costs, or (2) it will not be worth the cost of acquiring the preliminary information to determine whether the main information would be worth its costs. Where information is not worth its cost, or where it cannot be known in advance whether it would be, there is no escaping essentially intuitive decisions. This is the point at which there is no substitute for intelligence and experience—where intuitive decisions are more rational than "rational" ones.

Maximum versus Satisfactory Goals

Some interesting repercussions flow from the above relation. A major question in connection with decision making concerns the goal of the decision. Is the objective to reach the largest possible value, or merely a satisfactory one? This is another important aspect of decision making for which there are no significant rules, the decision maker presumably knowing which he prefers to do.[8] The question now arises whether in

---

[8] Herbert Simon uses the term "satisficing" to indicate the process of working toward a satisfactory, as contrasted to a maximum goal, as in his *Models of Man*, p. 205, and in March and Simon, *op. cit.* I agree with one of the early readers of the present volume that "satisficing" is a "particularly revolting neologism," and have successfully avoided it for the present discussion.

many circumstances the goal which is described as "satisfactory" may not coincide with the maximum rationally attainable if decision costs are considered. The two do not coincide in all cases, witness the many instances where a decision maker clearly knows how to increase a certain value (and hence is not deterred by decision costs), but prefers not to increase it.

This path leads still further. Except by accident, it would rarely be possible for either an individual or an organization to maximize more than one value simultaneously, such as income, or security. It is also rare that anyone, in or out of organizations, holds only a single goal, and wants to maximize it without regard to its effect on any and all other goals, the concept of economic man to the contrary notwithstanding. This means that the maximum *total* satisfaction will rarely coincide with the maximization of any one value, which means further that decision makers will rarely seek to maximize any one goal. Among other things, one lives in a society. To achieve an absolute maximum on one goal, regardless of cost, will almost certainly alienate other persons, and prevent the maximizing of other goals. In fact, it seems doubtful that we can define "maximizing" precisely. To maximize means to make one value as large as possible regardless of cost in other goals sacrificed. As soon as any limitation at all is acknowledged—such as "the most I can get without ruining my health or going to jail," then multiple goals are acknowledged. This is a clear recognition that the supposed principal goal is to be made satisfactory at some level consistent with other goals, rather than maximized. If maximization accepts such contraints as the goals of maintaining health and staying out of jail, the *logic* of maximizing is not changed if we also add such constraints as the goals of relaxation and freedom from excessive worry. When we try to define it precisely, the goal of maximizing slips through our fingers and seems to leave us with a goal of reaching a satisfactory goal.

This is closely related to another problem. We have seen that decisions are not isolated. Each instead is a subset within some larger set, while simultaneously having subsets within it. Except by rare coincidence it is also not possible to maximize some value for the whole of some set while simultaneously maximizing the goals of each of its subsets. In the business firm, for instance, only by extremely rare chance would the subgoals of production, sales, purchasing, accounting, research and development, and maintenance all be maximized at the same time, since the optimum position for one usually requires something less than optimum for another. The question of *which* set or subset to maximize thus becomes of major importance.

A conceptual question also creates further difficulty. All values are in the final analysis subjective. Rational decision making consists of selecting the highest priority item from a preference ordering. In the hope of getting an operational definition, we earlier defined preference as being reflected in the overt choice actually made. If the choice actually made represents the highest value, and the selection of the highest value is rational, have we defined ourselves into accepting all actual choices as rational?

We may note the following. A choice involves both preferences and opportunities. As to the latter, we can recognize the possibility of obvious error in acquiring or using information, as when we pour molasses instead of oil into the crankcase or trust the circus parking attendant to return with the change for our twenty. At the moment of decision we can also suffer lapse of memory of something long known. Further, emotions or strong motives may block or distort perception or memory, temporarily or permanently.

As to motives, we can conceptualize our motives, and reason about them even when a particular motive is not being currently experienced. Even as with opportunities, our memory of motives can be faulty, and longer run motives can be submerged in the strength of some intense but short run desire. In each of these situations involving opportunities or motives preferences, as well as in possible others, we can make decisions which more careful thought or wider perspective would clearly indicate to yield less satisfaction than available alternatives. Any such decision may be thought of as irrational.

In all these cases, however, the judgment of irrationality can be made only on the basis of some larger knowledge or perspective than that available at the moment of decision. All in all it seems doubtful if we can formulate a meaningful definition of irrationality without reference to such wider information. By extension, it is obviously possible for one person to judge the behavior of another irrational, in the context of the information and preference system of either.

We next move from the problem of rational vs. irrational choices to that of objective vs. subjective rationality of choice. Where subjective elements alone are involved, the choice is unavoidably subjective. Even in choices which involve important subjective elements it is often possible to make objectively rational decisions if the subjective elements are reasonably identical for all alternatives. For example, the manager of a store may feel that personnel policy, though highly subjective, is also very important. But if three alternative inventory policies all allow the same personnel policy, the decision on inventory policy can be made on the basis of such objective factors as floor space, investment in stock, and delay time, without regard to the subjective factor of personnel policy.

The similarity of nonobjective values among objectively different alternatives is the saving grace of a variety of systematic, objective techniques of decision making which now go under the general heading of Operations Research. Without going into detail, these techniques explore the V/C rations of numerous alternatives, by means of statistical probabilities, game theory, linear programming, and systems analysis. Sometimes called "scientific" decision making, decision processes at this level do parallel some broad aspects of scientific development. Among other things, the complex reality of the actual problem is reduced to a model which includes the major elements of the situation. All other elements are ignored, and the solution is computed on the basis of the model rather than of reality. With the aid of computers it is possible to explore numerous alternate solutions within a given model, and to select the optimum one within a given set of parameters.

In summary, it is possible to make highly systematic objective decisions within prescribed areas. But while systematic decision techniques are highly useful tools within those areas, they do not make good decisions by themselves any more than good saws, planes, and chisels turn out a good cabinet. The decision techniques do not themselves set goals, determine the scope of the decision, formulate the alternatives in the set (though they may help discover some alternatives), determine the weights for different kinds of costs or values, determine which decision technique to use, or determine whether information is worth its cost. Systematic decision techniques can thus greatly assist decision makers, but never supplant them.

V. TRANSACTIONS

Chapter 17

POWER IN TRANSACTIONS: THE BASIC MODEL

PREVIOUS CHAPTERS have dealt with preferences and opportunities, and their interaction in decisions. Decision was seen as a quasi exchange, in that it requires the giving up of one set of values, called costs, to receive another set.

Decision making is concerned with the general rules about preferences and opportunities—about costs and values—without regard to whether the opportunities lie in our own hands, in the natural environment, or in the hands of others. In moving to social analysis, however, we enter the realm in which one person's wants are satisfied through others—in which one's opportunities depend on others. To return to the psychological base, we have traced human behavior from the formation of concepts and motives through decision making, noting the nature of adaptive behavior in seeking the more rewarding opportunities and avoiding the less rewarding. The next step is to examine how these same basic forces operate in the relationships of two or more persons. This will be done by diagnosing the *transaction*, which has already been defined as any exchange of goods between two parties, and the accompanying negotiations. The analysis of the transaction thus is made the analysis of the adaptive behavior of the individual toward other persons who control opportunities to satisfy his wants.

We now shift focus slightly from the processes of satisfying wants to the ability to do so. For this purpose we will introduce the crucial concept of *power*, which will be defined as the ability to satisfy one's wants through the control of preferences and/or opportunities. Power can also be defined as the ability to satisfy one's wants through the control of wants and/or wanted things. The term presumably could be defined simply as the ability to satisfy wants; the reference to control of preferences and/or opportunities is added to focus attention on the ingredients of power, any change in which would bring a change in power, and on the possible conscious effort to affect power. As will be seen, this definition encompasses things referred to elsewhere as influence or control. It also includes the ability to satisfy wants for oneself, which aspect will be reviewed briefly before we move to *interpersonal* or *social power*.[1]

In the physical sciences power is the ability to do work. If we assume that the major work of human beings is to satisfy wants, then the definition of power as the ability to satisfy wants is apparently the closest equivalent for behavioral analysis of the concept of power in the physical sciences.

To clarify the definition, the "want" can be any want for any good. If fine distinctions are needed, it would be the same as a gross preference defined in Chapter 14, but this degree of refinement is seldom necessary. The good can be anything from a word of encouragement to the winning of a war, with onions or automobiles, haircuts or law enforcement thrown in between. For purposes of the definition it makes no difference whether the want is intrinsic or instrumental, or even whether the want is that someone else's desires be satisfied. Power itself is often desired, and therefore can be a good. In that case we are dealing with the power to get power, an important aspect of instrumental behavior.

"To satisfy" means to acquire or accomplish the wanted thing, or more simply "to get" it. This means to acquire the automobile or haircut, to receive the word of encouragement, to win the war, or to become more powerful. For present analysis our concern is solely with *getting* the wanted thing; we are not concerned that, once acquired, it may turn out to be less rewarding than anticipated, or more so.

To "control" preferences or wants means to change their position in a preference order, either one's own or someone else's, since either change will bring a change in power. In psychological language, to control a want means to strengthen or weaken the reinforcing value of some good. The change may affect the intensity of the desire, its frequency of occurrence, or the quantity of the good which is desired.

The final item in the definition is the control of opportunities, or wanted things. This control has four facets: to *produce* or to *destroy*, and to *grant* or to *withhold*. To produce or destroy means to transform goods so as to make them more valuable or less so. Producing obviously requires productive resources, but we should not lose sight of the fact that destroying may also require resources. Producing a nonmaterial good

----

[1] The present definition of power has been formulated after study and comparison of numerous other definitions. These include, among others, the approaches used in: Bertrand Russell, *Power: A New Basis of Social Analysis* (New York: Norton, 1938); Charles Edward Merriam, *Political Power* (New York: Whittlesey House, 1934); Harold D. Lasswell and Abraham Kaplan, *Power and Society* (New Haven: Yale University Press, 1950); Robert A. Dahl and Charles E. Lindblom, *Politics, Economics, and Welfare* (New York: Harper & Bros., 1953); and Neil W. Chamberlain, *A General Theory of Economic Process* (New York: Harper & Bros., 1955). Articles in various periodicals and parts of other books, including those of Max Weber, were also consulted. No attempt will be made here to state, compare, or critically analyze these definitions. Nor will any attempt be made specifically to justify the present definition, and it is hoped that its subsequent analytical usefulness will provide its justification.

means transforming some state of affairs, such as calming Aunt Susie's nerves, enacting a piece of legislation, or giving medical advice. Destroying nonmaterial goods includes such acts as inflicting pain or injury, ruining a reputation, destroying a sense of well-being, or causing distractions so others cannot enjoy a concert. Acts of destroying goods can also be referred to as *negative goods*. "To grant" is to transfer ownership of, use of, or access to some good to someone else, or to give him permission to perform some act. "To withhold" is to deny these things. As we shall see later in connection with strategy and tactics, the controls we are speaking of extend to include controls of alternate opportunities, as well as beliefs about any of the factors which go to make up power.

EFFECTIVE PREFERENCE AND PERSONAL POWER

Effective Preference is the degree of capacity to get some desired thing plus the will to get it rather than to satisfy conflicting desires. Effective Preference (which will hereinafter be abbreviated as EP) is a key concept in analyzing power, either in satisfying wants through one's own efforts or in satisfying them through others. Both preferences and opportunities are included in the concept. It is the logical equivalent in the small of effective demand as defined by economists, including, as it does, both the desire for a good and the purchasing power to make the desire effective.

We will now distinguish between (1) desires for things which fall within the available opportunities, and which can therefore be satisfied if one is willing to forego conflicting opportunities, and (2) desires whose satisfaction will more than exhaust the total available opportunities, and which can therefore be satisfied only by enlarging the opportunities. A parallel distinction appears in power. *Particular power* refers to the ability to satisfy any particular want which falls within the set of opportunities actually available, while *total power* refers to the totality of wants one is able to satisfy. The concepts of particular and total power apply to both the satisfaction of wants through one's own efforts and to their satisfaction through an interpersonal relation.

The Lone Individual—Particular Power. We shall first discuss the particular power of one person to satisfy a particular want through his own efforts. We will designate this person as A and the desired good as Y. In particular power Y is assumed to lie within A's opportunity system, which means that he is capable of acquiring it. The thing(s) which A must give up in order to get Y will be designated X. Y thus represents the objective good which is desired, while X represents its objective cost. If Y is a chair, for example, then X is the combination of time, effort, wood, glue, sweat, frustration and so forth, required for A to make the chair.

Whether A will in fact make the chair cannot be discerned from a simple comparison of the chair and its costs, Y and X. The choice depends instead on A's *valuation* of Y and X. We will designate the value of X

in A's preference system as AX, and the value of Y as AY.[2] If A prefers Y to X, this fact can be expressed by saying that AY exceeds AX, or that Y occupies a higher position than X in A's preference system. It also means that in a rational decision A will make the chair, whereas if AX exceeds AY he will not. We can also say that the greater the excess of AY over AX, the stronger is the decision to make the chair and the greater the likelihood that it will actually be made. In terms of these values we can then say that A's particular power to get Y varies directly with AY and inversely with AX. Because cardinal values can be assigned to preferences only under limited circumstances, to be seen later, these relationships are to be understood to refer only to the direction of any change in AX or AY, and not to the magnitude of the effect.

Using these symbols, and continuing the assumption that Y lies within A's available opportunities, we can now describe A's effective preference for Y as $AY-AX$. This is the same as the final net value of Y in a choice between X and Y. By comparison, should AY equal AX it would be a matter of indifference whether A made the chair or not, in which case his EP for the chair is zero. This means that he is no more likely to get the chair than he is to get any other good that might be made with the same or equally valued resources.

To deal with that aspect of power which lies in the control of preferences, anything which raises A's desire for Y or decreases his desire for X brings an increase in A's power to get Y, and the converse. Depending on the convenience in handling any particular piece of analysis, these relationships can be described in either of two ways. We can maintain the focus on the separate components of EP, and say that the power to acquire Y varies directly with AY and inversely with AX. Or we can focus on the net effect of AX and AY and say simply that the power to acquire Y varies directly with the EP for Y.

But the EP is determined not only by the subjective desires, but also by objective opportunities. As noted earlier, changes in opportunities depend mainly on changes in productivity, whether these latter changes involve tools, skills, environmental circumstances, investment, or other factors. Let us assume first that an increase in efficiency occurs in producing Y. This is the same as a reduction in the amount of X required to make Y, and produces a reduction in AX. If some or all of the components of X must themselves be produced before they can be used to produce Y, then any increase in efficiency in making them will also reduce AX. Any increase in productivity, whether in producing X or Y, thus reduces AX and raises A's power to get Y. Any previous investment which makes available a stock of X for current use contributes to the same result by raising A's current productivity in making Y, at least until the stock is consumed.

---

[2] Since X is something already possessed by A, we need not consider the costs of acquiring it. AX is therefore the same as the gross value of X, and AY is similarly the gross value of Y to A.

Although any increase in productivity of making X or Y will itself enlarge A's opportunities, the ensuing increase in A's power to acquire Y does not depend on that fact, but on the change it brings in preference among the existing opportunities. In fact the change would be even more marked if A's productivity in making other goods were to decline. This fact would raise Y in A's net preference scale relative to those other goods, since the costs of Y would be declining while the costs of the other goods would be rising. In brief, when A is seeking to produce Y for himself, and Y is a particular good, the effect of a change in productivity makes itself felt through a change in preference rather than through a change in opportunity *as such*.

The Lone Individual Total Power. Continuing the problem of A's satisfying his wants through his own efforts, we now shift from his particular power to his total power. This is the shift from his ability to acquire Y which lies entirely within his total opportunity set to his ability to acquire $Y + Y_1 + Y_2 \ldots Y_n$, the total of which more than exhaust his total present opportunity set. In this situation the power to acquire the larger set of goods depends solely upon improving A's productivity so as to enlarge the total opportunity set. This is done by the methods previously described, such as learning improved skills, finding superior materials, investing in more or better tools, and so on, or simply by working harder and longer. In brief, total power of the lone person depends on his total productivity. This depends on the decision factors, his preferences and opportunities, the latter consisting of his environmental conditions taken in conjunction with his skill and energy in using them. This is in marked contrast to particular power, which depends mainly on preferences alone.

EFFECTIVE PREFERENCE
AND INTERPERSONAL POWER

Having finished our preliminary skirmish with the power of the individual, we now move to the core of the problem—interpersonal power. Following the patterns described in Chapter 3, we will start by defining the elements of the simplest analytical model. After examining its behavior, we will modify it successively to see how the modifications affect the behavior of the basic model.

The initial model is as follows. We will at first examine only particular power in transactions. Particular power has the same meaning in transactions as for the lone individual, referring to the ability to satisfy any particular want, without inquiring whether few or many other wants must be sacrificed in the process. Except for a brief analysis of fixed-term transactions, particular power in transactions will be seen to depend on the same forces as bargaining power, though it is not itself the same thing. Total interpersonal power will be introduced in a later chapter.

Second, the basic model will deal only with positive goods. Only after the rules for transactions of positive goods have been clarified will we look at negative goods, such as pain and destruction. Third, the model will assume selfish transactions, by which we mean that each party attempts to receive as much as possible, and to give as little as possible in return. Generous bargains, in which one tries to give more in return for less, will come later. Fourth, the initial model will assume complete and accurate information by the parties, uncertainty being introduced later in connection with tactics. Fifth, both parties will be assumed to be principals bargaining in their own interest, not agents bargaining for someone else. Bargaining through agents will be discussed independently later. Sixth, we will assume that only two parties are involved in the transaction.

Seventh and finally, we will assume that the transaction is *unique*, independent. This means that neither party is concerned with the effect of this transaction on any subsequent transaction, with either the same or different parties, involving either the same or different goods. Nor does there exist any recognized ratio of exchange, at or near which the parties are impelled to trade. For instance, there exists no clear market price for the things exchanged, and no law or strong custom establishing the terms of exchange. Further, the unique transaction is defined to include only two goods, one given by each party and received by the other. For example, the union and company in a "model" transaction might be bargaining about vacations, with no reference to seniority, wages, or other issues. The customer and furniture dealer would be bargaining only about a chair, with no reference to tables or lamps, and so on. Importantly, no preferences about anything other than these two goods are involved. In the model, the parties bargain only for the best terms on the goods, with no feelings of hate, spite, friendship, or simple pride in driving a good bargain. In short, the unique transaction depends solely on the desires of the two parties relative to the two goods to be exchanged, as of the moment of exchange, with no foreseeable effect on the terms of any other transactions or satisfactions significant to the parties. This aspect of the model will also be relaxed later when we move from unique transactions to interrelated transactions.

As a part of the idea of uniqueness, the model will also assume that the transaction is explicit, in that each side knows and agrees what is to be given up and received in the exchange. Later discussion of implied bargains will relax this assumption.

Some Traits of Transactions. We have indicated that the goods involved in transactions can cover the range from the casual exchange of a smile for a nod to the exchange of $7.2 million for Alaska. Although casual goods merit only casual interest, there is no reason thus far to assume that they follow different rules. Illustrations below will often be couched in terms of commodity exchanges, first because such exchanges are easier to illustrate, and second because the basic rules of exchange were first formulated in that connection. It should nevertheless be noted that Emerson has found the same four factors of transactions to be described below, in the same relationships, by observing children at play—strongly supporting the alleged universality of the present analysis.[3] And Simon has noted that almost any action of one person on another produces some "feedback," the action and feedback being potentially construable as exchange in some of the less formal types of transactions which will be described after the main model has been examined.[4]

We will continue to refer to the person on whom our interest is centered as A, and will now add B as the one from whom A seeks satisfaction through exchange. Expressed in symbols, a transaction is any relation in which A gives X to B in exchange for Y, and the problem is to examine A's power to acquire Y from B. Although the problem of transaction is simpler than that of decision making, in that we need deal with the preference ordering of only two goods, it is more complex in that we must deal with the preference ordering of two persons simultaneously, and the interaction of those two preference orders.

In a decision, A will choose X at the cost of Y if AX exceeds AY, and he will choose Y if AY exceeds AX. A transaction, however, requires two decisions: A's decision to give up X for Y and B's decision to give up Y for X. In the simplest case, a transaction requires opposite preference orderings. If A and B both prefer Y to X, then A will be willing to offer X for Y, but B will refuse. If both prefer X to Y, B will be willing to give Y for X, but A will refuse. But if A prefers Y to X, and B prefers X to Y, then exchange is possible, and both sides will feel they have gained. A transaction is nevertheless possible when A and B have the same preference orderings, so long as they show a difference in their relative valuations of X and Y—as, for example, if A values X and Y at a ratio of 4 to 1 and B values them at a ratio of 5 to 1. *A difference in the relative valuation of each of two things to each of two parties is the basis of all exchange, and (as we shall see) of all bargaining power.*[5]

One source of difference in relative valuations is simple preference. A may like apples better than oranges, while B likes oranges better. A

---

[3] Richard M. Emerson, "Power-Dependence Relations," *The American Sociological Review*, Vol. 27, No. 1 (February, 1962), pp. 31 ff.

[4] Herbert A. Simon, "Notes on the Observation and Measurement of Political Power," *Journal of Politics*, Vol. 15, No. 4 (November, 1953), p. 504. See also the footnote on Leslie White, p. 332, below.

[5] Economics includes several other analyses of different relative valuations. International trade is based on differences in relative valuation (comparative costs) of two goods in two different nations. Gresham's law deals with the difference in relative valuation of two different monies in two different uses, monetary and market. Speculation involves differences in relative valuation of two things at two different points in time, and arbitrage involves differences in two currencies at two points in space. All are variants of the fundamental proposition that a gain can be made from exchange whenever two things show different relative valuations in two persons, places, times, or uses. If there is no difference in relative valuations, there is also no basis for gain through exchange.

This basic relation is applicable to a wide scope of human relationships. The analysis of trade might also be pursued as an entropic function, in which differences in relative valuation are construed as differential energy levels, which are reduced by flows of goods until the energy levels are uniform throughout the relevant area.

second difference is technical, rising from different uses of a good. A may want a light, rust-proof metal while B wants a heavy, strong one. In this case A will prefer aluminum to steel, and B the reverse. Third, the difference in valuation may reflect different production costs. If A's land is good for grapes but poor for rice, while B's is the reverse, this difference may bring an exchange of grapes for rice. Or A may have a knack for growing begonias but be clumsy at fixing lamp sockets, while B possesses the reverse set of skills. Whether the difference in costs lies in skills or environment, it provides a basis for exchange. Fourth, a difference in valuation can arise from the mere fact of specialization. Even though A and B might show identical results if both did produce both goods, once they have specialized each prizes things made by others more highly than things made by himself. With the knowledge that the basis of trade lies in a difference in relative valuations, we can now examine A's power to acquire Y from B.

The Set of Symbols. The symbols AX and AY have been used above to refer to A's desire for X and Y respectively. The parallel symbols for B's desires are BX and BY, and all four will be required to diagnose interpersonal power. The four symbols and their fuller meanings can be summarized as follows:

AX: A's desire for X. If X is a commodity, AX is A's desire to keep it, or the value or utility of X to A. If X is a service rendered to B, AX is A's desire *not* to perform it, or his reluctance to perform it. If X is some state of affairs under A's control, AX is A's desire that it continue rather than move to the state desired by B. If and when X is exchanged for Y, AX is the cost of Y to A.[6]

AY: A's desire for Y. If Y is a commodity, AY is A's desire to acquire it, or the expected utility of Y to A. If Y is a service or state of affairs to be effected by B, AY is the desire that B perform or accomplish Y, or the expected utility of Y when effectuated.

BX: B's desire for X. With appropriate substitution of symbols it is parallel in detail with AY.

BY: B's desire for Y. With appropriate substitution of symbols it is parallel in detail with AX.

FIXED TERM TRANSACTIONS

Before looking at bargaining power itself, we will examine the first and simplest case of power to acquire a good from someone else, which arises when the terms of the exchange are fixed by some outside force, and A and B have no choice in the terms of exchange. Here A's power to acquire Y is determined in the same way as if he produced Y for himself, and depends solely on whether his EP for Y is strong enough to justify giving up X for Y. For example, if the government has decreed that the price

---

[6] It is the *value* to the giver of the thing given up, not the thing itself, which constitutes the cost of the thing acquired. This usage is valid when X is a commodity. It is indispensable when X is a service, for then the thing received by B will probably never coincide with what A gives up—as when B receives a vote and A gives up a clear conscience.

of corn shall be \$1 per bushel and the price of wheat \$2, and if *A* grows corn, he then can acquire wheat for corn if his EP for wheat is strong enough to cause him to give up two bushels of corn for one of wheat. If the social code prescribes that the price of a bride is three cows paid to the girl's father, then *A* must both possess three cows and prefer the wife to the cows. In symbols, if *X* represents the three cows, and *Y* the wife, then *AY* must exceed *AX* if *A* is to acquire the wife.

We might toy with the prospects of what would happen if the social code were to prescribe that one always buy a man a drink when he praises one's work. A drink for a compliment would then constitute the fixed terms of this type of transaction. *AY* would represent *A*'s desire for a drink and *AX* would be his desire to withhold words of praise for *B*. If *A* likes drinking, the chances are that *AY* would exceed *AX* by a wide margin, *A*'s EP for *Y* being sufficiently strong to guarantee that he would acquire *Y*. We might expect that *B* would shortly become drunk with praise while *A* would become just drunk. Unless the code were to forbid reciprocal action, however, we may assume that *B* would return compliment for compliment until *A* and *B* were both very drunk, with neither gaining anything on the cost of the drinks. Such a practice would not only shortly be self-defeating, but would fail to meet the first requirement of exchange—namely, that *X* and *Y* occupy reverse positions in *A*'s and *B*'s preference scales. By contrast, a "thank you" in return for a compliment involves an exchange of two things of approximately equal cost. It is more easily executed than buying a drink, and less subject to exploitation by persons of low social conscience. Further, even though the thanks are normally conceived as largely a formality, there is a distinct possibility that if we examine the underlying feelings in such an exchange, a real case of opposite preferences, and hence a real transaction, will be found.

In summary, these three fixed-term transactions show that *A* can have a bushel of wheat for every two of corn he can command and is willing to give up; he can similarly have a wife for every three cows, and thanks for every compliment. If the society is so inconsiderate as to limit him to one wife, then he has the power to acquire that one as soon as his EP is strong enough to meet the stated price. The important characteristic of fixed-term transactions is that *A*'s power to acquire *Y* depends on his own EP alone, and varies directly with it—just as is the case when he produces *Y* for himself.

BARGAINABLE TRANSACTIONS: THE BASIC MODEL

The fixed-term transaction was discussed as an intermediate situation between producing for oneself and exchange, the role of the EP being the same in both cases. We now move to transactions in which the terms are completely within the control of the two parties, and in which all the other aspects of the basic model prevail, as outlined earlier. Here *A*'s power to acquire *Y* depends not on his own EP alone, as compared to a fixed price, but on the interaction of *A*'s EP with *B*'s. Within the scope of this relationship *A*'s EP can be thought of as *A*'s preference function and *B*'s opportunity function, while *B*'s EP can be thought of as *B*'s preference function and *A*'s opportunity function. The interaction of the two EP's is shown in Figure 17-1, an adaptation of a diagram by Boul-

Figure 17-1

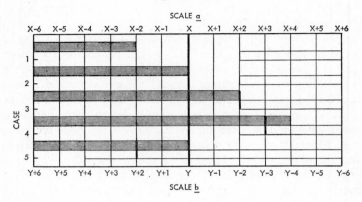

ding.[7] In this diagram *A*'s EP for *Y* is represented as a solid bar starting at the left and extending toward the right, while *B*'s EP for *X* is represented by an unshaded bar extending from the right toward the left. The longer the bar, the greater or stronger is the EP it represents.

Scale *a* in Figure 17-1 represents the value of *Y* to *A* expressed in terms of *X*, while scale *b* represents the value of *X* to *B* expressed in terms of *Y*. The line at the middle of the diagram is labeled *X* on the *a* scale and *Y* on the *b* scale. It represents the point at which *X* and *Y* are of equal value, and could exchange one for one. If *A*'s EP extends just to this line, then *AX* is equal to *AY*, and since *A*'s EP is defined as *AY−AX*, his EP is then zero. That is, *A* is indifferent as between *X* and *Y*; he might be willing to make the exchange, but it would bring no gain or loss. An exchange on these terms would be an *even exchange* of *X* for *Y*.

The first vertical line to the right of the center is labeled *X* + 1 on scale *a*. Since this scale represents the value of *Y* in terms of *X*, *X* + 1 means that *Y* is one unit more valuable than *X*. (The meaning of a "unit" will be discussed shortly below.) On scale *b* the same line is labeled *Y* − 1, which means that *X* is one unit less valuable than *Y*. To say that *Y* is one unit *more* valuable than *X* is equivalent to saying that *X* is one unit *less* valuable than *Y*; hence, the *a* and *b* scales are different statements of identical values. Similarly, *X* + 2 means that *Y* is two units more valu-

    [7] Kenneth E. Boulding, *Economic Analysis* (3d ed.; New York: Harper & Bros., 1955), p. 32. In his *Conflict and Defense* (New York: Harper & Bros., 1962), p. 18, Boulding extends his previous diagram more explicitly to the bargaining situation, but without most of the analysis which follows below.

able than X. This is equivalent to $Y - 2$, which means that X is two units less valuable than Y. The same relationship prevails to the left of the center line, but in the reverse direction. On the a scale, $X - 1$ means that Y is one unit less valuable than X, which is equivalent to the b scale indication that X is one unit more valuable than Y. Other vertical lines are read in the same manner.

A "unit" is any relevant unit of value. It may be one of the two goods involved in the transaction, some third good, or money. To illustrate a third good as a unit of value, suppose A inquires, "Will you give me your water pistol for this pocket knife?" and B replies, "No, but I'll give the pistol for the knife and two bars of candy." If the knife is X, the water pistol Y, and a bar of candy is a "unit," then A has offered X for Y, but B has asked $X + 2$ for Y. A compromise at $X + 1$ would mean giving the knife plus one bar of candy for the pistol. In the reverse, an offer of $X - 1$ would mean that the knife minus one bar of candy is offered for the pistol, more easily described by saying that the knife is offered for the pistol plus a bar of candy, or $Y + 1$.

The units could also be money, whether pennies, nickels, dollars, francs, or yen. If X were $5 and the units were dimes, then $X - 1$ would be $4.90, $X + 1$ would be $5.10, $X + 2$ would be $5.20, and so forth. If A is a customer contemplating the purchase of some indivisible good, Y (such as a table), and B is the seller, we would need only a single scale. This would show various prices of the table, extending from low prices on the left to high ones on the right. A long EP for A would mean that he would be willing to pay a high price for the table, and a long one for B would mean that he would be willing to accept a low one—that is, to give much table for little money.

The units on the scale could also be units of one of the commodities. For example, if X is a bushel of corn and Y is a bushel of wheat, then $X + 1$ might represent two bushels of corn, one bushel being X and the second bushel being the additional "unit." Three bushels of corn would be $X + 2$, four bushels $X + 3$, and so on. If smaller units were desired, X could stand for one bushel of corn, while each unit on the scale would stand for a tenth of a bushel. In that case, $X + 1$ would represent 1.1 bushels of corn (for a bushel of wheat), $X + 2$ would stand for 1.2 bushels and so on, $X + 10$ standing for two bushels.

We can now examine the nature of the relationships. In Case 1 the bar representing A's effective preference extends only to $X - 2$. This means that, considering both his desires and his resources, A is willing to give only $X - 2$ for Y, or that he will not give up X for less than $Y + 2$. At the same time B's EP extends only to $X + 2$, which means that he will not give up Y for less than $X + 2$, or that he will give only $Y - 2$ for X. A's EP does not meet B's minimum terms, and he must do without Y. B, of course, must also do without X. If we think of $X + 2$ as the minimum price at which Y is available to A, then view A's problem as a simple decision, A prefers X to Y by a margin of two units (with an EP of

$X - 2$), and in a simple choice will take X rather than Y. Even less (by another two units) would he be willing to give $X + 2$ in order to get Y. Similarly, B prefers Y to X, and is unwilling to meet A's minimum price, so he will have to do without X. Hence, in Case 1, no transaction could take place, since each party prefers to keep what he has. While recalling that all transaction situations are two-sided, we will hereafter confine our attention to A's ability to get Y.

In Case 2, A's EP has risen to X; he will now give X in return for Y instead of only $X - 2$. This is still inadequate to reach B's EP at $X + 2$, and the transaction still does not take place. A question now arises whether A's power is greater than in Case 1, since nothing happens in either case. We will say arbitrarily that it is, since he now requires less additional EP to close the gap and acquire Y.

In Case 3, B's EP remains unchanged but A's is now $X + 2$. Since B is willing to part with Y for $X + 2$, the transaction can take place on those terms.

Case 4 introduces a new element. Here A's EP is now even stronger than in Case 3, extending to $X + 4$. This is not merely enough to induce B to part with Y, but is two units more than enough. For convenience we will refer to the limit of one party's EP as his *threshold, reservation price*, or *minimum terms* on which he will exchange. Once he has passed B's threshold A has the power to acquire Y. Further, his power is greater than in Case 3. Whereas B was just barely willing to give up Y for $X + 2$, he will be more willing to do so for $X + 4$. Just as we have said that any increase in A's EP *toward* B's threshold is an increase in power, since it leaves less of a gap, so will we say that any increase *beyond* B's threshold is also an increase, since it reduces the likelihood that B will refuse to part with Y, and increases A's assurance of getting Y. Therefore the generalization previously reached for fixed term transactions and for producing for oneself still remains: namely, that A's particular power to get Y varies directly with his Effective Preference for Y.

A highly important new element in Case 4 is that once A's EP crosses B's threshold, the farther it goes the higher will be the price A will be willing to pay. To return to Case 3, B could not get more than $X + 2$ out of A, since A would do without rather than give more. In Case 4, however, B *might* be able to get as much as $X + 4$ out of A, since A is willing to give that much if necessary. It still remains true that A *might* pay no more than $X + 2$, since B *is* willing to sell for that amount. In brief, in Case 4 the terms of settlement might be as low as $X + 2$, as high as $X + 4$, or they might fall at any point between. For the time being, we will assume that the actual terms are a compromise at the midpoint, which in Case 4 is $X + 3$.

In Case 5 the two EP's have changed markedly, A's EP dropping from $X + 4$ to X, and B's EP rising from $Y - 2$ to $Y + 4$ (which is the same as from $X + 2$ to $X - 4$.) A now might be able to get Y for as little as $X - 4$ (or get $Y + 4$ in exchange for X), and B might induce A to pay as much as X. Assuming a settlement at the midpoint, the terms will be $X - 2$.

We can now see four aspects of this problem: (1) the *fact of overlap* of EP's, (2) the *position of overlap*, (3) the *amount of overlap*, and (4) the *position of settlement within the overlap*. For convenience we will refer to *any* contiguity as overlap, even if the two EP's just barely touch at the thresholds. These four aspects of the problem will now be discussed in order.

The Fact of Overlap. The fact of overlap determines whether there can be a transaction. If an overlap occurs, a transaction can take place; otherwise not. If the two parties are already in contact, overlap means the transaction will probably occur. If they are aware of each other but not in contact, they will tend to seek each other out. If the thresholds do not touch, parties already in contact will not complete the transaction. If the thresholds are far apart, the parties will drop contact, and if they are not already in contact, they will not seek it. Since the study of interpersonal relations deals mainly with the transactions that *do* occur, we should be aware that the vast majority of all possible transactions do *not* occur. Far more potential customers pass the store's window than buy. We cultivate as friends only a tiny minority of our acquaintances. Far fewer kinds of material goods are produced than remain unproduced, few voters seek personal favors from their senators, and so on. Under the concepts formulated above, all existing and continuing relationships of persons are *prima facie* evidence of overlap of EP's.

Position of Overlap. To refer to Figure 17-1, the position of overlap can be described roughly by noting whether the overlap lies toward the left, middle, or right side of the diagram. Regardless of whether the overlap is long or short, its position will be measured more precisely by its arithmetic mean, the mean terms being used hereafter as the arbitrary definition of position. The mean terms are indicated by heavy lines in Figure 17-1, at $X + 2$ in Case 3, at $X + 3$ in Case 4, and at $X - 2$ in Case 5.

The farther to the left the mean terms fall, the better they are from A's point of view and the worse they are from B's, and vice versa. The term "bargaining power" is widely used to describe the ability of one party to achieve terms favorable to himself. For this reason the totality of forces which determine the position of the overlap will be called *bargaining power forces*. Depending on the amount of detail one is interested in pursuing, these power forces can be said to consist of the EP's, the components of the EP's (AX, BX, AY, and BY), or the factors determining the components. Most of the discussion in this volume will deal with the EP's and their four components, greater detail being useful mainly for the initial introduction of the power forces.

It is customary to assume that a person with strong bargaining power gets good terms, while the person with weak power gets bad ones. The terms good and bad are misleading here, and we will refer to particular terms only as "better" or "worse" than some other terms. While this assertion of relativism could be made about any value judgment, it is important to see why it is made here. To begin with, *any* transaction not made in error is "good," in the sense that each party receives something whose value to him equals or exceeds the value he gives up. (We are still speaking of the model, as defined earlier.) This is the same as saying that the transaction takes place within an overlap of EP's, and that if there were no overlap the transaction would not take place.[8] But this fact provides no guidance to the relative goodness or badness of terms, which depend on the circumstances of the case. If a thirsty man were charged a dime for a glass of water in a drug store, he would consider it a bad bargain. But if he were thirsting deep in the desert, and happened on another man with a meager supply of water, he would consider ten cents an incredibly good bargain. To the English traders two centuries ago, a beaver fur in exchange for ten beads seemed a good bargain. But to the Indians who could trap beavers readily, but who had to spend painstaking hours to make a bead, two beads for a beaver fur seemed an excellent bargain. To one who digs stones from the ground, fifty tons of stone might seem a low price to pay for a new automobile if the stones are ordinary gravel, while an ounce might seem an atrociously high price if the stones are diamonds. Because such vast discrepancies in exchange ratios can be found, there is no way of labeling any particular ratio as good or bad in itself. There are, however, two different kinds of bench marks from which we can measure the relative goodness or badness of any particular transaction.

One bench mark is the consensus of what goes on around us. If the customary price of a glass of water is a "thank you," then to pay ten cents is a poor bargain. If the customary price of a wife is three cows and two years' courtship, then to get a wife for two cows and one year's courtship is an excellent bargain—if the wife and cows are of standard quality. As will be seen later, the consensus plays an extremely important role as a measure of what is properly given in exchange for what. For the moment we will simply note that it is one standard for measuring the goodness or badness of a particular bargain.

The second bench mark is a tentative proposal by one of the parties. If a Yankee offered two beads for a beaver fur, then to the Indian five beads would be better terms than the proposal, and one bead would be worse. If a father proposes that his son be allowed to go out two nights a week if he gets a B average at school, then three nights for a B, or two nights for a C, would be better terms from the son's point of view. If B offers $X + 2$ for Y, then X for Y represents better terms from A's viewpoint. In each case the proposed terms are the standard compared to which other terms can be labeled as relatively good or bad.

Thus far we have defined bargaining power forces, but not bargaining

---

[8] Coercive relationships have not yet been discussed, but it will be seen later that the same principle applies there as well.

power. The simple view is that bargaining power is the ability to get good terms. But we have just seen that "good" terms are not definable. The obvious next suggestion is that bargaining power is the ability to get "better" terms. But better than what? Again the simple view is to suggest that we compare A's bargaining power with B's, and say that A's bargaining power is greater than B's if A gets better terms than B. The difficulty here is that we must evaluate A's bargain through A's eyes and B's bargain through B's eyes, which takes us into the dubious area of interpersonal comparisons of utility. Both parties can leave a transaction feeling that they have made a wonderful deal, or both can feel they have made a very bad one. For example, if the EP's just barely touch, as in Case 3 of Figure 17-1, neither A nor B will feel elated, since each receives something he values just about equally with what he gave up. In Case 5, however, both may be delighted, since a settlement at the midpoint of a long overlap gives each a large gain.

Hence, no attempt will be made to measure whether A has greater or lesser bargaining power than B, except under some limited circumstances to be described later. On the other hand, should there be two different A's (whom we will call A and A') who deal with the same B, it is feasible to compare the bargaining power of A with that of A'. A comparison of Case 3 and Case 4 in Figure 17-1 will illustrate. Suppose that B's EP is $X + 2$ whether he deals with A or A'. But suppose that the EP of A is $X + 2$, as in Case 3, while the EP of A' is $X + 4$. A will pay no more than $X + 2$ for Y, whereas A' will probably pay $X + 3$ and might pay as much as $X + 4$. We can now say that in dealing with B, the bargaining power of A is greater than that of A'. We can also say that B has more bargaining power when dealing with A' than with A.

The measurement of bargaining power can be illustrated more broadly if we assume that in Figure 17-1, Case 3 represents a bargaining relation between A and B, Case 4 represents one between A' and B', and Case 5 between A'' and B''. If X and Y are the same goods throughout, we can say that among the A's the greatest bargaining power is possessed by A'', the next greatest by A, and the least by A', as judged by the mean terms in each case. The bargaining power of the three B's takes the reverse order, being greatest for B', second for B, and worst for B''. In brief, while it is not meaningful to compare the bargaining power of A with that of B, it is meaningful to compare the bargaining power between A and A', or between B and B'. It is also meaningful to say that the bargaining power of A is above or below the average of all A's.

If differences in EP produce differences in bargaining power, then changes in EP will produce changes in bargaining power. If we include only cases where overlap exists, it is clear from Figure 17-1 that the stronger A's EP the higher is the mean price of Y, and the stronger B's EP the lower is the mean price of Y. To generalize, assuming overlap, A's *bargaining power varies inversely with his own EP, and directly with*

B's. B's bargaining power also varies inversely with *his* EP, and directly with A's.[9]

In diagnosing bargaining power, it is often useful to break the EP's into their components. In that event A's bargaining power varies directly with those components which reduce his own EP or raise B's: namely, AX and BX, respectively. A's bargaining power varies inversely with the factors which raise his own EP or reduce B's: namely, AY and BY. The effect of each factor on B's bargaining power is the reverse.

The influence of these factors can also be stated directly. The stronger A's desire to retain X, the more will B have to give for it, and the stronger B's desire to get X the more will he be willing to give for it. A's bargaining power therefore varies directly with AX and BX. The greater A's desire for Y the more will he be willing to give for it, and the greater B's desire to keep Y the more will he insist on getting for it. Hence, A's bargaining power varies inversely with AY and BY. B's bargaining power is the reverse, varying directly with AY and BY and inversely with AX and BX. From these relationships it can be seen that A's bargaining power rests in the desirability of the goods he holds, while B's rests in the desirability of the good *he* holds.

As already noted, the power relation between A and B can be measured against the bench mark of a specific proposal in a particular transaction. To return again to the situation in Case 3 of Figure 17-1, suppose that in the course of bargaining A had proposed an even exchange of X for Y. Given the strength of the two EP's in Case 3, it is clear that B would have the ability to pull the terms in his favor to $X + 2$. On the other hand, if B, during the course of bargaining, had proposed a settlement at $X + 4$, then as measured against the bench mark of *that* proposal A would have the ability to pull the terms in *his* favor to $X + 2$.

The eventual terms are the same, whether the initial proposal is X for Y or $X + 4$ for Y, the terms being determined by the two EP's. Since the settlement is the same regardless of which proposal we start from, it seems poor usage to say that there is a difference in *power* between the two proposals. However, it is useful to have some word for the ability to move the terms from some proposed position. This can be called *bargaining advantage*, or the *balance of bargaining power*. For example, in Case 5, if the terms of $X + 2$ are proposed, then A would hold the bargaining advantage, or balance of bargaining power, since he could pull the terms in his favor by no less than two points, probably by four points, and possibly by six. If the proposal of $X - 6$ were made, however, then B would hold the balance, since he could pull the terms in *his* favor by no less than two points, probably by four, and possibly by six. No shift in power occurs between these different proposals, but merely a shift in the

---

[9] This generalization is the logical equivalent in its most general form of the principle of reciprocal demand as enunciated in international trade—that that nation receives the greater gain from international trade whose demand for the other nation's product is the less insistent.

point of reference. By analogy, we can describe the tenth floor as four floors above the sixth or five floors below the fifteenth. The location of the tenth floor remains the same, but the direction and distance to it differ with the point of reference.[10]

Amount of Overlap. The amount of overlap of two EP's is determined by the EP's themselves, just as is the position of overlap. If the overlap is minimal, the EP's just touching, there is only one set of terms on which the transaction can take place. In Case 3, for example, either the transaction takes place at $X + 2$ or it does not take place. But in Case 5 the terms can lie anywhere between $X - 4$ and X. The longer the overlap the greater is the uncertainty as to where the terms will fall, but the greater is the likelihood that the transaction will take place. If the EP's just touch, any minor obstacle can cause the transaction to fail. But where the overlap is large, much can be gained from the transaction, even if

---

[10] This particular point should be contrasted to that in Neil W. Chamberlain's *A General Theory of Economic Process* (New York: Harper & Bros., 1955). Although the Chamberlain volume is a highly useful contribution to the study of bargaining power, its definition of bargaining power as "the capacity to effect agreement on one's own terms" (p. 81) leaves this important point obscure. When there is a long overlap of EP's, for example, there is no unique point which constitutes "one's own terms." The objective of bargaining is to get "better" terms, and bargaining power must be measured as a direction of push, not a point to be achieved. There is rarely a bargain that could not have been better had the necessary bargaining power existed.

Chamberlain also measures A's bargaining power against B's, which seems improper for reasons cited earlier. Further, Chamberlain measures A's bargaining power in terms of A's ability to get agreement on the terms he offers, and he points out (p. 82 and *passim*) that a concession by A raises A's bargaining power since it raises the likelihood that B will accept the terms offered. This approach seems contrary to the customary meaning of bargaining power, which is the ability to get *favorable* terms. Chamberlain, however, implies that the worse the terms one is willing to offer, the greater is his bargaining power—a confusing formulation. What Chamberlain calls bargaining power is here called bargaining advantage, which measures the direction and distance to a particular point from the movable base of a proposal. The term bargaining power here refers to the forces which determine the point toward which the bargainers gravitate.

It may also be noted that the present formulation of transactions contains the same elements presented by Leslie A. White, in *The Evolution of Culture* (New York: McGraw-Hill Book Co., Inc., 1959), pp. 242 ff. White shows two parties, A and B, and two goods, I and II. Making the simple substitution of X and Y for I and II, White's relationships correspond to the AX, AY, BX, and BY relationships described above. White does not attempt to analyze bargaining power between A and B, however, and views these four items simply as *relationships*, rather than as intensity of desires. On the other hand, White strongly emphasizes the relations of the *persons*, A and B, as the elements of one kind of system, and the relations of the *goods*, X and Y, as the elements of another. What White calls personal relationships would be covered by the intertransactional aspects of the present analysis. These deal with the fact that A and B may engage in many transactions other than the immediate one, and that the terms of the immediate transaction may be governed more by those interrelations than by the power factors of the moment. This analysis appears in the next chapter. White's relationship of goods seems to correspond to the idea of consensus terms, to be described below. In either White's approach or the whole of the present one, six ingredients can be observed in any transaction. Four represent the values of each of two goods to each of two parties, the fifth being other transactions involving the same parties, and the sixth being other transactions involving the same goods.

costs must be incurred to effectuate it. As will be seen later, there are socially important differences between "threshold" transactions and those with long overlap.

For the moment we are accepting the EP's as we find them, assuming that a person's EP's at any one moment are the product of his culture, personality, and circumstances. Within any one transaction, *A*'s Effective Preference is *B*'s opportunity, while *B*'s EP is *A*'s opportunity. But either *A* or *B* may have other opportunities available outside the transaction. This is crucial to the transaction, since *A*'s best alternative outside the transaction places a limit on the EP he will show within the transaction. This in turn places a floor under *A*'s bargaining power and a ceiling on *B*'s. For instance, if *A*'s EP for chocolates would make him willing to pay $2.00 a pound, but he can get the chocolates from *C* at $1.50, then $1.50 per pound would be the limit of *A*'s EP in a possible purchase of chocolates from *B*—assuming equal quality, convenience, and other factors. When a political party negotiates with a prospective candidate for its slate, the best alternative candidate puts the floor under the party's bargaining power and the ceiling on the candidate's. If a fraternity wants to tap an outstanding student, the student's EP to join that fraternity (and hence the floor under the student's bargaining power and the ceiling on the fraternity's) is limited by his best opportunity available from some other fraternity. The alternatives may take many forms, all being substitutes with varying degrees of similarity to the thing substituted for. If one can find an alternate brand of granulated sugar, the substitution is precise. If he can find honey or saccharine, the substitute is less precise. But going without sweetening altogether is also a substitute for sugar, and if the price asked for sugar is too high, abstinence may be the best alternative which puts a limit on *A*'s EP in bargaining with *B* for sugar. Generally speaking, the more definite and obvious the available substitute, the more definite and obvious are the limits it places on bargaining power.

A fuller discussion of the limits on power will appear in Chapter 19. The present stage of the discussion requires, however, that we note the limits on an EP *inside* a transaction as lying in the best alternative opportunities *outside* the transaction, which place floors and ceilings on the bargaining power of the parties.[11] These alternative opportunities, which set the limits on the EP's and hence on bargaining power, will be referred to hereafter as *power limits* in the transaction.

Settlement within the Overlap—Tactics. The fact, position, and amount of overlap tell us whether a transaction can occur and the range within which its terms will lie; they do not tell *where* the terms will fall within that range. *Any* point within the overlap is better for both parties than no settlement at all, and the introductory assumption that the settle-

---

[11] In the language of systems analysis, the limits on the equilibrium position achievable within the transaction system are set by the parameters consisting of alternate opportunities available in the environment of the system.

ment would occur at the midpoint must now be opened to question. The analysis thus far shows that this aspect of the settlement is not determined by the power forces, and we must look for other explanations.

To give the process a name we will say that the settlement between the power limits results from *tactics*. The direct or indirect purpose of most tactics is to influence the other party's beliefs about power positions in such a way as to achieve a settlement most satisfactory to oneself. The details are almost infinitely varied and subtle, but the major rules are reasonably obvious. Suppose that *A* is willing to pay as much as $200 for an old used car possessed by *B*, who in turn is willing to sell it for as little as $100. We will assume that both *A* and *B* have already investigated alternate cars and customers and that the power limits of $200 and $100 are firm. The EP's overlap by $100, and the problem is to determine where between $100 and $200 the price will fall.

If *A* and *B* are experienced bargainers, neither will state his true limit —at least not at the outset—and the problem of each is to guess the other's true limit without revealing his own. If *B* can somehow learn that $200 is *A*'s maximum price without revealing his own minimum, he can hold out for that sum with confidence that he will get it. This conclusion follows from the fact that *A* is willing to pay that much but does not know that *B* will accept less. To make the proper impression *B* might "insist" on getting $250, and then make a "big concession" to a "rock bottom" price of $200.

On the other hand, if *B* does not know *A*'s maximum price he runs the risk of holding out for too much and losing the sale. It is easy to say that *B* should wait until *A* starts to walk out before he makes a concession, but in the absence of knowledge *B* cannot tell whether the walkout is sincere or merely a countertactic. *B*'s tactical problem is to set his own *apparent* minimum price as high as possible without exceeding *A*'s maximum price. An error in underestimating *A*'s maximum (say, at $180) means a loss of potential income equal to the amount of underestimation ($20), while an error of overestimation means loss of the sale. *A*'s task meanwhile is to try to discern *B*'s minimum price and to refuse adamantly to pay a cent more.

There is almost no limit to the number and combinations of gambits which can be used to "outtactic" an opponent. The essence of all is the same and can be stated in several ways. One statement is: to appear as "hard to get" as possible without crossing the thin line into the region of "too hard to get." A second statement is: to try to discern the other party's threshold, and then to represent one's own threshold as being at or just inside his—that is, to pretend there is no significant overlap. In Case 5 of Figure 17-1, for instance, *A*'s tactics will be perfect if *A* discerns that *B*'s threshold lies at $X - 4$ and then convinces *B* that *A*'s own threshold also lies at $X - 4$. In the automobile purchase *A*'s tactics will be perfect if he discovers that *B* will sell for as little as $100 and then convinces *B* that $100 is the most he will pay.

Because an important ingredient of tactics lies in misrepresenting one's own true position,[12] the making of a concession can have an ambivalent effect. Let us suppose that in the previous case *A* has been offering $100 and *B* has been insisting on $200. If *A* now raises his offer to $125 either of two contradictory effects may follow. First, although $125 is not world-shakingly good from *B*'s point of view, to reject it involves greater risk than to reject the lower offer, in two respects: (a) If he mistakenly rejects *A*'s offers, *B* stands to lose $25 more in rejecting $125 than in rejecting $100; (b) *B* knows that, whatever *A*'s maximum price may be, the higher offer is closer to it than the previous offer, and that in rejecting the higher offer he therefore runs a greater risk of losing the sale. For both reasons a concession by *A* weakens *B*'s willingness to hold out for further concessions. Since *A* is presumably aware of this effect, his position is simultaneously strengthened.

In the opposite direction, however, *A*'s concession demonstrates that his original offer of $100 was purely tactical, and suggests to *B* that the offer of $125 is also movable. Should *B* take this interpretation, *A*'s concession may convince him that if he holds tight to the $200 price *A* will eventually meet it. A concession may thus either increase or decrease the likelihood of a counterconcession, depending on how the second party interprets it.[13]

The problem of tactics is far too complex to be treated in detail here, and the bare introduction above is presented with three main objectives. The first is to clarify the distinction between tactics and power forces. The second is to show why the outcome of tactics is by nature unpredictable. To amplify this point slightly, tactics are highly personal, subtle, and evanescent; their outcome depends on the correct (or incorrect) interpretation of any one or more of many behavioral cues, which may themselves be genuine or pretended; and the net effect often involves such complex interactions as what *A* thinks *B* thinks about what *A* is thinking. The third reason is to show the way in which tactics reflect the nature of power forces. For though tactics themselves operate within the area of overlap where power forces do not reach, the essence of tactics is to *create beliefs about power*. Actual power lies in effective preferences, while the value of tactics lies in the ability to create beliefs, either about one's preferences or about one's capacity to make them effective, or both.

---

[12] It should be recalled that the entire present discussion deals solely with the single transaction between two parties. As will be seen below under the heading of "interconnected bargains" the tactical value of misrepresentation often declines rapidly when the same parties deal with each other repeatedly, or have mutual connections with the same third party.

[13] The double-edged effect of concessions is discussed more fully in Allan M. Cartter, *Theory of Wages and Employment* (Homewood, Ill.: Richard D. Irwin, Inc., 1959), p. 122, and in Thomas C. Schelling, "An Essay on Bargaining," *American Economic Review* (June, 1956), pp. 291–92. The Schelling article should certainly be read by anyone seriously interested in tactics.

In brief, the terms of transactions depend upon power forces and beliefs about power forces.[14] Sometimes terms reflect the fact that one side "just doesn't care" about the price. But not caring is indifference, which is equal preference, and therefore a power force.

Tactics represent the first relaxation of the assumptions of the model transaction, as outlined earlier in the chapter. The fourth assumption, about complete and accurate information, does not apply in the area of tactics. We may note here a distinction between the position of the bargainers in the transaction and that of the analyst. The bargainers themselves may not know the location of their opponent's EP, whereas we, the observers and analysts, assume that we do know them. The analyst can confidently say that the range of indeterminacy to be settled by tactics lies only between the power limits. But the bargainers do not themselves know where those power limits are, at least for the opponent, and may therefore believe the power limits to be either closer together or farther apart than they are in fact. Hence, when we say that the settlement is indeterminate between, but not beyond, the power limits, we are speaking as analysts, not participants.

STRATEGY

Having made clear that tactics operate within but not upon the power forces, we must now add that negotiations are by no means confined to tactics. Along with attempts to maneuver within the power limits many bargainers try to change the limits themselves. One way to do so is to alter the opponent's preferences. If B can convince A that the car is in better shape than A originally thought, AY will rise, and so will the ceiling on B's power. If A can convince B that the car is in worse shape than B thought, B's view of such alternatives as keeping the car or finding other customers will deteriorate—unless he thinks other customers are unlikely to spot the defects. Or if B can be convinced that the whole used car market is in bad shape, his vision of alternative customers may collapse, and with it his asking price.

Bargainers may not stop with trying to control the other party's preferences by controlling his beliefs about alternate opportunities, but may also try to control the opportunities themselves. Attempts at monopoly, whether in business, politics, religion, or social life, seek to improve bargaining power by restricting the other side's alternatives. Jealous restrictions on a mate or the quiet poisoning of a love rival may have the same effect. Bootleggers often support prohibition to eliminate the competition of legal whisky. Politicians sometimes try to get poor candidates nomi-

---

14 The whole area of threats, coercion, and physical violence is dealt with in the next chapter under the heading of negative power. As will be seen, the present generalizations about tactics and power are valid for negative power as well. More broadly, the use of strategy and tactics are matters which are studied most extensively under the heading of "game theory." Game theory goes into far more detail in these matters than the present introduction can encompass.

nated by the opposing party so as to lower the voters' best alternative. Whether so intended or not, any behavior by parents or friends which increases the dependency of others on them increases their power over those others.

We will use the term *strategy* for all bargaining maneuvers which work *on* the power limits, in contrast to tactics, which work *within* them. Although it is easy to make this distinction in the abstract, strategy and tactics mingle promiscuously in practice, so that it is often impossible to tell which is which in any actual bargaining situation. The realistic bargainer is always alert to both possibilities, to which we will return later.

SOME RULES ON BARGAINING POWER

Having surveyed the determinants of power in our model of the transaction, we can now summarize the rules for achieving power in such transactions, from A's point of view. Although many of the rules remain the same for multiple or repeated transactions, the rules are formulated at this point only for the model.

Since the terms of settlements are based partly on EP's and partly on tactics, the rules must be framed accordingly. Within the sphere of the transaction, B's EP for X constitutes A's opportunity to acquire Y, and the stronger B's EP the better is A's opportunity. The first rule, then, is that from among all the available B's with whom A might conduct his dealings, A should seek that particular B who either has, or can be induced to have, the strongest EP for X. Having found the best candidate, the next move is to raise his BX as high as possible. In psychological terms this means to strengthen the reinforcing value of X, either in fact or in prospect. In sales jargon it means giving X a good buildup. These moves can be supplemented by "tearing down" the alternatives to X, or by trying to make those alternatives unavailable in fact. Political candidates, salesmen, suitors, job applicants, and hosts of others regularly use both approaches to BX when they seek to make the X they have to offer seem like the answer to the voter's, customer's, maiden's, or employer's prayer, while making alternate sources of X seem fit stuff only for nightmares.

The second and related rule is to do business with B's who have, or can be induced to have, a low EP for Y. The techniques for reducing this value follow those for raising BX, but in reverse, and include belittling Y and pointing out satisfactory alternatives. If you want a friend to accompany you on an afternoon trip, but learn that he is thinking of attending a firemen's parade and picnic you say, "You don't want to watch a funeral procession through that mosquito-ridden park, and if it's beer you're after I'll buy you a couple."

Having pulled B's EP as far to the left as possible, A's next problem is to restrict his own EP to the smallest overlap which will nevertheless not endanger the transaction. This again is the problem of being hard to get, but not too hard—in fact rather than merely in appearance. It is the problem of manipulating one's own wants, which is partly a matter of will power and partly one of arranging alternatives.

Contributing to this end, the third rule is to raise AX. So long as we are dealing with unique transactions, it would seem that most of the raising of AX must be done before the bargaining starts. On the whole one's basic values, reflecting one's so-called moral training, are perhaps of greatest general usefulness here. Such habits as those of thrift and of thorough study before making large commitments also support AX in many situations. A high value attached to personal integrity, and to reputation for competence, maintains AX high in many others. Strategically placed attention cues may help, as when the spendthrift keeps his family's picture in his wallet to remind him when he reaches for money that it is badly needed at home. Some people reinforce their will to save by authorizing a payroll savings deduction. This is a form of negative attention cue, since it keeps the savings out of the line of sight. Before entering negotiations, a simple reminder of the value of what one has gives it recency and psychological strength, so that one will not lightly part with it under the spell of an opposing bargainer.

The fourth rule, of course, is to keep AY down. By strong odds the most effective way to accomplish this result is to be alert to and to arrange for alternatives, both subjective and objective. As to the subjective, one can train himself to enjoy, or at least to live at ease with, a wide variety of goods, conditions, and people. To do so often adds much to bargaining power. One's best alternative is the floor to his power, and the more alternatives he has cultivated the more likely he is to have a good one available in any particular case. The wider the scope of one's likes and enjoyments the wider is his perceived opportunity list, and the less his dependence on any one alternative. To illustrate objective alternatives, the more skills one has learned, the less dependent he is on any one occupation or employer for income, or on any craftsman, serviceman, or firm to produce the things he wants. Finally, the gentle art of learning to do without—gracefully— can often be a potent booster of bargaining power.

Having done all he can to control the preferences and opportunities reflected in AX, BX, AY, and BY, and having thus moved the position of overlap as far to the left as he can, A's fifth and final step is to achieve the best settlement tactically possible within the overlap. A's rule is simple in the extreme: to try to learn the position of B's EP (which usually means using as many clues as possible to guess it) and then to represent his own EP as lying the shortest safe distance inside it. Since tactics often involve deception, an interesting point arises here. Deception does not deceive unless believed. But being believed is best achieved by not deceiving. Our main interest in this fact comes later, with interrelated bargains. For the moment, it suggests that, however simple in principle, successful tactics may require high skill indeed.

CO-OPERATION AND CONFLICT
IN THE MODEL TRANSACTION

In cooperation two or more desires can be satisfied by the same act, while in conflict one desire can be satisfied only at the expense of another. Examining transactions in this light we find that the *fact* of a transaction is cooperative but that its *terms* are in conflict. The transaction will not take place unless at least one, and normally both, parties receive more value than they give up. Since both achieve added satisfaction, the definition of cooperation is fulfilled by the fact that the transaction takes place. The terms, however, are in conflict, since the better they are from one side the worse they are from the other. When diagrammed, terms farther to the right are better for *B* and terms farther to the left are better for *A*.

In most political or commercial transactions the statement that terms are in conflict needs no further comment. In many personal situations of life, however, there is no feeling of conflict, and the statement needs explaining. In most such situations analysis will show that conflict is *apparently* absent because custom or habit decrees the terms, because the costs are too small to argue about (and because good manners call for absorbing small costs), or because sympathy has transformed the motives. The effect of sympathy will be examined later, but one small transaction between friends can delineate the cooperation and conflict, and show how habit, manners, and small costs keep the conflict out of view.

Suppose two friends discover they will be downtown on the same day, and decide to have lunch together. The gain to both from this transaction is companionship, which provides the main cooperative feature. But some costs are almost inevitable, and to a certain degree are almost necessarily in conflict. Except by chance, any one time and place of meeting will be more convenient to one person than to the other. The two may, of course, find some spot which divides the inconvenience equally, but equal division is one way of compromising conflict, not the absence of conflict. If conversation fails to reveal a true compromise spot, they will probably agree to go where they or their friends have gone before, the person on whom this places the greater cost probably accepting it for want of a better suggestion. An often unstated conflict revolves around who arrives first, for he must either wait or try to hold a place for the other, thus incurring a cost for the other's benefit. Small as they are, these various costs can be shifted from one to the other, and hence are in conflict. Since they are small, the rules of courtesy provide that they should not be complained of. Should these small costs be repeatedly one-sided the person on the "losing" side will probably seek or readily accept a change, or discontinue the arrangement.

Now I would be the first to insist that the costs and values in such a situation cannot easily be listed or neatly catalogued, and a novel might be a more appropriate place than this book to make the attempt. As noted earlier, the costs and values must be judged by each person in his own preference system and what seems an onerous wait to one might seem a refreshing breather to the other. It also seems reasonable to insist, however, that in making the arrangements as to when, where, and whether to meet the parties *are* negotiating a transaction, and that it has elements of both cooperation and conflict. It may also contain some sympathetic help of one by the other—a matter for the next chapter.

Chapter 18

POWER IN TRANSACTIONS: EXTENDING THE MODEL

CHAPTER 17 established the model for bargaining power in transactions, its seven conditions limiting the model to particular power, positive goods, selfish approach, complete information, bargaining by principals, two persons, and unique transactions. The latter part of the chapter relaxed the assumption of complete information in connection with tactics, all other conditions of the model continuing throughout. We will now relax the remaining assumptions one at a time, and observe the effect on the power relationship.

The model of the transaction differs in an important respect from most models used in economics. Economic models are deliberately oversimplified versions of reality. By contrast, except for some possible reservations about information and uniqueness, the model described in the previous chapter is a very real description of a transaction situation widely found in human affairs. Relaxations of the model are important not so much to add realism as to extend the analysis to additional types of transactions.

INTERRELATED TRANSACTIONS

In line with the model's prescription of uniqueness, each transaction has been examined thus far on its own merits, as if nothing that happened before or after had any influence on its terms. The rest of society was ignored, except as background scenery in which the parties might discover alternatives lurking with which to undermine the opponent's power. In the original model the parties were also rather bloodless creatures, without loves, hates, spites, or gloatings to sully their relationships. Few goods in transactions appear in such splendid isolation, and we will now relax these assumptions of uniqueness by examining interrelations of transactions and of satisfactions.

MAIN AND SUBSIDIARY TRANSACTIONS

We will first look at interrelations in what we may call main (or major) and subsidiary bargains in continuing relationships. These can also be thought of as sets and subsets of bargains. The terms do not imply that the main bargain (or major bargain) is larger than the subsidiary, or necessarily more important. They imply only that the major bargain is logically prior, or primary, and that the subsidiary bargain is logically dependent on it, or derived from it. To illustrate, a major bargain may provide that a manufacturer deliver 1,000 radio transformers per week at a price of $3. Subsidiary bargains would then have to be reached about such details as whether to repair or replace faulty transformers; whether to repair them at the customer's plant at the seller's expense or ship them back for repair; how to rearrange the shipping schedule when the trucking company is on strike; or how to handle the customer's desire for a redesign before the contract expires. In a major bargain a man may allow the neighborhood children to play in his vacant lot if they will keep the grass cut, subsidiary transactions covering such details as how often or carefully the grass is to be cut, whose mower is to be used, or who is responsible for sharpening the blade. A major bargain that a son is allowed to go fishing on Saturdays if he does his weekly chores without grumbling may include subsidiary bargains as to what constitute the chores on any particular Saturday, or whether a mumbled inquiry why his small brother can't help constitutes grumbling. A major bargain that a government may use military bases in another nation may involve subsidiary bargains over the currency in which local employees of the foreign government are to be paid, and what local spots are ruled off-limits to the foreign troops. Since few agreements about a continuing relationship are completely self-enforcing, and since it is seldom possible to foresee all possible details when the major agreement is reached, subsidiary agreements are often inescapable. Although their terms are negotiated independently of the major agreement, they are nevertheless related to it.

The negotiation of the major agreement itself follows the general rules of bargaining power already discussed (or to be filled in below), and requires no separate discussion. The main feature of the major bargain is that without an overlap of EP's there will be no bargain. By contrast, in most cases the subsidiary bargain *must* be completed; it cannot fail. This feature can be seen most sharply if we assume either that the major bargain is enforceable by law, or that it is so important that neither party would give up the major bargain in a dispute over details. Under these circumstances *some* decision must be made about the subsidiary bargains, such as those listed above. This does not mean that every subsidiary agreement is openly discussed, or even explicitly recognized, and some may be settled on the basis of "anything you think is right is OK with me." But terms nevertheless *are* reached in each subsidiary transaction, even if the "agreement" represents nothing more than an action taken by one party and not challenged by the other.

Subsidiary transactions are often inescapable for several reasons. First, some are instrumental to executing the major bargain, in the sense that an agreement about grass cutting cannot be performed without at least a *de facto* agreement about whose mower is to be used. Second, some parts of the performance may deviate from the terms of the major agreement, as when a shipment of transformers is faulty or late, at which point the parties must agree what remedial action to take, if any. Ignoring the deviation is, of course, a settlement, presumably in favor of the less injured party.

If, as suggested above, the stake of each party in the major bargain is so great that either would accept the worst possible terms on the subsidiary transaction rather than terminate the major bargain, then agreement in the subsidiary transaction is assured.[1] The desire to continue the major bargain guarantees an overlap of EP's in the subsidiary transaction. Perhaps the key difference between the negotiation of a union-management contract and the negotiation of contracts between businessmen or other parties is that the former constitute subsidiary transactions under a continuing agreement of the employer to hire and the employees to supply labor, whereas the latter are major bargains which, if not consummated, leave the parties free to go their separate ways. The result is that for all practical purposes, the union and management representatives *must* reach an agreement on a new contract when an old one expires, whereas the negotiators of most other kinds of contracts need not do so.[2]

We can examine first the bargaining relation in a particular subsidiary transaction of so small importance that neither party would remotely consider terminating the major agreement in a dispute over the minor one. The EP's overlap to such an extent that either party is willing to give the other everything he wants in the subsidiary transaction if this should seem necessary for preserving the major transaction. This is another way of saying that the EP for the subsidiary agreement becomes the same as that for the major one, if agreement on the minor one is seen as essential to the continuance of the major. Several possible sets of forces may determine where the settlement will occur within this wide overlap. First, it could be settled entirely on tactics, with one or both parties trying to outwit the other. These have already been discussed. Second, it could be settled on an intertransactional basis, with each party paying attention to the effect of his behavior on future subsidiary bargains as well as on the present one. Since these intertransactional relations of subsidiary bargains are essentially the same as those of major bargains, to be discussed below, we need not analyze them further here.

On the other hand, if the minor transaction is important enough for one or both parties to terminate the major relationship rather than accept bad

---

[1] By "worst possible terms" in the transformer contract would be meant either that the buyer would accept the late delivery or faulty transformers without asking for any adjustment, or that the seller would replace the faulty items entirely at no expense to the customer, or compensate the buyer for losses due to late delivery. "Worst possible terms" means absorbing the whole of the cost of the instrumental act or deviation in question.

[2] Additional details of the nature and consequences of this distinction are found in my *Labor: Institutions and Economics* (New York: Rinehart & Co., Inc., 1956), chap. 8.

terms on the subsidiary one, a new factor enters. Now either side's bargaining power in the subsidiary transaction varies inversely with his stake in continuing the major one, the stake in the major bargain constituting the EP in the minor one.

Although the principle itself needs no elaboration, it is a matter of high importance in such continuing relationships as friendships, marriages, union-management relations, and international politics. For it means that the side with the smaller stake in the overall relation—the one perhaps characterized as the less responsible[3]—has the bargaining power advantage in the subsidiary transaction. The spouse more willing to accept divorce, or the government more willing to accept war, has the greater power to exact concessions in return for continuing the marriage or keeping the peace. This does not mean that the other party is helpless, since a variety of strategic and tactical devices are available, as reflected in: "So you think I can't live without you," "Who else would take care of you the way I do?" or "We'll wipe you off the map if you start something." All such moves can be resolved into acts of (1) increasing the other party's stake in the major relation, or decreasing one's own, (2) decreasing the attractiveness to the other party of the alternatives to a continued relationship and increasing the attractiveness of one's own alternatives, or (3) creating beliefs as indicated in (1) or (2).

Parties who place small value on self-respect, friendship, or the respect of others sometimes get a long series of concessions by careful changes of tactics and strategy. They get many concessions in subsidiary transactions, until the other party is just about to give up the overall relationship as not worth the many subsidiary concessions. Thereupon they express great interest and hope for its survival, concede just enough to make the expression credible, and then proceed to exploit the replenished supply of bargaining power. This alternating sequence has been the theme of many a marriage in fact and fiction, of some rather conspicuous instances of international relations, and of other relationships too numerous to mention.

PROMISES

In many simple transactions the two goods are transferred simultaneously between parties, or so nearly so as to create no problem. In other instances, however, A may give up X long before B gives Y in return. If X is a service rendered for B, or a material good produced to B's order, A will incur costs on B's behalf before he is paid for these costs. In reverse, B may order X and pay for it before he gets it. In these and other instances, one party incurs a cost for the other's benefit in return for only a promise, implicit or explicit. The giving and acceptance of the promise is a transaction subsidiary to the one over the goods themselves, and requires separate attention.

---

[3] The word "responsible" in this context has essentially the same meaning as that used later in connection with the discussion of authority and responsibility.

Whether the promise covers minutes or years does not matter to the principle, the central question being why one party will be willing to incur costs on the basis of nothing more than a promise. This hinges in turn on the question of why promises are kept.

We will state three general rules of promises, and then elaborate them: (1) a person will fulfill a promise when he has a greater stake in fulfilling it than in not fulfilling it, (2) a person will normally incur costs on the basis of another's promise only when he is convinced that the second person has a greater stake in fulfilling the promise than in not fulfilling it, and (3) if a person wishes to acquire value on the basis of a promise he must be able to demonstrate convincingly that he has an adequate stake in its fulfillment. All three of these rules can be deduced from the earlier discussion of decisions, and the reader can presumably discern for himself the value and cost ingredients in each.

The "stake" in fulfilling a promise is the value the promisor will lose if he does not fulfill the promise. By a greater stake in fulfilling than in not fulfilling the promise is meant that the promisor finds the value to him of fulfilling the promise greater than the value of not doing so.

The most obvious form of stake occurs when the promisor puts something of value in the hands of a third party, not to be returned until the promise is kept. A contractor may post a bond, to be forfeited if he fails to complete a building on time, or a person under arrest may put up bail which he will lose if he does not keep his promise to return for trial. To be effective the stake must be large enough so that, when added to other costs the promisor would suffer, the loss from failing to fulfill the promise will ge greater than the cost of fulfilling it.

The stake need not be advanced before the promise is made, but may consist instead of the promisor's knowledge that costs can be imposed retroactively if he fails to perform. Because it requires so little experience to recognize that human society is impossible without the reasonably reliable fulfillment of promises, even the most primitive societies impose some kind of penalties on persons who break promises. These have apparently not been systematically reported, but seem to consist mainly of social pressures of the sort to be described below in Chapter 20. Since it must first be ascertained that a promise was in fact made before that promise can be enforced, some investigative procedure normally precedes the penalty—a phase of the problem which need not detain us here.

The usual procedure of courts in Western societies is to require the promisor to compensate for losses reasonably attributable to his nonfulfillment, in addition to paying the court costs of settling the dispute. The state reserves the power to impose further costs, such as fine or imprisonment, if the award of the court is not obeyed. In most cases it is cheaper to fulfill the contract than to lose this retroactively imposed stake—which is the basic nature of contract enforcement in modern commercial practice.

In the numerous relations of everyday life the stakes to be lost from not keeping promises are such things as reputation, friendship, credibility, self-respect, and similar valued things. Among friends and close associates the accounting is less precise than in formal contracts, but its essential nature is the same. Someone may object, "But I am an honorable person, and have been trained from childhood to keep my promises, even if it is infinitely more costly to keep them than not," or, "I couldn't sleep at night if I welshed on a promise, and it is insulting nonsense to suggest that I won't keep a promise unless I have some stake to lose." The reply, of course, is, "You are entirely correct. But you are not really denying that you have a stake in fulfilling promises; you are merely identifying your stake as your honor or your conscience."

It is so commonly felt that personal relationships or matters of "honor" follow rules unrelated to those of business and politics that it must be insisted again that such things as reputation, self-respect, a clear conscience, affection, and many similar thing *are valuable things*. If they can be lost through failing to make good on a promise, they provide the stake which helps ensure that the promise will be kept. That these things cannot be transferred like diamonds or real estate does not reduce the severity of their loss to the person who forfeits them. With this explanation we can now return to the rule that a person will fulfill a promise if he has a greater stake in fulfilling it than in not fulfilling it, and note that the rule is valid whether the stake is some transferable good deposited as a bond, liability to legal action, or the possible loss of honor or conscience.

In addition, of course, we all are creatures of habit and culture. As to habit, we make many decisions without serious examination of alternatives, and most of us are reliable in most of our relationships because we have developed the habit of being reliable. In this respect our keeping of promises is no different from scores of other things we do. And as creatures of culture, many of us develop these habits from the outset because we are trained to, perhaps never giving them really serious thought. Granting all these things, even if we do nothing less we probably sense that we would feel "peculiar," or suffer embarrassment, if caught violating the code. If so, our desire to avoid these feelings is our stake. Again, it is important not to confuse differences in *kinds* of value with differences in *rules* about value.

If this first rule of promises is valid, the second follows directly: that one person will rationally incur costs in behalf of another on the basis of a promise only if he is convinced that the other person has a greater stake in fulfilling the promise than in not fulfilling it. In many commercial relationships the stake is a transferable good which goes directly to the promise in the event of nonfulfillment, thus serving simultaneously as the promisor's motive to fulfill and the promisee's compensation in the event of nonfulfillment. Mortgages, security for loans, and posted bonds are examples, and if the security is large enough to cover any possible loss from nonfulfillment, little or nothing need be known about the personality of the promisor.

At the other end of the scale are the nontransferable stakes, such as reputation or conscience. These are the stakes the loss of which "not enriches him but makes me poor indeed." Here the promise has value only to persons familiar with the promisor, for no one else knows whether he has a reputation or conscience to stake. If the promisor is a stranger, he does not even stand to lose reputation, friendship, or credibility with the promisee, and his only apparent stake is his conscience. Hence, the widespread caution toward promises of strangers.

In a humanitarian spirit, some persons feel they ought to trust even those whose promise seems dubious. The motives for so doing may be various, but do not invalidate the rules. This point can be clarified by distinguishing between promises, in which repayment is expected, and gifts, in which repayment is not expected, and which have not yet been discussed. When something is given in return for a dubious promise, the relationship is part promise and part gift, in indeterminate ratio, following the rules of promises to the extent repayment is expected, and the rules of gifts to the extent it is not.

The third rule of promises follows from the first two: if a person wishes to acquire value on the basis of a promise he must create conviction that he has a stake in fulfillment. Among persons who are known to each other, no special action is needed; the person's known habits or reputation are his bond. In other circumstances it may suffice to explain what loss will follow from failure to perform. When explanation or personal knowledge is insufficient, the ability to put some transferable value in bond may produce the necessary conviction. No further discussion of this problem seems necessary at this point, though some interesting problems of promises in connection with negative power will appear below.

This discussion has dealt only with the general rules about the effect of promises if they are believed, and provides no guidance in the applied science of creating belief. Some promisors are honest while others are liars, and some promisees are unbelievably gullible while others are impenetrably obtuse. Telling one from the other is a practical art for which we will not pretend to be able to give recommendations.

SEPARATE BUT INTERACTING TRANSACTIONS

Several kinds of interactions occur between technically independent transactions, by which we mean that nothing in one transaction is explicitly contingent on some other transaction. Such technically independent transactions can affect each other through interactions of persons or interactions of goods, or both, and the interactions may affect the power limits, tactics, or both.

To speak first of interactions of goods, the terms of any particular transaction are affected strongly by the terms on which similar goods are being transacted by persons with whom the parties might deal. The boot-legger cannot get more for his moonshine than the price of legal whisky, and the state will have difficulty recruiting new industry on a "normal" basis if a neighboring state offers tax-free land. The "price" of any one good available elsewhere in the society places a distinct limit on the terms of exchange in any one transaction—a matter for detailed investigation later.

Second, after a person has completed one transaction he may show either a stronger or weaker desire to make a second transaction in the same goods. For example, the transformer manufacturer may have been in desperate need of the first contract, and hence had low bargaining power in negotiating it. But if that contract meets his most urgent needs, his financial position is improved, and so is his bargaining power in negoti-ating a second contract. In the reverse direction, the first contract might meet the fixed costs of his plant so that he can produce additional trans-formers for little more than their variable cost. This result can be de-scribed as a reduction of AX, AX in a business firm consisting mainly of the costs of production. A lower AX, of course, brings a reduction in A's bargaining power in the second contract. Whether the subject of negotia-tions is picnics, shoes, social security legislation, wages, or technical assist-ance to a foreign power, the prior existence of one agreement normally produces a difference in bargaining power in negotiating a second, since it normally affects AX, AY, BX, or BY. Other kinds of power interactions undoubtedly exist between present and subsequent transactions between the same two parties, but these three illustrate the main problem.

In addition to interactions of goods, or of intensities of wants for goods, there also exist interactions of persons among transactions. These interac-tions may take many forms; we will cite two major ones. One involves information about the desirability of dealing with a particular party, while the second involves information of tactical value in negotiating with him.

If B deals with A on several occasions, and finds him prompt, reliable, and courteous, B will undergo an increased desire to deal with A in the future, rather than with C, who is tardy, unreliable, and nasty. The effect is the same as if BX were to rise by an amount equal to B's increased preference to deal with A, and constitutes increases in A's bargaining power with B in subsequent transactions.

As regards tactics, when two parties deal with each other on one oc-casion, each may learn something about the other's desires or goals, which knowledge will affect subsequent transactions. Suppose A owns several pieces of property in an area which B wants to acquire for a factory site. The cost of the land will be a small fraction of the cost of the total instal-lation. Hence, although B will prefer to acquire the land cheaply, he will be willing, if necessary, to pay a high price, and his problem is to acquire all of A's lots without letting A know why he wants them. If A succeeds in getting a high price from B on the first plot, A will have a clue to the intensity of *B*'s desire, and bargain for an even higher price on the second. This can be called a *forward* interaction. If *B* knows the nature of this forward interaction, he will bargain harder for a low price on the first plot than is justified by the merits of that transaction, taken by itself. Whenever it is known that one transaction will have a forward action on a second, knowledge that the second is to take place has a *backward* interaction on the first. The forward interaction constitutes a *precedent*. Although precedents have other strong supports, such as habit, inertia, and apparent fairness, an important aspect of a precedent is that it reveals the power positions of the parties, and makes it more difficult thereafter either to hide them, or to pretend they are something else. If a person knows the forward influence of precedent, and expects similar transactions in the future, he will not settle any one transaction on its own merits, but will try to settle only on terms which he is willing to accept in subsequent transactions. Parents dealing with children, and administrators with subordinates, often learn to take great care in these matters. Having granted a given concession once, they find it difficult to maintain that the same concession is unacceptable the next time. If the subsequent transactions can be dissociated from the first, however, by being made "different," these interactions can be minimized. In buying the properties, *B* may purchase successive plots from *A* under different names and through different agents so that *A* will not suspect the connection. The parent may insist that extra dessert when grandma is visiting is "different" from extra dessert at other times, so as to dissociate the two events and avoid a precedent.

In addition to the tactical interactions of revealing EP's, successive transactions also interact by revealing tactics themselves. If a bargainer in one negotiation takes a firm position at the outset, and adamantly holds it to the bitter end, his initial position in subsequent negotiations will tend to be taken seriously. If another bargainer makes grandiose initial demands from which he later makes equally grandiose retreats, his initial position in subsequent transactions will probably not be taken seriously. Numerous manipulations of tactical interactions are evident on all sides. One person may hold fast to a position he does not really want, so as to impress others that he does not retreat. Another may give way readily to argument in some transactions, to give the impression he is reasonable, so that when he takes a solid position later it will be assumed he really means it. A person may also make concessions in one transaction so he can say in the next, "It's your turn to give a little."

The effectiveness of any one tactic on subsequent negotiations depends on a host of subtleties of personality and circumstance, which need not detain us here; our interest centers on the *fact* of such interrelations, and their general nature. Interactions are not confined to the same persons. Human beings talk, and a man's reputation as a bargainer goes before him. Hence, one's performance in some transactions may affect the behavior of others toward him in relationships seemingly far removed.

TRANSACTIONS INVOLVING MULTIPLE GOODS

In the original model, the unique transaction was defined as including only a single good given by each party. Many transactions—in the broadest sense, probably most—involve more than one good moving in one or both directions. The company and the union bargain over wages, union security, company security, seniority, and health benefits in the same set of contract negotiations. The parent and child bargain about the child's school work, recreation, family chores, discipline, and sleep in short succession. The furniture dealer and the customer dicker over an end table, sofa, and lamp. Whenever two or more items are joined into what is essentially a single transaction, the terms on which any item is settled are usually influenced by the terms on which others were, or are to be, settled.

Here, too, the interrelationships can affect either power or tactics. The power interrelation is most obvious when the parties negotiate on a "package" basis, the main consideration being the size of the total cost or gain, with its breakdown being relatively unimportant. If a company is willing to accept a ten cent increase in costs in negotiations with the union, it will readily accept a six cent contribution to a pension fund if the union is willing to accept only four cents increase in the pay envelope, or a ten cent contribution to a health insurance plan if the employees will agree to no increase in the pay envelope. Less sharply, if one party has a certain EP for the net effect of all items in the negotiation, then to achieve good terms on one item will allow him to be more generous in another. That is, to have achieved high power in one detail may reduce bargaining power in the next, and vice versa.

Tactical interactions would tend to be the opposite. If in negotiating one item it becomes apparent that the opponent is a poor bargainer, one may be encouraged to press him even further on the next item. Questions of *agenda* become crucial in some negotiations. Since the agenda determines the order in which multiple issues are discussed, it will also affect what one party is able to learn about the EP's and tactics of the other. One sequence will reveal different information at a different stage of negotiations than will another, and may determine the outcome of the most serious items. Decisions on agenda also determine whether two items will arise in the same set of negotiations, in which case one can be played against the other, or in separate negotiations. The varieties of interaction of power and tactical factors in agenda are almost limitless; again, we can merely indicate the nature of the problem.

When we recall that goods are anything capable of providing satisfaction, transactions are seen to involve multiple goods in a second sense. In addition to the goods which are the subject of bargaining, the bargainers receive satisfactions or dissatisfactions from the bargaining process itself. If an opponent angers or frustrates, a bargainer may get satisfaction from the mere act of getting even, even if this means worse terms on the agenda items. In addition, negotiations may become a game, in which a bargainer may become more intent on "winning" than on achieving the most reasonable terms. A strong desire to "win" negotiations increases bargaining power. To A it constitutes an increased reluctance to give up what he already has, which is an increase in AX. The loves, hates, jealousies, and gambits which affect power in transactions are almost limitless, just as are the intertransactional relationships with which they mingle. We can note these things, but not analyze them all.

IMPLICIT BARGAINS

All bargains similar to the model transaction are explicit. Each party knows whom he is dealing with, and what he is giving up and receiving. Although explicit bargains are widespread, there probably exist a larger number whose terms are never discussed or negotiated, and whose terms have never been explicitly agreed upon. Yet the relationship may proceed smoothly and regularly on the basis of "I will do this if you will do that." These may be referred to as implied or implicit bargains, quasi bargains, or spontaneous coordination.[4] Implied bargains can occur between persons who meet face to face but do not explicitly discuss terms. They can also occur between persons who are fully aware of each other's identity and of their reciprocating actions, but who never meet or communicate directly. And they can even occur between parties who do not know each other's identity, but merely know in a reasonably dependable way that "If I do this, someone out there will do that." Knowledge of identity is sometimes one-sided, in the sense that A may know who B is but B may not know the identity of A. Interactions of this sort will be construed to be bargains or transactions only when each side has knowledge that a response is occurring, and deliberately engages in the action which brings the response because the response is more valued than the cost which must be incurred to bring it about.

Although we are concerned only with interhuman transactions some relationships between persons and other animals illustrate the implicit bargain. The seal and his trainer have an implied bargain that if the seal balances the ball the trainer will toss him a fish. If the seal does not perform as trained he will get no fish, and if he gets no fish his performance will in due time decline. To return to human examples, opposing troops during war have often reached implicit agreements to avoid fighting on Sundays, or to allow each other unmolested access to a mutually accessible water supply. Supposedly competing companies in numerous industries have tacit agreements of the sort, "If you don't cut prices we won't either."

Ordinary living would be more difficult without implicit agreements. As an example, A is a Florida resident who owns a summer cottage in Maine. Shortly after arriving there for his second summer he is informed

---

[4] These terms are all used in William Fellner, *Competition Among the Few* (New York: Alfred Knopf, 1949), pp. 15–16 and *passim*.

by *B*, a permanent resident nearby, that *B* has kept an eye on the cottage during the winter, chasing away children who showed belligerence toward windows, and fastening back some flapping shutters. The following Christmas *B* receives a crate of oranges from the Florida neighbor—and the pattern continues over the years. Though each thanks the other for his "gift" the two may never openly acknowledge the *quid pro quo* nature of the relationship, and it certainly was never openly negotiated. Under some social codes it is a breach of etiquette even to hint that the two acts are mutually contingent. Even where overt reticence prevails, the true nature of the transaction is often frankly recognized within the privacy of the separate families, where one may question whether he is giving or receiving fair value.

In the above instances each party knows who the other is, and the difference between these and the openly recognized transactions is not in the basic transaction but in the technique of communication. To say that the agreement is implied does not mean that the parties have never talked about it, but that verbal communication was not necessary. A clear agreement on price leadership can be achieved if one company promptly and uniformly follows every price change made by a competitor. If one army fires a spectacular salvo of shells ending abruptly at midnight Saturday night; if it follows this by an equally conspicuous silence until midnight Sunday, when it fires another large salvo; and if the enemy does the same the following weekend (while the first side repeats), the communication of an offer and acceptance is as clear as if phrased in impeccable grammar.

Although the terms in the above instances were arrived at without overt verbal communication, they are nevertheless explicit, each side knowing what is exchanged for what. Understandings of this sort merge into those in which no *specific* exchange is agreed upon, even tacitly, but the exchange does tend to balance, at least roughly. Here contributions are made essentially as gifts. But custom recognizes a return obligation. Many social relationships are of this sort, as evidenced by such phrases as "We owe the Browns a dinner," or "The Greens might do *something*, considering all we've done for them." If such relationships become heavily one-sided they tend to wither away. One of the important reasons why socializing stays for the most part among persons of the same general income level is that the lower income person is unable to return the kind of hospitality to which he is treated, and embarrassment to one or both may ensue. Nonincome factors, such as personality and mutual interests, may, of course, maintain relationships indefinitely despite income discrepancies.

QUASI BARGAINING AND OPEN END TRANSACTIONS

A large and complex society, unlike a small and compact one, includes many transactions between persons and groups who are only vaguely aware of each other's identity. In this position are many persons who deal with the public. Producers of commodities often estimate how much they can sell at a given price. They then set a price and observe the buying public's response. If the sellers do not like the result, they may change the price, and again observe the result. Although the persons who determine what price is offered and those who buy may not have the slightest idea of each other's identity, and although the buyers simply accept or reject rather than making counteroffers, the two sides engage in a quasi-bargaining procedure. As in any other bargaining, the terms of the exchange result from the interaction of the EP's of the producers and the customers.

Elected officials engage in quasi bargaining with constituents, of this sort: If I vote for you, will you support these policies?" and "If I support these policies, will you vote for me?" Both the political candidate and the seller of merchandise set and announce their terms. When the sales or votes are counted each knows how many people have accepted his offer, even though he does not know who. So long as there is a *quid pro quo,* a transaction is taking place.

Beyond the cases of quasi bargaining lie open end transactions in which one party provides some commodity or service to another in return for nothing more than a promise—perhaps only a hope—that the recipient will some day do something comparable for someone else. The parent, the boss, or the teacher do many things for the child, the subordinate, or the student, not in the expectation of specific repayment, even in gratitude, but in the hope that the recipients will similarly pass on help to *their* children, subordinates, or students. Sometimes the recipients are clearly informed that this is expected of them. The broadest concept of open end transactions is that if everyone helps whom he can when he can, within reason and without counting, the net result will be a reasonably even exchange among the population as a whole. Though the doctrine is difficult to test empirically, in order to teach the members of society to behave in this way it is probably useful doctrine that those who give more than they receive achieve the greater satisfaction. The effects of this kind of relationship are most closely observable in friendship, to which we now turn.

GENEROUS BARGAINS AND FRIENDSHIP

The chapter thus far has relaxed the assumption of uniqueness in its various aspects, admitting a wide variety of interactions between and among transactions, and among the parts of multicomponent transactions. It was assumed throughout, however, that the transactions were selfish, and that each party tries to receive more and give less in the transaction. Only toward the end of the discussion, in implied and open-end transactions, did something like generosity appear. We will now relax a second major assumption of the model, and deal with the *generous transaction* in which one or both parties try to give more and receive less.

Continuing the use of operational definitions, we are defining "generous" in terms of what persons *do,* without asking the essentially unanswerable question whether their actions are *really* unselfish, rather than a roundabout and farsighted method of increasing their own satisfactions. We can explore this problem further while noting the main conditions under which generous bargaining occurs. First are those conditions described as love, sympathy, empathy, or related states, in which we suffer when others suffer, and receive pleasure from their pleasure. Here one person clearly receives satisfaction from helping another, and it is pointless to debate whether the act is *really* unselfish in some deeper or grander sense. To return to the psychological terminology, such behavior is presumably rewarding, all things considered, or it would be discontinued.

Some acts of generous bargaining are clearly designed to make another person's mood or attitude more favorable to ourselves. When we go out of our way to prepare Cousin Penelope's pear pie precisely as she prefers it, she may turn from frowns to smiles, to the great benefit of herself and all around. In more somber tones, we may befriend a man so he will recommend us for an undeserved promotion, or relax while we steal his wallet. Such transactions can be considered an investment toward getting better terms in future transactions.

Still other generous bargains are designed to build, operate, maintain, or salvage a friendship, a desired thing in itself, which will be discussed below.

BARGAINING POWER IN GENEROUS TRANSACTIONS

We do not customarily think of bargaining power in connection with generous transactions, which often are sheer gifts. Having made the analysis of selfish transactions, however, it is interesting to inquire what significance that analysis has, if any, for generous transactions. With minor modifications of the model, some meaningful conclusions about selfish bargains can be applied to gifts and other generous acts. We will not alter the meaning of bargaining power in this connection, however. High bargaining power will continue to mean the ability to receive more or give less than under low bargaining power. Bargaining power in receiving a gift may refer either to the quantity one will receive, if the item is divisible, or to the likelihood of receiving it, if not divisible. We will deal with quantities rather than likelihoods, since they illustrate the problem more fully.

We will also omit tactics for the moment from the analysis of generous bargains, and return to them later. The absense of tactics means either that A and B are both completely candid about expressing their desires, or that each has reliable, independent information about the other's desires. We will also deal at first with unique transactions.

Exchanges and Gifts, with A Generous, B Selfish

We will start with a gift offered generously by A and accepted (or bargained) selfishly by B, a relation common between parent and child. Suppose that parents, A, consider offering to pay for piano lessons for their child, B, along with the additional possibility of providing his transportation to the lessons and of relieving him of some chores. AX is the parents' desire *not* to do these things—which means to keep their money, *not* to take him for his lessons, and to have him continue doing all his chores. Taken by itself, AX has the same effect in generous transactions as in selfish: the higher the value of AX the lower is B's power to get X, and the greater is A's ability to get larger concessions in return.

Taken by itself, BX also has the same effect as in selfish transactions. The larger the child's desire for piano lessons, the greater will be his willingness to provide his own transportation, or to do more chores, if his parents will pay for the lessons. If his desire is strong enough, he may even be willing to pay part of the lessons' cost.

In the gift, there is no Y, in the strict sense, since no good is offered in exchange. If a Y does enter the transaction—and the child's doing his chores would constitute a Y in this case—it behaves as in the double selfish transaction. The more the parents want the child's services in his chores (a higher AY), and the more reluctant he is to do them (a high BY), the more will the parents have to give to get the chores done.

The chief distinguishing feature of the generous transaction is that not only does B want X, but A wants B to have it. A may have various reasons for this desire, such as his own satisfaction (parental pride when Junior plays for the neighbors), sympathetic response (the child's pleasure is pleasure for the parent), or a sense of parental obligation for training the child. Regardless of the reason, the effect is the same as a reduction in AX. We can describe this by distinguishing between the *gross value of AX*, which is A's actual desire to keep X, in the same sense the term has been used thus far, and the *net value of AX*, which is the gross value minus A's desire that B have X. To deal with the sympathetic aspect of the generous relationship, the greater the child's desire for the piano lessons (a higher BX), the greater will be the parents' sympathetic desire that he have them, and hence the lower will be the *net* value of AX.

Omitting the AY and BY factors as not present in the gift, AX and BX have the same effect as in selfish bargains, a higher value of either enhancing A's bargaining power. But we must now deal with the *net* value of AX, which under A's generous response will tend to vary inversely with BX. As a result, the parents' potential bargaining power which resides in the child's high desire for lessons may disappear in the fact that the more he wants lessons the more they want him to have them. Whether AX will drop at the same rate BX rises, or faster, or slower, depends on the persons and motivations. It is clear, however, that if the net value of AX falls by less than the amount BX rises, A's bargaining power goes up—and the reverse. Similarly, if the net value of AX falls by the same amount that BX rises, no shift in bargaining power occurs. The important point is that if we deal with *net* values, the influence of AX and BX is the same in generous as in selfish bargains.[5]

---

[5] It is, of course, possible to reorient the whole analysis of generous bargaining so that *more* bargaining power would result in giving more and receiving less. This has a certain common sense appeal, in that *giving more* is the presumed objective of

Gifts, with Both A and B Generous

We move now to the gift offered generously by A and accepted (or perhaps we should say rejected) generously by B. We still have only AX and BX in the transaction, since it involves only one good. We have seen in the bargain which is generous by A but selfish by B that a high value of BX, though it adds to A's bargaining power directly, may detract from it by reducing the net value of AX. The new feature added when B is also generous is that B will insist that A's interest in him shall not work to A's disadvantage, and that the transaction shall take place at or near terms reflecting the gross value of AX, rather than the net. In short, the unbalance which arises when one side is generous and the other selfish tends to be cancelled out when both sides are generous. This force is reflected when B says to A, "Look, Honey, I know how fond you are of that rosebush, so you just keep it and enjoy it."

Mutual Exchange, Both A and B Generous

When both sides are generous and *two* goods are exchanged, *both* parties occupy a position like that of the parents in the first case. We now distinguish between a gross value of BY, B's actual desire to retain Y, and the net value, which is the gross BY minus B's desire that A have Y. We have now returned full circle to a transaction of two persons and two goods. Even when both are generous, the same four factors apply as in selfish transactions, and in the same way, the difference being that both AX and BY are now net values. Each is reduced by the amount of generous interest each has toward the other. As common sense suggests, the more generous of the two parties gives relatively more and receives relatively less. In power terms, if A is the more generous, AX will decline

---

generous bargaining, and the power to give more should therefore be construed as the greater power. Since such an orientation *can* be formulated, the main question is whether it would clarify or muddy the analysis. Having toyed with both approaches, I am convinced it is far simpler conceptually, and more manageable, to maintain the concept of bargaining power unchanged through both generous and selfish analyses, particularly since it is also possible in this framework to leave the four power factors unchanged in both nature and effect. The other formulation would require that the power factors be reversed in either content or effect, along with a reversal of the meaning of bargaining power itself. The result would be two systems instead of one, and would be extremely difficult to follow in transactions which are generous on one side and selfish on the other. The present arrangement requires nothing more than acknowledgment of the interaction of BX on AX (and later of AY on BY), and the introduction of only one new concept, the net value of a power factor. None of the power factors would have different influence under the other formulation, only different names.

It is also possible to describe A's sympathetic desire that B have X as an increase in AY, having the same effect as a decrease in AX. We might also say that in the gift, BY is B's desire to maintain the status quo. Assuming a desire by the parents that the child take lessons, the less his desire for lessons, the greater is his desire to maintain the status quo, and the greater his ability to get concessions from the parents if he will take them. Although AY and BY thus *can* be introduced into the gift, I feel it is simpler, and logically as complete, to deal only with AX (gross and net) and BX.

more from the generous attitude than will BY, and will thus push the overt terms in B's favor.

In short, perhaps contrary to what might have been expected, we need not throw out the rules of bargaining power when we move from selfish to generous transactions. We need merely change the magnitudes of the power factors to allow for the generosity, and proceed as with selfish bargains. The bargaining power of A still varies directly with AX and BX, and inversely with AY and BY, while B's power does the reverse.

Tactics in Generous Bargaining

One might assume that tactical misrepresentations are confined to selfish bargains. Anyone who observes, however, will quickly discover tactics in generous bargains as well. But the items are reversed. Whereas under selfish bargaining A will pretend that AX is high and AY low, under generous bargaining he will pretend that AX is low and AY high. If your positively favorite niece loves nothing more than the little chair you inherited from your great-grandmother on your father's side, and wonders if you would take her worn doll carriage in exchange, you may suddenly find yourself expressing indifference toward a prized heirloom, and great desire for a decrepit baby carriage.

An interesting contrast arises here. With or without tactical misrepresentations, under selfish bargaining no transaction will occur unless both sides gain—or at worst, one side breaks even while the other gains. But under generous bargaining, if one party believes the other is reticently misrepresenting his true position, an exchange may occur which brings a loss to both. This could happen, for example, if you mistakenly think that your niece craves the chair, but is reluctant to say so.

Friendship

A unique generous bargain which does not have ulterior selfish objectives is cooperative, in that A's gift to B gives satisfaction to both. But generous transactions, like selfish ones, are interrelated, and behave differently when interrelated than when unique. A continued relationship between persons in which bargains are typically generous is the main overt manifestation of friendship. Whether such a relationship is the central core, or definition, of friendship need not be debated here. Friendship also generally has major and subsidiary transactions, the former being a general understanding, however nebulous, that the two persons are friends, and the latter consisting of the various things they do for or with each other.

The overall relationship, or major bargain, is normally not explicit, and usually cannot be, considering its many subjective and indefinable dimensions. And while individual subsidiary transactions within the friendship may typically be generous, the overall relationship need not be so. In fact, unless the rewards exceed the costs for both parties, the friendship will cool, and by action or inaction come to an end. If so, then however vague and indefinable the content of the exchange, the fact that each receives more value than he gives up fulfills the minimum conditions for a selfish transaction.[6]

Like other desired relationships, a friendship may require investment. One may make overtures in the form of acts presumably rewarding to the prospective friend, such as compliments, expressions of interest in his work, small favors, or an invitation to a party—though the precise acts appropriate to this purpose vary tremendously from culture to culture. If the friendship is desired for its own sake, these compliments and expressions of interest can be real, since if a person's activities do not deserve sincere praise or interest, one will presumably not seek his friendship. If these overtures are accepted but not returned, a decision arises much like that in drilling an oil well: if the hoped-for result does not appear after a given investment, one must decide between writing off the sunk cost as a bad investment, and adding to the investment in the hope that it will eventually produce results.

Aside from the mutual enjoyment of each other, an important quality of friendship is the relaxed, nonconflicting quality of the subsidiary transactions. "You bring the ham and I'll bring the potato salad and dessert," or "We can go in your car and I'll pay for the gas" are terms which can be arranged without counting who is getting the better bargain—though some persons can be more objectionable in driving generous bargains than others are in selfish ones. If one party reverses the field and starts bargaining selfishly in subsidiary transactions while the other continues to bargain generously, the overall relationship will no longer be balanced, and will probably cease—unless the latter partner has a stronger emotional investment in the friendship. In this overall respect the friendship is not markedly different from the selfish major-subsidiary relationship. Even in the selfish relationship one party may be willing to take "bad" terms in the subsidiary transaction (an act closely related to the willingness to bargain generously) so long as the overall relationship is worth continuing.

An important value of friendship is the high candor it permits. So long as persons are engaged in selfish transactions, they cannot reveal their true feelings without risking a loss in tactical position. Friends, by contrast, discuss many things they never negotiate as opponents. They can thus be completely honest, confident that their frankness will not be used against them. The actual content of friendship is not confined to non-

---

[6] These statements about friendship are not so much assertions of fact as clarifications of the present concepts. In Chapter 14, choice was defined as the selection of the higher over the lower value, the higher relative value being defined as the one actually selected. This can be described in technical language as an operational definition of preference, and in layman's language by saying that actions speak louder than words. At this point the same operational definitions are being applied to friendship. It is asserted that a friendship will not continue unless its values exceed its costs. But if the very performance of any act is by definition the evidence that its values exceed its costs, considering all the facts of the case, then to say that this generalization is also true of friendship is not to reveal anything new about friendship, but merely to illustrate the application of the concepts to this additional area.

conflicting relations, of course. Human beings get satisfaction from such multifarious things as danger, excitement, wrestling, blackjack, arguing, or being insulting; hence friendships and generous bargains *can* be built on such improbable bases as argument and mutual insult.

Loyalty is related to friendship, and may be said to exist when one values a friendship, or a friend's welfare, more than he values the things to be gained by injuring the friend or friendship. Loyalty which continues after a friendship is developed is a fixed cost of that friendship; loyalty before the friendship is developed is an investment. Like other behavior, loyalty can be culturally acquired, and can become habitual, and hence may be practiced without any real thought to its costs and values in any particular case. By a line of reasoning parallel to that used with honesty, one might conclude that *any* breach of loyalty is more costly than the gain, because of the resulting destruction of confidence. There is an important difference, however. It *is* possible to be honest at all times. But it is not possible for *A* to be completely loyal to both *B* and *C* if *B* and *C* are opponents.

Friendship has been discussed above as a transaction, on the assumption that it is terminable when its costs exceed its values. However, many friendships occur within organizations, where persons are not always free to cease dealing with each other. Here the friendship is subsidiary to the whole of one's relationship with the organization. It cannot then be evaluated solely on its own merits, but only as a component of the larger relationship to the organization. We will discuss this point in later chapters on organizations, including the family.

In closing this discussion of generous bargaining, I am aware that some readers will be annoyed at this way of describing things. They may feel that I seemingly try to represent as cold, calculating, and narrowly dimensioned those human relationships which are in fact warm, spontaneous, and infinitely dimensioned. No such thing is intended. If the biologist makes the coldly dispassionate statement that during a lovers' kiss the blood pressure rises by ten per cent and the pulse rate quickens by fifty, he in no way implies that the kiss itself is cold and dispassionate. On the contrary, his statement is one measure of the intensity of the passion. Similarly, if I make the coldly analytical statement that a child's bargaining power rises in proportion to the strength of the parent's sympathetic interest in him, this statement in no way implies that the parent's interest is itself cold, analytical, or unspontaneous. As with the kiss, this statement is itself a description of the change in behavior which occurs when a relation is warm and sympathetic instead of cold and selfish. I have mentioned earlier that Emerson has found these same bargaining power forces among children at play, where all the activity was spontaneous and uncalculated. A geologist's coldly analytical description of an eruption does not imply that the volcano is cold. It merely implies that the geologist's interest in the phenomenon is scientific, not poetic or literary.

Further, we are not attempting to analyze the *whole* of the relationship of friendship and generosity. We are not, for example, dealing with the psychological or emotional aspects. At the moment we are dealing solely with the terms of the overt exchanges which occur under the conditions of friendship and generosity. This is an attempt at scientific analysis, and it is a matter of indifference whether the reader is pleased or offended by it. The only question is whether the analysis is valid or invalid, and whether it increases or decreases our understanding of the particular phenomena it deals with. As with other science, if rules are to be formulated, they must be stated within the context of explicit assumptions or conditions. The present model of transactions and its subsequent modifications attempts to formulate such an explicit context within which rules can be made.[7]

NEGATIVE POWER

The model of the transaction thus far has dealt solely with exchanges of positive goods, in which *A* and *B* get something from each other by offering some positive value in exchange. We now change the model by examining the effect on transactions of negative goods. This does not require a modification of the definition of power, since the "control of wanted things" on which power is based includes the destruction as well as the creation or transfer of goods. Negative power lies in the ability to diminish and destroy goods—the term "good" still meaning anything capable of satisfying a human want.

In everyday language, positive power lies in the ability to provide rewards and negative power in the ability to provide punishments. Also in everyday language, transactions involving positive goods are voluntary while those involving negative goods are coerced. In psychological terms, positive power utilizes reinforcers while negative power utilizes extinguishers. Although each of these sets of terms adds something to the understanding of negative power, each alone is inadequate. The distinction between voluntary and coerced settlements, while useful in everyday affairs, will be seen to be rather meaningless when examined closely. The distinction between rewards and punishments is useful, though the distinction between reinforcers and extinguishers is more precise. If *A* provides *B* with a positive reinforcer he raises *B*'s satisfaction level, whereas if he provides a negative extinguisher he lowers *B*'s satisfaction level. For the present the discussion of negative power will be confined to its role in particular power, the discussion of total power not yet having been opened.

---

[7] If we are to develop reasonably definite generalizations about human behavior we seem tied for the moment to the psychological tautology: human beings repeat and strengthen those behavioral responses which are rewarding and discontinue those which are not, our measure of "rewardingness" or its opposite being the fact that people do, or do not, give certain responses. The social scientist is in no different position here from the physical scientist, when he says, for instance, that for a given voltage (pressure), the magnitude of an electrical current varies inversely with the resistance through which it flows, when the only measure of resistance is the amount of current moved by a given voltage.

Because it is shorter, the term "negative power" will be used widely below. Strictly speaking, it is more accurately described as power based on negative goods, since it is the goods which are negative, not the power. As will be seen, negative power, like positive power, depends upon Effective Preferences.

We may note in passing that some persons get satisfaction from destruction itself. Certain unusual and dramatic destructive events, such as fires and storms, are evidently widely reinforcing, since many people go to great lengths to witness them. For anyone who wishes to create this sort of satisfaction for himself the same rules of power apply as for the person wishing to provide positive goods for himself. He must have a sufficiently strong EP to create it, the EP including both the "productive" ability to create the destruction and the subjective preference for it, rather than for other things which could be produced with the same resources. However, a complication arises in most such cases. Except perhaps to get rid of an imperfect or displeasing creation, and in the play of children, it is a rare person who enjoys destroying useful goods which he himself has produced, if the thing is of sufficient magnitude to create much of a spectacle in the destruction. Hence, the urge to destruction is usually directed at the goods of others, who take a dim view of the process and attempt to stop it. The costs of such destruction therefore include the punishments that may be received if the destroyer is caught. Persons who commit arson, murder, or other destructive acts apparently for their own sake fall into this category—although they may have additional motives, such as revenge or a desire to outwit their fellows. This problem need not be dealt with further; the point is that the ability to acquire satisfaction from destruction depends on the strength of the EP, just as with positive goods.

Destruction for its own sake, although extremely distressing at times, is rare compared to the use of negative goods to increase bargaining power in transactions. Injury to persons, destruction of property, and blackmail are some of the more obvious types of negative goods, and most societies try to prohibit their use. To invade a competitor's cherished market, to throw political support to another candidate, to alienate a fiancee's affections, or to shut off a tenant's utilities are also negative goods to the affected persons, since they reduce existing satisfactions or goods. Negative power may also lie in the ability to destroy peace of mind, status, self-esteem, the enjoyment of poetry, and similar intangible values. The use of these and a host of similar negative goods is normally allowed by society, partly because such negative goods often have useful concomitant functions, and partly because their prohibition would be unenforceable.

Just as with positive power, interpersonal power based on the destruction of existing value requires an overlap of EP's. For example, suppose A wants B to give up a million-dollar business which has been cutting into A's territory. And suppose A threatens: "Sign the business over to me, or I'll pull up your favorite rosebush—by the roots!" Obviously this negative "offer" no more reaches B's threshold than if A had offered to buy the business for a rosebush. The negative power of a threat to destroy certain goods is roughly equal to the positive power of offering to provide those goods if they were not already possessed. Whereas with positive power A must be able to *give* goods of value to B no less than that of the things A wants in exchange, with negative power A must be able to *take away* or destroy goods having that amount of value to B.

Having established this basic point, we can now state that in negative power, as in positive, the fact of a transaction depends on the fact of overlap of EP's, and the terms depend on the position of the overlap. The EP to destroy B's goods depends on both the physical or technical ability to accomplish the destruction (the effective aspect) and the willingness to use it (the preference). The ability to ruin a reputation, for example, requires the possession of deleterious information, skill in its use, and/or considerable reputation of one's own. The ability deliberately to destroy another person's self-esteem requires knowledge of him and of the things that are important to him, as well as status in his eyes as one whose opinion counts. To inflict personal injury may require strength, skill, scheming, certain psychological attitudes toward suffering, and the acceptance of certain physical and legal risks. Whether positive or negative goods are used by A to get Y from B, A must have the necessary EP. This includes the effective ability to accomplish the destruction and the preference which permits him to use it.

In negative power the factors AX, BX, AY, and BY remain the basic power forces, but with an important qualification. Because X is now a negative good the content of AX and BX is reversed (i.e., the "signs" are changed), as follows. Since a negative good is almost necessarily a "service" rather than a commodity, AX and BX must be thought of as referring to services. In positive services, AX represents A's desire *not* to perform the service, while BX is B's desire that it *be* performed. When these are reversed in negative goods, AX represents A's desire *to* perform the destructive service, which is perhaps better expressed as his willingness to perform it. His willingness is greater if he is sadistic or enjoys destructive behavior, and his willingness is also greater in proportion as his costs and risks are lower. To trace this latter point, since A's bargaining power varies directly with AX, and AX varies inversely with the cost of performing the destruction, the lower A's cost of inflicting a given loss upon B the greater is A's bargaining power—which is a widely recognized maxim of bargaining power.

To move now to BX, whereas with positive goods BX is B's desire that A perform his service, with negative goods BX is B's desire that A *not* perform it. This desire is equal to B's loss at A's hands. Since A's bargaining power varies directly with BX, it therefore varies directly with the amount of loss A can inflict upon B.

In order to keep the illustrations from becoming too complex, we will assume that A alone is using negative goods in the transaction. In that event AY and BY have the same content and effect in negative goods as in positive. The larger the value of AY the greater is the likelihood that A will succeed in acquiring Y, but the worse are the probable terms on which he will get it. In the case of negative goods, A's terms are worse if he must incur a larger cost or risk in doing the requisite harm to B. The larger the value of BY the greater is the harm A must be capable of doing to B before B will capitulate—that is, the more difficult will it be to make B give in.

In brief, with negative goods A's bargaining power varies directly with AX and BX, and inversely with AY and BY, just as with positive goods. The difference is that X is a negative quantity, which brings the reversal of content in which AX becomes A's willingness to destroy X and BX becomes B's reluctance to have it destroyed. The effect of these factors when viewed through their effect on EP is basically the same as with positive goods. The fact of A's acquiring Y depends on the fact of overlap, which depends on the total strength of both A's and B's EP. Assuming overlap, the terms then depend on the relative strength of the two EP's, being bettter for A when his own EP is weak and B's strong, and worse when his own EP is strong and B's weak. To illustrate with the previous example, the terms would be excellent from A's point of view if B *would* sign over his business in response to A's threat to pull up the rosebush. They would be much worse from A's point of view if B would capitulate only in response to a threat to poison his wife, kidnap his daughter, or blacklist him from the country club.

Negative goods often enter transactions in conjunction with positive. Let us assume the following transaction as it would appear without a threat, in the upper half of Figure 18-1. A would be willing to give as much as $X + 1$ for Y, and B would be willing to give as much as $Y + 1$ for X. With equal tactical skill the terms of exchange would end at X for Y. Suppose A now threatens to use some negative good which would bring a loss of 3 to B, but which costs A only 1 to employ. The new position after the threat will be as in the lower half of Figure 18-1, for the following reasons.

To begin with B's situation, since A has threatened to impose 3 units of cost on B if he does not give Y for X, a settlement at Y for X becomes 3 units more attractive than it was before the threat. That is, B will lose 3

Figure 18-1

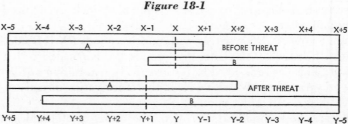

units if he does *not* give Y for X, which 3 he will save if he agrees to those terms *before* the threat is executed. Any other terms agreed to without having the threat executed are also now 3 units more attractive to B than before the threat. Hence, B's EP is extended by three units, from $Y + 1$ to $Y + 4$. Viewed as a union-management relation, if the company was willing to settle for as much as $Y + 1$ without a strike, and the strike is estimated to cost the company 3 units, the company would now be willing (ruling out other factors) to offer as much as $Y + 4$ to avoid a strike.

By similar logic, if the execution of the threat costs A one unit, then A will be willing to concede one more unit to avoid executing the threat than he would have done in the absence of the threat. In union-management terms, having threatened a strike whose cost to the union is estimated at one unit, the union will now be willing to concede one unit more to the employer (such as more work, relaxed seniority clause, or a stronger management security clause) in order to avoid the strike.[8] Hence, A's EP is extended by one unit to $X + 2$.

Viewing the transaction as unique, the threat thus does two things. First, it widens the scope within which a settlement can fall, by extending the EP of both parties. Second, it shifts the mean terms in favor of the party which would lose less if the threat were executed. Since the threat in this case costs A two units less than it costs B, bargaining power is shifted in A's favor. The shift in *mean* terms is half the difference, and the mean terms drop from X to $X - 1$.

Negative Power as Tactics

In positive power we have dealt with the power factors at three different levels: (1) the power factors at the outset of negotiations, (2) changes in power factors due to strategy, and (3) beliefs about power factors arising at the tactical level.

A distinctive feature of negative power is that its most significant aspects are tactical, and depend on the creation of beliefs. A second feature is that, despite its negative setting, the actual power lies in its positive aspect, even as with positive power. These two features are closely related, as follows.

Negative power arises in either of two circumstances. In the first A threatens that if B does not do as requested, A will impose some cost on B. In the second A imposes a cost on B at the outset, in the form of a

---

[8] The reason A may be unwilling to withdraw the threat reflects a tactical intertransactional relation to be discussed below. If A decides that he absolutely cannot fail to execute the threat because of the effect of his apparent weakness on subsequent transactions, then the cost of executing it behaves like a sunk cost in the present negotiation, and hence is irrelevant to it. A's EP then returns to its original position at $X + 1$. If B similarly decides he will not give in to the threat, it behaves like a sunk cost to him, and ceases to be relevant to the present transaction. Some of these problems will be discussed below, but the whole area is far too complex to allow more than a rough introduction here.

distressful situation, and then promises to relieve the distress if B does as requested. The first form will be called the *threat*, and the second will be called either *distress* or *promise of relief*, depending on which seems most meaningful usage in the case. The distressful circumstances behind the latter include such things as pain, fear, hunger, frustration, or confinement. The threat or the promised relief can be applied to B directly, or indirectly by applying it against persons with whom B has sympathetic attachments.

Before going further we should distinguish between the use of physical force to eliminate an obstacle and its use in a transaction. In the former A may be fully capable of doing what he wants, but finds B attempting to stop him. If A can physically immobilize B, as by killing or injuring him, tying him down, or locking him up, A can then proceed without interference. In the transaction, however, A seeks to get B to perform some desired act, such as revealing a secret or granting some concession. This calls for B's agreement, and the threat or promised relief is used as the leverage to bring forth that agreement. The distinction may not be entirely clear when A seeks B's agreement to stop being an obstacle to A's efforts. For example, if A punches B for blocking a doorway there may be a point at which there is doubt whether B allows A to pass in order to avoid another punch, which is an act of agreement, or because he was physically incapable of stopping A. In many instances, including warfare, the points of agreement and physical incapacity coincide. But in all disputes other than those over blockage itself, the distinction between agreement and the simple removal of blockage is clear. The present discussion is confined solely to transactions, and the possible use of physical force as a means of getting better terms.

In both the threat and distress the real power lies in the positive value of an offer of improvement. This is a promise in the ordinary sense, and the fact or threat of destruction is useful only to provide a base from which to make that promise look appealing. If you are on the first floor and want to stay at least that high, negative power either (1) puts you into the cellar and then offers to return you to the first floor, or (2) offers to let you stay on the first floor instead of putting you into the cellar—the fulfillment of either offer being contingent on your making some concession. Instead of tapping the desire to get ahead, negative power relies on the desire not to be set back—while simultaneously providing the means to execute the setback.

To look first at the case of torture, it is not the pain which brings the concession, but the promise that if the concession is made the pain will be relieved. The pain suffered up to any given point is the same whether the tortured person gives in or not. It is a sunk cost at that point, and irrelevant. The only relevant thing is whether the torture will cease or continue in return for conceding or refusing it. It is the positive value of promised relief, not the negative value already imposed, which B sees as possibly justifying concession.

The threat at first glance may seem wholly negative. But it too holds all its value in its positive aspect. It is not the threat which contains the power, but the implied promise not to carry out the threat if the concession is made. If *A* threatens to club *B* if he does not turn over the contents of his bulging wallet, it is not the clubbing or threat thereof which produces the cash but the promise that the cash will stave off the club. In both the threat and the promise the fact or threat of destroying value contains no power in itself; it merely lowers the base from which values are measured so as to make the *status quo ante* worth paying for.

Being based on promised relief, negative power gets nowhere unless the promise is believed. If the subject believes that the torture will go on or the threat be executed regardless—just for good luck—he then has no motive to concede, and the negative bargaining power disappears. This brings us to the second important characteristic of negative power: namely, that it depends heavily on its tactical aspects. If the promise is believed it produces its results whether it would actually be carried out or not. If it is not believed it does not produce its effect, again whether it would actually be carried out or not.

Although the actual execution of a threat holds no power in itself, it is sometimes effective as a means of creating conviction. Suppose a young man threatens to break my right arm unless I give him permission to keep my daughter out past midnight. I refuse and he breaks my arm. Now the bargaining power of his threat lay in the implied promise *not* to break my arm if I granted the permission. The value of this implied promise has now vanished, since I can now no longer save the arm by granting the permission. The broken arm is a sunk cost to me, and hence irrelevant to my decision thereafter. The broken arm is relevant, however, to my belief about his intentions when he next threatens to break my left arm. The effect of executing a threat lies not in the harm it inflicts but in the credence it lends to the next threat. That is, the threat is executed only after the transaction to which it was applied has failed, and its value is solely that of a tactical intertransactional investment in the next negotiation. The display of a wrestling trophy or flexed biceps might have been equally convincing, and have saved both my arm and his effort.

It is the belief in the opponent's *effective* preference that counts. Suppose instead of breaking my arm the young man locks me in the cellar, promising to release me when I grant permission. But suppose he then accidentally drops the key down the register where it is inaccessible to both of us. I now know that he cannot let me out even if he wants to. His promise of relief is valueless and his bargaining power nil. Again the power lies not in the distress but in the belief that it will be relieved in return for the concession. The successive increases of distress by torturers not only raise the value of the promised relief but provide repeated reminders of their ability to provide it.

Assuming that the practitioner of negative power has made his promise credible, his remaining tactical problem is the same as with positive power: namely, to represent his power position as stronger than it is in fact. For *A* this means appearing more willing to engage in the negative acts than he actually is, and for *B* it means appearing less likely to be harmed by them than he actually is. Even second graders sense this relationship intuitively, as when the bully exaggerates his fearsomeness, and the victim pretends it doesn't really hurt. Incidentally, although the rule of sunk costs was discussed above only with reference to *B*'s decision whether to concede under pressure, the same rule also applies to *A*. To impose costs on *B* normally involves some cost to *A*. Having incurred any given amount of cost without producing a concession, *A* must logically consider the costs up to that point as sunk and irrelevant. His only question is whether the additional costs from that point forward will bring commensurate concessions.

WHAT IS COERCION?

Since the outcome of tactics is indeterminate, and negative power is mainly tactical, the outcome of negative power is essentially indeterminate. Like tactics in general, the success of those involving negative power depends very much on the personalities involved and the numberless subtleties which determine whether a given threat or promise will be believed. Like any other promise, that used to effectuate a threat or promise has increased force if the party making it is in a position to demonstrate convincingly that he will keep it. One of the devices for so doing is to show that he cannot afford not to, as when a union leader claims that he will lose the next election if, without striking, he settles for less than a 10 per cent raise, the businessman who says he will become the laughingstock of the industry if he accepts the cancellation of his lease without a fight, or the senator who alleges that it will kill him politically if he does not filibuster a civil rights bill.

Since threats and promises depend so heavily on beliefs it is interesting to examine precisely what is meant by coercion, and the common distinction between voluntary and coerced agreements. Despite the usefulness of the distinction in everyday language, the above analysis suggests that the terms should perhaps be dropped from critical discussion.

There are tremendously varying degrees of power in interpersonal relationships. If *A* has the physical capacity to immobilize or incapacitate *B* it is common to say that *A* has coercive power over *B*. But such a situation merely assures that *B* cannot stop *A* from doing what he wants, whereas coercion normally means the ability to get *B* to do something *A* wants him to do. In the language of the earlier description, coercion has an unequivocal meaning when applied to physical blockage. It is when the term is applied to transactions that we run into difficulty.

For example, the threat of physical injury by club or gun in order to gain a concession is usually viewed as coercive. But so long as *B* is conscious, it does not necessarily follow that he is powerless to resist a demand, even though he is trussed up, a pistol at his head. For instance, despite such apparent helplessness, if B happens to know that A is not stupid, and that he (B) is far more valuable to A alive than dead, instead of capitulating B may say, "Don't be silly." A man may point a pistol at a hulking gas station manager who is closing up for the night, and walk off with the day's cash. He may try the same thing a few nights later to a frail woman closing a restaurant. But she may scream, throw a milk bottle, and send him scampering empty handed. One person may be "coerced" into revealing a secret by a mild hair pulling, while another may undergo fantastic tortures without talking. Examples of this sort raise the question: is coercion coercive if it does not coerce? It also raises the related question, does coercion refer to the pressures applied or the results achieved?

The latter question is particularly relevant to persons who make tremendous concessions under no physical threat or pain at all. To avoid the loss of a treasured heirloom, to save a child from knowing that his father died in disgrace, or to hold a valued leader in an organization, people have been known to give up much more than if they had been "coerced" in the normal sense. Assuming that the threat is believed, "Give it to me or I'll break your arm" may be highly coercive if "it" is a dollar and not at all coercive if "it" is a hundred million.

These are the more explicit reasons why, for the purpose of serious analysis of power, it seems better to drop the distinction between voluntary and coerced settlements. Whether positive or negative, power lies in the hands of those who control things desired by others, and the strength of the power lies in the strength of the preferences and the value of opportunities. If a beautiful woman clad only in a diaphanous negligee strolled casually in front of a lone workman in her house, most juries would conclude in effect that he had been "coerced" into rape. If a professor on meager salary is offered $150 a day for industrial consulting he may feel "coerced" into accepting it as part-time work. If the union and company will suffer about equal losses from a strike, neither side feels coerced. But if the employees' losses would be huge and the company's slight (as during slack season, or when the company has a large inventory on hand), the employees feel "coerced" into settling on the company's terms. In reverse, if the union strikes during the Christmas rush, or when a perishable crop is just ripe, the employer may feel coerced.[9] Coercion does not

---

[9] In the previous chapter it was indicated that it does not seem conceptually useful to try to determine which of two opposing parties has the greater bargaining power, but only which has the bargaining advantage relative to some set of possible terms which can be used as a point of reference. The power positions which would exist without the application of negative goods can be used as such a point of reference from which to measure the power of negative goods. In cases where negative pressures are dominant, as in a strike or a threat of death, it might be feasible to state meaningfully that one side has "more bargaining power" than the other. However, since the term "bargaining advantage" established earlier for the general case seems adequate for this one as well, I see no point in modifying the general terminology for this special case.

mean that one party has no choice, but that bargaining advantage is so obviously one-sided as to leave little doubt of the outcome.

The present discussion of coercion deals only with the unique transaction of two parties. In the next chapter, and again in Chapter 33, we will see how the power of government, of coalitions, and of other devices may be introduced to limit obvious unbalances of power.[10]

---

[10] In a paper delivered at the convention of the American Economics Association, December 29, 1962, "The Economics of Threat Systems," Kenneth Boulding suggested that the three major types of human relationships may be those of threats, exchange, and love. Re-expressed in the present language I would assume that these would correspond respectively to selfish transactions involving negative goods, selfish transactions involving positive goods, and generous transactions. Boulding then listed submission, defiance, counterthreat, and integrative behavior as the possible responses to threat. Analysis of these four items can, I believe, be subsumed within the present approach, but involve details of tactics, strategy, and game theory far beyond the scope of the present introduction.

Chapter 19

POWER IN TRANSACTIONS: CONCLUDING THE MODEL

INFORMATION IN BARGAINING

A TRANSACTIONAL relationship between two parties involves a decision by each. Each decision reflects that party's preferences for the opportunities currently available to him through the transaction, as compared with those available from alternate sources. Thus far the model has acknowledged that one party might improve his bargaining power by changing the preferences or opportunities of the other party, but has not specifically discussed the methods or consequences. Except at the tactical level, where we accepted possible ignorance or misrepresentation, we assumed that the information and motives on the basis of which each party accepts or rejects an offer are not influenced by the other party. We now relax this assumption to include the possibility that one party through communication may influence what the other party judges to be in his own best interest.

For this analysis we will define *moral power* as the ability to control or change preferences, and *intellectual* (or *information*) *power* as the ability to control the conceptualization or awareness of opportunities. Although the definitions include the ability to control these things in oneself, we will focus attention on controlling them in others. These definitions refer only to the *type* of thing being influenced, not the desirability or undesirability of that influence. A person will be construed to exercise *moral* power, even if he uses it for purposes which society considers immoral, and *intellectual* power even if he conveys falsehoods or mistaken conceptualizations. Expressed in the language of Chapter 10, intellectual power is parallel to the communication of information, and moral power to the communication of motives, but with an added emphasis that the communication effectively influences the receiver's behavior or thinking.

The number of possible ways of doing these things is vast, and we can merely illustrate a few. The dictator who can keep his people unaware that democracy is a feasible form of government, the church which can convince its followers that there is only one road to salvation, or the parent who can convince the child that there is no money for candy, improves his (its) bargaining power. Since full access to information might reveal information or beliefs to the contrary, one way of maintaining a bargaining advantage is to curtail the flow of information about the matters bargained about. For a whole society this can be done by ownership or censorship of the press and other news media. Where one is himself the main source of certain information, as with the parent's knowledge about the family's income, he may merely withhold the information, or misrepresent it. Where the flow of information cannot itself be controlled, one may nevertheless mold attitudes and beliefs in such a way as to determine what will be perceived from certain communications. In an announcement that the President has urged additional social security legislation, one person may perceive a government conscientiously striving to meet the needs of its citizens, while another may perceive a power-hungry bureaucracy seeking to enlarge its power. In a philosophy professor's searching questions one student may perceive an effort to stretch the mind and enlarge understanding, while a second may see a despicable effort to undermine religious faith. Any communication which molds perceptions is an important aspect of intellectual, or information, power.

In the opposite direction, any communication which leads to broader horizons and awareness of wider or more numerous opportunities also reflects intellectual power, by decreasing the sense of dependence on any one opportunity. As will be seen in the next chapter, such information typically leads to an increase in freedom. Since information of this kind does not normally increase the bargaining power of the person providing it, except in the case of advertising, it is usually given by persons who have a generous interest in other persons, or in the welfare of the whole society, as by parents, friends, and public spirited citizens; or by those specially set aside and paid by society for the purpose, as in the case of teachers or ministers. The term "knowledge of opportunities" is used here in its widest sense to include all those things perceived as possible, whether or not they are related to particular decisions or transactions.

Whether used to improve one's own position or not, intellectual power depends in part on the ability to present ideas clearly and interestingly. It also depends on access to means of communication and an audience, whether through TV, newspapers, town meeting, totem ceremony, confessional, or classroom. Since it also depends upon communication, moral power depends on roughly the same ingredients, though, of course, with the emphasis on motivation rather than information as such. Whereas in controlling information the dictator might try to keep his people unaware of democracy, in controlling motives he might try to convince them that they are better off to do his bidding without question. For reasons of this sort it is almost universal for groups holding power in any society to use communication to create concepts and motives favorable to their continued power.

At lesser levels, control of communication can be used to assist the child's bargaining power when he refrains from mentioning that he broke the milk pitcher. Employees try to see that certain information about themselves gets to the employer while other does not, and the employer similarly selects information for the reverse flow. The elected official wants his successes reported fully and his failures squelched, and so on through much of the society. Anyone in a position to circulate, hold back, or distort the flow of information holds a position of power. He may or may not use this to enhance his own bargaining power. But any analysis of the location of large power in any society must give serious attention to the controls of communication, be they tribal rituals or mass media.

BARGAINING THROUGH AGENTS

We have assumed thus far that all bargaining over transactions is done by persons representing their own interests. Long before Priscilla Mullins responded to John Alden's courtship speech on behalf of Myles Standish with, "Why don't you speak for yourself, John?" people have been aware that transactions conducted through an agent may turn out differently from those conducted by the principal.

The agent may be a better bargainer than the principal, or a worse one. He may be more inclined to give concessions, or less so. He may be a stronger arguer, or weaker. The effect of such differences is obvious, and does not require discussion. By contrast, other differences grow out of the fact of agency itself, and deserve to be discussed.

To speak first of power differences, an agent almost inevitably has goals of his own, which differ in some respects from those of his principal. The citizens and higher officials of a government may want justice in their courts. But the district attorney who is their prosecuting agent may be more interested in victory than justice, since in his private practice he sells his services to people who want victory. An occasional shop steward negotiating with the plant manager on behalf of an aggrieved employee may be more interested in demonstrating his promotability to the company than in defending the grievant. An antitrust lawyer earning $12,000 from the Department of Justice for prosecuting a case against a large corporation may be interested in demonstrating to the company that he would be worth $50,000 to them as a defense attorney. A salesman may try to sell that which will provide him the largest commission, a purchasing agent may order from the firm which provides him the largest Christmas gifts, and the personnel manager may try that system which will gain the most attention in the personnel association. An agent may not hold out for the best possible deal because he is hot and tired and wants to get home.

Further, the principal can never know the details of the negotiations as the agent can, and by exaggerating the skill of the opponent the agent may make his mediocre bargaining sound like a brilliant victory. In these and many other ways, bargaining through agents may produce different power positions than if bargaining had been done by the persons in interest.

These examples do not imply that agents are generally not conscientious, but only that they have motives of their own. These may differ from those of the principal, and dilute the achievement of his goals. At other times the agent may have the opposite effect, and fight harder for another person than he would for himself.

The use of agents also affects tactics. The secretary in the outer office who says, "I am sorry, but Mr. Plethora has left strict orders not to be disturbed" can turn away visitors the boss himself would not dare to reject. If a property owner wants an extortionate price for his plot; if he knows the buyer will pay it if necessary; if he also knows that his conscience could be appealed to; he may instruct his agent not to budge on the price, and then take off on a hunting trip in the wilds of Canada until the sale is concluded. On returning he can express regret that his agent was so hardhearted. A particularly strong position is to be "absolutely inaccessible" to everyone except one's agent.

Expressed in the language of bargaining power, the principal can decide what Effective Preference on his part is likely to give him the best terms in a transaction, and instruct his agent to that effect. Even though the opponents might give the agent arguments he cannot answer, he can still reply, "I am acting on instructions, and am powerless to concede." The agent may add: "I'll talk to him about it, but I doubt if he will change his mind."

If both sides deal through agents, the bargaining may be minimal. Each agent may be willing to reach a "reasonable" settlement with minimum effort, after which both will regale their principals with tales of how they fought every step of the way. Other agents may defend their principal's interest more vigorously than he himself would do, perhaps because they exaggerate the importance of the transaction, perhaps because they get satisfaction from a good fight, or perhaps because they hope thus to demonstrate their loyalty and promotability.

There is no need to delve further into the many repercussions of bargaining through agents. It is enough to note that it does make a difference, to both power and tactical positions.

CONSENSUS TRANSACTIONS

Consensus Terms and Determinate Bargaining Power

In the initial model each transaction was assumed to be unique, its terms dependent solely on the four bargaining power factors in that transaction. Other possible transactions involving the same parties or the same goods were assumed to have no effect on the transaction, either through power or tactical interactions. We have already relaxed this assumption by admitting several kinds of interrelationships, such as those of multiple goods in a single transaction, and the participation of the same persons in two or more transactions.

We will now allow another relaxation by shifting attention from interactions of *persons* among transactions to interactions of the *values of goods*, or *terms of transactions*. In doing so we shift from *unique* transactions to *consensus* transactions. In a pure, or perfect, consensus transaction, the terms of exchange of X for Y are universally known to and accepted by a particular group of people who exchange X and Y. We will first examine the effect of consensus on bargaining power, and then look at the source and nature of consensus.

In Chapter 17 it was observed that the strength of one person's EP sets the limit to the bargaining power of the other. It was also seen that the strength of that EP in dealing with one person is limited by the best alternatives available from other sources. If B is a seller of corn, and many other sellers around him are offering corn of equal quality at $1 a bushel, then any one customer, A, will have an EP of no more than $1 in dealing with B, since he has innumerable alternatives which are that good. Similarly, if there are many A's who are willing to pay as much as $1, then B's EP for $1 is no greater than one bushel of corn, which is another way of saying that he will accept no less than $1 per bushel, or give no more than one bushel for $1.

This situation, known in economics as a purely competitive market, and here referred to as a perfect consensus, performs an extremely important social function, in that it makes bargaining power, and hence the terms of any given transaction, determinate at the consensus. This it does by eliminating overlap of EP's, so that the EP's just touch at the consensus valuation. This can be illustrated by a diagram like that used in Chapter 17. Scale (a) at the top of Figure 19-1 represents the number of dollars A would be willing to give for one bushel of corn, ranging from $0.70 on the left to $1.30 on the right. Scale (b) represents the amount of corn B would be willing to give for $1.00, ranging from .7 bushels on the right to 1.3 on the left. If A can find many other suppliers who will sell at $1.00 per bushel, and B can find many other buyers who will purchase at $1.00, then the EP of each in dealing with the other extends just to the midpoint. Here the *same* best alternative is available to each. Either party can pull the other *to* these terms, but neither can pull the other *beyond* them. Assuming that neither party has motives beyond those of getting the best possible overt terms of exchange, under a perfect consensus it can be reliably predicted that any one transaction will take place at the consensus terms, or it will not take place at all. Under perfect consensus we can therefore say either that bargaining power is determinate, or that the terms of the transaction are determinate. Our main interest is in the latter wording—that under perfect consensus the terms of particular transactions are determinate at the consensus.[1]

Figure 19-1

EFFECTIVE PREFERENCES OF *A* AND *B* FOR CORN AND DOLLARS, RESPECTIVELY, UNDER PERFECT CONSENSUS

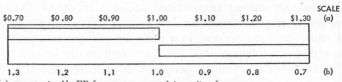

Scale (a) represents *A*'s EP for corn expressed in units of money.
Scale (b) represents *B*'s EP for money expressed in units of corn.

Perhaps because economists have studied transactions in more detail than other social scientists, there is a widespread impression that transactions occur only in marketable goods. The past several chapters should dispel this impression, and extend the notion of the transaction to cover virtually any interpersonal relationship other than that of organization, to be discussed in later chapters. With the extension of the concept of the transaction, the effect which economists have found in the perfectly competitive market is also found in any kind of perfect consensus, whether the goods are marketable in the traditional sense or not. Suppose that in a particular subculture the tradition is strongly established that a girl does not allow a boy to kiss her until their third date. If these consensus terms are widely recognized and accepted, the consensus automatically provides the terms of any individual transaction. Any boy will refuse to go with any girl who insists on more, and any girl will refuse to concede for fewer. Neither party can find any better alternatives elsewhere, and the absence of better alternatives limits the bargaining power of each to the consensus terms.

In the above examples, the consensus works overtly. The consensus terms are accepted by both parties because neither sees any better overt, objective alternative. Consensus terms can also operate subjectively, or internally. This will occur if both parties adopt the consensus valuation into their own personal preference systems. In the case of corn, this might happen if the price of corn has remained unchanged long enough

---

[1] There exists here a small, but, I believe, important change in wording from conventional approaches. Economists normally say that a perfectly competitive market reflects the complete *absence* of bargaining power. Under the present approach bargaining power exists in all transactions, and the perfect market represents the conditions of *determinate* bargaining power, not absence of bargaining power. This distinction in wording can be illustrated clearly in connection with union-management bargaining, where it is customary to say that wages are determined partly by market forces and partly by bargaining power forces. Under present terminology it would be said that wages are determined entirely by bargaining power forces, some of which are market forces, and some of which are nonmarket forces, such as unionization or legislation.

for both parties to accept one dollar as the "right and proper" price. In highly static, nonmarket cultures many goods come to have such a "just price," which may continue unchanged for generations. No one under such circumstances would pay more or accept less because he would consider a different price "wrong," and perhaps immoral. Similarly, three dates as the price of the first kiss may be enforced subjectively if both boy and girl believe that other terms are brash, cheap, daring, stingy, indecent, or immoral, and both refuse other terms because they are "wrong."

The subjective pressure toward consensus terms may not always be as effective as the objective, since in the latter neither party has any better overt alternative. The absence of overt alternatives is equally effective in bringing individual transactions into line with the consensus whether or not the consensus is felt to be "right," whereas the subjective is fully effective only if every particular bargainer accepts the terms as "right." If the group feels the terms to be right but the individual does not, and violates the group standards by taking advantage of some weak bargainer, other persons (or even the disadvantaged bargainer himself under other circumstances) may retaliate in other transactions to penalize the miscreant, and hence help to enforce the consensus. The techniques for doing this will be discussed later below.

The Sources of Consensus (Kinds of Consensus)

In a sense and in part, each of the three major social science "disciplines" deals with one particular kind, or source, of consensus. Economics deals with a consensus developed through exchanges in markets, a perfect *market consensus* existing when there are large numbers of persons engaging in transactions of identical goods. Under these circumstances, the terms on which any particular good is exchanged (which terms are the price of that good, the prices of all other goods being what they are) reflect the influence of all persons' desires for that good relative to other goods. As described in economics, the totality of desires of all persons for any particular good is reflected in the demand for that good, while the totality of its costs are reflected in the supply. The relationship between Effective Preferences and the supply and demand curves will be examined in a later chapter.

The *political consensus* is one of the things studied by political scientists. Elections and other means of public decision making are a second major technique by which individual preferences can be aggregated into a consensus. A political consensus can be enforced by promulgating certain terms, and applying the negative powers of government against those who do not conform. It can also be enforced by regulating the techniques, goods, or "weapons" used in transactions. The techniques of forming and enforcing political consensus will also be discussed in later chapters.

Sociologists give much attention to what they call *social norms*, which will be referred to here as instances of social consensus. The differences among the political, market, and social consensuses are not in the types of things to which the society attaches values, but in the technique by which the consensus is achieved and enforced. In the present context we will define a *social consensus* as one formed by the cultural process, which is the set of relations described in Chapter 12 under the title of "Culture as a System." It is the system in which the overt manifestations which we call the culture are the environment which form the motives and concepts of the people, whose behavior then forms the culture, in endless succession.

In the broad sense the system of culture is an all-encompassing, general-purpose process of developing consensus. It exists in all societies, and any consensus developed directly by the culture system may be thought of as a social consensus. To speak of valuations (rather than concepts) of things, these may include such general valuations as the relative positions of skill, education, physical strength, a large house, or high office in the preference ordering of the society. It may also include such explicit valuations as the exchange ratios of corn and wheat, or of wives and cows.

In addition to making direct valuations, the culture system may develop sociofacts in the form of market or political techniques for forming additional consensuses. A society's acceptance of any particular market or political process as a system of making collective evaluations is itself a consensus within that society.

The encompassing role of the social consensus in the analytical scheme does not mean, however, that the social technique of forming consensus necessarily dominates the other two in practice. Any one can have a compelling influence on either or both of the other two. It is difficult to know the source of any particular social consensus except to trace the history of the society, and its relation to its physical environment.

Numerous techniques of enforcing social consensus are in use. Since an important one, the coalition, has not yet been discussed, we will incorporate the discussion of enforcing social consensus into a broader examination of social controls in the next chapter.

The Great Middle Ground

For many years economists spent much effort analyzing the conditions of pure competition and pure monopoly. As with many other concepts, these represent ends of a spectrum, and are sharply definable. In parallel fashion, the discussion of transactions thus far has dealt only with unique transactions (though with some intertransactional relationships) and perfect consensus transactions. In actuality, the vast majority of transactions do not fall at either extreme—just as the majority of market purchases take place under conditions which are neither pure monopoly nor pure competition. Instead, they take place under circumstances where *some* consensus exists, but not a perfect one. Alternative sources of goods do exist, but not in sufficient numbers for any one person to be sure he can find as good an alternative source if he rejects a current offer. For the young swain in the large city there may in fact be thousands of young ladies whom he might date. But at any given moment there may be only three with whom he is actually on datable terms. This is roughly equivalent to the condition known by economists as oligopoly.

Second, the three girls are not exactly alike. As the economist would put it, they are not perfect substitutes, but instead show product differentiation. Given both conditions, the young man is not in a position to say: "Kiss me on consensus terms or you will never see me again." If he must judge them from the selection actually available to him, he may not be sure what the consensus terms *are*. Indeed there may be none within this trio, as all three girls may have different preferences, both about kissing and about the young man.

The point of all this is simple, and extremely important. In most relationships between pairs of parties, there is some latitude for the terms of the relationship to reflect the preferences of those parties, as distinct from the preferences of the surrounding culture. At the same time, the fact that other transactions of the same or similar goods are taking place in their environment places a limit on the range of terms within which a given transaction will be conducted. This limitation operates through overt alternatives, subjective preferences, or both. The conditions formulated by economists for marketable goods seem to apply in many kinds of nonmarket transactions. Namely, the larger the number of available alternatives (up to the point where they are "readily available" to anyone), and the more readily substitutable the alternatives, the more closely can the consensus be discerned, and the narrower will be the range of deviation of actual transactions from the norm. In reverse, the fewer and less readily substitutable the alternatives, the less precisely can the norm be defined, and the wider is the range of deviation around the norm.[2]

To illustrate once more, so long as the young man has many young ladies in his date book, and no emotional attachments to any one, he cannot be readily bargained (if he is alert) into any important concessions. But let him fall blindly in love! Suddenly the number and substitutability of available alternatives dwindles to the vanishing point, while his Effective Preference for this girl seems infinite. If the girl is not in love too, and if she also has no conscience, she can now get the most extraordinary concessions. Whether she will actually do so, depends on many other factors, strategic, tactical, and intertransactional. The important thing is that to be blindly in love makes the relationship highly unique, and re-

---

[2] A specific application of this line of reasoning to the determination of wages is found in my article, "Toward an Integration of Wage Theory," *The Southern Economic Journal* (July, 1959), pp. 13 ff, with special reference to Hypothesis #2.

duces the ability of alternatives to keep the terms of the relationship near the norm. Fortunately for young men, some young ladies do have consciences, while others suspect that the blindness may not be so complete or permanent as to make the alternatives irrelevant.

If both fall in love (with each other, that is), the overlap of EP's will now be much greater than if neither was in love. Hence, the range of *possible* terms of the relation also increases greatly, and the terms may shift toward one extreme or the other, or perhaps alternate spectacularly. (We are speaking now of possible shifts *within* a given set of EP's. Additional shifts are likely if the preferences themselves undergo change.) On the other hand, if both are about equally in love, no significant change of overt terms may ensue, since the overlap grows in both directions, and may not change the mean terms at all. Even unilateral love does not necessarily bring a marked change in overt terms, if the party with the increased bargaining power does not take advantage of it. Thus the advent of love *allows* marked changes in the terms of a relationship, but does not make them inevitable.

The above discussion was phrased as if some sort of general, average set of boy-girl relations exists in a given society, from which the arrival of love makes the relation more unique, and may or may not bring strong changes in terms, depending on the EP's of the particular parties. In a static, homogeneous culture this may be the case, as the terms of boy-girl relationships are rather standardized. In such societies, however, the terms of the relationship which follows love or courtship may also be highly standardized, and be enforced by social pressures of types to be discussed in the next chapter. In that case the advent of love will not make the relationship more unique, but merely shift it from consensus terms appropriate to couples not in love to a different set of consensus terms appropriate to those who are.

To generalize about all kinds of relationships, no conclusions can be made about particular cases until the facts of the cases are known. The great majority of human relationships, however, are neither so unique that their terms are unaffected by consensus, nor do they occur in so perfect a consensus as to leave the parties no choice about the terms. In addition, of course, the preferences and opportunities in many relationships are multidimensional in the extreme, and highly subjective to boot. In such situations it is impossible to predict what decision *one* party will make about the transaction, much less to predict the resulting interactions of *two* persons' sets of decisions. It does seem safe to say, however, that, other things equal, the greater the degree of consensus in a given culture about the terms of any one kind of transaction, either (1) the greater is the likelihood that the terms of any one transaction will take place at the consensus, if at all, or (2) the narrower will be the range around the consensus within which the terms of any one transaction will fall, or both.

To summarize, under perfect consensus the terms of any one transaction are determinate, at the consensus. The less perfect the consensus the greater is the importance of the desires of, and the alternatives available to, the particular parties involved.

MULTIPLE PARTIES

Thus far the model of the transaction has dealt explicitly with only two parties at a time. Others may have been lurking in the background, influencing or being influenced by a transaction under consideration, or being part of a consensus. But they were not explicitly brought within the frame of the picture. We will now modify the model further by bringing more than two parties directly into the analysis—in competition, coalitions, and collective bargaining. As with some previous modifications of the model, we cannot hope to trace all possible kinds of relationships, but we can look at enough samples to illustrate the nature of the analysis.

Competition[3]

In the analysis thus far, a transaction might or might not take place between two persons, depending on whether the EP's overlapped. The analysis did not specifically deal with the possibility that either party would consummate a transaction with someone else—though the presence of others did place limits on bargaining power. As we now broaden the analysis to include competition we must examine not only the *terms* of transactions, but also *with whom* they will occur.

In this connection "complete knowledge" will mean that all parties know the power limits of all other parties, but it will not mean that anyone knows what tactics anyone else is using. "Lack of knowledge" will mean that the power limits are also unknown. Although the term will be used with broader connotations elsewhere in the book, *competition* here means that two or more parties on at least one side are simultaneously seeking to acquire the good available through a given transaction. The practical effect is the same as saying that two or more want to conclude a given transaction. The analysis at this point will be confined to competition on one side only.

If we assume one A and several B's, the effect on bargaining power can be seen in Figure 19-2. A's EP for Y is assumed to extend to X. Four different B's are shown: B, B', B'' and B''', whose EP's extend to $X - 4$, $X - 2$, X, and $X + 2$ respectively. Assuming that each B would like to complete the transactions at any terms within his own EP, and assuming complete knowledge by all parties, the result is clear. The EP of

---

[3] In discussions of social relationships the term "symbiotic" is sometimes used to refer to cooperative relationships, and "commensal" to refer to competitive ones. These terms are not used here. First, "competition" seems adequate for its purpose, and I see no point in substituting a less known word. Second, "symbiotic" lumps together as "cooperative" things which are here treated as different in highly significant ways: namely, transactions and organizations, or exchange and joint production. As already seen, exchange is part cooperation and part conflict, a fact not reflected in the term "symbiotic."

B''' is too small to touch that of A. No transaction with B''' is possible, and he will drop out of the picture. B'' will recognize that his case is probably hopeless, and drop out. B' can see that he is not the strongest competitor, but that he might get the transaction if B muffs his strategy.

Figure 19-2

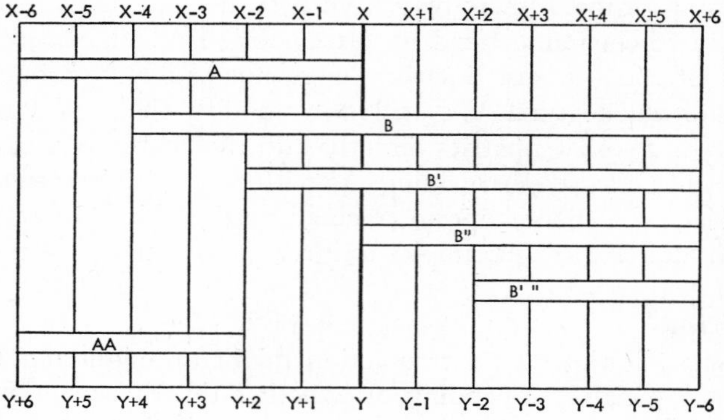

The real question, of course, lies between A and B. Although in itself A's EP extends to X, as soon as A becomes aware that the alternative of $X - 2$ is available from competitor B', his EP in dealing with B shrinks to that figure, as shown in the lower left of the diagram at AA. If we continue to assume perfect knowledge, from this point the negotiations behave like a two-person transaction involving the EP's B and AA, except that B would offer terms just below $X - 2$ in order not to lose the deal to B'. Since "complete" knowledge does not include knowledge of tactics, the terms remain power indeterminate between $X - 2$ and $X - 4$, to be settled by tactics.

If A's EP is known only to himself (i.e., is uncertain to all of the B's), but the EP's of all the B's are known to all, including A, unless one of the B's makes a tactical blunder, the deal will again take place with B at some figure between $X - 2$ and $X - 4$. There is the slight uncertainty not present under complete knowledge that the transaction might fail completely if B, B', and B'' all mistakenly held out for too high a price in the belief A's EP is greater than it is.

Let us next assume that none of the B's knows the EP of any other, but that A's is known. The bargaining position of any one B is now weakened. We can illustrate by contrasting the tactics of B if he knows the EP of B' with his tactics if he does not. With knowledge B is assured of the deal if he sets any price less than $X - 2$, and can therefore bargain with confidence to get a price as near that figure as possible. Without knowledge, however, he can make either of two mistakes. First, he might underestimate the strength of EP of B' and insist on $X - 1$. B' might then underbid him at $X - 2$ and get the deal. Second, he might overestimate and bid $X - 4$ in order to be sure of not being underbid, thereby receiving worse terms than if he had known his closest competition is $X - 2$.

If all parties are ignorant of anyone else's EP, the result is unpredictable. If A should start negotiations with B''', and the remaining B's were to overestimate A's EP, the transaction might fail entirely. If A were to continue shopping, however, taking each bid from a B to other B's, the shopping process itself would gradually reduce the ignorance, and if continued long enough would produce the same result as complete knowledge.

There is no need to examine other degrees of initial or final knowledge here, as our concern is with the broader aspects of competition. When two or more persons compete for the good available through a given transaction, under perfect knowledge the one with the strongest EP will get it.[4] If we look first at the "preference" aspect of Effective Preference, ignoring the "effective" aspect for the moment, this means that the competitor with the strongest net desire for X will get it. This is readily evident at an auction, where the good goes to the highest bidder, who is the bidder with the strongest desire for the good relative to his desire to keep his money. In competition among sellers the sale will be made and the money acquired by the competitor with the lowest price, who is the one with the highest desire for money relative to his desire to keep the good.

In generous bargaining the same principle would apparently also apply: if the donor of a gift must choose among recipients he will presumably select the one with the most intense desire for it. In negative goods the prisoner with the most intense desire for relief from torture will tend to be the first to talk.

In situations intermediate between selfish and generous the intensity of desire also seems to apply. Among equally capable students the one with the most intense desire for the lead in the school play will tend to get it, both out of generous consideration and because he will be willing to work hardest. All these illustrations are subject to the usual disclaimers of "all other things equal" or "unless offset by other forces."

Contests are competitive transactions in which the "effective" aspect dominates the "preference" aspect, and in which emphasis is placed on ability to produce the thing to be given in the transaction. Whether the contest is javelin throwing, limerick writing, or auto racing, the prize goes to the person with the greatest ability to produce the thing competed in. The role of preference lies in influencing the amount of time, energy, or other resources which will go into preparation for the contest. The

---

[4] To keep the terminology straight, the *strongest* competitor is the one with *least* bargaining power. To reverse the emphasis, in Figure 19–2, A's bargaining power is greater when he deals with B than with B', B'', or B''', which is the same as saying that B has the least bargaining power among all the parties on his side. Although the strongest competitor has the weakest bargaining power, he may or may not turn out to have the greatest *total* power—a matter to be discussed in Chapter 20.

thing received in exchange may be money, medals, or status, which may be offered for either selfish or generous reasons.

Coalitions

Coalitions can be used to increase bargaining power in a transaction of positive goods, or to increase total power. The first will be discussed here and the second later. A coalition may be desired for the simple goal of getting better terms in an ordinary exchange. It may also be a defensive measure under more dramatic circumstances where a single individual possesses a much needed good—like the farmer who has the only pair of sheep surviving a flood, or the bank with the only pool of liquid cash following a crash. Coalitions relative to negative goods also have a high significance which will be discussed separately later.

A coalition will normally be most desired by the weaker competitors on one side of a transaction.[5] To return to Figure 19-2, we have seen that B has the strongest competitive position among the B's, and, barring ignorance or poor strategy, he can get the transaction. Suppose that B' now suggests a coalition between himself and B, assuming complete knowledge. If formed, the logical move for such a coalition would be to set a price just below X. This is the maximum they can get without either killing the transaction or running the risk it will go to B''. If the coalition thinks of a floor on its price as well as a ceiling, this would be at $X - 2$, the lowest price at which B' could deal.

The coalition is a pure disadvantage to A, the *top* price available to A from B without the coalition now becoming the *bottom* price available with the coalition. The coalition is a mixed blessing to B. Without the coalition he was certain to get the business, but at a price no greater at $X - 2$, and probably less. With the coalition he has only a fifty-fifty chance of getting the business, but at a price no lower than $X - 2$, and probably more. The coalition, however, is pure advantage to B'. Whereas he formerly had no chance of getting the business, he now has a fifty-fifty chance, and on acceptable terms. This illustrates why strong competitors are usually restive under coalitions, while weak ones support them.

This coalition could be extended to include B''. The lowest price now acceptable to all three is X, which is also the most A will pay. Each member now has a one-in-three chance of getting the business. This is pure improvement for B'', who had no chance without the coalition. The addition of B'' decreases the likelihood of getting the business for the other two, the offsetting factor being the assurance of a higher price if they do get it.

---

[5] For the same reason that it is dubious practice to speak of one side as having *more* bargaining power than the other, it is equally questionable to speak of the *weaker* side—unless some clear standard exists for comparison. It is unequivocal, however, to speak of the weaker parties on one side, these being the ones with the smaller EP's, and the weakest competitive position.

No coalition is possible which would include B''', since any price acceptable to him would be unacceptable to A, and the transaction would fail.

Under uncertainty about the EP's, the question of whom to include in the coalition and what minimum price to set is conjectural. If the B's should overestimate A's EP at $X + 3$, for example, they might include B''' in the coalition, set the coalition price at $X + 2$, and lose out entirely, If they should underestimate A's EP at $X - 3$, then B would refuse to join a coalition, assuming that either he would get the business or no one would.

Viewed strictly on the merits of the individual transaction, any one party would join or remain in the coalition only if he found its advantages to outweigh its disadvantages. If the parties have continued or repeated relations, however, all the principles of interrelated transactions apply, and each member would have to think of advantage over the longer run. This problem is essentially the same as that of affiliation or disaffiliation with an organization, to be discussed in subsequent chapters.

However, a coalition of B, B', and B'' could enforce a minimum price of X on all its members if each were to make a deposit of five units with the coalition, to be forfeited if the member sold at less than the agreed price. The strongest competitor is B. If he were to sell for less than X, his receipts minus the lost stake would net him less than $X - 4$, which is less than he is willing to accept. If a deposit is able to hold the strongest competitor in line, it will automatically hold the weaker ones.

The coalition, formal or informal, appears widely through life. If mother is willing to give the child candy for fifteen minutes' work while father would insist on an hour, a coalition of parents may raise the price to a half hour. If some professors have been giving good grades for very little work, a coalition in the form of a faculty rule may establish the minimum the student must provide and reduce his ability to "shop" for easy courses. A coalition of customs inspectors can keep tourists from getting through a check point promptly without a tip, and a coalition of priests can keep parishioners from getting forgiveness without repentance. A coalition widely observed merges imperceptibly into a consensus, as in the cases in some societies of no food without work, or no sex without marriage. At other times the coalition becomes indistinguishable from organization. At this introductory level we will not tangle with borderline cases, but try to understand the logic of the pure form. A strict bargaining coalition, as above, differs from an organization in that it does not jointly produce anything, but only raises bargaining power by limiting the opponent's alternatives—i.e., by reducing competition. It is a form of bargaining strategy.

COLLECTIVE BARGAINING

In a simple bargaining coalition of B's, as above, A negotiates with only one B at a time. He completes a transaction with only one, and the purpose of the coalition is to improve the bargaining power of the B's. By contrast, in collective bargaining, A actually completes transactions with two or more B's. These B's could negotiate terms with A independently, but our present concern is with a collective negotiation in which a single agent or committee negotiates the terms for all. Before discussing collective bargaining, we will mention an intermediate state between the coalition and collective bargaining, which we might call coalition bargaining. Here A will complete a transaction with only one B. But instead of the B's forming a coalition and agreeing on a minimum price, the B's join together and send a joint representative to negotiate on behalf of all. The effect is essentially the same as in a tight coalition, in which any one negotiator is in effect speaking for the whole group.

The best known example of collective bargaining is that of unionized employees, B's, dealing with a common employer, A. When the same A purchases multiple units of the same thing he will inevitably encounter diminishing utility, as described in connection with decision making, and will be willing to take a larger number only if he can get them at a lower price. Even though the negotiations deal only with wages as such, a high wage will generally mean fewer sales to that employer for the time being (less employment), and the converse. In such negotiations the union as collective bargainer faces the problem of *how many* transactions will take place as well as the terms of each. Given a choice between quantity and terms, since the union is an agent, not a principal, it will presumably select the alternative which will make its action as agent look best to its constituents. Unions bargain on wages, not volume of employment, and therefore tend to do what looks best in the wage dimension. Given a choice between a union-negotiated increase in wage and an employer-controlled increase in employment, the union will normally choose the former. The increased wage looks to the members like a union accomplishment, while the latter looks like an employer accomplishment, particularly if it arrives gradually, and without obvious relation to the restraint on wages. Given a choice between a union-negotiated wage reduction and an employer-controlled reduction in employment the union will choose the latter. This looks to the members like the employer's fault, especially if it, too, is gradual, and not obviously related to the wage agreement.[6] Were the union to negotiate simultaneously on wages and employment it might well give employment the greater weight, since jobs are more important to members than high wages.

---

[6] Allan M. Cartter, *Theory of Wages and Employment* (Homewood, Ill.: Richard D. Irwin, Inc., 1959), chap. 7, analyzes this "wage preference path" of the union, though without the specific rationale stated here. We are, of course, speaking solely of the employment effect of a particular union dealing with a particular employer at a given moment in time, though allowing sufficient time for the response of consumers to a possible change in price of the product. This is strictly a problem in microeconomics. The total employment effect of all unions dealing with all employers over a longer period is an entirely different problem, reflecting the forces described in macroanalysis.

Depending on the circumstances, collective bargainers may or may not face a problem found in the coalition, in that a particular settlement may not be acceptable to all members of the group. If the B's in Figure 19-2 are members of a union, a union-management settlement at X would leave member B''' highly disgruntled, and he might leave the job or the union, or agitate to get the union leadership changed.

In the United States coalitions (agreements among parties to *one* side of a transaction) are generally not enforceable, and in the sale of goods are widely prohibited. Collective bargains (agreements between *both* sides) are generally legal and enforceable if they deal with legal subject matter.[7] In England a union-management agreement is not enforceable. It is not considered a contract, on the grounds that the union itself neither buys nor sells anything, and the employer does not commit himself to buy labor, but merely to pay a certain price if and when he does buy it.

Collective bargaining has numerous ramifications we cannot examine here. But its important distinction from the coalition is its explicit agreement between both sides to the transaction, and the fact that the *number* of transactions is involved (at least implicitly) as well as the terms.

COALITIONS AND NEGATIVE POWER

Although coalitions in transactions of positive goods are widespread, coalitions against violence in transactions are probably of greater overall importance. The original basis of social organization beyond the family, and particularly of government, probably consisted of coalitions formed to limit this form of negative power. The reasons for such coalitions are clear as soon as we contrast the use of positive and negative goods in transactions.

In transactions of positive goods, X and Y, A's bargaining power is limited by B's ability (1) to do without X, (2) to find alternate sources of X (including producing it for himself), and (3) to form a coalition with other B's in dealing with A. However, when A employs negative goods (threats or distress and promised relief), only the third limitation applies. Since the "good" is something B does not want, doing without it is something A does not allow him to do, and finding alternate sources is hardly an intriguing prospect.

If B can maintain destructive power sufficient to impose costs on A equal to or greater than the value of Y to A, he may deter A from using his negative power. But many persons lack the strength or other prere-

---

[7] Whatever its other merits, the proposal that antitrust legislation be applied to unions on the ground that they are parallel to employer monopolies is not logically valid, since the activities prohibited to employers are coalitions, whereas those engaged in by unions are collective bargains. Monopolies by producers would be parallel to collective bargaining by unions only if producers collectively negotiated the price of their product with some kind of collectivity of consumers, which of course they do not do. Unilateral wage fixing by union coalitions is already illegal, just as is unilateral price fixing by coalitions of producers.

quisites of creating sufficient deterrent power, and have no alternatives but coalition or capitulation.

Although the social disadvantages of negative power are intuitively obvious, some explicit difficulties seem worth spelling out. First, of the various possible checks on positive power, only the coalition is available for negative. Hence, negative power is less self-limiting. Second, in exchanges of positive goods both sides gain, or at worst one party breaks even while the other gains. The transaction thus creates a net increase in value, the equivalent of what game theorists refer to as a positive sum game. In transactions under negative power there is at most a transfer with no change in value (a zero sum game), and if the threat is carried out or distress is applied a decrease in value will probably result (a negative sum game). Measured on a scale of positive values, the *least* that can be accomplished by a selfish exchange of positive goods is the *most* that negative power can create. (We are not considering essentially generous threats in which *A* forces *B* to do something in *B*'s own interest.)

Third, negative power tends to be destructive indirectly. It destroys motivation, since goods laboriously produced may not be retained to be enjoyed. It similarly reduces the motivation to save and invest.

Fourth, negative power typically produces a highly unstable and unpredictable relationship, for a variety of reasons. (a) If *A* threatens or executes injury to *B*, there is a tremendous range of indeterminacy in the terms *B* will agree to in order to avoid the injury. He may be stubborn and give nothing, even preferring death to concession, or he may give all he owns. (b) The outcome of negative power is highly uncertain because of its largely tactical nature. *B* may refuse to concede, not because he does not want relief, but because he has no confidence that *A* will grant it. (c) Negative power may shift tremendously in short periods. If *A*'s threat is a pointed gun, *B* might get the gun, if *A* relaxes attention, and reverse the threat. (d) There is almost no limit to the amount of distress *A* can provide *B* at almost no cost to himself (in contrast to the limited value of positive goods which *A* can offer), and hence no limit to bargaining power. (e) Negative power may involve costs to produce weapons or strategic advantage, which costs may exceed the gain from the transaction. (f) Finally, if *B* gives up a good under threat, he will tend to feel entitled to use violence to get it back as soon as he is able. The transaction is thus not construed as final, but as lasting only so long as the wielder of negative power can make it stick.

Given these obvious disadvantages, the use or threat of violence can hardly be tolerated in a community. If one strong man attempts to take all because he can beat up any other man, the obvious recourse is coalition. A logical second step is to develop a strong disapproval of violence, and readiness to form a coalition whenever it occurs. A third step is to delegate the coalition function to a permanent specialized group, which then constitutes a police force. A police force thus represents a permanent coalition within some group, formed in advance of any particular use of force to counteract such force if it occurs.

Once such a coalition is established to keep the peace, its functions can be added to. We will not pursue that problem until later, in connection with government. We will observe an important point, however. A coalition to control violence is to an important degree a technique for regulating terms of transactions, and only partially to avoid violence, as such. Without coalitions the balance of physical power would often be so clear that no actual violence would occur, the threat alone being sufficient. Police thus not merely prevent violence, but greatly strengthen the bargaining power of the weak in dealing with the strong.

Violence to strengthen bargaining power may be allowed to certain persons other than police, such as parents or guardians, slave owners, medicine men, and possible others, depending on the culture.

Violence and destruction are not the only negative goods employed to affect transactions. Insults, shame, taunts, threats to reveal secrets, strikes, interrupting a nap or a party, warming the beer, and innumerable other disliked things are also negative goods, and can be used in major or petty ways to get concessions. Most of these are beyond formal control, and in any event do not normally bring disastrous concessions or leave the ordinary individual helpless. The use of negative goods (other than violence) by coalitions is one of the most pervasive techniques of social control—to which we will turn after a discussion of total power.

Chapter 20

TOTAL INTERPERSONAL POWER, AND FREEDOM

TOTAL OR ACCUMULATED POWER

THE DISCUSSION of the transaction was focused on *bargaining* power, the ability to get good terms in a transaction. It also dealt with *particular* power—A's ability to get Y. Both the ability to get Y (i.e., to consummate a transaction for it) and the terms on which he will get it depend on A's Effective Preference taken in conjunction with the EP of the B with whom he was dealing. If A's EP touches or overlaps B's, A can acquire Y; otherwise not. The farther it overlaps, however, the less will be A's bargaining power, and the greater will be the amount of X he may have to give for Y.

At the beginning of Chapter 17 we discussed the total power of the individual who satisfies all his own wants, without exchange. Total power was defined as the ability to satisfy the desire not only for Y, but also for $Y_1, Y_2, Y_3, \ldots Y_n$. For the lone individual, total power depends upon his ability to produce all these things. We now move to the problem of the total power to satisfy wants from others, total power still being defined as the ability to satisfy a *series* of wants. Unlike bargaining power, which is the ability to get *one* thing on *good* terms, total interpersonal power is the ability to get *many* things (or more highly valued things), whether the terms of particular acquisitions are good or bad.

To illustrate, suppose that a rich man and a poor man each wants a motorcycle. The poor man finds a dealer in urgent need of cash and gets the motorcycle for $350. The rich man buys from a dealer who will not handle motorcycles unless he gets a good markup, and pays $500. Although the poor man had greater bargaining power in the one transaction, he is now financially exhausted and can buy no more. Having greater total power, the rich man can go on to buy a launch, a summer cottage, and a trip around the world. The politician who gets a whopping concession for supporting a candidate for governor of Kansas displays more bargaining power than the man who gets a smaller concession. But if the first politician can go no further, while the second also gets similar concessions in Nebraska, Ohio, Maine, New York, and California, the second has the greater total power. Similar statements could be made about achievements of honors, victories in battles, or molding of opinion. Higher cost of a single achievement represents lower bargaining power, but total power is reflected in the total achievements. For goods purchasable by money, a greater sum of money represents greater power. It is difficult to compare different kinds of power, such as political power, money, ability to mold opinion, and military power. Present attention will be directed toward the means of accumulating power, not toward measuring it across discrepant fields.

One clarification is needed before we start. Power was defined as the ability to satisfy wants, or to acquire wanted things. Interpersonal power is the ability to satisfy wants through the efforts of others—to get others to do or give what is wanted. In line with our earlier discussion of psychology and decision making, a want can be either instrumental or intrinsic; it can be an overall goal, a subset, or a sub-subset. Power for an executive or general is therefore not merely his ability to satisfy strictly personal wants, as for banana splits or affection, but also the ability to get his subordinates in the organization to do as he instructs. As noted earlier, it is beyond the scope of this analysis to inquire whether the acquisition of wanted things actually produces satisfaction. The measure of power is whether they are acquired.

To review briefly the basic sources of goods to a person, if one produces for himself, the total goods he can have is determined by his productivity, which depends on his energy and skill taken in conjunction with the available resources. If he produces by himself, and exchanges, his total depends on both his productivity and the terms he gets in exchange.

No matter what the kind of power or how complex the combinations, the ability to acquire wanted things depends on the same two factors—productivity and terms of exchange—and the way to acquire more is to become more productive, to get better terms, or both. Large accumulations of power almost necessarily depend upon both, usually in some kind of alternating sequence, as we shall see, and usually with the help of organizations.

Accumulations of Money Power

Because money is perhaps the most widely recognized means of acquiring things from others, and because it is unidimensional and quantifiable, we will illustrate first the accumulation of money.

It can, of course, be inherited. This technique is widely preferred (I am told), but it hardly helps analyze how the money was accumulated in the first place. The unaided productive efforts of unusual individuals can produce moderate accumulations. But these are ineffectual in acquiring *large* wealth (of, say, a million dollars or more), since even our most ambitious and competent men are simply not that productive. If the lone individual by plan, accident, or invention finds some good which is scarce and highly valued, he may sell it on good enough terms to make him wealthy. The discovery of oil or diamonds on his property, or some valuable invention, would be examples. This wealth arises from bargaining power, not productivity, however, since he could have discovered gravel, or spent equal ingenuity inventing an unwanted device, and remained poor.[1]

A lucky or well-managed series of transactions, however, can make a man wealthy if he can arrange to make them on favorable exchange ratios. The basic technique is to buy things at a time or place of low value and sell them at a time or place of high value. If one buys tea in Sumatra where it is cheap and sells it in England where it is dearer, he can accumulate the difference. If he reinvests this gain into more tea, and so forth, he may in due time build a fortune. He can do the same by buying real estate when it is cheap and holding it till the price rises, reinvesting the earnings in more real estate, and so on. He might also shift from real estate to tea, to corn, to farm machinery, and continue to make money so long as, on the average, he holds things whose value is rising. Success in this process normally requires better-than-average ability to predict movements of prices, since other people are also trying to do the same thing. Better-than-average knowledge of race horses can also bring in money.

Unless the gains from each transaction are fantastically high, however, this process is slow and relatively ineffectual. Even at the comfortable return of a 100 per cent a year it requires five years to raise $100 to $3,200 (assuming that the whole increase is reinvested, and none spent), another five years to cross the $100,000 mark and another three to reach a million. (In short, all you have to do to become a millionaire is to invest $100 at a guaranteed 100 per cent return, and leave it for thirteen years at compound interest—without paying income tax on any of the increase.) Transactions of sufficient magnitude to accumulate much wealth will probably require the cooperation of other people as employees or consultants. If so, we are moving out of the realm of individual activity and into that of organization. Although the main discussion of organizations does not start until Chapter 21, some aspects must be opened here.

Whether the organization exchanges, produces, or both, it can often do so more efficiently than the individual. If ten persons could each produce ten units of a good per day working alone, but the ten working as an organization could produce 150, the additional 50 units represent the greater efficiency of organized production. Depending on other costs

---

[1] As economists define their terms, applying ingenuity to a wanted invention is more productive than applying it to an unwanted one. The present discussion reflects the change from economic definitions noted earlier: namely, that in economics exchange is included within the definition of production (the creation of possession utility), whereas in the present framework production and exchange are sharply separated.

and the state of competition in the labor and product markets, the entrepreneur who formed the organization could get all or some part of that additional 50 units for himself. If the organization is large, the entrepreneur can receive a large income even if he gets only a small return per unit.

The important fact about power in the organization is that the entrepreneur, executive, supervisor, or other authority controls the flow and use of productive force and resources of the organization rather than merely his own. Whether he is dealing with subordinates within the organization or with vendors or customers outside, such a person can grant or withhold large amounts of desired goods, which is the essence of large power. The usual definition of a supervisor, for example, includes the authority to hire, fire, promote, transfer, or discipline a subordinate. All these acts grant or withhold things highly desired by the subordinates. To be able to get work from a subordinate by granting or withholding these things therefore provides bargaining power in one transaction. To be able to do the same thing for many subordinates allows an accumulation of power, or a rise in total power. The position occupied by the supervisor or executive thus constitutes a switch which controls the flow of larger power than that of the executive himself, and the organization chart is a graphic display of a set of switching mechanisms.[2] As we move up the hierarchy, each successive level of switches has more power, since each directly or indirectly controls all the switches below it. In an organization of ten thousand employees and five levels of supervision the top executive is the master switch which, through five successive sets of switches, controls the productive energies of ten thousand producers. This series of successive switches (or valves) *amplifies* the power of the executive according to the normal pattern of amplification. Instead of being used directly for production, the executive's energies are used to control the flow of energies from a larger pool or reservoir. Most large power in any society belongs to those who control switching mechanisms in organizations.

The organization itself can accumulate money through the same techniques as the individual. It must produce much, conclude transactions on favorable terms, or both—usually the latter. The greater the productivity and the better the terms of bargaining, the greater and more rapid will be the accumulation.

The personal income of those connected with the organization depends on the organization's income and on *their* bargaining power with it. For example, the executive's bargaining power with the organization depends on such bargaining power factors as the strength of his desire for the job, the organization's desire for him, alternative jobs available to him, and alternative executives available to the organization. Since the

---

[2] Organizations also contain important switches not shown on the chart—a matter for later chapters.

organization's desire for him depends on his productivity to the organization, we again find that his ability to acquire much money depends on some combination of productivity and bargaining.

Accumulations of Nonmoney Power

The acquisition of power other than that of money also depends on the ability to produce desired results and to consummate transactions on favorable terms. In the political party, power resides with the party worker or candidate who can produce votes, contributions, or other things desired by the party. To the extent that he can do this by his own efforts he builds his own power. As in business, however, he will probably not accumulate much power unless he can control some switches within the party organization, and direct the activities of many other persons toward goals which he specifies. Also as in business, his power will depend on his bargaining power with the political organization, its bargaining power with those outside the organization, and the productive efficiency of the organization itself.

The entertainer's power is greater in proportion both to his ability to produce entertainment for others and to his bargaining power in dealing with them. His power in most cases will rise if he provides entertainment through an organization, such as a motion picture or broadcasting company, and with the more explicit use of such other persons in his organization as script writers, managers, musicians, directors, booking agents, and stage technicians. The productive power of a civic leader depends heavily on his ability to produce ideas and sets of interpersonal relationships which bring desired results. These are social inventions, or new sociofacts, roughly equivalent in their field to mechanical inventions, or new artifacts. Power of this sort usually is built on top of some accumulation of other power, such as that of money or position in business, church, government, or labor union organization.

Intellectual power in a professional field depends upon the productive ability to create new ideas in forms acceptable to others within the profession. This, too, is increased by organization, the officials of professional organizations determining what subjects will be discussed at professional meetings, and by whom, what papers will be published in professional journals, what research projects will be undertaken, what programs of study will be given in colleges, what qualifications must be met to teach or practice in the profession, and so on. The bargaining in connection with intellectual power is found in the ability to get one's writings published, to get fellowships and research grants, and so forth, in return for a given amount of time or effort.

ACTUAL TOTAL POWER, EFFECTIVE POWER, AND STATUS

In studying bargaining power, or the ability to get good terms in transactions, we have distinguished between the actual power limits, as measured by the EP's, and tactics, which involve beliefs about power limits. In connection with total power we must also deal with the same two kinds of things—a person's actual power, and other persons' beliefs about his power. A person's bargaining power is enhanced if his opponent believes his EP to be smaller than it is, so long as the opponent believes an overlap exists. However, if the opponent should believe there is no overlap, when in fact there is (as through tactical error), the transaction may not be completed, and the person loses his ability to get the good. So, too, in total power can a person's actual power be either enhanced or diminished by other people's beliefs.

The total power of a person is a phenomenon which has been studied primarily by sociologists, who thus far have not developed a uniform terminology on the subject. To select the particular formulation which fits most closely with the other analysis in this volume, we will define several terms, as follows.

Actual total power will mean the ability to get other people to do as one wants, as measured by actual accomplishment. This may be referred to more briefly as *total power, actual power,* or simply as *power*. At the level of total power, this is parallel to the actual outcome of bargaining at the transaction level. In terms of poker it is measured by the actual gains or losses. *Status* will mean other people's beliefs about one's total power. This is the power one is perceived to have, the total-power equivalent of tactical position in bargaining, whether deliberately manipulated or not. In poker it is the hand the other players believe one holds.[3] *Effective power* is *real* power. It is what one could do without status, parallel to Effective Preference in bargaining power or the actual hand in poker. As with numerous other concepts, these are defined at the ends of the spectrum, or as "pure" specimens. Many actual cases are difficult to classify, as in cases where the status is molded closely by the effective power, or where the effective power depends strongly on status.[4]

To illustrate, your actual ability to drive a burglar away will depend

[3] The poker analogy applies only to the *fact* of belief, not its direction. Depending on the circumstances, it may be desirable to have other players believe one's hand is either better or worse than it is in fact.

[4] As to the lack of standardization, Kahl observes: "Regarding terminology, . . . "status". . . has so many other meanings in contemporary sociology . . . that it seems better to use a less ambiguous term." (Joseph A. Kahl, *The American Class Structure* [New York: Rinehart & Co., 1957], p. 17.) Merton follows Linton in regarding status as "a position in a social system occupied by designated individuals." (Robert K. Merton, *Social Theory and Social Structure* [Glencoe, Ill.: The Free Press, 1957], p. 368.) Homans, by contrast, uses the term "status" to mean "the stimuli a man presents to other men (and to himself)"—that is, "what men perceive about one of their fellows." (George Casper Homans, *Social Behavior: Its Elemental Forms* [New York: Harcourt, Brace & World, Inc., 1961], p. 149.) In connection with status, as with the later analysis of organization, I have followed Homans more closely than others.

The distinction between actual power and apparent power, or reputation for power, is widely recognized, as reflected in William V. D'Antonio, Howard J. Ehrlich, and Eugene C. Erickson, "Further Notes on the Study of Community Power," *American Sociological Review,* December, 1962, p. 848.

on whether your gun is loaded (effective power), whether he believes it is loaded (perceived power), or some combined effect of the two. Your actual ability to prevent a competitor from cutting prices will depend on whether you are able to drive him out of business, whether he believes you can, or some combination. Your actual ability to get a good room in an overcrowded hotel without a reservation will depend on whether you are rich enough to buy the hotel, whether the manager thinks you are, or both. Whether the ability to get others to do things depends on the ability to bring them votes, dollars, bombs, half-nelsons, social invitations, knowledge, or status, the *actual power* over them rests on the *effective power* to deliver these things, *perceived power*, or both.

Whether one's status or his effective power will do more to determine actual power will depend much on individual circumstances, including the possibility of creating beliefs contrary to fact. We have seen that in individual transactions negative power is to an important degree tactical. In parallel, short of an actual fight negative total power would seem to depend mainly on status. With positive power, the power of status alone will depend in part on the likelihood that the effective power will actually have to be delivered. To acquire title to a yacht one must actually have the money, even if borrowed or stolen; to get a demonstration ride he must merely seem to have it. Where appearances are important, the actual short term results are probably based mainly on status. In the longer run, however, status itself will tend to conform to effective power, which is thus the long run determinate of actual power. The boxer who has won the heavyweight title does not maintain that status indefinitely unless he periodically defends it. The political manager who steers an unlikely candidate to victory will be listened to for a while. But he must produce some additional successes or his status will eventually drop. An economist who correctly predicts a spectacular drop in the stock market will have high status reflecting his good performance. But if his next few predictions are wrong, his status will adjust downward to match his now lower effective ability.

Status is perceived power. Like all other perceptions it depends upon cues. To those who know a person well these cues are knowledge of his actual performance. If a person is widely known to have effective power, then merely to identify him is to know that he has power, and his face or his name is the cue which carries his status with him. Much of the problem of status revolves around providing cues for those who are otherwise unaware of a person's status. For this purpose more generalized cues are widely recognized, and are familiarly known as status symbols. These include such things as clothing, automobile, jewelry, manner of speech, deportment, free spending, and name dropping. In the organization such things as size and location of office, size or newness of desk, convenience of parking, hours of arrival and departure, or number of secretaries are reliable cues. Depending on the culture, almost any kind of cue can be used, whether headgear, badges, nose rings, duelling scars, location of dwelling, or number of servants.

In the chapter on concepts we noted that almost anything can be perceived differently by different persons. The same is true of status, which is perceived power. The successful boxer may have high status in the sports world, and perhaps in cafe society, but little in an academic circle which does not know the cues because it pays little attention to this phase of sports. The status of a given individual also depends on the angle from which he is viewed. He may have high status to one who looks up at him from below, and low status to one who looks down from above. His status also depends in part on the value system of the observer. The same practices which make a man highly regarded as an astute bargainer by one audience may cause another group to view him as a crook.

Deference is a kind of behavior which symbolizes the perception of status. Deferential behavior is the evidence, outcome, or measure of status in the eyes of the particular person or group which gives the deference. Without specifying all details, we may say that deference takes the form of providing for wants and generally smoothing and expediting the path of the person of status. Status tends to receive preferred treatment. The pleasantest rooms, the finest foods, the best wine, the most courteous treatment are brought forth by status, as are also entertainment, gifts, attentiveness, praise, and imitation. To the extent that deferential responses are not received in explicit exchange for value given, they constitute a sort of bonus for status, being actual power in excess of effective power actually utilized.

By contrast, absence of status cues can bring actual power below effective power, as when a person of wealth happens to be without cash where he is unknown and cannot establish his identity.

Some types of aspects of status have wide currency, others narrow. Large money wealth probably has the widest currency, since money is a strong generalized reinforcer throughout much of the world, as well as being its own cue. It is a highly portable form of self-identifying, effective power. The status of a good photographer, poet, or scientific specialist is normally confined to a smaller group of persons, often to his own field of specialty. In some fields the main evidence of status is that a person is sought after for advice or information, and that his pronouncements or suggestions carry great weight. In others status consists of a reputation for good work, which brings customers and patrons. In the arts, status brings attention to each new painting or composition, often when an identical product by someone without status would command no attention at all.

Power of almost any kind tends to be self-accumulating after a certain point has been reached. Money can be reinvested to help produce more money. Once a scientist has acquired a certain amount of reputation, other scientists consult him, he receives research grants, speaks at meetings, and otherwise comes into situations which make it easier for him to acquire still further skill and reputation. Once the entertainer has achieved a certain status he is sought after to do more engagements, which bring him still more status, and so on. Like money, almost any other form of power can be reinvested to bring still more power, in a continuing upward spiral.

Given the power of status, it is understandable that many with effective power take the trouble to keep their cues in good order, while some without effective power nevertheless make a point of acquiring the symbols—sometimes with great success. Because status is perceived power, and perception is a psychological phenomenon, status can be pychologically manipulated. When two things are regularly perceived together, perception of one suggests the other. Hence, persons who regularly associate with those of status tend to be perceived as having status. Since status *is* the perceived condition, to be perceived as having status is to *have* it. Hence, the frequent coterie of hangers-on around persons of status.

Status and Bargaining Power

Status is a form of total power. Depending on the circumstances it may add to or detract from bargaining power in particular transactions. Again to start with money, the wealthy person normally finds a given amount of money less valuable than does the poor man. In making a purchase this is the same as a smaller value of AX, which brings lower bargaining power. The rich man generally is not as inclined to haggle—though he may do so. Further, in numerous places prices are geared formally or informally to ability to pay, and the rich will pay more for the same thing than the poor.

On the other hand, the rich are valued customers, and sellers will go out of their way to see that the best merchandise is set aside for them, and that they receive excellent service. Having money to spare, the rich can also stock up when prices are low, get quantity discounts, and jump at unusual opportunities. If they threaten to make trouble when a purchase is unsatisfactory, they are more likely to receive concessions. In general they tend to have more flexibility in selecting transactions where their bargaining power is good and avoiding those where it is bad. On the average, greater total power probably raises bargaining power, enhancing total power still further.

We have seen that some power is widely applicable, other narrowly so. Certain kinds of desired things can be acquired from others only by giving very specific things in exchange, which is another way of saying that power in these areas is very narrowly applicable. The affection of a wife, the confidence of a child, and the respect of close friends can usually be gained only by behaving in very particular kinds of ways toward those particular people, and money, skill, or power in other directions will not "buy" these things. Despite the partial interconvertibility among different kinds of power, some kinds scarcely convert at all. Still others are at least partially incompatible, so that an increase in one direction brings a decrease in another. For example, where "eggheads" are suspect, an increase in intellectual power in an academic field may decrease a man's power as a political candidate. Nontransferability is the reason why a person may reach a peak of power in one field and yet remain frustrated and seemingly powerless in another.

A particularly large amount of power can be acquired by a person who can build and articulate a strong goal held by more or less the whole of a society, and simultaneously get the society to perceive him as the sole channel for achieving it. These seem to be the two main ingredients in the *charismatic leader* portrayed by Max Weber. The founders of major religions seem to occupy this dual role, even if it is sometimes their followers rather than themselves who claim exclusiveness. Given the fact that eternal salvation can sometimes seem more important than life itself, a church which develops an intense desire for salvation among its followers, while simultaneously presenting itself as the sole source of salvation, can have tremendous power. It has large bargaining power with each follower, and also can have many followers. The Reformation greatly weakened the power position of the Protestant churches in this respect by proclaiming that the individual had direct access to God and salvation. The full effect has not been felt, since some denominations do not accept it, and others, while admitting it in theory, insist that the unaffiliated believer's chances are rather slim. The church can also hold power by providing other satisfactions, whether these be bingo, picnics, or social crusading.

Political leaders can acquire this power if they come to office when some strong ground swell desire is afoot, or some crisis is at hand, and provide the leadership for meeting it.

The Problem of Undesired Results

If power means the ability to achieve wanted results, a problem arises about the person who produces tremendous effects on others, but none turns out as he wants. Does he possess power?

We will distinguish first between a person who does things of his own volition which have strong undesired effects, and one who simply becomes the focus of forces not of his own making, like Alfred Dreyfus or the Scottsboro boys. Our present interest is solely in the former, such as the political candidate whose electoral compaign produces only antipathy for him and victory for his opponent, or the general who leads his army to spectacular defeat.

It seems most sensible to construe such persons as having more power than if they produced no effects, since they do achieve certain instrumental steps toward a goal. After all, becoming a candidate or commanding an army is more than most men accomplish. At the same time the failure reflects less power than success would have done. The further question whether a man fails because of too little power or too great an obstacle will be dealt with later in connection with power and freedom.

Status, Role, and Class

In the chapter on personality we discussed the nature of role in interpersonal relationships. Many socially defined roles include important power components. These may be effective power, as when a mayor or a church deacon is put in charge of certain switching mechanisms. Or they may be status, as when the role specifies certain deferential behavior from persons occupying other roles in the society. Here the person's own effective power rests on his ability to be selected to occupy the role, after which the power assigned to the role is also available to him. Where roles are inherited, the crucial factor is the child's wise choice of parents.

Within a society many persons will fall into any one general level of total power, the group at any level being known as a *class*. Within broad limits, merely to belong to a particular class carries with it the status of that class, one of the consequences of which is that many people try to appear to belong to a higher class than they actually do. Needless to say, along lines indicated in connection with motivation, status in many societies is a powerful generalized reinforcer. Hence, people often do not ask what good it will do them to have status; to many status is its own reward. Some other effects of class upon power will be examined in later chapters in connection with the whole society.

ON THE NATURE OF "SOCIAL" CONTROLS

We have seen the importance of coalitions of the weak in controlling the power of the physically strong—important because of the almost limitless bargaining power in superior physical strength. But power based on positive goods can also be cumulative for those who get a head start, particularly if they can get a monopoly on some much desired good, like salt, science, religion, medicine, funerals, or building materials. The less powerful therefore have a clear interest in keeping any individual or group from acquiring too much positive power.

There are, of course, limits placed on power by not wanting, by competition, and by consensus. But these do not always work, and when other methods fail the coalition seems the most widely usable device. Whether done formally and collectively or informally and more or less individually, the coalition can be analyzed as follows, in what we will call *retaliatory bargaining*.

Suppose that *A* takes advantage of superior power in some relationship to achieve terms of which others (whom we will designate as *B*'s) disapprove. *A* may have foreclosed a poor widow's mortgage when all but two payments were made, mistreated his wife and children, or failed conspicuously to follow the amenities of normal politeness which symbolize equality of power, and the *B*'s want to bring him into line. Because of their disapproval of *A*'s actions, the *B*'s will undergo a diminution of their desire to deal with *A*. The magnitude of this diminution will be said arbitrarily to equal the amount of disapproval of *A*. For example, suppose that in some transaction (other than the one disapproved of) the relation between *A* and one of the *B*'s would have been as indicated by the first two bars in Figure 20-1. These show an overlap from $X - 1$ to $X + 1$,

Figure 20-1

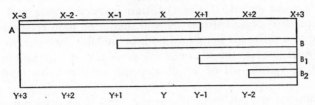

with mean terms at X for Y. Let us say that because of *A*'s actions, *B* feels two units of disapproval. Although *B* still wants X from *A*, the act of giving Y to *A* is perceived as helping *A*, which *B* does not want to do. *B*'s desire to deprive *A* of Y has the same effect as an increase in *B*'s desire to keep Y. This means an increase of BY by two units, which reduces *B*'s EP from $X - 1$ to $X + 1$ (or from $Y + 1$ to $Y - 1$), as at B_1. Assuming that all the *B*'s behave similarly, they constitute a coalition which reduces *A*'s bargaining power. This reduction may extend to all subsequent dealings with any *B*'s on any topic. If *A* wants to be nominated for president of the PTA, he will now have to work harder or give a larger contribution. If he wants to continue in the car pool he will have to drive more days per week (because it suddenly becomes less convenient for the others to drive). Although *A* continues to pay the same prices, the deliveries from the neighborhood grocer become slower.

Retaliatory bargaining of this sort can, of course, be done by one person as well as by the whole group, and if the relationships with that person are important to *A* this alone may have a disciplinary effect. Retaliation is analytically the opposite of generosity, the former bringing a contraction of EP and the latter an expansion. To illustrate, if the *B*'s find an *A* they would like to help, they can form a coalition of sympathy instead of retaliation, which will increase the bargaining power of that *A* in his dealings with all the *B*'s.

To return to the retaliation, disapproval gives all the *B*'s better terms in their relations to *A*, and makes *A* "pay" for his disapproved gains. If the disapproval is even stronger, however, the EP's of the *B*'s may shrink to $Y - 2$ in Figure 20-1, as shown in the bar marked B_2. These other transactions can no longer be completed, because the EP's do not overlap, and a *boycott* now exists. At this stage *A* cannot get nominated for PTA president even if he works harder, the car pool can no longer accommodate him even if he drives four days a week, and the grocery boy completely forgets to deliver his groceries. *A* will not be invited to parties, and invitations he extends will not be accepted. His application for membership in the club will get misfiled, and even his smiles may not be returned. Thus does the value of social approval become evident, as does also the disutility of "social pressure."

As with other coalitions, the effectiveness of retaliatory ones depends on how well disciplined they are. If some *B*'s do not join, the result may simply be a narrowing of the circle of the *B*'s with whom *A* deals, with no worsening of terms. If the coalition is very severe and tight, the relationships may cease entirely. *A* will then seek new relationships, perhaps move to a different neighborhood, or possibly become an outlaw or hermit. Or, of course, the *B*'s may overlook the *A*'s deviations if he has compensating virtues—all of which depends on the value system of the society.

If *A*'s actions are felt to be intolerable, and if he does not respond to coalition action of this sort, negative power may be brought into play, at the level of the vigilante and Ku Klux Klan, at the level of the law and police, or in some other fashion. In this connection, the role of government as a regulator of power will be seen in later chapters.

Concluding Notes

To summarize interpersonal power, whether based on effective power, status, or some combination, large total power is the ability to consummate many (or large) transactions in which others do or give what is desired, including (in the case of moral and intellectual power) changing their concepts and motives. We have talked thus far mainly of explicit transactions, and should now recall that these taper off into implied bargains, quasi exchanges, and open-end transactions. As the form of the transaction becomes more amorphous, so, too, does the visibility and effect of power.

The earth, living things, human psychology, and interpersonal relationships display infinite variations. Any attempt to select and classify certain types from among this infinity inevitably overemphasizes some varieties and underemphasizes others. The present analysis is intended to further the scientific understanding of interpersonal relationships. It therefore concentrates on groupings of phenomena which show the most reliable relationships, and have the highest information content, as discussed in Chapter 3. This does not mean that this is the way society *is*. It merely means that this seems a potentially fruitful way of describing it at this stage of knowledge. The present power analysis provides relatively little information about open-end and other types of transactions which are not precisely definable in the present model, and either a different model or supplementary models are needed if they are to be fully described.

POWER AND FREEDOM

If power is the ability to satisfy wants, it is inescapably related to freedom. Among many definitions of *freedom* the one most usable in the present context is Russell's: "the absence of obstacles to the realization of desires."[5] His statement that "complete freedom is . . . possible only for omnipotence" is also necessarily true of complete power. So, too, is his observation that complete freedom (and therefore complete power) cannot be possessed by two persons simultaneously, since there cannot be two omnipotent individuals in the world.[6] Morgenthau concurs in the reasoning behind his conclusion that "universal and absolute freedom is a contradiction in terms."[7] The problem is something like the traditional irresistible force and immovable object, which by definition cannot exist simultaneously.

The problem of freedom was implicit in the whole preceding discussion of power, and must be made explicit before we leave it. If power is the ability to satisfy wants, and freedom is the absence of obstacles to satisfaction, a brief analysis will show this relationship to be similar to some basic formulations of physical relationships. In mechanical, electrical, and hydraulic phenomena, among others, a basic relationship is that *work* accomplished, or effect produced, is directly proportional to *effort* (or force) applied and inversely proportional to *resistance* encountered.[8] Stated as a formula this becomes:

$$\text{Work} = \frac{\text{Effort (or Force)}}{\text{Resistance}}$$

In the human problems we have been analyzing in previous chapters, the work to be accomplished is satisfaction of wants, and the effort or force applied to achieve it is power. Resistance was not explicitly discussed, but was implicit in the "effective" aspect of Effective Preference, which by definition included the ability to overcome obstacles. If we incorporate the obstacles explicitly, the formula for human affairs becomes:

---

[5] Bertrand Russell, "Freedom and Government," in Ruth Nanda Anshen (ed.), *Freedom, Its Meaning* (New York: Harcourt Brace & Co., 1940), p. 251. I join Robert Dahl and Charles Lindblom (*Politics, Economics, and Welfare* [New York: Harper & Bros., 1953], p. 29) in preferring the Russell definition over the many others in the Anshen volume. It is probably no coincidence that the definition of power used in the above analysis is also closer to Russell's than to any other, his definition being "the production of intended effects." (*Power: A New Social Analysis* [New York: W. W. Norton & Co., 1938], p. 35.)

[6] "Freedom and Government," *ibid.*, p. 258.

[7] Hans J. Morgenthau, *Dilemmas of Politics* (Chicago: University of Chicago Press, 1958), p. 105.

[8] We are here dealing with an elemental notion of the determinants of the amount of a given type of effect which will be accomplished by a given set of forces. We are not attempting to define "work," and in physics the force applied is itself part of the definition of work. In short, we are here using a kind of analysis which appears widely in the physical sciences, but we are not using precisely parallel concepts.

$$\text{Satisfaction} = \frac{\text{Power}}{\text{Obstacles}} \text{ , or Satisfaction} = \frac{\text{Power}}{\text{Resistance}}$$

Since we do not have fully satisfactory words in our language for the next steps, some circumlocutions are necessary, but are nevertheless unequivocal.

If freedom is the absence of resistance, or nonresistance, resistance itself can be called nonfreedom. The equation now becomes:

$$\text{Satisfaction} = \frac{\text{Power}}{\text{Nonfreedom}}$$

Freedom is the reciprocal of nonfreedom, and we can therefore substitute freedom for nonfreedom if we simultaneously move this component from the denominator to the numerator. This produces:

$$\text{Satisfaction} = \text{Power} \times \text{Freedom}^9$$

Some sail "boats" have been built for water and others for ice. Neither will move if there is no wind, and no power means no work. Assuming equal sail area, however, a given amount of wind will move the ice boat (say) ten times as fast as the water boat. We can therefore say that the ice boat has either one tenth the resistance or ten times the freedom. We could also say that the water boat has ten times the resistance or one tenth the freedom. If we now try to explain why the water boat moves more slowly, we will see why it is easier to comprehend the problem if it is couched in terms of resistance, not freedom.

To begin with, resistance is negative—it prevents accomplishment. Freedom is psychologically positive, a desired thing. It is also logically positive, but only by virtue of being a double negative, the *absence* of *resistance*. It is logically valid to say that the water boat moves more slowly because it has less freedom. Conceptually, however, the statement is a triple negative, reflecting (1) *less* (2) *absence* of (3) *resistance*. The fact that freedom is conceptually a double negative, and a reduction of freedom a triple one, is perhaps part of the reason why freedom has typically been such an elusive concept. However glorious the history of the word "freedom," we will therefore drop it from the main relation, and say simply that work accomplished (including human satisfactions) varies directly with power and inversely with resistance.

The Problem of Measuring Freedom

Logically and conceptually the relation between results, effort, and resistance is no more difficult in human affairs than in physical ones. Nor,

---

[9] For those interested in a physical analogy, electrical theory is useful. Ohm's law states that current (I) equals electromotive force (E) divided by resistance (R), or $I = \dfrac{E}{R}$. Electrical theory also uses conductance (G) in its analysis, conductance being the reciprocal of resistance, or $\dfrac{I}{R}$. Conductance is thus the electrical analog of freedom, as is seen in the formula: $I = EG$.

therefore, is the notion of freedom. When we come to the technical problem of measuring the ingredients to be put into the formula, however, a vast gulf appears between the human and the physical phenomena. In the human problems we do not have (at least thus far) units for measuring satisfaction, power, and resistance—although the *logic* of measurement remains the same.

Suppose I put two boxes on a table, equal in size, shape, and surface texture, but of unknown weight. I push one with a measured force and it moves two feet. I then push the other with equal force, and it moves four feet. To simplify the problem we will assume that resistance to movement in this example is determined solely by weight. If I know the pushes are equal, I can deduce that the first box weighs twice as much as the second, and so on through other relations. Given the relation of force, resistance, and work in the formula, as soon as I know any two, I can compute the third. The great advantage of mechanics is that it has independent measures of all three variables, while the human problem has no accurate measure for any of the three.

This does not mean, however, that the human analysis is meaningless. Although we do not have cardinal measures, we often have ordinal ones. I cannot say how many units of satisfaction I get from a cup of hot, strong coffee, but I can confidently say that it is more than I get from weak, tepid coffee. The whole analysis of decision making is based on the assumption that we can distinguish the more desired from the less desired. It also assumes that we can measure costs in meaningful degree, costs being one way of conceptualizing resistance. Thus, although we cannot put absolute measures on these things, we often can know the *direction* of change of power or resistance, and hence can know the direction of change of the result. Further, at some points the units of analysis are goods, not satisfactions, and many of these are countable. If the worker of known capacity consistently produces twice as many plunkets on machine A as on machine B, or the salesman consistently sells twice as many encyclopedias in the suburbs as downtown, we can say that machine B and downtown have twice the resistance of machine A and the suburbs, respectively.

Whether some change of circumstance is one of force or of resistance often depends on how we wish to view it. Suppose a box requires a 40 pound thrust to move it one foot forward. We now install a fan in the box which exerts a 10 pound backward thrust, while removing enough weight so that the whole assembly weighs no more than before. We now find that a 40 pound external thrust moves the box a foot and a quarter (assuming a linear relation for simplicity). We can now say that the box has one fourth less resistance (more freedom), since the same 40 pound thrust has pushed it one fourth farther. Or we can say that the resistance is unchanged but that the force has increased by one fourth. The choice of terminology depends entirely on how we define the problem. If we are interested solely in the external push, we would say the fan provides decreased resistance. If we are measuring the thrust against the work accomplished in order to compute the total mass of the box and contents, the fan must be viewed as an increase in thrust.

Similarly in human affairs, if I have decided to go swimming, but then learn that I will have to change a tire first, and decide to play gin rummy instead, have I changed my behavior because of greater resistance (less freedom) or reduced desire (less power)? As measured by the result, it makes no difference which way we classify the flat tire. It does point to the fact, however, that a *problem* in freedom may not be so much a question of fact as of how that fact is perceived. Let us look first at some concepts about freedom, and then at the problem of perceiving it.

POWER, FREEDOM, AND COSTS

We have seen that in an exchange a person's ability to get something depends on an overlap of Effective Preferences. This depends on the extent to which A's EP extends toward B, and also on the extent to which B's EP extends toward A.

We can now personalize this situation and say that a person's freedom lies in the degree to which the EP's of his environment, so to speak, extend toward him. To the extent that A's environment consists of other persons who wish to exchange with him, A's freedom varies directly with the length of the EP's of those persons. The longer those EP's, the lower is the cost to A of acquiring things from B's, and freedom is thus seen as the inverse of cost. That is, the "free" in "free goods" is the same kind of thing as the "free" in "freedom." The housewife has more freedom to have servants if they charge a dollar a day than if they charge two dollars an hour. In all cases, the longer B's EP, the smaller can be A's EP for Y without denying him Y. To shift from the particular to the total, the larger the number of EP's which extend toward A the greater will be his freedom to acquire many things. Particular power and total power thus have their counterparts in particular and total freedom.

Similarly, if nature is prodigal in providing fish, berries, lumber, or minerals we can say (1) that these things have little cost, (2) that we have great freedom in acquiring them, or (3) that nature figuratively has a long EP extending toward us, so that we need give her little in return. Freedom again is the reciprocal of cost. The maximum possible freedom would occur if the EP's of our human or natural environment extended all the way to our own EP of zero. This is another way of describing free goods, whether gifts of nature or of other persons.

In many instances one person's freedom can increase only to the extent that another's declines, in the well-known conflict between "freedom to" and "freedom from." A can have freedom *to* dump sewage into the river, let smoke rise from his chimney, raise pigs in his backyard, and hold noisy parties, only by destroying B's freedom *from* filth, stench, and noise. In these cases, part of the cost of A's satisfaction is borne by B. B can be relieved of these costs only if A is prohibited from polluting water and air, from raising pigs in the city, or from throwing raucous parties, in which case part of the cost of B's satisfaction is borne by A. So long as people live in juxtaposition there is no way of avoiding the fact that some satisfactions to some persons bring costs to other persons. Nor is there any general theory by which we can decide which costs should and which should not be passed on to others without restriction, particularly in light of the difficulties surrounding interpersonal comparisons of utility. It is important, however, to see that the problem of freedom *among* persons is a problem in interpersonal allocation of costs. (A prohibition of some act is an incompatibility cost.)

Some Aspects of Interpersonal Costs

It is common to propose a rule that each person should have freedom to do as he likes, so long as he does not impinge on someone else's freedom. Restated in the present language, he should be free to do (or refrain from doing) as he likes so long as he does not impose costs on others. By reciprocal action, such a rule would automatically assure each person against costs imposed on him by others. Since it is impossible for persons living in association to avoid imposing some costs on others, a society can hardly avoid establishing rules about these things. Such rules about interpersonal costs are an important part of governmental activity, to be examined later.

The above instances of interpersonal costs are essentially accidental or incidental. In other cases costs may be imposed by some explicit arrangement, voluntary or involuntary. A government can impose costs on a citizen, in such forms as taxes, condemnation of property, or prohibited or required actions. A private organization also can impose costs on a member so long as he values continued affiliation more highly than the costs it brings him. These costs can take the form of fines, fees, or requirements that certain behavior be avoided or performed. In such instances the individual loses some of his freedom (that is, he accepts costs) by being the citizen of a government or the member of a private organization. His loss of freedom is encompassed in his accepting the authority of the organization, a matter we will examine in the chapters on organizations.

A person can also accept restrictions on his freedom through a continuing voluntary contract. In return for certain receipts he can promise to pay certain costs for another party, or to engage in or refrain from specified behavior. If he has a stake in the promise sufficient to bring its performance, there is no way of avoiding these costs, which are essentially the fixed costs of protecting the stake.

An individual can lack freedom because he is a slave. If he has sold himself into slavery, the contract of slavery is the major transaction, and the acceptance of the master's authority is the cost he has agreed to accept under it. Under involuntary slavery, acceptance of the master's orders is the cost imposed by the rules of the society. Slavery, too, is a problem in interpersonal costs, or interpersonal freedom. The power factors in slavery will be examined in connection with the later analysis of government, without whose help slavery could not exist in most societies. Problems of freedom usually referred to as those of civil and political liberty will also be studied in connection with government.

The Sense, or "Problem," of Freedom

Things of the sort illustrated above can sometimes happen without necessarily being thought of as problems in freedom. To return to an earlier illustration, to change my flat tire is certainly an increased cost of going swimming, and hence is a decrease in my freedom to do so. (To those about to object that I will have to change the tire whether I go swimming or not, I should note that if I wait until my son comes home I may be able to get him to change it.) Yet this kind of thing might not be thought of as a problem in freedom. What are the conditions under which something is (or is not) thought of as involving freedom?

The reason why some increases in cost are thought of as impingements on freedom and others are not apparently hinges on the expansion and contraction of aspirations, described in Chapter 8.

To illustrate, of all conceivable ways for me to get to work, my first choice would be to spread my arms like Superman and take off at supersonic speed. The method is quick, scenic, and low in fuel and maintenance costs. But I do not feel any impairment of freedom because I have to drive, at higher cost in time and money, since I never (while awake) considered the Superman technique among my opportunities. The key to discerning the conditions under which higher costs are perceived as a decline in freedom can be seen in the fact that anyone has full freedom to do anything he wants, so long as he does not want anything that he cannot do. "One does not speak of liberty at all unless there is a disposition to act."[10] Our goals and aspirations expand and contract with what is perceived as possible, and we perceive something as a restriction on freedom when our aspirations have not yet contracted to match the opportunities.

In the opposite direction, we have a feeling of increased freedom when the opportunities are discovered to be greater (the costs are less) than anticipated. The *sense* or perception that a problem of freedom exists thus lies in the gap between expectation and reality. At the level of freedom among persons, one feels his freedom to be infringed when he must accept costs (of either his own or other people's satisfactions) when, in his expectation or aspirations, those costs should be borne by others.

With this background we now return to the statements which opened

---

[10] Ralph Barton Perry, "Liberty in a Democratic State," in Anshen, *op. cit.*, p. 265.

the discussion of freedom, and strengthen them somewhat by saying that absolute freedom and omnipotence are the same concept in different verbal clothing. Omnipotence (in light of our definition of power) would be the ability to accomplish any and all wanted things. Omnipotence without complete freedom would mean the ability to overcome all costs. But cost is defined as the denial of some satisfaction(s) in the course of achieving others. To achieve *all* satisfactions thus presupposes that *none* has costs. This is the same as complete and absolute freedom—in the present model.

At levels more modest than omnipotence, when two EP's extend far enough toward each other to touch, a want can be satisfied. To modify the definition of power slightly for the moment, we can think of one's own EP as his power, and the one extending toward him as his freedom. The ability to acquire something thus depends on both power and freedom, in reciprocal relation. To state as a sort of motto the requirements for achieving a given result, the more freedom one has the less power he needs, and the more power he has the less freedom he needs. To return to the original definition of power, although in many circumstances one's power is directly proportional to his EP, power is defined in the present model to include the effect of freedom. Power is the ability to acquire, whether based on one's own EP, that of others, or both. The accurate paraphrase is thus a soupy rewording of the above ringing motto: the more freedom one has the less EP he needs, and vice versa. The whole model could, of course, be reconstructed to save the motto. But I strongly doubt that the reconstruction would be analytically as useful, which is another way of saying that I already had too much investment in the present model when I discovered its relation to freedom.

VI. ORGANIZATIONS

Chapter 21

ORGANIZATIONS: MODEL OF THE SIMPLE ORGANIZATION

DEFINITION AND NATURE OF ORGANIZATION

SOME GOODS are free—such as air, sunshine, and sometimes water—and afford man's first level of opportunity to satisfy his wants. But they are not numerous. Some goods can be produced by one person alone, such as combing one's hair, growing carrots, or mending a hammock. These are on man's second level of opportunities. How much of these things he can have depends on his Effective Preference for them, which means the strength of his desire for some goods, taken in conjunction with the ability to produce those goods and the strength of his desire for competing goods. The third set of opportunities lies in producing for exchange, the amount one can acquire by this route depending on his productivity and the terms of exchange.

But some things cannot be produced by one person alone, such as conversing, playing tennis, carrying a piano, singing in harmony, running a railroad, or making love. If such goods are to be produced, there is no choice but that two or more work together. Many things *can* be produced alone, but can be produced far better by joint effort. Joint production constitutes a fourth set of opportunities through which we can acquire either goods which an individual cannot produce, or larger quantities of things for which joint production is more efficient than individual production. This fourth set of opportunities utilizes *organization*, which is any relation of persons for joint production. The breadth of this definition includes relations as small, short, and casual as a game of tennis or the joint carrying of an injured friend, and as large, long, and formal as a national government or an international church.

Among these four sets of opportunities, free goods are not of concern to the analysis of society. Nor are the productive activities of the lone person, since social analysis necessarily involves more than one person. Transactions and organizations provide the two remaining opportunity sets. When taken in conjunction with the accompanying communications, transactions and organizations are the analytical lenses through which all interpersonal relations—all analysis of society—are viewed in this volume. The past four chapters have dealt with transactions, and we now move to the analysis of organizations. After the basic examination of organizations has been completed, the remainder of the volume will deal with the whole of society as an organization, including the transactions and communications it entails.

Both an important distinction and an important relationship exist between transaction and organization. To illustrate the difference, in a transaction *A* gives up cheese and receives bread, while *B* gives up bread and receives cheese. In organization, *A* gives up cheese, *B* gives up bread, and both receive cheese sandwiches. As with most other definitions, the two concepts overlap at the boundaries, especially where services rather than material goods are involved. A conversation or a game of tennis, for example, might fit the definition of either exchange or organization, and we need not dwell on these borderline cases.

An important aspect of organization is immediately evident from the bread and cheese illustration—namely, that organization necessarily embodies exchange as well as joint production. This is true in the sense that the inputs which any one participant contributes to the organization are different from the outputs he receives from it. It is also true in the sense that some bargain must be reached, overtly or implicitly, as to what each participant will contribute to and withdraw from the organization.

Since organization necessarily embodies transactions, we can say that organization consists of transaction plus joint production, even though joint production alone is sufficient to define it. This leads in turn to the observation that production and exchange—transformation and transaction—remain the sole sources of goods other than free goods. Organization thus adds only one new basic ingredient to the previous analysis, *joint* production. It also adds many complications. Since organization includes transactions, the whole analysis of bargaining power automatically applies to transactions in and around organizations. These include transactions (1) between organizations, as between a church and a city council, (2) between organizations and individuals outside themselves, as between a firm and its customers or between a mission church and a prospective convert, (3) between an organization and individuals inside itself, as when a charity hires a social worker, and (4) between individuals within the organization, as when a foreman gives a worker a raise for good performance.

In earlier chapters a complex decision was seen to include sets and subsets, all of which followed the same rules despite the complex interrelationships. A complex transaction also includes sets and subsets of agreements. A complex organization similarly includes sets and subsets of transactions, all of which follow the same rules, despite the complexity arising from the large number and multiple dimensions of their inter-relations. However, to say that both an adding machine and a threshing machine can be reduced to and understood in terms of gears, wheels, eccentrics, levers, and so forth does not mean that there are no important differences between adding machines and threshing machines, or that we understand either just by understanding gears, wheels, and other components. To understand any complex relationship requires that we understand both the components and the particular relationships of those components.

The organization consists of transactions and joint production. Many aspects of the joint production revolve around physical ingredients—machines, materials, electricity, and so on. These are of no concern to the present volume except to the extent that we must acknowledge their necessary presence. All *human* aspects of joint production consist of communications and transactions, which we have already discussed. We might thus say that we have already completed the presentation of the basic building blocks, or the basic mechanics, of social analysis, and that in organizations we are moving by analogy from the gear and lever stage to the adding machine and threshing machine stage—from the components to the larger configurations of those components.

This does not mean that physical aspects will be ignored. In the first place they do much to determine *which* transformations and transactions can occur. To return to the cheese sandwiches, in a straight transaction it is feasible for *A* and *B* to exchange one pound of bread for ten of cheese, or ten of bread for one of cheese. But the exchanges which take place in organization are constrained by the technical fact that acceptable sandwiches are compatible with only a limited range of bread-to-cheese ratios. In the second place, physical operations and decisions must be made by human beings, who must be selected, trained, supervised, and motivated, and who sometimes disagree over technical matters. Thirdly, there is no sharp dividing line between physical and human problems, especially in an organization which produces services rather than commodities. The sales director, the parish priest, the parent, the supervisor, or the diplomat is often limited by his own physical environment, and he must deal with others in terms of their relations with their physical environment. We can summarize by saying that our analysis will work around and among physical factors, rather than *with* them.

Joint production, as such, is a cooperative act. Two persons attempt to satisfy wants through the same joint production. Organization also encompasses exchange, which is part cooperation and part conflict. Whether two cooperative and one conflicting aspect in the organization make for more cooperation than conflict is a matter we shall not attempt to decide. Joint production is also cooperative in that it does not depend on opposite or different relative preferences, as does exchange. Both *A* and *B* can prefer bread to cheese or cheese to bread—a condition under which pure exchange would not be possible—so long as each prefers sandwiches to the ingredient he supplies. It is also possible in organization for both parties to contribute the same kind of input (e.g., the labor of raising chickens) but to take different kinds of output (e.g., eggs and fryers). It is also possible, of course, for both to contribute different kinds of input and take different outputs—perhaps the most common situation in organizations.

THE BASIC MODEL OF ORGANIZATIONS

Following the pattern used in transactions, we will establish a simplified model of organization, and examine its characteristics. Like the model of transactions, this one is not necessarily unreal, but merely the simplest possible version of organization. We will then modify the model in several ways to encompass other behavior found in the richer variety of organizations around us.

The basic model of organization is a two-person, unique, selfish, terminable-at-will, equal-authority relationship. "Two person" needs no explanation. "Unique" and "selfish" mean the same as in connection with transactions, meaning absence of consensus, and of generous bargaining, respectively. "Terminable-at-will" means that either party is free to leave the organization at any time, with no contractual obligations, investments, fixed costs, or capital accumulations to impede the separation. That is, an organization fully terminable-at-will has only variable costs. "Equal authority" means that all decisions about their methods of operation are mutually agreed, and that no difference in rank exists between the two.

Characteristics of the Model

In essence the basic model of organization is the basic model of transaction, plus the ability of two persons to produce better than one. Whether the two are more productive through division of labor, added strength, or the inherent necessity of two persons for the operation does not matter. As with decisions and transactions, we will analyze organizations with quantified units of value and cost, not because the rules apply only to such instances, but because nonquantified items are difficult to illustrate. We will sometimes refer to the "contribution of the organization" to production. This does not mean that some new entity does something when two persons join together, but merely that their joint productivity is higher than the sum of their separate productivities. We will assume at the outset that the inputs and outputs are divisible, and can be shared in any proportion. We will return later to cases where the output is not divisible.

Since the organization is joint production and transactions, and there is no profit in examining production problems in the social analysis, the present analysis of the model is confined to transaction aspects, and particularly to those aspects of transactions which are peculiar to organization.

Suppose that *A* and *B* separately can each catch 8 fish per hour, but together they can catch 24. Measuring the costs and values solely in the quantifiable inputs of hours and outputs of fish, the organization of *A* and *B* is more efficient than the separated *A* and *B* by 8 units per hour.

A fascinating aspect of this relation is that employer and employee points of view become evident at the outset. Either party views his own contribution to the organization through the eyes of an employee, and the other person's contribution through the eyes of an employer, as we can see by drawing the EP's.

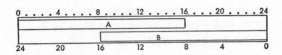

We will assume for the moment that each person has only the alternatives of fishing with the other or fishing alone. In the organizational relation, the EP's differ slightly from those in straight transactions. In this model *A*'s EP is not his desire for *B*'s good, *Y*, expressed in units of his own good, *X*, but his desire for *B*'s services in the organization, expressed in units of the good jointly produced—in this case, in fish. *B*'s EP is his desire for *A*'s services expressed in the same good, and indicated on the bottom scale.

A's EP extends to 16. Given a joint catch of 24, and *A*'s ability to catch 8 alone, *A* will be willing to let *B* take any number of fish not in excess of 16 in return for *B*'s services. If the "organization" (which, without *B*, is *A*) has to pay *B* more than 16 it will be better off without him. At 16 *B*'s participation will be indifferent, and below that point it will bring a net gain. If, for instance, *B* can be induced to work with *A* for 10 fish, then *A* will have 6 more than if he worked alone. Looking at *B* through the eyes of an employer, *A* will be willing to hire *B* at any wage up to but not exceeding 16 fish.

B meanwhile sees himself through the eyes of an employee. If the organization pays him more than 8 fish he is better off to work for it. At 8 he is indifferent, and at less than 8 he will work alone. (As noted, the model contains no costs or values other than hours and fish.) Since their positions are factually identical, each person is capable of taking either view. In the alternate view, *A* will be willing to work as an employee if he receives 8 fish or more, and *B* as employer would be willing to hire him for a wage of 16 or less. Whether we think of the maximum either would pay as employer, or the minimum he would accept as employee, we can express the EP's of each as extending to 16 on each man's own scale.

If neither side has any bargaining advantage, the two will rationally join forces and divide the catch equally, each thus gaining 4 fish. An overlap of EP's means that the fact of organization makes a contribution, which may tentatively be thought of as profit. Any output less than 16 fish represents a loss. The costs of the organization are the opportunity cost of the 16 fish A and B could produce alone. To produce less is to destroy value, not create it, and the organization would then rationally be dissolved.

The decision of the two to fish jointly can be called the *major bargain* of affiliation with the organization. It is the agreement between the individual and the organization that he will join it and it will accept him. In this model, if the bargain is settled at the midpoint of the overlap, each will agree to fish for the organization in return for 12 fish per hour. Transactions which settle details of the relation as it subsequently proceeds are *subsidiary bargains*. Major or subsidiary bargains can cover either the input contributions by each party or the division of the output. Until we examine the difference between the effects of fixed and residual contributions later, there is no need to discuss bargains over contributions as a separate problem, and we can assume either equal contributions or a division of output in proportion to the differential inputs.

The model shows the basic relation of the parties. The organization is cooperative, in that the two can produce more together than separately. The *fact* of organization thus satisfies desires of both. Once the organization has produced, however, the parties are in conflict over the division of returns. More for one necessarily means less for the other. This relation is independent of the nature of the organization. Thieves may be highly cooperative until their "production" is complete, whereupon they may dispute over the division of the spoils. "Conflict" also does not necessarily mean fights or unpleasantness, but merely that more for one means less for the other.

We can now examine some of the bargaining power factors in the simple organization. AX and BY in the bargain of affiliation are the desires of the parties not to work in (for) the organization, whether because they do not want the good it produces, because they can produce better for themselves, or for other reasons. AY and BX are the parties' desires for the services of the other in the organization, which in the simple model is the same as the desire to join the organization. The same rules apply as in other transactions, A's bargaining power varying directly with AX and BX, and inversely with AY and BY. Suppose that A has a large family to feed and no stock of food ahead, and he thus urgently needs fish. B, on the other hand, has no family and a plentiful stock. Since A urgently needs B's help, he may be willing to join B for any amount over 8. But B has no urgency and may refuse to work at all unless he receives a large return, in which case the catch might be divided with 15 to *B* and 9 to *A*.[1] Other changes in *AX*, *AY*, *BX*, or *BY* would also shift the power position, and need not be detailed.

Changes in objective alternatives would also affect bargaining power. Without moving to full consensus conditions, we can imagine other potential partners with whom *A* or *B* might join if they cannot reach satisfactory terms between them. Suppose the technique is so standard that virtually anyone fishing alone will catch 8 fish. Whenever *A* joins anyone else but *B* the total rises to 28, whereas whenever *B* joins anyone except *A* the total rises to only 20. In a partnership of *A* and *B* this would tend to sustain a claim by *A* that he is responsible for more than half the product, and ought to get more than half the product. Whether this claim is in fact true in the *A-B* relation, it does strengthen *A*'s tactical position by lending credence to it. It also strengthens his power position. For if *A* can split 50–50 with any others with whom he works, thus getting 14 fish, he presumably will refuse to work with *B* for less. If *B* splits his catches when working with others than *A*, he normally gets 10, and lacks the overt alternatives necessary to pull up his bargaining power with *A*. A catch of 24 by the team of *A* and *B* would thus presumably be split on a 14–10 basis.

To illustrate the next point, let us return to assumed equal contributions by *A* and *B*, divided equally. Solely by his own effort and ingenuity, but by methods which are of no value when he fishes alone, *B* now raises the total output of the pair to 28. Since *B* is solely responsible for the increase, will he get the whole extra amount for himself? No. *A* is now more valuable to *B* than he was before, since *B* will now lose more by producing alone. Being more valuable to *B*, *A* now has more bargaining power, and hence can share the increase due to *B*'s efforts. If we redraw the chart to show an output of 28 units instead of 24, the EP's now extend to 20 in each direction. Each party will still insist on no less than

```
0 . . . 4 . . . 8 . . . 12 . . . 16 . . . 20 . . . 24 . . . 28
                        A
                           B
28 . . . 24 . . . 20 . . . 16 . . . 12 . . . 8 . . . 4 . . . 0
```

8 fish, since each could produce that much alone. For the same reason, each would be willing to give the other as much as but no more than 20 for his services in the joint effort. Although the improvement brings a longer overlap, in itself it provides no reason to push the point of settlement away from the midpoint of the overlap, at which point *A* and *B*

---

[1] The reader not fully accustomed to analytical models may wonder why *B* is represented as such a selfish, unprincipled brute, unwilling to share his providence. The answer is that we are examining a selfish model, in which, by definition, each party seeks the most possible in return for the least possible. The model and the reader may relax together when we come to the generous model later.

will each take 14 units. The increase, even though due solely to B's efforts, is divided equally.

However, if B's improvement enabled him to produce 4 extra units, or 12 in total, when he worked alone, the situation would be different. Although A's EP would still extend to 20 on the a scale, B's would extend to only 16 (28–12) on the b scale. The midpoint of this overlap would give A 12 and B 16. This is in accord with the previous analysis of transactions: barring other influences, if one EP changes, the midpoint terms will change by half that amount.

Along similar lines, employers often express frustration when workers get increased wages from improvements in efficiency created solely by the employer, even though the improvement lightens the work and reduces the skill requirement. The simple fact is that as soon as the employer improves the productivity of the worker, the worker's bargaining power goes up. If other employers are also increasing the efficiency of *their* workers, and workers are free to move, workers will continue to be able to share this increase, even if they did nothing themselves to create it. The relation works in both directions, of course. If through greater skill, education, or training the employees become more productive in ways which they cannot use when working alone, the bargaining power of the employer rises, since the employer is now more valuable to the worker than before.

This is a reflection of the relationship found in previous chapters. The length of the EP depends on productive ability (now in the organization) as well as on preference, and is the measure of a person's particular power. But the longer one's EP (and particular power) the greater is the bargaining power of the other party. In organizations as well as straight transactions, one's power is greater when he deals with others of much power than with others of little power.

Assuming that the major bargain on the division of the catch has been concluded, most of the subsidiary bargains over details of the model are concerned with contributions to various aspects of the work. Although we will not go into questions of production techniques as such, a difference in the way the two parties conceptualize the production process can shift bargaining power on contributions. Suppose as B is loafing around and A is busy cutting bait A says, "How about helping with this bait, or we're not going to get much of a catch," to which B replies, "It's the movement of the net that attracts them; the bait doesn't do any good." Although B has the same desire for the fish as before, he has no desire to accomplish the bait cutting, since he does not see it as instrumental to acquiring fish. So long as A sees bait as instrumental to catching fish and B does not, A will suffer a decline in bargaining power, and will have to do a disproportionate share of the work of bait cutting. Once again, the person with the lesser stake has the greater bargaining power, and the result follows even if the lesser stake is based on a different concept rather than a lesser desire for the product. *B*, of course, might mend nets while *A* cuts bait, thus keeping the contribution more nearly equal.

Any person who fails to perceive the relation between work and results over a wide range will be generally "shiftless." He will not accomplish much in total. But his bargaining power in keeping down his contribution on details can be remarkably high, and extremely frustrating to those who want to "get things done." A stubborn refusal to understand things, or an alleged inability to do them, can often raise bargaining power to keep down one's contribution. In the reverse direction, sheer habit of doing things may cause *B* to cut the bait without ever questioning whether it is useful.

If *A* and *B* have different skills, bargaining power will also be affected. If the net gets snagged ten feet under water, and *A* can swim while *B* cannot, *A*'s bargaining power to avoid unsnagging the net is low indeed. On the other hand, *A*'s ability to swim might enable him to get better terms on the main transaction.

The discussion thus far has dealt with divisible products. Some results of joint action cannot be divided among those who help create them, like an orderly home, a well-kept lawn, an unpolluted stream, or good government. When joint goods of this sort are used by a relatively few persons, they are often known as *shared values*, and when used by essentially a whole society they are known as *public goods*. In the simple model production of shared values would occur if the two men went fishing for recreation rather than food, or if they got together for conversation, tennis, chess, or to fill a gully the rain had washed across their adjoining properties. For joint goods of this sort there can be differences in contributions to input, but not in division of output. Here the greater bargaining power lies in the lesser stake in the outcome; the one who most wants the orderly house, and so forth, puts in the most work. The same reasoning applies to a divisible product where the shares are agreed on in advance. If *A* and *B* are to split the catch evenly, and if *A* is desperately in need of fish while *B* has plenty, then *A* will have less bargaining power over contributions, and may find himself doing more of the work. This problem is closely related to fixed and residual shares of contribution and product, which has some relevance here, but will be discussed below in connection with organizations not terminable-at-will, where it is a highly important factor.

The organization is like the individual in an important respect. Instead of producing the particular good its members want, they may produce some other good and exchange it. The two-man fishing team may not want fish, but corn and pumpkins, or money. They can catch fish and barter them for corn and pumpkins, or sell them for cash. No basic change in the model or its problems arises from this fact; the partners still have to bargain over their inputs and withdrawals. The only difference is that the withdrawals now consist of corn, pumpkins, or money.

MORE THAN TWO PERSONS

The first relaxation of the model is to add more people. Suppose we start with the duo of A and B, splitting their catch of 24. C joins the organization, whose total output rises to 33, or an increase of 9. If the increase attributable to C is only 9 because C is a poorer worker, if all hands acknowledge this fact, and if C is willing to take only 9 while A and B continue to get 12 each, no problem arises. A and B are no worse off, and C is one unit better off than if working alone for 8.

On the other hand, diminishing productivity may have set in, the smaller contribution from C being due to the fact that a third man on the team is not as useful as a second, even though he is as good a worker. For example, if efficient fishing requires one man to handle the boat while a second handles the nets, two will be far more efficient than one. But while a third may help, his contribution is by no means as essential as the second man's. Here the logical arrangement is to conduct all fishing in pairs, not trios, the case of any odd man being referred to the tribal chaplain. We can examine what might happen, however, until it is discovered that pairs are most productive, as the same problem appears in permanent form in larger organizations with investment and fixed costs.

Let us assume that C is added, and he accepts only 9 fish, because that is all he adds to the total. One day A is sick, however, and C discovers that he and B together get 24 fish per hour. It is now evident that C's output is normally only 9 because he is the *third* worker, not because he is a poorer worker. The plot now thickens. *Any* one of the three is a *third* man, because if any one is removed, two will be left, who will be able to get 12 units each. C will soon sense that something can be done about his 9 fish. He might approach B with a coalition plan to put A out of the organization unless he will agree to work for 9, whereupon C could take 11 and leave 13 for B—an increase for both. If B should accept, A might make the counterproposition to B that they put C down to his former 9, give A 10, and leave 14 for B. By this time B may have an inflated ego, and figure that he should have 15 while A and C get 9 each. At this point A and C may conclude they are no longer enemies, and form a coalition to take 12 each and give B 9. As pure tactics, these coalitions are unpredictable, and are cited merely to illustrate the situation.

As hinted above, if other pairings are available with D, E, and so forth, then any one of the trio who is asked to accept fewer than 12 would presumably leave to make a two-man team with someone else, and the problem would be solved.

Suppose that a third man would show increasing instead of diminishing returns, and raise the output by 15, from 24 to 39. Would C now get 15 while A and B continue to receive 12 each, or would they divide equally at 13? The division would presumably be equal, for two reasons. First, if C insists on more than 13 he will motivate A and B to form a coalition against him, which coalition may be followed by others as seen above, the only stable position being equal division. Second, if other trios are available in which *A* or *B* might work, a threat of either to leave would bring *C*'s anticipated contribution down to 12, and a threat of both to leave (which is polite for throwing *C* out) would cut *C* down to 8, as he produced by himself. Hence, equal division seems the most probable permanent division—barring status differences arising outside the organization.

The kinds of forces at work are made visible by adding a third man. The quantities but not the principles change as a fourth and more workers are added. More workers can be added if they increase the average product, but not if they decrease it. This statement is valid, however, only so long as the members of the organization are on an equal authority status. A different set of forces operates when one is clearly employer and the other employee—a matter for the next section.

NOT TERMINABLE-AT-WILL: INVESTMENT, CAPITAL ACCUMULATIONS, AND FIXED COSTS

An organization which is terminable-at-will in the present model is an organization with only variable costs. None but the simplest organization can long continue without (1) inputs of investment from outside the organization, (2) accumulations of investment inside the organization, and/or (3) fixed costs to prevent disinvestment of items (1) or (2). Once any of these things has happened, the individual cannot leave the organization at will without either forfeiting his share of the accumulated investment (which we will call capital), or disrupting the productivity of the organization by taking his share out of it. This observation is equally true of a fishing partnership, a government, a corporation, or a scout troop, as each accumulates things which in effect belong to the organization. This fact leads to the study of organizations with longer commitments. There each participating individual who either makes or contributes to investment will want assurance either (1) that his affiliation with the organization will continue long enough for him to recover his investment or (2) that he will be able to withdraw his investment if he leaves.

If the organization uses only equipment which belongs to its individual members, the second technique is feasible. Each partner brings some of his own equipment if *A* and *B* join forces, and takes it away if they break up. Problems arise, however, when (1) equipment supplied by one is worn out, lost, or broken in the joint effort, as when *A*'s fish baskets are washed overboard in a storm, or when (2) an indivisible piece of equipment is produced by joint effort, as when *A* and *B* spend two weeks building a boat. Other complications arise, but these two suffice to indicate that any person following the General Rule of decisions will not make investments in the organization either when he joins (as by contributing nets) or while he is in it (as by helping to build the boat) without some commitment from the other partner about the duration of the relationship, the division of the investment in the event of a breakup, and the meeting of fixed costs to prevent deterioration of his investment.

Whether in organization or out of it, the effect of investment and fixed cost is to give a longer time range to decisions. This means not merely an agreement about how much each is to contribute when he joins, and how much he takes when he leaves, but also about his contributions to fixed cost and to further investment. To the extent these things can be agreed in advance, they are terms of the major bargain of affiliation with the organization. Since any organization will almost inevitably have to face problems not forseeable when the organization is formed, it must also have some provision for making decisions about these things as they arise—as, for example, whether all decisions will be made jointly, unilaterally, or by some other arrangement. There must be some understanding about *authority*, whether it be a relation of equality or subordination. In later chapters we will examine questions of bargaining power in and between the major and subsidiary bargains, and also the question of authority as such. Our main concern at this point is merely to note that the presence of investment and fixed costs necessitate some kind of decision process and authority relation.

Fixed and Residual Contributions and Withdrawals— and Control

The parties could agree to make contributions and withdrawals on an equal basis, on a three-to-one basis, or any other basis they chose, contributions including obligations toward fixed costs and possible further investment. Two important things happen, however, if an agreement is made that one party will provide some stated, or *fixed*, contribution, while the other party provides all remaining contributions, or *residual* contribution. First, the decision and bargaining forces will tend strongly to bring the withdrawals parallel with the contributions, the person making the fixed contribution taking a fixed amount of product, and the person making the residual contribution taking the residual amount of output. Second, the person making the residual contribution (and taking the residual withdrawal) will control the organization.

The reasons for these results can be seen by examining a situation which violates them. Suppose that A and B agree that A will provide two nets and four baskets and keep them in repair (the stated, or *fixed*, contribution), and that B will provide all other equipment for the joint venture, as he sees fit (the *residual* contribution). In return the catch will always be divided equally. In addition, either party will be free to terminate the relation at any time, and take half the organization's capital. No agreement, expressed or implied, is made about the amount of B's contribution, not even a minimum, since any such provision would make B's contribution no longer strictly residual.

This being a selfish relation, A would logically refuse such an arrangement, since B might do or provide nothing at all, and still take half the catch and walk off with half the equipment. However, if A knows B to be an ambitious fellow, he might be willing to take that risk. But then B would presumably refuse. *B* might have in mind an operation with boat, dock, hatchery, and a dozen nets, all of which he would provide. But he would be unwilling to do this under an agreement in which *A* would get half the product and freedom to take half the assets at any time. *B* might also suspect that this arrangement would kill his own motivation. By contrast, it would be reasonable to both if *A* were to get some fixed number of fish for his contribution, and freedom to take back his nets and baskets, while *B* would get all fish and capital over that amount. Thus, fixed and residual contributions are logically related to fixed and residual withdrawals. This does not mean that other arrangements never occur, but either that they are irrational, or that they involve other factors beyond the scope of the present model.

The second important point is that if *B's* contribution is truly residual, *B* will control the organization. If he decides to make no contribution, the assets of the organization will consist solely of the two nets and four baskets contributed by *A*. But if *B* decides to make a large contribution, *A's* contribution will be dwarfed to insignificance. By determining what other equipment is to be used in conjunction with *A's*, *B* also determines how productive *A's* contribution will be. In short, because he controls the residual contribution, the organization for all practical purposes *is* what *B* makes it. In consequence, the amount of output *A* can create is determined by the amount and quality of *B's* contribution, which means that *B* can do much to determine *A's* output. Being able to control to a large extent the productivity of *A's* labor and *A's* equipment, along with controlling the size and asset composition of the organization, *B* is in charge. Incidentally, this is not an ethically or legally oriented statement that the residual contributor *ought* to control, but a logically deduceable proposition that he *will*.

This proposition seems applicable to larger organizations as well. Although in large corporations the locus of control is sometimes hard to find, the problem there is not whether the residual contribution controls, but who controls the residual contribution. Despite frequent fuzziness about the *real* locus of power, the formal structure of corporations recognizes this distinction, by giving votes to stockholders, who make residual contributions and take residual withdrawals, but not to bondholders, whose contributions and withdrawals are fixed. This arrangement is also related to the definition of power as lying in the control of wanted things. Productive assets are wanted in the organization. The person who commits himself to make a fixed contribution loses power because he is no longer free to withhold wanted things, whereas the residual contributor still has that freedom. Either way of viewing it, control lies with the residual contribution.

ORGANIZATIONS WHICH ARE NOT UNIQUE

We have seen in Chapter 18 that transactions interact with each other in numerous ways. Organizations can conduct transactions with other organizations, or with individuals, and the organizations and individuals with which they deal will also have transactions with other organizations and individuals. To give a few examples, if A has an agreement to give C fish for firewood, A's desire for wood will indirectly influence his desire for fish, and hence his bargaining power with B. If A has worked assiduously with the tariff lobby while employed by a firm manufacturing watches from domestic parts, his relation to the lobby will change if A moves to a firm which manufactures watches with imported Swiss movements. A man may use his position on the job to further his chances of marrying the boss's daughter, or he may use his marriage to the boss's daughter to further his power on the job. A procurement contract signed by a corporation with one supplier increases its bargaining power in negotiating a supplementary contract for the same materials with another supplier—and so on. Any or all of these transactions may interact on any others, either on power limits or on tactics. There is no need to trace all of these relationships; all the rules already formulated about transactions and interrelations of transactions apply equally here. But because consensus terms have a special effect on organizations, we will examine that aspect.

The basic model of the organization spoke of the individual's ability to produce for himself as the main floor on his bargaining power in dealing with the organization, where A's ability to catch 8 fish for himself made it possible for him to bargain for not less than 8 from any organization he would join. If production of certain goods generally takes place in organizations, and is much more efficient than individual production, then the individual's ability to produce for himself ceases to be the best floor under his bargaining power. Instead, the floor in bargaining with one organization is the best he can get from some other organization. For example, if the individual can catch only 8 fish working alone, but can catch 50 with the organization, his ability to work alone is an unsatisfactory bargaining alternative. A's bargaining power with B then depends on the terms he can get from C, not what he can get working alone. The more highly industrialized the society, the less able is the individual to produce satisfactorily alone, and the more does his bargaining power with one organization depend on what he can get from others. If there are many organizations, the terms of the bargains between individuals and organizations will tend toward a consensus. Even if the consensus is not perfect, it will nevertheless set upper and lower limits on the pay.

In large organizations most persons give only fixed contributions of time and effort, in connection with residual contributions provided by those who control the organization. At this point the employer-employee points of view are no longer mutual, as they were in the original model. Now the contributor of the residual share becomes solely employer and the contributor of the fixed share becomes solely employee.

Several other things also happen. In the simpler organization in which labor was the only significant input (or in which each member of the organization brought with him an equal share of all other inputs, such as land or tools), the size of the organization would be that which produced the largest possible return per member, or the largest average output. When the contributor of the residual share controls the organization in his own interest, he will seek the highest return for *his* contribution, whether it be land, investment, labor, or some combination.

We have seen in connection with decisions that only rarely is it possible to maximize more than one value at a time, if, indeed, there is any real meaning to the attempt to maximize even one. Since the employer is not even motivated to maximize the income per employee, which is what the employees want, it seems unlikely that this result will be produced— though if there is competition among employers for employees the employer will have to maintain wages and productivity at competitive levels. Hence, the presence of consensus terms on wages, taken in conjunction with unequal control, makes it possible for the employer (i.e., the organization) to have goals other than those of the persons who do its work, who want the largest income per worker. This conclusion is valid whether the organization is a business, charity, government, or church, and is one of the most fundamental problems to be analyzed in succeeding chapters. If there are many employers and employees, there will also tend to arise a set of consensus terms on authority relations, a matter we will also discuss in later chapters.

The kind of consensus which arises when many of the model organizations exist in contiguity is essentially a market consensus. In many societies, particularly primitive ones, contributions to and withdrawals from organizations, as well as the authority relations within them, are fixed by a social consensus built into the organizational structures. Most production is done by families, clans, or communal work groups. Affiliation with such groups is typically made or dropped by birth and maturation, marriage, death, or other clearly definable events. In joining such a group there is no question that one's affiliation will last long enough to justify his contribution toward its capital and fixed costs, since he will normally remain there for life. The child growing up in the family inherits access to such accumulated tools as the family possesses, and leaves them to his children when he dies, meanwhile making his contribution to the fixed costs of maintaining them or to the investment of an increasing stock. Within the family, of course, much generous bargaining takes place, to be discussed just below.

Upon marrying, a person often leaves one productive organization and joins another. Depending on the consensus, he may leave his share when he leaves his own family, and receive access to the capital of the family into which he has married. Or he may take a share with him in the form of dowry or bride price, producing a net loss to one family and a net gain to the other. If the families are large enough, there will be movements in both directions, and the gains and losses will tend to offset each other.

Under strong consensus of any type there is little discretion about terms, as all affiliations are made at or near the consensus. In a traditional society the distinction between fixed and residual contributions, and hence the question of control, is less likely to arise, since the contributions all tend to be fixed in the sense the term is used here. Control is itself also likely to be determined by the pattern of the traditional consensus.

Under any kind of society, but particularly a strongly traditional one, certain status groups may receive preferred treatment. This problem has been partly introduced in Chapter 20, but will be examined more specifically later, in connection with the use of broad social controls to enforce special privilege or social handicap.

FRIENDSHIP AND GENEROUS BARGAINING

Just as many transactions outside of organizations are generous, so are many in organizations. The whole of the organization may have a generous purpose, such as a charity, and perform this purpose generously, even though the employees of the organization bargain selfishly with it. This relation is possible as soon as the employer-employee functions become clearly differentiated on the basis of fixed and residual contributions. Generous organizations as such will be discussed later; our present concern is with generous transactions within organizations.

The major effect of friendship and generosity is that it increases overlap of EP's, and hence extends the range of possible terms of exchange, for two reasons. To return to the original model in which two fishermen got a total catch of 24, under selfish bargaining the terms could have fallen anywhere between a division of 8–16 and 16–8. However, if the fishermen enjoy each other's company to the extent that either would be willing to sacrifice 2 fish per hour to avoid working alone, then the reservation price of each in the organization drops to 6. The EP of each would then extend to 18 on his own scale, and the terms of the transaction would be indeterminate between 6–18 and 18–6. The midpoint of the overlap, however, remains unchanged, and there may be no change in actual terms.

If the desire for companionship is not mutual, the change in EP's will not be symmetrical. *A* might want *B*'s company enough to sacrifice two units for it, whereas *B* might have a two-unit preference for working alone. In that case *A*'s reservation price would be 6 and *B*'s 10. The power limits would now be 6–18 and 14–10, and the midpoint would shift from 12–12 to 10–14. A one-sided feeling of friendship may thus change the overt terms—though the original 12–12 still lies within the acceptable range, and might continue if *B* does not wish to press his position. If the desire for companionship is stronger, it would, of course, shift the possible range of settlements even further.

In addition to companionship, one party might have a generous desire to help the other. We noted earlier the case in which *A* had a large family to feed and desperately needed food, while *B* supported only himself and had a plentiful stock. Under selfish bargaining these conditions provided *B* with great bargaining power. If *B* takes a generous interest in *A*, however, he might shift the terms strongly in A's favor. He might possibly give A the whole of the catch in a 24–0 division, and could conceivably make it 30–0 by reaching into his own store to augment the flow to A.

Purely aside from the desire for companionship, B's generous desire to help A would increase his desire to work as an organization instead of alone. Working alone, B could produce only 8 fish for A, whereas working with him he can produce 16, and thus double his generous contribution to A.

As we move into the broader analysis of organizations in later chapters, we will see that the major bargains of affiliation of employees with organizations are seldom generous. But in subsidiary transactions on a day-to-day basis, and in numerous transactions with and between subgroups of the larger organization, friendship and generous bargaining are widespread. The model of economic man has distinct usefulness in describing and analyzing the bargains of affiliation with organizations. It has rather little use in trying to understand the details of day-to-day relationships.

The analysis of friendship and generous bargaining is perhaps the most appropriate place to round out the discussion by noting the variety of influences on transactions with and within organizations. In the initial model we assumed one-dimensional, quantifiable values and costs (fish and man hours, respectively), since without one-dimensional, quantifiable measurements of values, it is extremely difficult to establish a manageable model. We have now added two other dimensions, friendship and generosity, related to each other but quite different from the initial dimensions. Although these new dimensions bring a modification of the model, they do not require us to discard it, and the model, in fact, helps us to understand the nature of the effects of generosity and friendship.

Having come this far, we can also broaden the model to include other factors. Perhaps A hates the smell of fish, B gets sick in boats, C loves to be on the water, and D feels that fishing carries status in his group. Unlike man hours and fish, the "quantity" of these feelings cannot be counted. Hence, the outside observer cannot predict the power limits when subjective considerations of this sort are introduced into the relaxed version of the model. Nevertheless, as soon as a given *kind* of preference is known to exist, the *direction* of its influence can be predicted. If enough observations are made, by noting deviations from the position which would prevail if objective alternatives alone were operative, it might even be possible to state the approximate magnitude of the effect of some subjective factors. This relationship is somewhat similar to that in economics, where, if we know what the competitive price of a good would be, we can measure the degree of a monopoly by the size of the difference between the monopoly price and the competitive one. Every variable that we learn to measure is a potential tool for measuring still another variable, with which to measure still others, in an ever-widening circle.

Chapter 22

ORGANIZATIONS: TYPES, AND SPONSOR-RECIPIENT RELATIONS

In the simple organization, like the fishing partnership for fish or for recreation, two or more join to do what can be done better together than separately. There is no investment or fixed cost, and the relation is therefore terminable-at-will, with each person free to leave at any time he feels he can get more satisfaction outside the organization than in it. Organizations of such casual and simple nature are extremely widespread, and it is important that we understand their basic rules. At the same time, especially in more advanced industrial and metropolitan societies, hosts of organizations exist on a more formal and permanent basis, replete with offices, staff, meeting halls, recreation rooms, factories and warehouses, and other facilities appropriate to their purpose. Many such organizations have goals quite independent of the goals of the persons who do their work, and continue through many changes of personnel.

This raises a question whether the organization is the set of persons or the set of relations. An organization is a *relationship* of *persons*, which means that by definition it does not exist if either persons or relationships are absent. Like the influence of heredity and environment on personality, both are indispensable, and there is no point in debating which is *more* indispensable. By analogy, are *you* the set of molecules which compose your body, or the particular set of relationships among those molecules? You are both. If all your molecules were rearranged in a straight line, we would have the substance of you, but not you. If we had all the relationships but no molecules, we would have the idea of you, or a set of plans, but not you. The organization is a system, as defined earlier, which means a set of *components* in some *relation*. The indispensable components are persons; the organization may also have other components, like buildings, books, or bowling balls.

But suppose all the persons leave an organization over the years and are replaced by others, is it still the same organization? Suppose all the molecules in your body are gradually replaced over the years, is the ensuing collection still you? This is a philosophical problem (though with organizations it can sometimes raise nasty legalities), since "same" and "different" are acts of classification, not of fact. Nothing in the universe is the same now as it was five seconds ago, and "same" or "different" are descriptions of our responses to things, not descriptions of the things. You and organizations remain the same even if all components change, so long as you and the organization are still classified as the same thing. Since many organizations *are* construed as the same even after undergoing many changes of personnel, we have no choice but to answer the question in the affirmative. The ability of an organization to maintain its identity through such changes is the basis of the layman's statement that it has a life of its own.

Whether an organization has goals of its own is a different matter. In the simple organization the goals normally are the same as those of its members, and in the larger and more durable organization the goals are typically independent of those of its members. We are interested primarily in the latter type of organization, though all large organizations contain suborganizations of the former type (often called informal organizations), which are extremely important to the performance of the larger unit.

THE BASIC TYPES OF ORGANIZATIONS

As we have seen in connection with concepts and communications, things can be classified in numberless ways. Organizations are no exception. Among others, they can be classified as good or bad; profit or non-profit; public or private; large, medium, or small; producers of commodities or producers of services; centralized or decentralized; primitive or advanced; or as educational, industrial, governmental, religious, philanthropic, or fraternal; and so on and on. No system of classification is "better" in any absolute sense, its usefulness depending on the purpose at hand. The present social analysis is focused on transactions and organizations, and the main emphasis in organizations is on their transactions. In this context the following classification system seems to have more analytical value than others.

First we will distinguish three types of roles, or relationships of persons to organizations, by identifying three groups or persons who stand in those relations, as follows:

1. *Sponsors:* Those persons whose desires originate and/or continue the organization's existence. Where the terms are appropriate, these will be the persons who control the residual contribution, and who perform the employer function.

2. *Staff:* The persons who actually produce the commodities or services created by the organization, or who actually perform its main work. In the

typical continuing organization these are the employees, who may or may not personally share the goals of the organization.[1]

3. *Recipients:* The persons who receive the commodities produced, or who are the direct objects of its services. These are the persons at or toward whom the work of the organization is directed.

The two persons in the basic model of organization occupy all three positions, since they originate the organization, do its work, and receive the product of its joint activities. In most small and simple organizations, the same persons typically occupy at least two of the three positions, and in the family all grown members are normally all three. These multiple relations indicate why these should be thought of as *roles* rather than as groups or persons. In the large organization, however, the three are more typically distinct, subject to later qualifications. Other persons may be affected by an organization, even though not occupying any of the above relations, and will be lumped into the catchall category of "other affected persons." The main analysis need not include the latter group, though it has distinct importance for other stages of social analysis.

As does the individual, the organization incurs costs and produces values, but with certain complications. Its employees incur personal costs in the form of time and effort, discipline of getting to work, and so on. These costs, however, are normally compensated to the employees by the organization. When we ask who carries the costs *of the organization*, we want to know who provides the compensation for the employees, or for materials, building, telephones, and so forth. Similarly, values are received by the staff and other suppliers in the form of pay and other satisfactions. But the values *of the organization* are the achievements of the organizations goals, the values to its employees being incidental. Except where the context indicates otherwise, when the terms costs and values are used in connection with organizations, they will refer to those of the organization itself, not to the incidental ones to staff and others.

The staff creates a series of problems in any organization, and four later chapters will be devoted to them. But the staff problems are largely independent of the nature or purpose of the organization. Hence, we will not distinguish among organizations on the basis of staff relationships, but solely on the allocation of costs and values as between sponsors and recipients, as follows.

The *cooperative organization* remains closest to the simple original model of organization—two or more join to do something better than they can do it alone. In contrast to the other three types of organization, the cooperative organization does not correspond to any particular type of

---

[1] Persons familiar with the subject and literature of organization will note that this is a different usage of the word "staff" than is customary, where *staff* is traditionally distinguished from *line* organization. I would prefer to avoid a different meaning for such a firmly established word. But no other word seems to do the job satisfactorily, and "staff" often is used in a looser sense to mean about the same thing it is defined to mean here—the collectivity of persons who do an organization's work.

Table 22-1

**FOUR TYPES OF ORGANIZATIONS,
BY ALLOCATION OF COSTS AND VALUES**

Type	Costs	Values	Transactional Base
Cooperative	Recipients	Recipients	None (Production for Selves)
Profit	Recipients	Sponsors	Selfish
Service	Sponsors	Recipients	Generous
Pressure	Sponsors	Sponsors	Third Party Strategies

transaction. It is instead the group equivalent of producing for oneself. If the organization grows in size it will have to hire a staff, even as any other organization. The cooperative is different from the others, however, in that sponsors and recipients are the same group, and the question arises whether they pay the costs and receive the values as sponsors or as recipients. The recipient role is chosen for two reasons. First, when the members of a cooperative receive the organization's benefits, they clearly do so as recipients—the persons to or for whom the organization's activity is directed. Since they pay the costs in order to receive the benefits, the costs are also borne by them as recipients. These roles will be clearer after the profit and control organizations have been examined.

In our society the major examples of cooperative organizations are the family; legitimate government (run in the interests of its citizens); consumer and producer cooperatives; trade and professional associations (to the extent they provide services to members, in contrast to promoting their advantage against other groups); social, fraternal, sports, hobby, and similar organizations; and church congregations (insofar as they serve their members, in contrast to performing charitable or missionary activities). Large cooperatives (like other organizations) may have divergent interests within the sponsor group. These are accommodated by essentially political techniques to be discussed in later chapters. Such conflicts aside, the persons who bear the costs in these cooperative organizations are collectively the same as those who receive the services. Although a cooperative may engage in transactions with organizations or persons outside itself, such transactions are instrumental to the objective of serving its members, but are not basic to the cooperative relation itself.

Profit organizations are the organizational expression of the selfish transaction. By means described in Chapter 20 for accumulating total power, they try to arrange successions of transactions on terms which will provide their sponsors an accumulation of goods. In business lingo, they try to sell things for more than they cost. Business firms are the chief example of profit organizations, and they deal solely in positive goods. Everyday usage distinguishes between trade, which buys and resells without physical transformations, and manufacturing, which makes physical transformations. This distinction, along with such further categories as agriculture, services, finance, transportation, utilities, and so forth are unnecessary for the present analysis. Virtually no profit organization resells precisely the same thing it buys, if only in the sense that part of what it buys is labor, which it does not resell as such. The profit organization may, of course, make losses (negative profits), but we have defined it in terms of its goals, not its accomplishments, and it remains a profit organization.

The customers of a firm are the recipients of its goods. When the firm is running according to plan the recipients pay the whole cost of operating the firm, plus the profit, which is the basis for saying that the costs of the profit organization are paid by the recipients.

Rackets and some other criminal groups are also profit organizations, with the distinctive characteristic being that they employ negative power to improve the terms of their transactions. Organizations other than firms often take on profit characteristics. Many a church, government, school, charity, fraternal organization, or cooperative has been converted in whole or part into a profit operation for the benefit of some official(s) or jobholders. Although we are currently speaking of types of organizations, our main interest is in the types of behavior they manifest. Any organization can at one time or another show all four aspects, and some show all four simultaneously. The purpose of classifying actual organizations at this point is mainly to clarify the meaning of the classification system, not to sort the organizations themselves into conceptual bins.

Service organizations are the organizational equivalent of generous transactions. The sponsors bear the costs, and the benefits of the organization are directed toward the recipients, essentially as gifts. The major examples are charities, the missionary and charitable aspects of churches, subsidized education, nonprofit research organizations whose findings are freely released, and groups which provide free legal aid, defense of civil liberties, relief of emergencies, and the like. Although the line is sometimes difficult to draw between service and pressure functions when the organization seeks to remold society according to its own plan, we will consider it a service organization if the sponsors would receive no more than the common share of benefit if their efforts were successful. To illustrate, if a group of consumers organize to raise tariffs in what they think is the national interest, we will consider them a service organization; whereas if the textile manufacturers organize to raise tariffs on textiles we will consider them a pressure organization.

The *pressure organization* directs its activities toward recipients who neither receive the benefits of the organization nor pay its costs in any direct sense. This does not mean that the recipients receive no value or incur no cost, and they may or may not, depending on the nature of the pressure organization's activities. The pressure organization's purpose is not to gain from transactions with the recipients, as such, but rather to influence the recipients in a roundabout strategy designed to change the power factors in some other transaction of interest to the sponsors, which transaction may be selfish or generous. To focus on A in a basic transaction between A and B, the relationship is at least triangular, as when pressure is put on recipient C in such a way that the relation between C and B will change in ways favorable to A in the basic transaction. It may be much more roundabout, on which A tries to influence B through C through D through E, and so on. We will use a model in which P is the pressure organization, seeking to further A's position relative to B. P may be A's agent, in which case we will consider A as the sponsor of P. Or P may have an ideological or other interest in A's position. In the model, P in some way influences someone at least as far away from the A–B relation as C, and possibly much more remote.

Before going into the analysis, we can identify pressure groups as including lobbies, political parties, labor unions, trade associations (to the extent they are not cooperatives), and propaganda agencies. To deal again with the muddy line between service and pressure organizations, a veterans' organization seeking to improve the lot of veterans only by improving the lot of the whole population would be a service organization, while one seeking additional bonuses or medical benefits for veterans would be a pressure organization. This classification reflects the objective relations between costs and benefits, not the wisdom of the proposals; that the goals of the pressure organization might be more sound and just than those of the service organization would not change the classification. The triangular relation of control appears when a labor union uses its influence on an employer to alter the terms of transactions between the employer and the union members; when a television station asks its congressman to use his influence with the Federal Communications Commission (via legislation or persuasion) to improve the TV station's relations with the FCC; or more roundaboutly when the TV station works on its audience to influence votes, to change the Congress, to change the legislation which determines the authority of the FCC over the station. As we shall see later, such controls may work directly on the terms of transactions or on the bargaining rules of transactions.

To illustrate the multiple roles of a given organization, a labor union is a pressure group when it negotiates with employers or lobbies for safety legislation for workers. It is a cooperative when it conducts picnics, gives classes in ceramics, or operates summer resorts for its members. It is a service organization when it sends representatives abroad to advise foreign unions in newly industrialized nations, and a profit organization if some officers raid its treasury or influence negotiations with employers for their personal benefit. A business firm is a profit organization in its normal operations, a service organization in some of its community activities, a pressure organization in its lobbying and some of its institutional advertising, and a cooperative in its nonprofit cafeteria or bowling team.

That the same organization falls into several categories simultaneously is not a defect of the classification system, but a reflection of the diversity of organizational phenomena. No other system would avoid this difficulty. For example, if we use a system which distinguishes between business and educational organizations, what is a school owned and operated by a private oil company for the children of its employees in the Middle East? If we distinguish between profit and nonprofit, what is a nationalized railway which turns all its profits into the public treasury? If we distinguish between public and private organizations, what is a college whose expenses are paid equally by students, private donors, and taxation?

The present definitions are essentially operational. The classification system seems to contain more information than other systems, in that to know that a given organization or suborganization is a cooperative or pressure organization will do more to predict the distinctive features of the *human* relationship within it than to know that it is a religious, public, nonprofit, or labor organization. The system also follows the rule of parsimony, in that it seems to be the conceptually simplest system of classifying organizations in ways which contain information about their interpersonal aspects.

PREVIEW

We are now at a point where we can sketch the outlines of the whole problem of organization as it appears within the present frame of analysis, and indicate which details will be filled in and which omitted in succeeding chapters.

To begin with, organizations engage in all sorts of transactions with other organizations, and with individuals not associated with the organization as sponsor, staff, or recipient. Any of the four kinds of organizations can lease property, protest a tax assessment, make a contract for trash removal, or buy fire insurance; and any can lobby for favorable legislation or engage in other pressure actions. Although the ingredients of such transactions will differ from one type of organization to another, as well as within types, the general rules are the same for all, and these aspects will not be discussed separately.

Among the three groups related to an organization there can be relations of sponsors to staff, sponsors to recipients, and staff to recipients, as well as relations among sponsors, among staff, and among recipients. Further, any one relationship can be that of transaction or communication. Of these, the relation of sponsors to staff is important to the ability of the sponsors to get the staff to work toward the sponsors' goals, and this relation will be examined. The staff-recipient relation can raise numerous questions in detail. But if we assume that in general the staff does what the sponsors want, the staff are the agents of the sponsors, and the underlying relation is between sponsors and recipients. Since the sponsors and recipients are the groups who bear the costs and receive the values of the organization, this is an important relation, and it will also be examined. In the sponsor-staff and sponsor-recipient relations, both the transaction and communications aspects will be treated, with such emphasis as the circumstances seem to require.

If the sponsors are to formulate goals for the organization and instruct the staff to perform them, the sponsors must act with essentially a single voice. This requires a decision among possibly conflicting interests within the group—a matter of group decision making, which will be explicitly discussed later. On the other side, the recipients need not deal with the organization as a unit, and seldom do. The general principles of transactions and communications apply between the organization and recipients, but no special ones. Hence, we will not discuss relations among sponsors or recipients as part of the problem of organization, though they may engage in competition, coalitions, mayhem, or other assorted strategies.

By contrast, the real core of the "problem of organization" occurs within the staff group. In a large unit the staff consists of sets, subsets, and sub-subsets of organizations, seemingly without end. Some are formally established and recognized in the organization chart; many are relatively spontaneous and unrehearsed, making up the so-called "informal organization." As noted, the term "staff" in present usage refers to the collection of persons who do the organization's work, and has no implication whatsoever that they serve in a "staff" as contrasted to a "line" relationship in traditional usage. The nature and uses of line and staff relationships have been widely analyzed for many years, and will be discussed below.

Organization in the present model consists basically of joint production and transactions. But in the myriad interrelations within the continuing large organization we find transactions about joint production, communications about joint production, communications about transactions, and transactions about communications (not to mention joint production of communications about transactions, or of transactions about communications)—not only between large units within the organization but within and between individuals and suborganizations, formal and informal. It is not possible to trace all of these in detail, but we will spend four chapters trying to sort out the main ingredients. We will then have completed discussion of the four main components of the social analysis—communications, decisions, transactions, and organizations. The major emphasis will be on the location of power in all these relations, rather than on techniques of accomplishing them. The remainder of the volume will deal with the whole of society viewed as a single organization, again in a framework of communications, decisions, transactions, and organizations, and again with emphasis on the location of power.

SPONSOR-RECIPIENT RELATIONS

Since the allocation of costs and value between sponsors and recipients is the basis of the present classification system, we will examine those relationships first. The cooperative will not be discussed in this respect. The sponsors and recipients are the same persons, and the interpersonal problems revolve around group decisions, not transactions, the former to be investigated at a later point.

For the same reason that it is easier to analyze selfish transactions before generous and interconnected ones, we will analyze profit organizations before service and pressure ones.

Profit Organizations: Firms

The sponsors of a profit firm are those who hope to benefit from the profit, and who control the residual contribution. In the individual enterprise, the enterpriser is the sponsor, as are the partners in a partnership. Sponsorship in corporations originally lay with the joint stockholders. According to legal conceptualizations, sponsorship still rests with the stockholders, who, through an elected board of directors, supposedly determine residual contributions by adding to or withdrawing from the corporation's capital.[2] In many large corporations it seems more likely that this control now lies in a more or less self-perpetuating group of top officers and board members, and may be difficult to locate in any particular corporation.

The recipients are the customers who buy the firm's goods. Between the sponsors and the customers are the staff who produce and sell the goods. As we shall see, the task of getting the staff to do what the sponsors want is sometimes formidable, and failure to keep the staff in line often distorts the goals of the sponsors. Despite this very real problem, the general contours of the sponsor-recipient relation are clear, and can be diagnosed without explicit regard to staff.

Ubiquitous and taken for granted as they are in Twentieth Century Western civilization, profit organizations are by no means common to all cultures or ages of man. They are largely absent from hunting and fishing, pastoral, and primitive agricultural societies, including the American Indians, Eskimos, and the tribal societies of the South Seas, Australia, Africa, Latin America, and the Far East. Although common in Greek, Roman, and other early Mediterranean civilizations, they diminished markedly during the Middle Ages, except for some traders, bankers, and a few craftsmen organized into guilds—though many of the early national governments were more nearly profit than cooperative organizations. The high importance of profit organizations in Western civilization got its impetus from about the time of the Renaissance.

Bargaining power as between firm and customer, like bargaining power in any other transaction, depends on the EP's of the two parties. We will speak in the context of a money economy, so that values can be expressed conveniently. To look first at the EP of the customer, the "preference" aspect is the intensity of the customer's want for the firm's good relative to his want for other goods, and the "effective" aspect is his purchasing power. If there is to be a transaction, the customer must have enough money to meet the seller's minimum price (the effective aspect)

---

[2] The terms sponsorship and residual contributions are those of the present analysis, not the law. The latter uses such terms as ownership, control, and property rights. A fuller translation will appear in a later chapter, where property rights will be expressed as rules of transactions.

and be willing to give it for the good (the preference aspect). Effective Preference is the equivalent in the individual of effective demand of the group in economic analysis; the latter includes both desire and purchasing power to make it it effective.

Where and why a person comes to have a particular want is essentially unexplainable, beyond some general principles outlined earlier in connection with motives, concepts, culture, personality, and decision. However, the customer is the person who receives the ultimate utility value from a good, since it has only income-earning instrumental value to the persons who produce and sell it. As the person who receives the value, the customer reflects the traits of values as outlined in Chapter 15. His desire for a good will be greater if it is complementary than if it is not—if he already possesses the thing it complements. Not to have gasoline or film means to forfeit use of the car or camera. Replacement parts for large pieces of equipment show high complementarity, and the customer may, if he has the money, pay a high price for such items. If the transaction is unique, as when there is only one supplier of replacement parts, the bargaining power of the seller is extremely high.

By contrast, where the customer has many other substitutable goods which would give him about the same amount of satisfaction, his EP for one good does not extend beyond that for others, and the seller cannot bargain him far above the price of the substitutes. The most perfect substitute is another seller of identical goods, and if the buyer is reasonably alert he will not pay any one seller more than the price charged by other sellers, assuming reasonable equality of such other factors as convenience, dependability, and credit facilities. Perfect substitutes would normally be found either in different sellers of the same brand of merchandise, or different sellers of homogeneous commodities, like granulated sugar. As identical products taper off into highly similar products, moderately similar products, and so on, the less is the customer's EP precisely determined by alternatives, and the greater is the room for the seller to bargain.

The distinction between absolute and relative wants may also affect bargaining power. The more nearly absolute the want, the easier it is for the buyer to know what he wants and how much he wants it. The greater its relativity, the greater is the opportunity of the seller to manipulate the customer's wants. The variety of techniques for doing these things is far greater than we can discuss here, and covers virtually the whole scope of advertising, merchandising, and salesmanship. The seller may bargain with individual customers over price. Or he may apply his selling techniques to the whole group of potential customers to raise their desire as high as possible, and then charge the same price to all. Bargaining with the individual customer then consists solely of trying to get him to buy.

Faced with a given income, the customer's job of spending is largely that of formulating a net preference ordering among various goods. This is a highly subjective task, and easily influenced by suggestions, attention cues, and the other paraphernalia of sales technique. In this area perhaps the main defense of the consumer against any one seller is the competition from other sellers using similar techniques.

Compared to that of the customer, the firm's EP is highly objective. Making its profit by selling things for more than they cost, the firm knows that any selling price above cost will bring a profit, and any price below it will bring a loss. Thus in bargaining with customers the firm has its costs of production as the reservation price below which it will not go. The reservation price thus determines the firm's EP.

Although the firm's reservation price is thus almost certainly more clearly definable than the customer's, it is subject to all the discussion of Chapters 15 and 16 about the nature of costs. This includes the General Rule of decisions, and the irrelevance of sunk costs. This leads us into some economic generalizations about time ranges of costs, and the firm's bargaining power in different time periods.

Over the long run, a firm can go into business or out of it, and it can expand or contract its productive facilities. It can make or not make investments, or it can disinvest. For the long run, the firm can view itself as standing at the bottom of the cost pyramid, with no costs yet expended, and the selling price of the product as the value to be achieved at the top. From this position the firm will not go into or remain in business unless the prospective value received covers total costs: investment, fixed costs of maintaining the investment, and variable costs. Once the firm has made the investment of acquiring plants and equipment, however, the fixed costs of these things are actually or contractually sunk. From that step of the pyramid the firm will improve its position if it produces any unit which it can sell for more than the variable cost, which is that portion of cost not yet expended. Once *all* costs have been spent and the product is already completed, *no* costs remain in the future. The firm will now gain if it sells the product for any price in excess of those costs still remaining—namely, any price greater than zero.[3]

Since every product at the point of sale already has all its costs expended, and none still ahead (except transaction costs), why, if this rule is valid, do not all things sell at or near zero?

First, although the seller will be better off to take any positive sum, however small, rather than leave a finished good unsold, he nevertheless will try to get as much as he can. To sell the good to one customer at a very low price incurs the opportunity cost that he cannot sell it to another customer who might pay a higher price. Competition among customers, or demand, may thus make it possible to get a higher price.

---

[3] For simplicity I have used the traditional economic analysis here, which uses a highly oversimplified cost pyramid, having only the bottom, first step, and top. Any real firm of respectable complexity has many steps to its cost pyramid. Varying write-off periods for different pieces of equipment reflect various degrees of fixity or variability of costs, and materials in different stages of processing also represent successive steps of the pyramid. The two-step analysis of economics is useful to introduce a line of thinking, but not to formulate an actual price list, or to predict one.

Second, the materials of some goods may have scrap value. The alternative of selling it for scrap is still in the future, being a partial recovery of sunk costs, and hence relevant. To sell a product to a customer for next to nothing thus incurs the still-future opportunity cost of losing its sale as scrap. Scrap value thus sets the minimum price the seller will accept.

Third, if the seller expects to stay in business, he will have to keep his stock replenished. If it will cost him $10 to replace an item, that $10 is still in the future at the moment of sale, and relevant. Except for minor modifications to simplify bookkeeping, so long as a type of good continues to sell, and will have to be replaced when sold, a firm will not rationally sell any unit for less than the cost of replacing it. Under the General Rule of decisions, this is the main factor which keeps the day to day price of finished goods high enough to cover their costs.

By contrast, witness a discontinued item which will not be replaced after it is sold. If the consumer demand for it is not great enough to cover its cost to the firm, the firm will be willing to cut the price further and further until it *does* sell. If the product is perishable, like fresh strawberries, the seller's bargaining position is very poor as he approaches the end of his selling day, and he may almost give his merchandise away.

A fourth factor is the intertransactional relation between a present sale and future sales, known as "spoiling the market." If the customers for strawberries learn that the price becomes ridiculously low at the end of the day, they may deliberately wait, and the seller will lose sales at regular prices. To sell some durable merchandise at distress prices may lead buyers to expect lower prices in general, and they may hold off regular buying. A seller may therefore refuse distressed sales desirable in themselves, for fear they will haunt his future. If the seller, however, can avoid spoiling the market he may unload distressed goods at the low prices. He might "dump" it abroad, change the label, describe it as shopworn, or move it to an area associated in people's minds with inferior merchandise.

A customer can usually find some firm which will produce anything whose costs he is willing to pay. However, if the firm is to produce goods no one has ordered, in the hope that someone will buy, it must make sure there exist customers with sufficient EP to cover the costs of production. If some firm were to produce mink-lined violins, steel-bristled toothbrushes, or chocolate-coated sardines, no customers would pay the costs, and the firm would stop producing.

Despite these complexities, the majority of firms probably have a rather definite idea, objectively determined, of the price below which they will not sell. By contrast the consumer faces a far more subjective decision, and on the average is more manipulable by the strategies and tactics of the firm. The typical consumer further has no specialized training in dealing with salesmen, whereas salesmen often have specialized training for dealing with consumers. Through advertising the firm can partly mold consumer wants, but the consumer has no comparable reciprocal device. Further, when items are complex, as are many household appliances, the consumer has little ability to judge their quality or probable durability. Often even the characteristics of less complex things are difficult to tell when bought, like the color-fastness or laundering characteristics of a dress or shirt, or the quality of construction of shoes.

Where the customer is another firm, as in the selling of machinery and materials, the bargaining factors are more equalized. Here the buyer also has specialists for determining the quality of what he is buying, and relatively objective standards for determining what he wants.

In dealing with the ultimate consumer, however, the firm has the bargaining advantage in numerous ways, though some customers can be highly demanding and get away with it. In particular the position of the firm is more objectively known, more rationally determined, and more skillfully defended. Even though consumers may eventually acquire more information about products, as through consumer testing services, or government protection in accuracy of labeling or advertising, this basic difference seems likely to continue. Lacking objective criteria of what is wanted, the consumer position tends to be more subject to manipulation by the seller.

There nevertheless are numerous situations in which the customer may have the bargaining advantage. Because people often shop around for large and expensive items, the prospective customer for an automobile, for example, may have a clear idea of the maximum price he will offer any one dealer, based on the price available from other dealers. At times, and particularly when a new model is to appear shortly, the dealer may have only a hazy notion of his most advantageous reservation price. At that point nearly all his costs of a given car are already sunk, and he may be better off to sell the car for less than he paid for it than to take a chance on receiving a still lower price later. For somewhat the same reasons that a firm's performance may be difficult to evaluate (as we will see in a later chapter), its costs may not be so precisely determinable as the preceding paragraphs suggest. When and to the extent that this is the case, the customer may have leeway to manipulate the EP of the seller.

Profit Organizations: Crime

Crime in Positive, but Illegal, Goods. When two or more criminals join, they constitute a criminal organization. Criminal organizations fall into two main groups: those which deal solely in transactions of positive but prohibited goods, and those which use negative goods in transactions. In the United States we can illustrate the first with the bootlegging of alcohol, traffic in narcotics, and prostitution. An organization which offers to provide these things is a firm, as defined, since it sells goods for more than they cost. Although organizations providing these goods have been legal at many times and places, their distinctive feature in the United States at the present time is that they are illegal.

We shall not examine why, whether, or to what degree it is socially desirable to outlaw these goods, but will merely discuss the effect of the illegality on the sponsor-recipient relation.

The obvious effect of illegality is to increase costs of production. To operate an illegal distillery requires all the normal equipment. In addition, illegality frequently brings such costs as extensive camouflage, remote location, surreptitious transportation, confiscation of equipment, jerry-built construction, off-beat communication techniques, and payoffs to maintain secrecy. Aside from the tax, there is little doubt that legal distilleries could promptly drive out illegal ones in open competition, since unaged grain alcohol is produced and sold legally for about a dollar a gallon, or fifty cents per gallon of hundred proof beverage alcohol.

To some extent illegality incurs higher wage costs to compensate for higher physical and legal risks, and for certain losses of status, and of freedom to move later into the world of legal business. However, once a person has been definitely aligned with illegal operations this loss of status is a sunk cost, and he loses his bargaining power to be compensated for it. A person in illegal operations also opens himself to possible blackmail, though with reasonable diligence he may garner enough counterthreats to defend himself.

Illegality also brings certain added costs (or lessened utility) at the consumer level. The customer for legal whisky has high assurance that the bottle contains what the label says, which can hardly be said for the illegal product. While recourse against misrepresentation is difficult enough to get for legal products, it is virtually impossible for illegal ones. Depending on the channels of distribution, the customer may also find illegal buying less convenient, and open himself to risks of being caught in a raid, or of having to appear as witness in a trial.

Higher costs of production and lesser protection to the consumer seem to apply to the narcotics trade and prostitution as well. As with alcohol, all the costs of legal production are present, plus the extra costs associated with illegality. To make prostitution illegal also virtually eliminates the possibility of maintaining health and sanitation, since no one has yet found satisfactory techniques by which a government can regulate an industry through one bureau while simultaneously trying to eliminate it through another. Nor is there much likelihood that conditions approaching perfect competition will appear in illegal industries, thus allowing monopoly costs as well. Whether these increased costs to consumers bring greater income to the producers is problematic, considering their higher costs of operation. Precisely how illegality affects the bargaining relation between a particular seller and a particular customer depends greatly on the individual circumstances.

Crime in Negative Goods. If the above types of illegal business successfully evade detection, nothing about them requires violence or threats. By contrast, the second type of criminal activity does use violence to enable the criminal to get much for little. Armed robbery is an obvious instance, along with murders, mysterious disappearances, blackmail, kidnapping, and rape. Unlike the situation in bootlegging, dope traffic, and prostitution, in which the recipients gain from voluntarily giving up one thing for something they value more, under the use of violence the recipient is clearly worse off than before, and often gives up much for little or nothing he did not possess before. The bargaining power in such circumstances follows the analysis of negative power in Chapter 18.

There are almost all conceivable degrees of difference between the purely voluntary transaction and those involving abject helplessness. The racketeer may threaten violence to get protection money from a small business, but give certain monopoly privileges in return which seem worth their cost. The racketeer labor leader may receive valuable "gifts" from an employer, in return for signing a "soft" contract on wages. Another racketeer may be paid to assure that acid will not be spilled on the clothing manufacturer's merchandise, and the tavern owner may "tip" the juke box service man to keep the machine in "good working order."

The power relations keep rackets focused largely on small businesses, many of which operate on a narrow margin under intense competition. If several truckloads of his merchandise "happen" to burn and inconvenience important customers, or if his plate glass window "happens" to break several times a year, the small businessman may find it easier to "protect" himself than to fight these things, particularly if the police show faulty vision for the racketeers. If the recipient is an individual enterpriser, there is no sharp division between his personal money and business money, and he can make payoffs directly from his pocket or cash register.

By contrast, the amount of merchandise or other property a racketeer would have to destroy before seriously hurting a large corporation is beyond his fondest dreams. Further, payments from a corporation do not come out of a pocket or cash register without having to clear a battery of accounting hurdles. The corporation may also have its own police, and it certainly has access to private ones. Unlike some small businessmen, corporate executives can utilize these police with little likelihood of physical retaliation for doing so.

As in positive power, the racketeer must have sufficient EP to bargain what he wants from his victim. This means not only the desire for what the victim can provide, but the effective means of meeting the victim's EP. The racketeer can provide enough destruction or sufficiently effective threat to meet the EP of the tavern owner or small clothing manufacturer. But he cannot provide enough to meet the EP of the large corporation. If there is no meeting of EP's, no transaction follows.

Whether it uses positive or negative goods, or both, the illegal profit organization faces the same decision logic as legal ones. In the long run their total receipts must equal or exceed their total costs, or they will be better off to go out of business. In the short run they will logically be willing to sell at any price above variable costs, and once all costs have been incurred they are better off to sell at any positive price rather than not to sell. On the whole, we must presume that they will decide to stay in business so long as values exceed the costs, and will go out of business when costs exceed values. If the law wants to eliminate a certain kind of business, it must therefore make its costs exceed its values. The two obvious prongs of attack are to raise costs or curtail income. If enforcement techniques were sufficiently effective, the costs in fines, lack of freedom, confiscation of assets, and increased cost of operation would bring the decision to discontinue. But if the chances of getting caught are low, those costs multiplied by their probability are not sufficient to terminate the business.

Reducing the income of the organization can take either of two main forms. One is to reduce the patronage by making contacts with customers difficult—as by eliminating the use of public wire services for gambling operations. The second is to establish legal competition on terms the illegal organization cannot meet. This is the approach to the narcotics trade used in England, where the government makes narcotics available at a price so low no criminal can compete.

The approach through decision factors can also be applied to the recipients. The social disapproval of alcohol is typically expressed by putting high taxes on it. In the United States the tax amounts to half or more of the retail price, and discourages its use. The costs of other disapproved aspects, like driving while intoxicated, are raised by fine and imprisonment. Increasing the cost is closely related to the punitive approach to disapproved behavior, and perhaps coincides with it if the analysis is carried far enough. The other approach is to decrease the value of disapproved goods to the recipient, and is related to the remedial approach. Here the disapproved good is made less rewarding. Making persons aware of the disapproval may itself have some effect in this direction. In the case of drug and alcohol addicts, the reduction in value may be accomplished by reducing the desire, as by altering the psychological states which led to addiction, or by reconditioning the person to do without. Other such actions can similarly be interpreted as remedial, as in reducing the desire of juvenile delinquents to steal or destroy property by building a system of alternative satisfactions in approved recreation and constructive activities.

Service Organizations

The service organization is the organizational equivalent of the unilaterally generous transaction. It incurs costs for the benefit of others, while expecting no payment, or only partial payment, in return. Whereas some persons might anticipate that power analysis does not apply to generous transactions, we have seen in Chapter 18 that it does.

Service organizations, like others, differ tremendously in size, duration, and scope, and may range from several families arranging a Christmas basket for a hard-hit neighbor to the Red Cross or the Ford Foundation. The assistance they render may be direct, as when a charity pays the rent for a destitute widow, or diffuse, as when a church seeks to improve the moral environment of youth by curtailing indecent literature. We will concentrate attention here on a private charity giving direct aid to specific recipients. The sponsors will be construed to include those who give time, effort, or money to the charity, and who, by selecting cases or formulating rules, determine who shall receive aid. We will use the bargaining power analysis of generous transactions, A being the sponsor(s), B the recipient(s), AX the sponsors' desire to keep their time or money, and BX the recipient's desire to receive help, which for illustration will take the form of money.

To recall the factors in the unilateral generous transaction, AX and BX have the same initial effect in generous as in selfish bargains, increasing A's bargaining power. But in the generous transaction A *wants* B to have X, and we must deal with the *net* value of AX, which is the original AX (A's desire to keep what he has) minus A's desire that B have X. The result of this relationship is that a high BX increases A's bargaining power in a direct sense. But it may reduce the net AX indirectly through an essentially sympathetic response, or because A sees B's receipt of X as instrumental to a better society, or to some other goal which A holds.

To start with the original (or gross) AX, the larger A's income the lower will be AX, and the easier will it be to get charitable contributions from A. If the A's are wives who have maids, they will also be more willing and able to contribute time. The bargaining power of the recipients thus varies directly with the incomes of the sponsors, and is enhanced by the tax deductible status of charitable contributions.

Several broad attitudes also affect power. A culture or religion which condemns selfishness or preaches that hellfire awaits the stingy helps the bargaining power of recipients. Oppositely, a belief in rugged self-reliance, or a conviction that charity degrades recipients and weakens society, increases the gross value of AX. Many a man has minimized his contributions by voicing the latter sentiments.

Giving time or money carries prestige in some subcultures, where not to have one's contribution publicized would be highly punishing, and doing charitable work is the easiest way to get one's picture on the society page. Charitable work may be partly rewarding in itself, in new experience, companionship, or release from routine. Such factors increase the power of the recipients. They are offset, of course, where giving is anonymous, or the work is dull and demanding.

The factors favorable to recipients would not bring assistance, however, unless the sponsors wanted them to have it. Such desires can originate from numerous sources. Generalized sympathy is one. Personal contact with deserving cases is another, and in organized campaigns dramatic cases are publicized to create a feeling of personal involvement. As with other aspirations the goal must be big enough to seem worthwhile, but not so big as to seem hopeless. Along these lines, sponsors may give generously if 1 per cent of the population needs help, but be reticent about giving at all if 50 per cent need it. For related reasons charitable drives publicize mainly the hopeful, successful cases. Expressions of appreciation from recipients are also feedbacks of success, and reinforce giving.

The interaction of BX on AX in the generous transaction sometimes creates interesting outcomes. In gross terms, a low BX raises B's bargaining power, and enables him to get more. In the generous transaction a low BX means a small desire for the charity's help. In the simplest generous transaction, A wants B to have X because B wants it, and the more B wants it the more satisfaction will A get from giving it. Sometimes in charity the sponsor wants the recipient to have help, but the recipient does not want it, perhaps because he feels a stigma is attached. A low BX of this sort might considerably strengthen B's position, because the sponsors feel that if they can show B a really worthwhile gain he will accept. A reluctant recipient may get more than the one who wants help. Sponsors, in fact, sometimes become quite frustrated when the recipients do not seem to want what the sponsors think they ought to want (which often turn out to be middle class standards), and the sponsors then incur extra expense to make them want it. "The damned wantlessness of the poor" which Lassalle complained about is sometimes the complaint of the charity, and can raise the bargaining power of recipients if they have the wit and will to use it.

Other recipients know the bargaining power of appearing to need, and utilize the tactic of seeming to be more in need than they really are. In addition to tactical misrepresentations, some recipients use negative power. By appearing appropriately miserable at selected times and places they can destroy one's calm of conscience. They can also destroy satisfaction through nuisance value. Either type of negative power can sometimes bring large concessions, though the tactic may backfire if suspected.

To illustrate the effect of a low BX in another type of service organization, the scientist who really wants a research foundation grant may get less than one who has to be coaxed to take it.

In a wider scope, the leader of a great social reform faces some problems similar to those of the charity in enlisting co-sponsors of his movement. He must dramatize the need, and make his potential followers *want* the world to receive their program. He must predict success, even if hard to win and long delayed, while he pictures the gratitude of unborn thousands for the sponsors' vision and sacrifice. Through praise, lieutenancies, and medals he must also provide present rewards to supplement the visions of distant success.

Finally, the power of alternatives, or competition, is the same in service organizations as elsewhere. If a recipient is eligible for help through two or more organizations, his minimum power with one depends on his best alternative. The Red Cross may be told "Why, the Salvation Army will do better than that!" And the foundation may hear, "Why should I come to you when the Ford Foundation will give me a hundred thousand?" In reverse, the power of sponsors to give to the most worthy is enhanced by competition among recipients, where many applicants increase the likelihood that a scholarship or other offering will be given to a person who will benefit greatly from it.

To this we may add a disclaimer: society need consider generous behavior no less worthy by virtue of its being amenable to power analysis.

Pressure Organizations

The fourth possible allocation of costs and values is that the sponsors bear the costs, while the organization has certain effects on recipients which are nevertheless designed to benefit the sponsors. This is the relation in a pressure organization.

Virtually all organizations of significant size engage in transactions outside themselves. In doing so they may apply strategy or tactics to the other party to improve their position against him. Because of the complex interrelations among parties and transactions, organization A may also find it useful to influence B's position through some third party. This third party might be a pressure organization, P, sponsored by A to influence B. Or this third party might be C, who already has existing or potential relations with B, and A may operate on C to change his relations with B in a way favorable to A in the A-B relation. Any such action may be designated third party strategy, roundabout strategy, or pressure. If A attempts to influence the B-C relation only by operating on B, we will include this under the heading of direct strategy, and not discuss it here.

Much greater degrees of roundaboutness may be used. A might operate on C through D, or still more remote parties. Or A might use P for any or all of these relations instead of acting himself. For purposes of analysis we will examine P operating on recipient C for the benefit of A in the A-B relation. P may be a suborganization within A, like a public relations or lobbying division, or a separate organization like a labor union or the Chamber of Commerce. Such a relation is not a coalition with C against B (except by accident), since P normally has no transactions with B on P's own account. Although P is a single organization, its sponsor(s) may be one or many persons or organizations, and so may its recipient(s). In an antitrust contest between the electrical manufacturing industry and the government, if P is a lobby, A might be one company or the whole industry, using the lobby to influence the government's action toward one company or toward the whole industry. At a different stage of the antitrust case, if the main relation is between electrical companies (A) and their private customers (B), A might use the lobby (P) to influence the government (C) to formulate a policy for settling the A-B dispute.

Such relationships are common. A lobby in support of minimum wage legislation is a simple case, where the workers use their union (P) to influence Congress (C) to pass legislation which requires employers (B) to pay higher wages to workers (A). The pressure organization may seek to control the *terms* of the A-B relation directly, as does minimum wage legislation. Or it may seek to influence the *bargaining process*, as when the National Association of Manufacturers asks the Congress to outlaw secondary boycotts by unions. If students (A) enlist the help of the alumni association (P) to get the college cafeteria (B) to reduce its prices, the pressure organization operates on *terms*. If students get the alumni association to strengthen the student council for better bargaining with the cafeteria manager, it operates on the *bargaining process*. In both cases the cafeteria administration would be the recipient of the alumni action.

The influence of P on C can take place through a transaction, a communication, or both. The secretary of the alumni association may approach the president of the college as follows. "We have been discouraged in our efforts to recruit new students for the college because of persistent complaints over the prices in the cafeteria. If you could manage to bring the prices down about a third, I think our people would be willing to work harder in the recruiting campaign next year." This is a proffered transaction, in which the alumni offer more support for the college in return for lower cafeteria prices. Bargaining power is determined by the usual factors: the intensity of the alumni's desire for lower prices, and of the college president's desire for alumni support, along with the desire of each party to keep what it has. The roundaboutness is seen in the fact that the parties to the basic transaction are the students and the manager of the cafeteria. The reserved language of the alumni secretary in part reflects the ritual of our culture regarding certain kinds of transactions, as well as the possibility that he cannot yet commit his members. At the end of the discussion the college president may say: "Good! I'll do what I can to get the cafeteria manager to reduce his prices, and you see if you can swing the alumni into a stronger campaign next spring." In this sentence the conjunction which connects the thing given with the thing received is "and." This is a ritual switch in syntax prescribed by our culture, the more accurate transactional conjunction being "if." Certainly each side sees his own action as contingent on that of the other. Each will feel definitely let down if the other does not perform as indicated, and if either *is* let down he will want more explicit assurances of performance before making further agreements. Like much everyday courtesy, the politeness of phrasing hides the power relationship—a matter of importance we will deal with later.

The alumni visit also shows components of moral and intellectual power. Even if neither party agrees to *do* anything, the secretary has informed the president that cafeteria prices impede recruiting, and has perhaps motivated him to act. By communicating information, motivation, or both, the alumni may exercise power. The college may ultimately benefit from this and other alumni actions. Within the limits of the illustration, however, it is the students, not the alumni, who sponsor and benefit from the alumni pressure.

In the United States there are 100,000 or more organizations which regularly or in special circumstances may exert pressure.[4] The actions of many are directed at the government as recipient, some relatively directly through visits to congressmen or testimony before legislative committees, and some very indirectly by trying to mold public opinion to accept or demand certain legislation. The role of pressure organizations in the whole nation will be examined in later chapters; the present discussion is merely to describe their nature and power components. As with all interpersonal relations, the power of pressure organizations is exercised through (1) transactions and (2) communications of information and motives. These two power forces show no distinctive traits when used by pressure groups, and discussions of them elsewhere will suffice.

---

[4] John P. Roche and Murray S. Stedman, Jr., *The Dynamics of Democratic Government* (New York: McGraw-Hill Book Co., Inc., 1954), p. 66.

Chapter 23

EVALUATING ORGANIZATIONS: THE SPONSOR-STAFF RELATION

THE ORGANIZATION has goals of its own, distinct from those of its staff. The staff may be pleased with their personal relationships with and within the organization, including their pay, which means that their personal goals relative to the organization are being satisfactorily met. But to meet the goals of the staff is by no means the same as meeting the goals of the sponsors, which are the goals of the whole organization as a unit.[1] In making decisions about the organization the sponsors must specify goals to the staff, and give at least a general outline of the methods to be used to accomplish them. To make and effectuate decisions covers the first three stages of adaptive behavior, which constitute the performance half of the adaptive process. The adaptive half includes an evaluation of the performance from feedback and modification of behavior on the basis of the evaluation. If the organization is to adapt successfully, it cannot avoid the evaluative stage, which means it must examine performance on occasion to determine whether it is satisfactory.

If anything less than perfect performance is found at the step 5 evaluation, it is necessary for accurate adaptation to discover whether the difficulty lay in the stimulus identification at step 1, the response selection at step 2, or the performance at step 3. The distinctive feature of evaluating organizations is that the decision is often made at step 2 by one person or group and performed at step 3 by another. When sponsors evaluate the whole organization, they must therefore separate the effects of their own decisions from the effects of the effectuation by the staff. The sponsors

---

[1] We shall see later that persons within the staff sometimes get control of the organization and operate it in their own interest, at which point one might be inclined to say that the staff has taken control away from the sponsors. To keep the concepts straight, we will note that the sponsors were defined as those "whose desires originate and/or continue the organization's existence." Under this definition it is logically impossible to "take control away from the sponsors," since whoever holds the control and directs the organization toward his own goals *is* a sponsor. The appropriate phraseology is thus to say that the staff take over the sponsorship.

thus evaluate themselves and the staff simultaneously, while also evaluating the desirability of the organization as a totality.[2]

At this introductory level we cannot detail how these things are done, any more than we could detail the techniques of making actual decisions in earlier chapters. We will, however, try to delineate some of the special problems of evaluation in the four main types of organizations.

Despite some complexities to be seen later, evaluating an organization has two simplifying elements not faced in evaluating individual behavior. First, except for government and the family, which we will not discuss until later chapters, any one organization has only one goal or a limited range of goals, whereas the individual may have hundreds of goals. As was clear from the discussion of decisions, it is far easier to determine whether one goal has been reached satisfactorily than some combination of a score or a hundred. Second, it is at least theoretically possible to draw up a balance sheet of *all* costs and *all* values of an organization, and to contract or terminate the organization if costs exceed values, or to expand it if the reverse is true. With the individual, the desire for life so dwarfs all other desires that the question of deliberate liquidation does not often arise, and there is no individual equivalent for the organization's "contracting" or "expanding." The organization thus faces a narrower scope of things to evaluate, and a wider scope of basic quantitative responses. Among organizations, only families and governments normally have a potentially limitless scope of goals, which is a reason they are treated separately below.

We shall discuss evaluation of independent organizations only. In a business firm this means the whole company, not a department or a subsidiary. An independent organization is a unit which can expand, contract, or disband on its own, not on orders from higher authority. To illustrate, a local union of the United Automobile Workers can vote itself out of existence, but the research division of the same union cannot.

An evaluation is a decision process, and uses the same main ingredients —costs, values, and a comparison of the two. We will examine a few of the main traits of evaluations in the four kinds of organizations already discussed.

THE PROFIT ORGANIZATION

At first glance, evaluating a business firm seems simplicity itself. According to the economic model of the firm (which many laymen accept to a larger degree than they know), all costs are paid and all incomes are received in money. In the model we thus have a single dimensional, quan-

---

[2] Because the main relation of staff to sponsors is to receive instructions on major policy and report back results, the process of evaluation is inextricably tied to the sponsor-staff relation. This is why the evaluation of the organization and the sponsor-staff relation are joined in the present discussion. The transactions and communications between sponsors and the top levels of the staff are not essentially different from those between upper and lower levels of staff, and will be treated as part of the within-staff problems in later chapters.

titatively expressible measure of costs and values. We subtract expenditures from income, and the remainder is (in the model) an infallible index of the organization's performance.

Two important comments are in order. First, it is true that in general the business firm is the most easily evaluated type of organization. No other type even approaches it for the single dimensionality and quantifiability of its success criterion. Further, businesses keep detailed records of receipts and disbursements, according to rather strict rules.[3] Second, despite this clear superiority, the evaluation of the firm is far more difficult and subjective than the economic model suggests and the average person believes. Because straightforward money values are so obviously objective, we will not discuss them further, but will deal with some often unsuspected subjectivities in evaluating a firm.

Many firms, especially farms, are individual proprietorships, in which there is no sharp distinction between the finances of the firm and those of the proprietor or his family. The proprietor often does not charge the organization for his own time, land, or investment, and his accounts therefore do not show these costs. The farmer may take $12,000 "profit" out of the farm (excess of cash income over cash expenditures) and think his farm is a profitable business. Yet he might be able to hire himself out as a manager of some other farm for $10,000, and also get $5,000 in rent for his own farm and equipment, in which case he is taking a $3,000 loss by running his own farm *as a business*. This does not mean that he should go to work for someone else, since he may strongly prefer his independence. It does not even mean that he ought to be told that his independence is costing him $3,000 a year, since he may be happier not to know. It does mean, however, that the farm *as an organization* does not reflect all its costs in its books.

When we move to the corporation things become clearer, in that the corporation normally pays for all factors in money, and all appear on the books. If so, does not the profit and loss statement provide in one figure the measure of how well the firm has done? By no means. To understand why not, we can examine the conditions under which the statement *would* be unequivocal. If a firm should come into existence January 1; if the sponsors should put a total of $50,000 into it during the year (whether for investment, fixed costs, or variable costs does not matter); if the firm should liquidate completely on December 31 and return to the sponsors a total of $60,000 from all sources, then we could state unequivocally that the firm had earned $10,000 during the year. The time period could be ten years instead of one. The point is that we can never reduce *all* the firm's costs or income to money terms until all assets have been actually converted into money—which seldom happens to profitable firms. A parallel at the consumer level is that one can never know the *actual* total

---

[3] The fact that all inputs and outputs of the firm can at least be conceived as measurable in money units seems almost undoubtedly the reason why economics was the first of the social sciences to develop a highly systematic analysis.

cost of operating an automobile until he has sold it and included the loss of capital value in its costs.

Any firm which states its profits or losses at any time other than after complete liquidation includes some highly subjective evaluations in its statement, except in the extremely unlikely case of a firm having only variable costs. Not only does a firm take in and put out money, but its assets are continuously changing in composition and value. Buildings and machinery depreciate and become obsolete as well as requiring repair, reconstruction, and improvements. Inventories of raw materials, semi-finished parts, and finished products rise and fall in quantity and in value per unit. These facts give rise to subjective evaluations of the following sort.

A firm purchases a machine for $20,000. Judged by sheer physical durability it might operate for 40 years. Under moderate technological progress it may be obsolete in 10 years, and under rapid progress in 5 years. Disregarding 40 years as unlikely (though many machines that old are still operating), an appropriate write-off period must be selected. Also disregarding taxes, interest, and scrap value, if it is decided that the machine will be good for 10 years, the firm charges itself $2,000 a year for its use. If 5 years seems more appropriate, the company charges itself $4,000 a year. Now although informed guesses are better than uninformed ones, the simple fact is that when the machine is bought nobody knows how long it will last, and what it will be worth when discarded, and the life expectancy chosen for accounting purposes is a guess containing some highly subjective elements. (The accounting department itself may use some objective average for this purpose. But this fact merely pushes the subjectivity back to the persons who decide whether the average ought to be used at all instead of a machine-by-machine actual estimate.) This means that something as simple as a change in the accounting procedures for one machine may change the firm's costs, and hence its profits, by $2,000 a year. It may also be decided that the price of these machines will rise to $30,000 by the time the present one is discarded, and that the company should charge itself replacement cost, not actual cost. In that case the machine would be assumed for accounting purposes to cost $6,000 a year on a 5-year basis.

Suppose that a new highway is built next to a company's plant, and because of improved transportation the value of the property rises by $100,000. If the company were to sell the property, this sum would increase its profit through capital appreciation. Even if the company does not sell, its capital value has nevertheless risen by this amount. Now the company may or may not show this appreciation as a profit, depending on what the people responsible for the accounting procedures *want* to show. If they are under pressure to show profit, the appreciation will show up in the corporation reports as an additional $100,000 of profit—probably undistributed. If they are not, and if they want to build a cushion against hard times, they may keep the value of the property unchanged on the books, and the appreciation will not show. By an amount of $100,000 the size of the company's profit is thus not a matter of fact, but of preference.

The same would be true in reverse if a different change of highway reduced the value. Substantial as it is, the amount of discretionary leeway in cases of this sort is small compared to that in mergers, separations or "spin-offs," major refinancing, sale-and-lease-back, or comprehensive reorganization of subsidiaries. The problem is not that the *figures* on the balance sheet are themselves subjective, but that the process of arriving at them incorporates numerous subjective judgments. The problem is that the firm's assets consist of hundreds and thousands of tangible and intangible items, and that the process of trying to reduce this thousand dimensional set of values to a single dimension of dollars *is* subjective, and often highly so.[4] Needless to say, the procedures are not infinitely flexible, or no firm would ever go bankrupt.

The point is not that financial reports are meaningless, but that they are not the whole meaning, and any sponsor who wants to know how well his firm has done had better know more about it than is expressed in dollars in the financial reports.

Assuming that the sponsor supplements the financial statements enough to have a realistic picture of the amount of profits, does he now know whether the firm has been well or poorly run? No. No matter how thoroughly understood, profit is a statement of the *net value* of the organization's activities for the year, and what is needed for an incisive decision is the *final net value*, defined in Chapter 15 as the net value minus the net value of the best alternatives. Freely translated, the question is not only whether the profit was a positive figure, but whether it was the largest possible figure.

To put it mildly, the problem of determining the maximum is at least "several orders of magnitude more complex"[5] than that of determining a satisfactory level. Economic theory has for years talked glibly of profit maximization, as if this were some sharply definable goal which businessmen work for. But Boulding[6] observes that this quantity which is supposed to be maximized does not really exist, and in the latter part of Chapter 16 it was suggested that maximizing one value in a multidimensional context is an illusory goal. Aside from these rather philosophical difficulties, some highly practical ones appear. One can never know in retrospect whether his decision was the best possible unless he can know what the outcome would have been had he done something else. This is

---

[4] This point is well discussed by Kenneth E. Boulding, *The Skills of the Economist* (Cleveland: Howard Allen, Inc., 1958), chap. 2. Of profit Boulding says: "It would be unkind to call it a figment of the accountant's imagination but it is certainly a product of the accountant's rituals." (p. 56) The accounting procedures also perform a great deal of what will later be referred to as "uncertainty absorption."

[5] James G. March and Herbert A. Simon, *Organizations* (New York: John Wiley & Sons, Inc., 1958), p. 141.

[6] *Op. cit.*, p. 56.

usually not knowable. Would the automobile company have made more money if it had put out compact cars two years sooner? Would the railroad have fared better if it had made a monumental effort to recover passenger traffic instead of discouraging it? How much more would the textile firm have earned if it had concentrated on broadcloth and plaids instead of madras and checks? Only after the sponsors have computed what their firm *could* have earned if it had done everything right can they tell whether they have maximized their potential profit. Economic theory provides discouragingly little guidance in the task.

The market place, however, does provide at least one significant benchmark of successful performance, a comparison with competitors. In a reasonably competitive industry, all firms are free to buy materials, labor, and other factors in the same market; to use manufacturing processes of their own choice; to sell in markets of their own selection; and to use such marketing and merchandising techniques as they deem best. Under these circumstances, the firm with the highest rate of return on its investment[7] is not necessarily doing the best *possible* job under all the circumstances of the case. But it definitely is doing better than anyone else in the field. This is perhaps the best measure actually possible, since in any area of human endeavor, of brain or brawn, we can judge good performance only by comparison with what others have done.

Although the monopoly has greater bargaining power with its customers, and should be more profitable, its sponsors have greater difficulty evaluating the quality of its performance. The transit company or the electric utility usually has no competitors in the same market. The electric company may be earning 8 per cent, and seem to be doing reasonably well. Yet its management might be grossly inefficient, and good management might have earned 30 per cent if the utilities commission would allow, or 8 per cent with much lower prices to consumers. The transit company might be barely breaking even, and seem to be doing poorly. Yet it might have required spectacularly good management just to keep the firm out of bankruptcy. As one writer (whom I cannot now recall) once put it, the monopoly has only technical criteria for evaluating its performance; it can never know whether its total job is good, since there are no comparisons with others doing the same thing under the same circumstances.

Although the business firm comes closer than any other type of organization to having a single dimensional, objective measure of performance, the profit statement is only the beginning, not the end, of the evaluation, which includes numerous other dimensions, some highly subjective. The evaluation is a decision in hindsight, after the feedback is in. If the original decision involved nothing less than an infinite number of variables, then

---

[7] Because it represents the residual contribution, and hence control, the sponsors seek the highest rate of return on the factor they provide, namely invested capital. If workers or landowners were the residual contributors and exercised control, presumably they would seek the highest return per unit of labor or land.

so does the evaluation, which means that all but a few of the most conspicuous factors must be ignored. In part, the process tends to be self-validating. For if the sponsors overlooked some important factor in making the original decision, unless it has been forced to their attention, they may overlook the same factor for the same reason in making the evaluation.

THE COOPERATIVE ORGANIZATION

The thing here called the cooperative organization includes cooperatives in the everyday sense, both producer and consumer, as well as clubs, fraternal organizations, and others seeking to perform a service for their members, at the members' expense. Among these we will discuss consumer cooperatives and clubs.

If a consumer cooperative operates in a competitive economy among profit firms producing the same goods, the sponsors (who are also the recipients) have a reasonably objective rough measure of their organization: does it provide them goods at lower prices than do profit enterprises? If so, the cooperative is worth continuing from the sponsors' point of view.[8]

But like the fact of profit in the business firm, this demonstrates only a positive net value, and gives no indication whether performance is the *best* possible. Also as in profit firms, the computation of the latter is several orders of magnitude more difficult, and we are faced again with the necessity of disregarding all but the few of the most significant variables.

In a wide variety of fraternities and clubs the evaluation may or may not be difficult. The officers must be concerned that the club does not spend more than it takes in, and in this respect they face much the same problem as do sponsors of profit organizations. That is, they must arrange a set of cost transactions in operating the club whose total is equal to or less than the set of income producing transactions with the members. Instead of maximizing the difference between the two sets, however, since the organization is a cooperative they may use any accumulated difference to increase services or reduce fees.

If the members pay their fees in money they are in much the same position as a consumer of other things. They make an outlay in money, and receive goods whose value to them is measured in satisfaction. This comparison cannot be objective in itself. If alternate clubs exist which provide similar services, it is possible to make an objective determination as to which is a "best buy." But it still remains a subjective decision whether even the best is worth buying. If the member pays his costs in

---

[8] It is argued by some profit enterprises that many cooperatives show lower costs only because of tax advantages. If so (and we are not accepting or rejecting the point), this fact might reduce the relative desirability of cooperatives to the whole society; but it in no way reduces their value to their members.

contributions of work or commodities, his costs as well as his receipts
are subjective.

This subjectivity in no way invalidates the decisions, since all costs and
values are ultimately subjective, and in the cooperative these are judged
within the preference system of the same persons. The members can
therefore determine whether the organization is worth its cost *to them*.
If persons can join or leave at will, the mere fact of sufficient continued
membership to maintain the club is evidence of positive net value. If
initial membership fees are large, however, members may not be able to
move to another similar organization without great loss, and continued
membership does not necessarily indicate success during any one period.

All the previous discussions about satisfactory as contrasted to maximum performance apply here with equal force. In addition, competition
does not provide the same incisive measure of a club as of a firm, since
even clubs doing nearly the same thing may have widely divergent goals,
one emphasizing growth, one quality, one vigor, one an easy pace, and
so on.

THE SERVICE ORGANIZATION

Evaluating the service organization is quite a different matter. The
organization is controlled by the sponsors, who also pay its costs. But the
values are received by the recipients, who are a different group. Normally
the charity does not give to the persons who contribute, and the missionary division does not try to convert heathen in the home congrega-
tion. This means that in its most basic relation the costs and values of the
service organization are not measured in the same preference system. Of
the four basic types, the service organization is therefore almost certainly
the most difficult to evaluate.

The service organization gives gifts, and the mere fact that people
continue to accept scholarships, payments of their rent, or turkeys for
Christmas is no indication that their value to the recipients equals or exceeds the cost to the sponsors. In fact, this crucial comparison cannot be
made, since it requires the acknowledgedly impossible interpersonal comparison of utility. The result is that if the sponsors are to evaluate the
service organization they must determine the *value to the sponsors* of the
things done for the recipients, and compare this with the *costs to the
sponsors*. In short, it is not the satisfaction received by the recipients but
the satisfaction received by the sponsors from giving help that becomes
the relevant criterion. This does not mean that satisfaction to recipients
is irrelevant, since their satisfaction may strongly influence the sponsors'
satisfaction. It does mean that only that part of the recipients' preferences
which filters through to the sponsors' preference system affects the organization's policies. This can sometimes be remarkably small. This situation is apparently inescapable. Whatever its merit on other scores, it does
get the decision process on a rational basis, by having values and costs
measured on the same preference scale.

The practical result is that the goals and accomplishment tend to be stated operationally, in relatively objective terms. Instead of the non-objective "We improved the health in the lower East Side," the operational statement is "We reduced new cases of tuberculosis 18 per cent and treated all emergency accident cases not able to pay." Instead of "We brought great happiness to the blind," the operational expression is "We taught 64 persons to read and write braille, and provided 15 seeing-eye dogs."[9]

Many of the main decisions of service organizations consist of establishing categories of persons to receive help, on the general assumption that if help is given only to persons in those categories, its value will exceed its cost. To specify that scholarships should be given only to persons within the top 5 per cent of the class, or financial assistance only to mothers of young children with no source of income, and then to see that assistance goes only to persons meeting the specifications, technically assures the sponsors that each contribution is worthwhile. A major task of the staff in administering the work of the service organization is to classify actual instances as falling or not falling in the categories established by the higher levels in the organization—that is, to make accurate "perceptions" about applicants.

Although operational statements of accomplishments are themselves objective, they are no more the whole story than are the profit statements of a firm, and much subjective judgment is inescapably embodied in the objective-looking statistics of the service organization. Should the little girl who sobbed frustratedly through all the classes be included among those who were "taught" braille? Should the delinquent given psychiatric treatment by the youth center, but who later became a major criminal, be counted as one "helped" by the center? Just as the alert sponsor of the firm needs to know more than the figures in the corporation report, so does the alert sponsor of the service organization need to know more than the statistical report of the agency.

THE PRESSURE ORGANIZATION

In the pressure organization we return to the condition in which costs and values are assessed in the same preference set. The accomplishments may be fairly explicit, as when an industry lobby gets a tariff which permits a 10 per cent rise in prices, or a union lobby gets a 25 per cent increase in the minimum wage. Or the accomplishment may be quite diffuse, in a changed public attitude toward legalized gambling or public sympathy toward church operated schools.

---

[9] March and Simon, *op. cit.*, p. 194, make the point that the goals at the top level of the organization are not operational. This is true for the service organization as for others, the goals of the sponsors being to relieve distress, improve society, and similar nonoperational wordings. It would seem to me at the moment that the relative vagueness of service goals would tend, as a practical matter, to push operational statements further up in the hierarchy than in profit and cooperative organizations, though investigation might reveal the contrary.

A fundamental difficulty in evaluating the pressure organization is that the desired result must be accomplished indirectly through others. If pressure is exerted and those others do as hoped, there is often a question whether they would not have done so even without the pressure. There is also the possibility that the pressure may generate resentment, and produce worse results than without the pressure. No other kind of organization faces quite the same question: to decide whether it might have accomplished more if it had not existed.

A pressure organization's transactions probably have more definitely measurable effects than its communications, as when an oil company lobby agrees to support the election of a congressman if he will oppose federal regulation of pipe lines. Although communications to specific persons may have clearly observable effects, the influence of communications on broader groups is difficult to measure, and the cost of measuring them is often greater than the cost of mistakes. As with the service organization, a frequent device is to use operational criteria: the number of circulars distributed or phone calls made, the number of articles planted in mass magazines, the number of square feet of billboards covered with advertising, or the minutes of spot announcements on TV. Such criteria sometimes encourage waste. If persons who distribute brochures are rewarded on the basis of the number distributed, rather than on their effect, they are likely to send them even to places where the chance of response is small. Although there are measures of effectiveness of certain kinds of communication, they are by no means complete or reliable, and often the sponsors themselves have only the haziest notion whether their efforts are worth their cost.

CONCLUSIONS

Regardless of the type of organization, when the sponsors attempt to evaluate the feedback from the organization's operations they must try to differentiate between the effects of their own decisions and the effects of the staff's performance. We cannot describe here how this is to be done, but can merely indicate that it must be done if the sponsors are to evaluate either the staff or the whole organization. The ability to evaluate the staff is crucial to the sponsors' ability to control the staff, as we shall see in subsequent chapters, and evaluation therefore takes on added importance.

The overall conclusion is that evaluations under most circumstances are quite imprecise, even in business firms which have the relatively single-minded goal of making money, and in which all values are potentially expressible in money. There is much leeway in interpreting the meaning of a profit statement for a given year. We have not even hinted that much thinking and planning for an organization is done in terms of several years, and even several decades. Some of our lumber and paper companies, for example, are planting trees which they do not expect to harvest for another 50 to 80 years. This means that companies are incurring expenses now, and therefore showing lower profits now, as an investment toward improving their position in future years.

All of which brings us to the conclusion that an evaluation of performance during a period just past is not merely a redecision in retrospect about events recorded in pages of the organization's books. It is part of a continuing decision process in which the plans sketched out on the pages ahead are just as important to an evaluation of last year's performance as are the now-closing pages on which that performance is written. This is the fuller meaning of an earlier statement that the performance stage of one decision is in important part the adaptive stage of previous decisions, and that the subsequent adaptive stage of present decisions will merge into the performance stage of later decisions.

This means in turn that, in a continuing organization, evaluative decisions are full-scale decisions. As such, they entail all the decisional dimensions of magnitude, time, quality, and probability, and are subject to all the same complications. For the period just past, some things previously unknown have by now become known. But this is not always the case, for in many respects our ignorance about what *did* happen can be quite as profound as that about what *will* happen.

Chapter 24

STAFF: MODEL OF THE
COMPLEX ORGANIZATION

THE MODEL of the simple organization described in Chapter 21 contained the fundamental ingredients of all organization, joint production of goods, and transactions over inputs and outputs. It also revealed the elemental logic of the employer and employee points of view.

The simple model did not at the outset distinguish major from subsidiary transactions between member and organization—a distinction which was added as we moved from terminable-at-will relations with organizations having only variable costs to not-so-terminable relations where fixed costs and investment are at stake. The initial model included no authority relation, the partners having equal voice. Decisions about production methods were not explicitly included, but the ability of either party to leave (and hence dissolve) the organization at will forces a presumption of mutual agreement on all items, or mutually agreeable division of decisions. Subsequent analysis showed control to lie with the residual contribution, if any, thus laying the base for an authority relationship. As we move to the larger organization, the sponsors are seen to control the residual contribution, and hence to hold the ultimate authority in the organization. The simple model did not include any reference to communications, about either joint production or transactions. Nor did it say anything about motivation, either instrumental or intrinsic.

The two chapters since the simple model was introduced have added ingredients in preparation for studying the larger and more complex organization, and have classified organizations by the relationships of costs and values among sponsors, staff, and recipients. The core of the problem of complex organization lies in the staff. This problem is essentially independent of the basic type of organization, and the next step is to draw a model of the staff, which will serve as the basis of the major analysis of complex organization. Following the established pattern, the present chapter will outline the beginner's model of complex organization. The next two chapters will relax the model and add enough detail for the intermediate kit. The advanced, or professional, model is beyond the scope of this book.

Like the simple one, the complex model hinges on transactions and joint production, but adds detail. One such detail can be described by analogy with the approach to motives in Chapter 6. There it was said that an organism must have separate mechanisms for controlling the amount and the direction of energy release, in parallel with the accelerator and forward-reverse gear of the automobile. Like the person and the machine, the organization, too, must have energizing and directing components. Perhaps the propulsion and guidance systems of the space rocket provide a better analogy for the organization than does the automobile, in that both the rocket and the organization are guided mainly by the controlled release of propulsion energy.

Our interest here is confined to the human aspects of organization, for which the "propulsion" is the motivation of persons to do the organization's work. In the model this is provided through transactions. The staff are motivated to provide inputs of time, effort, thought, and so forth, in exchange for which the organization provides them certain rewards.

If the motivation is provided by transactions, the first step of guidance is to provide rewards for performance directed toward the organization's goals, and unrewards or punishments for performance not so directed. But to hitch energy to a motive is only the first step of an individual's guidance system, the second being to further direct the energy release toward the motivated goal by means of information. The same is true in organization. It is not enough to get the employees to want to work toward the organization's goals. Their efforts must be guided by information about the materials and circumstances with which they deal. In line with the formulation of earlier chapters, the information aspects revolve around concepts, perceptions, and cues.

The overall performance is thus seen to lie in the amount of energy the organization is able to release and in the accuracy with which that energy is directed toward its goals. The amount of energy release (which is closely associated with morale) is effectuated in the model by transactions, and the direction of its release is controlled by both transactions and communications of information. The interrelations of these forces among each other will be reserved for the intermediate model of the next chapters.

TRANSACTION ASPECTS

Goals of the Sponsors

In the model the goals of the sponsors are those of the organization. These may or may not be the same as those formally displayed in the organization's charter, constitution and by-laws, annual reports, or manual of operations. Any formal statements of purpose may, of course, influence the sponsors. And if any such statements are part of the legal or contractual obligations of the organization they act as constraints on the freedom of sponsors to do as they please. But it is the goals, or motives, actually held by the sponsors which control their behavior, and the formal statements have influence only if and to the extent that they enter the motive and concept systems of the sponsors.

By controlling the residual contribution the sponsors hold the master switch in the organization's switching mechanisms. They thereby control not only their own contributions, but also the values created by the organization itself. The excess of the total value created by the organization over that contributed by the sponsors is largest and most evident in the profit firm. Here the costs are paid by the customers, and the sponsors control the disbursement of the entire amount provided by the customers along with controlling their own contribution. With this sum they have the power to hire and reward employees, as well as to acquire advice, materials, or equipment from outside. These things provide the power for the top level control of the employer function.

Having decided upon major goals, the sponsors select top level members of the staff. These may be a board of directors, trustees, president, executive secretary, or others, depending on the organizational structure.[1] The top levels of staff select second levels of staff below them, who select a third level, and so on. The sponsors communicate their statements of goals and broad outlines of implementation to the top levels of staff, under whose direction the whole staff perform the implementation. Thereafter the sponsors evaluate both their own instructions and the staff's performance, as outlined in the preceding chapter. Since the sponsors deal directly only with the top levels of staff, who in turn control the lower levels, the sponsor evaluation is really an evaluation of the top level only. If the staff performance is satisfactory the top officers are rewarded, with praise, prestige, pay, power, renewal of their appointments, or other wanted things, and if it is unsatisfactory opposite things happen. In business firms the pay is often tied through a bonus system to the profit performance. Whatever the techniques, obvious or subtle, the fundamental relation is that the sponsors control the top staff by granting or withholding rewards in proportion as the staff do or do not perform satisfactorily.

Goals of the Staff

At this point we are interested only in the motivational aspects of this relation, in which the energies of the top executives are released by the rewards which lie within the control of the sponsors. The staff may or may not share the goals of the sponsors, and the effect of their holding sponsor goals will be examined later. Members of the staff hold personal

---

[1] We are continuing to use the term "staff" as defined in Chapter 22, to include *all* persons who do the organization's work, whether line or staff according to traditional terminology.

goals, such as for pay, power, companionship, and the satisfaction of accomplishment. These obviously are not the goals of the organization.

The first aspect of this transaction is the major bargain, which is also called the bargain of affiliation, and in layman's language, the employment contract.[2] When a staff member, high or low, accepts employment he agrees to become an instrument for the organization, which means to do as it instructs toward the achievement of *its* goals. The organization agrees to give him in return things that will help him reach *his* goals, principally pay. Since there is no way of knowing precisely what tasks may need to be done over the years, only the general nature of the employee's work can be agreed on in advance. This must be accompanied by an understanding that details of work, and such changes of status as a transfer, reassignment, change of duties, job training, and so on, will be worked out as the relationship continues, along with possible changes in compensation. Depending on their scope and significance these may be thought of as subsidiary bargains under the major bargain, or perhaps as modifications of the major bargain. Even the acceptance of instructions to do specific tasks may be thought of as a bargain, as we will detail below.

Authority and Legitimacy as Relationships of Transactions

The bargain in which the employee agrees to accept future instructions from the sponsors or their agents in return for his compensations is the basis of authority. It is an inescapable ingredient of the major bargain between the employee and any organization above the rather simple level, and is one of its most significant features. We will define *authority* as the ability to grant or withhold rewards for the performance or nonperformance of instructions,[3] and *responsibility* as the position of the person on

---

[2] James G. March and Herbert A. Simon make the distinction between major and subsidiary transactions very sharp in their *Organizations* (New York: John A. Wiley & Sons, Inc., 1958), p. 48.

[3] The general approach to transactions and organizations resembles that of George C. Homans more closely than any other approach I am aware of, in his *Social Behavior, Its Elementary Forms* (New York: Harcourt, Brace and World, Inc., 1961). Although he does not define authority in these words, he notes that "a man's authority finally rests on his ability to reward and punish." (p. 292).

The present definition is based squarely on the concept of the transaction, and seems to include the most significant features of both the traditional and the newer approaches to authority. In the traditional approach, authority was viewed as the superior's right to give orders, along with the idea that the subordinate is under obligation to perform them. The newer, or "Barnard-Simon" approach is effectively described in Chapter 8 of Herbert Simon, Donald Smithburg, and Victor Thompson, *Public Administration* (New York; Alfred A. Knopf, 1950), and the contrast between the two approaches is succinctly described by Albert Rubenstein and Chadwick Haberstroh, *Some Theories of Organization* (Homewood, Ill.: The Dorsey Press, Inc., 1960), p. 171. The newer approach minimizes attention to the rights of the superior and emphasizes the response of the subordinate. In the latter view, authority exists when the subordinate does, in fact, accept and perform the instructions.

In the present model of authority as a transaction, we may identify *A* as the

whom authority is exercised. A person who holds authority thus both gives instructions and controls the flow of rewards. If A exercises authority on B, it is not necessary that the rewards actually flow through A's hands, so long as those rewards will be granted or withheld upon A's instructions.

A long expounded principle of sound organization is that one's authority and his responsibility must coincide—or must be coterminous and coequal. Within the context of the present stage of the model, and subject to substantial modification and reservation when complexities are added later, the reason is easy to see. Suppose A supervises (has authority over) B, who supervises C. B is responsible to A for getting certain work done, which means that his rewards will be withheld by A if he does not perform. But certain of the work for which B is responsible is to be performed by C. If B cannot withhold rewards from C he has no bargaining power to get C to follow *his* instructions. If C were an astute bargainer he might refuse to follow B's instructions unless B gave him part of his salary. Even without this aspect, B will presumably refuse any major bargain in which his rewards are contingent on the performance of other persons over whom he himself cannot exercise authority. Nor will the organization rationally give authority to any person without holding him responsible for its use, for to do so would (1) enable that person to use the resources assigned to him for his own personal use, and/or (2) deny to some other person the authority necessary to meet his responsibility.

The present discussion deals with limited purpose organizations, which a person may or may not join as he sees fit, and we will not deal with the complications arising from involuntary membership, as in the family (involuntary for the children, at least) and the state. In limited purpose organizations of this sort, the individual voluntarily accepts authority as part of the major bargain, or he remains outside the organization and its

---

superior, B the subordinate, X the rewards which A can grant or withhold, and Y the performance by B of A's instructions. To clarify the model we might introduce the notion of *effective authority*, and define it as the condition in which the transaction is completed—that is, in which B gives Y to A in return for X.

"Authority" in the Barnard-Simon approach is apparently the same as "effective authority" as defined above. It might be feasible in the present model to view authority as the EP of the superior for Y, and responsibility as the EP of the subordinate for X. I have not yet carried that phase of the analysis beyond the present suggestion, and it is not explicitly used subsequently in this volume.

The present approach resembles the traditional to the extent that it puts authority back into the hands of the superior alone. It simultaneously incorporates the newer approach by shifting from emphasis on the superior's *right* to get conformance to his *ability* to do so. To pursue this aspect somewhat further, and in line with the initial analysis of Effective Preference, we would say that (among other things) the superior's authority varies directly with the magnitude of the rewards or punishments he holds. Even if these are insufficient to cross the subordinate's threshold, a larger reward leaves less gap to be crossed than a small one, and is closer to bringing performance.

As with other concepts used in this volume, the main justification for the present deviation from accepted usage is to gain maximum unity with the rest of the analysis.

authority. Whenever the authority exercised on an individual conforms to that accepted in the major bargain, the authority is *legitimate*. That is, *legitimate authority* is *accepted authority*, and *legitimacy* is the condition in which authority is accepted as conforming to the major bargain. This does not mean that authority is always explicitly discussed in the major bargain, since it is often so thoroughly understood as not to require discussion.

We can illustrate legitimate authority best by its absence. It may be understood when a secretary is hired that she may be required to type letters, but not to scrub the floor. It may be left indefinite whether she is also expected to deliver emergency mail across town by bus. If she accepts such an instruction, the major bargain is filled in by practice, and her acceptance legitimizes it. But if she responds, "I wasn't hired to deliver mail" she is labeling the instruction as illegitimate, and also implying that her rewards cannot be withheld for refusing it. If her boss insists that she deliver the letter, he is asserting that the order is legitimate, and that her rewards, including all future pay, may be withheld if she refuses.

A clear record of the employment agreement would presumably settle the problem. If no record is available the two may negotiate a compromise—she will deliver letters by taxi but not by bus.[4] The other alternatives are discharge, resignation, or capitulation by either side. The bargaining power follows the usual pattern: the party with the lesser stake in the major transaction has the greater bargaining power in the subsidiary one. Intertransactional influences also arise in the form of precedents, a matter for the next chapter.

The degree and type of authority a person will accept when he joins an organization presumably depend upon much the same bargaining power factors as in any other terms of the relationship: namely, the best available alternatives. An employee may have to accept a highly authoritarian relation if he has little opportunity to work for himself, or if authoritarian relations are common in all other organizations around him. If opportunities for self-employment are good, or if alternate employers have more relaxed relations, then the employee's bargaining power to achieve relaxed relations is good. "More relaxed" or "less authoritarian" means that the scope of unchallengeable orders is narrower, and the scope of "bargainable" ones wider. On a particular job the more relaxed version also gives the employee more latitude to determine his own "program," as that term will be used below.

---

[4] As nearly as I can discern it, standard practice for secretaries is to accept the obligation to deliver letters by bus in order to get the job. The first four times the problem comes up the secretary finds a good reason why the delivery should be made by taxi, and offers to pay the fare herself. (If she cannot think of four good reasons, she is not worth keeping.) By the fifth time either the boss has forgotten that buses exist, or the secretary exclaims indignantly, "I always took taxis before! Why do I all of a sudden have to start riding the crumby bus?" Anyone who does not understand these things will make a miserable supervisor, and had better study bargaining tactics in more detail than is proffered in this book.

JOINT PRODUCTION ASPECTS[5]

Decisions

The transaction aspects of the organization motivate employees, and provide the propulsion and part of the guidance system. We now move to the joint production aspects, in which lies the rest of the guidance system, including most crucial details. All decisions come in sets, subsets, and sub-subsets, seemingly without end. So do the processes of effectuating goals, and any major goal must be broken into subgoals, which must be divided into sub-subgoals, and so on. The tasks must similarly be divided, both among different levels of persons in the hierarchy, and among different groups at any one level.

On the whole there is almost necessarily some division of sets and subsets of decisions along lines parallel to the division of tasks. It is not possible to make complete decision sets at the top level of the organization. The clerk or factory worker must make some decisions himself about carrying out his work, if only about when to refill his fountain pen or whether to cross the factory aisle before or after the materials truck. If the sponsors of a foreign mission decide to convert the Moovians, the board of directors in Kansas City cannot know where are the best spots in Moo for missions. A central director of all Moo missions, located in the country's capital, might make this decision. But the central director cannot decide which of the early converts ought to lead the singing in each of the five districts' evening services. Only the missionary on the spot is well enough informed for that decision.

The amount of discretion allowed at lower levels differs greatly from one organization to another. But since it is simply not possible to decide everything at the top, the large organization necessarily consists of sets and subsets of persons making sets and subsets of decisions for effectuating sets and subsets of tasks.

To return to the transactions for a moment, these sets and subsets of persons are not hired directly by the sponsors. Instead each set is hired in a transaction with the set just above it, with varying degrees of advice and consent from still higher sets. In the present stage of the model, each person gets his instructions from the same superior with whom he

---

[5] In a broad sense the "Joint Production Aspects" of organization in the present framework deal with the kind of materials which were the subject matter of traditional or "classical" organization theory. That phase of organization theory essentially took for granted that everyone wanted to achieve the organization's goals, and dealt mainly with the way in which tasks and decisions were divided and subdivided for efficient operation. In the last several decades attention has shifted markedly toward the "human relations" aspects of organization, and the problems of motivating, consulting, psychoanalyzing, and otherwise attempting to mobilize the desire of the employee to work and cooperate "as a team." This in a rough way is the area covered here under the heading of "Transactions Aspects." The equivalence is only rough, however, and the present model does not correspond closely with either area as it is usually handled.

has made his major bargain. This means that the organizational sets and subsets of transactions correspond to the sets and subsets of decisions, tasks, and persons, and guidance in the form of instructions comes from the same person who motivates through rewards. Although subject to modification in later stages of the model, this coincidence of the sources for motivation and instruction is a central aspect of organizational relations.

Communications

Because many decisions are not performed by the persons who make them, communication is inescapable. Communications in the organization include both information and motivation. We will concentrate for the moment on those information aspects which are essential to meeting the goals of the sponsors. This will be done in the context of the same information model used earlier in the chapters of psychology.

The first half of the communication problem is that of getting instructions from supervisor to supervised, or the so-called downward flow of communication. If the staff member is to receive and perform instructions, he must possess information concepts, performance concepts, or both (usually both), along with knowledge of the cues which allow him to perceive the information or release the performance. In somewhat the same sense that motor concepts can be developed by less complex mental processes than information concepts, performance concepts seem simpler to deal with in organizations, and we shall present them first.

A performance concept is widely known as a *program*. It consists of a series of acts in some sequence which will accomplish a given result. If a chief mechanic is instructed to prepare a 707 for a flight to Bermuda, the program is the series of checks, tune ups, refills, and so on which he performs. A particular employee may learn his main programs from his supervisor, from a fellow employee, from formal training on the job, from experience and experimentation, or from former jobs or education. When an organization hires a trained employee it in effect "hires a program" or set of programs as well as hiring the person.

The process of learning programs falls under the general heading of job training and education, whether the job is as simple as shoveling sand into a bucket or as complex as designing complete equipment for a trip to the moon. We will not deal with job training, or program learning, as such, even though training instructions and performance instructions are much intertwined in practice. In a smoothly functioning organization the programs most regularly used are stored in the heads of employees. Lesser used but important programs may be described in writing, and the file or manual can be pulled out when the occasion requires. Some will also be remembered by older employees who have performed them before. Still less used programs, including most of those required only once, are developed as needed.

In the chapters on psychology we have seen that both performance and information concepts are released by cues. Assuming that the employee already knows a particular performance concept, or program, he will perform it upon receipt of the appropriate cue. At the simplest level the supervisor decides when and whether a program is to be released, and issues the cue to his subordinate. The cue may be verbal, as "Deburr those six pans of castings," or "Give Senator Oxgored a two-column buildup next Tuesday." It can be a flashing light signifying that furnace No. 6 is to be tapped in ten minutes, a siren instructing the volunteers to report to the firehouse, or any other prearranged sign. Assuming that the cue is unmistakable, all discretion whether the program is to be performed is held by the supervisor, the subordinate being responsible solely for executing the program. At this level the supervisor gives instructions by a simple *performance cue*.

Perceptual cues leave some discretion in the hands of subordinates, and can range from relatively simple to highly complex. Here the supervisor does not actually give the sign to perform. Instead he specifies a *perceptual cue* for the subordinate, and instructs him to perform a program if and when the cue is observed. An instruction for this purpose might take the form, "Whenever the inventory level falls below two months' normal consumption, place a reorder for four months' supply," or "Whenever a claimant turns down an offer of appropriate employment, terminate his unemployment compensation as of the date of refusal." Such instructions, of course, are not confined to organizations, as in "When Joe's head gets that little tilt that shows he's groggy, give him a left jab to the jaw."

The employee might be given a subprogram for discovering the cues, as in checking all bins every third day to find how much material is still in stock, or placing a red flag on the file of every claimant who turns down an employment offer. Or the organization may provide the employee a flow of information. He is to scan this for the prescribed cues, and to perform the program whenever the cues appear.

If a person has the responsibility to maintain some variable in the organization at a more or less constant level, his function is that of a homeostatic governor of that variable, and he must utilize some kind of homeostatic cues. The inventory instruction above is essentially a homeostatic cue, which, assuming one month delivery time, will always keep inventories between one and five months' supply. Product inspection is also a type of homeostatic control, in which corrections are instituted whenever the product falls beyond specified tolerances.

The most advanced level of instruction is that in which the supervisor merely designates certain broad activities or goals for the employee. At this level the employee is sufficiently trained in his field to know what cues to look for and what responses to give.

The other half of the communication process is feedback of information to the supervising authority about the performance of the persons supervised, the so-called upward flow of information. This can take innumerable forms, such as a count of units produced by a machine operator or of cases processed by a case worker, sales by a salesman, a corporation report to stockholders, an auditor's check of accounts, or an article published by a researcher which informs a sponsoring foundation of his progress. Feedback need not always come through channels within the organization established for the purpose. Reports on quality of performance can come from such other sources as the customers who use a company's product, the chief of state of a nation in which an ambassador resides, simple failure of a result to occur, or accident resulting from improper performance. In parallel with the relation between staff and sponsor, the feedback can determine whether the employee followed the instruction satisfactorily, whether the proper instruction was given, or both.

The essence of this relation is the same for the sponsors dealing with the top level of staff, for the top level dealing with the second level, or for the next to bottom level dealing with the bottom level. To anyone at any level of the hierarchy, the person above him represents the sponsor interests as subdivided and interpreted for his level of performance by whatever persons intervene between him and the sponsors. His reports of progress represent his accountability to the sponsor interest.

The terms "policy" and "effectuation" are often used in this area of discussion. They do not seem necessary in the present model. But they should be mentioned, and seem to have the following application. A policy may be thought of as a programmed pattern of response to some category of recurrent situation, as contrasted to a situation occurring only once. A policy of paying extraordinary medical expenses for employees means that when the cue of an extraordinary medical expense is presented the program of paying it is invoked. A policy of putting all important policies in writing means that whenever the cue of a change in policy occurs the program of printing it up for employees is activated. To distinguish between policy and effectuation, in the present model we might say that a program for some category of cues or stimulus situations constitutes policy to a person who receives the program as an instruction from above him in the hierarchy. The decisions he makes and passes to his subordinates for performing the program constitute effectuation to him, and policy to his subordinates.

In closing, we may note again that the model is not a description of reality. Any actual organization, like any actual decision, involves an infinite number of variables. The ability to understand organization depends on selecting the most significant variables and understanding the relation among them. The simple model of Chapter 21 dealt with the most universal components, and we have now added others, though only by narrowing the focus from *all* organizations to larger and more complex ones. In the next two chapters we will add still further detail and achieve still closer approximation to reality. But given an infinity of components, any reality itself is forever indescribable. In any event a complete description would apply only to the individual case, and one can have a science of organization, of decision, or of anything else, only by ignoring individual differences and concentrating on the uniformities.

Chapter 25

STAFF: REFINEMENT
OF THE MODEL

THE BEGINNER's model of the complex organization was described in the preceding chapter. As we move to the intermediate model we both add more items and make more complicated arrangements of them. The main complication is the interaction of production and transactional aspects, and the main new ingredients are suborganizations, and transactions about production. As was indicated earlier, there can be decisions about transactions, transactions about decisions, communications about transactions, transactions about communications, and so on almost endlessly. Among all these possible interrelations we will try to delineate a few of the most conspicuous, in the hope that if these are clear the nature of the remainder will at least be hinted.

INFORMATION ASPECTS OF DECISIONS

As described in Chapter 24, major decisions were emitted from sponsors to top levels of staff. These were broken down into major implementation goals, and were issued to the second level of staff. This second level broke down the goals still farther, issuing instructions to their subordinates, and so on.

Although this kind of relation is part of the decision, communication, and production process, it is by no means all of it. One addition is that the top executives, and perhaps the sponsors, need much information from lower echelons. The first step in formulating their decision sets is to list the possible alternatives. Except for routine matters (which the top levels presumably should not decide in any event), unless the top executives receive information from the lower levels they may include alternatives in their decision sets which are simply not possible, while others which are possible may not occur to them. They also need to know the costs of various alternatives and the values they will produce. To the extent that these things concern the relations of the organization to its outside environment, the top executives may be better judges than lower ranks, although persons at lower levels in purchasing, personnel, public relations, or sales divisions might also possess pertinent information about outside relations. But to the extent that these costs and values depend on factors internal to the organization, important information about them can be learned only from the organization's own lower levels. Further, a major decision may bring major changes in the day to day working relations or authority structure of the various divisions, and affect their ability to work efficiently. Although they need not necessarily follow suggestions from below, the top levels do need information from below about the probable impact of their decisions on these workaday relationships and productive efficiency.

A top decision to improve performance in one division of the organization may inhibit performance in another. To illustrate from different kinds of organizations, to capture the farm belt vote a political party might contemplate a platform plank to double farm income. But the city divisions may expect their voters to bolt the party as they visualize skyrocketing food prices. A decision to broaden the second floor men's wear division of a department store might cut heavily into the sales in the basement division. The stainless steel parts which the engineering department considers ideal may be too hard to fabricate in the production department or too expensive to sell by the sales department.

Since any major decision may have numerous repercussions in any or all parts of the organization, a sound decision requires either (1) that the top decision makers possess tremendous information about the details of all the subordinate parts, or (2) that information from each such part be brought to the point where the decision is made. Given the limited scope of the human brain and the almost unlimited scope of potentially relevant information, the second is by far the more dependable method with normal executives under normal circumstances. This does not mean that poorly informed top executives will do as well as well-informed ones, but that even the best must have their information supplemented from other divisions and lower levels.

Numerous ways exist for tapping this information, but two main types are effective. One is a conference in which representatives of all affected divisions participate directly. The second is a decision made in tentative form at top levels and circulated among affected divisions for study and comment in light of its probable effect on the division. Following receipt of the feedback comments, the top officers then make the final decision. If the comments suggest substantial change, a second tentative proposal might be submitted for comment. This process is an application to decision making of the basic technique of successive approximations. Either this method or the conference achieves important upward flows of information to the decision center.

These techniques simultaneously perform important downward communicative functions. We have seen in the chapters on communication that possible doubts about an instruction may be resolved if the receiver knows the purpose as well as the content of the instruction. When persons who are to effectuate a decision participate in making it, they are intimately familiar with its objectives, and can carry out subsequent implementing instructions far more intelligently. Not unimportantly, participation also gives experience in decision making to the group from which future executives may be selected, and makes the heads of various divisions more explicitly aware of the effects of their actions on other divisions. Some additional aspects of communication are discussed in the next chapter in connection with decisions which change the major bargain.

MOTIVATION ASPECTS OF DECISIONS

Participation in decision making does more than improve the information at all levels. It also has strong motivational effects.

The first is a straightforward communication of motives from top officials to lower ones during discussions. For one thing, enthusiasm is contagious. For another, better understanding of the organization's goals increases the motivation of the lower officers as they see the instrumental connection between their actions and overall accomplishment. This instrumental motivation, incidentally, does not require that the lower executive share the organization's goals, so long as he does not oppose them. It requires only that he see some point to his performance.

Second, if a person has himself advocated a policy, or at least accepted it, he acquires a stake in its success. Its success confirms his judgment, and its failure indicts it. Hence, a person will tend to work hard to carry out a policy he has helped formulate. Lack of participation reverses the effect. A lower executive is often in competition for promotion. He competes mainly with others at his own level, but partly with the present higher-ups. If someone else has made the decision, or if it has been made over his objection, a person may have some stake in making it fail, since failure confirms his judgment and impugns that of his competitors. Further, not to consult a man affected by a decision suggests that his opinion is not worth asking, and hardly improves his morale. Participation in making a decision does not guarantee agreement or acceptance, and runs some risk of strengthening disagreement. On the average, however, it tends to work in the direction of greater agreement, or at least a more complete understanding of the logic of opposing positions and less cocksureness about the superiority of one's own.

Third, for a subordinate to participate in a decision which he will later receive instructions to effectuate unquestionably legitimizes the instruction. Not only has the subordinate accepted a *general* obligation in his major bargain to perform instructions from his superior. He has also accepted the particular instruction, by virtue of having helped formulate it. Although not essential to the definition of legitimacy, this is a more detailed application of it, and is highly useful where full acceptance raises the efficiency of performance. It is also related to a statement sometimes used in modern organization theory that there is no authority except by consent of the governed. This proposition is virtually true by definition in special purpose organizations. If the individual is free to avoid orders by leaving the organization, his remaining there gives consent. He may not necessarily like the terms. But the problem of transactions over authority is like that over transactions of goods. One or both parties may dislike the terms, and prefer better ones. But if both accept them as better than the best alternative (no negative power being used), the transaction is "voluntary" and "accepted."

Despite some weaseling of words around the edges, as a consequence of both the information and motivation factors, modern organization theory strongly recommends that persons who are to effectuate decisions participate in formulating them. This is not an ethically oriented view that wider participation is more democratic or moral, though it certainly has ethical repercussions, and seems (at least for persons reared in our culture) to provide a generally more satisfactory way of life for the staff. In the context of management theory and of the present discussion it is a hardheaded conclusion that widespread participation in decision making provides better management *for the sponsors*.

This does not mean that the technique has no disadvantages, the most obvious one being that it takes longer, both in elapsed time and in man hours consumed. The problem here is akin to that described in Chapter 16. The major advantage of wide participation is that it increases the information content of the decision. But here as elsewhere, information for decisions is not always worth its cost, and it will be more rational to make a quick decision at the top if the cost of a wrong decision is less than that of assuring a right one. If the motivational and legitimizing effects of participation are not to be lost, however, it would seem wise as a practical matter that the top executives make clear when and why decisions are made without consultation.

The above discussion assumed that the decision-making authority remained at the top, the participation of lower level persons serving to increase the upward and downward flows of information as well as motivation. Since the top levels in this model listen to, but are not required to follow, suggestions from below, participation should not decrease the wisdom of decisions if the top levels have more sense than the lower. If motivation is not to be killed, however, explanations should accompany rejected suggestions.

By contrast, some organizations give actual decision powers to a committee which includes lower-ranking officers. Unless combined with careful sponsor authority over the committee, such an arrangement can shift sponsor control to the staff. The merits of such procedures must be judged on criteria beyond those we are able to discuss here.

DECISION ASPECTS OF INFORMATION

Good decisions obviously require information. What is not so obvious is that something which is presumably pure information often has a decision already embodied in it. We have seen in connection with decision making that a person may possess well-established responses to particular stimuli. The organization similarly may have well-established programs for particular cues. In some of the less usual situations the problem is not to know what response or program to give to which cue, but to know what the cue is. Was that noise an explosion or a sonic boom? Was that eye movement a blink or a wink? Was the riot political or athletic?

In some complex situations the identification of the situation is often the only significant problem. The Taft-Hartley Act, for example, defines a certain cue to be a strike or strike threat which "imperil(s) the national health or safety." The act further specifies the program the President is to follow whenever he perceives that cue. When some large strike occurs the President is neither unaware of its existence nor unclear about the program prescribed by the law. He nevertheless faces an important and sometimes difficult decision in attempting to determine whether a particular strike does or does not constitute the cue for releasing the program. Does or does not the strike imperil the national health or safety?

In a different context, does or does not the pattern on the radar screen constitute the cue for total nuclear retaliation?

We have seen that decisions are often not carried out by the persons who make them. Similarly, programs are often not performed by the persons who identify the cues, and communication is required in both cases. Much of the information relevant to an organization's operation flows into it in relatively raw form, and is digested before it is passed to those who use it. This process of digesting, or recoding, is often essential, in that the persons who need the information may not have the time or special skills to understand the original form. The recoding process, however, may incorporate an unwitting stimulus identification. If a company's sales are off 15 per cent, one person might be inclined to say "It's a buyer's strike," another "It's an inventory recession," a third "The competition is getting very aggressive," and a fourth "Our quality control has gone to pot, and the public has finally found it out." The 15 per cent decline in sales might thus call for any one of four programs, depending on which cue is extracted from the raw information.

The body of evidence for making the correct interpretation is presumably too complex to discuss in the company's memos. Instead the person(s) who process the company's information may make the diagnosis on their own, and report nothing more than: "Overstocked warehouses bring 15 per cent drop in sales." If this inventory interpretation goes unchallenged, the person who processes information, but who has no ostensible decision authority, actually makes the major decision. March and Simon describe this action as "uncertainty absorption," stating that "Uncertainty absorption takes place when inferences are drawn from a body of evidence and the inferences, instead of the evidence itself, are then communicated."[1]

Whether the nominal decision maker is a chief of state receiving information from his intelligence division or a sales manager trying to remedy a consumer lack of interest, the point at which uncertainty is absorbed, or cues are identified, is the one at which the most important aspects of the decision may be made. Whether he recognizes it or not, the executive who asks that information for all his decisions be reduced to a two-page memo, and who relies on that memo, has delegated important and often crucial parts of the decision to those who prepare the memo. There is presumably nothing wrong with the technique if it is understood, and is appropriate to the situation. If the executive has independent information and uses the memo only to focus discussion, he may, of course, remain in full charge.

Information about events inside or outside the organization may move through prescribed or incidental channels. Departmental budget estimates of a firm or charity, reports on the enemy from the intelligence division of the army, conferences, and notices on bulletin boards are prescribed channels. Two or more may supplement and check each other. The government uses both military and diplomatic reports from abroad; unemployment is measured by both census samples and claims for unemployment compensation; and a firm's output is measured by both production reports and shipping reports. Channels of information may be unprescribed, as when anyone who observes may report a needy family to a charity or a flying saucer to the air force. Unprescribed channels within the organization include gossip, rumors, "leaks," "grapevine," planted hints, and the other equipment of the informal organization.

TRANSACTION ASPECTS OF PRODUCTION

We initially discussed joint production and transactions in organizations as if they were separate entities. In fact they influence each other in numerous ways. We will discuss first the transacton aspects of production, then the production aspects of transactions.

Suppose a salesman dashes breathlessly to the production manager some afternoon and says, "I can cinch an order for a $100,000 left-handed parameters if you can finish production in three months. How about it?" After some computations the production manager replies, "With present equipment and work schedules it's not possible. But if you could get the president to authorize six new Monstrosity machines and a couple of high speed Peripatetics, along with adding a third shift and

---

[1] James G. March and Herbert A. Simon, *Organizations* (New York: John Wiley & Sons, 1958), p. 165.

allowing about $50,000 for overtime and expediting, I think I could get them out in sixteen weeks."

Now although the actual decision will have to be made by someone with authority over both the sales and production departments, such as the president, negotiations will take place between sales and production divisions somewhat along the following lines. Sales will start with the request for a three-months' deadline because the customer asked it, although the salesman suspects that the customer will accept a six-months completion date if shipments can *start* in three months. The production manager will behave similarly. If he thinks he can probably finish the order in three months he at first will insist it will take at least four. Further, he may insist on the Monstrosities and Peripatetics because he has long wanted them, even though the job might be done on the old multiple spindled Philanders.

The two parties start with an actual substantial overlap of EP's on the time schedule, the production manager thinking he can probably meet a three-month date and the salesman being willing to accept a later one. But for tactical reasons the sales department overstates the urgency of the deadline and production overstates the difficulty of meeting it. Each provides some cushion for bargaining and possible errors.

Under different circumstances the salesman might reverse his initial tactic. Suppose three months really *is* the deadline, but the salesman expects that the production department will almost certainly refuse to commit itself to so tight a schedule. At this point the EP's of sales and production do not touch, much less overlap. The salesman's tactics now are to inquire whether the production department could give a five-months delivery promise if the management would authorize additional equipment. With visions of Peripatetics dancing before his eyes, the production manager might agree. Having generated this enthusiasm, which provides an apparent overlap of EP's, the salesman may then whittle the production manager down by degrees till he gets the necessary three-months promise. The salesman's strategy enlarges the production manager's aspirations (a larger BX if the salesman is A), and then capitalizes on it to get better terms than were initially possible.

The salesman in this situation may occupy several different roles, simultaneously or sequentially. In bargaining with the production manager over delivery dates he acts as an agent for the customer, having no power to accept any commitment longer than three months. As salesman for his own company he may receive a commission or status if he makes the sale. In this role, however, he has an intense desire to complete the sale for what it does for him, independent of its importance to either his own company or to the customer. Finally, as a member of his own company he wants to increase its income or prestige, or to avoid the sale if it might do the reverse.

No organization of any kind can long function without hosts of transactions of this sort among all its various divisions—production, sales, purchasing, public relations, labor relations, accounting, legal, maintenance, or planning. It might be objected that these are not transactions in the normal sense, since the parties do not give and receive personal values, and have no final authority to conclude a deal. Under the simple model described in the preceding chapter, some higher officer would listen to both sides, and then tell the salesman to refuse the order or the production department to produce it. Three aspects of that model need refinement.

First, although it is the company's machines and money which the salesman and production manager bargain about, each has a personal stake in the outcome, since his prestige, promotability, and possible immediate income will be affected. For his own future good the production manager must not get the company in trouble by making delivery promises he cannot fill; nor must he cause the company to lose business by refusing to make promises he might be able to meet. The salesman wants to bring in business; but he also wants to avoid a reputation for irresponsible promises. This means that the bargaining *is* important to each party's future with the company, and is not outside his own personal value system.

Second, the fact that an executive has authority over those below him does not mean that he does not need to bargain with them. The president is *not* the production manager, and unless he is prepared to take over the job himself he cannot get things produced except through the production manager. If the latter, after careful study, asserts that a three-months commitment cannot be met, no amount of presidential authority can get him to make the commitment. If the president wants the business he must bargain, on such basis as: "The company has got to land this order. What do you need to get it out on time?" Unless the president is sure the production manager is overcautious or incompetent, he cannot improve his position by threatening the man's job or future. In short, to have the formal authority to say, "Get that order out in three months or else" does not mean the order will get out. In fact, if the production manager feels he cannot easily be replaced, and if the president should proceed to make a delivery commitment without his consent, he might prefer to demonstrate the correctness of his position by *not* getting the order out on time. Except under highly unusual circumstances, however, the president would not make such a commitment.

Third, although there is no question about the president's formal authority, if the salesman and the production manager find a mutually satisfactory arrangement the president cannot lightly upset it except for reasons other than those affecting sales and production. To do so would presume that he knows more about production problems and the customer's needs than they do. This may occasionally occur, but would not be normal. It might be suggested that the salesman go first to the president, to keep the location of authority straight, and that the president then talk to the production manager. This is a shortcut to overburdening the president and burying action in red tape. This would mean the salesman could not get even a rough preliminary idea of a delivery date, nor could the production manager even start thinking about the problem until the president had found time to confer with both men. It might also be suggested that the salesman clear the matter first with the president before talking with the production manager. This keeps the lines of authority clearly visible. But if the two are responsible persons, the president is apt to suggest, "Why don't the two of you see what you can work out, and let me know how it shapes up." With or without the intervention of the president, since the essential problem lies in the relation between the customer's needs (taken in conjunction with the needs of other customers) and the production department's capacity, sales and production departments will be the chief negotiators.

Thus, although we originally introduced joint production and transactions as two distinct phases of organization, we now see that the production aspect itself is filled with transactions—not about personal goods, as such, but about relatively pure production problems. Transactions of personal goods are also closely tied to production problems, however, which is our next problem.

PRODUCTION AND INFORMATION ASPECTS OF TRANSACTIONS

The effects of production on the transactions aspect of organization hinge partly on production itself and partly on information about production, and we will discuss the two together. The core of the matter is that productivity, of both the worker and the whole organization, has much to do with the amount of reward each can receive, and the terms of the bargains between organization and staff member. Information about productivity is necessarily communicated through the organization in connection with the production process. The result is that information which is indispensable for directing and reporting upon production tends to influence the bargaining power between organization and staff in their transactions over contributions and withdrawals. Since this influence is at least subconsciously evident, both sides tend to introduce biases into their communications about production so as to produce the best tactical effect on their bargains. They may also manipulate some of their production transactions so as to have the best intertransactional strategic effect on those bargains.

The communications effect is perhaps most obvious. An individual's pay and progress depend significantly on the quantity and quality of his performance. If he were personally to inspect and report the quality or quantity of his own work, the reports would presumably contain an upward bias in his favor. This expected bias is almost universally recognized, and where possible each staff member's work is evaluated by someone else. In many circumstances, however, the staff member works on a more or less individual basis—like the case worker in a social agency or the adjuster for an automobile insurance company. Here the organization must depend heavily on the employee's own reports. Only limited inspections are feasible to determine whether the reports are accurate, and on the basis of occasional, sometimes accidental, feedback from other sources the supervisors must attempt to determine not only the quality of the work, but the accuracy of the reports, and accept or discount the latter accordingly thereafter.

Actual levels of performance have a two-edged effect on the individual's bargaining power with the organization. Suppose a production worker has been averaging 100 units per day. By dint of greater effort, skill, or ingenuity, he then raises his output to 140. In the direct sense his bargaining power goes up, since he is now more valuable to the organization. If he is on piece rates this fact will be reflected in an immediate 40 per cent increase in pay. But this is not all.

There is no such thing as a permanently definable "proper" level of output. The background assumption, which in part is inescapable, is that the worker is always to give his best. A "fair day's work for a fair day's pay" presumes no withholding of effort or initiative. As soon as the worker turns out 140 units he destroys the previous presumption that 100 units is a fair day's work, and his supervisors now want to know, "If you could do 140 today, why not every day?" Or "If Jim can do 140, why not Joe?" Given the indefinability of a "proper" amount of work, these questions cannot be answered convincingly.[2] In many places (or at least in enough places to create a conviction among workers that the practice is widespread) the worker will end with less pay per unit—immediately, by a rate cut, or eventually by a restudy or re-engineering of the operation. His total pay, however, will probably be more than before. If the new technique to increase his productivity becomes known to management, the worker who developed it will get only tenuous and fleeting bargaining power from it—like a firm with an invention not protected by patent.

In order to encourage new ideas which will increase productivity some firms give substantial bonuses to workers who develop them, providing at the worker level a reward something akin to the extra income from patent protection at the company level. Guarantees against rate cuts are also used in part, especially under union contract, but they tend to produce badly aligned wage structures, and some adjustment in rates must eventually be made on those jobs where productivity rises faster than on other jobs. This relationship reflects in the small the bargaining power factors outlined earlier—that an increase in productivity initiated by either management or workers increases the bargaining power of the other party to share that increase.

Having observed or heard rumors about the practice of cutting piece

---

[2] I am aware that some industrial engineers believe they can define a "proper" amount of work rather closely. Even if we accept that position for the sake of argument (and I do not), it still leaves open the question of increases in productivity due to ingenuity rather than effort.

rates, workers generally produce only up to a "safe" level. If they happen to produce more, they will not report it, perhaps putting the extra output into a "kitty" to draw on when things go badly. Although information about increased productivity can be hidden from higher management for a time, the safest way to hide the information is not to produce more. Restriction shows the same bargaining power factors as high production, but in reverse. Restricted output strengthens the worker's tactical position in the immediate bargain, by seeming to justify a higher rate per piece. But it weakens his position in the longer run by making him less valuable to management. The precise effect in any one case will, of course, depend on a series of other bargaining factors as well, and we are describing only the isolated effect of this one force.

These observations apply to any kind of organization, but are most conspicuous in the business firm. A parallel situation appears on the management side—again in all organizations but more evident in firms. To raise their own rewards from the sponsors as high as possible the top staff executives want a profitable and/or efficient organization. But a report of high profitability or efficiency lowers the management's bargaining power with the workers in trying to keep their wages down. Although this is by no means the only factor in the case, profitable firms generally do pay higher wages than unprofitable ones. Even the cooperative, service, or pressure organization may feel the same influence. If its ratio of output to input is high compared to similar organizations (whether the ouput is flood relief, propaganda bulletins, or services to members), the staff's bargaining power to get increased compensation is raised, regardless of whether the higher output is due to the staff's or the sponsor's efforts.

An important part of all motivation is feedback which reports success. The supervisor therefore wants to be able to tell the subordinate that his work was well done. But praise indicates the subordinate's high value to the organization, raising his bargaining power and lowering the supervisor's. Parents face the same problem, when the positive motivational effect of praise may seem to the child to justify relaxation of effort. Since the total power of both parties is increased in the long run by an increase in productivity of either, it seems better strategy in the long run to use the positive motivations of praise and perhaps of increased tangible rewards. As always, we are speaking of "production" as the creation of any desired thing, whether it be a material good or habits of thrift or politeness. The basic position is reflected in the ever present "You are doing fine. Now see if you can't do better."

Supervisors should always be alert to the possibility that rewards to stimulate performance may bring changes in reporting rather than in performance. If the organization gives awards or citations for good safety records, minimum breakdown time on machines, or few employee grievances, the foreman may fail to report some accidents, understate the time lost from breakdowns, or make undue concessions to stall off grievances.

Because of the value of tactical misrepresentations to bargaining power, the very process of motivating subordinates may encourage distortions of the information needed to run the organization.

Sometimes management cannot let its employees know its plans without disastrous loss of bargaining power. If a company is planning to close a plant in six months, and cannot use the employees elsewhere, it would normally be most efficient to close the plant gradually according to plan. But if the planned closing is announced, the employees' stake in the major bargain shrinks dramatically, and their bargaining power in day to day relations rises with it. An employer's strongest discipline is discharge. But now every worker's job will end shortly in any event, no matter how good his performance. Only a larger than normal loyalty or conscience will prevent employees from quitting without notice, leaving tasks unfinished, or resisting unpleasant instructions. Severance pay or bonus may keep some workers performing satisfactorily to the end, but the odds are against orderly termination. Hence, we find a tendency to secrecy about plant closing until the last minute. Even if employees are to be transferred to another division, because of the personal nature of recognition by superiors, morale is apt to deteriorate unless persons expect to work under the same supervisor after transfer.

Although they do not use the terminology of this chapter to describe it, most staff members of most organizations are aware of the bargaining power effects described here, and tend to hide, gloss over, or play down certain kinds of information, and to point up, overemphasize, or exaggerate other kinds. In short, most persons sense bargaining power factors intuitively, or shortly learn them from others in the situations where they are useful. Sometimes the tactics lie in selecting the medium of communication or method of coding the message. Suppose a foreman is under standing instructions to "report any unusual incidents of interest to management." A bitter argument arises over a man's wife in which one worker would have bashed the other's skull if the foreman had not arrived just in time. The foreman may feel that he could have prevented the scene if he had been more alert to keep the two out of contact. Must he report the incident? It would seem to be a "matter of interest." But then no blow was struck, so nothing really "happened." Besides, the whole thing may blow over if left alone, but could turn very nasty if a point is made of it. The foreman decides to report—but how? Shall he write a memo, report it by phone, or discuss it face to face? Shall he put it in a communication all its own? Or does this make it too important, and suggest that he tack it as an afterthought on a note about some other topic? Should he call it a brawl, fight, argument, disagreement, misunderstanding, incident, or what? Sometimes these things are of peripheral importance; sometimes they are at the core of things. The possible details are numberless, and we need not follow them. But to be unaware of them is to fail to understand much of what makes the organization tick.

Although all these factors are very real, so are the intertransactional factors described in Chapter 18, which operate in transactions within organizations as well as outside them. The effect of tactics declines drastically as the same persons deal continuously or repeatedly with each other. Persons who have long or continued relationships (or who have elsewhere learned the long run usefulness of being a "square shooter") short cut the "gamesmanship" and deal with realities at the outset. Such a straightforward approach is particularly fruitful in transactions over production, and greatly increases efficiency. So does a fair quota of generous bargaining. Both these aspects will be dealt with below in connection with groups, or suborganizations.

Transactions over production can take place in a completely, or almost completely, cooperative relation, both parties being interested in getting the job done. Transactions over the wage and terms of employment, however, always involve some conflict, since the income to the employee is a cost to the employer. Except where superior and subordinate are on unusually close terms, it is difficult for tactics over *major* bargains to be dropped completely. We will next examine some aspects of that bargain.

SOME DECISION FACTORS AS POWER DETERMINANTS IN MAJOR BARGAINS

In Chapter 22 we examined some of the power factors in the broad relations between sponsors and recipients. In somewhat parallel fashion we will now examine some power factors in the relation of sponsors and staff, with emphasis on the decision aspects. Until near the end, the discussion will assume that the sponsor-staff relation is within the control of the parties themselves, and is unaffected by unions or governmental controls.

Viewing an employment relation from the point before any agreement is reached between employer and employee, neither side will accept the relation unless its values exceed its costs as anticipated over the whole lifetime of the relationship. The investment the organization must make in the relation is the cost of recruiting, hiring, inducting, and perhaps training the new man. These costs may be relatively small (perhaps the equivalent of a week's pay for the man) for unskilled or semiskilled labor who apply directly for jobs. They may run into many thousands of dollars for scarce technical and managerial skills.

To the employee the investment costs of getting a new job are those of discovering and evaluating job opportunities, filling out application blanks and waiting for interviews, possible traveling for interviews, and perhaps moving his household and breaking many friendships. There may also be unemployment costs between jobs. Finally, contemplating a new job may entail long discussion and mental anguish, for in the employee's life the decision about a new job is often of comparable magnitude to that of a major reorganization in the employer's life.

Under the General Rule we find that any investment already made by either side is irrelevant to the decision and to bargaining power. If the employee has already incurred ten weeks of unemployment, or the employer has already spent a thousand dollars making contacts with prospective employees, these are sunk costs. However, the larger the amount of the investment not yet made by one party, but still remaining to be made if the employment agreement is to be concluded, the greater will be the reluctance of that party to conclude the agreement, and the greater his bargaining power. The employee who would have to move his family halfway across the country if he accepts a job will hold out for more than for a job five minutes from home. The employer who will have to invest heavily in training the employee will hold out for better terms than if the applicant is already trained. In the opposite direction, any costs to either party which will continue into the future only if the agreement is *not* concluded, reduce that party's bargaining power. Examples would be the employee's continuing to be unemployed, or the employer's continuing to search for additional applicants.

No obvious persistent bias inheres in the above relation, and the balance of bargaining power shifts greatly from circumstance to circumstance. If the applicant is unemployed, the pressure of continued lack of income can be very intense. For the head of a family this pressure is only partially mitigated by unemployment compensation, which in the United States averages less than half of normal previous earnings. For this reason an unemployed applicant may accept a job paying less than his previous one. On the other hand, if he is being recruited while he is still employed elsewhere, his bargaining power is excellent, and he normally will not leave for less than about 15 to 25 per cent increase in pay. Obvious shifts in bargaining power occur as between prosperity and depression, employees being scarce in good times and jobs in bad times.

Once the person has been employed, a new set of decision factors sets in. Some occasional persons are employed on fixed term contracts, and some work under severance pay or other agreements which inhibit termination of the employment relation. Otherwise the employment is terminable by either party when he sees its costs to exceed its values to him. Although certain key employees have large bargaining power, for the routine employee, particularly the one on hourly wages, the bargaining advantage is sharply on the employer's side, for several reasons.

First, hourly rated labor is a relatively strict variable cost. When the employer does not have enough work to keep a worker busy, he sends him home (or does not call him in) for a day, a week, a month, or indefinitely, and pays him nothing during the period.[3] On short layoffs the chances that the employee will get another job are relatively slim,

---

[3] With rare exception, employer contributions to unemployment compensation funds, public or private, are arranged on a variable cost basis. The employer pays a percentage of wages into a fund while the worker is working, but stops payments when the worker is laid off. The contribution thus has the same effect on the employer's cost structure as an addition to the wage.

which means that the employer has no recruiting or employment costs when the worker is recalled. Except for the original employment costs, which are now sunk, the great bulk of the cost of utilizing the worker are in the future, and the employer will not continue to use him unless there is work for him to do which to the employer equals or exceeds the wage cost. The employer has almost no fixed costs with respect to the worker already on his rolls, and the cost of using his services is almost entirely variable.

The worker's position stands in marked contrast. He has very small variable costs of working, such as transportation to work, and any extra cost for food and clothing over their cost if he stayed home. Few of the worker's costs decline when his job stops. Rent or mortgage payments, property taxes, heat, utilities, food, clothing, and medical expenses remain unaffected. On a strict money basis the worker will be better off to work for any wage which exceeds his variable costs of getting to work, rather than not to work at all. Since a day not worked is forever irrecoverable, his position is almost like that of the farmer who has already paid all the costs of raising and picking his strawberries, and who will be better off to take any price greater than zero, rather than not to sell at all. Further, all the investment costs of bringing the worker into the world and raising him to maturity are now sunk, as are any investments he has made in his own training.

During prosperity the bargaining power factors show no marked advantage for either side. Workers can find other jobs, and firms can find other workers. The fixed and variable costs of both are being met and the fixed-variable ratio has no significant influence on their relative power positions. During depression, conditions are less satisfactory, and both firms and workers may have to sell their offerings for less than their normal total cost. The General Rule indicates that either will be better off to sell at any amount more than the variable cost of making the sale. It is a rare industry whose fixed costs amount to half or more of total costs, and a fifth to a third is more common. This means that if the firm closes down for a month or two and sends its workers home its costs decline by half, and perhaps by two thirds or more. If it cannot get a price for its product which covers at least its variable costs, it will not produce and sell. If conditions show no signs of improving, the firm can sell its assets and liquidate. It may lose some of its investment by doing so, but it thereby permanently eliminates *all* future costs. There thus exists a price which is a relatively high fraction of total costs below which a firm cannot be bargained to sell—a matter we observed in a different context in connection with decisions.

If the worker and his family could go into hibernation when he is out of work, and cease all expenses for food, clothing, heat, and other variables, and if he also were free to liquidate the family and eliminate all future costs when things looked bleak, his bargaining position would be roughly comparable to that of the firm.

The fixed costs of a biological entity are relatively much higher than those of the typical organization, and the variable costs much lower. Since variable costs are the floor under bargaining power, the bargaining power of the biological entity is typically weak. It is no accident that the one major industry producing biological products, agriculture, also shows low bargaining power—along with some other difficulties.

Although workers do not rationalize it in the above language, they sense their position intuitively. The result is an almost desperate desire by working class people in industrial nations for measures to maintain their bargaining power, or at least their wage rates, during depression. Unions, minimum wage legislation, and unemployment compensation are the chief devices for this purpose, along with continued support for measures designed to maintain prosperity. These devices do considerably soften the disastrous effects of depression on workers' bargaining power. However, the ability to maintain wage rates does not maintain income for workers laid off for lack of work. Although handled in part by some of the same devices, the problems of maintaining full employment and of providing income during unemployment follow a different logic from that of bargaining power, and are beyond the scope of the present discussion. Whether unions and legislation have partially offset the worker's weak position, just offset it, or more than offset it is a question about which it is easy to make sweeping assertions, but difficult to measure objectively.

Chapter 26

SUBORGANIZATIONS AND GROUPS

ALTHOUGH PASSING reference has been made to groups and suborganizations, these have not been incorporated into the analysis, which dealt thus far only with relations of individuals. We are now about to enter a magnificent new complication of organizations. The large organization is not only a collection of sets and subsets of decisions, persons, tasks, and goals; it is also a collection of sets and subsets of organizations, each fulfilling the definition of an organization as a relation of two or more persons for joint production.

In recent decades a spectacular volume of literature and experimentation has been built around the heading of "groups," one important batch under the heading of *"small groups"* and a partly overlapping batch (plus much discussion) under the heading of *"group dynamics."* Hare provides an excellent introduction to the study of small groups,[1] including extensive coverage of the empirical research in the field, and Bonner[2] has performed a somewhat similar function for group dynamics. The definitions of a group are almost as numerous as the authors writing in the field.[3]

Whenever a widely used analytical term is given many and discrepant definitions, it is wise to ask whether the concept is, in fact, a useful one, and whether the subject matter grouped around it might perhaps be rearranged around a different conceptual framework. The concept of the group, with its frequent focus on persons, is perhaps a case in point. To the extent (and it is fairly large) that the study of the group is focused on persons, it violates the approach to systems analysis reported in Chap-

---

[1] A. Paul Hare, *Handbook of Small Group Research* (New York: The Free Press of Glencoe, 1962). This volume is an extension and updating of an earlier volume, A. Paul Hare, Edgar F. Borgatta, and Robert Bales (eds.), *Small Groups: Studies in Social Interaction* (New York: Alfred A. Knopf, 1955).

[2] Hubert Bonner, *Group Dynamics, Principles and Applications* (New York: The Ronald Press Co., 1951).

[3] Donald W. Olmsted, *Social Groups, Roles, and Leadership: An Introduction to the Concepts* (East Lansing: Michigan State University, 1961), p. 17, cites eleven "Representative Definitions of Social Groups."

ter 3, where it was suggested that the components of a system are variables (traits or states of persons), not entities (the persons themselves).

The present volume orients all interpersonal relationships and social analysis around communications, transactions, and organizations. These are sets of relationships, not sets of persons, and seem to fall within the prescriptions of Chapter 3. In this spirit the present chapter will deal with the group, but with a shift in emphasis. Instead of studying the group, as such, it will return to communication, transaction, and organization within the group setting, while noting that the group is simultaneously a subculture. Attention will be focused on a particular kind of group, namely, a suborganization within a larger organization, with special reference to its place in and effect on the organization. Although this focus does not bring out all facets of the group, it seems a useful introduction, and some other aspects will appear later in connection with the family.

To say that a group is a subculture implies that the concepts, perceptions, motives, decisions, and overt behavior of the members interact in the fashion described as the system of culture.[4] Personalities form a subculture, which subculture forms personalities. While in the main not consciously oriented toward the basic notion of culture as a system, the contemporary study of groups fills in many details of the interactions by which the system of culture operates. This large body of material is as yet quite diffuse, and we will pass over most of it, concentrating instead on a framework within which it can be viewed. All the interactions within the culture system, however, can themselves be analyzed as communications, transactions, and organizations.

We have seen that culture may be thought of as the personality of the society, and personality as a subculture of one person. The "personality" of the small group has been referred to as *syntality*.[5] Not unexpectedly, the same man who has delved deeply into the classification of personality types (Cattell) is also active in studying the syntality of groups. Without being given the same attention here, syntality may be viewed as parallel in an important way with personality. Although personality does not incorporate any principles of behavior not found in psychology, the simultaneous interaction of psychological processes within the individual which creates personality is nevertheless something distinct from the separate action of those processes. Similarly, although it might be said that the group does not include any principles of interpersonal behavior not encompassed in communication, transaction, and organization, the simultaneous combination of these things in any one group is a phe-

---

[4] Although the thought occurred too late to be incorporated in the earlier analysis, it seems possible that some aspects of communication and culture might be examined to determine the conditions and behavior of unique and consensus concepts and perceptions, in parallel with the conditions of unique and consensus valuations in transactions.

[5] See, for example, Raymond B. Cattell, David R. Saunders, and Glen F. Stice, "The Dimensions of Syntality in Small Groups," in Hare, Borgatta, and Bales, *op. cit.*, pp. 305 ff.

nomenon distinct from that of the separate ingredients. The classification of syntalities is at best no further advanced than the classification of personalities, and we will not deal specifically with that problem.

To tie the discussion of groups to that of organization, we will first examine a model of what may be called a pure formal suborganization. We will then jump to a model at the opposite end of the spectrum of a pure informal suborganization, under which heading will appear our main discussion of the group. Following the two extreme types will be an examination of the intermediate suborganization. This is a mixture of the formal and informal, and much more closely resembles the actual organization.

PURE FORMAL SUBORGANIZATIONS

By a *pure formal suborganization* we mean a group of persons, or a division within a larger organization, specifically designated by the sponsors or their agents to perform some subgoal or subtask instrumental to the goals of the whole organization. The larger suborganizations are departments, bureaus, or divisions, like the production department of a company, the Department of Agriculture or the Bureau of Roads in the government, or the appliance division of General Electric. Each major subdivision of the organization is broken down into smaller ones, like the grinding and stamping division of the production department, the statistical and insect control divisions of the Department of Agriculture, or the sales and accounting departments of the appliance division. These are broken still further, in perhaps several more steps, until at the bottom we find *groups*. These are pairs, half dozens, or scores of persons doing the same, similar, or related work, usually (though not always) in a given limited location under the direction of a single supervisor or group leader. Although all the intervening levels are suborganizations, as defined, we will confine attention almost entirely to the smallest group at the bottom of the structure.

In the pure model each such group, or suborganization, exists because it was established by the sponsors or by the top levels of the staff. The goals of the suborganization are specified by the top authority, as are at least the main programs of the group. All rewards and punishments are controlled by the leader or supervisor. The leader is designated by higher authority, and provides prizes, promotions, pay, or any other rewards to his subordinates out of the organization's resources, not his own. In the model no rewards of any sort are available from any source except the supervisor, and the group has no goals except those of the larger organization. Individual differences in personality and productivity are compatible with this stage of the model, and the supervisor may appeal to different motives to get different people to respond.

Such a group undoubtedly fills the definition of an organization when it operates as a coordinated team. In a team, tasks are subdivided within the group. Each person's task is important to the whole, as in a crew of four operating a large press, where two men feed sheets of metal into the press on one side and two others remove them on the other. A crew of men installing telephone poles, a congressional committee, the crew of a boat, or all the men along an assembly line are also teams—and organizations. A dozen men in a department, each operating his own machine independently, are not a team or an organization, since there is no jointness to their production. If we add their supervisor, these men are an organization, however; their joint efforts produce something, or produce more efficiently, than any one could do alone. The dozen may or may not also be an informal organization, as will be seen.

INFORMAL SUBORGANIZATIONS

At the opposite end of the spectrum is the *pure informal suborganization*. This is a relation of two or more persons within a larger organization for the joint production of some satisfaction *of their own*. The members of this informal group may or may not coincide with those of a formal group.[6]

In such a suborganization the members are the sponsors, and the two most common organizational types would be the cooperative and the pressure organization. Service or profit types of operation undoubtedly occur, but are rare enough to ignore here. Cooperative goals include friendship, opportunities for conversation, status, a context for generous relationships, and other normal human contacts. In a shop the members of the group might also assist each other in various ways, as by lending tools, giving advice, helping an ailing fellow, and generally smoothing the path of industrial life. The combat group in the army would share food, help each other to get some sleep, treat the injured, warn of danger, and otherwise try to make things livable. Although some such activities may contribute strongly to formally prescribed programs, in the informal model the members do these things *for each other*. Within the model (and realistically within wide limits in the armed forces) it is simply irrelevant whether the overall organization is helped or hindered by such actions.[7] As was noted, the culture effect will go on simultaneously, as the members of the group develop more similar motives and concepts at the same time.

The informal suborganization may also serve as a pressure group or

---

[6] The suborganization might share the goals of the larger organization in whole or part. This situation would not violate the definition if the group's "own goals" happen to coincide with those of the larger organization. To sharpen the model, however, we will assume that the group goals are *not* those of the larger organization.

[7] *The American Soldier* is a report of detailed studies of social interactions made by the Research Branch of the Information and Education Division of the War Department. Two volumes were published by the Princeton University Press in 1949 under numerous authors, and provide highly useful information about the group. Present interpretations of those data are from Robert K. Merton, *Social Theory and Social Structure* (Glencoe, Ill.: The Free Press, 1957), pp. 225 ff.

coalition[8] to improve its members' bargaining within the organization, especially with the higher levels. The group may support the bargaining of an individual member, or may bargain collectively for less work, more pay, better tools, stronger materials, tastier food, fewer calisthenics, greater justice, or cleaner rest rooms. Whether these transactions deal with production or rewards, their purpose is to improve the position of one or more members relative to the large organization. In many ways, a labor union is a formal expression of the kinds of activities performed by the group.

Since there are no absolute measures for these things, how good a set of terms one group can achieve depends on such forces as consensus and reference group factors. External consensus forces come into play if the individual is free to move easily from one group to another within the large organization, or to move to other organizations with more satisfactory terms. In that case the availability of overt alternatives may help pull low groups up toward the consensus. Overt consensus forces are by no means all-powerful, however, since they can operate only between groups which are the same or similar, and the various subgroups within a large organization differ greatly in many ways. The group's attention is usually focused on some other group(s) to which the given group for some reason (often obscure) feels that it is or ought to be comparable. Within the more restricted area of wages these are what wage theorists call "comparable groups." With modifications they are also a sort of extension to the group level of what some sociologists call the "reference group" of the individual. Without its being so named, the rough equivalent of the "reference group" has already been described in Chapter 13 as any one of the subsocieties with which an individual has contact, and which, by his acceptance or rejection of its concepts and values, helps mold his personality.

Whether we call it a "comparable group" or a "group reference group" for the present purpose we can think of it as a second group with which on an internalized basis a first group feels it shares or ought to share consensus terms. Any treatment which is less good than that received by the second group is felt to be "inequitable," and on the face of it ought to be corrected. Even small discrepancies from the standards of the second group loom large in people's thinking, whereas large differences from other groups which happen not to be accepted as "comparable" make little impression. The phenomenon apparently involves some kind of group perception about what makes a similar group. A reference group can also have higher or lower status, in which case it is felt that some particular amount of differential, rather than equality, ought to prevail between them. Although numerous studies have shown the effect

---

[8] A pure coalition is not an organization, since it engages solely in joint bargaining, not joint production. Since the group which acts as a coalition within the larger organization nearly always produces some of the cooperative forms of satisfaction as well, we will refer to it as an organization.

of intergroup comparisons on the thinking and sense of fairness of groups within organizations, relatively little is yet known about why one and not another group is selected as a point of reference for any one group.[9]

Membership in the Informal Group

Whereas a person becomes a member of the formal group when he is assigned to it by the organization, he does not automatically become a member of the relevant informal group. At first the cooperative and pressure objectives of the group will be communicated to the new man, by example, anecdote, expressions of attitudes, and many other means. An important problem to many groups is that of production quotas. Suppose that a new young employee, eager to show his stuff, is assigned to a utility pole installation crew. For years the crew has averaged five poles a day, in the feeling that this number neither overtaxes the crew nor short-changes the company. After several months the recruit begins to suggest ways to raise the installations to six or seven. By one technique or another (probably several) he will come to understand that, while the crew appreciate suggestions that lighten their work, they do not welcome any act which may cause the management to expect a larger daily quota. He may even learn to sound a warning whenever a higher level supervisor approaches so that everyone may be appropriately busy.

We do not mean that every group is a permanent conspiracy to keep down production, though within limits the tendency to defend themselves against what in their judgment represents overwork is a reliable component of the typical work-group's activities. The point of the moment, however, is that the new man does not become a member of the informal group merely by being assigned to the formal group. He becomes a member only when he conforms to patterns of behavior which are seen to serve the group goals. His membership is more fully confirmed when he also verbalizes those goals.

We have previously said that a person becomes a member of an organization when he accepts an authority relation in which he agrees to work toward the organization's goals in return for certain rewards. Now although the bargain with the informal group may be far less explicit, the same rationale applies. When the new man accepts the group's goals, whether or not they seem best for him or the larger organization, he has made his major bargain and is a member. In return the group will provide him rewards in such forms as advice, generous bargaining, assistance in difficult tasks, status, and support in his disputes with outsiders and superiors. If he does not conform, the group will assert its authority by withholding these rewards, attempting to bring conformity by the means described in Chapter 20 as "social pressures."

Responsibility has been defined as the position of the person on whom

---

9 Robert K. Merton, *op. cit.*, has an extended discussion of reference groups in Chapters VIII and IX.

authority is exercised. If the group is in a position to exercise authority over an individual by withholding rewards, it follows by definition that the individual *is* "responsible to" the group. If the individual himself accepts the group goals internally, he may be said to *"feel* a responsibility" to the group. Such behavior is parallel to the way in which persons may accept consensus terms of transactions because they feel them to be "right," even when no overt pressures are exercised.

However, if a person's own value system differs from those around him, he may refuse to support the aims of the group on the ground that he has "a responsibility to himself." In this case he is following the authority of his own conscience, which will punish him if he does not do as it instructs. A person may also feel a responsibility to society. This responsibility is overt if the larger society withholds rewards, such as status or votes, from a member who follows subgroup goals in conflict with those of the larger society. The societal authority is internal if a man believes that he should work for the larger society, and his conscience bothers him if he does not. More broadly, any person or group can be a "reference group" whose standards are accepted by others, and deviation from which is perceived by those others as unrewarding in and of itself. A person may thus refuse membership in one informal group if joining it conflicts with a more highly prized membership in some other group.

Since groups or their members often engage in outside transactions, part of the group's activity is to maintain its members' tactical positions against outsiders. One technique is to defend the member against criticism by outsiders, even though within the group he may be much criticized. Such behavior has a broader effect on the group. Status is apparent power, and is transferred by association. The group therefore acquires status if it contains members who have status, while the other members simultaneously acquire status if the group has it. Every member is thus diminished a little by criticism of a fellow, and to defend him is partly to defend oneself.

These observations apply, of course, where the group members provide mutual support. By contrast, to the extent that the members are competitive, group goals give way to individual goals, and if they are entirely competitive presumably no organization is possible, only coalition. Along these lines numerous empirical studies have been made of groups, the interactions within them, the conditions for being accepted and not accepted, the degree of cohesion, and other aspects. March and Simon have performed a monumental task in assembling and correlating these studies,[10] along with summarizing empirical work about other aspects of organizations. Some of these findings have been incorporated implicitly into the present model, with the result that the "empirical finding"

---

[10] James G. March and Herbert A. Simon, *Organizations* (New York: John Wiley & Sons, Inc., 1958).

is tautologically deduceable from the model. March and Simon report, for example, that "The greater the extent to which goals are perceived as shared among members of a group, the stronger the propensity of the individual to identify with the group."[11] Stated in the framework of the present model this would become approximately, "The greater the degree to which the members perceive their rewards to depend on cooperation and coalition, the greater will be their tendency to utilize cooperation and coalition." Another empirical finding is that "the greater the number of individual needs satisfied in the group the stronger the propensity of the individual to identify with the group." This, too, is essentially tautological in the present framework. Since motives are additive, the larger the number of needs which can be satisfied by a given alternative, the greater is the motivation to choose that alternative. The "empirical" finding thus is essentially, "the greater the motivation to identify with a group, the greater is the likelihood of doing so." In a model in which actual overt choice is the measure of motivation, the statement is logically inescapable once its terms have been defined.

Assuming that the goals are themselves desired, wherever conformity is important to the achievement of group goals, the group will have high power (or authority) to get conformity. First, the individual member will have a strong EP for belonging, since (if conformity is needed) he cannot achieve the goals outside the group. Second, the group will have a strong EP for his conformity, since nonconformity seriously reduces the entire group's chance of success. With a long EP for conformity from both sides it is very likely to be achieved. If the group achievement is an indivisible "shared value" which cannot be withheld from any one member (like a longer vacation for the whole group or the pleasure of clean windows), the group must withhold other things if it is to exercise its authority. Once a person accepts the goals and subculture of his group, he becomes subject to the distinctions between *in* and *out* groups described in connection with culture. These tend to reinforce the sense of unity of the group.

LEADERSHIP IN INFORMAL GROUPS

Except for small organizations with thoroughly known and accepted programs for all its activities, no organization performs automatically. Both its internal and its external activities must be controlled and coordinated through a continuing series of decisions, and for the most part these do not arise spontaneously. Whether in its internal or external relations, power (bargaining or total) can be possessed by an organization, and the same general rules of power apply to the organization as to the individual. An additional problem rises in the organization, however. Whereas power in an individual refers to his ability to satisfy *his* wants, when a person acts for the organization he attempts to satisfy *its* wants.

---

[11] *Ibid.*, p. 66.

These may not be the same as his own. For the organization to have power as an entity it is necessary to achieve joint action. Defined with reference to the group (which can have coalition as well as joint production functions) *leadership* is the function of directing a group toward the achievement of the group's goals, and a *leader* is anyone who performs this function. Where the group goals are not already clear, leadership includes the function of forming or clarifying the goals.[12] Since groups can have both internal and external relationships, leadership both coordinates the activities of members and conducts transactions between the group and outsiders.

In this section we will examine leadership as it functions in an informal group. Here the leader holds his position "on his merits" rather than by appointment by a superior authority. In the next section on intermediate suborganizations we will look briefly at the conditions of formal leadership, and the relations between formal and informal leadership.

If the group is a coalition, the chief function of leadership would presumably be that of getting good bargains, and if it is an organization, the function would be mainly that of directing joint production. We will deal first with what may be called pure leadership, in which the group action is directed solely toward group goals. Here the leader receives only the common share of benefit from the achievement of the goals, as such. Any other satisfaction is incidental to being leader, and the group activities are not directed in any degree toward *his* satisfactions as such. We will later note the complications which are added when the leader directs the actions of the group in some part toward his personal goals.

Leadership itself is sometimes divided among several persons, as a group function. Such a division creates an additional problem of analysis. Multiple, or group, leadership will not be discussed here, since it does not seem to change the nature of leadership itself, which is a transactional and communicational relationship with the followers.

Since the leader does or provides certain things, he must have certain abilities. First, he must have instrumental ability. He must know how the actions of the members of the group can be coordinated to reach the goal. If the group is to build a house, he must know how houses are put together, and if the group is to fight a public utilities case through the courts, the leader must know the courts, the law, and the kinds of procedures which are likely to win. If the group function is to bargain with outsiders, the leader must be a good bargainer. Competence in the task to be accomplished is the first requirement of the leader. If he tells the

---

12 Many definitions of leadership include nothing more than the ability to get other persons to do as one wants. That concept is here referred to as interpersonal power. If the term "leadership" is to have any meaning distinct from that of interpersonal power, it would seem to be the focus on group accomplishment. As the subsequent analysis will reveal, all the normal components of interpersonal power can be used in leadership, the unique additional feature of leadership being the application of power toward a common goal.

group to push when it ought to pull, or to buy when it ought to sell, the group will cease to accept his leadership—unless everyone else in the group is even worse. Part of the instrumental ability is that of giving clear communications. Unless instructions are communicated clearly, the work may not get done effectively.

Second, the leader must be able to motivate members. The leader may motivate through communication, as by clarifying goals and showing why they will bring satisfaction—an exercise of moral power. He may also motivate through transactions by giving desired things in return for the member's contributions—an exercise of authority. In the informal group the authority rests upon rewards available within the group, not on rewards provided by the larger organization.

The transaction aspects can be summarized by listing the chief ingredients of the power relation between leader and followers. If A is leader and B the followers, AX represents the costs to A of acting as leader. These include such items as extra effort, thought, worry, and the tension of taking responsibility. They also include the risks of making mistakes, of generating antagonisms, and having to defend the leadership against possible rivals. Leadership may also bring loneliness and a cooling of relations with other members of the group. As Homans reports, the popular worker who is elected shop steward is apt to complain, "No one is your friend any more."[13]

AY in this relationship is the leader's desire for his share in the results of the joint action of the group, along with the recognition, status, appreciation, sense of accomplishment, or other rewards he may get as leader. BX is the members' desire for A's leadership, along with such individual rewards as they might receive in the form of advice, help with their tasks, status by association with the leader, or praise. The more competent the leader and the sounder his advice, the larger is the magnitude of BX. BY is the members' desire to be free from orders or instructions from A (that is, to be free from having to accept subordinate positions as followers), and their desire not to make the contributions to the joint effort which A assigns.

In his relations with members the leader faces problems of bargaining power in particular transactions, and of total power over a series of transactions. To examine bargaining power first, the greater the magnitude of AX and BX the greater will be the contributions the leader can get from the group. Taken by themselves, the greater AX and BX the more effective will be the leadership in accomplishing the group task. The AX factor, which is the cost or reluctance to be leader, may come into the open only if the leader threatens to walk out unless the group

---

[13] George C. Homans, *Social Behavior: Its Elementary Forms* (New York: Harcourt, Brace & World, Inc., 1961), p. 311. The present discussion of leadership is patterned rather closely after Homan's Chapter 14, "Authority," which the interested reader should consult.

performs better. The larger the AY and BY factors, the more will the leader have to give in return for a given amount of response, and the less effective will be the leadership within the scope of the single transaction.

However, the leadership function is not one, but a series of trans-actions. The total accomplishment of the leader will depend not only on his bargaining power in any one transaction, but on his total ability to consummate leadership transactions continuously and repeatedly over a period of time. For total power, a greater AY will cause the leader to complete more transactions with the members, and get more done in total, even though he may get worse terms in particular transactions. This is another instance in which the greater the stake in the major bar-gain (which in this case is that of being accepted and recognized as leader), the less is the bargaining power in the subsidiary transactions. But the ability to consummate many transactions depends on the ability to produce things which satisfy others. Hence, continuing power in leadership, like large or continued total power elsewhere, depends mainly on the ability to "produce."

Many studies have been made of the phenomenon of leadership, and the person seeking practical advice should consult them. One rather strong conclusion is that leadership is *not* some set of personality traits, and certainly not an inborn set. Effective leadership lies in certain kinds of behavior, which behavior can be practiced and learned.[14] With respect to the "productive" aspect, the leader must know how to achieve the task, and how to communicate. As to the transactions aspect, he must be able to see to it that the members of the group see their participation as rewarding, and use such rewards as are available from him personally and within the group. Rewards may be things provided individually to members, or they may lie in the collective satisfaction of seeing the goal accomplished. To do these things successfully the leader must know his people, their strengths, weaknesses, and desires, for both the productive and the motivational purposes. One person, for instance, may feel in-secure after being told a dozen times that his performance was mag-nificent, while another may be ecstatic over a single "not bad."

The overall rules of leadership do not change when we move from the "pure" leader to one who directs the organization toward his own personal goals. But the content of the components changes, and depends much on the kinds of rewards the leader wants. If he is content with praise and signs of deference, these may be easily arranged. If he wants personal services, money, or material goods from the group, then pre-sumably he will have to satisfy rather substantial wants for his follow-ers. In the typical suborganization this kind of thing is likely to occur only if the leader diverts some of the rewards of the larger organization to motivate the people in his group to satisfy *his*, rather than the organi-

---

14 See Donald W. Olmsted, *op. cit.*, p. 39, whose position reflects that found in many other sources.

zation's, goals. This can be done most easily by a leader in the formal structure, like a foreman or superintendent, who takes kickbacks for easier or better paying jobs. Otherwise an independent organization, like a club or a gang, is more likely to be able to provide rewards of this sort to the leader. In the normal suborganization the leader's rewards will be mainly status and his share in the group accomplishment.

Like other types of power, leadership can be self-reinforcing. As one acquires the power of leadership in the group he is able to influence more persons more strongly than before he became leader, which influence can be reinvested to strengthen his leadership, and so on.

INTERMEDIATE SUBORGANIZATIONS

We have examined the model of a pure formal suborganization. This is a pure "line" structure, with all leadership, rewards, and goals being controlled by the successive steps of the hierarchy toward the goals of the overall organization. We have also examined the pure informal suborganization, whose leadership, rewards, and goals are all controlled from within the group, and not at all by higher authority. We now move to the intermediate situation, where leadership, rewards, and goals are controlled partly by the larger organization and partly by the group. This is a much more realistic situation than either of the pure forms.

As we move into this area, we may recall that transactions range from the extreme of highly explicit exchanges of goods to the opposite extreme of vague exchanges called open-end transactions, with interrelated transactions, quasi exchanges, and implied bargains in between. It is not necessary to trace all the details, but transactions within organizations, including transactions which exercise authority, also range from the highly explicit to the highly vague and tenuous.

Staff Relationships

A major deviation from the pure formal, line relationship is the staff relationship. Within this section the term "staff" will be used with the meaning customary to studies of organization, which contrasts staff with line, rather than with the meaning used elsewhere in this volume, which contrasts staff to sponsors and recipients.

The staff relation is conceptually an extension of informal assistance to the formal structure. Suppose that a shipping clerk forgets how to handle some problem in keeping his records. He can, of course, go to his boss, who is his formal leader. But the boss is the man who writes the clerk's merit ratings and recommends him for raises or promotions. The boss might think the clerk stupid for forgetting his instructions—or at least the clerk is afraid that he might—and besides the boss is busy. Hence, the clerk may go instead to the informal group leader, who may reward the clerk with the proper answer without lowering him in the eyes of the boss. The informal leader receives the rewards of attention, thanks, and the praise implicit in the clerk's turning to him for advice. For convenience or numerous other reasons—and not only when they have forgotten instructions—members of groups often turn to an informal leader for help in their problems. The important thing is that, although the members of the group remain formally responsible to the formal supervisor, *the informal leader has given instructions*.

In the complex organizations many kinds of specialized information are needed within a department which neither the formal leader nor his subordinates can be expected to know. Further, many specialized services may be needed which they cannot be expected to perform. When a particular specialized service or advice is needed in several subdivisions of the organization—like making blueprints, planning floor layouts, handling grievances, or recruiting new employees—a specialist in that skill may be employed. His advice and services are made available to anyone in the organization who needs them for his job. Such a specialist occupies a *staff* position, and if numerous specialists of his type are employed they constitute a *staff department*.

Although many staff departments spend their main energies performing services, our main concern is with the change in authority relations when they give advice. Suppose a foreman asks his superintendent, "What's the best way to teach these new men?" The superintendent replies, "I'm not sure, but there's a training specialist in the personnel department. Try setting it up the way he suggests." Although, according to the formal structure, the foreman is responsible to the superintendent, and is acting on the superintendent's instructions, those instructions have undergone a significant change. In exercising his authority the superintendent no longer says: "Do as *I* say," but "Do as *he* says." Further, the superintendent has no authority over *him*. Nor is the superintendent any longer in a position fully to evaluate the foreman's performance in his training role, since he himself is not a specialist in training.

As soon as we recognize that a person can "formally" be expected to accept instructions from someone not his formal line superior, we are prepared to recognize the many intermediate states where a man is *expected* to take another's advice, even though he is not *instructed* to. Whyte[15] cites the example of a plant manager who felt obligated to consult Harry, an older and much respected vice-president of industrial relations. Harry had no formal authority over the plant manager, and would have been careful not to say anything unless asked. But the plant manager knew that if he had made a decision either on his own or contrary to Harry's advice, and if it had not turned out well, he would be in a very embarrassing position when *his* boss asked, "What did Harry suggest?" In short, not only may informal leaders exist in addition to the line and staff relationship, but they may acquire semiofficial status and authority.

---

[15] William Foote Whyte, *Men At Work* (Homewood, Ill.: The Dorsey Press, Inc., 1961), p. 559.

Furthermore, many suborganizations performing direct productive functions evolve from experience, and are completely unacknowledged in the formal structure. A reporter, a photographer, and a lithographer may become a closely coordinated and highly efficient suborganization in a newspaper firm, and the editor may depend heavily on it, even though the organization chart and the files give no hint of its existence.

All large organizations are crisscrossed with informal and semiformal suborganizations of this sort, and could not operate without them. This fact has important repercussions on the concept of organization, and on authority and responsibility. Where line relations remain clear, authority and responsibility go hand in hand, as in the formal model. But if authority is the ability to grant or withhold rewards, and responsibility is the position of the person on whom authority is exercised in the real organization, the relation is not the single-minded thing shown in the traditional organization chart. Staff departments on an official basis, and informal leaders of all sorts on an unofficial basis, issue instructions, and often possess substantial rewards which they can withhold if their instructions are not followed. Hence, employees at various levels are also "responsible" to staff and informal leaders in a very real sense.

These modifications greatly dilute and sometimes directly thwart the sponsor control that supposedly operates mainly through the formal structure. Although the seasoned administrator will try to use the informal organization rather than fight it, he can by no means bring all of it to support the sponsor goals. The informal group has goals of its own, in congeniality, status, mutual help, and acting as a coalition to fight what in *its* opinion are excessive sponsor demands. As March and Simon observe, "employees are notoriously suspicious and cynical regarding announced performance criteria,"[16] and it is always difficult for sponsors to get more production than the group accepts as "fair."

In the actual organization, it is simply not true that the formal leader controls all the rewards. Substantial rewards, some more important than an increase in pay, lie with the informal leadership and group pressures. Holding rewards, they also possess authority. How well the whole organization can perform its sponsors' goals depends to a large extent on the degree to which it can keep the goals of the informal organizations in line with the goals of the formal ones. The satisfactoriness of the organization as a place to work also depends in part on the same factors, since a job can be frustrating and tension producing if the formal and informal authorities pull the employee in opposite directions. A still further complication is that an employee may be a member of two or more informal groups, and show divided or vacillating loyalties. An employee, for instance, may be a member of his office group, a work team scattered in several departments (like the reporter, photographer, and lithographer),

---

[16] March and Simon, *op. cit.*, p. 62.

a company bowling league, a plant safety committee, and the negotiating committee of the union.

The sponsor interest is presumably served best if the formal leaders show the leadership abilities which make good informal leaders. This is certainly the strongest position of leadership, since the formal leader has access to the organization's rewards in pay and position as well as the informal rewards. But rarely can one person perform both functions completely unless the suborganization is small. Leadership requires many areas of competence, and few persons possess them all. And there may be some hesitancy for employees to ask advice of the formal leader if asking may reveal their weaknesses. Since it cannot eliminate the informal structure, the formal organization will be better off to learn to live with it than to fight it.

Chapter 27

ORGANIZATIONS:
MISCELLANEOUS FACTORS

RULES, DECISIONS, AND BARGAINING

RULES IN an organization are much like habits to the individual—they reduce the decision process to the act of identifying the stimulus. They also produce uniformity among different persons. Uniformity often increases efficiency even if the uniform way is not itself the most efficient. Rules also prescribe the terms of certain transactions in advance and avoid the play of bargaining power over them. They do this primarily by making a supervisor at some level an agent for a higher level without power to change the terms. March and Simon point out that the legitimacy of supervisory power is enhanced if the power is less visible,[1] and that the holders of formal authority tend to conceal bargaining solutions (i.e., power solutions) to conflicts under the guise that the problem is analytical.[2] The reason for reducing the visibility of power can be seen if we visualize a line officer allowing decisions to be made on a bargaining power basis.

Suppose a position as squad leader is open, and Jack and Bill apply for it. They are about equally competent, and the foreman does not want to lose either man. Jack is known to have been eying a job in another firm owned by his cousin, and will probably quit if he does not get the promotion. Bill is tied down with financial troubles, and is unwilling to take any risks entailed in changing jobs. Jack has far more bargaining power, and under normal circumstances will get the job if the foreman can manage it without creating trouble. The foreman will tend to find or invent some principle regarding seniority, ability, age, or other factor to justify the choice. But he normally will *not* mention the implied threat of Jack's leaving, and if challenged will probably vigorously deny that it had anything to do with the case. Why?

The department would become a vast tangle of threats, counter-

---

[1] James G. March and Herbert A. Simon, *Organizations* (New York: John Wiley & Sons, 1958), p. 44.
[2] *Ibid.*, p. 131.

threats, strategies, tactics and assorted other bargaining activities as soon as employees sensed that their position depended on immediate, straight-forward bargaining power. Some employees would threaten to quit whenever they wanted to enhance their bargaining power, and the foreman would not know whether they meant it or not. If the threat brought no concessions, the employee would either have to leave or face a disastrous loss of bargaining power thereafter. The foreman would be forced to counter with hints, threats, and other tactical maneuvers. One of the great advantages of continued relationships is that the use of tactics can be largely eliminated. To acknowledge that particular settlements are based on bargaining power would prevent this efficient situation.

To take another example, suppose Joe is bored with his job in the Corroborating Department and asks to exchange jobs on a one week trial basis with a bored friend in the Bilking Department. The two jobs are not in the normal line of transfer, being quite dissimilar. Joe's fore-man objects that the retraining would cost the company money. Joe offers to accept a deduction from his pay of more than enough to cover any losses incurred from the trial. In a unique transaction Joe has sufficient bargaining power to get his request.

The foreman knows, however (or will soon learn to his sorrow), that the transaction is not unique, and that to grant it would be a precedent for all to see that any desired job transfer is negotiable if one offers the proper inducements. After negotiating permission on a similar basis, other employees might then transfer, dislike the new job, transfer back, be billed by the company for its losses, and then quit. The company might then refuse such requests unless the employee put up a bond for the amount of the probable losses. This in turn would lead to disputes over the actual costs to the company, and complaints that it was playing Shy-lock.

The foreman's position is simplified and strengthened immeasurably if he can reply at the outset, "Sorry, Joe, I'd like to accommodate you. But the company doesn't allow trials like that, and my hands are tied."

The Rule is the organization's defense against individual attempts to bargain for better terms. Under *The Rule*, the line officer is not a de-cision maker or bargainer, but an agent for his principal. He need not himself refute an argument, but merely report that "they" won't change the rule.

In addition to their role in simplifying decisions, rules also stabilize bargaining power relations. In the absence of such rules bargaining power and terms would not be the same in any two cases. Even more unstabiliz-ing, Bill's bargaining power would be different after Jack's bargain than before it, and so would the company's. The organization's life is compli-cated enough, and unless it can make many situations nonbargainable, the complication is beyond managing.

An unbargainable rule, however, also ties the organization's hands, as illustrated by mandatory retirement at age 65. Under mandatory retirement the deteriorating employee can be eliminated gracefully. Another, however, may be just reaching his peak of usefulness at 65. But the rule prevents the company from keeping him, since a single exception destroys the ability to say to the next man, "Sorry, but we can't keep you no matter how much we need you." To make one instance bargainable makes them all bargainable—or at least makes their bargainability bargainable.

If the visibility of the exception can be kept low, or if the exception can be categorized in a way that is not likely to be repeated, exceptions can be made without setting uncomfortable precedents. "Well, okay if you don't say anything" is the attempt to keep visibility low; and "Okay, I can't imagine that the problem will ever come up again" is the recognition of a unique situation which will cause no trouble as a precedent. Making exceptions with children can be particularly troublesome, since they do not recognize the finespun distinctions that make a particular situation unique.

Viewing the whole problem, we see that one of the major tasks in managing is to determine which transactions shall be bargainable and which not. The larger the number of bargainable transactions, the greater is the organization's flexibility to adapt to changing circumstances and personnel. But the greater, too, is the amount of time and energy that must be devoted to negotiating, and the more complex (probably in geometric ratio) is the number of intertransactional power relations of any one transaction. It is therefore a virtual necessity that many transactions within the organization be made nonbargainable. If these are clearly spelled out, and are made known to each person before he affiliates with the organization, they become part of the major bargain. It is not possible to make all relationships nonbargainable, of course, since this would be the same as complete lack of flexibility. The organization must therefore so arrange things that those transactions in which it wants to retain flexibility will remain bargainable. Those in which the cost of flexibility is too great must be covered by rules. The simplest avenue for accomplishing nonbargainability of these rules is to deny the bargaining agents of the organization (i.e., the lower levels of supervision) the authority to deviate.

Rules sometimes need to be changed. If the rules deal with subsidiary points over which the organization has acknowledged authority, no problem arises. But sometimes changes are needed which alter the major bargain itself. If the change affects only one employee, he can bargain about it with the organization, and either a mutually satisfactory arrangement will be made or he will leave. The real problem is that of a change in a rule which affects the major bargain of many employees, and it is not feasible for either side to have them leave. What happens to legitimacy at this point?

A change in organizational structure, such as the elimination, combining, or splitting of divisions, is particularly apt to cause difficulty. The management is apt to view it purely as a "production" problem, and therefore completely within its authority. But the employees in the affected departments are apt to view it as a change in the major bargain which seriously affects their immediate bargaining power, and as a possible threat to their jobs, status, security, chances of advancement, or salaries. It will almost certainly bring some rearrangement of group alignments, which will enhance the power of some and reduce that of others.

One path for the organization is to ignore these fears (or hopes) and simply announce and carry through its proposed changes, perhaps controlling some realignments and letting others fall where they may. If the organization up to that point has built an image of itself as legitimate, and as the protector of the interests of the staff, this move shatters that image, and makes it difficult to rebuild. Since the organization has used what the staff consider illegitimate authority to change the major bargain to suit its own convenience, a natural aftermath is for the employees to feel entitled to use illegitimate evasions of authority thereafter when these suit *their* convenience. The staff will tend to take an initial defensive stance toward *any* proposal from the organization until their own positions are assured. The organization's assertion of its freedom to make important changes without prior staff approval can therefore be expected to reduce the organization's flexibility in gaining ungrudging assent in the details of daily life thereafter. Single large, or repeated small, uses of illegitimate authority often lead to malingering, efforts to evade or thwart instructions, and a general unenthusiasm toward the organization's goals.

A second and opposite path for the organization is to accept its major policies and structures as part of its major bargain, mutually accepted by the employees and employer in the contract of affiliation. Even though these rules were initially drafted unilaterally by the organization, to construe them as a bilateral agreement means they cannot be changed in important ways without mutual consent. This consent can be obtained in several ways. One is for some formally recognized representatives of the employees, such as a union or an office committee, to examine the proposals and accept them, perhaps with modifications. A less formal way is to publish the tentative proposals for comment and possible revision. The legitimizing effect of the "trial balloon" is reflected in the perceptive homespun rule, "Never take 'em by surprise."[3] Other methods include discussions by supervisors at various levels, who will inform themselves about opinions within their divisions.

A major difficulty of getting comments from subordinates is similar to that of other information flows, but perhaps in stronger form. Since the future welfare of almost everyone depends on decisions by those above, many persons make (or refrain from making) comments more with an eye on their tactical effects on future transactions than on their

---

[3] The rule, of course, deals with continuing cooperative relations. The opposite rule applies to the unique bargain.

feelings about the immediate proposal. Even a highly objectionable proposal may thus be "accepted" if employees feel that their personal futures may be impaired by objecting.

Because of the many complications involved, those in authority rather uniformly try to hide the power base or content of their decisions. If they engage in a major change of policy with respect to employees they will try to make it appear (1) that no change in power is occurring, (2) that they are using only such power as was legitimized through the employees' acceptance of affiliation, or that (3) the change is bilateral, and hence legitimate, by virtue of being accepted by the employees through polls, discussions, or opportunities for criticism. It is a rare organization which overtly acknowledges that its employees may refrain from speaking their minds out of fear for their own futures. It is also a rare organization in which many employees do *not* hesitate to criticize administration proposals for precisely that reason.

This does not mean that executives are typically ogres who record employee comments in a little black book and reward only those who say the right things. It means that even the executive who most sincerely desires free expression from his subordinates has trouble getting it, because of certain psychological and tactical factors. Even highly objective persons are apt to feel that those who praise them show sound judgment, and feel intuitively that executives probably respond similarly. The superior presumably does not put forth a proposal unless *he* considers it sound. To criticize the proposal is potentially to label oneself of unsound judgment. Although this handicap to free upward communication can never be completely overcome, it can be minimized if the higher levels label their proposals as *highly* tentative, subject to serious modification or withdrawal upon receipt of comment—even if the upper levels have already given the proposal thorough study and can imagine no possible objection. Another technique, of course, is for the higher levels merely to state the problem, and let suggestions be initiated at the lower levels. Even then, however, some tendency exists to "sense" what the "brass" wants, and to suggest it. To avoid being surrounded by a group of "yes men" is one of the major tasks of the good executive. Although at this point we are speaking of the bargaining power aspects of decisions which change the major bargain, some of the observations are also pertinent to the information aspects of participation in decisions discussed in Chapter 25.

MANAGEMENT AS A HIERARCHY OF BARGAINS

Every supervisory person in the line hierarchy is a middleman. He receives instructions from above and passes them on with or without interpretation or modification to those below. He also bargains, in three main ways. (1) He acts as an agent for those above him when he bargains with those below, (2) he acts as an agent for those below when he bargains with those above, and (3) he bargains in his own behalf as a principal, mainly with those above, but occasionally with those below. These bargains show many interactions, and we will deal with only the more important ones.

In bargaining with those below, the supervisor acts largely as the agent for those above. He may act under explicit instructions: "These terms and no others." He may be given limited latitude: "Get the best you can, but accept no worse terms than these." Or he may have almost complete discretion: "Accept any reasonable terms." As with any other middleman, the terms he can offer or accept on one side affect, and are affected by, what happens on the other.

To oversimplify his position in the production structure, a supervisor concludes a bargain with the organization to provide it certain production results in return for which the organization provides him a budget and certain discretion in its use. To deal with the costs of staff, whether a particular bargain with those above will be acceptable to him depends on what kind of a bargain he can drive with those below. Conversely, his willingness to accept certain terms with his subordinates depends on the bargains he can reach with those above. These terms include pay, quantity and quality of materials, machines, personnel, and other items. If the supervisor does not think the budget is adequate to meet his responsibilities, he must insist on either (1) an increase in budget or a decrease in assignment, or (2) a contingency arrangement in which the organization will agree to accept added costs or decreased results.

If some change takes place on one side which leaves him an inadequate margin, or no margin, between the two sets of bargains, he will seek to modify the bargain on one or both sides. If subordinates claim their materials have deteriorated and they can no longer produce as well as before, the supervisor must either get them to accept the poorer materials or seek to get improved materials from above. Since his superiors *provide* the materials and the subordinates *use* them, he is an agent for the subordinates when he bargains above for improved materials, and an agent for his superiors when he bargains with the subordinates to accept what they have.

If the supervisor has adamant people on both sides, his position may be difficult indeed. Experienced bargainers know that they often strengthen their agent's hand by denying him any discretion. The superiors may therefore tell the supervisor that they absolutely cannot get better materials, while the subordinates meanwhile insist they absolutely cannot use what they have. Each will assume that if the supervisor is worth his salt he will get a concession from the other side.

Since the materials he is bargaining about are not his own, the supervisor can take the role of mediator, and avoid taking sides. He is not likely to be completely neutral in this role, however, though he can come close to it. He is paid from above, and his future is apt to be brighter if he bargains harder for his superiors against his subordinates than the reverse. This is not always the case, however. Some supervisors value a good working relationship with their men above their desire for advancement, and will do their hardest bargaining in their behalf. The result in actuality is often in the best, long run interest of the organization. The supervisor who fills the mediator role well can be unusually valuable. By dropping his role as agent he may gain confidential expressions from both sides from which to fashion a compromise acceptable to both.

Throughout all these negotiations the supervisor is also a principal defending his own interest, and the supervisory ulcer often reflects conflict among the roles of mediator, principal, and bivalent agent.

In addition to these bargaining positions, the supervisor is a middleman in an authority chain. Being himself an employee, he will be concerned that orders he receives are legitimate to him, in his own right. But he is also a supervisor who does not want to issue illegitimate orders to those below him. As noted above, to enforce an illegitimate order is to change the major bargain without the subordinates' consent. As such it seemingly relieves the subordinates of the obligation to meet their half of the bargain, and makes it more difficult for the supervisor to get their cooperation thereafter. If he senses his own position accurately, the supervisor will therefore protest as illegitimate *to him* any order which would necessitate his issuing orders which would be construed as illegitimate by those below him.

In several additional ways the demands of higher authority may weaken the leadership position of the supervisor. When the supervisor bargains on his own behalf, as for a promotion or raise, the rejection of his requests demonstrates him to be a relatively weak bargainer, or of relatively little value, and hence reduces his status with those below him. A reprimand or other punishment of the supervisor for presumed improper behavior will lower his status and bargaining power over his subordinates.[4] Measures of the opposite sort tend to raise status and power.

This set of relations often places the higher supervision in a quandary. The organization needs to maintain the status of its supervisors. But to do so increases their bargaining power with the organization. Conversely, the techniques by which the supervisor is kept within the control of the organization may reduce his ability to control those below him. In the authority area this relation parallels that in the rewards area: the organization gains by making an employee more productive, as by giving him training and experience. But as soon as he becomes more productive, his bargaining power rises.

We have discussed only three steps in the level of authority—the supervisor, those below him and those above. The larger organization may have five, six, or more levels, with the same relationships prevailing throughout. Whether the complications raised by multiple levels are addi-

---

[4] See March & Simon, *op. cit.*, p. 78.

tive, multiplicative, or offsetting requires more information or a more detailed model than need be discussed here.

In a very real sense the major job of top management is that of general supervisor of bargains.[5] Although people in organizations do not use the terminology employed here, experienced administrators understand the power factors in their positions, and behave accordingly. To display these power factors analytically may make them more explicit, but it does not reveal anything most seasoned executives do not already know. After all, we have seen that even the second-grader senses and uses some of the main components of bargaining power and tactics.

DISCIPLINE, INSUBORDINATION, AND REVOLT

Although each member of the staff accepts an authority relation when he joins the organization, questions may arise from time to time whether a particular exercise of authority is legitimate. Several problems of this sort may be explored in connection with discipline, insubordination, and revolt.

Discipline

Discipline is not a special phenomenon, but part of the day-to-day process of relating rewards to performance. Organizational life is complex, and it is not feasible to measure and reward each individual's performance separately every day, hour, or minute. Even where output is objectively measurable and employees can be paid on piece rates, the whole of a worker's performance covers more than units of output, and includes such things as regularity of attendance, adaptability to new tasks, and the observance of safety and other regulations. In day-to-day operations a wide band of levels of performance is considered satisfactory, and (again, except for pay for measured units of output) no attempt is made to relate rewards directly to performance within that band. If performance falls conspicuously above or below that band, however, rewards may be increased or decreased. Conventionally we refer to an increase as a reward or incentive, and to a decrease as a disciplinary action. The nature of the increase or decrease in reward depends on the nature of the deviation from normal performance. Positive rewards for unusually good job performance, as such, include in-grade raises in pay, bonuses, praise, a good merit rating, promotion, and so forth. Negative "rewards," or withdrawals of rewards for unusually bad performance include the withholding of merit increases, demotion, transfer to simpler jobs, or discharge. Certain actions are remedial, without positive or negative implica-

---

[5] Expressed in these words, this general idea appears in Neil Chamberlain's *A General Theory of Economic Process* (New York: Harper & Bros., 1955). The present volume accepts Chamberlain's proposition, though with much difference in overall context, a different definition of bargaining power, and the additional concept of total power.

tions, such as job training, or transfer of a person into jobs for which he is better suited, possibly at his own request.

Conformance to rules under the authority relation is essentially taken for granted, and no rewards are provided explicitly for conformance, although prompt and cooperative response may be considered an important criterion for promotion to more responsible positions. Nonacceptance or violation of directions and rules does call for explicit negative action, however, such as criticism, formal notice of violation, restriction of certain privileges, temporary disciplinary layoff without pay, or discharge. We can distinguish at the extremes between pure cases of poor performance (the worker tries hard but lacks the ability) and nonconformance to authority (the worker turns out good quantity and quality of output, but insists despite warnings on smoking in the no-smoking areas or putting his tools in the aisle where others stumble over them). Some cases are mixtures, as when the worker turns out poor quality because he stubbornly uses an unauthorized method, or poor quantity because he takes unauthorized rest periods. The main point is that so-called incentives and disciplinary action are parts of the total set of transactions which motivate workers to conform to organizational goals.

Insubordination

Some workers find assorted and devious techniques for evading instructions without seeming to reject them. *Insubordination*, however, is a conscious and clearly acknowledged refusal to follow an instruction, and is a rejection of the major bargain. As such it is typically construed to terminate that bargain, with the appropriate next step being discharge.

The details are not always simple, however. If the helmsman refuses to head the ship for an iceberg, if the factory hand refuses to operate an unsafe machine or ruin an expensive piece of equipment, is he punishable for insubordination? To take the last case as the simplest of the three, if the supervisor shortly learns that to have followed his instructions *would* have ruined the machine, the insubordination has saved the supervisor's skin, and he had better hope that the incident will be promptly forgotten —though the worker is "one up" on him thereafter. Any conspicuous failure of an important leadership function destroys the authority of the leader, at least for the moment and with respect to the individual and incident concerned. Repeated instances will get the supervisor into trouble with his superiors or subordinates, and he will have to be replaced if work and discipline are to be maintained.

The worker's choice is relatively simple in rejecting an order he thinks will seriously injure him, since he presumably would rather lose the job than accept the injury. But the question is whether he *should* lose it, or be otherwise punished. The answer could, of course, be spelled out in the major bargain, so that both sides would know what orders and refusals are legitimate and what illegitimate. It generally is not, and no fixed answer is at present accepted, though the practice of arbitration in the United States may provide some guidance. If a worker refuses an instruction not involving safety on the ground that it is illegitimate, the traditional position has been that the mere fact of insubordination is punishable. The employee is expected to perform the instruction, and later appeal to higher authority for clarification. More recently some arbitrators have ruled that the employee can take his chances in refusing an order. If later investigation shows that the order *was* illegitimate, no penalty ensues. If the employee turns out to be wrong, he can be punished. When an arbitration decision is handed down where the major bargain was previously unclear, the decision presumably settles the issue for all subsequent cases of like kind in the firm, and thereafter *is* part of the major bargain.

The degree to which instructions can feasibly be temporarily set aside at the discretion and risk of the subordinate would seem to depend much on the nature and goals of the organization. The greater the importance of detailed coordination of the parts, and of immediate performance of each detail, the less is the tolerance for this "tentative insubordination." In a machine shop or research laboratory where each person works independently, and where safety and haste are not involved, it might be feasible to investigate *any* disputed instruction for legitimacy before the superior insists that it be carried out. By contrast, no such prior investigation could be tolerated in the armed forces, and "perform now, argue later" is also necessary to avoid inordinate costs on assembly lines and other highly coordinated operations. Stated differently, the less the degree of subordination of the parts to the whole the less is the possibility of insubordination, and the less its cost.

Questions of legitimacy can arise in numerous areas. The area discussed thus far might be called "qualitative," in which a person objects that he has been asked to do the *wrong kind* of work. Quantitative illegitimacy would be asserted if an employee complained that he was asked to do *too much* work, and he might also assert that the *wrong person* was issuing orders. Even the removal of status symbols might be alleged to be illegitimate, and the employee might refuse to work until they are restored. The general observations above about the consequences of illegitimate action on power would seem to apply equally, regardless of the type of illegitimacy.

Revolt

When insubordination moves from the rejection of a single instruction by a single individual to the rejection of more orders by more persons, it becomes *revolt*. Revolt is most complete when all subordinates reject all instructions. This is tantamount to an insistence either that the organization itself be dissolved or that the leaders, rules, or goals be changed. Among the situations where it might be used, revolt is most appropriate to a general purpose organization in which membership is compulsory, like the state. It is least appropriate to a limited purpose voluntary organization, which one can leave if he does not wish to accept its authority. Revolt might make sense in the latter organization if the members have a large stake in remaining, such as a large investment, or no alternative organizations to affiliate with. Without going into questions of contractual obligations or possible illegal weapons, revolt might be appropriate action for coal miners in an isolated, company dominated, one-employer town, but inappropriate for workers in a small manufacturing firm in a large city.

A ship at sea is a total, if small, society and government, and is handled according to the same general rules as unlimited purpose government rather than limited purpose organizations. The crew or passenger of ship or plane cannot quit or be discharged in midpassage. The question of revolt is tied with that of legitimacy of government, which will be discussed in later chapters. Even in the limited purpose organization where termination of the relation is possible, repeated and widespread insubordination may bring an organization to question its authority structure, and possibly to revise it.

SIZE AND STRUCTURE OF ORGANIZATIONS

In some important respects organization is like a book. If it deals with one aspect of one topic it will tend to be small, and if it deals with many aspects of many topics it will tend to be large. Books have different internal structures, and even two textbooks of the same size on the same subject may have different numbers of chapters, in different sequence, and on different sets of topics. There are also differences in internal cohesion. Some have all parts closely related, while others are only loosely related, and sometimes consist of collections of essays by different authors.

The organization similarly has the major characteristics of size, arrangement of parts, and interrelation of parts. Size can be measured by number of employees or members; by amount of equipment, buildings, or land owned; by amount of money controlled; or by other possible measures. Structure has many facets, one being the degree of centralization or decentralization of control and another the arrangement of the sets and subsets of decisions, transactions, transformations, and persons. The whole question of the determinants of size and structure is far beyond the scope of this volume. We will confine attention here to the meaning of structure and to the way in which the determinants of size and structure could be categorized in the present framework.

In the organization, as in the book, the main aspect of structure is concerned with the arrangement of the main sets and subsets. For example, suppose a government provides credit for farmers, research for farmers, credit for housing, and research for housing. Assuming that we do not wish to operate all four independently, these four items can be arranged in either of two main relationships, as follows:

I	II
A. Farm	A. Credit
1. Credit	1. Farm
2. Research	2. Housing
B. Housing	B. Research
1. Credit	1. Farm
2. Research	2. Housing

Under the relationship at I, the farm supervisor would have line authority over a credit and a research function, and so would the housing supervisor. There could also, of course, be staff relationships to exchange information between the two credit groups and the two research groups. Under the relationship at II, by contrast, the credit supervisor would have line authority over farming and housing functions, and so would the research supervisor. Again staff relationships could cut across the two major divisions.

Neither arrangement is inherently better, and the relations of parts to whole and to each other depend on a series of factors to be indicated below. Complaints are often heard, "Why can't the government centralize all its lending operations in one agency so they can be run more efficiently?" The answer is that if this were done someone else could complain, "Why can't the government put all its farm activities into one bureau instead of having them scattered around in different agencies?" If the government provides multiple credit and multiple farm services, it is impossible simultaneously to have all credit activities in a credit bureau and all farm activities in a farm bureau. Like the author of the book, the government must put farm credit under the heading of credit problems or under farm problems; to "centralize" it under one heading removes it from related problems under the other. The problem is not unique to government, but is found in all organizations.

However they are arranged, all four subdivisions also have problems of personnel. Shall all personnel problems of all four be handled from a single center, should each subdivision have its own personnel department, or should there be one for credit and one for research, and so forth? Similar problems arise in connection with purchasing, printing, accounting, legal, and other staff services, and there is no inherent reason why all staff services should follow the same pattern. There are almost limitless ways the large organization can be put together, far more, in fact, than any one administrator will ever conceive. The actual structure is likely to reflect the pattern of its own historical growth as much as any total evaluation. Because of the complexity of both the organization and its environment, the structure of an organization well adapted to its environment is apt to look "messy" on paper. Good conformance to the facts of organizational life is rarely "neat," and the logical, symmetrical organization chart is apt to be better art than organization.

A reasonable simplicity of overall structure is nevertheless necessary if executives are to know what they are doing. For much the same kind of reason that a decision must ignore most potentially relevant factors in favor of a few dominant ones, so must the structure of the organization ignore many details to get the best relation among major parts. In addition, executives move from organization to organization, and the same person is often simultaneously on the board of several—business, charitable, cooperative, governmental, and others. Many executives study in the same schools, read the same management journals, and belong to the same clubs. Management thus becomes a subculture as well as a science or applied art. Organizational structures are sociofacts, and tend to show considerable similarity within a given management culture.

In line with the previous analysis, the problem of determining the most effective size and structure of an organization can be visualized as the analysis of a system whose main elements are communications, transformations, and transactions, both within the system and between the system and its environment. The system must be analyzed to determine the optimum position of some one or combination of values under different arrangements of internal and external elements. To illustrate, the external communications of the system will be at a minimum if they all flow through a central point. But the internal communications will then necessarily be larger if each subunit is to be in touch with the environment. By contrast, if each subunit communicates directly with the environment, external communications increase but internal communications (of external information) decrease, conceivably to zero. Similarly, if the organization makes all outside purchases of materials through a central agency, the number of external transactions is minimized, but numerous internal transactions are required as materials are disbursed to the various subdivisions. By contrast, all internal transactions of materials are eliminated if each subdivision does its own outside purchasing. Many additional factors are involved. But we have illustrated a central feature of the organization as a system: that internal transactions and communications tend to vary directly and external ones inversely with the degree of centralization. These opposite relationships provide the possibility of an equilibrium point.

The question of size differs from one type of organization to another. It is inappropriate to go after a mosquito with an H-bomb or a rhinoceros with a water pistol, and the size of the organization must be geared to the size of its task. The object of a profit firm is profit, and there is no logical limit to the goal, or the size of the organization which tries to achieve it. After making a large profit selling Sanskrit texts to the Eskimos, the imaginative enterpriser may go on to expand and make even larger profits selling steak knives to cannibals. Whereas the firm may have a single objective of unlimited size, a government, by contrast, may have no limit to the number of its possible objectives, though there may be limits to the size of any one of them. A professional society or a bowling club can remain limited in size; in fact it may lose its ability to perform if it grows. If the staff take over sponsorship, however, almost any organization may show signs of "wanting" to grow, since growth raises the prestige, security, and often the pay of the staff—which leads us to the next topic.

WHEN STAFF BECOME SPONSORS

A persistent tendency of human organizations throughout history is for the staff to take over all or much of the sponsor control. The hired hands become boss. Several strong factors work in this direction. First, in most organizations the staff have more stake than the sponsors. The pastor of a church, the manager of the automobile club, or the full time business agent of the union typically has more stake in his organization than any nonstaff member of the sponsor or recipient group. Although large stockholders in a corporation may have as much stake as the president, stockholders typically diversify their holdings so that the demise of any one corporation is not disastrous. This stronger stake exercised over many transactions and many years will tend to give the staff more total power.

Second, the staff often control major feedbacks of information to the sponsors. This does not mean that the staff can report anything they like and have it accepted, for sponsors are not necessarily fools, or devoid of independent information. An important check is that the auditors are normally hired by the board, not the staff. Nevertheless the staff are intimately familiar with the data of the reports, they sometimes initiate the classification system for the reports, and do much of the initial absorption of uncertainty. Top staff members are normally better informed about operations than the sponsors with whom they bargain. The sponsor with high stake can, of course, take an operating post and keep control. But it is important to note that in doing so he defends his sponsor interest by joining the staff.

A third factor is that in a battle for control, the staff often have access to the organization's resources to defend their position, while their opponents in the sponsor ranks outside must use their own resources. The officers of the "inside controlled" corporation can send out numerous illustrated brochures in full color on slick paper to half a million stockholders at no personal expense, while a group of stockholders who feel the officers have usurped control must dig deep into their own pockets to distribute even a simple mimeographed circular. The incumbents of offices in government, business, charity, labor union or other organization typically have superior access to the organization's prestige, mailing lists, and other channels of communication. Unless they make serious mistakes, channel conspicuously large favors to themselves, or use blatant methods, the top administrative officers of most organizations can defend their control against all comers.

This relationship is perhaps most likely to occur in the profit organization. Except for the period of initial formation, at which time the necessary funds are put up by the promoters or stockholders, the money available to the top staff officers arises from the organization's own activity. Unlike the officers of the cooperative, service, or pressure organization, the officers of the corporation get their money for day to day operations from the customers (recipients), not the sponsors. Once established, the officers of the inside controlled corporation make the crucial decision as to how much profit will be returned to the stockholders and how much will be retained for reinvestment. At that point the officers control the residual contribution, and there remains no doubt about who is in charge.

In one respect the problem of staff becoming sponsors is related to the problem of evaluating the organization's performance, as described in Chapter 22. Although the proposition needs empirical testing, it would seem probable that the greater the accuracy and objectivity with which the staff performance can be evaluated, the less would be the likelihood that the staff could take over sponsor control.

For all these reasons, the interests of the staff cause the organization to take on a "life of its own" in a more cogent sense than in the earlier statement that it is more than the sum of its parts. If the recipients do not want the service of the organization, the staff will spend great effort to make them want it. If the original sponsors no longer see any point to the organization, the staff will either try to revive their flagging interest or (in the profit organization) take over the sponsor control directly. In the long view of history, whether we look at governments, churches, schools, charities, corporations, clubs, professional organizations, or unions, the real control after a period of time tends to gravitate to the "professionals" who occupy the full time posts, and who thereafter spend the organization's own resources to create a demand by sponsor or recipient groups sufficient to continue the organization. Since their pay and prestige tend to vary directly with the size of the organization, they seek not only to continue it, but also to make it grow. This tendency to growth is augmented by the fact that size is one of the few objective measures of "success."

The logic applies to suborganizations as well as to whole ones. It is not merely government, as such, which tends to expand and perpetuate itself, but also the Department of Justice, the Interstate Commerce Commission, the armed forces, the tax bureau, and the courts. It is not merely the corporation which does this, but the sales department, the purchasing department, and the methods and research division. It is not merely the whole university which wants to expand, but also the chemistry department, the fine arts division, the humanities, the social sciences, the languages, and engineering. The tendency to expand and to secure the bailiwick of the organization permeates all the sets and subsets of the organization's structure, finally ending with the desire of many individual staff members to do the same.

A psychological factor helps to maintain the self-perpetuating relationship. Growth is perceived as instrumental to success in so many different situations by so many persons that it acquires intrinsic reward value. Whatever may be the case in other societies, in the United States growth certainly ranks along with money, acceptance, and status as an important generalized reinforcer. Growth of the organization is its own reward, and the booster is rarely asked to explain *why* he thinks the organization should grow.

*   *   *   *   *   *

In closing this discussion, I am surprised to discover that I have written seven chapters on organizations without the word *bureaucracy*. The omission was not premeditated or deliberate; but the analysis seemed to go forward without it. To the extent that "the bureaucracy" refers to people, the bureaucrats are the staff. To the extent that it refers to relationships and behavior, bureaucracy is perhaps all of the relationships described in connection with organizations, but most strongly the intra-staff relations and least strongly, if at all, the sponsor-recipient relations. I hope I have omitted no important aspects of bureaucracy, and some of the special problems of bureaucracy in government will be examined in later chapters. No problems of bureaucracy or bureaucrats have been changed by omitting the word; only the language is different. We are, of course, using the term "bureaucracy" in the technical sense as it appears in organizational analysis, not in the popular layman's sense, which generally implies red tape, inefficiency, and incompetence. The latter is a matter beyond the scope of the present discussion.

Chapter 28

THE FAMILY

SINCE PROCREATION and the birth and care of the young cannot be performed by one person alone, the family is an organization absolutely indispensable to the human race. Whether casual sexual relations should be construed as transaction or organization depends on the circumstances and the purpose of the analysis. Certainly the longer associations of husband, wife, and children common to all human societies fill the definition of organization, and it is as an organization that we will deal with the family.

In each type of organization studied thus far, the sponsors had only one or a limited range of objectives—to make money, to help others, to provide goods for themselves, or to influence the terms of other transactions. The family, by contrast, is an unlimited purpose organization. Actually or potentially it deals with any and every aspect of the lives of its members. This fact provides the family with a set of problems which need not be met by any other organization except government, to be discussed later.

The family is a group with which the individual is affiliated for a long period, often for life, and from which he cannot withdraw easily or at will. This fact has many repercussions, some of which this chapter will explore.

The facts of biology determine the membership of the *nuclear* or *conjugal* family, which consists of father, mother, and their children. From the parental view this group is called the family of *procreation*. From the view of the children it is known as the family of *orientation*, the group in which the child learns about and is attached to his society. In much of Western society the nuclear family lives separate from its relatives, and *is* the family unit. In other societies the nuclear family dwells amid grandparents, aunts, uncles, and cousins, all of whom may share a common dwelling and set of food facilities. Here the nuclear family is only part of a more extended family group, or clan.

Families differ from society to society in their basic structure, the distinctions between monogamy and polygamy, and between patriarchy and matriarchy, being among the more striking differences. In examining the family we shall look first at the consequences of its all-purpose aspect. The remainder of the chapter will examine the major and subsidiary bargains in the family, and their relation to the culture, family structures, and other factors.

THE ALL-PURPOSE ASPECT OF THE FAMILY

The family is a cooperative organization in its basic functions, although it can also be a profit, service, or pressure organization in part, or to particular persons. The family produces goods for its own members who, collectively, are simultaneously sponsors, staff, and recipients. Any servants the family may have are hired employees who augment the staff, although long-time servants may tend to become "part of the family," and participate in some sponsor and recipient functions.

Not all acts *in* the family are *of* it. Many are done by and for the individual alone, or are done with persons outside the family. This is true in the same sense that some activities within a business are unrelated to the organization, such as casual conversations, personal uses of the company's telephone, or getting a drink at the cooler. Proportionally more of an individual's time is spent on such personal activities within the family than within the business or other organization, partly because more time is spent within the family, and partly because other organizations often pay for a person's time, and expect it to be devoted to the organization's goals. It is usually within the context and locale of the family unit that we read, practice a musical instrument, collect stamps, cut our fingernails, bathe, sleep, build model boats, comb our hair, grow flowers, skip rope, or play solitaire.

When we say that the family is potentially an all-purpose organization, we do not mean that it actually *does* or *provides for* all kinds of human activities. The situation is most evident in the relation of parent to child in the nuclear family. The parent must take *total* responsibility for *all* aspects of the child's life, and we cannot say that any part or phase of the child's activity is none of the parent's business. The doctor or medicine man may be entrusted with the child's health, but the parent calls or does not call him in, take his advice, or look for a substitute. The school may perform a general kind of educational function, but the family teaches much that the school does not. It forms basic attitudes toward education and many other things, and can add to or subtract from the school's ability to teach him. Any one organization except the family deals with only part of the child's life; only the family deals with the whole of it. If the school does not provide dancing lessons, the parent can send the child elsewhere for them. But if the parent does not provide them, or prohibits them, the child goes without. The family does or does not do; it provides or does not provide; it encourages, allows, or prohibits. Among all these alternatives it *potentially* covers all possible actions or inactions of the individual, though the family's performance or controls may not *actually* be effective at all times. The family deals with the exigencies of births, marriages, deaths; of clothing, feeding, and healing; of motivating and training; of accidents, disease, unemployment, and old age; and generally of meeting the emotional needs of the individual. Although it may call on outside individuals or organizations to do many of these particular things, the family generally takes the responsibility to see that these outside agencies are utilized, and that the gaps between their activities are filled. This is the meaning of the potential all-purpose nature of the family. It has a parallel in the potential all-purpose nature of government, as will be seen in a later chapter.

More specifically the family must be prepared to meet needs for material goods, either by producing them or acquiring income with which they can be purchased, and it must allocate those goods among the members of the family. The family takes care of the sex needs of the adult partners, and regulates the sexual behavior of the children according to the mores of the society. It provides physical care of the young, and trains them in motor skills and body controls. As the chief vehicle for transmitting the culture to each succeeding generation, it also introduces them to the main concepts and values of the society.

THE MAJOR BARGAIN IN THE FAMILY

Marital Affiliation

Like any other organization, the family involves two main sets of transactions, the major bargain of affiliation and the subsidiary bargains of continued living together. As to the nuclear family, the bargain of affiliation is that of selecting a spouse (or spouses), of getting married, and later of deciding whether or not to stay married. Other major bargains determine when and on what terms the children leave home or remain. The questions of their being born into the family or remaining with it during childhood are normally not determined by bargaining.

The culture and subculture determine who is involved in the major bargain. In present American, Western European, and scattered other cultures, the marriage transaction depends on mutual acceptance of the male and female involved, on grounds weighted heavily by romantic love. In practice, romance seems to blossom most readily and deeply between pairs of approximately equal status: first because they are more likely to become acquainted, and second because their tastes tend to be adjusted to about the same scale of living, and third because great discrepancies in status leave a suspicion of mixed motives in the partner of lower status, and a possible later resentment over an "inequitable" bargain. In much of Western society, although the parents of the bride or groom sometimes strongly influence the selection of a mate, the norms prescribe that the overt choice remain with the partners, and couples of age can legally marry without the consent of the parents.

At the opposite pole are societies in which the partners themselves have no control at all, and may not even know whom they have married until the wedding is over. The nature of these arrangements will be discussed in more detail below.

All societies exert some control over the selection of mates. All have some form and degree of the incest taboo and/or marriage restriction, which means that brother and sister, parent and child, and various degrees of cousins may not marry. Most societies put minimum age limits on marriage, though in some the age is so close to that of puberty that the social limitation virtually coincides with the biological. In many societies the partners are actually selected many years before marriage, and the selection is sometimes made by parents at or before the birth of the child.

Caste cultures prohibit certain intercaste marriages, and allow marriages only within a caste, or between certain specified castes. In Western societies, nobility is generally expected to marry other nobility, and although this rule is often breached, the fact that exceptions are still considered exceptions demonstrates the continuance of the expectation. In many states of the United States, including all of the "South," marriages between whites and other races are prohibited by law.

As will be seen in connection with the incest taboo below, these various controls over mating must be construed as having social significance only, not biological.

The Goods Involved

Along with its glamor, excitement, pomp, and emotion, the marriage contract *is* a contract—and the process of arranging it includes bargaining. For the majority of the world's population, some kind of payments are made as part of the marriage bargain. Most frequent is the bride price, in which the man or his family pays for the bride, usually to her parents or larger family, in money, animals, or assorted gifts. In India, paying for a bride is a tradition of many centuries' standing. Although the government under its democratization program is now trying strenuously to eliminate it, the practice of bride purchase does not die easily. Among other obstacles to eliminating the practice, fathers of marriageable girls feel unjustly deprived of property (to use a Western phrase), and the girls feel insulted by the prospective groom if he will not pay. Among the Chinese peasants, payments were traditionally made by the groom's family to the bride's, as a part of the marriage arrangement.[1] Many African tribes have bride purchase practices, as do the Kwoma of New Guinea, the Alorese of Indonesia, and numerous other groups.[2] In some societies the groom gets a sort of guarantee, and can return the bride for a full refund if she does not bear children, or is otherwise unsatisfactory. In other cases a sort of downpayment is made upon marriage, and the remaining payment is not due until the wife becomes pregnant. Until the

[1] C. K. Yang, *The Chinese Family in the Communist Revolution* (Cambridge: The Technology Press, MIT, 1959), p. 25.
[2] Stuart A. Queen and John B. Adams, *The Family in Various Cultures* (Philadelphia: Lippincott, 1952), pp. 60, 66–69.

bride price has been paid in full, however, the girl is still the "property" of her own family, who will watch over her carefully to see that no harm comes to her.[3] In many societies the young woman is an important worker, and payment to the bride's family provides compensation for a real economic loss.

In other societies payments are made in the reverse direction. The Romans inherited the practice of the dowry from their early forebears and continued it through the Roman Empire. The dowry was not an outright gift from the wife's family to the husband's, however, but was conditional on continuance of the marriage. If the marriage were broken by death or divorce, the dowry was returned to the wife or her family. If a divorce was the wife's fault, however, the husband might keep part of the dowry.[4]

In numerous societies the wedding ceremony is elaborate and expensive. In this case, payment for the ceremony requires a large contribution to the marriage, even though it makes no money available to the couple for living expenses. In the traditional Chinese family, for example, the family of the groom prepares an elaborate feast and ceremony, attended by scores or hundreds of family and friends from the villages. The cost may equal a year's income or more; parents sometimes sell or mortgage their property for the purpose, and they may go into debt for life.[5] In the United States, by contrast, the major cost of the wedding is borne by the family of the bride.

Among the societies we know, the broad terms of individual marriage transactions seem to be determined very largely by social consensus. In societies having bride purchase, the actual net payment always flows in the bride's direction, even though in a unique transaction the husband might command a dowry. Similarly, in societies whose consensus prescribes a dowry, the bride provides one, even where her bargaining power in a unique transaction would command a bride price.

Despite these binding effects of consensus on the *direction* of flow, the *amount* within any given culture varies greatly from case to case, depending on the Effective Preferences of the two parties. Throughout the world the main factors in these EP's are apparently physical attractiveness, health, ability, and prestige. These factors receive different weights, according to their overt or subjective importance in the society. In an industrial society the ability of the husband to earn money is highly important to a family's success, while his physical appearance receives relatively little emphasis. Since the woman's ability to earn money is relatively unimportant, her physical attractiveness looms as a relatively much larger consideration. In most nonindustrial societies, the woman's ability

[3] *Ibid*. pp. 60, 61, 78.
[4] *Ibid.*, p. 144.
[5] Yang, *op. cit.*, p. 25.

to work is just as important as the man's, and her beauty takes a lower rating relative to her strength, health, and productive skill.

In some societies virginity of the bride is highly prized, in which case the virgin commands a higher bride price (or must pay a lower dowry) than the nonvirgin. Among the Kwoma the bride price is viewed as a payment to the girl's brothers for protecting her chastity, and they thus hold a vested interest in protecting her.[6] No such premium can be commanded in societies which do not value virginity. The reverse may in fact prevail, and in some societies a girl is not considered fully marriageable until she is pregnant. The Trobriand Islanders have the fewest known controls in this respect. Adults make no attempt to prevent intercourse among children, and a number of affairs prior to marriage are expected of everyone. Incestuous relations are strictly forbidden, however, as are relations between adults and children. Premarital pregnancy also is condemned, and, for reasons not yet known, is relatively rare, though contraceptives are not used.[7]

In societies whose marriages are presumably based on romantic love, the parties are often assumed to "give themselves" in an equal exchange. They do not bargain over price, since there is none in the straightforward sense. The factors which determine price in the societies that do make payments nevertheless have a definite influence. But instead of determining price they determine who will marry whom. As a general rule the girl who is beautiful, intelligent, and wealthy does not marry the boy who is ugly, stupid, and poor, or vice versa. If the boy shows serious interest in a girl whose qualities obviously do not match his own, the comments that he could "do better than that" circulate freely around and perhaps to him. The same would apply to the girl.

In matters of romantic love, preferences sometimes follow devious and unaccountable paths. The individual case may go far from the norm, and perhaps wisely so. In some seemingly unequal marriages one party may have a martyr complex, guilt feeling, enmity to parents, desire to rehabilitate others, or some other urge which leads him to marry a person "less valuable" than himself. The general tendency, however, is for marriages to take place between persons who are roughly equal in the total or average of desirable characteristics.

We should not leave the impression that bargains over material things are absent in societies which hold the romantic criterion. Marriages between the children of wealthy families often include bargains over who will contribute how much money to the joint pool, or who will accept which financial obligations. Bargains over heirlooms, jewels, house, or furniture often accompany middle and lower income marriages as well.

Even in Western nations where no formal payments are made by or to

---

[6] Queen and Adams, *op. cit.*, p. 61.

[7] William M. Kephart, *The Family, Society, and the Individual* (Boston: Houghton Mifflin Co., 1961), p. 350 f.

the bride's family, virginity has a value, which differs from nation to nation. The Scandinavians, for instance, show relatively low disfavor of premarital relations, particularly between a couple who plan to marry. The unmarried mother, while hardly lauded, is not deeply disgraced. By contrast, the Spanish place a very high value on the virgin bride, and it would be a source of great embarrassment and shame for a well-placed family to accept a daughter-in-law who had an affair before marriage, let alone an illegitimate child. Even years after the wedding, a Spaniard feels entitled to be angry with his wife, perhaps to abuse or divorce her (if religion permits) if he discovers she had had relations with another man before marriage. In the United States premarital intercourse by the female is more frequent and less frowned upon than it was two generations ago. The great majority of such relations reportedly take place between persons planning to be married, or between couples who are "going steady." Truly promiscuous relations are apparently confined to about 6 per cent of the female population.[8] By contrast, in no society, apparently, is a premium placed on the virginity of the male.

Ground Rules About Sex

Implicit or explicit in every marriage is an understanding about the terms of the sex relation. Of basic importance is the question, will there be only one husband and wife, and will either partner be free to have intercourse with other persons? Because marriage is such a basic social relation, a strong consensus on these matters prevails in each society. Strong efforts are usually made to bring all individual marriages into line with the norms, although rarely with complete success.

Monogamy is allowed and practiced in all known societies, and is the most common practice even in those societies which allow and use other types of relationships.[9] Polygamy, the practice of having more than one spouse, can take the form of either polygyny (multiple wives) or polyandry (multiple husbands). Polygyny is by far the most frequent nonmonogamous arrangement, and has been found in such widely varied times and places as among the ancient Hebrews, the Mormons until recently, the Moslems, most of tribal Africa, and the upper class traditional Chinese family. In many primitive tribes polygyny is allowed to the chiefs or the wealthy, even though it is not permitted or economically possible to the ordinary man. Concubinage is also relatively widespread, often as an accompaniment of polygyny. By contrast, polyandry is so rare as to be considered a curiosity, and is reported only among the Toda and the Marquesans.[10] Group marriage, with multiple husbands *and* wives, is not known in any human society as a permanent form of family arrangement.

Although there exists a wide presumption that sexual relations of mar-

---

[8] *Ibid.*, p. 350 f. The rise in the rate of premarital relations seems to be confined largely to soon-to-be-married couples.

[9] *Ibid.*, p. 68.

[10] *Ibid.*, p. 66.

ried persons will occur only between husband and wife, this rule is by no means universally enforced, and some societies do not seriously expect it to be. As a broad generalization covering the great majority of societies, we would say that the male is allowed considerably more freedom for sex outside of marriage than is the female. The same society which allows a divorce if the wife has intercourse outside of marriage may shrug off as unimportant a husband's relations with a maid, slave, prostitute, or mistress, particularly if such relations seem unlikely to break the marriage. Such extramarital affairs seem least frowned upon where the marriage itself is not romantically based. Mistresses are widely accepted in Europe, particularly in the upper classes where marriage often has heavy business and financial components, and in China, where marriage partners are typically selected by parents. Extramarital relations for the female are accepted on a controlled basis among the Eskimos, where a husband is expected to lend his wife to a male guest.

Many explanations have been offered for the wide dominance of monogamy, and many explanations have strong moral and religious foundations. All things considered, the basic bargaining power forces, including coalitions, seem to provide an adequate explanation. To start with, the number of male and female births is approximately equal in all places and ages, despite occasional significant local and temporary deviations. This means that if some individuals are to have more than one spouse, others must go spouseless—unless polygyny and polyandry should prevail in about equal amounts in the same society, which situation has apparently never been found.

Among nonhuman mammals the strong male often accumulates multiple wives, and leaves the weaker males mateless. But the ability of humans to communicate makes it possible for weak males to form a coalition against the strong to remedy their plight. "Together they could overpower the powerful, polygynous male in a single struggle, or, one by one, they could stand watch over him until he fell asleep and then dispatch him." In this way "cooperation led toward a uniform distribution of mates."[11] Weapons also reduce the dominance of the stronger male since the knife, sling, or poisoned dart eliminates much of the advantage of size and strength.[12] This explanation accords with the observations that monogamy is widely found in the most primitive societies of man, but not in the most advanced of the other mammals, including the monkeys and apes.[13] Nonmonogamous forms of marriage are found more among the relatively "advanced" than in the most primitive societies.

The terms of the major bargain about sex may or may not be explicitly discussed by the parties, and in any event will be strongly influenced by the terms of the surrounding consensus. The major bargain

---

[11] Leslie A. White, *The Evolution of Culture* (New York: McGraw-Hill Book Co., Inc., 1959), p. 74.

[12] *Ibid.*, p. 75.

[13] Kephart, *op. cit.*, pp. 47 ff.

will have much to do with the terms of many subsidiary bargains—a matter we will examine later in the chapter. Our present concern is that violation of the terms of the major agreement over sexual relations may be grounds for terminating the marriage itself. In the United States, for example, the courts almost without question will grant a divorce or annulment to a man whose wife refuses any intercourse, or to a woman whose husband is impotent, and in virtually all other societies the ability and willingness to have sexual relations is presumed basic to continued marriage. We have already noted that in some societies a divorce is permitted if the wife bears no children.

Despite many exceptions, according to the norms of many cultures, marriage provides exclusive, or monopoly, rights to sex relations with the partner, and either partner is entitled to break the marriage contract if the other engages in adultery. Adultery is the only ground for divorce recognized in all of the states of the United States, though all states by law or subterfuge also allow divorce on other grounds.

The Incest Taboo

In certain royal families brother-sister marriages have been allowed, or even required, as among the Ptolemies of ancient Egypt, the Incas, and the Hawaiian nobility. In the Azanda tribe of Africa the highest chiefs were required to marry their own daughters. And there is a possibility that in ancient Iran brother-sister, father-daughter, and mother-son sexual relations were permitted to the general population.[14] Aside from these few exceptions, marriage or sexual intercourse between close blood relatives "is one of the most rigidly enforced of all human behavioral proscriptions"—although many more such relationships apparently occur than is generally recognized, and in Western societies even those definitely known to the authorities are rarely publicly reported.[15]

The precise extent of the coverage of the taboo varies from one society to another, but the prohibition is universal (with the exceptions noted above) for relations between parent and child, sister and brother, and child and uncle or aunt. First cousins are usually forbidden to marry, though not always to have intercourse, and second and more distant cousins are also sometimes forbidden to marry.

The sources of the incest taboo are not agreed upon by anthropologists, although several explanations are now rather firmly rejected. First, there is no evidence of any innate, inborn disapproval, since (1) incestuous relations *do* occur with modest frequency, (2) there would hardly be any need for such strenuous social controls against incest if there existed an inborn revulsion, and (3) the concept of incest (as well as the concepts of mother, father, sister, brother, etc.) is learned, and it does not seem psychologically possible to have an inborn attitude toward a learned

---

[14] *Ibid.*, pp. 73 f.
[15] *Ibid.*, pp. 74 f.

concept. Second, it is highly doubtful that the taboo is designed to improve or maintain the biological quality of the human animal, since (1) inbreeding does not produce biologically or mentally inferior stock in general or on the average, and not often in particular cases, and (2) the taboo is just as strong among some primitive peoples who are unaware of the relationship between intercourse and pregnancy.[16]

The trend of thinking in recent years seems to be toward explanations of the taboo as social and interpersonal in origin. While agreeing that the above explanations are not tenable, White[17] traces some aspects of the problem back to the apes and other mammals, noting that sexual relations between mother and son would be the most obvious ones to be ruled out. Any attempt at such a relation by a son would directly infringe the sexual domain of the father, who, being the stronger and more dominant male, would not tolerate it. By virtue of the same dominance, the father would also claim first access to his daughters, and thus eliminate brother-sister relations. Two types of incestuous relations can thus be eliminated on the basis of male dominance alone, and their prohibition may be presumed to have developed at a very early stage of the transition from the male-dominant polygynous anthropoid society to distinctly human society.

Extensions of the incest taboo to other relations may be attributed to the practical necessity of building wider social contacts for production and mutual defense. In the absence of controls to the contrary, sexual relations would presumably tend to occur mainly between those already most intimate, affectionate, and accessible—the members of the same family. If the society insists, however, that unions take place only outside the immediate family, then each family is forced to extend its contacts, and a considerable network of interfamily relationships, common understanding, and cooperation arises. In short, *with* the incest taboo it is possible, according to White, to build a society of substantial size. Without it, the family would tend to remain like that of the apes: a male, the one or more females he can defend from other males, and infant offspring.

Other Terms of the Major Bargain

Many other items are normally included in the terms of the major bargain of marriage. Highly important is the question whether the bride and groom will reside alone, with his family, her family, or some larger family group. Most couples follow the dominant pattern of their culture. In the traditional Chinese family and many others the couple resides with his family, the *patrilocal* arrangement. The wife becomes an integral part of the larger family group, which usually includes nieces, nephews, grandparents, aunts, uncles, and cousins. In some other societies the groom

---

[16] *Ibid.*, p. 76.

[17] Leslie A. White, *op. cit.*, Chapters 3 and 4 on "The Nature of Social Organization" and "The Transition from Anthropoid Society to Human Society." The ensuing discussion is based largely on these two chapters.

goes to live with his wife's family, the *matrilocal* system, while in Western society, Japan, and India the couple normally set up a new residence of their own (*unilocal*) as soon as economic circumstances permit. As in other matters, the more cosmopolitan the society, the greater is the freedom of the couple to arrange matters to their own choosing, in possible contravention of the norm.

The question of who supports whom is also part of the major bargain. In nonindustrial societies it is usually necessary for both husband and wife to work a great deal, and the question is not so much that of support as of division of labor. This, too, usually follows the pattern of the culture. In industrial societies, where most income is received as money, the husband typically does the money earning and the wife the housework, since childbearing and rearing prevents the continuity of work attendance usually desired by industrial employers.

Social pressures are strong toward consensus division of labor. Even in such cosmopolitan cities as New York, London, or Paris, a man cannot keep house while his wife earns the money except for an emergency period, or for some obvious and compelling medical reason. If the relation is continued on a permanent and voluntary basis without justification, social pressures rise to embarrassing and troublesome levels, including ridicule of the couple's children by playmates. Only if enough persons choose some nonstandard arrangement to make up their own subculture is such diversity feasible. Strong identification with such a subculture, however, may restrict one's access to the dominant one, while simultaneously requiring fairly strict conformance to the pattern of the subculture.

On the main question of who supports whom, although latitude is possible by mutual consent, the society will promptly side with the one injured by a violation of the norm. Courts, for example, are strict and consistent in forcing the male to support his wife and children.

Rules of authority between husband and wife are part of the major bargain, and are also subject to the strong influence of the consensus. We have seen in Chapter 24 that in limited purpose organizations the terms of authority relations are subject to a sort of market consensus. Somewhat similar forces seem to affect the authority relation in the major bargain between husband and wife. Freedom to leave a spouse at will for another—like quitting one job and taking another—is not necessary for the "market" to have its effect. The girl can sound out suitors on their ideas about authority in marriage, and drop the domineering types. The latter will find desirable females elusive, and be forced to relax their authoritarian talk if they want wives. Unique sets of preferences may allow particular matches to deviate far from the norm, and almost anything can happen once the knot is tied. It nevertheless remains true that any one person will tend to avoid a match which seems to offer less than the consensus share of authority.

In China, Japan, and much of Europe the male is expected to assume the dominant role. The girl in such a society who seeks as much authority as is held by the typical American wife would have little chance, since each prospective husband could find other girls who would accept a subordinate role.

With respect to this authority relation, an intercultural marriage follows the rules of comparative advantage in international trade. For instance, if an American man marries a Japanese woman, each gets a better bargain on authority than is available at home. The male gets a wife who accepts more male dominance than the typical American girl, and the female gets a husband who allows more freedom than any she could probably find in Japan. When each is viewed through the eyes of the opposite sex, the United States has a comparative advantage in the position of males and Japan in females. With respect to this one trait, taken alone, the United States would therefore tend to "export" males and "import" females. If there were enough intercultural marriages of this sort, the eventual result would presumably follow the same pattern shown in the international exchange of commodities. Namely, if many Japanese brides came to the United States, and many American grooms went to Japan, the level of male dominance would rise in the United States and decline in Japan until it was roughly equal in both places. Exchange, of course, is not the only means of bringing similarities in culture, and diffusion and evolution have already brought a distinct move toward greater equality of status in the Far East.

The major bargain also includes other items. In many societies, consensus terms are sharply defined as to what happens to the remaining partner in the event of death of the other. In Western nations generally the widow or widower is on his own, to remain single or to find a new spouse. Under a practice known as the *levirate* duty, a brother of the deceased husband is required to marry the widow, and under the *sororate* duty a sister of the deceased wife is required to marry the widower. By extension, if no brother or sister is available, some other person in the family of the deceased is expected to fulfill the deceased's marital obligation.[18]

Another part of the major bargain involves the distribution of property at death. In societies with well-developed legal institutions such matters may be handled by a will, and the law provides for appropriate distribution to spouse and children if no will has been written. In patrilineal societies wealth, particularly land and animals, is passed on to the sons, and if the nuclear family lives as part of some larger family group, the property goes to the husband's family. In matrilineal systems the remaining property goes to the wife's family, and it may or may not be left to daughters instead of sons.

---

18 William F. Kenkel, *The Family in Perspective* (New York: Appleton-Century-Crofts, Inc., 1960), p. 46, and John J. Honigmann, *The World of Man* (New York: Harper & Bros., 1959), p. 388.

Like any other aspect of culture, the consensus rules about families undergo change. The American family, for example, in recent decades has reportedly been moving from authoritarian toward equalitarian control, and from an institutional to a companionship relationship, while granting more freedom to the indivdual family member to do as he likes.[19] At the same time, certain erstwhile functions of the family are declining in importance, especially economic production, education, recreation, protection, and religion. The functions which continue more or less intact are those of reproduction, the satisfaction of affectional and response needs, and the socialization and personality patterning functions.[20]

SUBSIDIARY TRANSACTIONS AND SOCIALIZATION PROCESSES

Any continuing organization shows not only the major transaction of affiliation, but also a series of subsidiary transactions which fill in its day-to-day operations. Far from being an exception, the family is perhaps the most conspicuous example. The major bargain is normally expected to be permanent, and even if not, distinct difficulties stand in the way of breaking it. Since problems and disagreements cannot easily be resolved or eliminated by disaffiliation from the organization, there is a stronger than usual pressure to stay and work them out. This is why the subsidiary transactions take on a heightened importance in the family. It is within the family that the individual experiences the multitude of interrelated transactions which lead him to soften and modify his demands in any one transaction in line with the interrelations of that transaction with others before, after, and around it.

This process has traditionally been referred to as "socializing" the individual, during which process he "learns to live with others." To redescribe the process of socialization in the present model, the individual learns that few transactions are unique. In the family the husband and wife learn these things more fully than they could possibly learn them as children, partly through the continued relationships with each other and partly through the necessity of maintaining a long, generous relation to their children. At the same time the parents try to inculcate an understanding and practice of these things into the child. Through both experience and the precepts already embodied in his culture, the child learns that his attempts to bargain selfishly in each situation bring selfish counterbargaining, and that generous approaches also tend to be met in kind. He also discovers from experience and social rules that many of his transactions must meet or approach consensus terms, as market, social, and possibly political techniques of enforcement make themselves felt if he attempts to deviate too far. It is mainly within the family that children

---

[19] Leonard S. Cottrell, Jr., "The Present Status and Future Orientation of Research in the Family," *American Sociological Review*, Vol. 13, No. 2, April, 1948, p. 124.

[20] *Ibid.*, pp. 126–27.

learn, and parents add to their learning, about multiple transactions with the same persons, and about transactions involving goods which are widely exchanged by others.

As we have already seen in the chapters on culture and personality, the family is the primary organization for transmitting other phases of the culture to the new generation, such as its main concepts and the value judgments attached to them. The obligation to do this is so obviously part of the major bargain that it is scarcely thought of, and the process of doing it is a substantial part of the subsidiary transactions which make up daily living. This transmission of the fundamentals of the culture is also a part of the "socializing" process.

Many of the largest transactions within the family carry out terms accepted in the major bargain. The basic division of labor between husband and wife, for example, is not repeatedly bargained, but is understood in broad contours before the marriage—normally along the lines of the social consensus. As we have already seen, although it is possible to deviate from the norm, serious deviations usually create difficulties within the family, and between it and others around it. When the husband and wife each make contributions to the common pool and withdrawals from the pool for their own needs, they are engaging in the kind of contributions and withdrawals that characterize all affiliations with organizations. In the family each for the most part contributes what he can within the limits of his abilities, opportunities, and the expectations of the society. And each mainly withdraws what seems reasonable in light of the amounts available, the needs and desires of the whole family, and the norms of the culture. On this score, the family follows the basic socialist principle, "From each according to his ability, to each according to his need."

To the extent that these transactions must follow the norms of the culture, and the extent is often great, it is pointless to ask whether they are generous or selfish, since the society allows no discretion on the terms.

Other Aspects of Bargains

Because of the large number and interrelated nature of the bargains within the family, it seems worth pursuing some a bit further, even at the risk of repeating some points made in Chapters 17–19.

In addition to the fact that every family lives within a culture, each to some extent develops a subculture of its own. This means that it has a set of values and concepts somewhat different from those around it, based on the interactions of the members of the family. In certain kinds of transactions the family also develops its own consensus terms. On this small a scale the market and social enforcements of consensus seem to coincide, in that the refusal of particular terms to one member from any other member of the family (market technique) probably depends on mutual agreement by the others that they will not "give in" to his terms (social coalition). Coalitions may be formed against any member of the family by the others to enforce a social consensus, as when the children and mother may join forces in dealing with a father who tries to drive too harsh a bargain. They may do this by withholding information from him, or some desired thing he is unable to obtain by exercise of parental authority, such as affection. Even in societies with high paternal authority, other members of the family are not helpless if they can mold the father's conceptualizations of situations, or his preferences about them.

Being unable to disaffiliate, young children occupy an inherently weak bargaining position. Some nevertheless discover some things highly desired by parents which they can withhold or destroy, and some unwary parents may find themselves making huge concessions to presumably helpless children. One such device is to trade heavily on the parent's desire that the child be happy. This has limitless possibilities if the parents do not catch on, since the child can withdraw this desired state from the parents as often or as completely as he chooses, and can also restore it at strategic moments. A second device is to work on the parents' desire to be a "good" or "unselfish" parent in the eyes of the rest of the family, friends, or neighbors. A third gambit uses the parent's desire to be loved by the child, which can be parlayed by some children into truly spectacular returns. The countertactics and strategy by parents is obvious once it is thought about, and consists mainly of parental willingness to be thought badly of in the short run, in the assurance that the long run result will move in the desired direction.

It is in the close relations of the family that one is apt first to discover the low usefulness of tactical misrepresentations in repeated transactions with the same persons, both because the rest of the family is apt to know him too well to be fooled, and also because it is much easier to relax and be oneself. It is here, too, that one is likely first to discover that a simple helping hand can cost little to provide, and be tremendously valuable to the receiver—the main lesson in learning willingness to engage in generous open-end transactions, whether or not they are considered at the the time to be investments with possible later returns from the same persons. The family is also the unit in which deep affections develop, that produce the kinds of transactions which, while strongly generous in overt terms, bring a large "gain" to the generous party.

What is perhaps surprising is that, despite the tremendous interrelations within the family, many transactions can remain selfish and relatively unique, such as: "If you wash the car this afternoon I'll drive you to the game tomorrow," or "If I let you use the garage for the ping-pong table will you keep the rose bed weeded all summer?" Because of their great importance, bargains involving sex are often strong indicators of the temperament and long-or-short-sightedness of husband and wife. The desire for sex is normally far stronger for the male than for the female.[21] Since

---

[21] Kephart, *op. cit.*, especially Chapters 2, 12.

it is a strong motive for the male, it holds strong potential bargaining power for the female. Some wives exploit this bargaining power, and get substantial concessions from husbands in return for sex, such as clothes or vacations. Others see it as an opportunity to grant a highly valued favor to a loved one, and consider bargaining over sex destructive to the whole husband-wife relationship. Where the sexual relation is highly desired and satisfying to both, it is a fully cooperative venture, and provides no basis for differential bargaining advantage. As with other relations, if the social consensus and the major bargain provide that the wife shall allow intercourse whenever desired by the husband, she loses her bargaining power in the individual case, since she is not free to withhold the desired thing.

As in any other organization, the party with the greater stake in the bargain of affiliation has the smaller bargaining power in subsidiary transactions. The spouse who is more in love with the other, more in need of the other's help or income, or less able to live satisfactorily alone or to find a new spouse, has the weaker bargaining position because he is less willing to dissolve the marriage. The one with the weaker bargaining power may have to do more work, accept more responsibility, tolerate infidelity by the mate, and generally take a subordinate position in the whole relationship—unless, of course, he finds some other kind of power over the marriage partner. This differential has no effect, however, unless the other partner is actually willing to terminate the marriage—or at least successfully to pretend that he is.

As we conclude this discussion it should be recalled that the above analysis is stated in the language of the observer and analyst, not of the participants. Persons who are in these various positions are often not aware of these forces, at least consciously, and they may prefer not to be. Bargaining power is often exploited intuitively, without knowledge of the logic or nature of bargaining power. In other cases it is not exploited at all, either because the person is unfamiliar with the process, or because he prefers not to use it. Here, as elsewhere in life, much action is performed out of habit or training, not out of thought about what is the most advantageous behavior. In very many instances the problems are so complex and the answers so difficult to predict that the line of conduct prescribed by the culture will be the safest to follow.

THE FAMILY AND OTHER ORGANIZATIONS

We have thus far looked at the family alone. In actuality the family both influences and is influenced by other organizations in the society. Among many other interactions, perhaps the most conspicuous are those with government, industry, and church.

In many simple societies the family *is* the government. The extended family, or clan, may consist of from dozens to several hundred persons. The great majority of the rules of the society are carried out by habit and training, and are enforced by social pressures. Where the rules are not clear, when new circumstances arise, or when some occasional individuals do not respond to social pressures, the case is submitted to the patriarch, chief, council of elders, or other duly recognized authority in the family. A decision is made, and appropriate enforcements are invoked. Within certain limits, the larger and more closely cohesive and effective the family organization, the larger can be the scope of the whole social relationship without the need of government distinct from the family.

In societies with formal governments, the law and the courts have significant influence on family relationships. Some of these have already been noted, such as the rules for marriage and divorce, of ownership and inheritance of property, and of support. For instance, if the law requires one to provide support for parents or children only, the effect on family relationships is much different than if the law requires one also to support a needy cousin, uncle, or nephew. Rules of primogeniture induce a different family structure than rules of equal division, and so on. There is, of course, the hoary dispute whether institutions make the law or the law makes the institutions. This is a particular case of the question whether the culture molds behavior or behavior molds the culture. A law normally does not come into existence until and unless there exists a set of concepts and motives to support it. But once in existence the law is itself a part of the body of culture, and thereafter helps to sustain and reinforce the concepts and motives which created it. As an act of the formal organization of society, the law is normally preceded by the development in the informal arena of the norms it espouses. (The distinction between the formal and informal parts of the organization of society will be discussed in later chapters.)

In the reverse direction, the family structure has repercussions on government. In China, the Middle East, some parts of Southern Europe, and scattered other places, the ties of family are strong and the family unit is large. Any one member of the extended family in a position to do so is expected to help provide income and favors for other members.

When a person with such family obligations attains a position in government it is taken for granted that he will put as many of his relatives as possible into government posts. An important factor which kept Chiang Kai-shek from establishing a satisfactory government on mainland China was that he filled important government offices on the basis of family ties, not competence. In doing so he was following his concept of his obligations.

The same extended kinship system can influence business. In some societies the man who gets a position of influence in a large firm feels obliged to put his relatives into other posts—a procedure not calculated to maximize efficiency. In smaller enterprises the structure of the organization is sometimes patterned to fit the size and composition of the family. Under this concept of family obligation the business may have to pay out all its earnings to the extended family, and be unable to plow back profits for expansion or modernization. If relatives are in businesses which supply raw materials or use the product, the transactions in these things often follow family lines, not those of maximum advantage to the firm. The extended family may not handicap the business, however, if it becomes a device for pooling capital and skill of numerous members of the family.

Industrial organization also has profound influences on family structure. In nonindustrial societies the production of the family's goods requires cooperative effort, and encourages large family groups among which the various tasks can be divided. In the industrial society each person enters the labor market and earns his living as an individual, largely without regard to whether he has a hundred living relatives or none. Industrial societies put the main responsibility for making an income on the father, which fact has repercussions inside the family.

On the whole the separate nuclear family seems better adapted to industrial societies and extended families to nonindustrial ones. A major problem, however, of the nuclear family in the industrial society is that until and unless the society develops some type of social insurance, the family is left destitute if premature death, ill health, accident, involuntary unemployment, or old age cuts off the breadwinner's income for an extended period. Where it exists the extended family "insures" the individual against these hazards, since each person draws on the income pool of a much larger family group.

The church may also influence the size or composition of the family. For instance, some Protestant churches consider family planning a "positive moral obligation" and urge or fully accept contraceptive devices as appropriate means to that end. By approving only "natural" means of birth control, in conjunction with a somewhat different attitude toward family size, the Catholic church, by contrast, tends to create a larger average size of family.

In these and many other ways the family acts upon other organizations in the society, and is acted upon by those organizations in turn.

B. The Whole

VII. THE WHOLE SOCIETY AS AN ORGANIZATION

Chapter 29

THE WHOLE SOCIETY
AS AN ORGANIZATION

A SOCIETY has been defined as a group of people having a common body and system of culture. The remainder of this volume will examine the whole of a society as an organization, the unit of a "whole society" for purposes of this analysis being the nation. The point is not to argue whether a whole society *is* an organization, but to explore what can be learned if we analyze it as one.

The earlier distinction between formal and informal organization will be followed here, where relevant. Government may be thought of as the formal organization of the whole society, and all nongovernmental organization as informal. The distinction is the same as within a corporation or other large organization, in which much activity is formally directed toward goals specified by the organization, but much other activity also goes on, some related to the formal activity and some not. The formal governmental organization will be considered *public* and all others *private*. We have seen that in private organizations we can distinguish pure formal and pure informal structures, but that in practice there is much admixture, in intermediate arrangements. So is there in practice both pure public and pure private organization. But here, too, there is an intermediate ground, in which the public organization explicitly recognizes and deals with private organization, as in controls of agricultural production and pricing and the regulation of interstate transportation. Some private organizations are semiofficially recognized to exist and function, as when the government acts to fill some gap not filled by private action, or decides not to act because some gap has already been filled. Different societies at different times and places in history show tremendous variation in the proportion of total activity which is brought within the formal structure. In some small primitive societies government is little more than the pronouncements of a council of elders in an extended family group, plus some arrangement for self-defense. Enforcement of decrees is carried out by social pressures. At the opposite extreme is the totalitarian dictatorship of an industrial society, where the government directly or indirectly exercises authority over a large fraction of all human activity within its borders.

GOVERNMENT, THE FORMAL ORGANIZATION OF THE WHOLE SOCIETY

The government is the formal organization of the whole society. The sponsors set up the governmental organization and use it to perform certain functions. For the moment we will bypass the question of who the sponsors are, or what the appropriate functions of government are, and define *sovereignty* as the authority to make and enforce decisions about any persons, transformations, communications, transactions, or organizations within a given geographic area. A *nation* will be defined as that geographic area, or unit of territory, within which a single sovereign authority exists, and a *national government* as that organization which exercises sovereignty in a nation. Except where a different meaning is indicated, the term "government" standing alone will hereinafter mean "national government." The *state* is a convenient term for referring to the totality of a nation, its people, and its government.

In a general way these definitions follow the contours of those used by political scientists.[1] However, the definition of sovereignty differs from customary ones, in that the content of its coverage is stated in terms developed earlier in the present volume, and not customarily used by political scientists. Further, the term "government" is given a somewhat different usage here, which requires explicit discussion.

No specimen of government having *actual* authority over the scope of things covered in the definition has ever existed or ever will. But like certain other "unrealistic" models used here and in other areas of science (such as the perfect market in economics and the perfect vacuum in physics), this concept is a sharply definable point of reference. Although all actual governments deviate from it, in important respects actual governments seem more clearly understandable as deviations from the model than they do without reference to the model. Except that it excludes nonhuman phenomena (such as those of physics, geology, biology, etc.) this definition of government coincides with that of complete power in Chapter 20. The simplest model of government is social omnipotence. We will not relax this model by stages, as has been done in some other areas, but rather indicate as we go along some of the limitations on omnipotence in practice.

We shall examine why only one model government can exist in an area, and why the area of jurisdiction must almost necessarily be defined geographically, the reasoning about the model being only slightly less cogent for the actual government.

It is obvious that only one model government can exist within any

---

[1] For example, see Robert Rienow, *Introduction to Government* (New York: Alfred A. Knopf, 1957), p. 12.

one area, one omnipotence by definition excluding a second. The geographic area covered by a government is a nation, or country. No feasible dividing line can be drawn between two sovereignties except on a geographic basis, as will be readily apparent if we try others. Suppose we try to divide sovereignties on a functional basis, one having total control of economic production, one of marriage, and one of justice. Both marriage and justice have economic components; economics and marriage have components of justice; and economics and justice may also have marital components. If divided on a functional basis, which of the three omnipotences would have jurisdiction over questions of economic justice in marriage? If one sovereignty were given control of communications, one of transactions, and one of organizations, which would control communications about transactions by organizations? One sovereignty cannot control persons over 21 and another control those under 21, since one or the other would have to give way in transactions between the two groups —which are rather difficult to eliminate. Either omnipotence has control over *all* persons and their relatonships or it is not omnipotence. Further, some transactions cover exchanges of land, and by the same logic the same sovereignty that controls land must control transactions. Although it may be difficult in practice, it is at least conceptually possible to cut off the people of one geographic area from all contact with those of another, or to insist that no intersovereignty relationships take place except on terms approved by the government. Walls can be built and border guards set up. Not even conceptually is it possible to set up a sovereignty of justice which could decree that there shall be no interrelations between economics and justice except on terms acceptable to justice. Presumably for reasons of this sort, sovereignties are defined geographically, not functionally. Religion is relatively isolable from other phenomena, and seems closer to achieving a functional sovereignty in some places than any other nongovernmental activity. The space age may make the geographic borderline less sharp in the future, but the geographic boundary will probably long remain a far sharper dividing line between sovereignties than any other.

Although the model government is unrealistic in the sense that no *one* government can ever exercise actual control over *all* transformations, communications, and so forth, within its jurisdiction, it is realistic in that historically we find few kinds of human activity that have never come under governmental regulation in some way, or may not be regulated in the future. The model of government represents the potential scope of any government, any time, anywhere, and this is conceived as limitless.

If we think of government in the same light as we earlier viewed the family, the limitless scope is true of actual government as well as the model. When we said that the scope of family activity with respect to its members is potentially limitless, we did not mean that the family *does* everything, since it obviously does not. We meant only that the family must inescapably deal in some way with the whole human being, including every phase of birth, life, or death. By action or inaction it must do, allow, provide for, limit, rechannel, or prohibit any kind of activity. If we similarly conceive the scope of government to include all its inactions as well as its actions, then by definition its scope is universal.

The subsequent analysis of government will lean on both the model and the reality. Government will be viewed as an organization which conceivably, or potentially, has the authority to control any human behavior within its jurisdiction. But not even the most dictatorial can come close to doing so in fact, and an important part of understanding actual government lies in discovering why it cannot do so.

WHAT KINDS OF THINGS CAN GOVERNMENT DO?

Authority to do *anything* is too broad to be informative, and we will start by subdividing it. Further, authority to do anything does not mean infinite activity, since even omnipotence may prefer to leave many things undone. If omnipotence is accompanied by omniscience, however, we would assume that its inactions as well as its actions are deliberate as its inactions.[2] Thus, both the omnipotent and the actual government will attempt to control something less than everything, the former because the preference half of its EP is limited, and the latter because the effective half is also limited.

Since we have defined government as having authority over persons, communications, transformations, transactions, and organizations, we will outline governmental functions under those headings. No distinction will be made at this point between democracy and dictatorship.

Persons

When we say that the government can control persons, we will mean only that it can permit or not permit them to be born, to continue to live, or to be free of imprisonment. We will assume that the government cannot directly control what goes on inside men's heads and emotions, even though control over communications and overt behavior can affect these things indirectly. Since all overt behavior can be construed to be a transformation, communication, or transaction, in or out of organization, all other government controls over persons will be classified under those headings.

Transformations

The government can itself engage in transformations, either productive or destructive. Virtually all except the simplest governments produce such goods as protection, justice, contract enforcement, and money

---

[2] If we wish to tie these things down, we might define a "deliberate" inaction as one which was listed in the decision set, but was rejected, and a nondeliberate inaction as one not listed in the decision set.

systems. Moderately socialized governments may produce such goods as water, electricity, transportation, and education; and highly socialized ones may also produce such goods as soap and pianos. Virtually none produce ordinary household services for families or the care of infants. At the opposite extreme, a government can destroy certain goods whenever it finds them; this is often done with narcotics or contaminated foods. In addition to producing or destroying, a government can allow or prohibit private production or destruction. It might, for example, allow the production of automobiles but not opium, and allow the destruction of flies and one's own chairs but not of wild rabbits in May or someone else's chairs. A government could also require certain production, as when conscripted soldiers or workers are required to follow orders or a parent is required to send his child to school. Various intermediate degrees of regulation can be employed, as in regulating the quantity, quality, timing, or sources of production, or in encouraging or discouraging production or destruction by taxation, subsidy, or communications of motives.

Communications

A government could control either the medium or the content of communication. As to the medium, the government could own or license newspapers, magazines, printing presses, telephone, broadcasting facilities, and other means of communication. As to the content, it could exercise censorship on political, moral, esthetic, or other grounds, in general or in particular cases. Although it is obviously difficult to regulate the content of conversations, a totalitarian dictatorship can be remarkably minute in its surveillance of intimate communications. As with transformations, a government can also permit communications without restriction, or exercise partial controls.

Transactions

A government can itself engage in transactions. It can buy or sell goods. It can tax, spend, borrow, and repay. As an organization it can also hire employees to perform its transformations, and become involved in all the intraorganizational transactions previously discussed. It can, of course, also make transactions with other governments, but we are concerned at the moment solely with its internal powers.

Government can also influence private transactions. It can directly control terms, as by setting the price of wheat, the minimum wage, or the allowable number of wives. The state can also regulate rules or weapons for bargaining. These will be detailed later, but include such things as the prohibition of force, monopoly, secondary boycotts, kickbacks, and blackmail. The government can establish procedures for settling disputes, such as a court, a ducking stool, a mediation service, marriage counseling, or a utilities commission. It may also establish criteria for settling transactions. The first squatter may be given first claim on the land, the nearest of kin may have the largest claim on the estate, and the number of children may be the criterion for determining how much alimony a man should pay.

In connection with transactions the significance of inaction by government can be particularly important. Transactions *are* going on all the time in a society. *Not* to intervene is to decide in favor of that power relation which evolves without government intervention. This is part of the significance of the earlier statement that the inactions of government may be quite as important as its actions, and that its scope is universal since its actions plus its inactions cover all possible actions. As a practical matter, it is never feasible for a government to refrain from all intervention in private power relations. The outlawing of force except for a few special uses (such as self-defense and perhaps by parents, teachers, or medicine men) is essential to the basic order of a society and to the government's own authority. And without some other regulation of power a small proportion of the population would probably gain substantial control of the whole society, probably including the government itself.

It may be asked in this connection whether inaction by government constitutes power. If "inaction" implies total absence of action or thought on some matter, the answer is negative. But if government intervention against some private interest is contemplated, the government may get substantial concessions in return for its promise not to act. This situation is essentially the same as the threat, as diagnosed in Chapter 18, and certainly constitutes power. Nonintervention where intervention is possible is an important determinant of the private power configuration.

Property.   The total set of rules about transactions are the *property rights* of a society. They must be accompanied by rules of evidence by which those who enforce the rules can discern whether a particular promise or transaction did or did not take place. The rules of evidence about transactions themselves become a significant part of the rules of property.[3] To take the most obvious case, if we could somehow prohibit the use of all negative goods in transactions, we would thereby assure that all selfish transactions would bring a net increase in utility, barring errors in judgment. We have seen (Chapter 18) that it is impossible in practice, and probably not socially useful, to outlaw all deliberate reductions of utility designed to increase bargaining power. We do, however, outlaw the use of physical force against the persons or material goods of others, and this (along with the outlawing of theft) is our most important rule of property.

---

[3] A problem arises when a particular kind of analysis is reconstructed in a different framework. The statement that the term "property rights" refers to the total set of rules about transactions and the evidence of transactions is true by definition in the present framework. A preliminary survey shows that most of the body of law conventionally referred to as dealing with property and contracts clearly falls within the present definition. To determine whether the two sets of terminology cover the same scope in total requires much more study.

Before someone can give a good in exchange it must first (in layman's language) be *his*. Since goods can be acquired through transformations or transactions, a person can demonstrate that a good is his by providing evidence of the transformation or transaction through which he acquired it. "Possession is nine points of the law" is a common way of saying that physical possession is accepted as evidence that a good was acquired through allowable transformations or transactions until and unless convincing evidence is offered to the contrary. "To own" something means to have acquired it by legal means, and to say that a thief does not "own" a stolen good means that he used illegal power in the transaction of acquiring it. Disputes over ownership revolve around kinds of transactions or evidences of transactions.

The rules governing transactions and the evidence of them are complex, making up a substantial, if not major, fraction of our law and of the work of our courts. Roughly, criminal law deals with prohibited goods, whether their production, exchange, or use as a bargaining weapon is prohibited. Civil law governing private controversies deals roughly with the terms and evidences of transactions, the enforcement of promises (contracts), and cases in which costs are imposed on a party without his consent. We will return to the control of transactions in connection with the fuller discussion of the functions of government in Chapter 32.

Organizations

Since organization consists of joint transformations and transactions, we need indicate only that the above discussion can be extended to organizations. No separate discussion of controls over organizations is thus needed, except to note that government can control internal affairs of organizations as well as external ones.

WHAT IS THE SOURCE OF GOVERNMENT POWER?

The control of a limited-purpose, voluntary organization resides with the residual contribution. The same conclusion does not apply to the model of a government, for two main reasons. First, the residual contribution is brought to the organization from outside itself. This concept is allowable for an organization which covers only a part of society. But it is not applicable to an organization of the whole society, since no person or human activity lies outside the organization to make such a residual contribution.

Second, the analysis of the limited-purpose organization assumed that violence to persons or property was not allowed as a bargaining weapon. No such limitation applies to the model of government, whose freedom to use force becomes a dominant consideration. In actual governments, which are not in fact all-inclusive, either public or private actions can be residual to the whole. In the United States, for example, both the private American Arbitration Association and the public Federal Mediation and Conciliation Service provide arbitrators for settling labor disputes. Private contractors build some mass housing projects and the government builds others. In each case we could say either that the private action fills the residual gap left by the government, or that the government fills the residual gap left by private action. If either were to disappear the other would probably expand.[4]

It seems almost certain that the power of government resides in its monopoly or clear dominance in the use of force. Without suggesting how real government actually originated, an area about which little is clearly known, we can observe some fundamental relationships.

A strong individual can dominate a group if he can outfight anyone else in it, and this kind of dominance is common among seals, sea lions, elk, and many other animals. Among reasonably alert humans, however, a coalition of the weak can prevent such dominance, and the control of the human group resides with the physically strongest coalition, not the strongest individual. The possible evolution from a coalition against violence to a police force was sketched in Chapter 19. In the normal, peaceful society the government represents the dominant coalition, and its police (supplemented by the army, if necessary) are the arm of force which is stronger than any other coalition within its jurisdiction.

This is the answer to the question at the heading of this section: the source of the government's power resides in its being the strongest coalition of force within its area. As soon as any rival coalition arises with any real possibility of challenging the dominant one, unless it is stupid or its hands are tied in other ways, the dominant one will promptly use its superior force to eliminate the challenger. Lest this suggest constant violence, let it be observed that a government can be guided by peace and reason only so long as its power position is unchallenged.

There is much muddleheaded thinking on this point, and it ought to be made clear. It is not that peace and reason make the presence of force unnecessary, but that the presence of clear and unchallenged force makes peace and reason possible. If 99 per cent of the population refused to have anything to do with force, the other 1 per cent would rule, and a general absence of violence depends on the readiness of rulers to use it when necessary. This does not deny the occasional great power of nonviolent resistance. But nonviolence is useful only against those with some reticence to use force and at least a latent sympathy for the nonviolent demonstrators. A Gandhi opposing the British is one thing. A Gandhi against a Hitler or Stalin is a different matter.

Legitimacy was described in connection with the limited-purpose organization as the condition in which an authority relation was accepted by those subject to the authority. The notion of legitimacy can readily

---

[4] Under the American value system, one would be more likely to say that the government fills the gap left by private action, and the reverse under the Russian value system.

be transferred from the employee relation to the citizen relation. Even though most citizens are not employees of the government, they are subject to its authority, but with an important difference. Whereas the individual joins and remains in a limited-purpose organization only if its value to him seems to exceed its cost, he is the subject of a government from the moment of birth, never making the decision to join it voluntarily. As he grows older he may have the opportunity to leave for another country. Although millions have done this at some time, the change is costly in money and emotional strain, and most dissatisfied people prefer to stay and improve their own government, if possible. Further, immigration and emigration are often severely restricted. Some of the countries whose people are most eager to leave will not let them out, and the places they want to go will not let them in. Although emigration can take care of some discontent, it never eliminates the need that a government come to terms with its own people. The question of who is allowed to use force, and for what purposes, is crucial to those terms.

The elements of the relationship can be seen if we return to the statement that a government's power lies in possessing the strongest coalition of force within the area. Suppose there exists a ruler (or ruling regime) in a country, and a rebel group tries to overthrow it by force. Some citizens support the ruler. That is, they join his coalition rather than the opposing one because they expect it to provide greater rewards. To some persons these rewards are privilege and power in the regime. To others they are government support in some private contest, such as between farmers and industrialists, employers and employees, or nobility and serfs. To still others the rewards are the promise of stable government, low taxes, or prestige abroad. Social pressures, bribes, and other forces may also help maintain support. If some feel coerced into appearing to support the regime when they would rather be with the rebels, their position is essentially the same as that of rebels after defeat, which will be discussed below. All others who support the ruler have voluntarily agreed to do so, even if only because he is the less bad of two unsatisfactory alternatives, and his authority over them is legitimate.

Whether the opposing coalition are rebels attempting to overthrow an established government or loyalists attempting to regain control for an ousted one, let us assume that the rebels are defeated and surrender unconditionally. Unless he is naively generous or virtually certain the opposition is over, the ruler will either kill or incarcerate those who oppose him, or at least their effective leaders, or liberate them only on condition that they accept his authority. The ruler's authority is now legitimate to the whole of the live, unjailed population. It was originally accepted by his own coalition. It is now accepted by the erstwhile rebels as the condition of their being alive and at liberty. In connection with this legitimizing bargain, we must recall from the discussion of bargaining power that a "voluntary" transaction does not necessarily mean that the parties are pleased with it. It means merely that it is perceived as preferable to the best alternative. Similarly, to "accept" a government's authority does not imply enthusiasm for it, but merely the absence of any perceived superior alternative.

Rebels do not always surrender unconditionally. If not, the agreement about government which the ruler makes as the price of gaining surrender is the major bargain that legitimizes the government's subsequent authority over the rebels.

Under unconditional surrender, it is easy to say that the support of the erstwhile rebels is coerced, not voluntary, and that they do not view the government's authority as legitimate. Two points must be observed. First, although the term "coercion" is useful for ordinary conversation, we have seen in Chapter 18 that its meaning can be highly elusive when we attempt to define it precisely. Second, although the rebels may superficially accept the ruler's authority because they lack the force to refuse it, they may be biding their time until they acquire the necessary force. At this point the authority is *not* legitimate in their eyes. They perceive a superior alternative and hope to achieve it, even if it is not available at the moment. The situation is one of *tension*, as defined in Chapter 14: a resolution of conflict accepted only until it can be changed. If the tension is strong the ruler must be constantly alert to his position. He will probably have difficulty enforcing his laws in dissident areas, just as the factory foreman will experience more-than-normal delays, breakdowns, and spoiled materials if his men feel he is using illegitimate authority. Without really thinking of overt rebellion, some groups seemingly never accept an authority. Some Frenchmen think of all governments since the monarchy as illegitimate, many American Southerners do not accept "Yankee" control from Washington as legitimate, and some European nobles regard everything since the feudal system as illegitimate. It is to be expected that there will always be some people in a nation who would revolt if they could, and the question is not whether a government is completely accepted, but whether it is sufficiently accepted to function satisfactorily.

For centuries political scientists and philosophers attempted to equate legitimacy with some morally superior qualities of government. They now tend either to abandon the term or to conclude that any government is legitimate which is, in fact, in firm control. The present analysis accepts the latter approach, which is not, however, without moral aspects.

The government whose acceptance is grudging is not in a strong position. Its staff meet with "accidents," and many of its lower functionaries do not perform well because they do not really believe in the regime. If a government is to be stable and reasonably efficient, it must get the former rebels to *want* the regime, which requires an exercise of moral power. The best way to develop this want is to get the people to conceive of the government as being run *in their interests*.

Many rulers throughout history have attempted to legitimize their rule as being authorized by the mutual superior of ruler and subjects, God.

This legitimization has worked with much success in some places, sometimes for centuries, and is difficult to refute by overt evidence. It is usually supplemented with more tangible methods of assuring dominance, such as police, since not even the most highly accepted regime, democratic or monarchic, is without *some* opposition. The most dependable, long run legitimization, however, lies in having the people believe that the government is at least trying to serve *their* interests, not the staff's.

Just as in psychiatry and mechanics, where normal behavior is often thrown into sharp relief by the abnormal patient and the malfunctioning engine, so in politics the nature of the "normal" bargain between government and people is perhaps never so clear as in the propaganda devices of the government which violates that bargain. The harshest Communist dictatorships are called "people's governments" and "people's democracies." The Hitler regime let the people "express their will" on ballots with only one "alternative," and the Russians "democratically elect" some leaders from a preselected one-party slate approved by the government. Even the most dictatorial modern governments (following the pattern of some ancient ones) rationalize their rule by constantly pointing out what they are doing "for the people." The grant of monopoly on force to the government in return for its use in the interests of the people is the major bargain of the model, and of most actual stable governments. That the bargain is often implied rather than explicit, does not change its basic nature, the same also being true in the bargain of affiliation with the private organization.[5]

The emphasis on force in the preceding paragraphs is meant only to indicate the location of the basic power ingredients in the event of challenge, and to denote the nature of legitimacy in its most elemental terms. Unless they are incredibly bad, almost any rulers can manage to develop in their people a reasonably strong positive EP for the government, so that it does not have to depend on the negative one of avoidance of death or imprisonment. Any but the most inept government can "engineer consent" from the people.

In Chapter 27 we observed that in special purpose organizations the major bargain must sometimes be changed *after* persons have become

---

[5] The *social compact* theory has long since been passé in respectable social science circles. The present approach conceives the original version as naive rather than on the wrong track. Citizens of the stable government *do* renounce the use of force against their government, and they *do* expect it to serve their interest in return. The history of mankind is replete with instances of citizens supporting their government so long as it could reasonably be construed to be serving the people, and of citizens indicating by open revolt that they feel free to drop their half of the obligation, and to use force against the government if the government fails its part of the obligation. The nature of the bargain is clear in Abraham Lincoln's statement about the "revolutionary right to overthrow" the government if it does not serve the people, and cannot by peaceful means be made to do so. The thing here called the "major bargain" between people and government, along with other details, is widely acknowledged in different words as the "obligation" of citizen to government and government to citizen.

affiliated. The problem of legitimacy then takes a different form than when major bargains are handled solely at the moment of affiliation. Because the government continues permanently, and because most citizens are affiliated by birth, the normal problem of public legitimacy resembles that of after-affiliation changes of the major bargain in the private organization. Where a written constitution operates, it is the major bargain, or an important part of it, and the procedures for amending it legitimize change. In a going government a large body of procedures and precedents are also part of the major bargain, and the main legitimization of change comes through announcing proposed changes and observing the response. Where protest is freely permitted, absence of marked protest presumably indicates acceptance.

SOME ORGANIZATIONAL ASPECTS OF GOVERNMENT POWER

A government normally has suborganizations within it, and simultaneously belongs to some kinds of larger organizations. When a sovereign state joins a larger organization, it does so as a member. Its authority relation with the larger organization is parallel to that of the individual's relation to a limited-purpose organization. The government accepts the authority of the larger organization so long as the value of affiliation exceeds its cost, and leaves the organization and its authority when costs exceed value. This relationship is generally known as a *federation*. In it a government may itself voluntarily accept the authority of the federation; but it retains sovereignty within its own borders. This means that the federation can give orders to the state but not to its citizens or to any suborganization within it.

To illustrate, the affiliation of the United States with the Universal Postal Union is one of membership in a federation. The United States has agreed upon joining this organization that it will accept the latter's decisions regarding international postal operations, even if the United States government opposes some of those decisions. This is the acceptance of an authority relation. If the United States does not follow its decisions, the Postal Union can curtail benefits to the United States or expel it. The fact that a postal union would be seriously handicapped without it gives the United States much power in the organization, but does not change the fundamental nature of the membership relation.

To effectuate the rulings of the Postal Union, certain activities must be carried out by employees of the United States Post Office. In performing these actions, however, even those postal employees who work entirely on jobs which effectuate rulings of the Postal Union are subject solely to the authority of the United States, and are in no degree under the authority of the Postal Union. No rules or regulations, no rewards or punishments can be applied to them directly by the Postal Union. Nor can the Postal Union by enactment or decree apply any laws, taxes, or fines either on the employees of the post office or on any other citizens of the United States. Should a citizen violate the regulations of the Postal Union he would be cited and punished by the government of the United States for violating *its* regulations designed to effectuate its international agreement—not for violating the regulations of the Postal Union as such. This relationship is implicit in the definition of government, since the government could not have authority to make and enforce *any* decision within its geographical jurisdiction if the Postal Union had authority to enforce *some* decisions within that area.

The authority of a model government includes complete power over all its subdivisions. A completely powerful government of the United States, for instance, could abolish, combine, reorganize, or otherwise shift the state and local governments at will. Not being like the model, an actual government may face distinct limitations on what it can do in fact. For example, the government of the United States evolved from a federation. Under the Articles of Confederation (from 1781 to 1789) the individual states retained their sovereignty, and would do many things only by their own consent.

By the acts of ratifying the Constitution in 1788, and the Bill of Rights shortly thereafter, the states voluntarily agreed to accept the superior authority of the federal government in many matters. A part of this initial pair of bargains, in which the Constitution and the Bill of Rights were accepted as the basic law of the land, is Article X of the Amendments, which reads:

The powers not delegated to the United States by the Constitution, nor prohibited by it to the States, are reserved to the States respectively, or to the people.

Precisely how much authority the states then conceived themselves to be ceding to the federal government, and how much they thought they were retaining, is disputable. The important fact is that the new central government did not arise from outer space, with powers to do as it liked. It arose only because the thirteen former colonies agreed to accept its jurisdiction in certain respects, under an agreement so worded as to indicate that the national government was not all-powerful.

The politicians, citizens, and legal authorities of different times and places have differing views about how much authority is reserved to the states. Nevertheless, if and when the federal government intervenes in matters which they consider to be reserved to the states (or to the people), these persons or groups construe the behavior of the federal government to be illegitimate. The techniques by which the government (federal or other) can be held to its presumed legitimate powers will be examined in later chapters.

In addition to the federal government's constitutional promise not to exercise certain powers on the states (and, by implication, on their subdivisions), the federal government also promised in the Bill of Rights not to exercise certain powers over individuals, such as to deny them freedom of speech, assembly, or religion. (Except for the First Amendment, the remainder of the Bill of Rights asserts the freedom of citizens from certain acts by *any* level of government, federal, state, or local.) Thus, although there is no *a priori* limitation on the power of government, a government must bargain with its citizens, and perhaps with prior governments, over the terms on which it can receive their support. Although his willingness to use force ruthlessly narrows the number of persons with whom a dictator must bargain once he is firmly established, he must also reach many similar bargains in his rise to power.

In some other nations, such as France, the national government operates directly in all areas. Political subdivisions are not areas which voluntarily affiliated with the larger government, but administrative subdivisions of the central government. In that sense the subdivisions have much the same relationship to the central government as the departments or subsidiaries of a corporation have to the whole corporation. The top levels can re-arrange, expand, merge, or eliminate the subdivisions as suit their needs. However, this does not mean that the national government can do any-thing it wants. Among other things, any long-continued practice comes to be accepted as "proper," and cannot lightly be abandoned without strong reason. In addition, thousands of employees at all levels have taken jobs on at least the tacit assumption that these jobs will continue, and they would consider large changes illegitimate. So, too, would citizens who have established relations with the various subdivisions of govern-ment.

Having started with the concept of government as potential omnipo-tence, we now see that any actual government comes into existence under some particular circumstances, in which the government must accept limitations on its power as the price of being recognized and obeyed by its people, or by the previous governments from which it was formed. These limitations are often substantial, and vary greatly from case to case. Up to this point we are speaking only of the major bargain in which the government's authority is accepted and legitimized. The still further bar-gains a government may have to negotiate to get its normal business ac-complished is another large area of restriction of its power, to be seen later.

What Kind of Organization Is Government?

Is government a cooperative, profit, service, or pressure organization? Insofar as we think of it as a government of a *whole* people, it cannot logically be viewed as anything except cooperative. In profit, service, and pressure organizations, one portion of the population, the sponsors, acts on some other portion, the recipients. By definition, none of these three types of organization can operate for or on the whole population. The whole population can hardly make a profit at the expense of the whole population, give generously to it, or exert pressure on it. When the whole population are both sponsors and recipients, the organization is necessarily cooperative.

But just as a limited-purpose organization can in some degree perform all four organizational functions, so can government. If a government is established by only a fraction of the population for their own benefit, it is a profit organization, later referred to as a profit dictatorship. It is also a profit organization if it operates primarily for the welfare of its staff, a situation described earlier as the taking over of the sponsor function by the staff. Even in the most conscientiously operated government some officials, petty or large, will fill their own or their friends' pockets at the public expense, which makes a profit organization out of part of the government. Most governments also perform and charge for certain services, such as issuance of passports, sewers, parks, turnpikes, or loans. Some of these operations bring in more revenue than they cost, and the section which performs them can thus be a profit organization.

An important part of the normal function of all government is to throw its support to some and against other private groups, which makes government a pressure organization for the favored group. If the government taxes the well-to-do to subsidize housing for the poor, it acts as a service organization (at least if the well-to-do support the move).

Government thus can, and usually does, perform all four kinds of organizational functions, just as many other organizations do in part. But a government viewed as acting *for* the whole people *on* the whole people— that is, in an essentially democratic state in which the whole population are both sponsors and recipients—is cooperative, and can hardly be anything else. The chief domestic problems of a government are those of running a large cooperative with diverse interest among its sponsor-recipient members. Where political subdivisions have considerable autonomy, and the local citizens decide local issues, all these same observations about the type of organization apply at the local, county, or state level as well as at the national level.

VIII. THE PRIVATE PRODUCTION OF PRIVATE GOODS

Chapter 30

THE MARKET PROCESS

A COMPLIMENT, a cup of coffee, a hat, or a bicycle produces satisfaction for one person. A radio, an automobile, a kiss, or a house can produce satisfaction for two or a limited group. Without attempting to state precisely the maximum number of people who can achieve satisfaction from any one good, we may say that goods of this sort are privately consumed, and will be called *private goods*. No matter what the nature of the system of social organization, many goods in any society are necessarily and by nature private, and are typically consumed by individuals or families. Some are also highly personal and give satisfaction to only one or a few people, like the faded boyhood snapshot of your grandfather hanging by his knees from the apple tree behind the old house on Sixteenth Street. An important aspect of private goods is that, within the limits of his income, a person can consume or not consume any one good according to his personal preference.

In marked contrast is a good such as the national defense. Although individuals can get satisfaction from having their nation defended, this kind of good can be consumed only collectively, or publicly. It cannot be divided up so that each person can have as much or as little as he likes. By the same token, the values and costs of these *public* (or collective) *goods* cannot be allocated to the same individuals. Although there is no sharp dividing line between private and public goods, such things as fire and police protection, a system of justice, a network of roads, a stable economy, a sound currency, and cleaning a polluted river are also public goods. A limited-access highway or a system of local trash collection paid for by tolls or fees of users is intermediate, showing some traits of public and some of private goods.

We have earlier distinguished between government as a public organization, and all others as private. We have now further distinguished between public and private goods. Between these two pairs, four combinations can be made: (1) the private production of private goods, (2) the public production of public goods, (3) the private production of public goods, and (4) the public production of private goods. Although the line of demarcation is not sharp in all cases, changing the baby's diaper or

559

raising and milking a cow for family use are clearly private production of private goods. The national defense and courts exemplify public production of public goods. The production of military rockets by business firms for the government is private production of public goods, and the production of civilian clothing in a state-owned Soviet factory is public production of private goods. The remaining analysis of the whole society will be grouped under these four headings. To name the alternatives, the public production of public goods is *government activity*, or plain *government*. The private production of private goods is *capitalism*, or a *private market economy*, and the public production of private goods is *socialism* or *communism*.[1]

The private production of public goods has no recognized name, and to the extent the term has meaning at all it refers to the sale of goods by private firms to the government for public use. It therefore can exist only in the context of a private market economy. In a stricter sense it may not be possible for true public goods to be privately produced, since such goods are not transferable. If we think of the public good as defense instead of rockets, as justice instead of the judge's robe, then perhaps only government can produce these public goods. For this reason we will give only passing attention to the private production of public goods, although some purchases by government from private enterprises are inescapable if the economy is private.

This fourfold division does not imply that any and all goods can be produced either publicly or privately. Daily living includes many transformations which could be publicly produced only by great stretch of that arrangement. Witness combing hair, tying shoe laces, caring for infants, mending, bathing, or preventing mayhem after Gerta drops an ice cube down her brother's back. Under any apparently feasible system these things seem destined to remain private goods privately produced—though state-supplied servants could conceivably provide them.

Despite the many transactions within families, any good produced within a family for its own members will be considered self-produced. In an advanced industrial economy many private goods are far too complex or specialized for self-production, such as radios, books, medical care, movies, rail transportation, or even pencils. People can have these goods only if they are produced by public or private organizations and given or sold to individuals who want them.

THE SOCIETY AS A DECISION SYSTEM
FOR PRIVATE GOODS

Steel is made, automobiles are assembled, animals are slaughtered, fish are caught, and corn is grown by approximately the same production

---

[1] The names for these systems have many and diverse definitions and connotations both beyond and in conflict with the present usage. I am not trying to define these much-used words, but to clarify the fourfold classification presented here by suggesting some rough equivalences with existing terminology.

techniques in a socialized economy as in a capitalist one. The degree of industrialization may be affected by the fact that an economy is public or private (a matter for later discussion), but the techniques as such depend on the degree of industrialization plus some peculiarities of local resources and history, not on the fact of public or private ownership. Although the assembly line technique originated with Henry Ford in Detroit, once it is known, it can be used in either public or private enterprise. Although public or private ownership may produce indirect effects on the technology of production, some of which may be highly important, they do so because they are different as *decision* systems, rather than because they are different as technical systems. Although we will return to some effects of these decisional differences on transformations in later chapters, our concern is with the difference between the market system and the socialized system as techniques by which a society makes decisions about producing private goods.

Five major decisions must be made, and can be stated as questions. First, what kinds of goods shall be produced, and in what quantity and quality? Shall the nation produce airplanes, Yo-Yos, and electric shoe polishers, how many, and of what design? Or should it perhaps import them, or do without?

Second, how shall they be made: of what materials, and with what combinations of productive factors? Shall a suitcase be made of leather, wood and cloth, molded plastic, aluminum, magnesium, or fiberglass? Shall a seam of coal forty feet below the surface be taken out by shaft-and-tunnel mining, or by removing the overburden and using surface mining techniques? Shall the material be loaded and carried away by shovel and wheelbarrow (much labor and little equipment) or by a huge mechanical shovel and conveyor (little labor and much equipment)?

This second question can be viewed in a different way. Given certain amounts of iron ore, land space, forest land, machinery, unskilled labor, skilled labor, and investable capital, how much of the iron (for example) shall be used for building, automobiles, cranes, toys, bathtubs, printing machinery, guns, or doorknobs? Shall a particular piece of land be used to raise corn, wheat, oats, vegetables, or lumber; to graze cattle or sheep; to lie idle, or to be dug up for the granite below? Which persons will work in the factories, and which in the offices, forests, fields, mines, laboratories, and classrooms?

Third, at what relative values shall the various goods exchange? Shall a medium quality automobile be considered the equivalent value of ten bushels of wheat or a thousand? Shall a ton of limestone exchange equally for one ton of coal? Or for two tons, or a half ton? If it takes exactly the same amount of total effort and machinery to produce a ton of each, shall they exchange equally even if coal is scarce and there are no substitute fuels, while the limestone is plentiful and has many substitutes? In an economy which uses money (and all complex industrial societies do), the ratios at which things are exchanged, or their relative values, are the same as their relative prices. This third question can therefore be stated more simply: at what prices shall various goods sell?

Fourth, how shall the total product be divided among the population? Since most people in an industrial society get their share of the total product by buying it with the money they receive for their contribution to production, the question can be rephrased: how much shall be paid to each person who makes a contribution to production? How much shall the plant manager be paid compared to the foreman, the machine operator, the typist, and the research engineer? How much shall go to those who contribute savings for investment, and shall the amount be the same whether the investment is used to produce steel or to produce hybrid tea roses? Shall wheat land get the same price as orchard land, or should land be paid for at all? As a final aspect of this fourth question, should anyone receive income except in payment for his contribution to production?

Fifth, how strenuous an effort should be put forth to make the total output as large as possible? To illustrate with labor, should the population work an average of 6 hours a day 5 days a week, giving relatively little goods and much leisure? Or should it work 10 hours a day 7 days a week, giving much goods and little leisure? Should children be put to work at 12 or continue education to 25, and should everyone retire at 55 or work until death or incapacity? Shall women work in industry, and if so, how many? As to the other factors, should factories, mines, farms, and offices on an 8 hour day per worker operate 1, 2, or 3 shifts? Whereas the second question asks *which* resources should be applied to some given total amount of output, this fifth question is concerned with *how much* resources should be used in total to produce *how much* total output of goods. The items listed here illustrate the question of general intensity of effort.

These five are by no means the only important decisions in the production of private goods. But they are sufficient to clarify the decision process. All must be made whether the social organization is private, public, or mixed. Further, if all these decisions are independently made, as in market economy, they have joint effects which are in no sense intended by the separate decisions, and may or may not be desired by the persons who make the decisions, or by the whole society. The main such joint effects are business cycles or their absence, the rate of economic growth, and stability or instability in the general level of prices. Such joint results of separate forces are often referred to as *synergic* effects, and the study of the whole system must consider these effects as well as the direct and immediate ones. A public system may or may not explicitly consider these joint effects in its main decisions about production. It can reverse the emphasis and gear its production decisions to the desired joint effect.

Decision is the process of selecting an item higher on a preference list than one rejected. Production is the process of transforming things so as to raise their position on a preference list. Transaction is the process of exchanging one good for another higher on a preference list. Organization is both transaction and joint production, and incorporates two phases of selecting the more wanted over the less wanted. The problem of making rational decisions for the whole society similarly requires that the less wanted be given up in favor of the more wanted. An important difference between the individual decision and the social decision is that in the former the alternatives are arrayed in a single preference ordering, whereas the latter must formulate some kind of summation, average, compromise, or other compounding of many preference orderings. The social decision could, however, represent the preference ordering of a dictator or planning agency for the whole society. Whatever the decision technique or criterion, the problem is that of deciding upon a *total* set of private goods for a *total* population. If the decision is to be rational, the total values of operating the system must at least exceed their total cost in the value system of the decision maker.

THE PROBLEM ILLUSTRATED IN THE INDIVIDUAL

The fifth decision, about the intensity of use of resources, seems a useful focus for introducing the problem of market decisions, and we will approach it first at the level of an individual producing for himself. First, we may recall that satisfaction is greatest at the point where marginal costs and marginal values are equal. The time of a person living entirely alone, like Robinson Crusoe, must be divided somehow between work and rest. If he prefers to work only a few hours a day and have many hours of rest, relaxation, and recreation, he will produce few goods and have much free time. But if he does produce little, he must in those few hours satisfy high priority wants basic to survival, such as food and shelter. If he should decide to work an additional hour to produce additional goods, these extra goods would necessarily produce less satisfaction than those produced in any preceding hour, since they go toward satisfying lower priority wants. To generalize, as he adds successive hours of work, the output of each successive hour will have smaller utility than will the output of any one hour of a smaller number.

We are, of course, speaking only of different totals of hours, not of the actual sequence of operations within a given number. Let us assume that food has first priority, and that building a hut has second priority. Suppose that in three hours per day he can get sufficient food, and that with an additional two hours per day he could build the hut within a reasonable period. If he works only three hours per day he will devote the whole three hours to getting food. If he works five hours the *extra two* go into building, and are the *additional* hours, even if in any one day he works on the hut *before* he goes after food. Just as successive hamburgers and milkshakes were seen in Chapter 15 to provide declining marginal utility, so will the goods produced in successive hours of work, if additional hours are devoted to lower priority wants.

A second factor also prevails. As more hours are worked per day, diminishing returns set in. (See Chapter 15.) Although other forces may also be involved, fatigue alone could account for diminishing output per hour as more hours are worked. The added value of working an additional hour thus declines because of both diminishing utility and diminishing productivity. The additional hour brings fewer additional units of goods, and each additional unit has less utility than any preceding units.

This set of relationships is shown by the line labeled D in Figure 30-1. The vertical scale represents satisfaction, expressed in utils, and the horizontal scale represents hours per day. The satisfaction of the first few hours' work is very high, and presumably would be almost infinite for the amount of time necessary to produce the minimum required to stay alive. Successive hours show declining marginal satisfaction. At 20 hours per day the additional satisfaction reaches zero, at which point we will assume that Crusoe is too exhausted to produce more. Because this line represents the desire for the product of work, we will call it the demand for one's own labor.

Figure 30-1

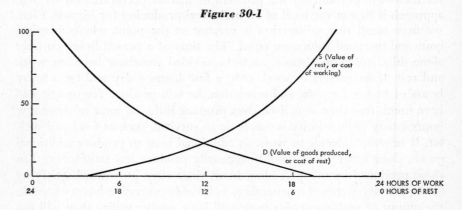

For at least a few hours per day, let us assume that work is preferred to rest or recreation. Up to that point (which we have shown at three in Figure 30-1), rest and recreation have no positive value. Stated the other way about, if our man has already had 21 hours of rest and recreation per day, he has no disinclination to spend the remaining 3 working, and 3 hours of work per day has no cost in his preference system. But beyond that point each successive hour of work leaves one less hour of desired relaxation. Each such reduction leaves every remaining hour of rest more valuable. The marginal value of an hour of rest is therefore shown on Figure 30-1 (the curve marked S) to rise as more and more hours are worked. The relation can also be expressed by the second horizontal scale. This is numbered from right to left, and is marked "Hours of Rest." On this scale we can also read the S curve from right to left, and see the declining value of each additional hour as more and more hours of rest are taken.

Since rest is what has to be sacrificed in order to work, the value of the rest and recreation thus sacrificed is the cost of working, or of supplying one's own labor. (For simplicity we are representing only the opportunity costs of labor, and ignoring the disutility costs.) The S curve is the willingness or unwillingness to work, and can be thought of as the supply curve of one's own labor. As in the demand curve, we are not concerned with the arrangement of hours within the day, but merely with the relative numbers devoted to work or rest.

The two curves can be thought of either as the marginal cost and the marginal value of working, or as the supply of and demand for one's own labor. Following the reasoning of Chapter 15, the maximum satisfaction will be achieved at the point where the two are equal, which is the point of intersection of the two curves. As can be seen from Figure 30-1, the intersection occurs at about 12 hours, where the extra, or marginal, value of the twelfth hour of rest and the twelfth hour of rest are equal, at about 20 hours.[2]

THE RULES OF MARKET SYSTEMS

Before we move from the problem of the individual to that of the production of private goods for the whole society, we must look briefly at the rules by which a market system operates.[3] Although the rules differ in detail from nation to nation, the main rules of a reasonably complete market system are as follows.

1. *Freedom to Produce and Consume.* With the exception of some occasional goods considered harmful to society (such as opium or beverage alcohol) anyone is free to produce, consume, or own any good he chooses. He may produce individually, or as an employee or sponsor of a private organization. He may sell or use any productive factor at his command through transactions of his own choosing in any firm, occupation, or industry. In a market system the government does not engage in any significant amount of production of private goods.

---

[2] This particular way of phrasing it seems most useful, and follows the traditional pattern of economics—though economists do not usually apply the terms supply and demand to the lone individual. The same logic applies if we reverse the language and view the two curves as the supply of and demand for leisure. The demand for rest is the same thing as the value of rest. The value of goods which must be sacrificed if one is to have rest is thus the cost of rest. This represents the willingness or unwillingness to rest, and can thus be thought of as the supply of rest. Whether it be thought of as the supply of and demand for labor or rest, the result is the same. This latter way of stating the relation will not be pursued further, but illustrates the flexibility of the analysis.

[3] This kind of system is known variously as a market system, price system, free enterprise system, capitalism, or the private production of private goods. No distinction will be made between those terms here, although later chapters will indicate that even a fully socialized economy can fruitfully make many decisions on the basis of prices, and operate in considerable part as a price system. That discussion can be better understood if we look first at the full, free market system.

2. *Freedom to Exchange.*   Anyone is free to exchange any good with anyone else for any other good on any terms of exchange agreeable to both parties.

3. *Power Forces.*   The use of force and violence are outlawed in private bargaining. Certain kinds of misrepresentation are also disallowed, either to or about one's competitors.

4. *Promises.*   Contracts are enforceable. Whenever it can be demonstrated from written records or otherwise that *A* has made a promise to *B*, and that *B* has undergone costs in *A*'s behalf based on that promise, *A* will be required to make good on his promise—at least to the extent of compensating *B* for the costs actually incurred.

5. *Competition.*   Except for certain limited circumstances (such as with patents granted to encourage invention, and the public utilities), the producer of any one good is prevented from forming coalitions with other producers of the same good in ways which will materially affect the terms of exchange of that good. In the words of the Sherman Antitrust Act, sellers (or buyers) may not "conspire" to fix prices, allocate markets, or otherwise avoid competition. Different nations differ greatly in the amount of monopoly they allow. Although monopoly in some industries will bring a different equilibrium of prices and income distribution, it does not disqualify as a market system.

Although joint efforts for bargaining purposes (coalitions) are restricted, joint efforts for productive purposes are allowed. Individuals may form partnerships or corporations, and hire staffs. Except when they unduly restrict competition, firms may grow, merge, buy other firms, acquire or sell off subsidiary companies, and integrate horizontally or vertically.

6. *External Costs.*   To a degree which is not easily summarized, firms are limited in their freedom to impose uncompensated costs on others, as by polluting rivers, leaving poisonous residues on food, or blocking highways. To the extent that a firm does impose such costs on others, the full costs of producing its goods are not reflected in its cost figures or prices, and the decision process of the system does not operate according to presumed market principles.

THE BASIC PROBLEM IN THE WHOLE SOCIETY

To return to the problem of decisions, in the individual, both the values and costs of goods are subjective, in the satisfactions achieved and the satisfactions denied. A Robinson Crusoe may keep count of hours of input and units of output, but it is the satisfaction they give (the utils in Figure 30-1), not their numbers, that are important. If his subjective valuations were different, the equilibrium point would be different.

We now move from the individual to the whole society. This stage of the analysis is definitely valid for a private market system. It is also valid in a general way for the whole population of a completely socialized system; it may or may not be valid for the decision makers, depending on how they go about making their decisions about socialized production. An important change now appears: in the industrial society, individuals do not produce for themselves. They work for an enterprise for wages or salary, helping to produce its goods. They then acquire wanted goods by spending their income, perhaps in part for things produced by their own firms, but mostly for goods produced by other firms.[4] Individuals thus remain both producers and consumers. But instead of demanding their own labor directly, they do so indirectly by demanding products from firms, which then demand their labor to produce those goods. A host of other complications arise, but the intermediary position of the firm between the producer and consumer roles of the same people brings the following set of relationships:

Consumer: *Values are subjective*, in utility of goods purchased.
    Costs are objective, in money spent.
 Firm: *Values are objective*, in income received from sales.
    Costs are objective, in money spent for factors.
 Factors: *Values are objective*, in income received from firms.
    Costs are subjective, in satisfactions denied by working.

In discussing the evaluation of firms (Chapter 23) and the bargaining power relationships between sponsors and customers of firms (Chapter 22), we noted the relative objectivity of the firm's position. The consumer spends money, objectively measurable, and receives goods, whose value is subjective. At the other end are the costs of giving up factors for productive use. These, too, are subjective, though with the following reservations. Once a system is in operation and prices of factors have been established, *any* factor can have objective opportunity costs when put to any one use. For instance, the farmer's working for himself has the opportunity cost of the $10,000 he could have earned as a hired farm manager. When we say that the factor costs of labor are subjective, we are referring to the disutility costs of effort, frustration, and the opportunity costs of recreation, and so forth, denied by work. The time preference costs of investment are similarly subjective. The risk element is partly subjective (worry) and partly objective (the statistical probability that the investment will not pay off). Here, too, however, the ultimate evaluation of even the objective risk is subjective. To say that you have a one-in-four objective chance of losing an investment does not bring an objective total decision if the cost of providing the investment is itself subjective.[5] Thus,

---

[4] The term "firm" or "company" refers to a profit organization in a market economy. The term "enterprise" refers either to a profit company in a capitalist nation or to the productive unit (such as a tractor factory) in a socialist one. That we are now using the term "firm" indicates that the ensuing discussion is oriented in a market economy, even if it might have some relevance for socialist ones.

[5] The distinction between net value and final net value in Chapter 15 seems relevant here, though without precise parallelism of wording. We must distinguish between (1) putting a factor to one use rather than another, in which one use is the opportunity cost of the other, and (2) not using it at all. When we speak of factor

at the top and the bottom of the scale, which represent the ultimate values and costs of the whole structure, we find subjective evaluations—in line with and illustrating the earlier statement that in the final analysis all costs and values are subjective. Under no type of organization of the society is it possible to eliminate this ultimate subjectivity.

The firm occupies a unique middle position, however. Its income and its expenditures, its values and its costs both take the form of objectively measurable money flows.[6] On the output side, despite the subjectivity of the consumer's decision within himself, once he has made it the result is objectively measurable by firms. He buys the shirt at $3.95 but not the one on the next counter at $5.95. Group pressures and status factors may determine whether wives in a particular neighborhood will buy automatic dishwashers, and the salesman has subjective leeway in which to influence sales. After all this is done, however, the firms which sell dishwashers do know how many they have sold and at what price, which is relatively precise information about consumer demand.

On the input side of firms, the workers face a highly subjective decision about what occupation to enter, how much training to acquire, where to apply, what jobs to accept, at what wage or salary. But the subjectivity is within the worker. Once he accepts a job at $150 a week, he is a highly explicit cost to the employing firm. If the wage includes another $25 of fringe benefits, these, too, are explicit to the employer, even if they do not show in the pay check.

Firms thus perform a central coordinating function in the production of private goods, which can be seen in the following way. Whereas the consumer and producer aspects of the lone individual are related through a *decision*, when the individual becomes part of a market system his consumer and producer aspects are related to each other through a series of *transactions*. In a broad sense the collectivity of all consumer interests strikes a series of bargains with the collectivity of all producer interests,

---

costs as subjective, we are referring to the distinction between using and not using the factor. Opportunity costs of alternative uses can come into play only after the decision has already been made to use the factor. Labor and investment do not exist unless a human decision is made to provide them. Land, by contrast, exists whether anyone does anything or not, and its use presumably has opportunity costs only. These can also be subjective in some respects, as when a pleasing pasture is turned into a gravel pit.

[6] We noted in Chapter 23 that the measure of profit is far more subjective than is generally suspected. This does not mean that income and expenditures are equally subjective. But how can income and outgo be objective without making profits equally so? The answer is that most of the difference is not held in the form of countable money, but is converted into tangible and intangible assets of many sorts, such as buildings, materials in process, good will, and so forth, whose value is a matter of judgment. I have argued elsewhere (*Labor: Institutions and Economics* [New York: Rinehart & Co., 1956], chap. 15.) that even when firms have strong non-profit motives, as for prestige or stability, they nevertheless seem both willing and able to achieve relatively precise balance between marginal costs and receipts in some details. This is possible only because the values and costs are measurable in money.

through firms as their intermediary. These are not collective bargains, however, between all consumers as one group and all producers as another, with every individual simultaneously a member of both groups. They are a series of individual bargains. Each person active in the system makes both consumer and producer bargains with firms, the one when he buys their goods and the other when he sells them some productive factor. This series of individual bargains, however, *is the decision process of the market system,* and its total joint effect is the social decision.

We will now break down this decision process into some of its more important components. Consumers and factor suppliers are collectively the same persons. Their desire for products is the demand to firms, and their willingness to provide factors is the supply of factors to firms. We will illustrate the relation in terms of labor. Guided by the demand for products on one side and the willingness of people to work on the other, firms act as the intermediary between the two phases, serving as the agent for each in dealing with the other. Through the mediating position of firms the same relation appears for the whole economy as for the individual: the desire for products is the demand for labor, and the willingness to work is its supply. Despite the inescapable subjectivity of the decisions in any one individual, the demand curve of the whole population for any one product and the supply curve of any one type of labor are relatively objective phenomena to which firms adjust. This objectivity permits far more precise decisions than would be possible under voting or other techniques of making public decisions to be examined later. When we say that the supply and demand curves are objective, we do not mean that they can actually be measured and plotted through any significant length. We mean simply that when a product is offered at a given price a specific quantity is sold, and that at one wage a firm may have difficulty recruiting employees but that at a higher wage it may get them easily.

Although firms may make errors of judgment, two forces tend to keep these errors from being serious in the total scene. First, where there are many firms the errors are presumably random and tend to average at the same level they would reach if all were precise. Second, where firms are in competition for labor, no one firm can pay too much less than the market rate or it will not get workers, and no firm can pay too much more or it will price its product out of the market. When firms are in competition for customers, no firm can charge too much for its product or it will not sell, or charge too little or it will be unable to cover costs of production. Competition for factors and customers prevents firms from abusing their position as agents between the production and consumption phases of the economy.

We should not infer from the above discussion that the system works with infallible precision. But a market system *does* operate along the general lines described, and these are very different from those of a fully controlled socialized system.

From EP's to Supply and Demand

The terms of transactions are determined by Effective Preferences. In a unique transaction, only the EP's of the two parties are relevant. We have referred to consensus transactions of various sorts, and our next task is to observe how a market consensus arises, and its relation to the concepts of supply and demand used in economic analysis. This can be done by extending the analysis of competition in Chapter 19 to include a larger number of persons. Figure 19-2 in that chapter showed one party, A, with a given EP, as he faced the possibility of a transaction with any one of four different B's, each with a different EP. By adding more A's and more B's a supply and demand curve can be derived.

Figure 30-2 below is the same kind of bargaining power chart used

Figure 30-2

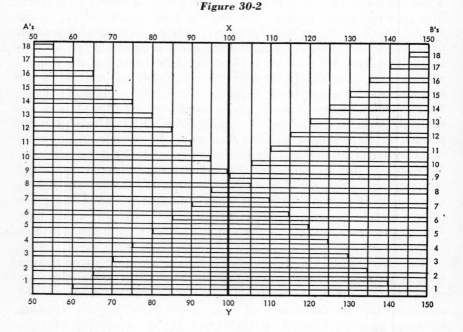

before, but with more EP's. As in previous charts, the midline is labeled X on the top scale and Y on the bottom one, indicating the point of equal exchange of X for Y as a point of reference. For easier reference this midline is also given a value of 100. This means that X is here defined as 100 units of value (say dollars), and Y as one unit of a good. The Y's wanted or offered by all parties are assumed to be identical. As before, the right side of the chart represents higher prices of Y (more money for a unit of Y) and the left side lower prices (less money for a unit of Y, or more Y for a given amount of money). That is, as we move from left to right we are dealing with successively higher prices of Y. The total range of prices shown here extends from 50 to 150. The EP's of 18 A's and 18

B's are shown, each identified by number. These are arranged in order of increasing magnitude on both sides. The *A*'s, of course, are buyers and the *B*'s sellers.

The *A*'s and *B*'s might come into contact in any of many different combinations, and we will illustrate two opposite extremes to start. We may note first, however, that *A*-18 cannot conclude a transaction to acquire *Y*, since his EP does not reach that of any *B*. Nor can *B*-18 sell *Y*, since his EP does not meet that of any *A*. Having eliminated those two, let us now take one extreme situation, and assume that by chance *A*-17 is paired with *B*-1, whose thresholds coincide at 60; *A*-16 is paired with *B*-2 whose thresholds coincide at 65; *A*-15 is paired with *B*-3 with thresholds at 70; and so on, ending with *A*-1 paired with *B*-17 with thresholds coinciding at 140. Let us further assume that each pair either is unaware of all others, or is somehow precluded from negotiating with them, so that each transaction is unique. The result would be 17 pairs of EPs, all just touching at the threshold. With no room for tactics, all would be settled at threshold prices. Each transaction would be settled on different terms, however, ranging from the transaction between *A*-17 and *B*-1 at a price of 60 to that between *A*-1 and *B*-17 at 140. Because each transaction is unique, no one would influence any other.

In the second situation all conditions remain as above, but the pairing is reversed. *A*-1 is now paired with *B*-1, *A*-2 with *B*-2, and so on through *A*-18 with *B*-18. Again we will assume no contacts among pairs, each pair representing a unique transaction. Let us further assume midpoint settlements in all cases of overlap. The *A*'s and *B*'s numbered 10 through 18 will not conclude agreements, since there is no overlap. *A*-9 and *B*-9 will agree at 100, their mutual threshold. All other pairs will also agree at 100, the midpoint in all cases. The total result is 9 transactions at 100 and 9 "no-sales."

We have illustrated only 2 of the 324 possible combinations of the 18 *A*'s and 18 *B*'s. Any other combination is possible. It is also possible that terms of particular transactions might not be settled at the midpoint. There is no need to examine the other possibilities.

The third case illustrates the situation in which a consensus price can develop. Here we will assume (1) complete information by each buyer and seller about all others, (2) complete freedom for any *A* to deal with any *B*, (3) as before, a good *Y* which is identical among all the *B*'s offering it for sale, and (4) a succession of transactions on different days, weeks, or other interval, in which *A*'s repeatedly buy *Y*'s from *B*'s, but in which any one *A* buys only one unit of *Y*.[7] When such transactions first start, any party on one side would seek out the low-numbered parties on the other. On the first round the outcome is unpredictable, though it

---

[7] These conditions plus a larger number of buyers and sellers are the specifications for the pure competitive model in economic theory. The number of buyers and sellers is omitted at this point, since we are assuming that each offers and buys only one unit in any one transaction period.

might be anticipated that about 9 transactions would be completed at a price averaging of about 100. The precise number and average price would depend on who dealt with whom, and in what order. If similar sets of negotiations were repeated day after day, the price of all transactions in the group would get closer and closer to 100. In due time 100 would become a price readily accessible to any *A* or *B*, any of whom would then refuse to pay more or accept less. Thereafter any *A* numbered 1 through 9 could buy from any *B* numbered 1 through 9 at a price of 100, and all *A*'s and *B*'s numbered 10 through 18 would drop out of the market. The interaction would then have reached an equilibrium relationship at a quantity of 9 units exchanged at a price of 100 each. This equilibrium price and quantity is the market consensus of this good among these persons. A line connecting the tips of all the *A* EP's can now be labeled the demand curve for *Y* among this group, and a line connecting the tips of the *B* EP's can be labeled a supply curve of *Y*.

Only two steps remain to complete the transformation from EP's to typical supply and demand curves of economics. The first is to reverse the scales so that price appears on the vertical axis and the quantity (which here is the same as the identification number of the *A*'s and *B*'s) appears on the horizontal.[8] The second step is to add the possibility that the *A*'s and *B*'s can represent either (1) different persons, or (2) the values of successive units of the same good to the same person, or some combination of the two. To illustrate the meaning of "successive units," one person might have the EP *A*-1 for his first unit of *Y*, A-8 for his second unit, and *A*-15 for his third. A supplier might be prepared to offer one unit for 70, a second for 100, and the third for 140.[9] He might also, of course, be prepared to offer a large number of successive units at the same price. This situation is not shown here, but could easily be represented.

By counting the number of bars that touch or cross any particular price line, it can readily be observed how many units will be available (effective supply) and how many will be taken (effective demand) at that price, and a supply and demand schedule can be drawn accordingly. The figures are shown on the following page.

In summary, the EP's of those who want a good and of those who can provide it constitute the power ingredients which determine the terms of transactions. If only two persons are involved, the transaction is unique.

---

[8] An upward-sloping curve represents a direct relationship and a downward line an inverse one, regardless of which variable is plotted on which axis.

[9] So long as the buyers show diminishing marginal utility and the sellers show increasing marginal cost, it is satisfactory to have the bars represent successive units for the same person or firm. The longest EP, which is the one most likely to bring a completed transaction, appears first in time, and is followed by shorter EP's. If an individual showed increasing marginal utility or diminishing marginal costs, we might find the analytically untenable situation in which an individual could complete his second transaction but not his first!

If Price Is	No. of Units Offered (Effective Supply)	No. of Units Taken (Effective Demand)
50	0	18
60	1	17
70	3	15
80	5	13
90	7	11
100	9	9
110	11	7
120	13	5
130	15	3
140	17	1
150	18	0

As more and more persons exchanging the same good come in contact with each other, the terms of any one transaction come to be determined less and less by the EP's of the parties to that transaction, and more and more by the consensus valuation set by the interaction of all persons who want and provide that good. When a large number of persons exchange the same good, their individual EP's can be added to form schedules of supply and demand. We can think of the two EP's in a unique transaction as the simplest possible interpersonal supply and demand. Or we can think of supply and demand in the whole market as total bargaining power components of a large, multiperson transaction. The effective demand of the market is the sum of the Effective Preferences of the individuals in that market. Be they many or few, EP's are the basis of the bargaining power which determines the terms of transactions.

Even when a general consensus prevails, some particular transactions can depart from it, in what was called in Chapter 19 the "great middle ground" between complete uniqueness and complete consensus. The fussy customer who deals with the local store whose manager gives her special care and service may be represented by *A*-5 and *B*-11, who might transact at midpoint terms of 115, despite a consensus of 100 around them.

The Slope of the Curves

If a system is to reach an equilibrium, it is necessary to have one direct and one inverse relation.[10] In a market system this relationship is provided in the supply and demand curves, in which supply varies directly with price and demand varies inversely.

We have seen why this relation exists in the lone individual. We may sense intuitively that the aggregate of all persons should show the same

---

[10] At the introductory stage of discussing transactions it was indicated that *A* and *B* must have opposite preference orderings for *X* and *Y* if they are to exchange. It was later seen that when *X* and *Y* are continuous variables rather than discrete units, the preference orderings need not be opposite, but only different in relative intensity. With supply and demand, too, opposite slopes describe the simplest case. But an equilibrium is possible under any slopes, if they do not coincide, and if they intersect in the first quadrant. Such an equilibrium is stable, however, only if the slopes are opposite.

basic traits as the individuals who compose it. The individual and collective curves do not have fully parallel meanings, however. The curves drawn for the individual represent the desires of *one* person for *all* goods, whereas the curves we are now talking about represent the desires of *all* persons for *one* good.

Demand. The downward slope of the demand curve can be seen in Figure 30-2. At a price of 55 all the *A*'s will buy, while at a price of 140 only *A*-1 will buy, with intermediate numbers willing to buy at intermediate prices. A downward slope means that the lower the price the larger the number of units that can be sold. When generalized, this inverse relation between the price and the number of units sold is known as the *law of demand*.

The reasons why the demand curve slopes downward are as follows. The first is *diminishing utility* within each person. Since the first units (within any given time period) satisfy the highest or most intense want under diminishing utility, beyond some point a person will not be willing to pay as much for additional units as he would pay for the first units.

Second, some goods have *multiple uses*, particularly raw materials and unspecialized finished products. If so, at a high price the product will be used only for high priority wants, but at lower prices it will also be used for lesser priority wants. If silk is very expensive it may be used only for scarves and neckties. But at successively lower prices it might also be used for shirts and suits, draperies and curtains, awnings and feed sacks, or as raw material for paper. The principle will have little effect on such specialized products as toothpaste and pianos, which have only one use.

Two other forces contributing to the downward slope of the demand curve are *different desires* and *different incomes*. The former represents a difference in the preference aspect of EP and the latter a difference in the effective aspect. To illustrate the first, some persons have a great fondness for oysters, and would buy them even at a very high price. Others have moderate and low desires, and will buy at moderate and low prices respectively, while still others would eat oysters only if paid to. If oysters are expensive they can be sold only to the first group. At medium to low prices they can also be sold to the second and third groups, while only if subsidized could they be "sold" to the last. Hence, the statement that the lower the price the larger the quantity that can be sold.

To illustrate the effective aspect of EP in different incomes, the poor can satisfy only their highest priority wants. Middle income groups can satisfy their high priority wants plus a quota of middle and lower priority wants, while the very wealthy can satisfy even the mildest whim for purchasable goods. Assuming equal wants, at a high price some goods will sell only to the rich, at a medium price they will sell to the rich plus the middle income groups, while at a very low price they will also sell to the poor.

Diminishing utility, different uses, and different preference orderings among individuals are almost certain to exist under any kind of economic system with any distribution of wealth and income. Different incomes, however, are at the core of conflicting views about a proper distribution of wealth, since the rich are able to satisfy very low priority wants while the poor may find even some of their highest priority wants unsatisfied. Although no problem arises if each individual satisfies *his* high preference wants before his low preference ones, in the absence of interpersonal measures of utility there is no way of knowing whether the market system satisfies the highest priority wants *of the whole society* if it satisfies the hundredth, or thousandth, priority wants of some before the second or third—perhaps even the first—priority wants of others. There is no doubt about the nature of the system, however. Of two equal EP's, one may arise from an intense desire coupled with low income and the other from a weak desire coupled with high income. The market makes no distinction, giving equal weight to both. The wider importance of this fact will be discussed later.

Taken together, these four factors explain why the joint effect of all the EP's of a whole population for a particular good show the relationship described in the law of demand.[11] That is, they explain why there are more short EP's than long ones, or more strictly, why more EP's cross a low price line than a high price line. Reduced to its most basic level, the law of demand states, in effect, that the number of long EP's plus short EP's is greater than the number of long EP's.

The Factors of Production. The other half of the decision process in a market system is supply. But supply is based upon costs, and costs go to pay for the factors of production. We must therefore specify more clearly what these factors are before attempting to analyze supply. The customary economic classification of factors as land, labor, investment, and enterprise is most useful, and will be followed here.

Thus far we have specifically spoken only of *labor*, which is any human effort expended for the purpose of making productive transformations or transactions. For the purpose of understanding the market system, we are interested only in that labor which is sold to organizations, and more particularly to firms for producing goods for sale.

The second factor is land. Following the definition of economics, *land* means all natural resources. This includes air, the fish of the sea, forests, sunlight, the power of falling water, or any other substance or energy not created by man. Any transformation requiring materials or non-human energy must utilize land, and in the broad sense even services require land, since their producer must at least have something to stand on.

The third factor is *investment*, which was defined as current costs in excess of those expended for value currently produced, the purpose of

---

[11] These four explanations of the slope of the demand curve were first reported by Raymond T. Bye, *Principles of Economics* (New York: Appleton Century), starting with the early editions.

which is to improve the future value-cost ratio. Investment in firms typically takes the forms of buildings, machinery, desks, and so forth, which enable more to be produced with a given amount of labor and land.[12]

Land, labor, and investment are very broad classifications, and each has many subdivisions. There are wheat land, corn land, coal land, and marsh land. There are skilled and unskilled labor, lathe hands, physicians, engineers, teachers, and pianists. Although all investment in production can be thought of initially as money, once it is in use it becomes machines, buildings, rails, mine shafts, or good will. For simplicity most of the discussion mentions only the main headings: land, labor, and investment. The actual decisions which make the system work, however, are all oriented around specific details: not how much investment and labor, but how many lathes and lathe hands—considering their cost.

The fourth factor, *enterprise*, is the function of buying and coordinating the other three factors, and in the present framework is the same as sponsorship of the profit organization.

It should be noted in this connection that profits—the residual amount left after land, labor, and investment have been paid for—go solely to the enterprisers. The amount paid to workers, land owners, or investors is no different (under perfect competition) for profitable firms than for unprofitable ones. Hence, the *profit motive*—that is, the desire for *profits*—applies only to the enterprisers. The earning of profits is the motive for which the sponsors form and continue or discontinue the organization.

Workers work for wages, not profits, and this relation is the same whether the sponsors are a cooperative, a capitalist enterprise, a state or municipal university, a charity, or the coal mine of a socialist or communist state. This point should be clarified, since there is often much confusion on it. It is the difference in *sponsorship* between a capitalist and a socialist enterprise which is basically different, the former being a profit organization and the latter presumably a division of a huge cooperative. For reasons analyzed in previous chapters, the relationships within the staff are essentially independent of the type of organization or the goals of the sponsors. As Max Weber put it, the bureaucracy will serve any master.

Supply. It can be seen from Figure 30-2 that the supply curve slopes upward. This is another way of saying that the quantity varies directly with the price, that the higher the price the larger the number of units which will be offered for sale. This statement is the *law of supply*. In

---

[12] It is widespread practice to call the third factor *capital* rather than investment. With the modification brought by my own definition in Chapter 16, I follow Bye (*op. cit.*) in calling this factor "investment," and in viewing the denial of current satisfaction to achieve greater future satisfaction as the essence of the problem, not the tangible equipment that may more appropriately be called capital. The emphasis on current satisfaction denied for increased future satisfaction also makes unmistakable that this third factor is something quite distinct from Marx's "congealed labor," and is as essential to socialist as to capitalist production.

Figure 30-2, at the low price of 60 only *B*-1 will be willing to sell, while at a high price of 145 all 18 *B*'s will be willing to do so.

Supply refers to a particular product, like the supply of grade #1 wheat, pine shelving, Swiss cheese, and so forth, and an upward sloping supply curve means an increasing cost per unit as more units are produced. When and whether the supply curve will slope upward depends on several considerations, including the product, the technique of production, the number of producers, and the time and quantity range under consideration.

To take the simplest case, if the total supply comes from many small firms, because of differences in skill, location, quality of resources, willingness to work, and other forces the costs of production will differ among firms. Those with high costs of production will show only short EP's, and those with lower costs will show longer ones. This fact would result in a rising supply curve, like that shown in Figure 30-2. Second, in the short run with a given set of plant and equipment, *any* firm will experience diminishing productivity as it attempts to turn out more and more in the same plant. Third, if the producers of any one product try to turn out indefinitely large quantities, while the production of other products continues unchanged, they will have to bid high enough prices to pull the factors away from other industries, and reduce *their* output. As described in Chapter 15, because of diminishing utility, each successive unit of good *Y* which must be sacrificed to make more of good *X* is increasingly valuable, and hence raises the opportunity cost of successive units of *X*. To describe the reaction in terms of factor prices, if industry *X* takes workers away from industry *Y*, the greater the number of workers who leave *Y* the greater will be the value to the employers of those who remain. Hence, if industry *X* continues to bid more workers from *Y*, it can do so only at successively higher prices, which will raise the cost of increased output to *X*. This is the same effect for the whole society as when Robinson Crusoe experiences increasing opportunity costs of more house building in the form of decreased food production. For these reasons it is generally assumed that the supply curve of any one product in the short run slopes upward. Over a long period, however, the costs of producing a product may go down because of technological change, and/or as increasing sales permit mass production techniques to replace custom or semicustom production.

THE WHOLE SYSTEM

The preceding pages introduce the general logic of a market system. Instead of a decision between the consumer and producer interests within an individual person, the market system makes a collective decision by means of a sort of mass bargain, which is actually a series of transactions, between the consumer and producer phases of the same group of people. The desire for goods is expressed in the form of a demand curve, which summarizes all the EP's of the consumers. The willingness to provide factors of production is expressed in the supply curves of the factors, which summarize the EP's of the factor suppliers. But this bargain is made through the mediation of firms. Hence, the customer who wants an automobile does not go to automobile workers, but to the automobile firm. And the men who want to build automobiles also go to the firm for jobs, not to the customers.

The general idea of this "mass bargain" can be visualized in a figurative way from Figure 30-2. The EP's originating from the left may be thought of as those of consumers for automobiles, and the ones at the right as those of the factor suppliers for income. Where EP's do not overlap, the ones at the left represent customers who will not buy cars at the price they must pay, and the ones at the right represent workers who will not take jobs with automobile firms at the existing wages. The cases of overlap represent conditions in which workers will produce and customers will buy. Profit to the firms arises from keeping some portion of the gain to both sides represented by the overlap. This description is figurative only, since supply and demand can meaningfully be applied to only one factor at a time, and since the supply and demand of factors and of products operate in a different plane, so to speak, as will be seen below.

All transactions in the system are voluntary, which means that each person receives something he values more than what he gives up. A person will not work for wages (or provide any other factor he may own) unless the value of the goods he can buy with the price he receives equals or exceeds the satisfactions lost in providing his labor (or other factor). The firm will not produce and sell unless the price it receives for its products equals or exceeds its payments to the factors. Finally, the customers will not buy any one good in the short run unless its value to them equals or exceeds the values of other things they could buy with the same money. They will not buy in the long run unless the goods acquired equal or exceed the costs of earning the income. The fact that value must be increased at each stage of the relationship, and that the customers are both consumers and factor suppliers, assures that the whole system will produce a net increase in value to the collectivity of participants.

The whole system, however, is a network, not a ladder, of decisions. The wages for labor are determined by the total supply of and demand for workers in *all* industries, not just one. The interest on investment and the rent on land are similarly determined by a single supply and demand simultaneously for all industries. The supply and demand of every factor cuts across every industry or product, and the supply and demand of every product cuts across every factor. That is, the price of every factor depends on its use in every product, and the price of every product depends on the price of every factor it uses.

In addition to these "cross" relationships between factors and products are a series of "parallel" ones. Because they are often discussed independently, the demand curves for products may perhaps seem to be logically independent. They are not. Suppose you have a yen to trade in your old car on a new one, and have the money (or credit rating) already in the bank. But a weekend at a lake gives you an even stronger yen for a boat at about the same price. Your EP for the car now goes down, first because its preference position has fallen below that of the boat, and second because if you spend the money for the boat your preference for the car will no longer be effective. Because of both the effective and the preference aspects, an EP has now shifted "sideways" from the demand for autos to the demand for boats. In consequence, the demand for factors by firms will also shift in part from automobiles to boats. If the relative amounts of land, labor, and investment are different in the production of the two items, the *total* demand for each factor may also change. Since any expenditure for one good changes both the amount of money left to buy others and the relative intensity of unmet desires among different goods, the demand for any one good depends upon (is a function of) the availability and prices of all other goods.

Similar parallel relations exist among the factors, both for firms and factor suppliers. Like consumers, firms try to produce their products at the lowest cost. If labor is high in price and machinery low, the firm may substitute machines for labor. It may also substitute labor for land, as by putting more men on a farm to cultivate it more intensively instead of spreading the same number of men over more acres. Parallel substitutions can also be made within each factor, as by using a punch instead of a drill to make holes in sheet steel, or by using laid-off production workers instead of painters to do interior painting in a factory.

Factor suppliers have similar choices. Within the clothing industry a worker may train himself to be a cutter, presser, or sewing machine operator, and the investor may put his savings into the Senescent Corporation or the Burgeoning Works. Each factor must make cross-industry comparisons as well as within-industry ones. Should the comptometer operator go to work in the steel, pencil, or insurance business? Shall the investor put his money in copper, aluminum, steel, or watchbands? Should the farmer plant his field in soy beans or lease it to a fortune cookie company?

The above description gives only the barest hint of all the possible interrelations and ramifications of the whole system. If we could stop all outside influences for a while, and consider it a "closed system," there would exist one set of relationships in which potentially every worker could be in that occupation, firm, and industry in which he could earn more than anywhere else. All labor, land, and investment could be distributed according to the principle of equimarginality (Chapter 15), so that each unit would earn the highest possible in the system, and each firm and industry could produce just that amount of output which would bring its marginal costs and marginal income into balance. This point is called a static general equilibrium. At the point of equilibrium every plant and factor is used in the place where it can earn the highest return. At this point the system will produce the largest possible difference between the value of finished goods and the cost of the factors. That is, it will maximize the satisfaction of the people in the society.[13]

Now no actual system can reach this equilibrium point in fact, since no system is in fact closed. Nor do all its people behave as the model prescribes. But the nature of the market system is such that its decisions tend toward this result. By this we mean that no collective decisions are necessary. All that is required is that each individual examine the alternatives open to him, and select the one that will bring him the largest return relative to its cost.

An important logical aspect of this system is that discrepancies of detail are self-correcting. If one industry has over expanded (by which we mean that it is producing more goods and consuming more factors than it would do in the equilibrium position), the excess of supply will force its prices down. Thereupon its profits will decline, producers will be discouraged from entering or remaining in the industry, and production will in due time decline again. If too few people have entered a particular occupation, its wages will rise above their equilibrium rate, more people will be induced to enter it, and, with the now increased effective supply, the wages will go down again. Throughout the whole

---

[13] A question long debated by economists is whether factors are price-determined or price-determining. That is, do the prices of products depend on the prices of factors, or do the prices of factors depend on the prices that can be commanded for the products? In the present framework the question is irrelevant. Both products and factors are goods—positive goods which provide satisfaction when received, and negative goods which provide satisfaction when avoided. To view the problem through the individual, all these values can be arranged in a single preference ordering. The individual will decide in favor of producing a particular good if the goods given up to create it have a lower total value than the finished good. An individual cannot make a decision for or against producing unless both the good and its costs are *already valued* in his preference system. The relation is not one in which one value determines the other value through the medium of production. It is rather a relation in which a comparison of the two values determines production. When we move to the market system we add the complication that the costs and values reflect the preference system of a collectivity of persons, not of an individual. As I see it, the problem is not whether values determine costs or costs determine values. The problem is (1) how the system makes decisions when the costs and values fall in the preference systems of different persons, and sometimes even in different subcultures, and (2) whether this is the most valid or useful method of making the decision. The element of interpersonal values does not seem to change the main relation, however, that both goods and factors must be valued *before* the production decision can be made. On the basis of a preliminary examination of the problem in the present framework it would seem that the exchange value of the product must lie somewhere between the subjective values of the goods and the factors. That is, the basic transaction is between customers and factor suppliers, with the firm as their mutual agent, and the price of the good must lie somewhere in the overlap of EP's of these two groups. Although the marginal analysis is indispensable to a theoretically determinate system, some aspects of the problem seem more manageable if viewed as a bargain between two collectivities.

system reactions of this sort go on constantly. The logic of laissez faire, or noninterference with the system by government, is that if let alone the system will automatically correct its own discrepancies. By contrast, interference by subsidy, price, or quantity controls supposedly prevents the adjustment from taking place, and impedes self-correction. To use an obvious case in the United States, if farm prices are unduly low because of excess production, price supports by the government tend to aggravate the condition. They keep prices up, thereby encouraging more production and discouraging sales, both results being the reverse of what is needed if equilibrium is to be achieved.[14]

Although the system is often thought of as subordinating all other considerations to the pursuit of money income, and although the theory shows this emphasis, this is not necessarily so in fact. When a man selects an occupation he may consider companionship, geographic location, or security of the job as well as its money return, and choose the one that brings him the largest combination of money and nonmoney benefits. In choosing its location a firm may put a factory on a site that is scenic as well as practicable for production, even if it is less efficient in overall money terms. Conventional economic analysis specifically allows for subjective considerations among customers and factor suppliers (since it can hardly avoid them), but not for firms. The fact that in its quest for determinacy economic theory omits nonmoney motives from firms does not mean that firms as well as consumers and workers cannot attend to subjective considerations, and attempt to maximize the total of objective and subjective ones.

Taken in total, the set of relationships described above is the technique by which a market system makes its decisions about private goods. As to what goods to produce, starting from any point, the system tends to produce those goods which will bring the highest profits. These are goods showing the largest gap between value and cost, and hence the ones whose production is most obviously advantageous to the society as well as the firm. As to the factors, firms will tend to produce with the factors having lowest cost. These will be the ones the use of which brings the least loss of satisfaction. Between them, these two forces tend to satisfy the highest priority wants by sacrificing the lowest priority wants. This is the essence of sound decision making. It is subject, however, to the earlier reservation about the interpersonal comparisons of utility in connection with the distribution of income.

The next question relates to exchange ratios, or relative prices. These are determined by supply and demand for each separate product, determined simultaneously with the supply and demand factors of all other products, and in light of the interrelation of all factors of production.

---

14 The basic market logic against intervention is clear. However, the particular case of farming is subject to reservations, to be seen in the next chapter, which makes clear that the straightforward market analysis is by no means adequate to deal with all supposedly "economic" problems.

To say that price is determined by supply and demand means that it is determined by an interaction of its value in use and the value of the factors that must be sacrificed to make it. The intersection of supply and demand curves determines the quantity simultaneously with the price. Any unit of a good produced up to that quantity has a value which exceeds its cost; beyond that point the cost of any unit exceeds its value. To set prices and quantities at the intersection of supply and demand curves is thus to achieve greater total satisfaction than could be reached at any other point.

In a market system, the distribution of income is the same as the pricing of factors. Except for profits, the prices of factors, like those of products, are determined by the interaction of their supply and demand. Supply reflects the willingness of people to make the factors available, and demand reflects the value of factors as contributors to production. Here, too, firms will continue to purchase additional units of each factor so long as the value of each exceed its cost, and will not purchase additional units whose cost exceeds their value. Any one supplier of a factor will continue to offer more units so long as the value he receives from selling it exceeds the subjective cost to him of providing it, but will provide none beyond that point. In the model of perfect competition at a position of equilibrium no profits would exist. Profits do arise, however, under dynamic conditions in which there are changes of values, fortuitous events, new products and techniques, differences in bargaining skill and information, and so on. According to the model, the presence of profits (or losses) in the dynamic model will induce enterprises to adjust their activities in directions which will move the system toward the equilibrium position.

Most market systems operate under the private ownership of land, so that landowners are among the factor suppliers who receive income. It is possible to build a market system on government ownership of land, as is done in Mexico. If the government attempts to get the largest rent it can from each piece of land, the result may be fairly close to that of private ownership in many respects. One of the outstanding questions of economic justice is whether any private person or organization should receive payment for land, since human beings did not produce it. We will not go into the controversy here, which is essentially a value judgment with relatively little logic to assist it. We can observe, though, that private ownership is a technique of administering the use of land as well as of distributing income.

The market system in itself does not provide goods to anyone who does not contribute some factor(s) to the productive process. Such receipts as those from gambling, theft, or gifts, including organizational gifts through service organizations, are outside the system, as such.

As to the general intensity of effort, each individual is presumed to give as much or as little of his contribution to production as he wishes.

The next chapter will indicate why the system is relatively insensitive in making this decision.

Other kinds of decisions about the whole system are incidental or accidental, as we shall also see in the next chapter.

THE MARKET AS ORGANIZATION AND AS A SYSTEM OF INFORMATION

The market system is an arrangement by which a society produces its private goods as part of its informal, not its formal, organization. Instead of engaging in such production itself, the government provides a framework of rules within which private individuals and organizations carry out production and exchange. The operation of the market is a system, as described in Chapter 3. Its main parameters are (1) the preference sets of the people for both goods and factors, (2) the "technical coefficients," or ratios of factors required to transform particular goods, and (3) the general framework of rules provided by the government.

Since the government does make rules for the system, the market process is formally recognized, even if not formally organized, as the technique for producing private goods. If we try to imagine the system in formal terms, we might picture a general manager for the whole people issuing the following instruction: "Under the following rules and with such resources as you can command, engage in those transformations and transactions, or form those suborganizations, which seem likely to produce the largest amount of income for you." Under a complete and undiluted market system for producing and exchanging private goods, the general manager for the whole society does not directly specify programs, provide cues, create the structure of suborganizations, or engage in transactions. What is more, there is no general manager.

The information system follows the same logic. If the market system is undiluted, each individual or firm is responsible for acquiring and interpreting its own information. No higher authority formally absorbs uncertainty by recoding original information into cues for releasing specific programs in firms. Government statistical services may do so informally, though firms follow these cues on their own initiative and at their own risk.

Perhaps the most outstanding feature of the market system is that its value systems and information systems are essentially the same thing. The same messages simultaneously communicate information and motivation. The main information is that of prices, for both factors and products, supplemented by information about quantities of both. Assuming that a firm knows its present costs, prices, and profits, then information about a change of price in either the product or factor market immediately alters the components of its decisions. If a rise in factor prices occurs, for example, unless the enterpriser can manage to make a compensating change in some other component he stands to take a reduction in profit. But he does not want such a reduction, and hence is not only informed but is also motivated to do something about it.

Information to workers that wages have gone up in an occupation to which they could easily move motivates them to consider changing jobs, and almost undoubtedly motivates persons just selecting an occupation to move toward the one with rising wages. Information to consumers that the price of pork has gone up and beef down motivates them to eat more beef and less pork. This effect is felt not only at the level of the consumer, factor supplier, and the whole firm, but within every department and subdepartment of an organization which has to work on a limited budget. The market system is one in which every individual is potentially a decision maker.

Considering the whole society as an organization, every communication about prices which flows through the system is a program cue from the "general manager" and a motivation as well as a piece of information. The ability to communicate information, instruction, and motivation in the same message probably represents the simplest conceivable technique for running an organization. This represents one of the greatest practical strengths of a market system, and its absence under a fully planned system creates some difficulties we will observe later.

The legitimacy of the system is high, since all transactions within it are voluntary, and the government exercises no formal authority. Its ability to evaluate managers is also high, as seen in Chapter 23, since many managers are doing roughly the same thing under approximately the same circumstances, and profits (despite their partial subjectivity) are apparently the best single measure we have of the overall performance of the firm.[15]

The basic logic of this system says in effect: "within the context of reasonable transactions rules, if everyone will but do what brings him the largest income, he will in those same acts be doing what is most advantageous to the whole society." A system under which intelligent selfishness leads the individual "as if guided by an invisible hand" to do what is good for his fellows and the whole society has strong rational appeal. To the extent that it is valid in fact, it also has great performance strength.

The system is sometimes described as making its decisions by "dollar ballot." Every time an individual spends or refrains from spending, he casts a ballot for or against the production of some good. Firms produce those goods which receive the most "votes" (relative to their cost), and stop making things customers do not "vote" for.

In this connection it may be well to survey the difficulty of the problem. Any industrial society must make decisions about goods—what to produce, with what factors, and so forth—for the whole society. This

---

[15] Profits as an evaluation of management will be discussed again in connection with socialized economies.

decision requires some sort of technique for aggregating many preference systems into a single preference system—at least in a society which pays attention to individual preferences. Viewed in this light, it is difficult to imagine any technique of social decision making which could give more continuous and detailed attention to individual preferences. Every EP of every individual is part of the demand curve for every product he is interested in. Every cash register is a "voting machine" counting dollar ballots. Every piece of merchandise sold depletes an inventory and influences a buying or production decision of a firm. Every time a person decides for or against a particular occupation, accepts or rejects a job, invests his savings, or lets out a piece of land, he is not only advancing his interest as he sees it, but is also making part of a social decision in a fashion that is objectively recorded and which has inescapable influence. In contrast to a political decision system, in which one is apt to vote not more than once a year and on only a dozen or so of candidates or issues, in the market system each individual is voting day in and day out. What is more, his vote carries influence whether it is within a minority, plurality, or majority. In many respects the individual can change his "vote" whenever his preferences change, without having to wait for an election.

The present chapter has described the general set of relations in a relatively pure, undiluted market system. For reasons to be seen in the next chapter, no actual market system is pure, and governments have found reason to impose numerous controls. That is, the market system is in fact more closely attached to and part of the formal organization of society than the preceding discussion suggests. In any event the market system is not the whole of the social organization, and cannot be, since it cannot by nature perform certain essential functions. Some important modifications, limitations, and restrictions of market systems will be examined in the next chapter.

Chapter 31

LIMITATIONS AND COMPLICATIONS OF MARKET SYSTEMS

THE LARGER LIMITATIONS: WHAT MARKETS CANNOT DO EVEN IN THEORY

THE LOGIC of the market system's decision process is strong within the realm of private goods. However, it can make decisions only about those goods which are privately produced and privately consumed, and are capable of being exchanged. Some very important goods cannot be privately consumed, and a market system, for example, cannot make decisions as to how much a nation should spend for its national defense, or what kind of system of justice or police protection it should have. A market system can therefore never provide the whole social decision process of a nation. It can supplement but never replace government as the organization of the whole society. Further, it by no means constitutes the whole of the informal private organization, which includes co-operative, service, and pressure organizations, which also produce private goods. These facts give rise to some limitations and complications.

This chapter and the previous one are intended together to give some notion of the specific potentialities and limitations of the market process. They do not pretend to provide an overall evaluation of the system, either alone or in comparison with other systems—a well-nigh impossible task. The later chapters on planned economies will be undertaken in the same spirit.

Public versus Private Goods

First, the market system cannot decide the proper allocation of the total national income between public and private goods, or between the public and private production of goods. Private goods can be offered for sale, and individuals can cast their dollar ballots for or against them. But public goods cannot thus be offered, dollar ballots cannot be cast for them by individuals, and the market therefore cannot make decisions about them. We cannot, for example, offer national defense or police protection for sale to individuals and let each person buy as much or as little as he likes.

For similar reasons, it is not possible to offer some particular combination of public and private goods to see whether the public will buy it or not, since the public goods themselves cannot be thus offered. That is, the people cannot decide whether 1, 10, or 30 per cent of the Gross National Product should be devoted to national defense by casting their dollar ballots—by buying or not buying as individuals any particular percentage. In consequence, the decision about the relative amounts of public and private goods must itself be a public decision, at least at the conscious level. In practice, the government decides how much it will spend, on the basis of political considerations. That amount is then the public share, all others remaining private.

One of the strong theoretical defenses of the market system is that it will allocate resources to those uses which satisfy the greatest total desires. Two modifications must be noted. One has already been stated—namely, that it is true only if we assume arbitrarily, for example, that the tenth or twentieth suit of clothes to the rich man brings as much satisfaction as the first suit to the poor man. This proposition can be neither proved nor disproved, since the values involved are entirely subjective. To say the least, the proposition is by no means self-evident on common sense grounds.

The conclusion that the system will satisfy the greatest total desires is also valid only if we assume that equal payments to factors represent equal costs to factors. That is, if two men receive the same hourly wage, we must assume that they both suffer the same cost, opportunity plus disutility, of providing the hour's labor. This point applies to factor costs the same general kind of reasoning as was applied in the preceding paragraph to product values. Like the former, this, too, involves interpersonal comparisons of utility, and can be neither proved nor disproved.

The distribution of income among a people also affects total satisfaction through the motivation to produce. Rewards in a market system are related to the increase in value which is produced by transformations and transactions. Persons are therefore presumably motivated to perform those transformations and transactions which bring forth the greatest rise in value. The total effect of a given distribution of income upon total satisfaction therefore depends on its sub-effects on consumer satisfaction on the one side and on producer motivation on the other. Although the proponents of various economic systems make glib and sweeping assertions about these things, we thus far apparently have neither models nor empirical findings which provide an objective conclusion to the problem.

Second, even if the market process does produce the best possible allocation of private goods, it is inherently incapable by itself of achieving (as contrasted to deciding) the best possible combination of public and private goods, since it cannot make decisions about public goods. The market can assist decisions about many public goods, however, by determining their cost. Since public goods require the same factors as private ones, and often use many privately produced materials, the cost of the public good is determined by the market prices of the factors and materials required to produce it. So long as public goods do not dominate the society, the cost of public goods can thus be market determined. Knowledge of cost is important to a rational decision regarding what public goods to produce, whether the decision is being made by a legislature, bureaucrat, or voter. How large the market sector must be relative to the public sector to perform the function of determining the cost of public goods is at the moment unanswerable.

Rules of Transactions

A market system cannot decide its own rules about transactions, including the important ones described earlier as property rights. Should trusts, cartels, price fixing, unions, collective bargaining, strikes, secondary boycotts, misleading advertising, bribes, or the cornering of a stock be allowed? When should contracts be honored and when not? These things cannot be produced and offered for sale, and hence cannot be decided by the market process. They must be decided by government, either by writing the rules or by not disallowing those which evolve in practice.

The market system cannot itself determine whether land should be privately owned, although private ownership is practiced in most such systems, and is normally assumed to be part of the market process. The system cannot make the fundamental decision whether incomes ought to be based on productivity. The system in itself produces that result, though most societies with market systems supplement them with charitable, governmental, or other techniques which assure that no one will be completely destitute if he does not produce. It is impossible for everyone to receive more than he produces, or (unless goods are destroyed) for everyone to receive less, since the total income of the society is the total goods produced. Whether a society would be "better" if some groups regularly receive more than the value of their production and others less is a matter which cannot be answered on objective grounds.

Aggregative Decisions

Certain kinds of synergic effects[1] are *produced* by a market system, but cannot be *decided* by the market process, because they cannot be offered for sale. The system can experience a depression, to take an im-

---

[1] Synergic effects, for purposes of social analysis, can be thought of as the unintended outcome of the joint presence of two or more intended actions. If action A causes X, and action B causes Y, then we can bring about X by doing A, and Y by doing B. If, however, the simultaneous occurrence of X and Y brings on Z, then Z may be referred to as the synergic effect of actions A and B. We are here concerned mainly with the fact that the sum total of many individual actions may bring a collective result not intended or sought by the individuals. So far as the definition is concerned, a synergic effect can be either desirable or undesirable. Since the latter cause "problems" and the former do not, the latter will receive the main attention.

portant example, which nobody wants and many would be willing to pay to avoid, if a market mechanism were available to buy prosperity. But no such mechanism exists, nor does any seem possible. For although depression is an outgrowth of the private market process, it is by nature a public, not a private good, albeit a negative one. There is no conceivable technique by which different amounts of national prosperity can be offered for sale, each priced at its respective cost, so that each individual can buy the particular amount he wants.

Not only are unaided market processes incapable of avoiding business cycles, but in many respects business cycles tend to be self-aggravating under market processes alone. If prices start down in an incipient recession, the movement might easily be halted if everyone would promptly expand his buying or withhold selling. But if prices are expected to continue downward the *private* interest of everyone is to do the opposite. Buyers are better off individually if they wait till prices go down further, and sellers if they sell promptly before they go down. Both actions tend to drive prices farther down. This is one example of the self-aggravating effect. The converse is true for upward movements into booms.

Now, of course, if everyone could be induced to behave contrary to his own apparent short-run interest, the good of all would be assured. The difficulty is that anyone who does so takes all the loss his behavior entails if the common effort fails, but gets only his common share of the benefit if it succeeds. By contrast, the person who refuses to participate saves all his share of the cost if the venture fails, but gets as much benefit as everyone else if it works. The odds are thus heavily against avoiding depressions by voluntary individual contracyclical action. Further, such action requires a reversal during recession of the whole logic on which the market system depends, and requires that people buy when prices are expected to fall and sell when a rise is expected. This is more of an adjustment than can reasonably be expected of the system, particularly if people disagree whether or not we are in a recession. For reasons seen in the previous chapter, disequilibriums of *details* of the system tend to be self-correcting. There is a widespread tendency to assume that the self-adjusting mechanisms of supply and demand for individual products also operate for the total supply and demand for all products. Neither theory nor practice suggests that this is so. If the price of any one good or factor goes down, the effective demand for it will be larger. More will be sold and the downward pressure on its price will be relieved. But since the demand for any one good reflects the relative preference as among *all* goods, no such balancing effect occurs if the prices of *all* goods go down simultaneously. The reverse tends to happen instead, and unbalances in the whole economy tend to be self-aggravating. The logic of laissez faire is strong when applied to self-correcting phenomena; it is meaningless for self-aggravating ones.

Depression may also be self-correcting in time. But in a highly interrelated modern economy, particularly if it is trying to show its superiority to socialist ones, a major depression may be considered intolerable. Whereas we now consider 7 or 8 per cent unemployment large, and 10 per cent unacceptable for even a short period, during the 1930's an unemployment rate of 15 to 25 per cent continued almost without interruption for 10 years. We now have techniques by which government can influence business cycles. But there is no technique by which the market system, as such, by market techniques can prevent, control, or provide dollar ballots for or against business cycles.

Economic growth and inflation follow part of the same logic. While a system may *have*, or synergically *produce*, a 4 per cent rate of growth or a 2 per cent rate of inflation, no market technique exists by which individuals within the system can assess the costs and values of each, and by market processes choose one rather than another. Like prosperity, these are public goods. There can be only one answer for the whole nation, and if a decision is to be made it must be public. Our knowledge of how to achieve these things is still imprecise. We therefore may not be able to accomplish a given result even if we make the public decision, in much the same sense that a decision to put a manned rocket on the moon within five years does not necessarily mean that we will do it. The public decision may not be effective or precise; but a private market decision is not possible.

Another kind of aggregative decision in which the market system shows weakness is that between the relative importance of present wants and those of a generation or two hence. To what extent, for instance, should the settlers of a hundred years ago have increased their costs by being less profligate with timber resources, so that we would now have better lumber at lower cost? How much cost should the current generation incur to insure parks and forests for our great-grandchildren? This is a difficult choice at best, requiring both intertemporal and interpersonal comparisons of utility, among other things.

Speculation is one technique through which future wants and resources are reflected in the present. If someone concludes, for example, that forest lands will be extremely scarce and costly a century hence, he can buy forest lands to hold against the expected rise in price. Forest lands will thus be taken out of current use and reserved for future use. The likelihood that private action will do this on a significant scale for long periods of time, as a century or two, seems remote, despite the thirty to eighty year thinking of some of our lumber and public utility companies.

The interest rate is also a technique for balancing present against future wants, through the supply of and demand for loanable funds. But although both interest rates and speculation take the future into account, and do so in ways which tend to allocate resources rationally over time, both do this in a fashion designed to maximize the returns to those now living and making the decisions. This by no means is necessarily the same as bringing the maximum satisfaction to present and future generations as viewed in the value systems of *both*.

The Cessation of Unwanted Goods

In discussing freedom we noted that the actions of some persons often impose costs on others, as when one family's raucous parties keep the neighbors awake. As a result, some of us would occasionally be willing to pay others to stop doing certain things. Billboards illustrate the problem. They have value to those who put them up, but disutility to many who use the highways. If the mechanism were possible, some private enterprise might make a profit selling *absence* of billboards to motorists. No such mechanism seems possible, however, as it would require paying for every billboard *not* put up. Although billboards themselves are private goods produced by the market system, the *absence* of billboards is a public good which can apparently be achieved only by government action. The same is apparently true in other areas as well, including physical violence. Whereas the presence of positive goods can be privately produced, the absence of negative goods requires public (or highly collective private) action.

SOME PRACTICAL LIMITATIONS ON MARKET PROCESSES

The preceding section dealt with public goods which are outgrowths of the operation of a private economy, but which cannot by nature be decided by market techniques. We now move into the area of private goods which *can* be decided by the market, but which show certain complications in practice which prevent market forces from operating as the model prescribes. The details are numberless, and we will confine attention to some general kinds of impediments.

"Natural" Monopolies

First are "natural" monopolies. In industries such as railroads, gas, electricity, water, and communication, it is not feasible to have the large number of competing companies on which the market system depends. The large fixed cost of distribution facilities is the main reason for the nonfeasibility of competition, although in radio the main factor is the limited number of channel frequencies. Since competition is the force we rely on to make firms provide good service at reasonable prices, and full scale competition is not possible in these industries, we typically allow monopoly or semimonopoly, and substitute public regulation for competition.

Semipublic Goods

It is possible to provide such things as roads, dams, bridges, or parks on a market basis. Private toll roads and bridges have been widely used in many places. Thousands once existed in the United States, and some still operate, along with many private ferries. Many private parks or lakes are similarly operated.

If such things are relatively small, private operation is feasible, but pure private sponsorship is almost impossible if such facilities are to be large. A few landowners at strategic points along a proposed highway could hold out for exorbitant prices, and either stop the highway or make its price excessive. A major road therefore requires authority to condemn property and force its owners to sell at a reasonable price. The same principle applies to large parks, dams, bridges, or other projects.

The government will presumably grant that authority only if the project is in the public interest. Such a decision can be part public and part market—market in that a private sponsor (such as railroad company) will not undertake it unless the receipts from sales are expected to exceed the costs, including a reasonable cost of the land, and public in that condemnation authority will not be given unless the project is publicly desirable.

Although long toll roads with few intersections are feasible, it is too costly to collect tolls if there are many intersections and short trips, as in the case of city streets. Streets and unlimited access highways are therefore generally built at public expense, and made available without charge. Such things behave partly like private goods, in that users could be charged a fee for service. They are also partly like a public good, however, in that it is difficult to allocate costs to individual users in proportion to the amount of value they receive.

Absence of Markets

It hardly seems necessary to state—though the point is sometimes missed—that a market system depends on markets, which often do not exist in undeveloped or underdeveloped areas.[2]

If left to its own devices the transition from an undeveloped to a fully industrialized market system may take a century or more. It typically starts with small handicraft industries, followed by light manufacturing of consumer goods, such as textiles, clothing, and simple housewares. In due time these justify the development of power and transportation, and the manufacture of light machinery for the light manufacturing. Finally heavy industry is added, including steel, cement, locomotives, and heavy industrial machinery. The process is slow, because for many decades the society is not productive enough to accumulate investment rapidly. Each successive stage depends on the prior one for a market, and market techniques are feasible.

Many undeveloped and underdeveloped nations now want to telescope

---

[2] An undeveloped area is represented by the Eskimos, the Australian Bushmen, or sections of tribal Africa, where no industrialization has occurred. Underdeveloped areas are those such as Korea or Burma, or much of Latin America, where some industry, mining, or relatively advanced agriculture are found, but where important natural and human resources remain untapped.

these steps into a short time by reversing their order. Whereas evolutionary market development starts with things for which there is an immediate market—light consumer goods—and work backwards to the heavy producer goods, a transition can be accomplished much more rapidly if it starts with the heavy industries for which no market yet exists in the country and works forward toward the consumer goods. If a nation is willing to make tremendous sacrifices for a time (for perhaps 30 years) and go deeply into debt to richer nations for capital lending, it may accomplish this rapid transition.

If this rapid course is chosen, it is not possible to make production or pricing decisions at the early stages by market techniques, since no domestic market then exists for the product of new heavy industries. Foreign markets are irrelevant except as a stopgap, since the not-yet-existent domestic consumer industry is the one these facilities are designed to fill. Whether local or imported, private capital will hardly be invested in heavy industry whose markets are decades away, when markets for light industries already exist and provide immediate returns. Capital is likely to be put in heavy industry only if some immediate return is guaranteed. In the absence of present markets, such a guarantee can be made only by the government, which, through taxes, can draw on any and all local resources to pay interest on the loans. At the time it was undertaken, the Tennessee Valley Authority was able to command capital for a project whose returns were farther distant than private investors would contemplate, and on a scale which private capital was unable to handle.

To make such a transition, it seems inescapable that a nation or region must start by taking stock of where it is, and of its potential resources both human and natural. It must then draw a blueprint of what it can be built to, along with sketches of the intervening stages. Sources with money to invest, domestic or foreign, public or private, may participate in formulating and effectuating these plans. Whoever the participants may be, however, the resulting decisions as to both ends and means are clearly not market decisions—unless we are to stretch the meaning of "market" beyond recognition. They are decisions made through, with, or around the government of the nation in transition.

By a sequence of events not yet widely visualized, it is possible through government planning to bring an economy from a premarket, nonindustrialized condition to a state of industrialization at which market processes are feasible, and then gradually to relax the government participation. A fairly large amount of such relaxation has taken place in Yugoslavia, and distinct glimmerings are visible in Russia, and will be discussed in later chapters. The relative inattention to the prospects or procedures of transition from the more socialized to the less socialized society probably reflects the wide dominance of and preoccupation with Marxist thinking. The Communists are only beginning to verbalize this movement within Russia, although Yugoslav officials reportedly discuss it rather freely. While loudly protesting its values, many Americans have accepted more Marxist concepts than they know. Discussion with a person who expresses deep-seated fear of "creeping socialism" often reveals that he accepts the basic Marxian doctrine that the movement from capitalist markets to socialist planning is a one way street with no turnaround. The intensity of his fear reflects the completeness of his agreement with Marx that the movement is irreversible.

Later chapters will examine whether there is perhaps a position on the centralization-decentralization spectrum which is dictated mainly by information and decision factors, and toward which point an economy will tend to move from either direction. If so, there is no more *a priori* reason to assume that every industrial economy must start decentralized and move toward centralization than the reverse. "Creeping desocialism" might well be a dominant feature of the next 50 years in nations rapidly industrialized through central planning. The immediate point is that market techniques cannot make decisions about such all-out transitions, and that central planning may produce the conditions for a later transition to a market system.

When Desired and Undesired Traits Are Not Separable

In the process of natural selection, if trait A has survival value and trait B does not, then A can persist and be strengthened while B disappears only if A can exist without B. Similarly, if consumers or factor suppliers in a market system want A to continue, but want B changed to C, they may be unable to express this preference effectively if A is always accompanied by B, but rarely by C. By the market technique it is difficult to make an independent choice about one item within a package if the package must always be accepted or rejected as a whole.

For most businesses, it is most efficient to operate a regular number of hours per week, with all employees working an equal number of hours. Except for unusual circumstances there are also advantages to having common, or approximately common, work schedules in different companies. Among jobs equally acceptable in other respects, the typical worker is unlikely to have a choice of work week, and hence cannot express his preference by the market method of accepting one and rejecting the other. The result is that decisions about the length of work week are typically made through nonmarket techniques, such as collective bargaining, administrative decision within the firm, or legislation.

To cite a well-known parallel in consumer goods, the consumer cannot express his preference for or against tail fins on automobiles unless he has a choice between two cars equally satisfactory in other respects, one with tail fins and the other without. Commercial television in the United States is also a sort of tie-in sale, in which the consumer cannot cast his dollar ballots independently for two things. If he likes a particular brand of soap but dislikes the TV program it sponsors, there is no way by which he can buy the soap without helping to pay for the TV show.

Where Dollar Ballots Are Not Available

A second aspect of television also differs from normal market mechanisms. The fact that the programs are allegedly "free" prevents the viewer from casting his dollar ballot for what he prefers. In a normal purchase the customer can buy low quality products at a low price, or higher quality products at a higher price. The viewer of TV programs has no such choice, since there is no mechanism by which he can get a better quality show by offering to pay its higher cost, or a lower quality by refusing to pay as much. He can, of course, choose Program *A* over *B* or *C*. But this is an exercise in gross preference only, whereas a sensitive rational choice must be based on net preference. (Gross and net preferences were discussed in Chapters 14 and 15 on decisions.) This does not mean that to choose *A* over *B* and *C* has no effect, since the number of viewers is a dominant criterion for determining which shows will continue, though the chances that any one viewer will be polled are small.

Since the sponsors are guided by the number of viewers, they do to this extent "give the public what it wants." This measure of what the public wants, however, is less sensitive than a market. To illustrate, every single time I go to a movie or a stage play, my $1.00 or my $3.50 is counted, and every single time I stay home the gross income from that show is smaller than if I had gone. By contrast, not once in the 15 years or so of television has my watching or not watching been recorded in any poll, nor has that of any of my family. Further, the polls of viewers record numbers only, not intensity of preference. In this respect the TV polls are like political elections, which give all votes equal weight, rather than market "elections," which measure the relative intensity of desires by the amounts of money each will command. The full market mechanism of choice would appear in television only if each viewer paid for each show or series at a price roughly proportional to its cost, and if viewers collectively paid the full costs of production.[3]

More explicitly, the market mechanism works only for profit firms. By definition, a profit firm makes its gain from selling a good to recipients for more than its costs of production. Since the sponsors pay for TV programs and the recipients do not, the particular suborganizations which sponsor TV programs are necessarily and by definition either service or pressure organizations. Since these suborganizations initiate, modify,

---

[3] The purpose in this and the next several chapters is to analyze a variety of techniques of making social decisions. I am not suggesting that different techniques would bring either better or worse TV shows, or that the market process is in fact feasible in television. Nor am I commenting on the quality of present TV programs. My point is solely that, although the television industry in the United States is "private enterprise," the decisions in selecting programs are *not market decisions*, since they are not paid for by the consumers of the programs. This conclusion follows inescapably from comparing the market technique with that of TV program selection. It is neither praise nor criticism, but simple diagnosis. In this connection, it would seem that the strong efforts made for many years by much of the television industry to prevent even the trial of "pay TV" are inconsistent with their alleged belief in a market process.

and discontinue programs on the basis of the value of the program *to the sponsors*, they clearly classify as pressure, not service, and their pattern is that of the pressure organization defined in Chapter 22. The sponsoring company (A) uses its advertising division as a pressure organization (P) to produce certain effects on customers (B) which will improve A's position relative to B—in this case by creating more or larger BX's. A nation can thus have a major private industry whose decisions are not made by market processes. We are speaking, of course, of the position of the sponsors. The broadcasting companies themselves operate as profit organizations, since the recipients of their services (i.e., the sponsors of programs) pay their costs.

Because it does not follow market rules, TV shows another interesting facet. It is often (correctly) pointed out that "free" services by government are not really free. All must be paid for by someone. All come out of the total national income, thereby denying us other things we could have had with the same money or resources. The same is true of TV. It is no more free than is public education or roads. Being paid for by the consumers of sponsored products, rather than by the viewers, TV represents an involuntary redistribution of income from the purchasers of the products to the viewers of TV, just as the public subsidization of housing represents a redistribution of income from taxpayers to the consumers of housing.[4]

Nonprice Competition

It is generally assumed that the influence of competition is to keep quality up and prices down. With respect to prices, a practice of considerable significance has developed in the United States, known as nonprice competition. One technique of nonprice competition is product differentiation. If these differences are significant, they contribute to consumer welfare by enlarging the range of choice. Often, however, the differences are insignificant sales gimmicks, or exist only in advertising, with no gain to the consumer. A second technique of nonprice competition is less likely to be useful to the consumer or the economy, and lies in increasing sales effort instead of cutting prices.

If a $5.00 item is not selling well, the vendor might cut the price to $4.50. Or he might keep the price at $5.00 and spend an extra 50 cents on promotion. In either case *his* net receipts per unit are the same, at $4.50.

---

[4] It is often argued that the enterprise who makes correct decisions does good for the whole people, since he directs productive resources into those uses which will satisfy wants. This conclusion was accepted in the preceding chapter as an important logical strength of the market system. But if so, then by the same token it is also true that the enterprise who uses resources for purposes *not* desired by the population brings a loss to the whole people. This proposition remains true even if the money loss from the poor decision is borne directly by the enterpriser. In a correct decision the people receive a good which can satisfy wants, while in the incorrect decision they do not. Further analysis of the feasibility of free goods will be found later in connection with planned economies.

But the customer pays 50 cents more under the second approach. This illustration is intended solely to clarify the meaning and probable direct impact of nonprice competition. The process may have indirect benefits which offset its direct costs, and an overall evaluation of nonprice competition is far beyond the scope of the present discussion. The point is that much competition in the United States seems to be moving from the price to the nonprice variety, and much more than simple market reasoning is needed to determine whether the net effect improves the utilization of resources or the reverse, since the immediate effect is a rise in costs of distribution.

Competition through sales effort has various effects, depending on the product, its stage of development, the marketing channels, and other factors. When a product is new, intense advertising is often able to build a mass market, and promptly achieve great efficiencies in mass production and marketing. This effect is important. It is also widely reported and easily understood, and requires no further explanation. An opposite effect is less well-recognized, and seems to be growing relatively with the passing years. This is the ability of intense advertising to build so strong a brand preference that better and lower-priced brands are driven off the market or relegated to insignificance, leaving the highly advertised ones to charge prices out of all proportion to costs. Although this result has occurred in several fields, it is probably most conspicuous and long standing in drugs and cosmetics. There it is common for items which cost 5 to 20 cents to manufacture (including packaging) to sell for 50 cents to $5.00. Chemists who purchase the same materials assure me that the ingredients in a typical 69-cent tube of toothpaste cost 10 to 15 cents at most, in which case the finished product could very probably be made to retail profitably for half or less of its present price. Realistically priced toothpastes have appeared on the market in years past. But multimillion dollar advertising by a few large firms has driven these lower priced but equally effective brands from the market and made them unavailable to consumers. The firms which came out on top in this battle were not necessarily the ones with the best product at the lowest price, but the ones able to spend the most for selling effort.[5]

By any reasonable standards it should be far cheaper to mass produce and merchandise a product than to have it made up to order. Yet I have had a prescription druggist make up an antiperspirant and sell it to me at a profit for one-fourth the price of a mass-produced, highly advertised, chemically identical product on his shelves. The effect of advertising here is not to reduce prices, but to enable the seller to get four times

---

[5] Until Procter & Gamble received recognition of its fluoridated toothpaste, the American Dental Association construed all toothpastes as cosmetics—i.e., materials for making tooth brushing more pleasant, not more effective. Despite wide and voluble advertising claims to the contrary, toothpastes containing chlorophyll, anti-enzymes, and other ingredients are considered by the Association to have no discernible effect in retarding tooth decay. This is the basis for the statement above that the lower priced toothpastes were "equally effective."

what his product is worth. Typically, an unadvertised brand of rubbing alcohol (70 per cent isopropyl alcohol) sells for 19 to 25 cents, while more highly advertised ones sell for 49 to 79 cents, and a somewhat larger discrepancy is customary for 100 aspirin tablets. (If one observes carefully, he will note that the highly advertised brands claim that they are the *best,* which is true. They do not claim that they are *better,* which is not true.)

This situation has for years been prevalent in drugs and cosmetics, but seems to be spreading widely in other circles, particularly in small items on which customers are not likely to haggle. For example, I find a small plastic insert to hold a wood screw in a plaster wall selling for 10 cents, though an experienced plastics manufacturer has estimated it to cost less than half a cent to produce. A stationery store charges 5 cents apiece for Number 1 (large) paper clips, even in dozen lots, and these, too, must cost the minor fraction of a cent.

These items show markups over manufacturing cost of 300 to 2,000 per cent.[6] Now such profit increments are not unexpected in a market system when products are new or are covered by patents. But the expectation is that in due time competition will bring the prices down to a modest margin over costs. In many instances markups of this magnitude, not covered by patents, have continued for decades, with no sign of coming down, and this raises the question, "Where is competition?" Such results are at marked odds with the expectations of a market system.

Lest it be thought that it is not possible to purchase materials, and to manufacture, package, ship, wholesale, and retail anything for small sums, all these operations are performed on toothpicks, kitchen matches, and sticks of chewing gum, which in the summer of 1962 sold at a profit for approximately a hundredth of a cent, a fiftieth of a cent, and a cent apiece, respectively.

The drug industry illustrates several other aspects of decision making in the market system, at least as presently constituted in the United States. A high markup on drugs is sometimes justified with: "If the customer doesn't pay a high price, he won't get any good out of it." While some logic in this statement is undeniable, it might be asked whether the sellers of drugs are the appropriate persons to engage in mass psychotherapy via their pricing policies, and whether they have a disinterested view of the patient's welfare in doing so. This kind of rationale is now widely heard in other industries, particularly in their merchandising and promotion divisions, to the effect that the company does not sell the customer a product, it sells him an image. The image (goes the argu-

---

[6] In an old but never satisfactorily duplicated study based on 1929 data, the average experience in the United States is that 40 per cent of the retail price of a good goes for manufacture and the rest for distribution. On this basis a retail price of $1 for an item costing 40 cents to manufacture would be "normal," and would show a markup of 150 per cent between the two points. (*Does Distribution Cost Too Much?* [New York: Twentieth Century Fund, 1939], p. 117.)

ment) is the thing that produces satisfaction, and the firm is really producing more consumer satisfaction by its efforts to build that image.[7] The argument may have fair validity for cosmetics, whose effect is largely subjective in any event. It is slight for household appliances, where the third frustrating bout with the repairman sets the consumer to wishing he had less image and more product.

The Multiproduct Firm and the Allocation of Costs

In the market model of the firm, described in the preceding chapter, it was implicitly assumed that each product is made by a different firm, and that unless the price it brings exceeds its cost the firm will go out of business. The model is far from the facts. Many firms turn out dozens, hundreds, or thousands of different products. Although many products will be closely related, they often require different raw materials, processes, and marketing channels—witness the generators, light bulbs, jet engines, tungsten carbide, and synthetic diamonds of the General Electric Company. Now many such companies isolate the accounts for each separate product, and their subdivisions add, subtract, and price products on much the same cost-value basis as independent firms. Certain costs are not separable, however, like those of the top management of the parent company, or of the research findings which contribute jointly to several products, and may be carried on the books as "overhead." With or without initially segregating the separate costs and incomes on their books, many companies use some of the income from some products to finance some of the expenses on others, or charge common costs unequally to different products on a more or less arbitrary basis. Such actions have definite implications to the nature of the market decision process. The discussion of drugs can be continued to illustrate this point.

Let us assume that a drug company greatly overprices its aspirin and uses the income thus derived to finance research in antibiotics. This is another way of saying that the drug company, on its own initiative, is charging the cost of research in antibiotics to the customers of aspirin. The question now arises, why should one have to pay for antibiotics research in order to acquire aspirin? Viewed more broadly, why should this expense be charged to aspirin users rather than to the consumers of bread or pogo sticks? To use another illustration, companies in the magnesium, aluminum, rubber, electrical, meat packing, glass, and dairy industries all have chemical divisions. Let us suppose that all seven companies are simultaneously doing research on a new type of plastic foam, and that each is using a comfortable markup on some other products to pay for this research. Among these companies we might then find the cost of plastics research being borne by the consumers of aluminum, magnesium, tires, electric motors, beef, window glass, and ice cream,

---

[7] This line of reasoning is taken seriously by many merchandising men today, though they would use more imagery in expressing it.

respectively. If the dairy company also had a subsidiary in the drug business, and if that subsidiary were also doing research in antibiotics and manufacturing aspirin, we might find customers for aspirin paying for research in foam plastic and customers of ice cream paying for research in antibiotics. The first and minor question in the case is, "Is the mere accident that products *A* and *B* happen to be produced by the same company a good social reason for charging the development costs of *A* to the customers of *B?*" Those costs might instead be paid by the customers of product *C*, by borrowed money, by a research foundation, by a trade association, by taxation, or by enterprisers.

All this leads to a further interesting question. Profit is traditionally interpreted as the reward for risk. To return to the drugs, if the cost of research in antibiotics is paid by consumers of aspirin, the financial risks of that research are also borne by those consumers, not by the drug company. If so, should the profits from the subsequent sale of antibiotics go to the purchasers of aspirin? If not, why not? It might, of course, be said that if the customers are so stupid as to pay that much for aspirin, they have no subsequent claim to the profits. The latter argument is more logically defensible in a market context than the one that aspirin finances antibiotics, though the drug companies may find it less useful for public relations purposes.

There is no obvious answer, and the purpose of the questions is to point up the fact that the market model is not a description of actual practices—which may or may not produce results similar to the model. The more diversified the structure of different multiproduct firms (and they are quite diversified in the United States) the greater is the likelihood that individual "distortions" of this sort will cancel each other out in the whole economy.

Plowback of Profits

A larger form of this same problem arises when profits are plowed back to expand a corporation. The nature of the problem can be illustrated if we start with an individual enterpriser, such as a one-man television repair shop. If this man puts back some of the business income, rather than taking it for personal use, no theoretical question arises, since he is both owner and manager.

Plowback of profits by a corporation raises a different problem, however. The assumption of a market economy is that those who receive income, including profits, will examine *all* possible places to invest their savings, and select the one which shows the highest expected return. The shareholder who wants to reinvest his dividends might or might not want to put them back into the company from which they came. However, when the board of directors withholds dividends from stockholders for reinvestment, the stockholders are forced to reinvest in the same company, even if investment in some other firm or industry would be more profitable. They are also denied the opportunity to spend this money for consumption instead of reinvesting it.

In making this decision the directors are by no means unbiased, since the plowback enhances the size and wealth of the corporation, and hence their power. Reinvestment *may* be all to the good. But often the stockholders and the economy would be better off if the money were paid out. According to the theory of a market system, if the corporation cannot induce its shareholders to reinvest their dividends in the same company after they have been paid out, the plowback of those profits is presumably not the most desirable investment under all the circumstances of the case.

It is not the point of the above discussions to criticize either the plowback of profits by corporations or the use of profits from one of a company's lines to finance research on another line—which is a variation on the same theme. The point is merely that these practices are definite departures from the theory of a market system, and illustrate further that the terms "private enterprise" and "market system" are by no means necessarily synonymous.

Cost Structures—Agriculture

Agriculture is another area in which the market process does not function smoothly according to its rules. Among numerous other reasons, the cost structure seems the main one, in both short and long run. We noted earlier that the biological nature of the human being gives him a bargaining disadvantage in selling his labor to employers, because so few of his costs go down if he stops working. Variable costs are the floor under bargaining power in the short run, and the worker's variable costs are extremely low. The farmer produces a biological product, and faces much the same situation. Whereas the manufacturing company can close its plant for a month if continued production would glut its market and push its prices down disastrously, the farmer cannot stop feeding his cattle and chickens for a month, or even stop spraying or cultivating his crops. Once started, his plants and animals cannot be "laid off" for a month without destroying his whole year's income, and for larger animals the commitment may extend into several years. Given the seasonal nature of his produce, he also cannot postpone the start of his year's production until the market looks right, or again he will lose production for the whole year, not merely for the period of the delay.

Once the crop is finished, under the General Rule he will be better off to sell than not to sell, even if the price covers only the costs of picking and marketing. In the short run, the stubborn inflexibility of things biological tends to keep agricultural products flowing to the market whether or not they are needed, and prevents the short run supply from adjusting to demand according to the presumed rules of the market.

The long run also does not behave as market theory suggests. According to the theory, if prices do not cover total costs some farms will go bankrupt, the supply will decline, and the price will rise high enough to cover total costs for the remaining farmers. This theoretically expected reaction clearly occurs in the incorporated factory. Most of the corporation's short run expenses, and virtually all of its expenses in the long run, require explicit payments in money, to bondholders, workers, suppliers, and others. If the cash income does not equal or exceed these cash outlays, the firm goes out of business. Not so the farm.

The great majority are family owned. The land, labor, and investment are supplied by the farmer and his family. Unlike the absentee landlord, the hired worker, or the bank, the farmer will not force himself into bankruptcy if he fails to pay himself adequate rent, wages, or interest. Instead of being forced into bankruptcy by low prices, the farmer takes a lower and lower rate of return for the productive factors he provides, but keeps on producing so long as he can pay his relatively low cash costs. In addition, farming is a way of life. Moving from the farm to the factory is not at all the same thing as moving from one factory to another, and reluctance to leave the industry adds to the difficulty. This does not mean that farmers never go bankrupt or move into industry, as millions have done so. It does mean that the process does not happen rapidly or completely enough to relieve the perpetual downward pressure on prices.

Through a combination of economic difficulties and political power, farmers in the United States have been able to get large governmental assistance. It is not our purpose to evaluate the wisdom or success of that assistance, but to show why normal market processes do not solve maladjustments in farming as well as in many other industries.

The Fixed Markup

Another deviation from theoretical market processes arises from the widely used practice of the "fixed markup." This occurs most frequently in retailing, and makes for tremendous inefficiency. Gasoline stations are a conspicuous example, though the problem appears in hundreds of cases. To use a convenient figure, let us say that the wholesale price of gasoline is 30 cents, including taxes. Let us assume also that an efficient gas station with high traffic volume could retail the gasoline at 32 cents and clear a modest profit on it. By contrast, an inefficient station with low volume might just be able to break even with a markup of 4 cents. If competition should follow the market theory, the retail price would be forced down to 32 cents by the efficient stations, and many less efficient stations would be forced out of business. But in gasoline, as in much other retailing, in many regions (and except during occasional price wars), it is common for nearly all retailers to use the same fixed markup, which must necessarily be large enough to permit the less efficient retailers to stay in business. In the case of the gasoline we will suppose that the uniform markup is set at 4 cents, with the uniform retail price of 34 cents.

The first consequence is that the efficient retailers cannot drive the inefficient out of business, since the consumer pays the same price in both. The second consequence is that still more stations are induced to open. The outsider looking for a place to invest concludes: "At a markup of 4 cents I'm sure I could make a profit." He opens a gas station, and adds another unit to an already overburdened distribution system. By the same act he also makes the existing stations less profitable and less efficient by taking away part of their business.

By contrast, if stations charged the lowest price that would cover their costs, the price would tend to be 32 cents, reflecting the costs of the efficient stations. Prospective investors would conclude, "Unless I'm darned good, I can't make a profit on 2 cents a gallon," and most would stay out. Without the fixed markup, and with price competition, the marketing of gasoline would follow the theory of market systems, and only the efficient could survive. Under price competition profits would be narrowed by cutting prices till they approached costs of operation. Under the fixed markup, profits are also squeezed. But they are squeezed by dividing the business among more and more retailers until few have enough volume to operate efficiently. The fixed markup is itself a deviation from a pure market system. The result it produces is also therefore a deviation, in which competition takes a form which tends to decrease efficiency, not increase it.[8]

Small retailers also share one of the problems of farming. Many are independent enterprisers providing their own labor, land, and capital, and are difficult to drive out of business even if inefficient, because their costs are implicitly paid to themselves.

External Costs

In connection with the discussion of freedom, we have seen that important costs can sometimes be imposed on others. This is as true of firms as of individuals. But unless *all* costs created by a firm are explicitly charged to it, there is no assurance that its successful operation means a net gain to society. To take a sharply defined situation, suppose a firm which is the sole large employer in a moderate sized town can save a million dollars by abandoning the plant. But suppose the effect is to impose costs of five million on the local community for moving, retraining, and loss of real estate values. On the company's books the value of the closing exceeds its costs by a million dollars. But to the whole society (including the firm) the cost exceeds the value by four million, and is a poor social decision. The general proposition that under market competition what is profitable for the firm also contributes to the society is valid

---

[8] The analysis of the effect of the fixed markup is based on Alfred Oxenfeldt, *Industrial Pricing and Marketing Practices* (New York: Prentice-Hall, Inc., 1951). The petroleum industry as a whole is highly efficient, from geological exploration to transporting the gasoline to the retail unit.

only if all the social costs the firm incurs are directly chargeable to the firm.

A second kind of social cost not charged to firms is deliberate obsolescence. The most conspicuous case is the annual model change in automobiles, which brings a typical decline of 20 per cent or more in the value of an automobile during its first year. Most of this decline occurs whether the car is used or not, and results solely from the subsequent appearance of a newer model. For a $3,000 car this means a cost of $600, entirely aside from the costs of fuel, maintenance, insurance, and so forth. Now some obsolescence costs cannot be avoided if progress is to be made. But the American automobile industry deliberately changes the model every year, whether to make progress or not. To take conservative figures of $500 per car and 5,000,000 cars per year, the annual model change imposes an obsolescence cost of approximately $2.5 billion per year on the consumers of new cars. This is in addition to the direct money cost of the factory changeover to produce the new models, which the consumer has already paid in the price of his car.

This is only one item of an extremely complex topic, laden with status, salesmanship, the American Dream, and other elements of high controversy. I open it with trepidation, knowing that I cannot properly close it, and only because it represents an important segment of market decisions. Unquestionably many buyers want a *new model*, not merely a car that is *unused*. Further, they are willing to incur the obsolescence costs—or at least to buy with knowledge of them (though some have remarkably little knowledge of anything but the down payment). The typical justification of present practice is that *people buy*, and this is presumably the ultimate test in a market system.

As a social decision mechanism, this is a weak indication, however. Our whole experience is based solely on the annual model change. We have no idea how people would react, how much status value would be gained or lost, or how much greater or less would be the obsolescence costs if the whole industry were geared to a three or five year model change, since the longer periods have never been tried. (The whole industry is mentioned, because competitive factors make it hazardous for one company to deviate too far.)

Another important omission in the choice mechanism is that (to the best of my knowledge) within the past 20 or 30 years no American consumer has had the opportunity to buy a domestically produced automobile *not* subject to these obsolescence costs, except, of course, for high priced custom cars. By this is meant that no American can buy a domestic car with assurance that it will not be outdated within a year by a model change. Although obsolescence may be inescapable during technological infancy, the industry is now mature enough to produce a car that should require no changes (except "debugging") for ten years or more at a time. And although it is often asserted that the American public does not want a nonchanging model, there is no recent experience to support the claim, since no such car has been offered in recent decades. The abandonment of the Model A Ford in the 'thirties may demonstrate that a long-continued model could not provide the bread-and-butter base of a major company's main large-volume car. It does not demonstrate that a stable model would be unprofitable as one of a large total line of cars. For a proper test, incidentally, any such car should be produced by one of the "Big Three," as cars released by the smaller companies suffer certain disadvantages which preclude meaningful conclusions.

Deliberate obsolescence is not confined to automobiles, but appears in appliances, clothing, furniture, and other goods. Its purpose, quite openly acknowledged by manufacturers and sellers among themselves, is to get consumers to throw out the old and buy the new, even when the old is still thoroughly useful. The social cost of model changes is particularly high when joined with another force. This is the fact that manufacturers, particularly of appliances, face strong competition in selling their main products—such as stoves, freezers, or washing machines—since customers typically shop and compare prices. By contrast, there is rarely competition in producing replacement parts. Many manufacturers and dealers therefore take comparatively little markup on new appliances, and depend on large markups on replacement parts for their profit. This fact produces a bias in the consumer with an appliance that needs repair. It means that the cost of repair is overpriced while that of a whole new appliance is underpriced, and the decision is uneconomically biased toward throwing out the old. Because of rapid model changes, replacement parts are sometimes hard to get at any price, which fact adds to the bias.

A still further cost of model changes is deterioration of quality. If producers assume that an item will be discarded in eight years because it is outdated, they tend to build it to last only that long, with the result that it starts giving trouble long before that time. Speaking from the background of an often exasperated consumer of a representative cross section of America's mechanical goods, I would say that one great weakness is outstanding. The glamour of a new appliance lasts for several months, perhaps a year. After that the question is, does it give good, trouble-free performance through normal use and some occasional inevitable abuse, and when it does give trouble, is it easy to repair? Despite accelerated use and aging tests, these things can be determined only by years of experience with thousands of units in actual use. But by the time this experience is accumulated, so that corrections could be made, the entire product has been basically redesigned and the experience is irrelevant. A wide range of mechanical goods are perpetually unreliable because new "bugs" are built into them faster than old ones are worked out. I add, with feeling, a suggestion that two years' experience as a repairman be an absolute prerequisite for designers of mechanical products. (This suggestion originated with an exasperated repairman.)

It is often suggested that deliberate obsolescence, and the accompanying waste, are necessary to avoid unemployment. This is an application to the company and the industry of the same make-work fallacy which motivates many workers and unions to engage in so-called featherbedding and make-work practices, and it is an open question whether deliberate obsolescence does not cause at least as much economic waste as output restrictions by unions. The rationale is the same in both cases—to make more work, respectively, for the company or the workers. This reasoning also assumes that the problem of unemployment can be solved at the level of microeconomic analysis of the industry and the firm. By contrast, the whole tenor of economic analysis of the past several decades indicates that the problem must be dealt with at the macro level of total income and total spending for the whole economy.

The Perplexed Consumer and Advertising

According to market theory, the consumer makes a rational choice among alternate goods, based on a clear preference among them. Grave complexities, however, face the modern consumer confronted by a half dozen to a score of different brands of complex products, and this difficulty has implications for the nature of the system. First, if when he buys it the consumer cannot tell which of six washing machines will do the best job and be most free of trouble, he cannot intelligently direct the economy to produce what he most wants. This kind of situation (and it often occurs) not only reduces the consumer's ability to get what he really prefers, but also weakens an important link in the logic of the market system.

The logic becomes even weaker, and is perhaps reversed, when advertising plays an important role in forming people's wants. The market system is theoretically supposed to produce what people want, and is guided to do so by their dollar ballots. In this relationship the producers are the servants or agents of the consumers. To the extent that advertising informs consumers about what is available, where, and at what price, it assists that relationship. But to the extent that advertising *forms* consumer desires, and brings them to want things they would otherwise not want, it reverses the relationship. The producers now are not the servants who provide what the master wants. Instead they control the master's wants, in the interest of the servants.[9]

The same thing can be expressed as an ends-means relationship. In theory the economic system is the means of producing things people want, their wants being the ends to be satisfied. Under want-creating advertising, however, the means take over the task of directing what the ends shall be. This latter point is seen clearly in the frequent assertions that without advertising to stimulate wants our industrial machine would slow

---

[9] This point has been strongly made in John Kenneth Galbraith, *The Affluent Society* (Boston: Houghton Mifflin, 1958), chap. 11, "The Dependence Effect."

down to a permanent depression. It is implicit in this assertion that a market system cannot successfully produce merely what people want; it must instead, or in addition, produce much they do not want, and then make them want it. In this relationship, the economic system ceases to be the means of meeting human wants, and human wants become the means of making the system work. The producers and advertisers who propound this argument often go on to tell the consumers how fortunate they are to have changed places with their servants—though in somewhat more elegant language. Although those who espouse this argument usually consider it a defense of the market system, its implications, if valid, suggest a fundamental weakness of the system.

Because a growing volume of advertising seems to accompany a market economy as it becomes more affluent, it may be well to examine briefly its uses and limitations. Although advertising in its broadest sense covers many things, the present discussion is directed toward publicity designed to increase sales, the content and cost of the publicity being controlled and paid by the seller. The term "advertising" does not include unpaid news articles about products in newspapers, magazines, or technical journals.

First, there is no reasonable doubt that advertising can increase the sales of one brand of a product relative to less advertised brands of the same product. Whether advertising can increase the total sales of all brands of a product depends on the nature of the demand. If it is highly inelastic—i.e., does not respond to changes in price—sales will probably also not respond to advertising. For instance, if the advertising of gasoline or table salt were to disappear forever, it is doubtful that the total quantity sold (all brands) would decline as much as 1 per cent. On the other hand, if the advertising of automobiles, cigarettes, books, or cameras were to cease, the sales of these products might drop dramatically.

Whether advertising increases total sales of all goods is a much more difficult problem, but it seems doubtful. Total consumer spending shows strong relation to income, employment, and expectations about the future, but no discernible relation to advertising. Most families are apparently competent to spend more than their income without help. Few outside the high income groups would find difficulty spending 50 or 100 per cent more than they have, and their spending is limited by their income, not their wants. If it is suggested that these wants are themselves created by advertising, it is then necessary to explain why through most of recorded history even the rich have been able to spend their all, and pant for more, even though advertising did not exist. If advertising *should* induce the whole people to spend more than their incomes, by inducing net borrowing, it would take its place beside the federal debt as a possible inflationary pressure (during full employment), and raise the question whether a public "good" of this sort should be left within private control. The latter question seems relatively unimportant, however, in light of the improbability that advertising does raise total spending. An important practical and theoretical problem is that as all brands of all goods come to be advertised, much advertising will go mainly toward canceling the effect of other advertising. Whereas competition in price and quality help the consumer and the economy, competition in advertising can be largely self-defeating.

Some Miscellaneous Differences Between Theory and Practice

Degree of Competition. Industries are not equally competitive. It may normally be expected that in the short run the complete or partial monopoly will charge higher prices and sell less than it would do if competitive. In the resulting general equilibrium, consumers' desires would be relatively undersatisfied in the monopoly industry compared to what they would be if that industry were also competitive. On the other hand, a monopolized industry might earn more profits, devote more money to research, and in the long run turn out more and better products at lower prices than if it were competitive. The highly competitive clothing and textile industries, for example, have for decades done relatively little research, much of the reason being that until recently no company was big or profitable enough to afford it. Monopolized industries do not necessarily do better, however; witness the steel and aluminum industries in the United States for half a century prior to World War II, which did unusually little basic research in their fields.

Three Types of Discrimination. For reasons which sometimes are and sometimes are not logically related to profit objectives, many employers refrain from hiring Negroes and persons over 40 or 45 years of age. These two practices are rarely paralleled by opposite preferences in hiring by other firms. The result is that many persons in both categories either remain more or less permanently unemployed, or are employed irregularly or at less than their full level of skill. Compulsory retirement at 65 also forces many fully competent persons into nonproductivity. All three practices lead to less than full utilization of productive labor resources. Although they occur *in* the market system, they are not a part of its basic logic, and bring less overall efficiency than the market analysis would call for.

As with deliberate obsolescence and make-work practices, these actions are sometimes rationalized as a means of avoiding unemployment. For reasons stated earlier, I regard that argument as fallacious. In any event, if the market system must accept deliberate waste of resources in order to keep functioning, this, too, is a serious weakness of the system.

Time Range of Decisions. Industries differ in the time range of their thinking. Electric utilities not uncommonly do at least rough planning for 25 to 50 years ahead, whereas some shoe and clothing companies may think they are doing well to plan for six months hence. Because many of their present plans become future facts of the environment to which those who did not plan then adjust, the industries which do long-term planning probably have more influence in the long-term decision processes of the society.

Mixed Decision Techniques. Sometimes the total social decision about some type of good is made by mixed techniques, with results of doubtful overall merit. A particularly mixed case is that of local passenger transportation in some of our large cities. The local public transportation, such as bus, subway, and trolley may be part privately and part publicly owned, and their roadbeds must be paid for wholly or mainly from passenger fares. Public controls of them are normally exercised by the municipal government. Railroads running commuter service in the same area are subject to the control of the Interstate Commerce Commission, and the cost of their roadbeds may be shared with freight shippers. The persons who drive may get to work over local streets, state highways, or federally financed throughways. These are paid for by taxation and decided upon by political mechanisms at three different levels. Part of the driver's costs, however, are for his automobile, parking, and gasoline, which goods are produced by private industry through decisions made on a market basis. This is only the beginning of the complications. But it would be a near miracle if a sound decision about the total transportation facilities could result from a series of largely uncoordinated decisions made by different basic techniques.

The Profit Unit of Decisions. Contractors often cut up a new subdivision into plots smaller than the buyers of houses would be willing to pay for. The reason is that they try to maximize the profit from the whole subdivision rather than the profit per house. The total profit from squeezing more houses into a given area is greater than from a larger profit each for a smaller number of houses. The motivation would be different if the contractor set his sights on either one house or many projects at a time.

Some Further Details. Beyond the broader questions above, any real market system displays an impressive wealth of practical details not contemplated in the model. These (as well as the broader problems) often call for actions not prescribed by the model, sometimes known as "institutional supplements" to the market.

The model does not provide for the contingency that a well on one man's property can draw oil from below another property, and that if both tap the same pool each will try to get out the oil before the other. For many years the result was a tremendous overproduction of oil, with disastrous slashing of prices and great waste of a valued resource. Government thereupon stepped in and supplemented the general rules for the whole system with special rules for the petroleum industry, in the form of prorationing. Because of the self-reinforcing nature of accumulated power, by the time the United States was a century old a dozen or more industries had come under the unquestioned control of one company each, and the federal government responded with the Sherman Anti-Trust Act of 1890. Because all men are not doctors but want health, unscrupulous men have been able to sell worthless and dangerous drugs and appliances. To protect health, the government has established a bureau to restrict the sale of drugs. Because both the supply of and demand for sugar are highly inelastic, and because much of the raw material comes from one-crop areas, fluctuations in the price of sugar tend to be drastic, chaotic, and ruinous—to American refiners, cane growers and beet growers, and to foreign suppliers. With the general consent of all parties (though with disputes on details) the government closely regulates, limits, and manipulates the quantities and prices of sugar used in the United States.

SUMMARY ON THE MARKET SYSTEM

To summarize and put the problem in perspective, if every decision "embodies no less than an infinite number of variables," then a complex society embodies an infinite number raised to an infinite power. And if the beginning of wisdom for decision makers is to realize that they can deal with only a tiny fraction of what is possibly relevant, the beginning of wisdom for students of society is to realize that social decisions, market, political, or other, can deal with an even tinier fraction of what is relevant. Viewed in this light, the model of a market system is an extremely sensitive decision process about human wants for private goods. "It incorporates a delicately calibrated system of penalties and rewards which records the preferences of individuals and creates pressures to honor those preferences."[10] It is theoretically capable of observing and responding to every want of every person for exchangeable private goods if the EP is strong enough to overlap that of others. Thus far no one has even imagined a more sensitive technique of social decision making, and it is difficult to conceive that one is possible. Theoretically it maximizes the satisfactions of the society within the area of private goods—subject to the reservations noted about income distribution and factor costs.

Even in theory the system is not able, however, to make decisions about public goods, about the relative quantities of public and private goods, or about its own bargaining rules. Nor can it make conscious decisions about its own synergic effects, such as business cycles, inflation, and rate of growth, or give consumers the opportunity to buy the cessation of negative goods. It assumes (but does not decide) that incomes shall be based on productivity, and that weak wants of persons with high income shall have as much decision power as intense wants of persons with low income. If the society wants to make decisions about these things, it has no choice but to use nonmarket processes.

Even with respect to those things the market system *can* do, practice

[10] Alfred R. Oxenfeldt, *Economic Systems in Action* (New York: Rinehart & Co., 1957, paper), p. 8.

is not the same as theory, and no living, breathing market system is like the model. In many particular times, places, and circumstances the necessary conditions for market responses are not present, or are insensitive or distorted. Even for a society which accepts the market as its preferred system, a choice must be made in such cases whether to leave the system alone and allow undesired results, or to achieve the desired results by modifying the system, as by government intervention. If government intervention is directed solely at actual conditions which differ from those of the model, it is entirely possible that real conditions, as modified by government, will come closer to the market model than will the real conditions if left alone.[11] Similarly, although government intervention is often denounced as a deviation from market processes, it is entirely possible that the results of the market process itself are "purer" with intervention than without.

To cite just one illustration, according to market theory the consumer is able to judge the quality of everything he buys, for otherwise he cannot direct producers to make what he wants. But because of their complexity many goods cannot be evaluated by consumers, and government intervention to require accurate and informative labeling would be more likely to move the system toward the market norm than away from it. In short, the nonintervention prescribed by the model makes sense only if real conditions conform to the model. In practice, no government has refrained from intervention, and none is likely to, since the results of a completely unregulated, actual market system would shortly be intolerable.

This analysis, of course, gives no clue to when or where intervention is desirable, whether it is administratively feasible, or whether the particular cure will be worse than the particular disease. It does not even suggest that intervention be confined to instances where the market system does not follow its own rules, a notable instance being the many ways in which the society by taxation, charity, and relief programs deliberately changes the distribution of income created by the market.

It should be noted that despite deviations from the model, whether they be "natural" (like monopoly) or governmental, the deviation changes the equilibrium position of price and quantity of particular goods, but the market process continues to function in other respects. If the government pegs the price of raw sugar at four cents when the market

---

[11] An instructive parallel here is Reynolds' discussion of union influence on wage structures. He cites wage determination (1) under theoretically perfect market conditions, (2) under actual, highly imperfect nonunion market conditions, and (3) under unionization. Reynolds notes the common tendency to decry the effects of unionization on wage structures because unionization (3) differs from theoretical conditions (1). He then suggests by contrast that the appropriate comparison is between items (3) and (2), not (3) and (1). On the basis of his studies he concludes that in some, but not all, respects (3) more closely approximates (1) than does (2). (Lloyd G. Reynolds and Cynthia Taft, *The Evolution of Wage Structure* [New Haven: Yale University Press, 1956], p. 193.)

would put the price at three, cane growers, raw sugar mills, refiners, and users orient their decisions around a price of four cents, not three. But *their* decisions remain market decisions, and are the same in most respects whether the price of four cents was itself determined by the government or the market. Similarly, import duties raise the prices of many products higher than they would be under the operation of pure market forces. But all the remaining decisions about the imported goods remain market decisions oriented around the partially nonmarket price. Obviously the market process would cease if the government intervened in all prices, and at this point we simply do not know how many such interventions are possible without changing the *whole* system rather than the part.

In previous chapters on psychology, decisions, transactions, and organizations the distinction between the models and reality is probably accepted with equanimity as an expositional device. This device is apt to arouse some readers' ire at the economic level, however. The model is a method of helping us to understand things by stripping away the many complexities of reality, and it is logically fallacious to prescribe *real* policies for the *real* system from the *theoretical* model. The ire may arise because many persons—including some very intelligent ones, and including some economists as well as laymen—unwittingly base their *real* social philosophies and votes on the analytical model of the market, not on reality.

For simplicity, we have talked as if the market and political processes were the only techniques of social decision making. This is a gross oversimplification, as a subsequent chapter on pressure groups will reveal. In a society whose government does not try to take over the whole of social organization—i.e., in a "free" society which remains largely informal—numerous other channels are available. If we think of the market system as an official but informal organization of profit organizations, there still remain cooperative, service, and pressure organizations. These can satisfy wants which the market and government do not provide for. They can also try to modify the behavior or effects of government or market decisions. Some can also work on a cooperative basis with firms or governments. Even within the area of private goods, therefore, we are not dependent solely on the market system, with or without its imperfections, and with or without government intervention.[12] The whole of the social decision process depends on the whole of the social organization. We have thus far discussed only the market, first in theory and then in practice.

As a final note, a market system of producing private goods is widely associated with the idea of a free society. The relation is close, in two ways. In the direct sense it would be improper to say that the market system *creates* freedom—freedom in this sense being a wide range of

---

[12] The word "imperfection" must be treated with care. It means only that facts differ from the analytical model, and in no sense implies that the model is "better" than the facts.

choice based on the absence of socially dictated obstacles to particular choices. Rather, the market system *presupposes* freedom. Freedom of choice of consumption and production activities is one of the fundamental rules, and we have seen that the market system uses, but does not determine, its own rules. Once the market system is in use, however, it does help to perpetuate the freedom which it depends on, by retaining much power in the informal organization. A government obviously has less power if it controls the production of public goods only, instead of the production of both public and private goods. The problem is more complex than that, however. Government is not the only possible source of power, or the only organization capable of depriving people of freedom, and large government may sometimes be the only means of keeping private power from becoming too concentrated. The market system is definitely related to the problem of freedom, but the relation is not simple or unidirectional.

IX. THE PUBLIC PRODUCTION OF PUBLIC GOODS

Chapter 32

THE NATURE AND FUNCTIONS OF GOVERNMENT

INTRODUCING THE FORMAL ORGANIZATION OF SOCIETY

THE MARKET system discussed in the past two chapters is the chief and most conspicuous piece of the informal organization of society. The discussion of other informal organization will follow, rather than precede, discussion of government, since much of it is devoted to influencing government. We now move to the formal organization of society, the government itself.

Having concluded earlier that the government of a whole society is a cooperative, at least if reasonably democratic, we will discuss it as such, and reserve for later the problems of a government used by one segment of the population as a profit organization for its own benefit. The sponsors and the recipients are the same people, namely, the whole society. We will see later that it is possible to operate a government dictatorially in the interests of the people, at least for a short period, but wherever relevant we will assume for the next five chapters that we are speaking of a democracy. In a very broad sense, however, the general nature and influence of government can be outlined without reference to the democratic or dictatorial status of the government. We will also assume that the society produces its private goods through a market system, and wait till we have examined socialist organization to examine the role of government in such a society.

As an unlimited-purpose, all-inclusive cooperative, the government faces a kind of problem not met in the limited-purpose, private cooperative. The latter is limited in the scope of both its kinds of activities and its numerical coverage. It performs only a limited number of functions for a limited group of people, and anyone not interested in having those functions performed in that way leaves the organization. He thereby avoids both its costs and its values. As a result, those who remain in the organization are likely to have a reasonably homogeneous set of goals for the organization. This does not mean that they always agree. But it

617

means that if some members turn a camera club into a bowling league, or a farmers' cooperative into a political party, those not interested in bowling or politics can drop out. The distinctive aspect of the government as a cooperative is that (1) it at least potentially serves *all* functions, and (2) no one can drop out and avoid its costs or its effects.

It is easy to say that the cooperative is an organization to do to and for the members what the members want. But to determine what the members want when their interests are highly diverse and no one can leave is a formidable problem. Only government faces it in this form, although the family faces something like it in a smaller and less permanent way. Lacking the mutually interacting selective effects of limited membership and limited function, government has no choice but to compromise as best it can a permanent divergence of aims among its sponsors. These divergences may be large, such as a difference over the nature and scope of government itself, or a disagreement whether different races shall receive equal treatment. They may be fairly explicit interests of groups, as when mine workers want stricter safety laws and mine owners want looser ones. When we view the *whole* society, the individual himself has conflicting roles and interests. As a consumer he may want strict control over insect poisons left on foods, but if he is also a cranberry grower he may feel the enforcement to be unduly strict on his product. Almost anything a government can do will please some citizens and displease others, or please a citizen in one respect and displease him in another. How these divergent interests are learned, made potent, and compromised is at the core of the study of government.

WHAT DOES GOVERNMENT DO?

The functions of government are many and complex. The mere listing of actions by a large modern government would fill a good-sized volume, and the major purpose of the present chapter is to classify those functions on the same basis as other interpersonal relations, so that the earlier analysis can explicitly or implicitly be extended to include government. The basic functions of government can be viewed as extensions of coalition and organization.

We have already seen the possible origin of government as a coalition of the weak against the strong, and the source of a government's power in holding the strongest coalition of force within its territory. One of the two major functions of government is an extension of the coalition concept, which affects the redistribution or allocation of power. We have also referred to government as the formal organization of the whole society, in which role, as a relation for joint production, it can do certain things collectively for the whole people that they cannot do as well, or at all, for themselves. Because a government which accompanies a market system produces public goods only, while a full socialist government produces both public and private goods, we can distinguish them in definition by saying that the functions of socialist government are the allocation of power and production of *goods*, while those of the nonsocialist government are the allocation of power and the production of *public goods*. The definitions cover the pure forms, actual governments usually showing some admixture. The present chapter will fill in details of these functions, and the next several chapters will examine the mechanisms by which decisions are made about which goods to produce and to whom to allocate power.

The term "public goods" will include two things: first, transformations performed directly by the government itself for the use of the people, such as roads, parks, navigable streams, and so forth; and second, certain broad or explicit conditions which increase the power or freedom of the people to satisfy more wants on their own, such as traffic rules or a stable money system. The first type of public good actually provides goods, the second facilitates people's ability to provide goods for themselves. Power can be allocated directly by taking it away from some and giving it to others, particularly money power, and indirectly by throwing the weight of government on one side in private disputes. We have already noted that government can influence the terms, tactics, goods, criteria, or settlement methods for private transactions, as well as to establish its own suborganizations to decide disputed transactions. It can also regulate communications and transformations in ways which influence the distribution of power. The allocative function can affect either bargaining or total power, or both. As we shall see, many government activities simultaneously and unavoidably perform both a production and a power allocation function. Further, what is clearly power regulation at the *micro* level may be considered a public good at the *macro* level—to extend these terms from their economic usage. A court decision in a private civil suit, for example, is an unequivocal act of power allocation to the parties involved. But the presence of the system of civil courts as a whole is an important environmental condition that facilitates the private satisfaction of wants through transactions, and can therefore be considered a public good. Similarly, the presence of a policeman on a street may be a dramatic allocator of power between a particular robber and intended victim, while the presence of police protection as a general thing is a public good. In the broad sense, the general fact that the government regulates power—which is an indispensable function to any society—can also be thought of as a public good. (Anyone not liking this extension of meaning may retitle the chapter, "Public Production of Public Goods, and the Regulation of Power.") This is another way of saying that in the small, the regulation of power is a coalition function, and in the large an organization function. This whole area of allocating power is generally known as "maintaining order." There is no need to abandon that term, so long as it is recognized that "order" is not something different from the allocation of power and freedom, but part of the process.

PUBLIC GOODS

The provision of public goods by government both creates goods and makes it easier for citizens to create them for themselves, the former being a transformation and the latter an increase in power or freedom of the citizen. We noted in Chapter 20 that the "free" in "freedom" is closely related to that in "free goods," and also that until and unless the social sciences develop independent measures of power and freedom roughly comparable to the independent measures of force and resistance in the physical sciences, we cannot say whether a particular increase in satisfaction results from an increase in power, freedom, or both. Although the *concepts* are sharply definable, we cannot measure which is which in any particular situation. Given the relation between freedom and free goods, the fact that a government has provided a park or highway for use without explicit charge can also be thought of by the citizen as an increase in his freedom to go places, or in his power to do so. Because our measures are not yet developed sharply enough to distinguish these things in particular instances, we will join them in a single discussion, and distinguish them from power regulation on the following basis. Any government act which shifts power from one segment of the population to another without increasing the total is unequivocally an act of power regulation, and any act that increases it without shifting it is unequivocally a public good. The ability to shift power without raising it is widespread, whereas raising it without shifting at least relative power, although theoretically conceivable, can hardly even be imagined in practice, since it would require a simultaneous and equal rise in the power of every person. That the two things are often inseparable in fact in no way diminishes the importance of separating them for analytical purposes.

Transformations made by government and directly accessible for individual satisfactions include parks, roads, water supplies, cleaned rivers, trash collection, sewers, pamphlets, statistics, soil analysis, maps, streams stocked with fish, advice on how to grow corn or run a small business, weather reports, assistance on traveling abroad, unemployment compensation, disaster relief, and (in some countries) medical care. Because the individual is so markedly less productive without than with them, health and education will be classified clearly as components of power (rather than freedom) of the individual. Free public education, other direct or indirect assistance to education, medical care, and the many activities of public health services (vaccinations, quarantines, sanitary inspections of restaurants and food factories, epidemic control, water pollution control, etc.) will therefore be considered techniques by which government assists in maintaining or raising the power of citizens by keeping them healthy and knowledgeable.

The major items in the area of increasing freedom are those which create a generally stable environment in which a person can go about his business of doing something or nothing in confidence, safety, and freedom from interference. In different ways and degrees the national defense, police protection, fire protection, protection of privacy and against disturbances of the peace are examples. Rules providing uniformity where uniformity itself facilitates accomplishment are also contributors, such as the regulations of auto traffic, rules about the transfer of property, and the requirement that in public males and females wear clothing that will not confuse their classification. A sound money system is similarly an important facilitator of private transactions and an indispensable tool of a market system. Interpersonal freedom is maintained within realistic limits by the general principle that for compensable losses, at least, no one is allowed to impose costs on another without his consent—although the principle is more of an ideal than an accomplishment in many instances. It is easy, for instance, to rule that I may not burn down my neighbor's garage or dig up his driveway, but not so easy to say whether I may disturb his sleep with an outdoor lamp that shines in his bedroom window or a dog that howls poignantly at every third full moon.

Although these things raise freedom (or power) in general, probably all can reallocate power to some degree in detail. Police and the laws against robbery change the relative power between robber and victim. The enforcement of contracts changes the relative power between those who would honor and those who would break them. A stable money maintains a constant power relation in one respect between creditors and debtors, whereas a money of changing value shifts their relative power—inflation in favor of the debtor and deflation in favor of the creditor. Parks and highways change the value of adjacent land, and hence the bargaining power of the purchasers and sellers of such land, and zoning and city planning do the same. Free public education decreases the power advantage of those who can afford private education relative to those who cannot, and free or subsidized medical care does the same. However, since education and health are effective mainly in maintaining productivity, their chief effect is to raise the *total* power of those served. This does not necessarily raise their bargaining power. Nor does it reduce either the bargaining power or the total power of others with whom they deal, and it may raise one or both. In transactions of positive goods one has more power in dealing with others of power.

THE ALLOCATION OF TOTAL POWER

Although government actions to increase freedom or power also almost inevitably reallocate power, that result is generally incidental and often fortuitous, as in the largely accidental effects of a new highway in raising the value of some properties and lowering others. This does not mean that these results are insignificant or lightly to be dismissed, but that they are not designed for that purpose.

In other cases, however, the transfer of power is deliberate—or at least is well recognized by the persons involved even if not verbalized and formally justified as a transfer. In dealing with such actions we move from the organization, or joint production, function of government to its coalition function. By this we mean that the government takes sides with one private group to raise its power relative to another. We will deal first with changes in total power, accumulations of which take such forms as money and positions of authority.

The main device for transfer of money power is to provide government benefits in different proportion from that in which taxes are collected. If taxes are raised mainly from the rich and used to provide schools or hospitals for the poor, a redistribution takes place from rich to poor. If taxes are collected more than proportionally from the poor, as by a sales tax on basic consumer goods, and the proceeds are used for extra police protection or better streets in high income neighborhoods, an opposite redistribution occurs. If the serfs are taxed on salt and flour, or forced to work one day a month, to build and furnish the manor, income and power are transferred from the serfs to the lords.

The filling of positions in organizations can similarly allocate power. If judges are recruited from the propertied classes—as they have been through much of human history—they hold an important position of power which enables them to settle disputes on terms favorable to their class. If high executive posts in government, business, and other organizations are typically given to one class or group, those persons themselves receive a grant of power. They also are in a position to use the power of the organization for the benefit of their class.

THE ALLOCATION OF BARGAINING POWER:
SOME BROAD BASES

In Chapter 20 we discussed status, as perceived total power, and class, as a group of persons having approximately the same amount and kind of status. Unless all individuals are to have equal power, which seems most unlikely in light of the individual differences in personality and the hierarchical structure of organizations, then classes are inevitable in any society. Even assuming that everyone is completely free to move up, down, or sideways according to his inclination and ability, at any given moment some persons will be in one class and some in another. The existence of classes in this sense does not mean that the society is discriminatory, but merely that persons are different, and that any society necessarily has different roles with different power. And however egalitarian the society may be in distributing its income, responsible high officials cannot serve the society well without wardrobes, travel allowances, relaxation, and relief from household chores.

But this is not the whole story. Power is self-sustaining and self-reinforcing, and once a given group attain a superior amount they normally also have much ability to hold and increase it. Because one has more power in a positive transaction when dealing with others of power, those in higher classes tend to deal more largely with each other than with those of lower classes. This simultaneously reinforces the relative position of the group and decreases the opportunities of those below to rise. Aside from luck, the main opportunities to rise from below lie in possessing the kinds of power which are valuable to those above and available to those below. These are mainly brains, specialized skills, and the ability to accomplish difficult tasks without constant prodding.[1]

There is thus strong reason to believe that distinct classes will arise, even under complete equality of bargaining rules. The higher classes will have a definite advantage in maintaining their position. At the minimum they will tend to be self-perpetuating in the sense that they will determine the criteria on which new members are accepted into the class. If in addition the society allows inheritance of rank and wealth, the classes become heavily hereditary, even if the rules of inheritance are the same for all, and only virtual confiscation of wealth at death, combined with drastic limitations on gifts, will break a hereditary class of wealth. Even where inheritance is not allowed or is severely limited, unless children are taken from their parents at an early age, they are likely to learn certain attitudes and skills about making decisions and exercising authority which will give them some advantage in an open competition with their contemporaries from lower classes.

Either to reinforce or to offset the self-perpetuating powers of a higher class, many societies establish different power rules for different classes. Codes that require the rich to feed the beggar, give more to the church, hire servants to do what they would rather do themselves, or pay higher prices than the poor—rules common to many cultures—create a bargaining disadvantage to the rich and help redistribute their power. Although informal rules of this general sort are to some extent found almost everywhere, they are most obvious in countries where rich and poor are conspicuously different, and the total effect is usually token rather than significant. High inheritance and gift taxes, of course, tend to weaken the hereditary continuity of classes.

Much more important are differential bargaining rules which give a permanent power advantage to one class in controlling the government, or in transactions with other classes. Some rules are related to competence, while others provide power, as such. Any set of differential rules must distinguish people in some way, whether by age, sex, citizenship, wealth or property, education, debtor or creditor status, race, religion, occupation, or status of parents. These categories can best be understood in connection with the rules themselves, which we shall now examine.

---

[1] This is commonly called the acceptance of responsibility. In the present framework every person in an organizational relation accepts responsibility. The question is therefore not whether the person accepts responsibility, but whether he is willing and able to accept it for long and complex tasks which involve risks and decisions, rather than solely for simple, routine tasks.

Some Areas or Kinds of Differential Rules

Voting qualifications are one technique of providing differential power. Not to allow a person to vote is to deprive him of an important type of bargaining power over elected officials, as well as to reduce his communication and decision power in government. It might also be said to bar him from the ruling coalition. An age limitation is universal wherever ballots are cast for government, twenty-one being the most common lower limit, and eighteen the apparent minimum anywhere. Perhaps on the supposition that they, too, were politically immature, women have not been allowed to vote in many places, and were given the vote in the United States only as recently as 1920. It is doubtful if voting restrictions by age or sex have much effect on the allocation of power among groups or classes, however, since they cut more or less equally across all class levels.

On the other hand, if voting qualifications are based on some criterion which itself reflects a difference in power, the power differential is widened, as in allowing the vote to property owners only. This practice has appeared often through history, and was eliminated in England and the United States only during the nineteenth century. Plural voting is not unknown (legally, that is); the last remnants of a second ballot for paying taxes on a business property or for a special representative from a university were eliminated in Great Britain as late as 1948.[2] A property qualification means that the whole sponsor control of government is exercised by property owners, and will presumably produce a bias toward property owners as recipients. Property owners presumably have higher average income than nonowners, which means that the richer run the government for the main, or at least biased, benefit of the richer. Universal suffrage tends to run government for the poor, since there are more of them, although important factors which offset this tendency will be seen later.

Racial qualifications for voting almost necessarily have a strong power content. Unless there already exists a strong status difference within a nation it is unlikely that there will be any racial qualification. Given the white dominance of most of the world in recent centuries, the most common differentiation has been votes for whites but not Negroes. The opposite relation has occurred in Liberia, whose constitution of 1847 (Amendment 3, article 5, section 13) provided that "None but Negroes or persons of Negro descent shall be eligible to citizenship in this republic."[3] A curious parallel limitation was adopted in Haiti. Under Jean Jacques Dessalines in 1804 the constitution provided that no white man could be a citizen or own property unless he called himself black. The

---

[2] Robert Rienow, *Introduction to Government* (New York: Alfred A. Knopf, 1957), p. 325.

[3] Nathaniel R. Richardson, *Liberia's Past and Present* (London: The Diplomatic Press and Publishing Co., 1959), p. 68.

practice of limiting votes to Negroes may grow with the emergence of formal governments in the recently created states of Africa.

The vote has been prohibited to Negroes by law, as in the Union of South Africa and in the southern United States before the Fifteenth Amendment in 1870. More frequently the restriction is implemented by subterfuge under superficially nondiscriminatory rules. A widely used device in the South is the "literacy" test. In many Southern districts all whites automatically pass, even if they never went to school, while all Negroes automatically fail, even those with advanced university degrees. The Negro's registration may be found invalid on grounds of a faulty signature or incorrectly spelled address, or be "misfiled"—while these same things do not happen to the white's registration. This discussion deals only with abuses of literacy tests. Properly applied, such tests could have significant usefulness in denying ballots to persons who would be extremely unlikely to have enough information to cast a meaningful vote. It could also introduce a class bias in nations where the poor are predominantly illiterate and the rich almost universally literate.

Poll taxes have kept Negroes from voting in areas where most have low incomes. Although high state and local officials may not openly advocate these practices, neither do they try to stop them. Private acts supplement those of voting officials. The Negro who tries to register to vote may be fired or evicted by his white employer or landlord. Further, the boss or landlord who does *not* take such action may find himself boycotted by the white community; and the "accident" rate seems higher for those who fight the system. This discussion does not mean that all sections of the South do these things, but that all of these practices have been widely and frequently found, particularly in the poor and rural areas.

Partly from active intervention by the federal government, the South has been undergoing a rapid change toward equality of voting eligibility, though full accomplishment may still be far distant. The obvious fact is that from the days when Negroes were first brought into the South as slaves, they have lacked political power because of their ineligibility to vote.

Although Negroes are not formally disqualified, in few districts can a Negro be nominated, much less elected, to an important office in the United States, and only recently have Negroes received high appointive office in the federal government. Religious qualifications have also been common for voting in many times and places, though not in the United States. No formal racial or religious restrictions are placed on candidates for federal office, but for all practical purposes the presidency has been achievable only by white Protestants until 1960, at which time the category was broadened to white Christians.

Slavery. *Slavery* is a condition in which one person (the owner or master) has complete powers as bargaining agent in all transactions conducted by the other (the slave), and the powers of agency are irrevocable by the slave. The sale of a slave is the sale of this exclusive, irrevocable agency.[4] Insofar as the rules are concerned, the slave can conduct no transactions in his own interest, presumably the lowest conceivable degree of interpersonal power. This does not mean, however, that the slave is totally without power. The slave owner may find it convenient to allow the slave to conduct transactions on his own, with other slaves or possibly nonslaves. Nor is he without bargaining power with the owner if he has wanted abilities which he can withhold. Since the slave owner can apply negative pressures to extract concessions, unless the slave is sure the master will not do this, his best way to withhold services is to hide his ability to perform them. The reaction is parallel to that of many workers in industry, who refrain from revealing their best so the boss cannot bargain more work out of them. Slave owners, dictators, and authoritarian parents find that negative power is a relatively poor motivator, and even the absolute master may sometimes give substantial concessions to bring forth greater effort. Any sympathetic identification of the owner with the slave, of course, raises the slave's bargaining power.

Slavery cannot exist without the acquiescence and active support of the state. Unless prohibitive expenditures are made for fences and guards, slaves can escape from the plantation, castle, army, or mine, and without cooperation by police and courts, it would often be impossible to capture and return them. If the system of slavery is to be orderly, it is also necessary that courts enforce contracts of the sale of slaves.

Just as the presence of slavery depends on government help in maintaining it, its complete absence also depends on government help in refusing to enforce contracts of an additional sort. Persons often get into such difficult straits, or want so desperately to help a loved one, that they would "sell their souls," by which we mean that they would sell total and irrevocable power of attorney or accept an unlimited authority relationship. Indentured servants in colonial America had done this for a limited period to pay their passage. But the practice is now impossible because courts will not enforce such a contract, and anyone who "sells himself" can break the agreement at any time without legal penalty. Nonslave status is thus made inalienable. On a nonenforceable basis, however, one can accept as much authority as he likes, or can be induced to accept. An individual can also sell to an agent exclusive control over some aspects of his behavior, such as his boxing, ball playing, acting, or piano playing. But while such contracts often give *exclusive* agency, they are not total, permanent, or irrevocable, and usually require the consent of the principal to any particular contract about himself made by his agent.

Right of Contract. We have already seen the importance of contract enforcement to the ability to acquire goods on the basis of a promise,

---

[4] Slaves are property, and according to previous analysis, all property rights can be stated as aspects of transactions. The present definition of slavery is therefore stated in those terms.

with the government providing the necessary stake through its willingness to enforce the contract. Refusal to enforce a contract is in effect a denial of the right of contract, since it makes the agreement of no value, and reduces the power of those so treated. Courts will not enforce contracts of minors. Hence, minors cannot normally acquire goods on the basis of promises whose stake depends on legal enforcement—although anyone willing to accept a minor's integrity (or the possible embarrassment of his parents) as an adequate stake can sell to the minor on credit.

Contracts made by the mentally incompetent are also generally not enforceable against them or their guardians, and contracts made by those in jail are subject to limited enforcement. Since the use of negative power in transactions is prohibited, contracts signed under "duress" will not be enforced. However, for reasons indicated in Chapter 18 the line between a "voluntary" and a "coerced" agreement is not always sharp.

Occupation. Some societies have had differential rules for entering various occupations, the limitation usually being the father's status or occupation. The population under such rules is normally divided into two or more classes, such as commoners and nobles. The commoners are typically restricted to occupations such as farming, trading, and the handcrafts, while the nobles fill all the positions in government and the arts and sciences. Stratification has also been practiced within types of jobs, as when commoners are allowed to fill all the lower level jobs in industry, the army, or government, but all top-ranking positions are reserved for nobility. Such regulation is more usually enforced by custom than law, though government could easily control the staffing of its own offices. Such controls are seldom completely impervious to penetration by commoners, since the occasional commoner with outstanding ability is too valuable to give up. Since the commoner must have far more ability than the noble to receive a given level of pay and position, he does operate under a differential set of bargaining rules.

Caste. One of the most conspicuous forms of differential bargaining rules is caste, as it appeared in India for centuries, and which the government is now trying to eliminate. Low caste is not slavery, in that no one is given agency controls over anyone else. A caste is a closed class, with no movement in or out except by birth or death.[5] Each person born into a given caste is expected to marry within that caste, work in the occupations assigned to it, and die within that caste, and his children follow the same path.

In many respects the various castes come into little contact. To this extent no question of relative bargaining power arises. A caste system follows rigid rules, many of which set consensus terms on such relations as do arise between castes. In India, many castes are oriented around a

[5] A. L. Kroeber, *Anthropology* (New York: Harcourt, Brace & Co., 1948), p. 276, and Mischa Titiev, *Introduction to Cultural Anthropology* (New York: Henry Holt & Co., 1959), pp. 25–51.

particular occupation, such as priests, clerks, fishermen, or streetsweepers,[6] who necessarily engage in intercaste transactions in rendering services or selling goods. One caste are often servants to another, in which case transactions are frequent. The consensus terms normally provide that the upper caste receive goods on very favorable terms, particularly personal services of servants and messengers, although these low prices are often reinforced by the market force of a large supply of the lower castes. In some East African tribes a caste of herders has forced the farming caste to render tribute and perform services from time to time, apparently without receiving any value in return.[7]

Not only are lower classes expected to render services to persons of higher caste, but certain deferential behavior, such as bowing, acknowledges the superior-inferior relationship, and is normally rewarding to the higher class.

As caste is defined, the Negro in the United States has occupied the position of an inferior caste, especially in the South—and has so been described by Myrdal.[8] The ban on marrying outside the Negro group is very tight, and is enforced by law throughout the South. The Negro is taught the "ceremonial system of scraping his foot, tipping his hat, and using self-abasing vocabulary and dialect, and generally being subservient and unobtrusive in the company of whites."[9] Whenever there is not space for both in some restricted area, the Negro is expected to stand back and wait for the white to pass. These transactions over time and deference are almost invariably settled in favor of the white.

Until the system was partially broken down in recent years under pressure from the federal government, the races were rigidly and universally separated in the South in schools, restaurants, theaters, and other places of contact, as well as in public conveyances. We have already seen the markedly inferior power position of the Negro in political influence and in the ability to get jobs at reasonable rates of pay. The Negro also has an inferior chance of getting justice in a Southern court, (and in many Northern ones as well), as juries are predominantly white. The basic ingredient of caste is evident here, in that the Negro can never move into the white group—except for a tiny minority with very light skins who "pass."

In many transactions the difference in caste makes no difference in bargaining power, as when the two shop in the same grocery or department store. Although declining, discrimination in employment is widespread. This represents lower-bargaining power, in that the Negro must generally

---

[6] Kroeber, *ibid.*, p. 750.

[7] Franz Boas & Others, *General Anthropology* (New York: D. C. Heath & Co., 1938), p. 318.

[8] Gunnar Myrdal, "The Dilemma of the American Negro," in Howard Becker (ed.), *Societies Around the World: Shorter Edition* (New York: The Dryden Press, 1956), p. 650.

[9] *Ibid.*, p. 651.

present superior ability to get a given level of job, and often cannot get certain good jobs regardless of his ability. His typical position of "last to be hired and first to be fired" represents lower-bargaining power in getting job security.

Miscellaneous Differentiations. Various groups are sometimes given differential treatment on other scores. One caste or class may receive tax exemption, or lack of enforcement. Some have superior access to public services, and can "demand" a passport or copy of a deed, while a different class must "request" and pay for such items. Such practices differ from country to country. The citizens of some nations take it for granted that government employees will provide "free" services upon request, while citizens of other countries take it equally for granted that they must bribe or tip.

During the Middle Ages, the church prohibited the lending of money at interest (usury) and wholesaling (forestalling) to Christians, with the result that Jews, the largest non-Christian group in Western Europe, became dominant in banking and trade. The dominance was by no means complete, however. The Lombards, for instance, earned large returns on loans from delinquency charges, and the Fuggards received large land grants and other favors for lending to royalty—neither return being "interest." Meanwhile Jews were widely forbidden to own land or belong to guilds, which greatly reduced their participation in farming and the handicrafts. Both sets of rules had marked effects on the total and bargaining power positions of both groups.

In some European university towns the officials of the university, rather than the local police, have sole authority over the behavior of students. In consequence, the power of the students as against that of the local citizenry is raised, since university officials will tend to dismiss as "student pranks" petty thefts or disturbances for which the regular police would put the students in jail.

THE ALLOCATION OF BARGAINING POWER:
DETAILED REGULATIONS

In addition to rules based on the broad categories above, any society complex enough to be formally organized will throw the influence of its government on one side or the other in innumerable private disputes—occasionally by taking sides in a particular dispute, but more usually by siding with certain categories of disputants. We have already observed that such regulation is a "public good" in a collective sense, in that it provides "order." "Order" is typically considered more efficient and tolerable than "disorder," even if some of its terms are felt to be unfair. The effects of such regulation on the power of particular parties—as contrasted to their order-producing effects—are numberless, and we can cite only a tiny sample. Probably the great majority of laws, ordinances, court decisions, and executive rulings deal mainly with the relative power of private groups, even though the word "power" is discreetly avoided in the rulings.

Aside from such obvious public goods as the national defense and highway systems, relatively little government action is taken out of context of some conflict of interest, in which the government assists one side against the other. This does not mean that all such conflicts are "selfish." Some of mankind's bitterest conflicts have revolved around opposing ideas of how to create an "ideal society," and governments often take sides between dedicated groups seeking the public good as well as between selfish groups, not to mention contests between one of each. That the Woman's Christian Temperance Union may consider its motives unselfish and those of the distilling industry selfish does not eliminate the conflict of demands by the two groups on government, or the necessity of the government to choose between or compromise them. Nor is there any *a priori* basis to assume that the allegedly unselfish interest is necessarily better for the whole society. What is put forward on an honestly unselfish and idealistic basis in this fashion is sometimes nothing more than an attempt to enforce the value system of a particular subculture on the whole society. In the United States the use of government power to prohibit intoxicating beverages (in the former Prohibition Amendment) and the restriction on information about birth control are among the more conspicuous examples of this relation.

To move to the more detailed regulations, almost any day's newspaper will report a half dozen government actions which alter the relative power of private groups. To cite several that occurred while this chapter was being written, the Interstate Commerce Commission approved a set of railroad rates for the "piggybacking" of truck trailers on railroad flatcars. This approval greatly increases the power of the railroads and decreases that of the trucking industry in their battle for medium and long haul freight business. The Secretary of the Interior recommended that electrical transmission lines connecting a series of federal power projects in the northern Rocky Mountain area be constructed and operated by the government rather than private utility companies. If eventually approved, the "yardstick" rates set by the government will increase the bargaining power of consumers of electricity relative to the private sellers in the area.[10]

The Federal Communications Commission for years has allowed the license of a radio or television station to *continue* from year to year (i.e., to be renewed automatically), unless the Commission acts to revoke it. The Commission has contemplated changing the rules so that the license

---

[10] This statement refers to the *particular* relation between the local consumers of electricity and the private suppliers. The consumers would gain power in that *particular* relation even if a lower government price were subsidized from taxation, and even if the total cost (price plus tax subsidy) were greater to the consumers than under private operation. A good total decision requires more information than that about the particular bargaining relationship.

automatically *expires* every year unless the station applies for and demonstrates that it deserves renewal. This is only one of thousands of cases where burden of proof is important to bargaining power. In the first instance the Commission must demonstrate that the station is doing a *bad* job before it can revoke the license. In the second instance the licence is automatically removed, and the station must demonstrate that it is doing a *good* job to get it renewed.

Even under the latter arrangement it is true that approval will tend to become routine. But the power relation is important mainly in contested cases, at which point a shift in the burden of proof makes a real difference in the power position. In the event of complaints about a broadcaster from the public, it is far easier for the Commission to hold up a renewal until the station explains or reforms than to convert the complaints into a case which will justify canceling the license. And if the Commission is inclined to let things slide, it has much more difficulty explaining to the public why it took the *action* of *renewing* a challenged license than the *inaction* of *not canceling* it, particularly since a cancellation usually requires extensive hearings and the marshaling of evidence.

A protective tariff on textiles increases the bargaining power of the domestic producers over both the foreign producers and the local consumers of textiles. It also increases the power of the domestic textile producers to bid resources away from other domestic industries, such as flour or machine tools and reduces *their* ability to export. The concomitant reduction of textiles imports also reduces the amount of dollar exchange which foreigners might use to purchase American flour and machine tools.

Laws against disturbing the peace decrease the power of those who like to be raucous as against those who want to quiet them.

When the Taft-Hartley Act enacted a provision that there should be no strikes or lockouts during the 60 day period preceding the expiration of a union-management contract, it automatically handed managements a partial no-strike clause without their having to bargain for it or give the unions anything in exchange.[11] When the Supreme Court in the *Lincoln Mills* case later ruled that any dispute arising between union and company during the life of a contract is arbitrable unless the contract specifically states that it is not, it automatically handed many unions a wider arbitration clause without their having to bargain or give anything in return. The first government action increased the bargaining power of managements, and the second that of unions.

No court in the United States will now enforce a restrictive covenant, which is a clause in a contract of sale of real estate that the purchaser will not resell to some specified category of people, such as Negroes. The effect of enforcing such clauses was to reduce the relative number of

---

11 This reference is to the unfair labor practice clause in Section 8(d) of Title I, which deals with *all* contracts, not to Section 206 covering national emergency strikes.

properties available to Negroes, and hence to reduce their bargaining power in trying to buy a house. Their power was reduced to zero for a house covered by a restrictive covenant. The covenant increases the bargaining power of the seller if the white customer wants restricted housing, while if the restriction is unimportant, it may decrease the seller's bargaining power by eliminating Negroes as potential customers. Covenants also increased the bargaining power of owners of those houses which were open for sale to Negroes, by reducing their supply. The refusal of the courts to enforce such restrictive clauses changes all of these bargaining relationships. As with caste, racial segregation, as such, brings a difference in total power, not bargaining power, between races, since in itself it involves no interrace transactions.

For many years some employers in the United States required all employees to sign an agreement that they would not join a union—the so-called yellow dog contract. The Norris-LaGuardia Act of 1932 made such contracts unenforceable, and thus decreased the power of employers to keep their employees from joining unions. By an indirect bargain, if a group of citizens persuade their traffic department to install a pedestrian light at a certain much-walked intersection, the pedestrians add greatly to their power to get cars to let them cross in safety. If a state raises from sixteen to eighteen the age at which one may marry without parental consent, the normal result is to increase the bargaining power of parents over marriage-hungry children for an additional two years. By making divorce expensive, the state raises the bargaining power of whichever spouse is more desirous of holding the marriage together. By having the social security agency reveal information of the whereabouts of a man who has abandoned his family, the government reduces the bargaining power of the deserter as against his family by reducing the likelihood that he can escape his financial obligations. Restricting the use of negative goods in bargaining reduces the power of those who would use them. Laws making persons liable for slander or libel raises the power of persons with socially approved conduct as against those without it.

Sometimes a question arises whether the government itself should compensate the "losing" party in some such regulation. For example, when the federal government in 1961 was conducting an investigation into air safety, it was recommended by some authorities that the government requires seats in passenger planes to face the rear of the plane, whereupon another suggested that in this event the government should help pay the cost.[12] It is common practice in the United States for government to help pay certain costs to families or firms which suffer from certain government actions in the good of others, as in installing equipment to control smoke, in moving a home or business for urban redevelopment, for advice or recruitment in ceasing racial discrimination, for research to improve

---

[12] *Cincinnati Post and Times-Star*, July 5, 1961.

the packaging of food so as to reduce disease or food poisoning, and the like.

The list could continue indefinitely. Whenever the government makes any kind of ruling, decision, enforcement, law, or regulation which directly or indirectly affects the cost to one party of acquiring something from another, or of getting him to stop something—that is, whenever the cost to *A* of getting *X* from *B* is increased as a result of government action —the government has brought about a shift in the power relation between the two parties. Any such action can be construed as an act of power regulation by government. Any such power shift necessarily involves a conflict of interests as among different groups of citizens, since a gain in bargaining power to one means a loss to another. An obviously important question is how the government decides whose side to support—to which we turn in the next chapter.

It should not be assumed, however, that the government's support is the only important power factor in these cases. Perhaps more often than not, as soon as government regulates one kind of activity so as to shift a power relation, the more strategically located side finds a new technique of accomplishing the same result as before. The refusal of courts to enforce restrictive covenants may be replaced by refusal of real estate agents to show properties to Negroes, by the refusal of loan companies to give mortgages, or even by an organization to purchase all houses that become vacant for resale to buyers of their own choosing. For many years after the antitrust laws forbade one company to hold a controlling share of stock in a competing company, the company would buy the *whole* competing company instead, and merge the two. Further (and this fact is lost sight of more often than seems reasonable), the presence of a law does not mean that it is regularly enforced. Price controls during war do not eliminate black markets, and a law prohibiting employers from discriminating between union and nonunion employees has not stopped thousands of employers (particularly small ones and those in the South) from systematically discharging everyone actively interested in unions. In public as in private organization, the informal organization does not necessarily conform to the pronouncements of the formal authority. Further, there may be no way to make it conform, existing or in prospect.

Chapter 33

SPONSOR DECISIONS:
ON SOCIAL CHOICE

DESPITE distinct limitations, market techniques can and do make decisions about private goods. But they cannot either in theory or in practice decide what public goods should be produced, or which collections of private power the government should augment or diminish. In short, the sponsors cannot use the market process to make their decisions about what they want the government to do, and if they want to make their collective wishes known, some other decision technique(s) must be used. These can be thought of as political, as contrasted to market, decisions, but since they include items not normally labeled political, we will avoid that term for the time being.

The basic problem is that of a huge cooperative whose sponsors must instruct the staff regarding goals, but in which the sponsors are much divided among themselves. The question is, which goals of which sponsors are to be adopted, in what proportion, and at whose expense? To clarify by contrast, in the market process every individual makes and effectuates his own decision. The total social decision is the net, interacting effect of the individual decisions. By their collective actions the people "instruct" the system what to produce, at what price to sell, and so forth. But although a collective *effect* is achieved, at no point is collective *agreement*, or decision, required. With respect to public goods and power regulation, however, the sponsors must collectively *agree* on what they want. Whereas two-thirds of the population can have large cars and one-third small ones, two-thirds cannot have large national defense and one-third small.

Not only must the decision be made, but it must be communicated to the staff, who must also be motivated to perform it. To the extent that sponsor decisions are made by ballot, the vote is simultaneously a decision and an instruction to the staff. By the "staff" we mean roughly all persons doing government work on government payroll, whether elected or appointed. The motivation to perform the instructions lies in the people's ability to grant or withhold rewards to the staff, which is the people's authority. Unless the people can control the rewards as well as make the decision, they lack authority, which will lie with those who *do* control the rewards. Within this outline of the problem, the present chapter will discuss the nature and meaning of collective decision. The actual mechanisms for measuring what the people want, and of motivating the staff to perform it, will follow in the next chapter.

One other item of background should be mentioned before we go on. The distribution of power in the society strongly determines who will control the instructions, or at least the motivations, to government staff. But by putting its weight behind one private group and against another, government to important degree determines what private groups will have most power. The basic relation is potentially circular, in that power con-

Figure 33-1

By permission of Walt Kelly.

trols government and government controls power. If this crucial aspect of social power and decision making is to be understood, presumably we need a model of this system. Its main components should be listed, and some attempt be made to diagnose the circumstances, if any, under which equilibrium may be expected. To the best of my knowledge, no such model has thus far been constructed, and I am not prepared to offer one. Its absence, however, seems to leave a major gap in social analysis.[1] It is hoped that subsequent pages will help identify some of the possible ingredients of such a model.

As a selection of the preferred from among a list of possible opportunities, a sound decision requires clear information about the alternatives and a clear knowledge of one's preference ordering. The same is true for a collective decision by a whole society, and the remainder of the chapter will try to delineate some problems of collective preferences and collective information.

SOCIAL PREFERENCE

Except for simple and clearly defined choices, any meaningful statement about an individual's desires takes the form of a preference ordering, not a simple dichotomy of wanted or not wanted. Further, the ordering must be of net, not gross, values. This requires that the person know the gross value of each item on a list as well as the cost of each—or at least have a reasonably good intuitive approximation of it. By extension, a social decision requires a selection from a list of alternatives on the basis of a preference ordering for the whole society, and the central problem of social choice is that of forming a composite preference ordering which meaningfully reflects the individual ones. Several monumental obstacles block this path, some theoretical and others practical, and we will try to outline their nature.[2]

First is the ugly head of interpersonal utility. It is valid to say that I prefer A to B, but not that I get more satisfaction from A than you do from B. There is simply no way of measuring whether my desire for an item fifth on my preference list is even approximately equal to your desire for the item fifth on your list, or first, or twentieth. One might observe the difference of intensity with which we pursue these items, but this might reflect differences in energy, available time, or temperament, not preference, and is hardly practicable by this criterion to measure the intensity of preference for tariffs, nuclear testing, and aid to Laos. The inability to measure interpersonal utility is an obstacle of the first magni-

---

[1] Anthony Downs, *An Economic Theory of Democracy* (New York: Harper Bros., 1957), has built a noteworthy model of the political party, which will be used later below. But he does not attempt to cover the particular area suggested here.

[2] A pioneering work in this field is Kenneth J. Arrow, *Social Choice and Individual Values* (New York: John Wiley & Sons, Inc., 1951), a Cowles Commission Monograph.

tude to achieving a social preference ordering, and there is no apparent solution in either theory or practice.

A second problem is that an individual's preference as one of a group is not necessarily the same as his personal preference. His preference ordering for decision purposes includes only that which he perceives as possible. But if the society operates by group agreement, the list of things which the individual perceives as possible must be narrowed from those which are technically possible to those which can be agreed upon. If your first choice is complete elimination of all tariffs and quotas in international trade, but you conclude that the people will not conceivably approve it, you may cross this from your opportunity list, leaving reciprocal trade agreements as your first preference in any actual contest or social expression. If your first choice is the Prohibition Party, but you feel it hasn't a ghost of a chance, you might vote Republican as your second choice so as not to waste your ballot. For reasons of this sort, your strongest personal preference may not be expressed at all, and may play no part in forming the preference of the whole society. In attempting to understand a social decision mechanism, we must therefore consider whether the individual preference is already modified by what is believed to be the social preference.

Weighted and Unweighted Preferences

In making many kinds of composite expressions of values (such as a price index), some kind of weighting must be used, implicit or explicit. To illustrate, let us assume two possible public goods or policies, X and Y, and five citizens, $A, B, C, D,$ and $E,$ showing the following positions:

Persons	Weighted by Utils		Weighted by Persons	
	X	Y	X	Y
A	10	9	√	
B	10	8	√	
C	10	8	√	
D	10	50		√
E	10	100		√
Totals	50	175	3	2

The figures under the X and Y columns in the set weighted by utils show an arbitrary measure of the relative utility of X and Y to each of the five persons. To simplify presentation the utility of X has been shown equal throughout at 10 utils. $A, B,$ and C prefer X to $Y,$ since X has more utils than Y to each. This preference is indicated by a check mark opposite $A,$ $B,$ and C under Column X weighted by persons. That is, in a decision in which each person is given a single vote of equal weight, the votes of $A,$ $B,$ and C will go to $X.$ However, these preferences of $A, B,$ and C for X are mild, since all three desire Y almost as much as $X,$ at 9, 8, and 8 utils respectively. By contrast, both D and E prefer Y to X. But their preferences are not at all mild, with margins of 5–1 and 10–1 and util valuations of 50 and 100, respectively. If the system of converting individual choices into a social choice asks merely which item is preferred, the choice is 3 to 2 for X, which becomes the social choice. But if the strength of individual preferences is considered, then the socially preferred good is Y, which shows a total of 175 utils, compared to only 50 for X. That is, if the preferences are weighted by units of value instead of units of persons, Y is the socially preferred good.

The alert reader will have noted that interpersonal utility, so indignantly kicked out the front door a few paragraphs earlier, has just been sneaked in the back way, by giving equal weight to utils between persons. This surreptitious re-entrance was tolerated only to illustrate the meaning of weighting by preference, and interpersonal utility can now be kicked out for good by noting that the inability to measure utils is probably the major reason why ballots use equal weighting. It should be clear that it is kicked out only because it is unmeasurable, not because it is unimportant, and any measure of social preference is grossly insensitive that does not reflect it. As noted, this is a dilemma of the first magnitude in making social decisions.

In this sense, the market is a more sensitive decision mechanism than the ordinary vote. In the market each individual has handfuls of ballots, so to speak, and can concentrate or disperse them as he likes. If he wants a good enough to pay the costs of custom production, he may be able to get it even if no one else in the society wants it. As we have seen, however, the number of ballots available to an individual is based on his earning power, not the intensity of his wants, and no technique is visible by which voters could be given more or fewer votes to reflect want-intensity, or utility.

Much the same may be said about information. On difficult issues one person may be twenty times as well informed as another, who is really only guessing. There is no apparently satisfactory way to reflect these differences, as by giving greater weight to "better-informed" ballots. Among other difficulties, if we were to give some people more ballots in proportion to their information on an issue, as measured by some test, the vested interests on any particular issue would often be the best informed and carry the vote.

Majorities

Given equal weight for all votes, a majority vote (or a plurality among three or more) is normally presumed to represent the group preference, or consensus. Although it unquestionably is a technique for measuring preference, it has some important limitations.

Except for a tie, a majority is inescapable in a selection between two alternatives, and the collective preference ordering between the two items represents the majority preference order of the individuals who voted.

When three or more items appear, the collective preference may or may not represent a majority of the individual preferences, depending on the relative numbers. Once the nature of the problem is seen, the reader can easily see how the collective preference could coincide with the majority (or plurality). We therefore need not illustrate that situation and will show only an example in which it does not. In the following choice among three alternatives, each person has one vote, which he casts for his first choice, and the largest number of votes wins the election.

Per Cent of Votes	Preferences		
	1st	2nd	3rd
40	X	Y	Z
35	Z	Y	X
25	Y	Z	X

Although X wins, with 40 per cent of the votes, 60 per cent of the voters prefer both Y and Z to X—the second and third groups. A run-off election between the top two contenders would not help, since the voters would have to decide between X and Z. Y would have been eliminated on the first ballot even though 65 per cent prefer Y to Z and 60 per cent prefer Y to X. Assuming that all the same persons voted with unchanged relative preferences, in a run-off between X and Z, Z would win with a 60 per cent majority.

In a single ballot among three or more choices, the social preference will reproduce a majority of the individual preferences only by chance. A preferential ballot, however, in which each voter records his whole preference ordering, is much more likely to reproduce the majority preference. For example, if each voter above were to have his first choice counted 3 points, his second 2, and his third 1, Y would win the election, Z would be second, and X last.

In circumstances now often known as "Arrow problems,"[3] there is no such thing as a majority preference, no matter how counted, and it seems dubious practice even to say that a social preference *exists*, counted or uncounted. Among alternatives X, Y, and Z, suppose the population is equally divided among preference orderings X, Y, Z; Y, Z, X; and Z, X, Y. Two-thirds prefer X to Y; two-thirds prefer Y to Z; and two-thirds prefer Z to X. What is the social preference? As Arrow puts it:

> If we exclude the possibility of interpersonal comparisons of utility, then the only methods of passing from individual tastes to social preferences which will be satisfactory and which will be defined for a wide range of sets of individual orderings are either imposed or dictatorial.[4]

---

3 Arrow, *ibid.*, p. 3.
4 *Ibid.*, p. 59. This conclusion is arrived at by a highly systematic logical proof. An imposed choice is one in which the preference cannot be expressed, and a dictatorial one is selected by one person without regard to the wishes of the people. (pp. 28, 30.)

We now come to the heart of the problem of social decision. If there is only one issue and two alternative answers, it is easy to form a single social position which corresponds to the preferences of the people. With one issue and three or more possible answers, some consensus may or may not exist, depending on the distribution of preferences, and if a consensus does exist it will probably require a preferential ballot to reveal it. As soon as we face multiple issues and multiple alternatives on each, the likelihood that a meaningful social preference can exist dwindles quickly to insignificance. And when we move from the textbook illustration to the dozens and scores of issues which simultaneously face any society, many of which have three or more major alternatives and endless minor ones, it seems safe to say that except for some miracle of coincidence a social preference does not exist, never has existed, and never will. Needless to say, if it does not exist, it cannot be measured, no matter how sophisticated the technique. Here we have many individual preferences, but no aggregate preference. In short, on one dominant issue with two clear alternatives the people can speak with a clear collective message. On the total combination of many issues with multiple alternatives, not only can they not speak; they have no message. Only individuals and interest groups can speak, normally with conflicting messages.

The obvious recommendation if there is to be a people's voice is to reduce the decision to two clear alternatives—a result approximated by a vigorous two-party system. This is the major practical solution, to be discussed further in the next chapter. But like the executive who wants all his problems reduced to a two-page memorandum, the voter who chooses between paired alternatives has had most of the important decisions made for him before he casts his ballot. The consequence is that the major decisions about government are made through a process of coalition formation, not group decision making through some collective preference. The main function of voting is to determine which coalition shall hold power, and to decide some occasional particular issues. These, however, are matters for the next chapter.

Where decisions are made by majority vote, the question arises whether the social decision should be measured by a majority of the whole population eligible to vote or by a majority of those voting. The general practice is to count a majority of votes actually cast, assuming that those who did not vote are relatively indifferent. Where a vote selects between two alternatives, where one or the other must be adopted, there is little choice but to accept the majority of votes cast. Where the alternatives are between a change and the status quo, it is feasible, though not necessarily desirable, to require something other than a simple majority. For example, treaties and constitutional amendments in the United States require a two-thirds majority vote in Congress, and ratification of amendments by the states requires a three-fourths vote. A union shop (in which all workers in a bargaining unit are required to join the union) cannot be established under the Taft-Hartley Act unless approved by a majority of all those *eligible* to vote.

Psychological Factors in Social Choice

Voting or any other activity related to social decision follows the same psychological laws as other human responses. Among the most obvious of these are the three major factors in learning—frequency, recency, and intensity. Other things equal, that which is experienced most frequently is learned most completely, and produces the most reliable response. This fact is reflected in many ways. Voters who have frequently in the past voted Democratic, against government borrowing, or for improved schools, will tend to repeat the pattern unless something relatively strong occurs to break it. A particular argument which is heard frequently (that tariffs are necessary to protect the jobs of American workers) produces a stronger impression on voters than the argument less frequently expressed (that a reduction in imports will lead to an offsetting loss of exports). Candidates try to keep their faces and names before the public, in the knowledge that sheer repetition will bring more votes. Slogans, catchphrases, and over-easy generalizations are readily learned by voters, and can be repeated on billboards, posters, speeches, and spot announcements. Logical arguments, by contrast, cannot be learned so quickly by voters nor repeated so frequently, and are relatively played down. In politics, because in psychology, repetition is power.

The psychology of recency makes the elected official more sensitive to public wants two months before election than two years before. Approval of an appropriation for flood control is more likely if a flood occurs just before election than if the last flood was thirty months before, even though the long run need is no different. The Congress is more likely to pass strong legislation for national emergency strikes if such a strike is in progress at the time. Two kinds of maneuvers are widely used in connection with the recency factor. If one can control the events, he tries to bring on (or avoid) an event which will help (or hurt) his cause just before or during the decision period. Or if he can control the timing of the decision, he will try to bring it into the best "recency" relation with the unfolding events. A "sense of timing" in politics relies heavily on the psychological factor of recency, and much power lies therein.

Intensity is also important. Citizens may complain frequently to the highway department about an extremely dangerous curve, without response. After years of futile petitioning, a nasty accident may bring a decision within a week to straighten the curve. Many safety regulations have been passed in the wake of some particularly frightful event. Barring actual incidents, the ability to dramatize an issue utilizes the intensity factor. Through plan or accident, these psychological factors do much to shape decisions by the public and the government.

SOCIAL INFORMATION

For citizens attempting to instruct their government, as for any other decision maker, the first step of adaptive behavior requires information about the alternative opportunities and the probable consequences of each, and the fourth step requires feedback with which to evaluate the original decision and the performance of the staff in carrying it out. It also, of course, requires sufficient education to understand the information when received, but the present attention is on the flows of information itself.

In addition to the question whether there can *be* a social preference in complex circumstances, a further crucial question about the people's ability to instruct their government toward their own ends can be sharpened by examining a hypothetical group of people whom we will call an "information group." Though not a part of the government, this group will be assumed to have complete control of all information mechanisms in the nation, including schools, press, and radio. By control of these mechanisms the information group convinces the people that they are receiving full and unbiased information, on the basis of which they make their decisions about government. Since the group succeeds in making its information *seem* complete and unbiased, the public sees no reason to challenge their control of information. (In the chapter on the "Information Needs of a Complex Society" we will see some inescapable chinks in such control, no matter how tightly organized. Meanwhile it illustrates an important point.)

By manipulating the people's perceptions of their opportunities, such a group might easily create majority support for programs which would greatly benefit the information group at the expense of the rest of the population. And by controlling the feedback of information the group could make the situation *seem* to be in the best interests of the whole people. Anyone with evidence to the contrary would be helpless to oppose the information group. He would be unable to communicate widely enough to create organized opposition, while the information group would have massive communications available to discredit him.

Under these circumstances the people would apparently have complete freedom to propose, discuss, and decide issues in full democratic fashion, with no sense of coercion or control. Yet the information group would in fact make all significant decisions, because it would control the people's decision sets, their expectations of the probable outcomes of their decisions, and the feedback for later evaluation of the decisions. Clearly, if the people in a democracy are to protect their own interests, they must have unbiased and reasonably full information, both initial and feedback, and any persistent bias in the flows of information weakens the fact of democratic control, even if the forms are intact. In the United States, certain biases seem large and persistent enough to deserve attention.

The Meaning of "Freedom of Press"

Before getting to specifics, we should note that "freedom of the press" prevails in the United States. Since many persons believe that a "free" press necessarily means an unbiased press, this important distinction should be clarified. The fundamentals of a free press are incorporated in the first article of the Bill of Rights, which reads: "Congress shall make no law . . . abridging the freedom of speech, or of the press. . . ." This provision is extended to other divisions of government by the Fourteenth Amendment, which adds that "No State shall make or enforce any law which shall abridge the privileges or immunities of citizens of the United States." The scope of the protection is rounded out by court decisions to the general effect that other branches of government may not by executive action or court decision achieve results which the legislature is forbidden to bring about by legislation.

"Freedom of the press" prevents the *government* from controlling the content of newspapers, which is another way of saying that the content of newspapers is exclusively a private decision. Freedom of the press thus does not guarantee freedom from bias. On the contrary, it guarantees the newspaper freedom to be as biased as it likes—to include everything it likes and exclude everything it dislikes, to lie, to distort, and to misrepresent. If I own a newspaper, I am completely free under law to print my own point of view exclusively and refuse to print yours, no matter how long or hard you beg me. Within wide limits I am even free to refuse your paid advertising. You cannot go to the courts and get a writ requiring me to print your point of view (except perhaps as advertising), since under our law this would be an infringement on the freedom of the press. If I print lies about you which demonstrably damage your reputation or income, you can sue me for libel, and perhaps collect. But if you make a speech in which you denounce the distortions in my paper, or the asininity of its editorial policy, I am free under law not to mention your speech, to report its weak points and not its strong ones, or to denounce your speech without reporting its content. Within an extremely wide range, I am even free to quote portions of your speech out of context in such a way as to leave the impression that you said the exact opposite of what you did, and to refuse to print your correction. In matters regarding your point of view (as distinct from your character or income earning capacity), I can misrepresent your position in large type on page one and print a correction (if any) five days later in small type on page 32. In all these things you have no *legal* recourse, for to prevent me from doing these things would infringe freedom of the press. Letters to the editor offer room for rebuttal, but these are inconspicuous compared to front page news and political cartoons, and can be omitted, or perhaps be edited, before being published.[5]

---

[5] I have written occasional letters to the editor. All but two have been published, some without change, some with moderate alterations which did not change their essential sense, but did leave me somewhat less able to defend my position, and in

Lest as author of a book I create grave distortions by describing the grave distortions I could create if I were editor of a newspaper, let me make the purpose of the preceding paragraph clear. First, it is *not* a backhanded suggestion that the government change its policy, and I would personally be adamant that the government should not intervene on any of these matters—though it might perhaps take vigorous action to prevent monopoly and encourage diversity of newspaper ownership and control, so that viewpoints excluded from one paper could find expression in another. Monopoly over the flow of information (which is something like the "information group") probably holds power second only to that of the government's monopoly of force, and it may in a sense be greater if it can mold the government's decisions. Second, the preceding paragraph is neither a description nor a criticism of existing practices (though instances of all things mentioned can occasionally be found), but simply an attempt to make unmistakably clear that the guarantee of a *free* press is in no sense a guarantee of an *unbiased* press. In practical terms, it guarantees that you can get your point of view expressed in a newspaper *if you own a newspaper*. Freedom from government control is assured by the legal "freedom of the press." Freedom from bias can be assured only by other forces, such as editorial responsibility and competition.

With the exception of motion pictures, over which our courts have rather consistently allowed some censorship, the general statements made here about newspapers apply equally to other means of communication, such as radio, television, books and magazines, art galleries, meeting halls, and the stage. They are subject to some modifications about "equal time" in broadcasting, about physical safety in meetings, about "clear and present danger" of overthrow of the government (and about obscenity everywhere), all of which are important, but are unrelated to the problem of bias at the level we are now discussing. The controls in broadcasting, incidentally, reflect the fact that the number of stations and channels is limited by the technical characteristics of radio waves. Whereas anyone is free to run a newspaper who can make a go of it, not everyone is free to operate a broadcasting station. This fact gives partial monopoly status to those who do, and seems to justify some intervention to attain multiple viewpoints. The intervention is modest, however, and does not prevent some stations and their sponsors from showing a marked overall bias.[6]

---

one instance an important point was omitted. In a recent instance of a touchy question on which I wanted my wording precisely as I stated it, I added: "P. S. Please do not change this letter. If it is too long, please return it, and I will cut it by the amount indicated." (The letter contained 217 words.) It was returned three days later by the editor, with his statement of policy: "We do not accept letters which cannot be edited, so I am returning yours."

[6] A useful short summary of government intervention and participation in communication in England, Canada, and the United States is found in James Burns and Jack Peltason, *Government by the People* (New York: Prentice-Hall, Inc., 1960), pp. 275–80.

Some Biases in Information Channels

Our next task is to examine in a broad way the actual state of affairs regarding bias in the United States. Again we will speak mainly of newspapers.

In the early days of the republic, the typical newspaper was small business, and anyone with strong interest and a little money could own and edit one. Newspapers reflected every shade of opinion and every level of journalistic integrity, and most communities of reasonable size had a reasonably representative group. If one newspaper had one bias, a second might have an opposite bias, and a third might be impartial.

By about the beginning of the twentieth century the small paper found it financially difficult to survive, while the large paper moved into the realm of big business, with a budget of a million dollars or more. Since then, newspapers have disappeared by the hundreds, through bankruptcy or merger, while many of the remaining papers are parts of nationwide chains. Two main results have followed. One is a strong tendency toward monopolization of news presentation. As of 1959, 1,233 cities in the United States had only one newspaper, and an additional 119 cities had two papers, which were controlled by the same persons.[7] In 1954, 970 cities had only one radio station.[8] Further, in 72 towns or cities having only one newspaper and one radio station, the newspaper held whole or majority ownership in the radio station, and minority ownership in 12 additional instances.[9] Of these 84 places, however, 12 are located in metropolitan areas, so that people have ready access to other newspapers and radio stations. Such situations tend to bring a monopoly on local news, and a distinct dominance in national and international news, since many people will patronize only a news medium which provides both local and national coverage. In many other cities two independent newspapers operate, but without distinct difference in broad point of view. More important than the statistics, however, is the question of how much and what kind of bias is to be found.

The quantity of bias is difficult to measure, but the type is fairly obvious, the dominant position being a business-employer orientation. The reasons are clear: chiefly, that newspapers are themselves big business with many employees, and that their main revenue comes from advertising by business. The business community itself is not a unitary thing, and has many internal differences. Among many other divergences, "business" includes borrowers and lenders, importers and exporters, dominant giants and small firms that fear them, manufacturers and retailers, selling firms and firms which buy

---

[7] Compiled from *1959 Editor and Publisher International Yearbook* (New York: The Editor and Publisher Co., Inc., 1959).

[8] Richard E. Chapin, *Mass Communication* (East Lansing: Michigan State University Press, 1957), p. 85.

[9] Figures compiled from public records of the Federal Communications Commission, taken in conjunction with *Broadcasting Year-Book 1961–62* (Washington, D.C.: Broadcasting Publications, Inc., 1962).

from them, those which receive help from government research grants and those which consider such grants unfair competition. To say that newspapers are "pro-business" gives no clue to a stand on issues on which businessmen themselves differ, and biases in this area are apt to be random or nonexistent. In three respects the position of business is much more nearly unanimous: all are employers, not employees; none like to be taxed; and few want the power of private business reduced relative to government. Of these three, taxes and government power are both related to government, with the result that the three items are reduced to two, which are reflected in a pro-employer, anti-union bias, and a pro-business, anti-government bias.

Newspapers themselves, of course, differ widely. Some show a deep, persistent, and blatant bias; with some the bias is seen as moderate and inconspicuous; others show at least superficial evidence of impartiality; and still others (but a distinct minority) show the opposite bias. The following observations, therefore, do not apply to every paper, and they apply in differing degree to those they do describe. But they do reflect a general and fairly deep trend of American newspapers on the average. Numerous studies of newspaper practices concur that they show a pro-business orientation, and none to the best of my knowledge has concluded the opposite—that the general trend of American papers is pro-union, pro-government, and anti-business.[10]

Several kinds of differential reporting can often be seen if the reader will be observant. One is the ingroup versus outgroup attitude described in the chapter on Culture. Good performance in business is reported as if normal, to be expected in the system, while sins or errors are individual, and happen despite the system. Good performance in unions and government, by contrast, is apt to be treated as individual and not quite the expected thing, while sin and error are viewed as regrettable developments to which these organizations are prone. These attitudes are more often implicit than ex-

---

[10] Among sources the interested reader might consult on this subject are Robert M. Hutchins, *Freedom, Education, and the Fund* (New York: Meridian Books, 1956); Robert M. Hutchins (Chairman), The Commission on Freedom of the Press, *A Free and Responsible Press* (Chicago: The University of Chicago Press, 1947); Nathan B. Blumbery, *One Party Press?* (Lincoln: University of Nebraska Press, 1954); Alfred M. Lee, *The Daily Newspaper in America* (New York: The Macmillan Co., 1937); Harold L. Ickes, *America's House of Lords* (New York: Harcourt, Brace & Co., 1939); Malcolm M. Willey and Ralph D. Casey, *The Press in the Contemporary Scene*, Annals of the American Academy of Political and Social Science, Vol. 19, January, 1942; Frank L. Mott, *American Journalism* (New York: The Macmillan Co., 1941); Allan Nevins, *American Press Opinion, Washington to Coolidge* (New York: D. C. Heath & Co., 1928); Upton Sinclair, *The Brass Check* (Pasadena, Calif.: published by the author, 1919); Ben H. Bagdikian, "Television—the President's Medium," *Columbia Journalism Review*, Summer 1962, pp. 35 ff.; and various books by George Seldes, such as *Freedom of the Press* (New York: Garden City Publishing Co., 1937), *Lords of the Press* (New York: Julian Messner, Inc., 1938), *The Facts Are. . . .* New York: In Fact, Inc., 1942), and *One Thousand Americans* (New York: Boni & Gaer, 1947). Hutchins observes the tendency of the press to react neurotically whenever any criticism of it is made, in his *Freedom, Education and the Fund*, especially pp. 54, 58.

plicit, which makes their influence both more pervasive and more difficult to detect. Socialists of any shade or degree are rather consistently treated as outgroup.

Semantics also show differential treatment. The words "socialist," "socialization," and "socialized" are reserved for acts of socialization which the paper disapproves. With respect to acts of socialization which the paper happens to approve (such as public schools, social security, a federal power project, or municipal ownership of a local transit system) these "dirty" words are avoided, and the "clean" words "federal," "social," "public," or "municipal" are used.

Both the Food and Drug Administration and the Federal Trade Commission issue frequent releases on companies charged or found guilty of such things as false advertising, misbranded products, and dangerous or unsanitary drugs or foods. Although this information would be highly useful to consumers (and damaging to some advertisers), it is generally played down or omitted through wide segments of the American press. During the 1930's no less than 60 newspapers refused to carry advertising for Consumers Union, an independent testing organization which reports the strength and weaknesses of consumer goods by brand name and model.[11]

A persistent type of antigovernment bias which most readers of this book have probably observed is that some papers seldom go for as long as a week at a time without a political cartoon which in some way depicts government as bungling, moronic, inefficient, and wasteful. (Within half an hour after checking this section of the manuscript, I picked up my evening paper and observed an important division of the federal government referred to by no other designation than "the spenders.") If a local government official commits some act of notable stupidity, the fact will be spread across the headlines and be duly condemned in the editorial pages, perhaps for weeks. If an important official of a dominant local industry makes an equally stupid mistake, and one equally costly to the welfare of the community, the chances are high that the paper will not touch it, and if it does it will mention it only once, discreetly on the inner pages, without editorial comment.

Now it is not easy to know how much attention *ought* to be given relatively to the weaknesses in government and business. And it would be rather surprising if an organization with a relatively single-minded objective like that of making a profit could not be more efficient in decision making and performance than an organization with a potentially unlimited number of conflicting objectives, like government. Whatever the differences may be in *fact*, the papers provide biased feedback. A normally expected consequence would be to push public preferences away from public goods and expenditures and (at least by residual effect)

---

11 George Seldes, *Lords of the Press*, p. 390.

toward private ones. It would simultaneously tend to raise confidence in action by private business and decrease that in public action.

An interesting example occurred just as this section was being written. In connection with a difficult local transit problem, a local newspaper discussed at length the success of the Cleveland Transit System, strongly commending the company and its officials. Nowhere in the article, however, was there any direct or indirect hint that the Cleveland system is socialized—i.e., owned by the city.[12] Although there is no way of knowing whether this *particular* omission represents deliberate bias, it is a *kind* of treatment which is common in American newspapers. The opposite "error" (of failing to mention the socialized status of a system that is doing badly) is a rarity indeed.

On the union-management front, even many newspapers which are generally fair show some occasional pro-employer bias. One is to throw in the term "union monopoly" at intervals when unions are discussed, whether or not the word "monopoly" is relevant to the particular discussion. A second frequently occurs in seemingly impartial editorials about strikes. The editorial (impartially) laments the loss to workers, company, and the public from the strike, and points out how many years it will take the workers at higher wages to make up the income lost by striking. The stated or implicit moral is that they would have been better off not to strike, which means, by implication, to have accepted the company's terms. Although I have seen this many times, and have been alert to the problem for years, I do not recall ever seeing a hint that the company could have avoided the strike by accepting the union's terms.[13]

A related kind of bias is reported in a particular strike by Liebling, who states:

> The union had rejected the company's proposition, and the company had rejected the trainmen's proposition. In newspaper practice, this situation, which occurs pretty often, is treated as a tie in favor of the company. It looked to me like a reciprocal rejection, but the union's was the only one mentioned in the *Tribune* story. . . .[14]

He concludes the article with:

> The truth appeared to be that neither side had got all it wanted, and that what newspapers call pigheadedness in a railroad conductor is what they call devotion to principle in a railroad president.[15]

---

[12] *Cincinnati Post and Times Star*, July 6, 1961.

[13] Editors sometimes agree with the union in a particular dispute, and state or imply that the employer was wrong. But although my personal sample is modest, I would be surprised if any reader of this book has seen the explicit suggestion stated above—that everyone would have gained if the management had avoided the strike by accepting the union's terms.

[14] A. J. Liebling, "The Wayward Press," *The New Yorker*, August 20, 1960, p. 86.

[15] *Ibid.*, p. 98.

The rather persistent unstated assumption that failure to agree is the union's fault—as in the first quotation above—takes other forms. As Liebling quotes the *Tribune* again (which was not his only target in this case):

> "We urge the strikers [not, I could not help noting, the management] to remember that this is a stoppage that hurts the entire community—the community of which unions [but not, apparently, railroad management] are a part."[16]

In the mid 1950's the McClellan Committee was investigating union and management practices for the Senate. Whenever unsavory practices by unions were uncovered, they were given great space, and often headlines, throughout the nation, particularly those of Dave Beck and James Hoffa in the Teamsters Union. However, the Committee also uncovered some equally unsavory practices by companies in their attempts to fight unions, particularly by one Nathan Shefferman and his Labor Relations Associates. The activities were of sufficiently unpleasant character to lead Senator McClellan to say:

> The activities disclosed before this committee reflect a great discredit on some business firms in this country . . . It came as a profound shock to me to see men acting on behalf of American business take the Fifth Amendment before this committee . . . In conclusion, let me say that it is elements in management which must take the heavy blame for the activities which have been unfolded before this committee. It was the services which management desired which created the need for Nathan Shefferman. It was management who paid the bills for the activities of Nathan Shefferman, and it was management which knowingly utilized the services of Nathan Shefferman with no compunctions or regrets until the revelations in recent months. They were aware of what they were doing and how their money was being utilized. These activities, . . . as well as those [of] dishonest labor officials with whom they connived, should be strongly condemned.[17]

In contrast to the heavy and almost universal coverage given by the papers to the misdeeds of unions, often with banner headlines, these findings and the senator's statements about business were generally omitted or played down in American papers.

Along similar lines, the abuse of stockholder interest in the Bellanca Corporation by its president, Sidney Albert, was hardly less flagrant or newsworthy than the abuses of the members of the Teamsters union by its president, James Hoffa, and investigations of both were under way at about the same time. Among many other actions highly detrimental to the corporation, Albert lent 5,000 shares of stock owned by the company to a friend for no reason related to the purposes of the corporation; he used 50,000 shares of stock belonging to the company to secure personal loans of $300,000, and on another occasion he had 10,000 shares

---

[16] *Ibid.*, p. 88.
[17] *New York Times*, November 6, 1957, p. 19.

deposited in escrow to help him purchase stock on his own account. He made false and misleading reports to the stockholders and to the Securities and Exchange Commission about these and other matters, and illegally omitted reports on still others.[18] But while American newspapers were making Hoffa's name highly familiar to most American citizens, they allowed those same citizens to remain in almost complete ignorance of Sidney Albert. To anyone who follows the newspapers regularly, and compares what they say and do not say with what is reported in the nonmass sources, it is difficult to escape a conclusion that much of the press has a clear double standard, one for business news and another for union and government news.

When it is pointed out that the *New York Times*, the *Christian Science Monitor* and the news (not the editorial) sections of the *Wall Street Journal* show a generally high level of fairness, it is sometimes replied that mass readers do not want a scholarly looking paper, but that sex, human interest, and sensationalism are what sell papers. The answer, of course, is irrelevant to the question of bias, since it is possible to be just as folksy, sexy, and sensational in favor of unions or government as against them.

On the whole, radio and television probably show less bias than newspapers, probably because too strong and persistent a bias may jeopardize their licenses, and because of their structure. Whereas everything in a newspaper except the paid advertising is subject to the control of the same sponsor interest, every change of program over the air brings a new sponsor. And whereas one may have to buy a whole newspaper to get his point of view presented in it (other than in a paid advertisement, which is highly suspect as "news"), he can sponsor a news broadcast reflecting his own views by buying only a small fraction of the station's time.

Tied to the pro-business bias is a fairly significant one in the producer-consumer relation, which is related to advertising, and is firmly institutionalized into the system. Anyone who cares to can misrepresent his product on the air by brand name, without lying, by the simple device of overstating or emphasizing its desirable qualities and understating or ignoring its weaknesses. But for all practical purposes it is impossible on a paid or unpaid basis for anyone, *by brand name*, to call attention to this misrepresentation over the air and correct it. Although competitors make counterclaims, and on rare occasion prick the balloon of the opponent's claims fairly pointedly, and although some comedians occasionally satirize commercials, virtually never does anyone state specifically over the air that a particular claim by a particular advertiser is false or misleading, or that his demonstration was rigged. Nor, except perhaps to report an action by the Federal Trade Commission or the Food and Drug Ad-

---

[18] *Securities Exchange Act Release No. 5706* (Washington, D.C.: The Securities and Exchange Commission, June 2, 1958), especially p. 17.

ministration, will a typical newspaper print a news story or accept paid advertising specifically describing the falsity of some advertising claim. Considering the way the claims and acts of public officials and candidates are open to the most complete dissection and criticism, the almost complete immunity of advertising claims from similar critical publicity creates a marked distortion in our communications system.

The following proposal might make an interesting experiment to test the relative power of producer and consumer interests in controlling information flows. Let us suppose that some heavily endowed, consumerminded foundation should buy a half hour of prime television time—say, from 7:00 to 7:30 Sunday evenings. Backed by a staff of topnotch script writers, actors, technicians, and lawyers, a well-equipped laboratory to run and televise its own tests, and a group of consulting economists and scientists to check its material for accuracy and fairness, this program would be devoted to pointing out the fallacies, inaccuracies, and omissions in advertising whenever found, in guarantees, and in selling techniques. (Actors useful for this purpose might include Mort Sahl, Henry Morgan, Bob Newhart, and Stan Freberg.) Among other things, the program would report by brand name the experiences of consumers in actually using a product, and compare the experience with the advertising. Frequency of repairs could be reported, and experiences in attempting to get repairs effectuated could be re-enacted. What is covered and not covered by guarantees could be described, along with enactments of attempts to get performance under guarantees—again by brand name. Tests of the comparative performance and durability of various brands might be reported or demonstrated, showing both the tests and the results under impartial conditions. Techniques of salesmen to manipulate unwilling customers into buying could be acted out, along with suggested countermeasures to be used against salesmen. If done with reasonable imagination and skill, the program could draw a large audience.

Without detailed study it cannot be known whether such a program would be socially useful, all things considered, and the taboos against mentioning brand names over the air are not without logical basis. Nevertheless, if a foundation were to conclude after thorough investigation that the program did offer high educational and economic value, the obstacles in its path would probably be almost insuperable, even if the foundation had demonstrable capacity to take full legal liability for possible law suits. Actual or anticipated boycotts by advertisers would probably cause the networks to refuse the program, even if the foundation offered two to three times the normal price, and numerous other obstacles, legal and other, might be expected.

Again, the point is not to evaluate the overall desirability of the existing situation, which is a long and complex task, but to use the suggested program as a device for focusing attention on the existing bias in our information flows.

Although it has little if any effect on the alignment of power, an almost universal atheism taboo seems worth noting. Although in appropriate places the mass media will allow presentation of religious views of almost any color, virtually all firmly and uniformly exclude statements affirming or attempting to justify an atheistic position. The situation is more evident in the Sunday supplements to newspapers and mass circulation magazines, where articles relating to religion are common, than in ordinary radio or newspaper news, which have relatively little occasion to discuss religion.

Mass versus Special Media

The above discussion of information biases is confined to the mass media, which reach all strata of society. Above and beyond these are a host of general and specialized, small-circulation publications which, along with books, are read by the minority of better-informed people. Although distinct partisanship appears in particular books, articles, or magazines, these publications taken as a whole show no persistent bias such as pervades the mass media. The difference is somewhat parallel to the earlier discussion of ritual in Chapter 11. The mass media in significant degree perform the ritual function, presenting the news in a context which reinforces the basic norms and values of the culture, and rather consistently supports the dominant power groupings. But those who do the more difficult thinking in the society need accurate information, whether it supports or contradicts the existing norms. Such information is available, and without it the society could not function well.

SUMMARY

To review the whole situation, the two major techniques we have studied thus far for making social decisions are the market and political processes, where individual preferences are expressed by dollar votes and ballot box votes respectively. In any power contest between rich and poor (to use the shortest words for the high and not-so-high income groups), the rich cast far more dollar ballots and the poor more political ones. As might be expected, the rich give strongest support to the market decision process, in which they have a relative advantage in numbers of votes, while the poor put more emphasis on the political process in which *they* have more votes. In a direct and unadulterated contest for control of government by vote, the rich would consistently lose, as they are a small minority.

But the rich also own and control most of the mass media, which are the main sources of information for most of the poor, and the sole source for many. The mass media reflect a persistent, overall bias against unions and government, which are the two main instruments of power available to the lower income groups. By means of this bias, the rich bring the poor to feel reticence, uncertainty, and some lack of confidence in their own instruments of power, and reduce the effectiveness of those instruments. Control of mass information thus seems to be a major factor in maintaining the status quo of the power structure in the United States. There is no way to know the magnitude of the effect, since we have no condition of absence of bias with which to compare it.

Chapter 34

SPONSOR DECISIONS:
ON MEASURING PREFERENCES

WHEREVER an organization has more than one sponsor, the sponsor-staff relation has two steps. The first is for the sponsors to agree on what they want the organization to do, and the second is to get the staff to do it. The second step usually requires both communication and transactions. A distinctive feature of government is the close relation between these steps, which in one sense seem to be joined in the single operation of an election. An important similarity between government and other organizations is that only top levels of the staff are selected directly by the sponsors, and are responsible to them. Lower levels of staff are selected by and responsible to the higher levels. The term "staff" will continue to include both the elected and nonelected workers in the government. But as in all other organizations, the sponsor-staff relation is directly concerned only with the top levels of the staff, who in the present discussion will be identified with the elected officials. Although we sometimes elect persons to fill routine operating posts, the subsequent analysis is directed only at elective positions with policy-making powers, these being mainly executive and legislative. First, however, we will examine direct policy decisions by vote.

THE REFERENDUM ON ISSUES

Presumably the most direct way to find what people want on some issue is to let them vote in a referendum. The method is appealing, but has many limitations.

First, a referendum can have clear meaning only if it is applied to a relatively isolable issue, whose marginal costs and value to the voters is clear. In a referendum on a new sewer system or high school building, for instance, the public can have a fairly clear idea of its cost, which can be stated on the ballot, and of the value it will create for the community. The issue is isolable, in that other activities of the community remain largely unaffected. Similarly, some large, overriding issue could also meaningfully be decided by referendum, such as to merge one's nation with another, or adopt a new, greatly changed constitution.

Many issues, however, cannot be isolated. The paving of a particular section of road is tied to other sections of road in a total network. A treaty with one country is tied to a total foreign policy, and cannot be evaluated out of its total context. A particular dam for flood control is part of a total system, and so on. To submit any one such issue to voters would not make sense.

Second, many issues are technical, and require far more knowledge than most voters possess. Third, some issues can be decided only by the top echelons of the government organization, as only they have the co-ordinated view of the information from all the parts. Further, in times of international tension, information essential to a decision may have to be kept from the people for security reasons.

Fourth, decisions which carry significant shifts in private power, such as that of allowing or prohibiting secondary boycotts by unions, are likely to be voted on the basis of emotional likes or dislikes, rather than on knowledge of the practical effects of the legislation.

Fifth, we have previously observed that in a selection between two alternatives, important parts of the decision must often be made before the issue gets on the ballot.

Sixth, it is virtually inconceivable that the people should attempt to decide all issues. A single session of Congress considers approximately 5,000 bills, and state and local governments add impressively to that total. Most are handled by committees which specialize in one area, and spend scores or hundreds of hours studying one issue.

Seventh, if a measure requires expenditures, should the decision about the taxes to pay for it be made along with the decision on the expenditure? Or will we have a more sensible tax structure if it is designed without regard to what the taxes are to be used for?

Finally, the referendum raises a basic issue of authority, because its decision is mandatory on the staff. Suppose the elected staff say: "Don't pass that measure. It will hamstring the government, and we cannot be responsible for the consequences." If the voters nevertheless pass it, it is difficult to evaluate officials when they come up for re-election, since they have been required to effectuate against their will a program they have insisted is unworkable.

All in all, although the referendum has distinct uses for some issues, it holds little promise as a general technique of public decision making.

POLLS OF PUBLIC OPINION

It is sometimes suggested that public opinion polls be incorporated into public decision making. The proposal has little merit. First, polls are samples. Even if the sample is truly random, the sampling error may run to 3 to 5 per cent, which is often enough to reverse a decision. If the sampling error is systematic (rather than random), as in the ill-fated *Literary Digest* poll which predicted the defeat of Roosevelt in 1936, no normal statistical technique can correct it or measure the size of the error. If polls were taken by interview, "watchers" would have to accompany each interviewer to make sure he correctly recorded the answers and did not influence the answers by his tone of voice or leading questions. If questionnaires were mailed, mail might be intercepted, or counterfeit answer sheets be printed. If polls were announced in advance, political parties might feel under pressure to conduct campaigns for every poll, and if not, the respondents might have to answer the questions without prior thought. In existing public opinion polls, the polling agency often "adjusts" the figures to "correct" certain biases in the polling technique. This is fine when polls have no official standing, but who would be trusted to "adjust" them if they did? Finally, if the poll covered a sample of only one-thousandth of the population, partisans would find it a thousand times as rewarding to buy or influence any one vote.

All in all, the poll can be useful so long as anyone is free to put as much or little confidence in it as he likes. Its chief advantage is that it can cheaply and frequently tap the general state of sentiment, or change of sentiment, on a wide range of issues. But it shows no prospect of taking the place of the ballot as a formal decision process. Further, it suffers most or all of the limitations already described for referendums.

VOTES FOR PERSONS

Because of the many unworkable aspects of referendums and polls, most formal decisions by the people take the form of elections of persons. For the moment we are interested in the election as a decision process. Its major characteristics are the same whether the voters are filling one post or many, and whether the posts are legislative or executive. For this stage of analysis we shall speak of *a candidate*, but the same general conclusions would follow for the totality of candidates in a party, particularly if it is tightly disciplined.

We have already indicated that the voters do not decide on objectives and then hire top staff employees to carry them out. The actual relation can better be described by saying that the sponsors entertain applications from two or more prospective employees, each with his own program. This kind of situation has already been described in Chapter 24 for hiring skilled employees, who have their programs already built in. The election does three things at once, in that it (1) selects the employee, (2) chooses his program over that of competing employees, and (3) provides the cue to release the program. Re-election does these three things, plus rewarding previous performance.

The major bargain between the candidate and the public is subject to ground rules spelled out by the Constitution and previous practice. The public gives the candidate its agreement to pay taxes in amounts decided by the candidate, to be spent under the control of the candidate for purposes decided in part by the candidate, including his own salary mutually understood in advance. The candidate, if elected, also receives the authority to hire and control subordinates, although, under civil service, he is to select only the top policy officials in the various departments, and to retain the permanent hired staff at lower levels, who will presumably perform as directed. The candidate also receives the important grant of the exclusive use of force, with which to require sponsors to pay taxes as well as to conform to such power regulation as the candidate shall promulgate. Though complex in detail, the bargain is nevertheless simpler than it would otherwise be, since the agreement implicitly assumes that previous government relations with citizens will continue unless the candidate's program calls for change. Significant changes other than those authorized by the election or justified for ordinary good management will probably be construed by the electorate as illegitimate, unless the candidate by other means ascertains that they are acceptable.

The rewards to the elected candidate are not essentially different from those of the top staff of any other organization: pay and expenses, prestige, the fun of the game, the exercise of power, and the candidate's opportunity to increase his own power permanently. In short, and more mnemonically, the rewards are pay, prestige, power, and pleasure. The rewards in pay are usually lower and those in power higher than in private employment. The public lacks such devices as merit rating and in-grade raises to reward its elected officials. But it can "promote" them by returning them to successively higher office, as they move from dog catcher to president. As an additional reward, each staff member is also a member of the sponsor group, and has some opportunity to apply his own ideas of what the government ought to do.[1]

Keeping Government Legitimate

The grant of power to the elected official is large—the right to tax, to spend, and to control the state's monopoly of force. In a going democracy, several important checks on this power are present. The candidate serves a limited term, after which his power automatically expires. When it does, the burden of proof is on him to show why it should be renewed, not on the people to show why it should be taken away. At election time he must defend his record against the programs of competing candidates, who will delight in displaying his errors and weaknesses.

If the incumbent has used his power illegitimately, this is the same as insubordination. In government, as in other organizations, this is imperative ground for removal, and competing candidates will be sure to report any such actions. Since serious illegitimate use of power in a democracy is more likely than any other one factor to bring defeat in the next elec-

---

[1] In important respects the present analysis follows that of Anthony Downs, *An Economic Theory of Democracy* (New York: Harper Bros., 1957). His model is intended primarily as a first approximation to the political party and candidate, and makes the maximization of votes the sole objective. The present analysis does not require so strict a list of motives, and hence includes some motives which Downs does not.

tion, the desire to avoid it is by the same token the most compelling influence on the official's exercise of power. All things considered, this is perhaps the most crucial aspect of the normal democratic process. Like the necessity of wearing clothes in public, this discipline in a well-functioning democracy is so strict and pervasive that it may hardly be given conscious attention. But it is precisely because legitimacy *is* so much taken for granted that attention at election time can be concentrated on programs and their performance.

Given the almost certain penalty at the polls for serious illegitimacy, the only way for officials to continue it would be to use the monopoly on force to seize power and rig, or do away with, elections. Other factors in an operative democracy prevent this. First, other members of the government are sponsors as well as staff. They would be sensitive to orders representing illegitimate authority, and probably refuse them. Second, since some lower officers are also elected, they would assume that to follow illegitimate orders would insure *their* defeat at the next election unless the *coup* were virtually guaranteed of success. This factor reinforces their resistance to illegitimate orders. Third, most democratic governments are constructed so that the cooperation of many separate parts is required before a would-be dictator can consolidate his position. The larger the number of separate groups which must acquiesce, the greater is the likelihood that his intentions will be conspicuously revealed long before he has consolidated his position far enough to abolish the elections which would oust him.

Together, the inability of elected officials to get a permanent grant of power *without* election, and the great resistance to permanent power *in* elections, provide the people's ability to keep the incipient dictator out of office, and maintain the core of the people's authority over government. However, if the voters feel such a sense of crisis that they condone illegitimate behavior, a rising dictator can eventually consolidate his position, as in Germany and Italy during the 1930's. In the United States there is presently concern in some quarters whether the sense of crisis has led the people to condone limitations on freedom of speech and political action which might make it easier to implement still further restrictions at a later date.

POLITICAL PARTIES

Except in small units of government, more than one office is filled by vote. Because it will facilitate running for office and executing programs once in office (among other things), noncompeting candidates for several different offices may form a joint program and run a joint campaign. The result is a political party.

Power Aspects and Some Notes on the Model

A political party is normally both a coalition and an organization. It will here be treated as a coalition, since its role in improving the bargaining position of those who wish to control government seems strongly to outweigh its efforts at joint production. The latter is done mostly by the government after the party gains power, rather than by the party itself. With recognition that a party *can* properly be considered an organization, we will nevertheless define a *political party* as a coalition of office seekers and their supporters designed to improve their power position in controlling the government. To *improve* means to make it higher than it would be without the coalition, which means in turn to get more for relatively less. The definition puts no limitations on what the party wants to achieve through its control of the government, and its desire may be a selfish raid of the public treasury, or a thoroughly unselfish improvement of the nation. The party may include citizens, candidates and office holders, and nonoffice-holding party workers, all of whose desires are part of the party's aims.

Under almost any degree of democracy or dictatorship the party coalition will improve the power of the top officers as against the subordinate staff. Under democracy it will also help to improve their power position with the electorate. In a dictatorship it will improve the power of one group as against any other person or group seeking to unseat it, either to establish democracy or to shift control of the dictatorship. In dictatorship it will also improve the power of anyone seeking to seize control from the ruling party.

This definition follows the lead of Roche and Stedman in distinguishing a political party from a pressure group on the basis that the former runs candidates for office, while the latter does not—at least not openly.[2] The present chapter will concentrate on the role of the party in democratic governments. To the extent that a political party can be considered an organization, it is clearly a pressure organization, since both its costs and its benefits are allocated to the sponsors. But even though the party is in significant degree an organization, its most distinctive features are those of coalition, on which aspect we will concentrate.[3]

---

[2] John P. Roche and Murray S. Stedman, *The Dynamics of Democratic Government* (New York: McGraw-Hill Book Co., Inc., 1954), p. 28.

[3] The above definition is similar to that of Downs (*op. cit.*, p. 240), but has significant differences. Downs defines a party as "a coalition of men seeking to control the governing apparatus by legal means." The major differences lie in his definition of *coalition*, which is essentially the same as *cooperation* in this volume, and in his absence of reference to bargaining power. Downs' restriction of "legal means" is useful for his model, but is not necessary here. The present usage in that respect is closer to prevailing usage, in that it includes dictatorial and revolutionary parties as well as democratic ones. Downs' second definition of the party as a *team* seems to have little greater significance than the definition as a coalition, and has no additional relevance to the present discussion.

Many political scientists use the term "party" without defining it. Some other definitions, which do not seem as useful for analytical purposes, are:

1. "The organized attempt of persons with competing beliefs and programs to win elections to public office." Robert Rienow, *Introduction to Government* (New York: Alfred Knopf, Inc., 1957), p. 246.

2. "An autonomous organized group that makes nominations and contests elec-

Although, according to one authority, the political party is at most three hundred years old,[4] and has performed an important political function for perhaps only half that time, it now seems so firmly established that it is very unlikely to disappear as a basic tool for controlling government, in either democracies or dictatorships.[5] Its analysis is essential to an understanding of government, and of the relations of the electorate to the government.

We will examine first the relationship where there are only two parties, each of which is a tightly knit and strongly disciplined coalition, and the electorate votes entirely by party lines—i.e., votes a straight ticket. The public's bargaining power is highest if both parties are vigorous and imaginative, since the public's power over one party lies in its ability to choose the other. If one party, however, has a much greater following and is unlikely to lose, the public's bargaining power drops dramatically. Such a condition may exist when for some reason the leaders in one party are incompetent but entrenched, so that the party cannot attract good candidates. Or it may occur because one party has been associated with some important historical event, whose psychological intensity is still strongly attached to the party years after the event is irrelevant. The continued attachment of the South to the Democratic Party a century after the Republicans aroused their ire during the Reconstruction is a notable instance. Or two nominally competing parties can cooperate, as in Austria.[6] The one which wins a majority assumes a few key posts, but gives the other party a more than generous share, so that neither is badly hurt if it loses at the polls. Here the bargaining power of the public declines to a low level, since it is deprived of meaningful alternatives.

Whatever its source, one sign of low bargaining power is large tax payments in return for government services, with tax money leaking into the pockets of officials, families, and friends, through government contracts and payrolls. Another sign is power regulation in which the power of the government is thrown heavily toward assisting the private transactions of government officials and friends.

Since the public's bargaining power depends mainly on competition,

tions in the hope of eventually gaining and exercising control of the personnel and policies of government." Austin Ranney, *The Governing of Men* (New York: Henry Holt & Co., 1958), p. 313.

3. "A group formulating comprehensive issues and submitting candidates in elections." Harold Lasswell and Abraham Kaplan, *Power and Society* (New Haven, Conn.: Yale University Press, 1950), p. 169.

4. "A body of men united, for promoting by their joint endeavors the national interest, upon some particular principle in which they are all agreed." Thomas Burke, quoted in Lasswell & Kaplan, *op. cit.*, p. 169.

[4] Karl Loewenstein, *Political Power and the Governmental Process* (Chicago: University of Chicago Press, 1957), p. 75.

[5] *Ibid.*, p. 77.

[6] Frederick C. Engleman, "Haggling for the Equilibrium: "the Renegotiation of the Austrian Coalition, 1959," *The American Political Science Review*, September, 1961, pp. 651–62.

where parties themselves do not compete, it may be possible to instill competition *within* the party. To a significant degree this has happened in the South. Knowing that Republicans are rarely elected, the people participate heavily in the Democratic primaries. Although the public cannot thus force the candidate to perform well to be *elected,* they can force him to perform well to be *nominated.* Although less evident, intraparty factions can perform much of the function of interparty competition, though the multiple-party arrangement is more reliable in general.

Political parties also provide stability and continuity of the major bargain between sponsor and staff. Without parties, a person in power not intending to run for re-election would hold a powerful bargaining position. With nothing to lose but his conscience, which might be expendable, he could raid the treasury and revise the power regulations to his own advantage during his final term. But the party *always* has another election ahead, and will therefore exert pressure on the individual to act as if he, too, faced another election.

In this same connection, we have seen that promises must be believed or they have no bargaining power. The way to get promises believed is to show a record of, and stake in, their fulfillment. Despite the common and sometimes well-based cynicism about election promises, the party does have a large stake in performing at least some important platform promises. The whole party therefore wants the elected officials to try to do what was promised. Without the party, government can easily become a succession of individuals who independently run for office on high promises, take their loot, and retire after one term. Having no rewards to withhold, the public then has no authority or bargaining power. But however single-termed the candidate's sights, the party must take a longer view. This fact increases the public's power over the party, and hence over the government staff.

This statement should not be misunderstood. The party pushes the shortsighted elected official to take a longer view of the staff's *relation to the public.* This may or may not coincide with a longer view of the public welfare, depending on the public's own view. If the public itself is farsighted, the party's long range interest puts pressure on the officials to respond in kind. But if the public is shortsighted, by bringing greater responsiveness to its will, the party may force the official to take a shorter view of the public good than he personally would do.

Before we look at decision processes of political parties, let us clarify the model we are using, which is similar to that of the market system in one important respect. The essence of the market system is that in no way does it expect or rely upon unselfish, socially oriented behavior. It so arranges things that the selfish decisions of the individual will collectively produce a socially desirable result. The present model of social decision making and the control of government also does not assume or expect unselfish behavior by any individual. In this respect it follows the model of organization in earlier chapters, and the approach of Downs[7] which consciously follows Schumpeter.[8] In this model the sponsors do not rely upon the staff's holding a sponsor interest, but upon a major bargain with the staff members that motivates them to aim for sponsors' goals.[9]

To say that the individual will work to satisfy *his* goals does not mean that his goals are always or totally at odds with those of the public. In government, as in private organizations, some members of the staff do share sponsor goals. In the first place, every member of the staff is normally himself a citizen, and may want good government as much as anyone else. Second, sympathy and a desire to feel useful are not uncommon motives. Just as the factory manager can get deep satisfaction from seeing his plant run well, so can an elected official get satisfaction from helping to provide good government.

When candidates are found who hold strong sponsor goals, the power of the public rises in at least two ways. First, these goals in the official lead him to socially desired behavior far more fully than does any formal reward system in the sponsor-staff bargain. Second, when the official has a large stake of his own in doing well, he has much lower bargaining power in *not* giving as much to the public. There *are* such things as dedicated public servants, who do a good job despite low pay and criticism, and the people get a good bargain when they elect them. The public will probably get more of them, however, if it rewards them more highly than undedicated ones.

Decision Aspects Within Parties

The preceding discussion indicates that there are two major steps in the political decision process. The first is the formation of the party platform and the selection of candidates, and the second is the choice between parties by the voters. The power effects of the second step have

---

[7] *Op. cit.*

[8] Joseph A. Schumpeter, *Capitalism, Socialism, and Democracy* (New York: Harper Bros., 1950), as noted in Downs, p. 29.

[9] Much of the teaching of government in public schools, and some in colleges, employs an implicit model which expects unselfish behavior by government staff. The government is expected to do things because they are "needed," or "in the public good." People who learn this model typically become disillusioned and cynical when they later learn the actual details of politics. By contrast, the present model does not expect anyone to do anything not personally rewarding. This model seems to give both greater understanding of reality and greater potential for plans to improve it.

Phrased in a different context, popular models of government expect a different morality or set of motivations than the popular models of business. By contrast, the present model follows the earlier chapters on psychology, in which all persons do only those things that are rewarding *to them*. This model does not, however, restrict behavior to selfish acts, since unselfish ones can often be highly rewarding. In this context the problem of achieving good government is that of creating organizational arrangements in which socially desired behavior will be rewarding to the individual in government.

already been seen. We will now examine intraparty decisions, and the interacting effects of those decisions and elections on the total social decision process. If the voters are to have a choice between only two alternatives, the formulation of those alternatives is a crucial part of the total mechanism. We will continue the assumptions of strong discipline and the presence of only two parties. For the moment we will also assume a single electoral unit, with no political subdivisions voting as blocs.

The party has been discussed thus far mainly in terms of candidates. Beyond them is a vaguely defined and changing group of pressure groups, party professionals, contributors, and interested citizens. Their motives are various. Pressure groups represented in party councils include manufacturers and trade associations, unions, retailers, racial and religious groups, veterans, and recipients of social security benefits—to mention only a few. The main interest of the pressure groups is to get the government to shift the power rules in their favor, or to increase their share of government output or decrease their share of input. Interested citizens may work in the party from a sense of civic duty, from lack of other activity, or from enjoyment of the companionship, power, or sense of accomplishment. Party "professionals" are often lawyers who feel the contacts will enlarge their clientele, contractors who hope to get better access to government construction, prospective candidates who want to build experience, or others looking for a source of income. The professionals may or may not be paid, but a party of substantial size will usually have some full or part time paid personnel, such as a county chairman or executive secretary, and some stenographers. The party workers typically rise to large numbers just before election and dwindle to a handful at other times.

Leadership in the party is largely informal, and depends on the factors described in Chapter 26. It gravitates to those who are willing to do the party's work. They determine how the details of work will be done, because they do them. They acquire the knowledge and skill of experience, and their voice thereafter carries more weight. They maintain contacts with the voters and learn how to influence their decisions. Hence, their assertions that "this policy will bring us lots of votes" are taken seriously. As with other informal leaders, their advice must work, or it will no longer be heeded. The party leaders may or may not themselves run for office or accept appointive offices in government, depending on their inclinations and abilities.

The central goal of the party organization is to win elections, and in the main the power of any individual in deciding what goes into the party platform depends on the value of his contribution of advice, work, or money toward that goal. In this combination, the contributor of money carries definite, but not necessarily controlling, weight. Money is necessary to pay for telephones, publicity, rents, and travel expenses. These all help to gain votes. But if a policy supported by a large contributor seems likely to lose more votes than his contribution can gain, his policy may not appear in the platform. If the reverse is true, the large contributor may be able to "buy" a plank in the platform, or at least a sharp rewording of an existing plank. Even those in the party who have no interest except the public good may agree to these modifications, in the feeling that the party can do more good if elected "with strings" than if defeated without them.

Votes are the dominating instrumental goal of the party. If a successful and popular incumbent seems almost certain to be re-elected if he runs, and if the party has no other candidates who seem likely to win, the incumbent holds tremendous power in the party, at least regarding the platform on which he himself will run. If his popularity is likely to rub off onto other candidates, who can "ride his coat tails," he can influence the platform for them as well. But if his popularity brings votes only for himself, he loses that power. A candidate strong enough to win without party help, but without the "coat tails" effect, may maintain only a loose affiliation with the party machine, which may write off its ability to control him but refuse to let him have much to say. Because most elected officials control some patronage, the party will nevertheless be reluctant to drop the relation entirely.

The detailed influences on party decisions about policy are endless. Someone in the active party group has a friend who knows the newspaper editor, who might swing his support to the party if it will weaken its platform on government medicine. Another knows a prominent citizen, and thinks he can be talked into endorsing the party if it will support a strong ordinance for zoning. A large industry might move into the high unemployment area if the tax or labor laws are changed. Or the Negro vote may be lost unless the party takes a strong stand on civil rights.

All of this is only the barest outline of things. But these are the kinds of forces which operate within the party to determine what it will support and what it will not. They are many, complex, uncertain, and mostly incapable of measurement. In detail these activities may seem little concerned with the public good. But they are seldom unconcerned with the vote—which is another way of saying that the vote and the public good may not be closely related. How far apart they can be depends, among other things, on the way in which one party responds to the behavior of the other, to which subject we now turn.

Decision Aspects Between Parties

The kinds of forces at work in one party are in actuality working simultaneously in both. Whether Mr. Wealthy will contribute to the party, or Mr. Influential endorse it, depends not merely on what this party does, but also on what the other one does. Whether the Italian vote will go for the party's Italian candidate will depend on whether the other party also nominates an Italian, and who he is.

This interparty relationship gives no advance knowledge of which precise details will have to be considered in any particular situation. But it does provide a rather reliable prediction of certain broad patterns of behavior. These are widely known among political scientists, and are often viewed somewhat deprecatingly by the public. Downs provides a useful analysis of them,[10] which we will summarize here.

To win, a party must assemble that combination of issues and candidates which will capture the votes of a majority of the *people*. Because it is difficult to generalize about the appeal of candidates, we will confine attention to issues. On first thought, one is apt to think that a party can capture most votes if it takes a majority position on every issue. Circumstances could exist where this would be the case, but they are so rare that they can be ignored. The group of people who make up the majority on one issue are not the same as those who are the majority on another. Further, not all people have the same intensity of feelings about different issues. To woo a *majority* of the *people*, the party must normally adopt the *minority* view on *some issues*. It is even possible, but unlikely, that a party could get the most votes with a minority position on every issue. How this could happen can be illustrated by a simple two-group, two-issue election. For the moment we will ignore the question of which party takes what stand, and examine only the sentiments.

Suppose a political unit contains 100 farmers and 100 city dwellers, and that the campaign hinges on two issues, farm price supports and prohibition. On the farm the price supports are a strong issue and prohibition a weak one, the situation in the city being the reverse. A *strong* issue is one which alone will decide a person's vote if the parties differ on that issue, all other issues being irrelevant to the voter. A *weak* issue is one which will determine a person's vote if, but only if, the parties agree on the strong issue and differ on the weak one.

Assume that the votes are distributed as in Table 34-1:

Table 34-1

		Rural Vote	Urban Vote	Total Vote
Price supports	For	80	10	90
	Against	20	90	110
Prohibition	For	80	40	120
	Against	20	60	80

The figures in Table 1 show majorities *for* prohibition and *against* price supports, and in separate referendums, prohibition would be adopted and price supports rejected. However, if people cannot vote separately on the

[10] *Op. cit.*, especially chaps. 2 and 3.

issues, but only for or against a party which takes a stand simultaneously on both, the difference in intensity between strong and weak issues becomes important. Let us examine which combination of issues will bring the largest total vote, as weighted by strong and weak positions. Table 34-2

Table 34-2

Platform	Issues		Votes		
	Price Supports	Prohibition	Rural	Urban	Total
A	For	For	80	40	120
B	For	Against	80	60	140
C	Against	For	20	40	60
D	Against	Against	20	60	80

rearranges the figures of Table 1 to show how the vote will go on a joint basis, assuming that the farm vote will be determined solely by the price support issue, and the city vote solely by prohibition. We now see that the largest number of votes is commanded by platform B, *for* price supports and *against* prohibition, which is the minority position among the whole 200 voters on both issues.

What a party is able to do depends on whether it is in or out of power, and on what the other party does. If a party is *in* power, and is planning to run on its record (instead of its promises), and if it has complete information on voter sentiments, it will presumably enact legislation incorporating the minority position on both issues.[11]

By contrast, if neither issue has yet been enacted, and both parties are campaigning on promises, things are far more complicated, and we can trace only a few cases to illustrate their nature. Seeing that the farmers show a heavier majority on their strong issue than the city dwellers do on theirs, both parties might endorse price supports. If so, price supports are no longer an issue in the farm vote, which now hinges on the weak issue of prohibition. If Party A is for prohibition and B against it, the farmers will give 80 votes to A and 20 to B. The city will give 40 votes to A and 60 to B. Since prohibition is the *only* question at issue, it will win for the party which adopts the majority position on it, which is A.

Suppose instead that both parties are more impressed by the majority against prohibition in the cities, and both take a stand against it, while Party A endorses price supports and B opposes them. By the same reasoning as before, with only price supports at issue, Party B will win the election, since it has endorsed the majority view on that issue. In both illustrations, the winning combination consists of one minority and one majority position, not the majority on both.

---

[11] Most readers will accept without demonstration that a party may get the most votes by taking majority positions. To keep down the number of examples, we are showing only the ones the reader is not likely to accept intuitively, namely those in which the most votes can be commanded by minority positions. To show that these are *possible* does not mean that they are *necessary*, and majority positions *can* win.

We now come to the complication of strategies. From Table 34-2 we can see that combination B commands more votes than any other. This might suggest that the party which adopts its platform first can pick that combination and leave the other party helpless. Not at all. Platform B would command more votes than any other *if only one platform were available to the voters*. As soon as one party chooses a platform that includes at least one minority position, the other party can then match it on all issues except on one minority position, and take the majority position on that issue. As seen above, if the parties are alike on one issue, the party that endorses the majority position on the other issue wins. If Party B were to select platform B, Party A could then win by taking the same position as Party B on *either* issue, and the opposite position on the other, since B has taken the minority view on both. If Party A were so stupid as to oppose B on *both* issues, however, it would lose, with only 20 votes from the farm and 40 from the city. Party B would win with what Downs calls a "coalition of minorities."[12]

We might now be inclined to jump to the opposite conclusion, that the party which adopts its platform last could always win, by matching the other on all points except one minority issue. This would be the case if the drafters of the platform had perfect knowledge of the voters' preferences on all issues, if voters did not change their minds, if no circumstance changed between platform drafting and election, if issues were solely relevant and candidates irrelevant, and if the campaign itself had no influence on voters—and we are hardly in imminent danger of this result. In fact, candidates keep tuned to voters' wave lengths as best they can, and typically keep "reinterpreting" their platforms up to election day. As further complications, many issues do not demand simple yes or no stands, but allow a party to take any of a dozen or more variant positions, including words that seem to say whatever the voter prefers.

Political platforms deal not only with affirmative or negative stands on issues, but also with stands of varying strengths. To give just one among many possible illustrations, if an issue is already a strong one and the opposing party has taken a majority position on it, the first party can then take a *stronger* stand on the majority side. The Communist issue has appeared in this role repeatedly in the past decade or so in the United States. Any party knows that if Communist subversion can be made to appear sufficiently menacing, it can readily be built into a dominantly strong issue. If it wishes to use this, the party's (or candidate's) first move is, by fear tactics or otherwise, to generate enough concern to make anti-Communism a dominantly strong issue. The second move is to take a stand which is conspicuously *more* anti-Communist than that of the opponents.

The same strategic logic applies to *any* issue which seems of potential

---

[12] The above examples are my own. The reasoning behind them is that of Downs, *op. cit.*, pp. 55–60.

overriding importance to an electorate. The inherent nature of the situation is such as almost inevitably to lead some party or candidate both to exaggerate the importance of the issue and to take exaggerated stands on it.

In short, a party must take a stand on many issues. In doing so it seeks a majority of *votes*, which can rarely be gained through a majority stand on each *issue*. Any party platform that hopes to win necessarily incorporates a coalition of majority and minority groups of the electorate. Only by accident will either the voter or the active party worker (including the candidate himself), approve of the party's stand on every issue. The party's posture at any one moment is a coalition of divergent interests designed to command the most votes, but not necessarily to please anyone in its totality. This is apparently the inescapable logic of public decisions through the two party system.

The Candidate, and the Subculture. The preceding analysis was couched solely in terms of issues. Candidates also are obviously important, and can be analyzed as follows.

The personal appeal of the candidate can be viewed in the same framework as if it were an issue in the election. To illustrate, if a person highly appealing to voters as an individual were to run on a pro-integration platform in Alabama or Mississippi against a highly objectional individual running on a pro-segregation platform, the latter would win. This is the equivalent of saying that the racial issue is dominantly strong, and that the personality of the candidate by comparison is a weak issue. However, if both candidates take the same stand on the racial issue, which is the strong one, the weak issue then determines the outcome, and the more appealing personality wins.

The strategy appropriate for party victory can be deduced from this relationship. If a party has a very strong candidate, its strategy for victory is to move close to the other party on all significant issues, so that the difference in personality is the only serious "issue" in the election. If its candidate is personally unappealing, however, it needs to take a majority position on some issue which is, or can be made into, a strong one, but on which the opposing party has taken a minority position.

If no important issues of policy arise in the campaign, the personality of the candidate by default will occupy the strong position, and determine the outcome. The one important distinction between candidates and issues is that the same candidate can be the more appealing in every major group in the nation. Except for those involving national survival, few issues have this degree of universality of appeal. For this reason political parties presumably give more attention to personalities of candidates than they otherwise would give.

As with other social phenomena, habit and culture have their influence here. For no other reason than sheer habit a person may regularly vote for the nominee of his party, regardless of who the candidate is or what the issues. He thereby also greatly reduces the information cost of his decision. To cast his vote, all he needs to know is the party label of the candidate.

Others take their cues from the particular subculture which is their reference group for matters political. This, too, keeps information costs low. All one needs for a decision is to ask how his friends are voting.

The Political Spectrum.   Under normal circumstances, the election of one party indicates that its coalition commands more votes than the coalition in the opposing party. This fact gives it the authority to mold the government in the direction desired by the component groups of that coalition, if they can agree what that is. (The winning party will normally make a more imposing statement about what its "mandate" implies, while the opponents will try to discount it.) On the other hand, if the election has featured one dominant theme, large or small, and the public and the parties generally understood that this issue was "strong" to most citizens, the election *would* be a clear mandate to carry out that program.

If a dominant issue or mood prevails in an electorate, some fairly reliable predictions are possible about party orientations regarding it. Let us assume first that the attitudes on the issue fall roughly into a normal distribution, with the majority bunched close to the middle and the minorities tapering off to the extremes, as follows:

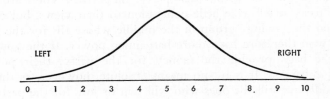

The height of the curve represents the number of persons at any one position, and the numbers along the horizontal scale are arbitrary points on the political spectrum. Suppose Party A should adopt a position well to the left of center, as at 3. Party B could then take a position between A's stance and the center, as at 4, with the certainty it would win. Most voters to the right of 4 might feel that B was too far left for their taste. But B is their best alternative, since A is even farther left. Assuming that the voters between 3 and 4 divide equally at 3.5, Party B would get all the voters to the right of 3.5, who are the large majority.

Now suppose instead that some members of Party B want to give the voters a real choice, instead of snuggling so close to A. If Party B were to follow this recommendation, as by taking a position at 7, it would drop from a sure victory to a 50–50 chance, assuming that A remains at 3. Whether we examine the professional politicians, who are interested solely in a winning platform, or that part of the party following who want to acomplish something in the area of 8, a victory with any platform to the right of 3 is better than defeat. This conclusion is based on the analysis of one election by itself. If voters take a longer view, those to the right might prefer to let A win, and adopt its program, assuming that the program will fail and push the voters farther to the right in the next election.

On the basis of this analysis, one party will prefer to push the other as far as possible to that party's side of center, and then to adopt a position between that point and center. The closer one party can get to the other while remaining distinguishably different, the greater is its likelihood of victory. The other party, of course, is guided by a similar logic, but is pushing in the opposite direction. Since either party puts itself in danger by moving far from center, the tendency is toward an equilibrium with both parties near center, but distinguishably different, at least oratorically. In this situation the voters can choose one party or the other. And they can force either party to take a stand on any issue. But there is no apparent method by which they can force one party to move very far from the other, even by abstentions, which can be effective under other circumstances to be seen below.

This situation can be expressed in the language of bargaining power. Voters toward the extreme of their distribution will not vote for the opposite party, no matter what. This is the same as having a large Effective Preference for the party closest to themselves, which gives them low bargaining power within that party. Since their votes are "in the bag," the party need make little concession to their views, but can concentrate on the "swing" group in the middle whose EP for the party is low, and who therefore have more bargaining power. If the voters who are "in the bag" provide the money for the party, their power, of course, is enhanced. It is by no means absolute, however, as the voters in the middle are still the ones who will win or lose for the party. Also, the professionals tend to hold the upper hand, with the proposition: "You may not like this, but if you don't accept it the other party will win."

Again the facts are more complex than the diagram. No one is sure where the precise center is, or whether the distribution is symmetrical around it. The diagram illustrates positions only along a single dimension of a problem, which is unrealistic, since most problems have many dimensions. Despite these reservations, this line of reasoning nevertheless does seem to describe the general facts of two-party behavior fairly well. One of the most frequent complaints of two-party elections is that the voter can hardly tell the parties apart.

If the population is split into two divergent groups (rather than being massed at the center), the two parties may follow the same pattern as the population. In countries with a distinct upper and lower class, with little middle class, one party may support each class. This is diagrammed by Downs[13] as illustrated at the top of page 671.

If Party A assumes a position at 2, then it might seem rational for Party B to take its stance at 3 or 4, on the assumption that all voters to the

---

[13] *Op. cit.,* p. 119.

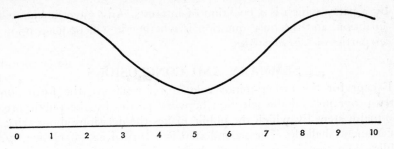

| 0 | 1 | 2 | 3 | 4 | 5 | 6 | 7 | 8 | 9 | 10 |

right of 3 (an obvious majority) would find B a better alternative than A, even though not a satisfactory one. However, some voters, say to the right of 7, might decide that the election of a party oriented at 3 will be so little better than one oriented at 2 that it is better not to vote at all. If they abstain, then Party A will win. This is no immediate consolation to the abstainers, but it may force Party B to move far enough to the right at the next election to attract the rightist group, perhaps to 7 or 8. Under this kind of population distribution the two parties will tend to remain far apart. The logic of each party is to move as far toward the center as it can without causing the extremists at its own end to abstain. If there are no abstentions, the pressure is toward the middle, as with the unimodal population.

Other distributions of the population can exist, and have different effects. We need not go into them, however, as we have come far enough to see the logic by which a party chooses its position.

More Than Two Parties

If the eventual social decision is somewhat ambiguous under two parties, it is more so under a multiparty system. Under, say, five parties, each will tend to cater to some one section of the population. Here each voter may find a party whose platform reflects his views fairly well. But when he votes for that *party*, he is very uncertain what kind of *government* he will get. In the legislature, no one party will command a majority, and the passage of any law will require a coalition. But who will coalesce with whom, when, and on what issues, depends on such shifting fortunes that the voter has no advance assurance what measures *his* party will actually vote for. To know when he casts it what the effect of his vote would eventually be, the voter would have to be able to predict (1) the distribution of votes among parties, (2) the coalitions which these parties would form after election, and (3) the compromises that would be necessary to achieve these coalitions. The professionals cannot know this, much less the average voter.

A comparison of the two-party and multiparty systems reveals an important conclusion. The people of a democracy face two major alternatives. They can be ruled by a government which is a coalition of parties, or by a party which is a coalition of interests. Any government will be by coalition, and the only question is whether it will be a coalition *between* parties or *within* parties.

SUMMARY AND CONCLUSIONS

Except for the rather minor role of referendums, the formation of party programs and the selection between parties by the public are the two major steps by which the public makes the decisions about what the government shall do. The second step is a formal act of choice by the public. The first is an informal decision by semiprivate groups about what the public is likely to accept. In a limited sense, the parties parallel the behavior of firms. First, the organizations try to find out what the people want, and produce it. Second, competing organizations offer their products to the public, which selects the one it prefers. In both the firm and the party, the first step decision reflects the wants of both the public and the organization. Also in both, the state of competition between organizations is the major determinant of how good a product the public can get when it chooses, and whether the public or the organization will benefit more.

The second stage is a collective decision. If the public chooses on a straight party basis between two parties, the preference ordering of the composite decision will be the same as that of a majority of the voters. If there are more than two parties, or if voters split their tickets, the resulting decision may or may not bear some meaningful relation to the preferences of the public. The first stage is not a collective decision, but a process of forming coalitions of divergent sponsor interests, in a competitive effort to find which coalition will command the most votes. This is the crucial process of narrowing the decision—of formulating the alternatives between which the public will choose. The party that assembles the dominant coalition of interests takes control of the government. As Schumpeter put it,

> The democratic method is that institutional arrangement for arriving at political decisions in which individuals acquire the power to decide by means of a competitive struggle for the people's vote.[14]

This is the main story, but a few other items seem worth noting before we leave it.

Of the various kinds of arrangements, the power of the people is probably greatest in a system with only two significant parties, both well-disciplined. Each must keep its ear well-tuned to public sentiment and the relative strength of its factions, and must perform well when in office, or it will not win. Referring to the British government, which is perhaps the sharpest instance of such disciplined, two-party government, Loewenstein observes:

---

[14] Joseph Schumpeter, *op. cit.*, p. 269.

Easily one of the most successful patterns of government of our time—and, possibly, of all times—it is predicated on the existence of two, and not more, competing and alternating parties, with the electorate holding the balance of power between them.[15]

For all practical purposes, when a party is given a victory in England, it can enact and put into effect any piece of legislation in its platform. Any member of parliament who does not support the party's proposals will not receive the party support in the next election, and will probably be defeated. If the Prime Minister does not get majority support on any important measure, he can dissolve the parliament and call a new election. The majority party *is in charge*. The government's successes are its successes, and the government's failures are its failures. Although evaluating a government is at best a difficult and highly subjective task, under disciplined, two-party government at least the voters know who is responsible for what.

The United States may best be described as multiparty government in two-party clothing.[16] Perhaps of greatest importance, there exists no significant, national party organization except just before presidential elections. Only in recent years have the parties maintained a full time, national party chairman, and his powers and functions are still somewhat vague and unstable. The solid bases of the parties are their state, county, and smaller divisions, which run candidates of some sort every year. These differ widely in geographical and ideological constituencies. For example, the Democratic Party in California differs far more from the Democratic Party in Maine or Georgia than it does from the Republican Party in California, and there is little the sporadic national party, including the President, can do to bring them into line. The result is that it is not uncommon for the President to have substantial majorities of what is nominally his own party in both houses of Congress, and still be unable to get enactment of key items in the national party's platform.

This kind of situation is virtually unheard of in England, and makes it difficult for the voter to know who is responsible for what. The core of the problem is that the members of the Congress are basically regional, not national, representatives, and often tend to vote the interests of their regions, not of the nation.[17] Again, the national party in the United States, unlike the ones in England, cannot assuredly stop re-election of a disaffected member of the party, and hence cannot discipline him. Considering that members of Congress are elected from a local constituency

---

15 Karl Loewenstein, *op. cit.*, p. 104.

16 *Ibid.*, p. 111.

17 As an illustration of the regional orientation, a couple of weeks before writing this section, I wrote to my Congressman. This representative was opposing a crucial item in the President's foreign policy on the ground that it *might temporarily* increase unemployment in *one* county in his district, and I wrote to suggest (in somewhat different language) that beating the Soviets in a no-holds fight perhaps calls for sterner stuff.

for essentially local motives, and that the national party has no effective disciplinary powers, "The remarkable thing is not that so few legislators will risk their local positions [to support the national interest], but that so many will."[18]

It is by no means certain, however, that the form is the essential difference between England and the United States. Disciplined, two-party government is possible in England because the population is relatively compact and homogeneous. The population of the United States, by contrast, is dispersed and diverse. Attempted discipline by the two major parties might bring *not* discipline, but defection, openly acknowledged multi-party government, and perhaps even less discipline than at present.

Blocks and Third Parties

In the United States, votes for president are counted by states, the whole vote of the state going to the winner within the state. This occasionally puts a president into office with less than a majority of the total vote. Its more significant effect, however, is to give tremendous political power to those in charge of the party apparatus in key cities in key states —such as New York, Philadelphia, Chicago, and Los Angeles. As a result, in these cities presidents sometimes endorse candidates they would rather drown. If it were desired to use more highly disciplined party government, an essential step would presumably be to reduce the power of the state parties by making the election of the president hinge on a majority vote of the whole nation, without regard to the division of the vote within states. This would require a constitutional amendment which must be approved by three fourths of the states, which means, in effect, by the state party machinery. This approval would hardly be given, since it would greatly reduce the power of these machines.

Even with only weak discipline in the two major parties, it seems unlikely that a third party will arise. A sharply left-wing party would pull most of its membership from the Democrats and assure Republican victory, which would hardly please the new party. Similarly, a sharply right-wing third party would draw from the Republicans and assure Democratic victory. This is the rock on which third party movements in the United States (except in local areas, notably New York City) have typically foundered, and seem likely to continue to founder. Should such a party by some strange circumstances beat out a major party, it would itself in due time move toward the center, by the logic described earlier.

The Definition of Party

Many pages ago in this chapter we defined the party, and we have not referred to the definition since. How or wherein does the subsequent

[18] David B. Truman, *The Governmental Process* (New York: Alfred Knopf, Inc., 1951), p. 533.

analysis follow the definition? As a coalition of office seekers and their supporters, designed to improve their power in controlling government, the party succeeds in several directions. Most directly, it gives the elected officials, and through them their supporters, increased power over the permanent employees of the government. The permanent staff could often ignore the lone elected officeholder with impunity. But if all elected officers are joined into a party, which selects all the top bosses of all departments and bureaus, such ignoring is far less feasible. And besides, though individuals come and go, the party goes on forever.

On the sponsor side, both candidates and supporters are more likely to get what they want, which represents an increase in their power. The lone voter, and even the lone pressure group, is lost in a mass of voters, and has little chance of electing its own representative. But if individuals and groups with mutually supporting interests join together, they may collectively be able to elect a representative of their point of view. Similarly, a candidate on his own among dozens or hundreds has only a remote chance. But if he can gather numerous voters and groups together and say, "I will do what all of you want if you will all vote for me, and help me get other votes," he greatly improves his chances. Both candidates and supporters thus raise their power. We have already mentioned that noncompeting candidates running simultaneously for different posts increase the effectiveness of their campaign by joining together. The description of the well-disciplined party shows the further advantage of being able to get legislation passed once the candidates are elected, which is an increase in the power of the supporters as well as of the candidates. The offsetting disadvantage is that, by joining with others, one will pick up their enemies as well as their friends, and sometimes be defeated when he otherwise would have won. Although this sometimes happens, and is a *decrease* in power, one does not join a party as candidate or supporter unless he *expects* it to help him. The definition accommodates this fact, by saying only that the party is *designed* to increase power, not that it necessarily does.

Although we have discussed only democratic systems, the party is even more the instrument for exercising control and raising power in the dictatorship, to be seen later.

Conclusion

We have tried to trace only a few of what seem to be the dominant forces which determine the nature and outcome of the decision process by which sponsors exercise their influence over the government organization. If the sponsors of this large cooperative are relatively homogeneous in their desires, they can succeed in getting something relatively close to what they want if there are only two significant, well-disciplined parties. If the population is more diverse, there simply is no such thing as a consensus set of desires, except on occasional issues of overriding importance with clearcut alternatives. Whether the population is diverse or homogeneous, each party is a coalition of at least somewhat discrepant forces, and the alternative to this situation is a government which is a coalition of discrepant parties. The latter is apparently the less satisfactory system. Other systems may show various combinations or permutations. But the ingredients are always the same—coalitions *within* parties, coalitions *between* parties, or some mixture. To revert to the language of earlier chapters, whatever may be the relation of the end product to the wishes of the underlying population, that end product may be referred to as *the political consensus*. Like the market consensus, it is the value actually produced, whether or not its ingredients can be traced after the fact.

Although we cannot say what the relation is between the consensus and the wishes of the underlying population, unless the system uses a highly complex multiparty arrangement, government by competing parties will normally detect, report, and promptly punish serious illegitimate action. It thus assures the continuance of the people's ability to turn a seriously offending government out of office. Whatever else it may or may not include, this is by large odds the most important single ingredient of the democratic process. The invasion of the rights of citizens by congressional committees investigating alleged subversion is perhaps the most conspicuous instance of illegitimate behavior in the United States in recent decades which has gone unpunished at the polls. The reason apparently follows the lines cited earlier—that the persons involved build the national safety into an overwhelmingly strong issue allegedly more important than legitimacy itself, and then take a *stronger* position on subversion than anyone else. The basic technique is the same as that by which Hitler and Mussolini rationalized the illegitimacies on which they rode to power. This problem is related to the crisis dictatorship, to be discussed in Chapter 37.

Chapter 35

SPONSOR DECISIONS: PRESSURE GROUPS

MOST PEOPLE are too busy looking out for their own interests to take care of the interests of others, with the result that anyone who does *not* defend his own interests is apt to find them undefended.

If people find their interests can better be served by changing the shape of the society around them, few have sufficient influence to accomplish such changes by their own personal efforts. The result of these two factors is that in advanced nations where persons are free to do so, they tend to organize to defend and promote their particular interests.

Viewed in the large, all private organizations are instances of coordinated action by citizens to achieve some goals. We have already discussed firms in great detail in connection with the market system, and have seen the general nature and purposes of cooperative, service, and pressure organizations. All are important parts of the informal organization of society, and perform important functions. The aggregate effect of the production and bargaining activities of all these organizations is an important part of the total decision process of the whole society, in the same sense that the aggregate effect of millions of separate decisions in the market produce a total social decision, though we thus far have no analytical system for studying these effects comparable to that of economics for studying markets. As to the private effects of these private organizations other than firms, there is little to say about them except (1) to describe particular organizations and their relationships in more detail, or (2) to leave them, with the observation that the general principles of their operation have already been covered in previous chapters. We will take the second route.

Pressure organizations perform more than private functions, however, as many spend much energy trying to influence government. Such behavior is a significant part of the total control of government, and must take its place alongside political parties and votes as part of the public decision mechanism.

The pressure organization, or pressure group, as it is more commonly called, follows the characteristics described in Chapter 22. Given a relation between A and B, A uses some group, P, to exert influence directly or indirectly on B so as to improve A's position in the A-B relationship. In this chapter we will think of A as some private individual, organization, or coalition. If A is dealing with the government, B, as in the case of a contractor building roads or selling materials to it, P might be a lobby for A trying to influence the terms of that relation. Or if A is dealing with some other private party, B, P might influence the government to throw its influence on A's side in the A-B relation. A might also be a taxpayer using P to try to get his taxes reduced, or a beneficiary of government action trying to get more of the benefits. In short, our interest in this chapter is in any relation in which A seeks influence on or by government to improve his relations with government or with others. Straightforward transactions between A and the government are not included, since they fall outside the definition of pressure operations.

Among the more prominent examples of pressure organizations are the Chamber of Commerce, the National Association of Manufacturers, labor unions and the AFL-CIO federation, trade associations, professional associations, the American Legion and the American Veterans' Committee, The American Civil Liberties Union, the National Education Association, and a host of others. Pressure groups can work on the government at any level from township and precinct to the federal government; on legislative, executive, or judicial branch; on the voters; on the parties; or on the Constitution. The remainder of the chapter will examine the nature of some of these influences in the United States.

PRESSURES ON PARTIES

In this country pressure organizations make relatively little direct financial contribution to political parties. Most have functions other than political pressure, and are chartered as nonprofit corporations, which could lose their tax-exempt status if they contribute. Corporations and unions are specifically prohibited by the Taft-Hartley Act from making contributions in connection with national elections, and others prefer to exert their influence in different ways.

Pressure organizations nevertheless often perform chores for the party, such as typing, duplicating, mailing, collecting information and preparing bulletins, running errands, making phone calls, arranging large meetings, and sometimes traveling. Employees of pressure groups often do these things on their employer's time and expense account. Many pressure groups maintain a panel of speakers whose topics, while technically nonpartisan, often mesh closely with the needs of the party. Republican parties can often find a suitable speaker for a meeting from a business, Chamber of Commerce, or trade association list, and the Democrats from these or a labor union list. During an election campaign in 1958 on the so-called "right-to-work" issue, for example, I appeared on several discussion panels with representatives of companies and unions whose time was paid for by their respective organizations. Although the talks were technically "nonpolitical," the firms and unions which provided the speakers were obviously spending money in support of a party position in an effort to influence votes. In these and many other ways corporations, unions, and trade and professional associations work parallel with party objectives, sometimes technically aloof, but nevertheless cooperating.

Where open connection with a party might embarrass an organization, some of its members may work in the party as individuals, and the organization may encourage and facilitate such "civic" activities. Though this encouragement may be overtly nonpartisan, employees of business typically work for the Republicans and of unions for the Democrats. The distinction is not absolute, however. Some unions are Republican in orientation, and some businesses Democratic. Further, neither group feels it safe to be completely unrepresented in *either* party, with the result that both groups have some representation in both parties.

Negative pressures may be applied as well as cooperation. "We have 5,000 members in our group, and most of them will vote against you if you do that" is a typical kind of pressure on the party organization.

PRESSURES ON LEGISLATORS

In addition to efforts to elect or defeat particular legislators, pressure groups work on them while they are in office. Since legislators, from township trustees to senators, make policies, the pressure on them is often intense.

An important way to influence legislators is to testify in committee hearings on a bill. Such testimony may range from a simple statement of preference to an extensive presentation of charts, diagrams, motion pictures, and printed research reports. On important legislation a group may send dozens of experts to testify. If the interested pressure groups include a wide variety of opinion they may do much to clarify the problem. If not, they may generate a highly biased view. Even if the bias is recognized, if no opposing views are presented it may still have a one-sided influence.

The life of the typical legislator is filled with "contacts" from special interests. They often attempt to rationalize their position as being in the public interest, though some simply state what they want. These requests may be accompanied by promises of votes or threats of nonvotes, gifts, or offers of personal advantage. The effectiveness of these pressures depends on many factors, such as the length of time until the next election, the size and political cohesion of the pressure group, the degree of understanding they display, and the number and size of opposing groups. With experience, legislators learn which groups they must attend to and which they can afford to ignore.

In total, pressure groups apparently overrepresent the special interest and underrepresent the general. The business, union, or profession which thinks that some legislation means millions of dollars to itself or members will readily spend thousands to influence it. Even though these millions of dollars may come from the general public in taxes, higher prices, or less government benefit, not enough will come from any individual or group to make it seem worthwhile spending for counterinfluence. Typically, producer interests (whether of business, labor, or investors) are more than proportionately represented, since they are concentrated interests, while the diffuse consumer interests are less than proportionately represented.

This does not mean that the concentrated lobby necessarily wins against a relatively diffuse larger interest. In 1961, for instance, lobbyists for the billboard advertising industry were extremely active in Washington against the control of billboards along interstate highways. Some miscellaneous groups, such as garden clubs and the American Automobile Association, fought for controls. Despite much heavier and more costly efforts by the billboard industry, the controls were voted.

Much lobbying is directed at legislative switching mechanisms, such as the Rules Committee, which determines whether a bill will be scheduled for debate, the committee that studies the bill, and particularly the chairman or uncommitted members of the committee(s). In committees as with the whole electorate, the uncommitted minority is the "switch" which determines the outcome.

INFLUENCE ON ADMINISTRATORS

The law is but the shell of policy. A strong law can be nullified, or a weak one made useful, by those who carry it out. Most of this work is done by bureaus, commissions, departments, agencies, boards or other divisions of government. An important aspect of administration is to classify cases as covered or not covered by the law. The federal law provides, for example, that the government will cover the medical costs of service-connected disabilities. Suppose a man had a knee injured while in service, which ten years later gives him much trouble after a slight accident. He applies for free treatment on the ground that the accident would not have hurt the knee at all but for the earlier injury. The government doctor denies the claim, and insists that any healthy knee would have behaved thus. A strong veterans' organization now intercedes with strong contrary testimony from *their* doctor. Even if the government physicians do not necessarily give in, the knowledge that every *yes* will be accepted while many *noes* will be contested tends to bias their decision.

Whether a government agency is assigned to require citizens to keep ragweed cut in their vacant lots, to regulate competition in the airlines, or to collect income taxes, the agency has dozens, hundreds, or thousands of instances where judgment must be exercised as to when, how, or whether to apply the law in the particular case. Any one decision may mean tens or millions of dollars to the interested party, and the pressure applied to the administrator is sometimes monumental. One form of genteel harassment is to present evidence in such large volume that the administrator cannot possibly read and digest it all. If no results are forthcoming, pressure may be applied to his superior, and so on up the line until an elected official is reached. Or the pressure group may go straight to the elected councilman, governor, or senator, and work downward. The pressure may be as subtle as: "Senator, we thought you might like to keep an eye on this case so you can see how that law you voted for last session is working out." As with pressures on legislators, those on administrators may be minute or massive; subtle or blatant. They often fail completely, and sometimes backfire by making the administrator more suspicious or more determined. On the average, however, they almost certainly place a bias on the administrative process in favor of those who exert the pressure. Regulatory commissions often seem to work more in the interests of the regulated than of those they are supposed to protect, for the simple reason that they are in so much closer contact with the former. Again, too, the regulated interest is concentrated, while the beneficiaries of the regulation are diffuse.

PRESSURES ON COURTS

On the whole it is much more difficult for pressure groups to influence the judiciary than other branches of government, but some pressures do occur. Perhaps the most significant pressure is on the appointments. Since prospective judges often have reputations as liberals or conservatives, strict or lenient, pro-civil rights or anti, pressure groups work for the appointment of judges with social philosophies or judicial practices which will do them the most good.

Pressures for or against a particular judge can be directed at the appointing authority, such as the President or governor, before a nomination is made. They may also operate indirectly, as by working inside the Bar Association to influence its recommendation. Although it has no official standing, a strong recommendation or objection by the Bar Association carries great weight, especially at state and local levels. Since appointments to the Supreme Court must be approved by the Senate, persons who object to an appointment can exert pressure at that point. Although most appointments eventually go through, knowledge that pressures can be expected there undoubtedly influences some nominations. The confirmation of John J. Parker, nominated for the Supreme Court in 1930 by President Hoover, was successfully fought by labor unions and the National Association for the Advancement of Colored People. Parker was opposed for having supported the "yellow dog" contract, and for other decisions, and the intensity of the campaign against him approximated that of lobbying on major legislation.[1]

---

[1] David B. Truman, *The Governmental Process* (New York: Alfred A Knopf, Inc., 1951), p. 492.

Pressure groups can take action at court to speed up or block administrative actions which affect them, as by writs of performance, taxpayer suits, injunction, claims of unconstitutionality, and so on. Measures can sometimes be held up for years while court hurdles are cleared. Pressure groups can also help to keep government actions legitimate. If an administrator apparently oversteps his authority, some pressure group may file suit or seek an injunction, and get a court ruling on the matter. Some organization of interested citizens, or a permanent organization such as the American Civil Liberties Union may provide money to defend individuals whose civil liberties seem to have been violated.

Perhaps the most significant and long-standing use of the courts to shift power in private disputes occurred from roughly 1800 to 1932. First with the so-called conspiracy doctrine and later with injunctions, employers rather consistently through this whole period could get the assistance of the courts to restrict or enjoin strikes.

Groups not party to a court case, but who feel they would be affected by the decision, often appear or file a brief in the case as a "friend of the court." For example, many companies, trade associations, and farm groups helped argue on both sides of the case in which the Supreme Court invalidated the first Agricultural Adjustment Act in 1936.[2]

PRESSURES ON THE CONSTITUTION

Pressures regarding the Constitution must, of course, be exerted on some group in government, such as the Congress or state legislatures which act on amendments. The three amendments to the Constitution which most directly affected private power interests were the Thirteenth, Sixteenth, and Eighteenth, dealing with slavery, the income tax, and prohibition, respectively. The issue involved in the first was an important factor in the Civil War—a fairly substantial pressure. The prohibition amendment can probably be attributed mainly to private pressures from temperance groups, which the opposing pressures from the brewing and distilling industries were unable to offset. After years of unsuccessful enforcement, the amendment was repealed in 1933.

The Sixteenth Amendment permits the federal government to levy taxes on incomes, instead of apportioning taxes among the states according to population. This is not only a means of raising revenue. Because of the way the Congress has graduated the income taxes, with no tax at all on very low incomes and marginal rates as high as 91 per cent on very high ones, this amendment permits important redistributions of income. Pressures on it were high.

An influential group with an interesting history started as the Association Against the Prohibition Amendment, and "included on its rolls the great financial interests that resented shifting tax burdens from the

---

[2] *Ibid.*, p. 495.

shoulders of beer drinkers to their own."[3] This group later became the American Liberty League, a well-financed and highly reactionary organization which distributed large volumes of literature during the 1930's. After the repeal of prohibition "the Association's objective was to scuttle the Sixteenth Amendment 'as an instrument to redistribute wealth, to communize the nation, and to confiscate the property of one man and dole it out to others.' "[4]

PRESSURE GROUPS AND THE PUBLIC

In the long run, probably the strongest force is the general state of public opinion. By this is meant not only the attitudes about certain issues, but a more deep-seated set of values about large institutions. Are government, business, unions, public expenditures, social security, advertising, and so on "good" or "bad"? If a wide, deep-seated feeling pervades the people in government as well as the voters that the government ought to "clamp down" on some group, that group is likely to be made subject to public restrictions. The many regulations placed on business during the thirties and early forties, and on unions during the late forties and the fifties reflect broad shifts in sentiment without which specific government responses to specific conditions would probably not have been possible. Public feelings about particular pieces of legislation can also, of course, be important. For these reasons important groups try to keep a favorable public image of themselves and an unfavorable one of opposing groups.

In the battle for publicity, many factors are involved, but in the long run probably the dominating one is money—to pay for mailing lists, advertising, speakers, pamphlets and brochures, propaganda agencies, "independent" research, broadcasting time, and so forth. It is difficult to know how much influence any particular kind of publicity has, and exactly how to classify the groups which release it. We might, however, take a broad division between unions, as representing one general class of the population, and business, as representing another. If we assume as a first approximation that the amount of publicity each group can buy is roughly proportional to the amount of money flowing through the respective organizations, the preponderance on the side of business is overwhelming. The total receipts and disbursements of all unions for all purposes amounts to approximately $1 billion per year, which is about two thirds of the net profits after taxes in 1962 of one American corporation, General Motors. Total receipts and disbursements of all American corporations run to about $800 billion per year,[5] and expenditures for

---

[3] Alpheus T. Mason, "Business Organized as Power," *The American Political Science Review*, Vol. 44, No. 2, June, 1950, p. 331.

[4] *Ibid.*

[5] Internal Revenue Service Publication No. 453, November 1962, *U.S. Business Tax Returns.*

advertising alone are about $12 billion. The total wealth of all unions, exclusive of the trust funds to be mentioned below, is perhaps $4 to $5 billion, as contrasted to about a hundred times that amount for total business assets. Substantially larger amounts, of perhaps $55 billion, are being set aside under various health, pension, and other benefits for workers under union-management contracts. But the great bulk of this money is in trust funds under management, or joint union-management, control, to be paid for the most part through the companies to individual workers, and in no sense can it be considered "union" assets.[6] On the whole, it would seem appropriate to put the financial resources of the whole American labor movement—whether in total wealth or annual flows—at about 1 per cent of that of the business community.

To jump from the extremely broad to the highly specific, although as a specialist in labor-management relations I receive more than a normal quota of mailings from unions, I would estimate roughly that of the unsolicited partisan "literature" sent me, that with a business-management point of view exceeds that with a union view by at least four to one, and my colleagues in the economics department who do not teach labor report receiving about three to five pieces of management-oriented literature per week, and none with a union orientation.

The effect cannot be measured by the quantity. It might be argued that there is a "natural" tendency for people to side with the lower-income group, and that a much larger volume of material in support of business is needed to offset this "inherent" bias. It might also be argued that people generally tend to accept the existing power structure as "normal," to identify with it, and that a disproportionate volume of material is therefore needed in the opposite direction to achieve reasonable balance. These things are difficult to tell. But there is no reasonable doubt as to which group holds the quantitative dominance of "communications," particularly when we add the position of the newspapers. At the same time, however, labor unions have one of the largest and most alert lobbies in Washington, and in many state capitols.

GOVERNMENT STAFF AS A PRESSURE GROUP

Pressures are not exerted solely *on* government, but sometimes *by* government. This pressure may be an exercise of leadership, or an attempt to further the interests of some group within the government staff, or of some related private group.

The leadership function as a pressure is perhaps most conspicuous in foreign affairs, although it appears in domestic issues as well. If the President, the Secretary of State, and important leaders of Congress feel that

---

[6] The estimates of wealth and income of American unions are based on reports in *Business Week*, November 19, 1949, pp. 115 ff; March 4, 1950, p. 114; and June 4, 1960, pp. 82 ff; and *U.S. News & World Report*, September 10, 1962, p. 50.

some action is important, but that the people are not prepared to support it, techniques have been worked out to gain approval. These include the "leak," the "plant," and the "trial balloon," which are unofficial releases of plans or information. They first appear to the public as rumors, or as statements from some lower official, in such a way that the top officers can deny any knowledge or responsibility for them if they are not well received. They open the way for discussion, and psychologically prepare the people for further moves in the same direction. Typically, during the 1930's the government was trying to arouse the people to the probable need for eventual involvement in stopping the expansion of the Hitler totalitarianism, and in the 1960's to restrain impetuous urges to action which might precipitate total nuclear war.

By speeches, press releases, and the dramatization of unusual cases, departments are sometimes able to swing public sentiment behind legislation to increase their authority or budget, particularly if the newspapers take up the case. The dangers of the drug Thalidomide, for example, in 1962 were widely publicized on the basis of actions by an employee in the Food and Drug Administration, and led to legislation that substantially increased the powers of the FDA over new drugs. Investigation by Congressional committees are sometimes televised—as were those of the Kefauver Committee on rackets and the McClellan Committee on improper behavior in labor unions, and led to widespread public support for new restrictive legislation.

A particular combination of government and private interests was forcefully called to public attention by former President Eisenhower in his farewell address on January 17, 1961. This is a "military-industrial complex," about which the President said:

We must guard against the acquisition of unwarranted influence, whether sought or unsought, by this military-industrial complex. This conjunction of an immense military establishment with a large arms industry is new in American experience.

He added that it "creates the potential for the disastrous rise of misplaced power," and "the weight of this combination" may some day "endanger our lives and democratic processes." Approximately 70 per cent of an annual expenditure of $20 billion goes to 100 firms, the largest five averaging about a billion dollars each. The 100 firms employ 1,400 retired officers from the armed forces, including 261 ex-admirals and ex-generals. Many belong to the Air Force Association, the Association of the Army, and the Navy League, which have considerable influence in Congressional and Defense Department thinking. Their companies engage in heavy advertising of the weapons, planes, boats, or missiles they produce, on occasion at the suggestion of the armed forces. A power bloc of this magnitude, tied to an activity for which appropriations are seldom withheld because of their essentiality to the national defense, and about which much information can be hidden under the cloak of "security," would seem to justify Eisenhower's deep concern.[7]

In short, in these and other ways the government staff are not always passive recipients of instructions from the citizens. They sometimes actively assist in forming the sentiments behind those instructions. Some divisions have extensive means of getting support, while others, perhaps with distinct public usefulness, have difficulty getting any hearing at all.

THE SIGNIFICANCE OF PRESSURE GROUPS

If dollar ballots in the market and political ballots in the polling booth are two major techniques for making social decisions, pressure groups are a major third force.

It is customary to view pressure groups, and particularly lobbies, as "unholy" deviations from the "pure" relation between voter and government in the privacy of the voting booth. Without for the moment passing judgment on the techniques or relative strengths of pressure groups, we might recall the techniques of making the public decisions as sketched in the past several chapters, including political parties. These do not seem so fully and accurately tuned to the people's wishes as to argue against supplementary flows of information, and perhaps of motivation.

To illustrate, along with being a voter, I am also professionally interested in education. Except to vote on occasional tax levies for schools, I have never been able to communicate my wishes about any educational problem through the ballot box, since education has never been a major issue in any campaign. Just as the dollar ballot cannot convey precise information unless desired and undesired factors are separable, neither can the ballot for a candidate convey much information about *one* issue if the election involves *several* issues, as well as several personalities. Although I do not always agree with their position, I nevertheless feel that it is important that several educational associations exist which approach legislators directly, testify before committees, and use other lobbying and pressure techniques. In other areas, if a change in postal rates could be disastrous for magazines, if a change in tariffs could wipe out the textile industry, if a change in tax structure could shift a billion dollars of business from railroads to trucks, if a change in labor law could make it impossible for unions to organize in the South, if a federal power dam could wipe out three private utility companies, and so on, it is demonstrably impossible for the ballot to convey the amount of information required if the affected citizens are to express their wishes on such matters.

To return to the opening sentence of the chapter, unless the maga-

---

[7] The particulars of this paragraph, including the quotations, are from Jim G. Lucas, Scripps-Howard staff writer, in the *Cincinnati Post and Times Star*, September 26, 27, 1962.

zines, textile manufacturers, railroads, unions, or utilities make some fairly strenuous moves to defend their own interests, those interests are not going to be strongly defended. It is hardly reasonable to believe that they will not try, or to argue that they should not be allowed to defend their interests. Until and unless the political decision process by ballot is capable of carrying more information than it now does—and the prospects are dim—the very least that can be said is that interest groups must be free to provide *information* about their positions before legislators, administrators, and voters, along with reasonable attempts at persuasion. In fact, organizations do not have any vote, as such, and are deprived of any voice if they do not communicate directly. And how can a citizen interested in having the Department of the Interior step up its activities for the preservation of wild life in national parks express this desire in a normal ballot?

Precisely where or how one can draw a line between information, persuasion, and pressure is not easily answered. Bribery can easily be ruled off limits, though complete enforcement of the rule is another matter. Threats to withhold votes may seem coercive. But "Do as I say or I won't vote for you," even if crudely put, is the heart of the major bargain between elector and elected, and can hardly be eliminated without cutting deep into the democratic process. All in all, it would seem that some substantial degree of pressure is an inescapable part of a democratic society, and the question perhaps is not whether it is desirable or should be allowed, but whether it can be kept in reasonable balance.

On this score, the "special interests" seem to get most of the attention, and the general interests little. But as Truman points out, even the special interest group is seldom monolithic. The human beings in both the Iron and Steel Institute and the United Steelworkers of America are also veterans, home owners, users of highways, consumers, parents with children in public schools, church members, vacationers in our national parks, and citizens expecting justice and national defense. Directly or indirectly each may be represented by two or three to a dozen or more pressure groups, some in conflict with others. "It is thus multiple memberships in potential groups based on widely held and accepted interests that serve as a balance wheel in a going political system like that of the United States."[8] To revive the language of earlier chapters, although one particular subculture may conflict directly with another, the members of both are simultaneously members together in numerous other subcultures, and accept many of the same cultural norms. And in the end, it is the *general* interests to which the government official returns for reelection.

All of this is not to suggest that pressure groups do not at times push the influence of government far in their own direction at the expense of the rest of the population, since they undoubtedly do. How large or

---

[8] Truman, *op. cit.*, p. 514.

how serious this effect is for the whole nation over an extended period, in light of the multiplicity of groups, is probably impossible to estimate, since we would have to compare the existing situation with one without such groups.

Viewing the whole picture, the formal ballot provides very little communication from citizens and private organizations to their government, and leads to supplementation in rather large ways. Pressure groups are the major supplemental technique. The conscientious legislator or administrator will, of course, want to know the probable effect of his vote or ruling on various elements in the population. As things now stand, tentative actions are communicated through the land, and those who feel an interest then speak up. Those who desire action where none is planned can also speak up. Despite obvious gaps, weaknesses, biases, and abuses, pressure groups as a system of communicating information and motives apparently fill an inescapable and essential role in the total social process. It could be improved and be better balanced, but its absence is difficult to imagine. In general, the citizen with some program to espouse will probably have more influence if he becomes active in a pressure group or political party than if he merely casts his vote, and this situation seems likely to continue.

To compare the three main decision techniques, the market gives one vote per dollar, and therefore much more influence to the rich. The ballot gives one vote per person, and many more ballots to the relatively poor. Given its monopoly on force, the government is the presumed boss in a conflict between the two decision processes, which would seem to give the dominance to the poor. But the holders of the money have a strong hold on mass communications, and on a larger number and wider variety of pressures on government. On balance, the behavior of the government in the United States more nearly resembles that prescribed by the mass media than that advocated by the limited-coverage trade union press. Whether the government thereby follows Truth and eschews Error, or the reverse, and whether the results are more than coincidental, are matters beyond our present scope. The farmers and some other groups occupy a position somewhat off to the side of this main conflict, receiving government assistance which is generally decried by business, but not vigorously fought, because business is not seriously hurt by it.

Chapter 36

GOVERNMENT, STAFF STRUCTURE AND DECISIONS

A GOVERNMENT is not one man. Both the kinds of decisions the government makes and the ability of the people to influence it depend in significant ways on the size and relationships of the parts of the governmental structure. The kinds of influences are many and diverse, and we will sample only a few to give some idea of the nature of the problem. As with other large organizations, the major bases for division are geographical and functional.

The general problems of organizational structure for performing tasks resemble those of other organizations. Some organizational structures are undoubtedly more effective than others for specific purposes, but it is doubtful if there is any such thing as one "best" structure. The staff of government has both a formal organizational structure and an informal one; it has both line and staff functions; and its supervisors are middlemen in an information, authority, and bargaining relationship. Its essential problems of selecting and motivating lower levels of staff are the same as in other organizations, although civil service regulations make the penalty of discharge more difficult to employ, and require that the supervisor rely more heavily on merit ratings, praise, transfer, and other types of rewards to motivate employees. These facts have some relevance to its ability to perform efficiently. In addition, and unlike other organizations, government has a monopoly on all but minor uses of force; it is at least potentially an unlimited-purpose organization; and the individual citizen cannot withdraw his membership and support if government does not meet his wishes. Government thus has many organizational problems in common with other organizations, and some that are distinct. The many respects in which government resembles other organizations need not be discussed independently, and previous analysis automatically applies. For the present chapter we will examine two major types of decentralization of government structure, geographic and functional, to see their effects on decisions and power relations.

GEOGRAPHIC CENTRALIZATION-DECENTRALIZATION

As Communication

The way in which an organization is divided has both power and decision components. When a single decision about public goods or power regulation has costs and values which cover more or less the whole nation, there is little choice but to make the decision at the national level, and assess its costs across the whole nation. National defense, foreign policy, nation-wide monopolies, or a postal system cannot be decided independently by Idaho and Georgia, or by Seattle and St. Louis, with each unit participating or not participating in effectuating the decision and sharing its costs. The wishes of the people on such matters must be directed to the central government, where this information is combined with others, for a single total decision.

By contrast, with respect to many other problems, all costs, values, and information are, or easily can be, local. If a thief is caught entering a house in Topeka, there is little point in sending all the information, exhibits, witnesses, and the defendant to Washington for trial and decision. The housebreaking has no national consequences, and requires no significant information from the national level. Similarly, whether Front Street in Harrisburg needs repairs, whether a block in Denver should be rezoned from residential to commercial, or whether the windows in Des Moines city hall should be cleaned this month or next can all be handled locally. Unless the national officials were to travel to the spot for information, and unless their decisions are to be highly arbitrary, they would have little choice but to do what is indicated by the information transmitted from the local scene. This is another way of saying that the actual decision resides with the person(s) who provide the information, and is, in effect, local. A central decision could bring only delay and dilution of the information.

Centralization and decentralization are also related to the amount of information citizens can communicate through the ballot. If, for example, at the national level they vote for one of two candidates each for president, senator, and representative, the ballot carries three bits of information. It is difficult to say how many bits a citizen needs to express his position adequately, but he would normally need at least two, and often four or five, for every issue, not merely three in total. Inadequate as the ballot is for conveying information regarding national issues, if decisions about local issues were decided at the national level, the voter would often have no voice at all, since such local issues would normally not be contested at the national level. By contrast, if votes are taken separately for local and national representatives—as between city councilman and senators—it is then at least *possible* for a voter to cast a ballot which will distinguish his desires on the local scene from those on the national one.

This line of reasoning seems to suggest that the larger the number of issues and candidates on the ballot, the greater is its information content. But if there are so many items on the ballot that the people do not know the candidates or understand the issues, the apparent information content is meaningless. Further, many issues are not isolable, and the authority relation between voters and representatives is muddied if the voters give too many explicit instructions. The important point, however, is that geographic decentralization of government does allow some control over local actions by local voters, and when one or two issues are central to a campaign, the voters may exercise a clear, controlling voice.

The Power Effects

The size of the governmental units affects the power relations as well as the communication and decision relations. Among the various possible effects we will examine three: first, the difference in decisions as between different sized decision units; second, the differences in sponsor-staff relations; and third, the differences in the power of pressure groups.

Size of the Decision Base. Suppose a picturesque and historic covered bridge carries a township road across a stream, and it is estimated that $5,000 could be saved over the next ten years if it is replaced with a steel and concrete structure. Artists, photographers, historians, and nostalgic citizens over several states would like the bridge preserved. But only a few of them live within the township. Since the whole cost of the bridge must be paid for by the township, unless the value of the bridge *to the township* exceeds its costs, it will be torn down. The values of the bridge to the many people outside the township are essentially irrelevant to the decision. True, a private "Save the Bridge" committee may collect voluntary contributions, and historic items are often preserved in this way. The technique is sporadic and unreliable, however. It is grafted onto the basic decision process, and often depends on the fortuitous appearance of some person with time, money, and energy to head the campaign. Hundreds of historic monuments have gone, not because their cost exceeded their value to the whole society, but because all the costs were levied on a smaller unit than that which received the values.

The local decision on bridges is apt to be irrational in a second sense as viewed on a larger basis, since it considers only one bridge at a time. A rational total decision might pose the following kind of question: Considering their condition, maintenance cost, location and accessibility, and scenic and historic value, which covered bridges in the United States are most worth saving, and which least? The fact that a national government *can* ask the question this way does not guarantee that it *would* do so, or that it would reach a sound conclusion. But the local government cannot even raise the question in this way. The point is not to suggest what the best decision unit is, but to indicate the way in which a decision can be influenced by the fact that the costs and values may cover different units of people.

Conversely, if the costs are spread more widely than the values, a decision may be made in favor of some project even though its costs exceed its values. This could happen, for instance, if the federal government on request were to pay half the cost of paving streets which have local value only, in which case the local decision would be to pave the streets if their value exceeded only half their cost. If the federal government confines its contributions to projects which have national as well as local interest, and contributes only to those which do, in fact, serve the national interest, then both local and national values and costs are represented in the decision.

A thorny problem in the United States involving decision units is that of the size and composition of metropolitan districts. Most central cities have one municipal government, and are surrounded by a multiplicity of suburbs. Each has its own local government, even though the person driving through the section often cannot tell when he leaves one town and enters the next. In metropolitan Cincinnati, for example, there are approximately 45 separate governmental units, each with its own town council or board of trustees, plus 39 school districts whose officials are elected directly by the voters.[1]

Many difficult metropolitan problems can be handled more effectively and at less cost if dealt with on a unitary basis for the whole area—such as water, sewers, garbage and trash disposal, drainage, local mass transportation, police and fire protection, and jails and courts. In addition, serious inequities occur if several large industries locate within one town, and none are set up in others. In the first town the taxes from these industries provide lavish municipal services while citizens pay very low taxes, and in the second high tax rates may be required to provide even skimpy services. These are only samples of the many problems which have given rise to a strongly felt need of cities for some kind of pooling of decisions, revenues, and expenditures for the whole metropolitan area under a common government.

In most or all states, suburban governments can be absorbed by the major city only by their own consent. This they usually will not give. The central city *must* deal with such problems as public transportation, slum clearance, and policing unruly districts. If the suburbanites retain their own local governments they obtain the benefits of the central city's actions, directly or indirectly, without having to pay any part of the cost. Typically, the higher-income groups pay more in taxes than low-income groups, because they have higher incomes and own more valuable properties. They also usually cost the city less for police, jail, court, and relief expenditures. When they move from the city to the suburbs they therefore leave the central city with only a high-cost, low-revenue population. The suburb by itself, by contrast, has the higher-income, lower-

---

[1] Doris D. and Thomas H. Reed, *The Cincinnati Area Must Solve Its Metropolitan Problems* (Cincinnati: Stephen H. Wilder Foundation, 1953), p. 9.

cost segment of the population, and hence levies less taxes than its citizens would normally pay if they lived in the city. But since these people use the city's facilities frequently—such as museums, theaters, places of work, recreation, and the attendant policing and control services—without having to pay for them, they vote to remain separate.

It is not the purpose of the present discussion to suggest a solution, but to point to the effects of decision units on the outcome of the decisions. If the central city had authority to absorb any suburb at its own discretion, or if it were required by state law to absorb any suburb of a given size or within a given distance, many decisions would be very different from the present ones.

Sometimes problems having a significant national interest are decided at the local level on the basis of local criteria. For example, Hessler argues that the relative inferiority of the United States compared to the Russians in technical education results in part from the decision unit, when he states:

> In part, it is because nearly every outlay for education, local or state, is subject to a decision of the voters, on a bond issue or tax levy. And the main body of voters do not see that they must pay for superior education if the United States is to have enough physicists and engineers and language experts for the cold war ahead.[2]

To the extent that decisions are made by school boards, rather than the voters, they, too, are subject to local election against local opponents on largely local issues. Individual communities, unless they are more than usually civic minded, feel their own local efforts are insignificant, and tend not to bother. Again, we are not suggesting that the decision unit be changed, but are simply noting a particular kind of effect of a particular decision unit.

Sponsor-Staff Relations

The smaller the decision unit, normally, the smaller will be the number of decisions and functions performed within the unit. Hence, the greater will be the voter control over decisions when they elect or refuse to elect the persons who make those decisions. It thus seems that the greater the amount of decentralization, the greater is the voter control over the behavior of government activity.

But the more decentralized the government, the larger is the number of officials and issues to be voted. We have already seen that the voter may then have less information about any one, and be less able to control the total performance of government, and less able to know whom to hold responsible. It is easy to note these two conflicting tendencies in public control, but not at all easy to know where the equilibrium point lies at which the public's power is greatest.

---

2 William Hessler, "Real Threat to U.S. Being Ignored," Cincinnati *Enquirer*, July 23, 1961.

The Power of Pressure Groups

The ability of pressure groups to influence government also changes with the degree of centralization of the government. Part of this difference is due to the experience of the government staff, and part to size. Most elected career officials start at the local level, and work up. Local officials are therefore on the average less experienced, which fact can have two opposite effects on their receptivity to pressure. One is to reduce the candidate's stake in being elected. If he has been in politics only a short time, he has less investment to lose by ignoring pressures. But his lack of experience may also make him easier to intimidate.

As to size, state and local governments are more homogeneous, and involve fewer divergent interests than the national government. Any one interest group therefore looms larger to its welfare, and exerts more influence. As to sheer size, a pressure group, such as a union, large corporation, or farm organization, looms much larger relative to state or local government than to national. In the small town, a mere hint that a large firm might leave sends cold shivers up and down councilmanic spines, and the simple word that some action displeases the company will often bring conformance. The large city or a state is less subject to such influence, although a large company in a small or thinly populated state may still carry much weight, as in the case of the DuPont Company in Delaware or Anaconda Copper in Montana. The plains states are not deaf to the will of farmers, nor is Michigan to that of organized labor. By contrast, even the largest pressure group is small compared to the federal government.

Pressure at the national level is most effective when applied to senators or congressmen in relation to their state and local base. No one pressure group, however, can curdle the blood of the *whole* Congress the way the local pressure group can do to a *whole* city council. When public regulation is in question, many industries or other groups argue for state rather than national regulation "in principle." The "principle" in their minds apparently is that they can dominate state governments more effectively than the national, since the same groups seldom object to federal action which helps them, or to federal regulation of their opponents.

Legislative and Executive Functions

Any kind of organization has three major sets of relationships, as outlined in earlier chapters. These are the sponsor-staff, staff-recipient, and within-staff relations. Within the present model, the sponsor-staff relation can be identified, at least roughly, with what is generally known as the legislative function, while the executive function can similarly be identified as the staff-recipient relation. If the two functions of government are classified as power regulation and the production of public goods, the legislative, or sponsor-staff, function is that of deciding (1) what public goods are to be produced, and (2) whose power is to be regulated, in what direction, and by what techniques. The executive, or staff-recipient, function is to carry out these decisions—that is, to produce the public goods or to regulate power.

It should be clear that we are speaking of *functions*, not subdivisions of government, since the functional division may or may not coincide with the nominal structural divisions. In the United States, for example, we refer to the President and his cabinet as executive and the Congress as legislative. Yet often the President and his aides formulate the major part of the legislative program, present it to Congress, and do much politicking to get it passed. Regardless of the name of his division, the President is thus performing crucial legislative functions. At the same time, the Congress often establishes the administrative bodies which are to carry out some of its laws. Although the heads of these agencies may be appointed by the President, in their day-to-day operations they are responsible more to Congress and its committees than to the President. Thus, important executive functions are actually within the control of the Congress.

In England, no such division of function into separate bodies is made; the Prime Minister and his cabinet are conspicuously responsible for both legislative and executive functions, and the Prime Minister will dissolve the Parliament if it does not pass important legislation he has asked for. Regardless of where they are formally placed, or how they are divided or mixed among two or more formal divisions of government, the sponsor-staff and staff-recipient functions are distinctly different aspects of the government performance. In the United States, if different parties control the Congress and the Presidency, it is difficult either to perform or evaluate either the legislative or the executive functions, since interparty conflicts exist within both. The separation of the two bodies in the United States was done mainly to achieve a functional division which would make dictatorial or arbitrary government more difficult. Whether the gain in that direction has been sufficient to justify the relatively clumsy government structure probably cannot be answered decisively, since we cannot know what course history would have taken under a different system.

The verbal distinction between legislative and executive functions is easier to make than an actual one. A piece of legislation can specify broad categories of goods to be produced, and provide money for producing them. It can also specify in broad terms what kinds of disputes the government is to exert its influence on, on whose side, and provide the money for doing so. In most cases the executive function retains much discretion to decide whether a given case should be prosecuted, whether a given private action falls within the scope of the legislation, and what particular public goods should be produced. For example, legislation about a highway program at the federal level cannot specify exactly how many miles are to be built, or exactly where. Nor can a law spell out the details of power regulation, since no one knows in advance what circumstances will arise to which the law will be applied. This is equally true whether the executive function itself takes the initiative in uncovering and prosecuting a violation, or whether it waits until someone complains. Criminal acts, such as murder, burglary, and arson, fall into the former category. Here the government attempts to discover the crime and punish the violator whether the victim complains or not. In the United States the government takes the initiative in prosecuting persons who violate such assorted laws as those against monopoly, misbranding or shortweighting, traffic control, smuggling, narcotics peddling, spying, perjury, and income tax evasion.

If the decision of the executive department is accepted by the person(s) whose power is regulated, the case ends there. In such decisions, however, the administrators for the government are not necessarily impartial. The contest takes place between the government and a private individual or organization. The status and promotability of the government administrator often depend in part on the percentage of wins and losses in the cases he handles. The executive branch therefore cannot in fairness be given final say in such contests. Hence, provision is made for judicial review, to which either the government or the private party can appeal.

The Judicial Function

In both the legislative and executive functions, the staff are themselves participants in bargains, or have vested interest of their own in the outcome, as seen above. It therefore is normally deemed necessary to have some authority which does *not* have an interest, or which has a minimal interest, to settle disputes whether sponsor-staff and staff-recipient activities are carried out according to the rules. This is the judicial function, performed by the courts. Courts also handle the enforcement of promises and the disposition of controversies in which costs are imposed by one party on another.

The function of the judiciary is often said to be that of administering justice. If we include power rules determined through political decisions as part of the "consensus," we can say that the function of the judiciary is to direct the authority of government to or toward the achievement of consensus terms or rules in particular disputed transactions, and that *justice* is the achievement or approximation of consensus terms.[3] In a "straight" decision, the court puts the government into a coalition with the winning party against the losing one. In a compromise or mixed decision, we might say that it aligns the government with one party on some terms and with the other party on others, or, simply, that it will join a

---

[3] According to Webster's New International unabridged dictionary, 2d ed., *justice* is "the maintenance or administration of that which is just; just treatment." The present definition follows Webster by referring to the *process* of applying certain kinds of terms. Neither Webster nor the present definition carries the implication sometimes suggested—that there is in justice some nebulous entity which exists above and beyond the "just terms" or the process of applying them. The consensus incorporated in the present definition may be derived from various sources, as will be seen below.

coalition with either party against another who refuses the court's decision.

Judges and courts are not the only ones who can be just, and the definition is broad enough to include cases where the parent, executive, teacher, or other authority "does justice" in the decisions under his control. A party to a transaction can himself be just if, having great bargaining power to get unusually favorable terms, he nevertheless settles at about the consensus. A legislature can do justice when it formulates rules governing private transactions, and the administrator can do justice when he executes those rules according their intent. An administrator may also be thought of as doing justice if he modifies an apparently unjust law toward consensus terms.

Although anyone in or out of government thus can act justly, we will confine our attention here to decisions made by the judicial branch of government in transactions whose terms are alleged by one or both parties to be unjust. As observed in Chapter 12, the terms which are thought to be "just" vary widely from culture to culture, which means that what is "just" can be defined only with reference to a particular culture. Since the judges are not themselves parties to the transactions they decide, they can presumably discern the consensus with less bias than others. Having discerned the consensus terms, they throw the power of government against the party farthest from the consensus. This is not the way judicial action is currently described by lawyers, judges, or political scientists, but the way it seems to fit into the present analytical framework.

Kinds of Transactions.   We will first discuss four kinds of transactions courts handle. Three revolve essentially around property, while the fourth covers questions of legitimacy, usually referred to as problems of liberty. We will then examine the sources of courts' information about consensus terms or rules. The following discussion roughly parallels Frankfurter's approach when he says:

> The Supreme Court marks the boundaries between state and national action; it mediates between citizen and government. This tribunal is the final authority in adjusting the relationship of the individual to the separate states, of the individual to the United States, of the forty-eight states to one another, of the states to the Union, and of the three departments of government to each other. The Court thus exercises essentially political functions.[4]

1. *Among Private Parties.*   A substantial fraction of the cases in our courts represent disputes over private transactions. Such disputes are handled by civil courts. An important aspect of their work is the essential one noted earlier of enforcing promises. The general rule is that if one party has incurred a cost on behalf of another on the basis of the latter's promise, then the latter will be required to pay those costs. The cost might be an actual outlay, or it might be an opportunity to receive value,

---

4 Felix Frankfurter, "Mr. Justice Holmes and the Constitution," *41 Harvard Law Review*, p. 122.

which opportunity was lost on account of the promise. If some payment has been promised, the courts nevertheless will not require any payment under it unless costs have actually been incurred, and/or the contracted good has been delivered. For example, suppose that a man contracts to have a $40,000 house built, that he then suffers financial reverses that would obviously make it impossible for him to pay for it, and that the contractor decides to finish off the relation at the stage actually reached. Suppose that up to that point the contractor has spent $2,000 for grading the ground, but no more. Although it is unsafe to predict what any court will do, or precisely what the law is on any particular point, the court would probably give the contractor an award of approximately $2,000. That is, it would compensate him for about the amount of his actual loss in the case. If he could demonstrate that he lost another job because he was tied up in this contract, the court might award an additional amount —again representing compensation for a loss actually incurred.

In a simple case where a buyer has received a good but has not paid for it, payment will be required. If failure of the buyer to pay, or of the seller to deliver as promised, brings costs to the other party of a sort not mentioned in the contract, the courts will generally require payment of that cost, or some fraction thereof—though particular circumstances are so various that broad generalizations are unsafe, and we can do nothing more than indicate a general type of reasoning.

If one party places unnegotiated costs on another, as by automobile accident, an untended fire, or bad aim in archery practice, courts will normally require the first party (or his insurance company) to make reasonable compensation. The court may itself determine the amount, or specify a procedure for determining it, as by designating an impartial appraiser or umpire. If some act would create an irremediable or irreversible cost (such as cutting down a stately oak or revealing a trade secret), and if there is doubt whether the act is legal, a court can enjoin the act until after a fuller investigation into who owns the oak or the secret.

2. *Between Private Parties, but Involving the State.*   We have already seen that the state generally approves of "voluntary" transactions, but outlaws certain "involuntary" ones, such as assault, theft, rape, murder, and some kinds of transactions involving monopoly and misrepresentation. Because the violation of such regulations is felt to produce a less-satisfactory society as well as to hurt the victim, the violation is handled as if it imposes a cost on the state, and enforcement proceedings are instituted, even if the victim files no complaint. If compensation is feasible, the violator is expected to make it. If not, or in addition, he is typically required to incur some loss more or less proportional to the loss he caused, this loss normally taking the form of a fine or jail sentence. Common parlance refers to the punished criminal as having "paid his debt to society."

The logic can be construed differently, however. Punishment can be seen simply as a negative feedback from society to the criminal for his behavior, in the hope that the unrewarding behavior will be extinguished. But unless detection, capture, and conviction are highly reliable, the criminal is apt to see the punishment as feedback to some carelessness which led to his capture, rather than as feedback to the commission of the crime. This result is psychologically expected under the principle of recency, since the act of getting caught is necessarily more recent than that of committing the crime. Not until the thought of punishment is strongly conditioned to the commission of crime, as such, will punishment be an effective extinguisher of criminal behavior. Other factors also enter, since many criminals apparently find the thrill of evading police and the limelight of a public trial intrinsically rewarding, and others are simply not adequately familiar with alternate methods of behavior. Jail does, of course, eliminate the danger of similar behavior while the criminal is confined.

3. *Between Private Parties and the Government.* Individuals and private organizations, particularly business firms, have many transactions with the government. Individuals, for example, may work in the civil service, pay taxes, or sell property to the government. Businesses may sell merchandise or services. The government may condemn land, buildings, or equipment for public use. Government activities may damage private parties, as when the sonic boom of military planes turns a farmer's prize bull neurotic, or the well supplying an army camp lowers his water table. A private party can damage government property. In all these instances the relations between private party and government can take forms parallel to that between two private parties. The government can do damage or be damaged; it can fail to keep a promise or be injured by the failure of a private party to keep his promise. Aside from the rule that the government cannot be sued without its consent (an assertion of sovereignty), the courts handle these problems according to the same general rules as apply to contests between private parties.

When a private party disagrees with some regulatory commission's ruling about him, he can appeal it to the courts. The courts will generally review such rulings for principle, if appealed, and may or may not review the commission's findings of fact. The courts may also review the legitimacy of the government's acts, a matter for the next section.

4. *Legitimacy: Questions of Political and Civil Liberty.* Sponsor-staff and staff-recipient are the two kinds of relations between citizen and government. The government staff might behave illegitimately in either relation, in which case we will say that one of the liberties of the citizens has been violated. We will apply the term *political liberty* to the ability of the people to control the government in the sponsor-staff relation, and *civil liberty* to their ability to remain free of arbitrary or dictatorial controls in the staff-recipient relation.[5]

---

[5] In examining numerous sources, I have not been able to find a sharp distinction between, or definition of, these terms. I think the present definitions are fairly

Under the heading of political liberty we find such things as the rights to register, vote, campaign, support candidates, form political parties, hold meetings, criticize government, and otherwise to engage in the various paraphernalia of political activity aimed at keeping the control of government in the hands of the citizens. If the government interferes with such political activities by citizens, the courts are the normal instrument for taking action against the government. If one group of private citizens interferes with the political liberties of another group, as in the nongovernmental pressures of whites on Negroes to prevent the latter from voting in the South, the courts would also be the channel for action. This does not preclude legislative, executive, or constitutional action. It does mean, however, that the courts will settle the question in the absence of clear legislated rules, or that they will rule on the constitutionality of such rules.

In the area of civil liberties, perhaps the most important aspect is the freedom of the citizen to do or not to do as he likes, until and unless the government, by legitimate exercise of its powers and in the presence of political liberty, controls or prohibits it. This is very similar to the concept of "due process of law," if that phrase is extended to cover other than transactional behavior included under the heading of property.

Because of the importance of information flows to all aspects of a free society, and of the importance to a dictatorship of curtailing information, freedom of speech, press, and other means of communication are normally guaranteed by democratic societies. This does not mean that complete freedom is always the most socially useful condition in every detailed situation. It means rather that to give the staff of government the authority to decide what may or may not be said or advocated is in itself a grant of potential dictatorial power. The reasons are approximately those described in Chapter 33 in connection with the "information group." The general logic of freedom of speech, short of "clear and present danger" of overthrow of the government, is that it must be treated *as if* absolute, because we know of no technique for enabling the government to control *some* ideas without running the danger of enabling it to control other ideas as well.

In this connection, an important aspect of the nature of freedom seems somewhat obscured in recent years in the United States. Any people in any society, no matter how dictatorial, are "free" to speak in support of the existing government, and to make minor recommendations for change. No real problem of freedom arises, however, except in connection with

---

close to customary usage, and are fairly close to those of Ralph Barton Perry in "Liberty in a Democratic State," in Ruth Nanda Anshen (ed.), *Freedom, Its Meaning* (New York: Harcourt Brace & Co., 1940), p. 274. The term "freedom," as defined in Chapter 20, is wider than that of "liberty," as defined here, the latter being applied solely to the relation of the citizen to government. As well as following roughly those of Perry, the present definitions seem to conform to the discussion by Bertrand Russell in "Freedom and Government," in *ibid.*, p. 250.

ideas which are considered unpopular or dangerous, and people either are free to advocate allegedly "unsafe" ideas or they are not free. We are, of course, speaking of *advocacy*, not of rioting, revolt, the collection of arms and drilling of troops, or the clear and present danger of these things. Freedom of speech is quite as important to political as to civil liberty, but since its curtailment would occur under the staff-recipient relation, it can be analyzed primarily as a problem in civil liberties.

Other major aspects of the Bill of Rights, such as freedom of religion and of assembly, freedom from search, trial by jury, and freedom from excessive bail are also restrictions of government in the staff-recipient relation. The Bill of Rights only implicitly deals with a second aspect of information freedoms, which is freedom of access to information. If someone else is denied freedom of speech, by that act I am denied the freedom to hear him. Attention to "freedom to hear" may sharpen the importance to a free society of the problem of freedom of speech. Some curtailment of free speech may strike some persons as not important, since they seemingly restrict only a small and unpopular minority. But they simultaneously deny to the *whole* population the opportunity to hear the minority view, and hence curtail the freedom of all. This is one facet of the oft-made statement that freedom is indivisible.

More broadly, whenever any citizens or private organizations feel the government staff has exceeded its legitimate authority over them—whether regarding constitutional rights, the denial of some minor legislated right (such as the ability to get a liquor license), or the implementation of some power regulation (such as allowing a competitor to make obviously false statements about his product)—an appeal can be made to the courts to review the staff's authority. The citizen can similarly appeal to the courts if he feels that the staff has *failed* to perform some duty, or that the legislature has exceeded its constitutional powers in passing some law. He can even appeal from the decisions of a lower court, the Supreme Court being his last appeal.

The problem of civil liberties in general parallels that of freedom of press (a particular civil liberty) as described in a preceding chapter. That is, the direct effect of guarantees of civil liberties is to prevent *government* from interfering with private rights. Generally, the Bill of Rights does not provide protection against *private* curtailments. So far as the law is concerned, an employer is free to discharge an employee for publicly criticizing the company, or for writing a letter to the editor stating political views the employer disapproves. More subtly, an employer may refrain from promoting someone who expresses unpopular views, or who lives in the "wrong" neighborhood. A friend in a Northern city, who works for a company doing business on an international scale, assures me that if several Negro families were to move into his block in a middle-class neighborhood, he would have to move or lose all chances of promotion in his company, since an address in a "Negro neighborhood" would be an automatic bar to high executive position. A number of unions effectively prohibited free expression about the unions by their members. The Labor-Management Reporting and Disclosure Act of 1959 has presumably reduced such suppression, but has no more eliminated it than the Taft-Hartley Act has eliminated discrimination by some employers against union members. The Ku Klux Klan for years suppressed rights presumably guaranteed by law. In short, the *kinds* of freedom dealt with under the heading of civil liberties can be privately suppressed, with little remedy at law unless specific legislation is passed. Thus, while liberty may be denied in some respects by government action, in others it may be denied by *lack* of government action.

5. *Intragovernment Disputes.* In addition, disputes often arise within the staff of government itself. For example, in 1961 the legislature of Ohio challenged the right of the governor to make certain appointments without the prior consent of the state senate. Upon appeal the courts ruled that he had the right. Certain executive departments of the federal government have challenged the right of congressional committees to subpoena their records, and the courts in some cases and with certain safeguards have upheld the congressional committees. In the antitrust case against the glass container industry in 1948, the Supreme Court ruled that the Circuit Court had exceeded its jurisdiction, and had usurped the powers of Congress by changing the patent laws when it declared certain patents invalid because they were obtained by illegal means.

Although most such actions are taken care of by the Civil Service Commission, in certain unusual circumstances an employee of the government may take a dispute with his boss over his pay or employment status to the courts for settlement. The courts can thus be seen to determine who has the authority to do what in many kinds of disputes within the government itself.

6. *Who Controls the Courts?* From the above discussion, one might get the impression that all disputes over the allocation of power are decided ultimately by the courts, since they decide disputes over transactions between private parties, between private parties and the government, and disputes within the government. If so, it would also seem that the courts are the ultimate determiners of power within the nation, and hence themselves the greatest and ultimate power. Although this conclusion is valid in a direct, short-run sense, it does not follow that the courts have limitless powers.

To begin with, the courts do not themselves control physical force. The police and the armed forces are controlled by the executive branch, which might not carry out the court decrees if the courts were to behave illegitimately. Second, the money to operate the courts is provided by the legislature, and could be withheld. Third, the judges in many municipal and county benches are elected for limited terms, and poor performance may be rewarded with a permanent vacation. Fourth, the Constitution itself defines the courts' powers, and thus provides criteria for judging the performance of the courts. Fifth, the courts do not select their own membership, since judges are typically appointed by the executive and confirmed by the legislative branch. And finally, the courts apply and interpret legislation, but do not make it. Although the power of interpretation is great, a given law cannot be made to mean just anything the courts happen to want. For all these reasons, the courts are not immune to control by other branches of government, or by the citizens.

Enforcing Court Decisions. In connection with nongovernment organizations we have seen that insubordination requires prompt disciplinary action if the organization is to be able to function. If the insubordinate person persists, he is usually removed from the organization.

Refusal to accept the decision of a court is insubordination to the government, and as such must be promptly disciplined. But unlike the limited-purpose organization, the organization of the whole society cannot so easily expel the insubordinate. Instead, we label any such refusal contempt of court, and authorize the courts to invoke any punishment appropriate for gaining compliance.

Sources of Consensus. If awarding justice is the process of approximating consensus, whence do the courts receive their information as to what the consensus terms or rules are? There are several sources.

Many consensuses are arrived at by the government itself, through social choice mechanisms already described. Legislatures specifically state the terms of many transactions, and/or the positive or negative goods which may or may not be used in bargaining. In these cases the courts apply the rules specified by the legislature. Since no legislation can cover all conceivable cases which will arise under it, the courts must fill in the gaps by applying the same kind of reasoning which seemed to guide the legislature. For maximum consistency, the courts must discern the direction in which the legislature seemed to be pushing power, and fill in the details accordingly.

The courts pass on the validity of administrative actions only when these are appealed to the courts by the government or the affected recipient. In such instances, the courts normally allow an administrative decision to stand if it seems reasonable to apply the intent of the legislature, and if neither the legislature nor the executive has exercised illegitimate authority. The legislated consensus is thus defined initially by those who execute it, and is upset by the courts only if it seems to violate the legislation to be implemented, or if the legislation itself violates the Constitution.

The market is a second important source of consensus applied by courts. Courts decide not only who violates the rules, but how much compensation he must pay to the injured party. Money damages usually represent the costs of repairing property, medical costs to an injured person, financial losses due to failure to perform a promise, loss of earning power, and the like. When courts make awards for such instances they accept the market value of the things to be compensated as their main measure of consensus.

But many cases come before judges where neither the government nor the market provides a significant guide. In such instances, the judges have little choice but to examine the society around them to find what is considered wise, prudent, sensible, or fair. If a husband wants a divorce on the ground that his wife does not contribute her "fair" share to the family's work, what is "fair" can be determined only with reference to the practices in the surrounding society. In present-day United States, the wife might be construed to be doing her share if she puts in six hours a day of light to medium housework, with the aid of appliances. In a different society her proper share might be considered to be twelve hours of heavy work at plowing, carrying water, and pottery making. In one society the courts might require a noble to compensate a farmer for cabbages trampled by the noble's horse, and in another society the courts would consider this a normal, uncompensable risk of cabbage culture. The judge has little choice but to be guided by the practices of the surrounding society, since these are the only practices he is normally familiar with. These are also the only terms which will meet acceptance by the society and its government. Whether a judge will allow a man to horsewhip his son for filching cookies depends on the surrounding society's attitude toward corporal punishment and parental authority.

A technique widely used by courts is to ask what a "normally" intelligent person, using "average" diligence and "reasonable" foresight would have done under similar circumstances, and then to hold the particular individual to those standards. The words "normal," "average," and "reasonable" focus attention on the general run of human behavior, and hence on consensus.

The jury system contributes to the same result by bringing the value systems of a dozen persons to bear on a case. Such questions as to whether a railroad train should stop for a pedestrian, or vice versa, are answered on the basis of what seems reasonable to the ordinary individual—another measure of consensus.

If judges are better educated and less provincial than the rest of the society, they may be guided by the standards of their own subculture. If we assume for the sake of argument that the better educated are more sensitive and aware than the rest of the population, the judges can move ahead of the population, and help to bring it along. If judges belong to a particular social class, they tend to bring the standards of that class to the bench—though experience may make them aware that their own values are not necessarily applicable to others. The judge from a social class in which a girl is forever disgraced by bearing a child out of wedlock, will have to learn a new set of values when he must decide the case of an unmarried woman with five children by five different fathers, who seems surprised that the court frowns on her behavior. If one subculture has consensus terms of no-sex-without-marriage, while another expects only a nominal connection between sex and marriage, both the courts and their clients will meet frustration if judges apply the standards of either group to the other. Probably the courts would cease to function at all in such cases, since the potential litigants would feel they could get a more "just" settlement out of court.

Although the courts must usually bring individual cases into approximate conformance with the consensus terms of the surrounding society, which means to enforce a particular bargaining power position, they do not ordinarily describe their actions in these terms. We have already seen in Chapter 27 that the possessors of authority normally attempt to hide the fact that particular decisions are reflections of the power forces in *that* case, and that their power is greater if they refer instead to The Rule. Where judges have a clear political or market consensus to apply, they face little difficulty. These consensuses are relatively objective, and can be demonstrated more or less unequivocally to anyone who asks. But when the judges apply a social consensus they are on less firm ground.

Given (1) the fact that in their regulations of power the courts are frequently applying their own personal concepts of what is right or fair, and (2) the weakness of the power position of the courts if they acknowledge that they are ruling on such a basis, the courts greatly strengthen their position if they can recast it so that each decision comes as a Voice of Authority rather than the voice of the judge. This they have done by creating a Consensus of Judges on which they can base their individual decisions. This (notably in the English system of courts, which is shared by England, the Commonwealth, and the United States) is done by a system of common law and precedent.

The rationale of the system is that whenever any judge has made a decision in a particular sort of case, all other judges are obligated to decide similar cases similarly, until and unless compelling reasons arise for changing. A "compelling" reason could be a new piece of legislation, or the discovery of a fallacy in earlier reasoning. Once this system is established, much attention in any one case is paid to previous cases of similar sort.

At its most highly developed state, this system can be highly rigid, so that an eminently sensible decision may be overruled by a higher court solely on the ground that it violates existing precedents. In its most rigid form, it is not enough for a judge to show that the existing precedent is itself not sensible, in light of information acquired since the principle was established.

In fact, much flexibility can exist in the system, if the judges understand the process they are dealing with. Over the years the courts hand down decisions in thousands of cases, no two of which are precisely alike. Every case has *some* elements in common with each of several *different* kinds of other cases. For example, a case covering the bankruptcy and reorganization of a railroad has some elements in common with other railroad cases, including cases involving rates, valuations, liabilities, condemnation of property, and so on, each of which in turn has elements in common with still other cases. The railroad bankruptcy case also has elements in common with other bankruptcy cases, including those in steel making, retail trade, telephone companies, or coal mining—and the same can be said of the reorganization aspect of the case. The alert judge can usually figure out what decision he thinks to be the most sensible, all things considered. Out of the whole gamut of existing railroad cases, bankruptcy cases, and reorganization cases he can then usually find *some* cases which he can cite as the precedents supporting his present decision.

It is difficult to generalize about the amount of discretion available to the individual judge, since much depends on his prestige, the temper of the times, and the prevailing views among the judiciary as a whole, as well as the amount of understanding possessed by the judge himself. Such outstanding jurists as Cardozo, Holmes, and Brandeis seemed particularly aware of the role of judges in reflecting the world about them. Of their many statements on the subject, two of Holmes' will suffice.

It is revolting to have no better reason for a rule of law than that so it was laid down in the time of Henry IV. It is still more revolting if the grounds upon which it was laid down have vanished long since, and the rule simply persists from blind imitation of the past.[6]

Holmes also observed:

I think that the judges themselves have failed adequately to recognize their duty of weighing considerations of social advantage. The duty is inevitable, and the result of the often proclaimed judicial aversion to deal with such considerations is simply to leave the very ground and foundation of judgments inarticulate, and often unconscious.[7]

Because of their control of the main switch in the judicial system, the practices and beliefs of the members of the Supreme Court are of great importance. At that point any one judge must convince at least three others of his point of view in order to command a majority.[8] This fact in itself is a reasonable guarantee that broad lines of behavior of the courts will not allow that which does not have fairly wide representation throughout the legal community, and through the wider society.

---

[6] "The Path of Law," an address by Oliver Wendell Holmes, 1897, on the occasion of the dedication of a new hall of the Boston University Law School, *10 Harvard Law Review*, p. 469.

[7] *Ibid.*, p. 467.

[8] If the decision is made by a full court of nine, five is a majority, and he must convince four others. Decisions can be made by as few as six judges, with decisions being carried by a majority of four. When we say that the Supreme Court controls the main switch in the judicial system we mean only that it stands at the apex of the organizational pyramid, and can hold all inferior courts to their appointed tasks and authority. Not all kinds of cases can be appealed to the Supreme Court. Cases over private transactions and ordinary criminal acts cannot go higher than the state court system, unless a constitutional issue is involved, which is rare.

Although the courts sometimes lag behind the general movement of things, and obstruct social change, in the long run if they do not permit the people and their government to mold society into new patterns, the judges can be replaced as they retire by others who do. It nevertheless remains true that for day-to-day operating procedures the judges' activities consist mainly of bringing particular transactions into conformance with the consensus terms or rules of the judicial system itself, the judicial system in turn having little choice in the long run but to conform to the broad values of the surrounding society.

GOVERNMENT STRUCTURE: GENERAL OBSERVATIONS

Any organization of more than insignificant size faces the problem of centralization versus decentralization, and the subdivision of its tasks. Generally speaking, any decision which affects substantially the whole of the organization, or which requires the close coordination of many parts, must be made at the center or top of the organization. Any decision which affects only a small part and has no visible ramifications elsewhere in the organization can (and for efficiency, should) be made far down in the hierarchical structure. Whether Sally, the file clerk, can have Friday and Monday off to get married, and what shall be done with Peter for shooting partridges in his neighbor's pear tree, are questions that can and presumably should be settled without consulting the top management. These generalizations about centralization are valid irrespective of whether the organization is public or private, democratic or dictatorial.

If a government is to be democratic, however, several factors seem to speak in favor of resolving questionable points on a decentralized basis. First, by contrast with the market system in which each person can take or leave any particular good, most government decisions apply equally to all persons. Hence, if different localities are to fit the government to their needs, some government units must be small enough to include themselves, but not a predominance of people with different ideas. Second, in contrast to the multiple firms which supply the market, and which allow for variety and experimentation in their methods, only a single, local governmental unit normally provides a given good or type of regulation. Although local governments therefore cannot compete directly with each other, if they are allowed considerable freedom from central control, they can each experiment along separate lines, and learn from each other's experience.

On the other hand, decisions which can be made on a local basis nevertheless sometimes have a national significance, and we have already noted the possible role of education in the "cold war" between the communist and noncommunist nations. If the local decision units can be made to understand the national problem, and desire the national result with sufficient intensity to be willing to pay its costs, the two sets of interests are both taken care of, with the decision remaining decentralized. Other techniques are also available for achieving this result, such as letting the national government pay that part of the cost which is attributable to achieving the national purpose, while the local government pays the cost of achieving the local purpose.

If the people are to remain in control of government, rather than the reverse, the most obvious requirement is that they maintain control over the use of force. One aspect of this objective is that the military must unqualifiedly remain under the control of civilians, who in turn are subject to election. A second aspect is that the various kinds of power be distributed among different parts of the government organization, with the government functions being divided on both a horizontal (functional) and vertical (essentially geographic) basis. In particular, the courts, which make the operating decisions as to where and on whose side the government monopoly of force will be used, do not themselves control armed forces of consequence. On the other side of the fence, those who do control force are subject to the decisions of courts as to where and on whose side the force may be used—except in cases of international conflict. The executive branch may, of course, use armed forces to quell a riot or for other emergency, but anyone who objects to any such action can petition the courts for an injunction to have the forces withdrawn. Any elected officials who ignored the court's finding would have to face the possible wrath of the voters at the next election for an illegitimate use of force.

A possible coup which would suspend elections and create a dictatorship is prevented (1) by so dispersing authority that the cooperation of large numbers of persons is required before the coup could be successful, including the civilian administrators of the armed forces, and (2) by filling these posts with many persons who have a high stake in preserving the democratic process.

So far as the structure is concerned, the legislative and executive functions are common to all organizations. However, except in government they are commonly combined in the same persons, so that the top officers of the staff, in conjunction with the sponsor representatives, are responsible for both functions. Such judicial functions as are performed in private organizations are handled as a part of the administrative process. The normal final appeal from an administrative decision in a private organization is to leave the organization, and if the organization as a whole ceases to perform satisfactorily, the sponsors can dissolve it.

But when an organization performs an indispensable function, and includes the whole population, it cannot be dissolved or withdrawn from. It therefore must be prepared to issue a final and binding decision about *any* dispute which arises within its borders, including disputes within the government itself. A refusal of the government to hear a dispute means that the person who can win on the basis of all power factors other than government remains the winner. If the government does hear the dispute, it throws the authority of the government on one side or the other, either supporting or overthrowing the outcome which would prevail in the absence of government intervention. When described in these terms, the role of the government as an allocator of power, with its backstop in the use of force, is clearly evident.

All in all, the power of government is a central feature in almost any complex society. Yet its power is subject to many limitations. In the United States pressure groups are strong. Many functions are performed satisfactorily by private organizations, and pressure is exerted to keep the government out of such areas. The mass media maintain a constant and pervading climate of opinion in which government action is considered bad, and private action good, more or less *per se,* and often with little regard to the merits of the particular problem. There are also many techniques for evading and escaping government regulation, and the actual behavior on a subject may or may not show much resemblance to the law. It is not easy to know where the power lies in this complex situation. As noted earlier, we have not yet developed even the first approximation of a model for analyzing the circular relation in which government controls private power and private power controls government. Much work remains to be done in this area.

FUNCTIONAL CENTRALIZATION-DECENTRALIZATION

We have already seen that it is more difficult for a would-be dictator to install himself if he must first get acquiescence of numerous subdivisions of government. This generalization seems to apply equally to geographic and functional decentralization. At the same time, however, decentralization may make it easier for one or a related group of pressures to control government in their own interest, by "picking off" and dominating one division at a time, particularly if these pressure groups also have substantial control of mass media of communication. What point on the centralization-decentralization scale provides the best balance of freedom from the control of both one-sided pressure groups and would-be dictators has not been determined, and may differ from time to time and case to case.

Chapter 37

SOME NOTES ON DICTATORSHIP

DEMOCRACY is often thought of as government which follows the wishes of its people, while dictatorship does not. While this definition may be satisfactory for introducing the subject in grade school, preceding chapters make clear that it is difficult to measure what people want, and more difficult to follow it. The pages below will also indicate that a dictator, even a ruthless one, is not completely free to disregard the wishes and wants of his people. In view of the techniques by which people in democracies actually make social decisions, it seems more fruitful to make the distinction in terms of certain overt behavior. We will say that a government can be classed as definitely democratic if *all* of the following types of behavior are allowed, and occur:

1. Open criticism of the heads of state and their major policies in the mass media.
2. Secret ballot elections, accurately counted, with one vote per person, in which members of all classes or interests may vote. Elections are held at reasonable intervals, as (say) no less frequently than every five years.
3. Organized opposition to the chief officers of the state, which opposition actively seeks, through election, to replace the current policies and personnel with its own. This opposition must be independent, not in collusion with the incumbents, and it must (a) have policies significantly different from those of the incumbents, and/or (b) mold the policies in its platform toward the position that will command secret ballot votes.
4. Withdrawal of the incumbents if defeated in election, in favor of the victorious competitors.

These requirements for democracy are compatible with Schumpeter's definition[1] and with MacIver's statement[2] that in democracy the people hold the balance of power between governments, while in dictatorship the government holds the balance between different groups of people. Considering that modern governments almost necessarily operate through political parties, a simple but effective practical indication of democracy is

---

[1] See Chapter 34, above.
[2] Robert MacIver, *The Web of Government* (New York: MacMillan Co., 1947).

a vigorous, functioning, independent opposition party. The main officers of the government can normally control their own party, so that whether elections are held or not, if there is only a single party, the government is in charge of the decision process.

If any of the above requirements is lacking, a lesser degree of democracy exists. There is no sharp dividing line between democracy and dictatorship, but absence of all four conditions would seem to indicate incontrovertible dictatorship. Perhaps the most compelling single evidence of dictatorship is the use of force by the state to prevent opposition to the incumbents.

It is not uncommon to distinguish governments as being ruled by one person, by a few, or by the many. As MacIver points out,[3] this distinction is not very useful in separating democracy from dictatorship. So far as major policies are concerned, all governments are run by a "few," who are the "top management" of the government. Given the limitations of the human brain, the most absolute-appearing dictator must have advisers and consultants who help form decisions. In reverse, the most democratic president, prime minister, or cabinet cannot consult an indefinitely large number of persons before deciding. Although the precise structure differs with the individual case, the normal pattern of top management in government resembles that in any other organization. There will usually be one top official, who will have from one to perhaps four or five close, general advisers, plus perhaps a dozen to a score of others who are called on for special kinds of advice. This pattern is basically the same in democracy or dictatorship, and the crucial question is not how many people make the important decisions, but whether the electorate can replace the decision makers.[4]

Anything so complicated as a government can be classified in many ways, and the same observation applies to the subspecies, dictatorship. The most useful division for present purposes seems to be the threefold distinction among profit, crisis, and "transition" dictatorships. The first is clearly run for the benefit of the rulers, the second for the benefit of the people during an emergency period, and the third at least allegedly (which accounts for the quotation marks) is designed to accomplish a major change in social or technological organization.

THE PROFIT DICTATORSHIP

As seen in Chapter 29, a normal legitimate government is a cooperative organization, in which the sponsors and recipients are collectively the same people. By contrast, in a profit organization these are two different

---

[3] *Ibid.*, p. 149.

[4] The separation of legislative and executive functions in the United States requires that the President include in his "outer group" of consultants the key members of his party in the Congress, and perhaps some members of the opposition as well. Where the President and the legislators differ, the above analysis applies most strictly to those functions which *are* within the control of the executive branch.

groups; the sponsors receive the benefits and the recipients bear the costs. It is possible in any kind of organization for the staff to take over sponsorship, and run the organization for their own benefit. Starting from a democratic government, if the staff thus take over control for their own good, the situation then fills the definition of a profit organization, since the sponsors receive the benefits and the recipients pay the costs. As with the business firm, this does not mean that the recipients receive no value, and they may possibly feel that they are receiving a good bargain. It also does not mean that the sponsors ignore the wishes of the public, in much the same sense that even the complete business monopoly may sometimes make more profit from selling a reasonably good product at a moderate price than by selling a poor product at an exorbitantly high price. It does mean, however, that it is the sponsors', not the recipients', evaluation of the governmental balance sheet which determines the government's behavior.

A shift in control to the staff is nevertheless apt to be a dramatic development in government. Since the people would be likely to vote out a staff which thus uses its power, the staff will at some point have to start using its control of force to keep itself in power. We will not examine the transition, but only the condition which exists thereafter.

Some dictators have seemed to get satisfaction from destruction and anguish, and have left their trails in fire, plunder, rape, and blood. Such actions are more adventures than governments, and need not concern us here. Whether the dictator himself seeks the prestige of office or access to the public treasury does not greatly matter. He will necessarily maintain his power position or fall, and even if he does not want wealth for himself, his family or followers will. The whole controlling group thus gets its rewards from exercising the power of position and acquiring wealth at the public expense. These rewards typically range from grandiose to routine, in proportion to the usefulness and loyalty of the followers.

Not all the wealth he uses need be personally owned by the dictator, who may be content to use publicly owned palaces, hunting lodges, yachts, and automobiles. If the dictator's control is uncertain, however, he is well-advised to take public funds rapidly, and send them abroad for safekeeping. If he is later overthown, with luck he can flee before he is captured, and retire comfortably. If the control is more stable, the dictator may make little distinction between the public property and his private property, since he can use the former at will.

MacIver observes[5] that the many Latin American dictatorships have been highly lucrative businesses. So have many sheikdoms of the Middle East, a variety of earlier monarchies in Western Europe, and countless empires and satrapies of many ages and places.

Loewenstein[6] refers to this type of relationship as *authoritarian*. By

[5] *Op. cit.*, p. 237.
[6] Karl Loewenstein, *Political Power and the Governmental Process* (Chicago: University of Chicago Press, 1957), pp. 55 ff.

this he means that the dictator controls the apparatus of the state, but makes no attempt to control other aspects of social or economic behavior except as necessary to stay in power. Such a dictatorship is not *totalitarian*, which type exempts no aspect of life from its control. Loewenstein's distinction between authoritarian and totalitarian corresponds roughly, but not completely, with the present distinction between profit and transition dictatorships. Assuming that the profit dictatorship is directed toward satisfying personal desires of the dictator, this limitation is rational. Operating any dictatorship is not easy, but running a totalitarian one is a strenuous task. Unless the dictator has an almost insane desire for wealth and position, control of the government alone can provide all that he and his supporters can reasonably want. To extend control to the whole of society would greatly increase the costs of the dictatorship and provide little added reward.

Being interested in controlling only the government, a profit dictatorship is compatible with a relatively free market. With reasonable luck it need not create military ventures or international crises to hold its position —a measure of freedom not always open to the totalitarian dictatorship. So long as no serious competitors are visible, the profit dictatorship may also permit a fair amount of open criticism.

Legitimacy and Tenure

Legitimacy has been construed as the acceptance of a major bargain between the rulers and ruled. At its most elemental level this is an agreement by the people to pay taxes and obey the government, in return for being allowed to stay alive and out of prison. No population is homogeneous, however, and the profit dictatorship seems to live most easily in a bimodal population, with many very poor and a few very rich. The dictator protects the wealth and income sources of the rich, and draws most of his top staff from that group. The rich therefore accept—that is, legitimize—his rule. With the government on their side, the rich have strong bargaining power with the poor, whom they hire in their farms and factories, and as servants. The poor accept the dictatorship because they see no alternative. Their bosses and the government have a coalition against them, and if they challenge either authority they may be jailed, fired from their jobs, or both.

There is nothing about wanting wealth and authority that necessarily deprives a man of sympathy, and a dictator *may* do useful things for the people, such as teaching them trades, giving them land, or building roads, hospitals, and schools. However, such moves will not be rational unless they are seen as strengthening, or at least not weakening, the regime. They may strengthen it by softening frustrations which might lead to revolt, or by providing a more productive population for the government to exploit. This is in line with the earlier conclusion that one has more power among others with power than among the weak. Not infrequently the dictator faces the dilemma that if he tries to keep the people down they are sure to revolt, while if he tries to improve their situation they may be less likely to revolt, but be better able to make a success of it if they do. So long as he can get away with it, his best technique is apparently to promise reforms to the poor at the expense of the rich, while quietly assuring the rich that he will not carry them out.

The threat to the profit dictator may come not so much from his subjects as from competitors who envy his position. Latin American dictators typically come from high army positions. Controlling the arm of force, they consolidate their position therein by promising government posts, power, and income to other officers who will support them. When the time seems right, the army overthrows the existing dictator, and installs the general in his place. His position is not stable, however. Since the dictator must spread his attention over all phases of government, he cannot keep in as close touch with the army as before. In due time another general forms a new coalition in the army, and the cycle is repeated.

It is, of course, possible that a dictator may develop a high sense of social welfare, and conscientiously try to rule for the good of his people. If he does so in a bimodal population of the sort described, however, he may lose the support of the rich, who might throw their weight behind a rival. The mere continuance of the successful profit dictatorship will itself change the structure of the society somewhat, by making a new class of rich out of high friends and supporters of the government.

Needless to say, any real profit dictatorship is much more complex than this brief outline suggests. There are not merely the rich, the poor, the army, and the dictator. There are also trade unions, newspapers, poets and dramatists, student movements, popular leaders left over from previous regimes, foreign corporations, neighboring states, distant world powers, and a host of other forces which can do disconcerting things just as the dictator thinks that everything is under control. The actual operation of a dictatorship, like the operation of any other major organization, is more an art than a science, and seems bound to remain so. Among other devices, most modern dictatorships conduct elections so as to keep the appearance of popular sponsorship and legitimacy. But they try to arrange the election districts, voting eligibility, party structures, propaganda, nominations, or the counting of ballots so as to assure their own continuance.

There are numerous intervening stages between the profit dictatorship and a full democracy, including societies whose people have accepted the notion that those who control government are expected to use it for their own benefit, and those which accept the doctrine that "to the victor belong the spoils." There is also no sharp dividing line between profit and transition dictatorships. If the profit dictatorship uses a reformist ideology, or actually institutes substantial reforms, either to help consolidate its power or to help the people, it takes on some of the character of the transition dictatorship, to be discussed below.

CRISIS AND TRANSITION DICTATORSHIPS

The profit dictatorship is operated in the interest of the dictator and his associates. In order to make its task of control easier the dictatorship may rationalize to the people that it is actually doing good for them, too—and it may actually do so. But as a profit organization, the dictatorship does for the people only what it needs to do *in its own best interest*.

It is at least theoretically possible that a dictatorship might be used in the bona fide interests of the people. The *crisis* dictatorship is one such instance. The most obvious example is a major war, which no nation can prosecute without substantially curtailing normal freedoms. The chaotic multiparty government of France after World War II was a lesser, but very real, crisis, which was met by deliberately giving "strong man" powers to de Gaulle in 1958.

At other times the informed members of a society might feel it desirable in the real interests of the people to bring about quickly some massive change which would otherwise take a century or two—such as rapid industrialization of a primitive society, or the elimination of a caste system or religion which inhibits individual and social development. A dictatorship to carry this out may be called a *transition* dictatorship. Despite a seemingly legitimate purpose, there is always the risk that, once installed, the dictatorship cannot or will not let go. This and other problems of crisis and transition dictatorships are the subject of this section.

Crisis Dictatorship

While recognizing that other types of crisis may be handled through dictatorial or semidictatorial powers, the present section will deal only with war. To focus the problem, it will deal only with the situation in well-established democracies.

There is no doubt that in a major war ordinary freedoms are drastically curtailed, and that the people widely agree to the curtailment. Men are drafted into the military and ordered to risk their lives. Many are frozen into or driven out of their customary jobs. Rationing places limits on what they can buy or make, while price controls limit the prices at which they can sell. They may be prohibited from striking, limited in their traveling, or forced by various pressures to work long hours and to buy government bonds.

In addition, the government directly and indirectly controls the flow of information. This does not mean that all news is distorted, since accurate information on many topics is important for prosecuting the war effort—as will be seen in the subsequent chapters on planning. It does mean, however, that what the public hears depends more on its probable contribution to victory than on its merit as history. The victories and heroism of one's own side are exaggerated, while its losses, stupidities, and defections are minimized or omitted. Lasswell has reported the typical in-group and out-group reactions, in which *both* sides represent themselves as moral, appreciative, protective, helpful, and certain of victory; while representing the enemy as immoral, insolent, menacing, destructive, and certain to lose.[7]

In long-established democracies, such as England, Scandinavia, and the United States, the totalitarian tactics of the secret police are not in evidence. But this is apparently a reflection of the low level of internal subversion, rather than absence of willingness to use such tactics. With respect to one obvious group that *was* deemed a security risk, secret police tactics *were* used in the United States during World War II. Without warrants or formal charges, thousands of Japanese-Americans along the west coast, many of them citizens, were suddenly arrested and placed in concentration camps. With relatively little regard for their individual loyalty or prior behavior, many were held until the war was over. Many were forced by the circumstances to sell their homes or farms under conditions where bargaining power was almost nonexistent, with the result that they were deprived of property without due process.

That democratic governments do not become even more dictatorial during war is determined by lack of cause rather than fundamental objection—and the reason is clear. Suppose during World War II the British or American citizen faced the question: If conditions reached the point at which we had to choose between complete dictatorship at home or loss of the war to Hitler, which would you vote for? Since most people would prefer a home-grown dictator to a foreign one, the practical effect is that war legitimizes dictatorship, even though it may not be fully utilized. This conclusion is not diminished if the war is started by the arrogance or blundering stupidity of one's own government.

Granted the impossibility of prosecuting a major war with full normal democratic freedoms, to give a government great power incurs the risk that the officials may use that power to dig themselves in permanently. What is the risk that the voluntary grant of dictatorial powers may be kept by the government when the crisis is over?

In a well-established democracy the risk is apparently slight. All the forms of democracy, notably the opposition party, continue undiminished. The opposition party is not merely tolerated, but is made an important part of the psychological structure. The minority party accepts the overriding importance of victory, and party differences largely disappear with respect to military operations and their most important domestic concomitants, such as rationing, production and price controls, and the draft. These things become national, not party, programs, and their full support by the minority party symbolizes the national unity.

Meanwhile the executive division engages in many actions far beyond its peacetime power. But the legislature passes laws formally granting these extraordinary powers, and the courts uphold their constitutionality.

---

[7] Harold D. Lasswell, Nathan Leites, and Associates, *Language of Politics* (New York: George W. Steward, Inc., 1949), p. 41.

Many such grants of power are tied temporarily to the war emergency, leaving their use illegitimate if continued after the war. Elections continue, even if the people do not "swap horses in midstream."[8]

The crux of the matter is that in a strong democracy the stringent controls are enforced mainly by self-discipline, not governmental controls. Very importantly, wartime distortions of news are carried out by the voluntary cooperation of the news media, not by the government's taking over the media. The return of democracy is assured because all its forms, especially an independent press and a functioning opposition party, are eager and ready for the task.

Although the curtailment of freedoms during a full blown war of limited duration seems relatively safe, the present cold war raises special problems, since it is a state of semicrisis which could continue for half a century or more. As a semicrisis it seems to many persons to justify restrictions on freedom which we typically associate with war, such as denial of the right to advocate ideas resembling those advanced by the enemy. At the same time, the long duration of the international tension means that the restrictions tend to take on a permanent, rather than emergency, character. The risk to freedom here is a possible permanent acceptance of government controls over the flow of political ideas, and the denial of freedom to organize for certain political goals. The problem is the long-known one, that a little loss of freedom makes it more difficult for the citizen to defend his remaining freedom, and that unless freedom is scrupulously defended at all times except in obvious emergency the curtailments can easily snowball.

Because of its great significance to the long-term status of freedom, this problem seems worth investigating in more detail. Let us first list some restrictions or disqualifications that many persons think may properly be applied to known communists because of the cold war relation. They may be discharged from public employment, "sensitive" private employment, or teaching. They may be denied federal funds for a National Science Foundation fellowship for graduate study, or a student loan for undergraduate study. They may be jailed for contempt of Congress if they refuse to answer questions. They may face various difficulties in their private work life, such as serious loss of reputation, promotability, and general personal power.

Second, we can list some kinds of persons or relationships of persons to the communist issue. *A* is a communist. *B* is not at all a communist. But he strongly believes in the Bill of Rights, and believes that freedom is jeopardized when *anyone* is prohibited from expressing his views, and therefore defends *A*'s freedom of speech. *C* is a college professor who has described *A* on a recommendation blank as competent, reliable, coopera-

---

[8] Under the constitutional amendment which prohibits an American president from serving more than two terms, an interesting question arises as to what would happen if the second term of a highly competent and popular president were to expire at a crucial point in a major war.

tive, and a loyal citizen (to the best of *C*'s knowledge), because these are the traits which *A* displayed to the professor.[9] *D* is an employer or college administrator who has hired, or granted a scholarship to, an applicant, relying partly on a recommendation by *A*, although *A* was not known personally to the employer or administrator at the time. *E* is an intelligence officer in the foreign service who years earlier recommended a policy which subsequently turned out to be advantageous to the communists. *F* is a person who has observed that merely to have one's name mentioned in connection with an allegedly subversive event can subject him to suspicion, harassment, and loss of promotability. Before a committee of Congress, *F* therefore refuses to name persons he is sure are noncommunists, but who were present at an allegedly subversive meeting.

We now have a list of some disqualifications or limitations that might seem to be legitimately applied to communists, as presumed enemies of the nation. We also have a list of six categories of persons, *A* through *F*, only the first of which represents a communist or a supporter of the communist point of view. Yet over a period of only a few months before this chapter was written (in the summer of 1961) instances were reported in which one or more of the disqualifications or limitations was suffered, not by communists (category *A*), but by persons in categories *B* through *F*. Now it is possible that some of the persons in the *B–F* group *were* communists. But the reports did not indicate that they were so charged, and the difficulties they faced arose solely from their status in the *B–F* group.

These instances illustrate the way in which suspicion and curtailment of freedom tend to spread from the subversive himself to those who have been in contact with him, to those who refrain from condemning without evidence, and, perhaps of greatest significance, to those who do nothing more than staunchly defend traditional constitutional freedoms. The problem is often difficult for the layman to understand. Because persons who hold conservative and "safe" views seldom have their freedoms curtailed, the defense of *freedom* typically takes the form of defending *persons* whose ideas are considered nonconformist, heretical, and subversive. If freedom is to be preserved it is imperative to understand that defending a person's *freedom* in no degree implies defense of or agree-

---

[9] Some interesting questions arise in this area. Suppose you are a professor, and feel the following statement to be justified: "Although I have no evidence of overt affiliations, I think from some things he has said that this student may have some slight communist leanings." Because you know from experience that government administrators get into great difficulty if a communist is discovered on their staffs, particularly if there is any prior indication of possible doubt of loyalty, you expect that to make the statement on a recommendation blank would kill the student's chances of getting a civil service job he has applied for, and for which he seems highly competent. Should you report your suspicion, even if you are quite uncertain about it? Or should you assume that loyalty, like honesty, should be treated as unquestioned until there is convincing evidence to the contrary? Among other questions, what are your respective obligations to the government, the administrator, and the student? What will be the effect on the feeling of students in general about freedom to inquire and express themselves if they know that their professors must answer questions of this sort?

ment with his ideas. We have learned how to defend freedom in normal times, and how to regain it after a relatively short emergency. How to maintain it during an indefinitely long semicrisis is a problem which we have by no means satisfactorily solved.

The "Transition" Dictatorship

In all past history, large changes in the organization or control of society have come through evolution, revolution, or external forces, such as foreign conquest. With increasing knowledge of social change and social structures, man has been giving increased thought to the possible conscious control of the direction and speed of social change. The Tennessee Valley Authority, city planning and slum clearance, and the legislated and court decreed changes in race relations are only three of the areas in which such controls have already been exerted in the United States. On a much larger scale, educated natives of primitive and impoverished nations now visualize the possibility of changing to an advanced industrial status in a massive, rapid movement. These changes are not revolutionary in the older sense that the poor seize power from the rich. Nor are they utopian in the sense that they seek some dreamy idealistic state. They are a pragmatic attempt to change from a known, existing, unsatisfactory condition to a known condition which already exists in workable form elsewhere in the world.

Such a transition involves not merely the economic and industrial changes which come through building roads, mines, factories, mechanized farms, and banks. It requires that tribal and extended family structures be replaced by urban relations, and that people be trained to new notions of time, regularity, and punctuality. They must learn about property, money, and credit. They must also learn new sets of in and out groups, new attitudes toward them, perhaps a new religion, and they must replace their magic with science. In short, the whole culture must be reconstructed, in what may be called the "social leap."

The leap may not be as long or large as indicated. Many nations of Latin America, Mediterranean Africa, the Middle East, and the Far East are neither savage nor completely undeveloped. Many of their people nevertheless live close to subsistence level, and receive little or no education. Here large changes are possible.

In the leap from savagery there is no way in which democratic techniques can be used to decide for or against the change, since only a small minority of educated leaders, including some who have spent time in advanced areas, can understand the nature of the goal and the problems of the transition. Nor can the market process make the decision, for reasons seen in Chapter 31. There is nevertheless a wide and deep desire in many places for *some* such leap to be made. The practical present question seems to be not so much *whether* it will be tried, but when, with what techniques, and with what impact on the advanced nations and the cold war. In semideveloped nations, as in Latin America, the decision might be reached by overtly democratic process. But the masses of un-educated people would have to vote on the basis of their feelings about particular leaders, rather than on policies which require technical educa-tion far above their level.

Democracy, Dictatorship, and Legitimacy

We shall not attempt to trace the details of the social leap. But it raises some important questions about the relationship between people and gov-ernment, both during and after the leap. In the first place, it is possible for a transition of major size to be accomplished without dictatorial con-trols, and Puerto Rico is a notable example. Its "Operation Bootstrap" was started in 1940. One of its originators was Luis Muñoz Marín, who has been governor since Puerto Rico became self-governing in 1952. Its in-dustry and agriculture have been diversified and rapidly expanded, urban and rural slum clearance has greatly improved housing, and real per capita income is doubling each decade. It is visited by representatives of unde-veloped nations from all over the world, who want to find what it is possible to accomplish under a democratic regime. The people reportedly show no interest in communism, which is not outlawed.

Few areas have the advantages possessed by Puerto Rico. So long as it was a dependency of the United States it had no problem of self-defense, and still has none. It long had the stabilizing influence of being governed from the United States, and of stable American markets for its produce. In recent years it has had tax advantages and labor costs which made American firms not merely willing, but eager, to settle there. Hence, Puerto Rico's example provides no assurance that other nations could necessarily achieve the same success without dictatorial controls. By con-trast, the strong ties of the Chinese to the family and the land, along with their ancestor worship and immobility, might make industrialization and efficient farming well-nigh impossible until these cultural traits are broken —a process that could take centuries by evolutionary methods.

In a broad sense, Soviet Russia is the prototype of the notion of dic-tatorship used for transitional purposes. Although the discussion that follows is not based entirely on the Russian experience, and is not an exact description of it, it does draw on that experience for important questions and observations. Karl Marx, the ideological progenitor of the Russian Revolution, and Lenin, Trotsky, and the others who brought it into being, saw themselves as the creators of a new society. According to plan, the managers of the Russian Revolution of 1917 formed a dictator-ship, designed to liquidate or incapacitate its obvious enemies, and to force its supposed friends into the pattern of the new state.

The alleged major bargain is that the people turn over all powers to the dictatorship. They agree to make great temporary sacrifices under the direction of the dictatorship, including possible harsh controls. In return the dictatorship will create a greatly improved society, and in due course return it to the control of the people. Since the new society is expected to be so obviously superior that virtually no one would oppose it, dictatorial controls would then be superfluous and democracy could prevail. Dictatorship is deemed necessary for the transition, however, because without revolution the owners of industry and land could prevent or sabotage the change, and because many of the people in whose interests the change is made may not initially recognize the potential advantages, and may therefore oppose the new system. Even if the change could be made by evolution, it would take 150 years, instead of 40 or 50 under dictatorship. These are the arguments used to legitimize the dictatorship. Because the change is so large that it affects every phase of society, we will consider the transition dictatorship to be totalitarian, not merely authoritarian.

Maintaining the Dictatorship. In a democracy if a man wants to serve his fellows in public office, he must first get elected. But if the voters do not see eye to eye with his program, the necessity of getting votes may cause him seriously to modify the program. Similarly, if a social leap requires dictatorship, those in charge must give first priority to maintaining the dictatorship, even if this requires actions which inhibit the leap. We will first examine some techniques for maintaining dictatorship, after which we will look at its potentialities as an instrument of rapid social progress.

1. The *political party* now seems to be the most effective technique of control between sponsors and government staff, in both dictatorship and democracy. Russia has maintained only a single party. Red China and some of the Soviet satellites have four to six parties. These reflect allegedly divergent points of view, but representatives elected by them vote the Communist Party line. They typically apologize for not yet having learned the true doctrine, and promise to work hard at the task. The sponsors of the dominant party(s) are the dictator and his immediate followers, and the party(s) reflect(s) their wishes, not the people's. And since the party is the agency which controls the government, it is the head of the party rather than the chief of state who is the real boss. This is parallel to the corporation, where the board of directors are the agents of the sponsors (or may *be* the chief sponsors), while the president is the "chief of state." In the event of conflict, the chairman of the board, not the president, normally has the final word. In both the dictatorship and the corporation, the same man may fill both roles, but it is in his role of chairman of the board or party that he exercises control.

To speak in terms of the single party in Russia, the party selects likely looking persons from the population, trains, indoctrinates, and gives party membership to them. The party roster is the pool from which the government draws its chief officers—though not all members of the government need come from the party. This technique assures that all persons in sensitive government posts will know the party ideology and techniques.

The party structure roughly parallels, but is separate from, the government structure. We have seen earlier that it is difficult to have prompt, accurate communication between the top and bottom levels of a large organization, because the bargaining and authority relations tend to distort the information, and to inhibit any by-passing of intermediate levels. The party short-circuits the structure by putting party members at strategic spots throughout the whole government structure. In reporting information to the party, the member is responsible only to the party, not to his boss in the government. In return, he carries party policies directly to his post. By this technique, party directives can reach the lowest levels of government undiluted by the long hierarchical chain of the government itself.

This same technique also permits the party to penetrate and control nongovernmental agencies. Whether it be the Soviet government's own farm or factory, or a private firm or club in Hitler's Germany or Mussolini's Italy, members of the party were there, and carried information efficiently in both directions. Party members similarly can be put into every technical or professional association, labor union, school, fraternity, fishing club, or charity. Thus, as the Soviet Constitution of 1936 puts it in Article 126, the party will be "the leading core of organizations of working people, both public and state." Because information to and from the party flows around, rather than through, the government and other organizational hierarchies, the party can achieve an all-pervasiveness which would be extremely difficult for the formal government structure.

Despite its effectiveness for dictatorial control, this arrangement brings a split loyalty for the authorities *within* any one organization, government or private. For example, in his line function a factory superintendent is responsible to the factory manager for all operations below his own level of authority. He may conclude that certain organizational changes at lower levels will bring higher production, and the manager may agree. But if the superintendent tries to put them into effect, one of his subordinates who is a party member may tell him to stop, as the practice is contrary to party policy. Although such conflicts can be worked out, the superintendent nevertheless faces two conflicting authorities. The conflict does not necessarily disappear if the superintendent himself belongs to the party, since belonging to the party does not remove his responsibilty to the manager.

This conflict is apt to be sharpest during the early days of the dictatorship, when both the party and the factory staff have much to learn. As experience increases, the party adjusts to many practical necessities of production, and the producers adjust to the practical realities of the party. The awareness of conflict also goes down, as the regulations increasingly take on the character of "spontaneous field controls,"[10] under which

---

[10] See Robert A. Dahl and Charles E. Lindblom, *Politics, Economics, and Welfare* (New York: Harper Bros., 1953), pp. 99–104 and *passim*.

people behave in certain ways for the simple reason that they are so thoroughly conditioned that it does not occur to them to do otherwise. That is, both sets of people develop a common subculture. For this reason, as the dictatorship matures, its harshness and apparent ruthlessness tend to decline. But the dictatorship is no less in charge.

2. Obviously, the dictatorship must control the *armed forces*. Before the field controls take over, the dictator may need special armed forces at his personal disposal, such as the SS Troops, or Elite Guard, of Hitler, and the Secret Police of Stalin. It is mainly these troops that are the "terror" in the dictatorship, and who "liquidate" its enemies without warning or trial. With the help of information from the party, these are the forces which make the citizen afraid to talk frankly to his neighbor, his fellow workmen, or even his family.

3. Despite these stupendous differences, the dictatorship's basic *internal relations* are similar to those of other organizations. The sponsors have certain aims. They select persons who seem competent to effectuate them. Flows of information go to the staff in the form of instructions, and feedback is returned for evaluating performance. Rewards are so directed as to encourage desired performance and punish the undesired. The positive rewards of the dictatorship are similar to those elsewhere—income, recognition, and opportunities to exercise power. The distinctive features are two. The first is the widespread use of negative power, not merely against those who violate important rules, but against those who simply fail to perform, or who criticize the wrong things. The second is the substitution of the dictator's will for broader-based consensus. "Due process" becomes the carrying out of the dictator's wishes, and "rules of evidence" are whatever influences his decisions. The dictator also has use for persons with stored-up frustrations, who are rewarded with opportunities to commit assorted indignities against other human beings. At the height of overt dictatorial controls, the dictatorship behaves like an overlarge racket.

So long as people remain who do not like the regime, the dictator will centralize as many decisions as possible. Even to the most extreme dictator, however, many things are largely irrelevant to his power. These can remain decentralized, and include the layout of streets, repair of sewers, administration of building codes, apprehension and punishment of ordinary (i.e., nonpolitical) criminals, and the physical techniques of production. If the dictatorship continues long enough, field controls may take over sufficiently to allow more local discretion. So long as the party remains ubiquitous and centralized, the actual administrative machinery of the dictatorship might conceivably be quite decentralized. This problem will be discussed further in the following chapter.

4. A basic power factor is control of *information*, not only of the mass media, but also of the professional and other journals with limited circulation. Foreign travel must be restricted, since it might provide "socially undesirable" information. If the control of information could be

absolute, the dictatorship might maintain itself by that means alone. Complete control of internal information is not possible, however, for reasons to be seen in the last chapter.

The dictatorship may effectively control foreign news. But even here, inconsistencies may reveal more than is intended, as is reported to some American visitors by ordinary Russians. "The government tells us that capitalism has failed, that millions of Americans are unemployed and starving, and that the factories are closed and inefficient. But later they tell us that we are progressing so rapidly that in ten years we can live as well as Americans." The Russians apparently feel that their domestic control is now secure enough, and that the people sufficiently accept the system and the government's information, that their citizens are now allowed much freedom to talk to foreign visitors. The government, however, does not seem ready to risk foreign travel except to a limited group of government representatives, spies, scientists, and artists.

5. A thorny problem of dictatorship is that of *succession*. In monarchies the rule goes to the eldest son, or to some other specified relation, while voting selects new rulers in a democracy. In case of death, in England the party selects a new Prime Minister (who is nominally appointed by the Crown), while in the United States the Vice President takes over until the next election. MacIver states the widely accepted conclusion that:

> dictatorship can invent no constitutional device for the succession to dictatorial power. If it were to achieve any such device it would become legitimate and in so becoming would cease to be a dictatorship.[11]

It is perhaps useful to reopen this conclusion in the present framework.

There is nothing conceptually difficult about the notion that a whole people might voluntarily give a government dictatorial powers to achieve a "social leap," even if there are grave doubts that the people can ever get the power back. But a stupid bargain over authority can still be a bargain, and therefore make the authority legitimate. Thus viewed the problem of succession in dictatorship seems not so much a problem of legitimacy (or constitutionality), as of the practical mechanics of transferring power without bloodshed. An absolute dictator, for example, might name his successor in his will. Or he might select an advisory council of five men who, after his death, are to select one of their own members as the new dictator, who would thereafter fill subsequent vacancies on the council. A game theorist may demonstrate that the successive coalitions within this council would be fearful to behold, or that the existence of the council would materially increase the dictator's risk of assassination. This is a different matter, however, from saying that dictatorship cannot create a formally recognized technique of succession. The crux of the conventional analysis seems to be that dictatorship itself is il-

---

[11] MacIver, *op. cit.*, p. 233.

legitimate, which conclusion automatically makes any device for dictatorial succession illegitimate and "unconstitutional." If we accept the notion that a particular kind of dictatorship might be legitimate, it is conceptually possible, even if not practically so, to have a legitimate succession. Perhaps the Board of Trustees of Harvard University provides the perfect model, in its power to appoint all its own successors in perpetuity.

Some Troublesome Trappings of Dictatorship. We have seen that, once in power, the dictatorship must necessarily give first priority to keeping its power, and that this may lead it into activities which inhibit the performance of its supposed main goal. Some of these activities may be minor nuisances and wastes. Others raise the question whether dictatorship other than for the short crisis can ever be worth its costs to the people.

First is the development of a personality cult around the dictator, and a tendency to deify him. This move greatly increases the distance between the dictator and his possible rivals, raises his monopoly advantage, and makes the people less likely to question his wisdom. The Russians have retroactively virtually deified Lenin, and Stalin made much of the personality cult for himself. However, the party presently seems unwilling to permit Khrushchev the same latitude.[12]

Second, the great leap is given an aura of mysticism and inevitability. While a semanticist might say that a planned social transition from state X to state Y is to be effected through the medium of dictatorship, such language does not make hearts pound or inspire dedication, and the goal is described instead as the ideal, irrepressible, great hope of mankind. Its alleged inevitability is a major psychological device. If the goal cannot fail, no work in its behalf is in vain, and any such work can therefore be neurologically rewarding.[13] A typical expression is the declaration of the Party Congress in Moscow in July, 1961 "Socialism (Communism) will take over from capitalism everywhere. Such is the objective law of the development of society."

Third, in order to have maximum psychological effect for support of the dictatorship, much of the promised future must lie beyond the present generation. If the dictator asks for sacrifices and discipline from existing people for their *own* future welfare, they may decide that their own later welfare is not worth the price, and insist on more in the present. But how much sacrifice may be asked for *future* generations? Interpersonal comparisons of utility are extremely tenuous, comparisons between generations are impossible, and the question is therefore unanswerable. By the same token, the government's assertion that future welfare *is* more important cannot be disproved. Moreover, the government makes its as-

---

12 See James Biddleford (pseud.), "Russia Returns to Collective Leadership," *The New Leader,* August 29, 1960, pp. 8 ff.

13 See Chapter 8.

sertion endlessly, while counterassertions are suppressed. Where objective decisions are not possible, assertion tends to carry the field.

Fourth, symbol and ritualism abound in dictatorships—parades, military reviews, songs, poems, flags, and mass meetings. One symbolic relation is particularly important in the early, uncertain, and violent stage of dictatorship—the oath of allegiance by devoted followers to the person or regime of the dictator, rather than to the nation or its government in the broad sense. The oath of loyalty is construed to take priority over any other obligation. In practice it becomes a commitment to spy and inform on anyone who opposes the dictator, even if this means to inform on friends, neighbors, and family. By such devices the dictatorship can minutely penetrate the society.

All nations have their heroes and dogmas. But the greater urge of the dictatorship to appear legitimate gives it a special need. The Marx-Lenin line is Bible and creed to the Russians. No matter how far they deviate from it in fact—and the deviations are frequent, great, and permanent —they never admit the discrepancy. They insist to the people that everything they do is in strict accord with the creed. Since the creed is accepted, to be consistent with it is to be legitimate. The Party Program of July 1961, for example, states that "The Communist Party of the Soviet Union follows the principle that the irreconcilable struggle against revisionism, dogmatism and sectarianism, against any deviation from Leninism. . . ." is necessary for strengthening the communist movement. Although such apparent dedication to Lenin probably does not prevent the government from doing anything it really wants to do, it often brings forth some tortuous rationalizations.

Fifth, the most troublesome of all dictatorial trappings may appear in the international scene. If the people show signs of disaffection for the government, they can be pulled into a coalition with it if the government can make itself seem their protector against a more fearsome enemy. In addition, even in the established democracy international crisis provides grounds for restricting criticism of government, and the dictatorship finds it a convenient, additional tool for legitimizing suppression. Now it is easy enough for a nation to have external enemies without really trying very hard. But the dictatorship often finds it expedient deliberately to generate enemies, and to create crises with them so as to justify the severity of its rule at home. The enemy must be made to appear power hungry and warmongering, since this situation rationalizes a military establishment and some occasional "pre-emptive defense" in the form of "liberating" small nations by invading them. Such action can be made more acceptable if the nation is simultaneously represented to have the world's finest people and social system, who therefore have a moral obligation to the rest of the world to control it.

Democracies are not totally immune to this problem. Under a state of continued international tension some candidate, elected official, or party can deliberately generate anger and war-like feelings toward another nation, in the hope of being swept into office by taking a stronger anti-enemy stand on this strong issue than the opponent. Despite some proneness of democracy to this behavior, the dictatorship's disciplined structure and control of mass information would normally give it the distinct superiority in the use of this technique.

Whereas the other trappings of dictatorship are mainly matters between the government and its own people, the militaristic and expansionistic aspects force other nations to spend huge sums in military preparation, to live in perpetual fear, and occasionally to fight real wars. The dictatorship may find it useful to develop an internal enemy as well, as Hitler did with the Jews in Germany.

Precisely which devices will be used to maintain any particular dictatorship depends much on the people, the dictator, the background and foreground facts, the strategic position of the nation in international politics, and a host of other factors. The important thing is that once in power, the dictatorship tends to follow the logic of its own survival, which may cause it to deviate far from what it was put into power to accomplish. As the industrialists who supported Hitler discovered, once the dictator is installed *he* is boss, and can liquidate his former friends as well as his former enemies. Hence, although the transition dictatorship may seem a logical means of achieving the social leap, its typical, troublesome trappings leave grave reservations about the technique. The question whether a totalitarian dictatorship over all phases of life can evolve peacefully into democracy is related to matters to be taken up in succeeding chapters, and will therefore be deferred until later.

A mutual interaction between goals and dictatorship can easily arise. The social leap may initially seem to justify the dictatorship. But if a dictator arises for other reasons, he may invent social goals to legitimize his control. In due time it may be impossible to tell whether the dictator exists for the goals or the goals for the dictator, and he himself may not know. In either case, maintenance of the dictatorship is the more immediate problem to the dictator, and takes precedence in his thinking.

To sharpen the problem and conclude the discussion, it might be speculated that a supranational government, such as a stronger United Nations, might develop a code for "legitimate dictatorship." Under it, a nation might file with the U.N. a timetable for the establishment and ultimate relaxation of transitional, dictatorial controls, simultaneously authorizing the U.N. to supervise and police the steps for the return to democratic controls. Such an arrangement would be a rough equivalent on a larger scale of the way in which a national labor union under the Labor Management Reporting and Disclosure Act is allowed to put a local union into a quasidictatorial trusteeship for a limited period of time. The law specifies the conditions under which the trusteeship may be exercised, and the timetable for relaxing it, while the Secretary of

Labor exercises a general supervision over the process. Such a program obviously could not work in a major nation, such as Russia, where policing would require a major war. It might conceivably work in the smaller emerging nations of Africa, Asia, and Latin America. This question is raised to help focus the nature of the transition dictatorship, not as a proposal, since the moral position of the U.N. would probably be untenable if it were, in effect, to endorse and "support" a dictatorship, even a temporary one.

X. THE PUBLIC
PRODUCTION OF
PRIVATE GOODS

Chapter 38

PLANNED ECONOMIES:
STATIC, KNOWN GOALS

In the view of the typical layman, socialist economic planning wipes out the profit motive. Further, as the layman sees it, it provides no incentive to save and invest, and no payments for land. If these things are so, then from the analysis of earlier chapters it would seem to follow that socialist planning also eliminates the only single-dimensional, quantitative measure of the performance of the enterprise and its managers, and that it probably has no mechanism for the efficient allocation of its land and its investment. To the person schooled in the market system, to expect a planned economy to perform under these circumstances is like depriving a farmer of sunlight and water and expecting him to grow crops. Yet planned economies do operate, and a current concern of many Americans about Russia's planned economy is that it may be producing alarmingly much, not that it cannot produce. The purpose of this and the next chapter is to examine the nature, role, and problems of planned economies.

We have seen that public goods must be publicly decided upon, whether in a planned or market economy. This means that the crux of the difference is whether *private* goods are publicly or privately planned and produced. Without arguing the precise meanings of these terms in practice, we will continue to consider the private production of private goods the same as the market system, or capitalism, and the public production of private goods the same as a centrally planned system, or socialism. Most actual nations have mixtures, not pure forms. Because it is easier to examine the pure cases first, this chapter will discuss the totally planned, public production of private goods, using Russia as the chief example, since it most nearly approximates that condition. Market systems which use much central planning, and socialist systems which use much market decision making will be examined in the latter part of the next chapter.

In important ways, the relation between a socialist government and its controlled enterprises is parallel to that between a large capitalist corporation and its wholly owned subsidiaries. We can think of General Motors as the planning agency and of Chevrolet and Fisher Body (two of the many divisions of General Motors) as the producing enterprises. The subsidiaries either (1) produce and exchange as instructed by General Motors, or (2) make their own decisions on these matters within limits allowed by General Motors. In fact, many aspects of managing a totally planned economy can be better understood by the capitalist-oriented reader if he imagines that General Motors were to buy up all productive enterprise in the nation, including agriculture and service industries.

Important differences remain, of course, in motivation. A private organization running the whole economy as a huge monopoly would presumably seek to make the largest profit, whereas a government may have other goals. Somewhat surprisingly, it makes little difference to the main outlines of planning, as such, whether the government is democratic or dictatorial. The staff function in carrying out the goals of the sponsors is largely independent of who the sponsors are, or what techniques they use for formulating their goals. That is, the goals sought by the government may be formulated by democratic or dictatorial political techniques, and they may be directed toward the welfare of the people or of the ruling clique. Once the production goals of the economy have been set, however, it makes little difference to the main planning process how they were arrived at in the first place, even though it would make a great deal of difference what the goals *are*.

Western libertarian socialists believe that central economic planning is compatible with much traditional capitalist freedom of consumer choice and occupational choice by workers. The possible validity of such proposals can best be judged at the end of the discussion of the totally centralized system, on which the main discussion will focus.

As to the possible goals of central planning, if the government's primary goal is military strength, its planning task, although still complex, is relatively direct. The goal is single-minded, and provides a criterion against which to measure all subdecisions—their contribution to the total military strength. The production of war goods is directly evaluable. And civilian goods are not measured by consumer welfare or desires, but by their ability to keep the civilian population in physical and mental shape to fight and produce. In any event, production for a military objective is essentially the production of public goods, not private. In the sense indicated above, in a war-oriented nation even private goods take on an essentially public character, since they are subordinated to a public goal.

The social leap discussed earlier has many facets, cultural, psychological, political, and economic. Within the economic sphere, its central theme is normally rapid industrialization and mechanization. Except in the agricultural sector, where the problem is more largely organizational, rapid industrialization means mainly the buildup of producer goods: factories, steel mills, railroads, mines, and power plants. Although these things are private goods in a capitalist system, they are not used by individuals and families. More importantly to planners, many decisions about producer goods can be made without too much regard for the ultimate set of consumer goods to be made, since any set will require a strong and reasonably balanced group of producer goods industries. As with a military objective, here, too, consumer goods are intended to keep the population in shape to create the industrial machine. Again, the planners have a relatively single-minded goal.

So long as the consumer is fed, clothed, and housed with the view to making him a more effective factor of production, it is feasible to speak of distributing consumer goods on the basis of *need*. If people are at or below subsistence level, needs can be biologically defined. The people need so many calories to work, so much clothing and shelter to be healthy, and so on. Even above subsistence, *need* may still have relatively sharp meaning if viewed as a means of getting the worker educated and keeping him mentally alert.

Whenever living rises much above the subsistence level, however, *need* ceases to have much meaning. A person may need transportation to work. But does he need a private car instead of riding the subway? He needs food, but does he need tender beef instead of tough? The man who does hard physical work needs more food than the sedentary worker. But once there is enough food for all, and people want frills, variety, and delicacies, how does one measure *need?* One needs water. But does he need running water? Hot as well as cold? In short, the typical communist and socialist references to distribution on the basis of need may be meaningful at the subsistence level. But above that level *need* is neither a measurable nor a useful concept. Plan or no plan, governmental goals or no governmental goals, dictatorship or democracy, as soon as the level of consumer goods rises from subsistence to relative affluence, there is no escaping the shift in production goals from what people *need* to what they *want*.

In this chapter we will examine some major problems of planning on the assumption that the planners have a sharply defined set of goals, whether for military goods or producer goods, and whether for subsistence or affluence levels of consumer goods. How consumer wants can be determined in an affluent planned society will be examined in the next chapter, along with the problem of changing goals. The present chapter will make a static analysis of the planned production of private goods, and the next one will take a more dynamic view. The present chapter will also assume complete knowledge by the planners of both their opportunity and preference functions, and will examine how these are converted into an actual operating system.

THE BASIC DECISIONS

What to Produce

The major decision areas are the same, whether the productive system is public and planned or market and unplanned, the first being the decision about what to produce, and in what quantities. Given their broad goals and objectives, the planners must break these into subgoals. At the very top they must decide on the relative quantities of public and of private goods, and then break each into its components, such as roads, parks, and military goods; and textiles and textile machinery, and so forth.

With What Resources, and What Distribution of Income?

Having decided to produce specified goods, the planners must decide what to make them with. A rational decision here requires first a cataloging of the available productive agents, such as agricultural land, petroleum reserves, workers, and locomotives. Although a long task, this is conceptually simple.

The next question is which combination of resources to apply to the production of any one thing, which question in a planned system is the same as has already been detailed for market economies. Shall steam be generated with coal, oil, or gas, and should house wiring be made of copper or aluminum?

At this point a completely planned system faces basic difficulties. The most elemental aspect of decision making is that it compares values with costs. If the planners are to make rational decisions about which resources to use, they must first place a *value* on each resource, such as coal, oil, and gas, or have no basis for making a decision among them. Here the planners are handicapped by the Marxist argument that land is provided free by nature, and that capital is only "congealed labor." Hence, neither land nor capital should be paid for, since all value is created by labor. Here Marx confused two quite different questions. The first is whether land and capital should be privately owned, with their owners receiving compensation. This is a value judgment, not the scientific judgment Marx claimed it to be, and the Soviets, or any other group, are free to express their preferences about it. Secondly, however, Marx assumed that the absence of payment to private owners is the same as absence of cost. This is an analytical judgment, on which Marx is wrong. The use of *any* factor entails costs, whether of scarcity, incompatibility, destruction, or disutility. The scarcity cost of digging coal from the ground is that it is not available to be dug out again a year or a generation hence. This scarcity cost prevails just as much in a socialist as in a capitalist nation. Similarly, savings invested in a power dam cannot also be used to make textile machinery. This Marxian error has caused the Soviet union great difficulty, from which it is just beginning to emerge.

Thus far, Soviet planners have expressed only vague awareness that land and capital *do* have costs. But they (including Khrushchev) have in recent years explicitly acknowledged that capital will be most productive if put into that use which has the shortest "payoff" period.[1] This is a definite, though backhanded, way of computing the cost of capital. As Campbell notes,[2] the payoff period of capital is nothing but its rate of return turned upside down. Omitting compounding, a payoff period of 5 years is the same as a 20 per cent return on investment, and a 25 year payoff is the same as a 4 per cent return. If money would pay a 10 per cent return if invested in one industry, then 10 per cent is its opportunity cost to the planners of putting it into another industry. The Marxist dogma prevents the Soviets from using this eminently sensible method of computing at least first approximation capital costs. Even more does it prevent them from using the far more sophisticated, full-fledged interest rate which reflects a much wider scope of supply and demand (cost and value) factors.

Thus far, the Soviets make no charge to the managers of an enterprise for the use of land,[3] and do not seem to recognize that its use does have real costs. They also rather consistently underestimate the costs of depreciation and obsolescence.[4] Until the planners place an explicit value on investment capital, on each piece of land and the resources extracted from it, and on the amount of depreciation and obsolescence, they can make only crude, rule-of-thumb calculations about how to produce any particular good at least cost. The fact that the government is both the owner and user of land and capital means there is no market in these factors, and hence no market price to determine their value.

At What Prices Shall the Products Sell?

Whether the system is socialist or capitalist, an automobile has more value than a match. For reasons to be seen later, it does not seem feasible for any but a few goods to be provided free of charge, since none is free of cost, and if goods are to be sold they must have prices.

The technique in market economies is to set the price at cost of production plus a profit, the amount of profit varying with the degree of monopoly, relative efficiency, bargaining skill, and other factors. The Soviets have adopted the same general principle of basing prices on costs, in accord with the Marxian doctrine of price as equaling "socially necessary cost." The particular concept they use is the "weighted average cost for the industry."[5] The government may charge more or less

---

[1] See Oleg Hoeffding, "The Soviet Reorganization of 1957," *American Economic Review* (May, 1959), p. 69.

[2] Robert W. Campbell, *Soviet Economic Power* (New York: Houghton Mifflin Co., 1960, paper), p. 103.

[3] *Ibid.*, p. 109.

[4] *Ibid.*

[5] Gregory Grossman, "Industrial Prices in the USSR," *American Economic Review* (May, 1959), p. 57. This is apparently the price which would seem most

than this sum, if it wishes to discourage or encourage the use of the product.

Although both consumers and producers can make rational calculations from these prices, the basic difficulty of the fully planned economy is that the prices of the factors, if they are priced at all, are themselves arbitrarily set by the planners. Hence, when a factory manager rationally chooses coal over oil, no one has any assurance that the lower *price* of coal represents a lower *cost* to the nation, particularly if the enterprises which produce them have not been charged for land or capital.

That scarcity costs of land and capital are not explicitly incorporated into the cost and price structure does not mean that the planners would be so stupid as to use a ton of diamonds from a freak deposit as if they had no more value than a ton of limestone which cost the same to extract. But where the difference in scarcity costs is not intuitively obvious, the Russians have no technique for incorporating this difference in their decisions, which fact seriously limits their rationality.

The same problem has been seen earlier in connection with *any* production of public goods, but is handled in capitalist and partially socialized countries by charging the government for factors at the prices determined in the market sector. The Soviets do somewhat the same by keeping their eye on prices in the surrounding capitalist markets, as reflected in the classic remark of Stalin that cotton must be more expensive than grain in Russia because this is the case in the world market.[6] Neither the Western nor the Russian economists seem impressed with this aspect of the Soviet system. Whether a totally planned economy can ever solve this problem satisfactorily without reference to surrounding markets is not yet known. The basic problem is that consensus valuations are determined basically by transactions. Since a complete socialist government is, in effect, both buyer and seller of land and capital, no exchange occurs in which to set these values.

By contrast, the Soviets use an essentially market technique to determine the price of labor, with the people as sellers and the government or its enterprisers as buyers. Higher prices are paid to induce people to learn scarce skills, to exert greater effort, or to move to understaffed industries or areas. Relative scarcities are thus reflected in the wage structure, which at least roughly resembles that of market systems.

THE PRODUCTION STRUCTURE

Any decision explicitly or implicitly involves sets, subsets, and subsubsets, and is in turn a subset within some larger decision. In an organization of more than a few persons, these sets and subsets of decisions are

---

applicable to the computation of the prices of goods to consumers. But the Soviets, according to Grossman, use as many as seven different types of prices, and it is not clear which is used for computing prices to consumers.
[6] *Ibid.*, p. 62.

made by sets and subsets of persons. There is no possibility that all decisions can be made by the top man, and "as an organization grows, it faces the problem of how—not of whether—to decentralize decision-making functions."[7]

Viewed purely as an organization, the planned economy faces many of the same essential problems as a large corporation—which it is. The first is that of horizontal integration. Assuming that it has decided to produce five billion bolts per year, shall they all be produced in one huge bolt works, or in a hundred small scattered ones? Shall all TV repairs for the whole nation be done in Minsk, or shall service be scattered so that no citizen is more than five miles from a repair station? Many factors enter a full decision on such matters, but the most obvious are transportation and communication costs and delays, and the relative efficiency of large and small plants. This latter problem, incidentally, illustrates an earlier point. Intuition alone will prevent obvious errors, such as centralizing TV repairs. Intuition not guided by prices cannot accurately answer whether electricity is more cheaply generated by water power or coal—a matter on which the Soviets admittedly erred badly.

Next is the question of vertical integration. Should an automobile plant merely assemble parts made in other plants, or should it make its own parts? If the latter, should it also make its own steel? Should it build its own assembly line and buildings? Starting from the other end, should the enterprise which mines iron ore also mine coal, make coke, smelt pig iron, and refine steel?

Third, what should be the product mix of a plant, and should it be oriented around factor inputs or product outputs? In the latter case all insulation products would be grouped in a plant, which might make glass wool, rock wool, glass foam, plastic foam, vermiculate, and aluminum insulation. In the former case, the product mix might be oriented around glass, and the plant would produce window glass, bottles, light bulb shells, and glass tubing. In a similar vein, should brass bolts be made in the same plant with steel bolts or with brass tubing? The number of such questions is almost limitless.

Perhaps because Marx wrote near the beginning of the industrial revolution, when larger plants seemed strikingly more efficient, and perhaps for dramatic effect, the Russians have displayed an almost idolatrous love of giantism.[8] By expanding plants beyond the limits of maximum efficiency, transportation costs included, they repeated toward midcentury the American mistakes of the early century, and are now learning the reversal to smaller, more scattered, plants.

We have seen in Chapter 27 that there is no such thing as one best

[7] David Granick's comment on Oleg Hoeffding's paper cited above, in *loc. cit.*, p. 81.
[8] Lazar Volin, "Soviet Agriculture Under Khrushchev," *American Economic Review* (May, 1959), pp. 16, 17, and 19 points to this situation in agriculture, and Campbell, *op. cit.*, p. 108 refers to gigantomania in industry.

structure for a large organization, and that different parts must have different structures if the whole is to be best adapted to its environment. The fact that the well-adapted organization is "messy" on paper, rather than neat and symmetrical, brings a direct conflict of goals at the top administrative levels. The top planners tend to prefer uniformity among the parts, because the greater the uniformity the fewer are the concepts they must learn in order to understand and manage the system. The top planners must almost necessarily think in terms of an over-simplified model of the system. But what seems more efficient in their model is apt to be less efficient in actual operation.

Coordination

The number of units of products must be coordinated in many ways, including two main ones. To illustrate, the total production of lead from all sources must be programmed to equal the total uses of lead, whether the lead comes from lead mines or as a by-product of zinc, copper, or silver mines. At the same time, the total inputs to the plants producing lead must be sufficient to achieve their planned outputs, these inputs including pencils, light bulbs, locomotives, and cranes. The input of any one component must be geared to that of other components, as in the automobile industry, where the number of motor blocks, transmissions, wheels, and windshields must all come out even. Finally, the total of planned inputs to all industries must be coordinated with the total resources available for the purpose. After a lag of perhaps 20 years, the Soviets are now apparently realizing that input-output analysis, linear programming, and other mathematical techniques for handling complex decisions through electronic computers, are potentially highly useful for their purposes.[9]

THE DECISION STRUCTURE

At the larger levels, the Soviet system must face the same problems as a capitalist corporation as to whether to arrange its subdivisions on the basis of product, process, materials, region, or function. If the major division is on one basis, the subdivisions must be on another, with provision for coordinating the parts. For example, if a major division is by product, and a function within each product division is that of wage setting, then the wage-setting divisions for all products must be coordinated, or a chaotic wage structure will arise.

The Russians have experimented with various arrangements, but dur-

---

[9] Herbert S. Levine, "The Centralized Planning of Supply in Soviet Industry," in Morris Bornstein and Daniel Fusfeld, *The Soviet Economy* (Homewood, Ill.: Richard D. Irwin, Inc., 1962), p. 106. Levine (p. 107) notes the irony that these highly useful techniques were long boycotted in Russia because they are too capitalistic, and in the United States because they are too socialistic.

ing most of its history the major divisions have been by product, or industry. At different times, the ministries of production normally numbered from 20 to 40,[10] each in charge of some area, such as agriculture, power, mining, or clothing. The manager of each plant, or enterprise, reported to a regional director for his industry, who reported to the national minister for that industry. Coordination among industries was done at the very top level by the ministries, under the supervision of *Gosplan*, the overall planning agency.

In 1957 a basic reorganization was made. Gosplan does not now work directly with the ministries of separate industries. The nation instead has been divided into regional councils, each of which is responsible for *all* the industries within its region. The chairman of the Council of Ministers of each of "the 15 Union Republics is now charged with the direction and supervision of the regional Economic Councils."[11] The reorganization seems to imply that coordination of industries within regions is more important than coordination of regions within industries. The reorganization followed years of wide and vocal criticism of the previous arrangement. One purpose was to eliminate "a *sub rosa* network of 'expeditors,' 'fixers,' and so on, who were well-rewarded for their ingenious and highly personal methods of getting for their employers needed materials and machinery."[12] A second purpose was to eliminate excessive duplication of technical and administrative facilities. For example, "In one case, where enterprises in seven different industries were using a raw mineral taken from one quarry, there were seven separate and distinct quarrying units in that quarry, each under the jurisdiction of a different ministry."[13]

As interpreted by Soviet experts in this country, the reorganization does not weaken central control, but rather achieves the " 'transfer of centralism nearer to the immediate production process.' "[14] The new arrangement more nearly parallels the organization of the Party, and hence is easier for the latter to control.[15]

Just as capitalist firms undergo periodic reorganization to improve their efficiency, the Soviet planning and control structure has been reorganized with great frequency over the past several decades.[16]

---

[10] *Ibid.*, p. 87.

[11] Hoeffding, *op. cit.*, p. 73. The precise number of these councils seems to depend on what kind of unit is being counted, and one source makes reference to approximately a hundred. (See Samuel Hendel, ed., *The Soviet Crucible* [Princeton, N.J.: D. Van Nostrand Co., Inc., 1959], p. 472.)

[12] William N. Loucks, *Comparative Economic Systems* (New York: Harper & Brothers, 6th edition, 1961), p. 484.

[13] *Ibid.*

[14] See Hoeffding, *op. cit.*, p. 70, and the strong confirmation of this interpretation by David Granick immediately following the article. Robert W. Campbell, *op. cit.*, takes the same view. The overall present discussion also draws heavily on David Granick's *The Red Executive* (New York: Doubleday & Co., 1960).

[15] Hoeffding, *op. cit.*, p. 75.

[16] Levine, *op. cit.*, pp. 87–88.

Planning Procedures

The technique of planning is complex in detail, simple in outline, and consists of a series of information flows, decisions, and bargains. The overall goals are formulated by starting from the existing situation, and modifying it in the light of hoped-for changes and new evaluations of the possible opportunities. Planning is done primarily in units of physical quantities of steel, coal, clothing, and so forth. After each goal is broken into its major input components, the rough plans are turned over by the Gosplan to the next lower authorities. These were formerly the ministries of production, and are now the regional councils, where the goals are broken into regional quotas, industry quotas, and finally into quotas for individual enterprises.

Important aspects of decisions and bargains are made at the level of the enterprise, which is the productive unit, roughly equivalent to the operating division of the large capitalist corporation. In consultation with his superintendents, the manager of the enterprise examines the proposed quota in light of his available equipment and manpower. Both for information to the manager and for increased cooperation, the plans may be submitted to the rank and file workers, and to their union, for comment. The tentative quota is then sent back up the same channels, with appropriate modifications and comments. These may be such comments as: "Ten per cent increase is impossible. But we should be able to do five, and perhaps seven." Or, "Quota can be met from existing equipment if we receive the following improvements in quality of materials and quantity of labor, plus additional housing for 50 workers." This set of discussions is simultaneously a decision process in making the plan and a production bargain between the planners and the plant managers. As these comments and modifications travel back up, they are re-coordinated with the modified forms of other details of the plan. As Campbell puts it:

> Only the most aggregative kind of coordination is carried on at the center. The whole plan is not drawn up in Moscow, but rather the entire hierarchical pyramid of Soviet economic organizations participates in the process. At each level people operate with different degrees of detail, subject to varying degrees of constraint. The whole plan is finally produced by a process of negotiation and reconciliation between the different levels.[17]

If the completed plan were to reflect perfect knowledge, it could specify every item of material or labor to be received in each plant; what plant, mine, or farm it would come from; and every item of output, and where it should go. For purposes of control (to be seen below), the values (in transfer prices) of these items would also be given. Since much of the output of one factory is input to another, the plan would also have to include delivery schedules—even as between Fisher Body and Chevrolet. If the plan were perfect, everything would then be produced as scheduled, with no shortages and no leftovers.

---

[17] *Op. cit.*, p. 94.

In actuality the plans cannot and need not be so precise, even aside from error, accident, or change of circumstance. For agriculture, inputs can be specified, but outputs are unpredictable. Building construction is done largely with local materials, and there is no need to coordinate the consumption of local sand, gravel, or bricks with an overall national plan. Steel, by contrast, must be planned on a national basis. If some materials or machines are needed from abroad, these must be incorporated in the plan, along with the exports with which to pay for them.

THE INFORMATION STRUCTURE

Internal to the System

We have already seen the flows of information at the planning stage, in which statements of broad objectives flow downward, and statements of plans for detailed implementation, along with possible suggested changes, flow back up.

After discrepant estimates from the various parts have been ironed out at the top, the production stage is entered. At this stage the downward-flowing information tells the factory manager what to produce and when, where to get his materials, and where to ship his output. Under flawless planning all else would be in his hands. The upward feedback flows are reports of actual performance in such forms as receiving and shipping records and statements of money receipts and expenditures.

If planning and execution were complete and perfect, there would be little or no need for horizontal communication between enterprises, since the higher levels of planning, in effect, do all sales and procurement work for enterprise[18] and could handle all the accounts. Planning is not so complete in fact, and need not be. Even as Chevrolet and Fisher Body can negotiate over production and shipping schedules between them, although both are subsidiaries of General Motors, so can Soviet enterprises negotiate directly over details. And just as the Chevrolet division is charged for all materials it receives from Fisher Body, so is the Soviet enterprise charged in money units for all its inputs and credited with its outputs, generally through its accounts in the bank.[19]

Information about plans and production can be expressed in physical units of goods, or in some combination of money and physical units. But they could not be expressed in money terms alone, in such form as "Ship 50,000 rubles' worth of output to the Vladivostok tractor factory." The results might be fascinating, but would hardly bring joy to Vladivostok. All instructions *could* be given in physical units from the planning board, and all must, in fact, be broken into physical quantities to be effectuated. A workable compromise is to state major items in physical terms ("Ship 2,000 tractor frames") and minor ones in aggregated money terms

---

[18] Gregory Bienstock, Solomon Schwarz, and Aaron Yugow, *Management in Russian Industry and Agriculture* (London: Oxford University Press, 1944), p. 62.
[19] See Campbell, *op. cit.*, p. 118.

("Ship 5,000 rubles' worth of miscellaneous small hardware, as specified by customer"), for both instruction and feedback reporting. In Russia thus far the basic planning and instruction are done in terms of goods, and so are the evaluations of the managers' performance. For both purposes, the price mechanism is grafted on top of the physical controls.[20] Under complete and perfect planning and performance it would make little difference whether instructions were coded in units of goods or money, except that the former requires far more information to be handled at the top. However, when the manager has discretion, under imperfect prior information it makes a tremendous difference which type of unit he is expected to maximize—as we shall see.

Adjustments to Externals

Both the goals of the plan and the natural resources from which it draws are external to the planning system itself. That is, they lie in the environment of the system, and are not components of it.[21] Under complete detailed planning, all adjustment to the environment would take place through the top levels of the planning system, and enterprise managers could operate satisfactorily in complete ignorance of available needs and resources. All information about the environment would come from the upper levels of the hierarchy, and all reports would go back to it. This does not mean that the enterprise manager would be a complete automaton, since he would still have to take care of the input-output relations within his own factory, at both the planning and the production stages. As in any other kind of organization, the greater the centralization of adjustments to the environment, the greater is the need for internal communication, and the less the need for external communication by the parts. Adjustments to imports and exports are also made at the top in the completely centralized system.

BARGAINS OVER VALUES

As we have seen in Chapter 26, the organization includes transactions over production and transactions over the flows of values between the organization and its personnel. Both kinds of transactions are present in a planned economy as well, whether it is run as a huge universal cooperative in the nation, as in democratic socialism, or as single profit or transition dictatorship.

---

[20] Grossman, op. cit., p. 61.

[21] The planning system is the "economic" part of the larger system. The footnoted statement is the equivalent for the planned system of saying that the demand curve on one side and the resources and technical coefficients on the other are "givens" for economic analysis in a market system. See, for example, Lionel Robbins, An Essay on the Nature and Significance of Economic Science (2d ed.; London: Macmillan Co., 1935), chap. 2. It is possible, of course, to plan the development of labor resources, as through training, migrations, and perhaps birth rates. And although the existence of natural resources cannot be planned, and lie outside the planning system, in the long run the exploration and use rates can also be brought inside the system.

The major bargain between the top planning authorities and the manager of the enterprise is the manager's acceptance of the job and the planning authority's acceptance of the manager. In that bargain the manager agrees to accept the authority of the planners, and to produce those things they direct him to produce. In return, the planners agree to provide him salary, title, other possible rewards, and authority over his subordinates. Subsidiary bargains over production have already been seen, in which the manager agrees to turn out specified quantities of products A, B, and C, in return for which the planners will provide him specified quantities of factors X, Y, and Z, or of money.

The manager can increase his rewards in either of two general ways, the one by doing well enough to get an increased salary or bonus for the existing job, and the other by increasing the size or importance of the job. In these respects the manager of the Soviet enterprise is no different from the functionary in any other kind of organization in any kind of society. In bargaining over the planned output for his plant, these motives tend to be reflected in two main directions.

First, the manager will tend to play down the amount his plant is capable of producing from a given input. This provides the cushion, so loved by administrators, which permits them to meet their quota with effort but not strain under normal circumstances, to meet it with difficulty (but still to meet it) if things go badly, and to outproduce the quota if things go well. In the bargaining over production, this is the tactical equivalent of understating one's own EP in a bargain over goods, in the attempt to give as little as possible in return for a given receipt. In his tactics what the manager proposes to produce must not be ridiculously small, however, or he will make himself appear incompetent or dishonest. The presence of managers of other enterprisers who may want to outshine him is the alternative which puts the floor under the bargaining power of the planners and the ceiling on the manager's. His best tactic is to try to minimize the amount they *think* he ought to produce.

Second, the manager can try to build his empire by urging the superiority of his product, his method, or his competence, so that more resources will be channeled to him. If his enterprise produces aluminum, he will urge its superiority over steel, copper, or plastic, and if it produces planes, he will allege their superiority over missiles or trains. He may also seek to show the superiority of his plant's location or other traits. His familiarity with his own product will often strengthen his own belief in its merits, and increase his ability to give advice about its uses and potentialities. If he convinces the planners, he may get a larger plant, or be promoted to a higher post.

In guarding against exaggerated claims by managers, the planners do not depend solely on competition from other managers, since the managers might form a coalition. In addition, the planners scatter party members through every enterprise, to make firsthand reports of loose operation or obviously understated capacity. Even this system is not foolproof. The party member may think he can improve his position more by being promoted on the job than by routine elevation within the party. In that case he is not likely to "squeal" on his boss unless the plant is so flagrantly mismanaged that his reports will bring assured glory within the party.

To return to the major bargain, even in a ruthless dictatorship the position of enterprise manager is essentially voluntary. Anyone wanting to remain an ordinary worker can easily hide his superior abilities. The planners have little to gain by putting incompetents into supervisory positions, and then shooting them if they fail to perform. Except in the early days of planning, when the planners might have to draft any likely-looking candidate, it is improbable that plant managerships will fall to persons who do not want them. In the long run, if the planners want competent managers, they must make competent people want to be managers.

In Russia the rewards for successful managers are substantial. They receive high salaries, personal automobiles, expense accounts, homes, resort vacations, and other advantages not purchasable with money because they are reserved for persons of special status. They also receive bonuses if their performance of the quota is good, plus special bonuses for particular kinds of performance which are of crucial importance at the time. A bonus of as much as 37 per cent may be received simply for fulfilling the plan, plus an additional 4 per cent for each 1 per cent of overfulfillment.[22] In this respect, the management incentives follow the same general pattern as those for workers and for some managements in the United States. That is, *some* bonus is given for *meeting* the quota, and an additional bonus for exceeding it. For excellent performance, the bonuses may be double the salary. Successful managers may also distribute bonuses to subordinate members of the managerial staff. Other rewards of high position are enjoyment of work, the exercise of power, recognition, the feel of success, and the sense of being socially useful.

American top managers who do not perform well are often eased into less responsible positions or are "kicked upstairs." Outright firing is usually reserved for those whose performance is spectacularly bad, or who are seen as a threat to the power or tenure of important persons. The Russians are more direct, and do not hesitate to discharge an unsuccessful manager. Given very poor performance (or perhaps the need for a scapegoat), managers may be accused of criminal negligence, and be imprisoned or shot. Fear of not making the quota may also lead the manager to violate certain rules, which opens another channel of possible punishment. These dire things apparently do not happen often enough, however, to leave the typical manager permanently apprehensive. While such matters are difficult to evaluate from a distance, the Soviet man-

---

[22] Campbell, *op. cit.*, p. 120. The present discussion of management incentives is based on Campbell.

ager's position is perhaps like that of the typical American automobile driver, who knows that he may be jailed for manslaughter if a lapse of attention leads to an accident. But this knowledge does not haunt his every moment of driving.

Negative incentives are generally ineffective, especially for managers. Positive rewards have not only a primary reinforcement value for the specific thing rewarded, they also have a secondary reinforcement value for a host of subsidiary activities. Rewarded activities tend to become satisfying in themselves. Positive rewards therefore have the potential for making the whole work situation enjoyable, and for eliciting "enthusiastic" performance. In brief, they reinforce work. Similarly, negative "rewards" tend to extinguish not only the particular actions punished, but the whole set of related work activities. The successful control of behavior requires discriminated use of rewards, with positive rewards being given for desired and negative ones for undesired behavior, but with a substantial overall balance on the positive side. Punishment or persistent fear is particularly inhibiting to a good manager, who must have enough confidence in his own judgment to carry out a decision without doubts and vacillation. The use of rewards that are positive, but variable in size, seems best suited to developing such attitudes.

The transactions between managers and workers follow the same general path. The Soviets use incentive rates very widely, even on jobs that American industrial engineers would put on flat hourly rates, on the ground that the worker has little control over output. Many Russian workers are paid on accelerated incentive rates, under which pay rises faster than output after the quota is reached. Outstandingly good workers receive sharply higher incomes than the average, plus special citations, superior housing, and vacations at special resorts. Skilled workers also are paid proportionally more than in the United States. For example, the skilled Soviet worker receives 3.5 to 4.5 times as much as the lowest skill in his plant, in contrast to a typical differential of 1.5 to 2.0 times as much in the United States.[23]

In the early days of the regime, and with renewed use during World War II, punishments were used against Russian workers, especially for

---

[23] These differences do not necessarily reflect differences in basic policy. Industrially mature areas generally show smaller relative advantages for skilled workers than do undeveloped or newly industrialized areas. The differentials may reflect supply and demand conditions, and may narrow as the Russian economy matures. If so, the Russians will probably then hail the change as part of their move toward equalitarianism.

Some authorities also argue that the real effect of these differentials is not so large as the money differences in wages, in that the government places very high rates of turnover tax on the "luxuries" which will be bought with the higher wages. Although I am not in a position fully to evaluate this argument, I would be skeptical that the effect of the tax in this direction could be more than minor. However, even if taxes should consume some of the real value of the higher wages, their incentive effect might by no means be lost, since the prestige value of the higher wage would still remain.

specific offenses against discipline, such as being late, absent, or drunk. Poor work might produce a pay reduction of as much as 25 per cent. The slave labor camps were primarily for political offenders—those who opposed the Communist regime—rather than for poor workers. Some of the laws penalizing poor work or absenteeism have subsequently been repealed, and the remaining ones are interpreted more loosely. For the same general psychological reasons as apply to managers, negative incentives are not productive over an extended period.

Much of a worker's normal bargaining power against unsatisfactory wages or conditions lies in his ability to leave one job and take another. The Soviets have sought to control this bargaining power by requiring each worker to have a work book. This he leaves with his employer when he is hired, and he cannot legally get another job without it. Thus his freedom to leave a job is substantially curtailed. However, managers eager to meet a production quota, but short of help, have at times resorted to wholesale pirating of workers from other enterprises, being eager enough for workers to overlook the question of the work book. Spurred by highly discrepant pay between enterprises, the quit rate of workers at one time ran extremely high, rising to a peak of 80 per cent from 1938 to 1940. That is, on the average, eight out of ten Russian industrial workers quit their jobs during the year. Although since 1950 the law prohibiting quits has not been seriously enforced, by 1954 the quit rate had been reduced to only about 20 per cent, apparently as a result of a more rational wage structure.[24] On the whole, it appears that negative motivations have now largely disappeared from Soviet industry, at both the managerial and worker levels. The parallel development within the government is that since World War II, the death of Stalin, and the advent of Khrushchev, officers of state who fall into disfavor are transferred to less responsible posts, but are not shot or imprisoned.

One aspect of voluntary incentives is linked in an important way with the alleged ultimate communist objective of equal or need-based incomes. The planners now use higher wages to induce workers to move to areas of labor shortage. The mere availability of work, incidentally, attracts fewer applicants than in the United States, because there is almost no unemployment in Russia. Higher pay similarly induces workers to prepare themselves for more skilled jobs. Such differentials are generally accepted as the only effective technique for getting labor to move without compulsion.[25] If the Russians expect eventually to achieve equalitarianism, then they must either be prepared to reinstitute coercion

---

[24] The figures on labor turnover are from David Granick, *The Red Executive*, pp. 215–16. That on work incentives, positive and negative, is from Campbell, *op. cit.*, pp. 134–38.

[25] See Emily Clark Brown, "The Soviet Labor Market," in Bornstein and Fusfeld, *op. cit.*, pp. 195 ff. An interesting question arises whether this technique will impart a more or less permanent inflationary push to the Soviet economy. The higher wages in the shortage area will have to be equalized after it gets enough workers, while the next shortage area will then have to pay higher wages. As Granick has pointed

for moving labor, or to develop more subtle forms of motivation than have thus far been effective. This problem parallels that outlined by Barbara Wootton[26] that free collective bargaining over wages is incompatible with the use of wage differentials for the voluntary allocation of labor.

The Soviets run into some of the same problems as managers elsewhere (including parents) when they want desperately to improve some aspect of performance. If they criticize or punish, they may ruin early enthusiasm before it blossoms into an intrinsic desire to do well. But if they praise, they may bring a relaxation of effort. In the apparent feeling that reinforcement is a safer bet, the Soviets have shown much willingness in recent years to follow that line. For example, the Central Committee of the Communist party apparently planned that awards be made at its December, 1959 meeting to a number of agricultural districts, even though their output had fallen considerably short of their goals.[27] One praises, not condemns, those whose cooperation he needs. The Soviets have, however, reportedly been taking stern measures, including the death penalty, against such violations of regulations as bribery, fraud, and embezzlement, for managers as for more lowly functionaries.

THE CRITERIA FOR EVALUATING MANAGERS

Of all the points at which motivation may count, that of the managers is perhaps the most crucial. We have distinguished between the income motive and the profit motive. The former is simply the desire for income, and is a motive for the staff members of any kind of organization—profit, cooperative, service, or pressure—under dictatorship or democracy, in public or private employment. Income reinforces any activity that the employee perceives as bringing him income.

Profit, on the other hand, is the excess of income over expenses for a business enterprise. If an individual owns the business, the profit becomes his income, in which case *his* desire for income is also a profit motive. If the top executives own shares in a corporation, their desire to increase profit so as to earn more on their shares is also a profit motive. If the top executives do not own stock, their desire for their salary is an income motive, not a profit motive. If the executive does not own stock but receives a bonus based on the size of the profit, he is nevertheless motivated to make a profit. To distinguish this from the case where he personally receives profits, we will say that this is not a profit motive, but an income motive geared to a profit criterion. In the Russian context, only the state itself could have the profit motive. But should they

out in *The Red Executive*, the Soviet authorities show no enthusiasm for cutting wages, and have consistently brought wage equalizations by raising low rates rather than cutting high ones.

[26] Barbara Wootton, *Freedom Under Planning* (Chapel Hill: University of North Carolina Press, 1945), chap. 7, especially p. 118.

[27] See Boris Nicolaevsky, "Agriculture and Khrushchev's Power Struggle," *The New Leader* (August 29, 1960), p. 11.

have reason to do so, the Russians could easily motivate their managers to earn a profit by gearing their salary or bonus to a *profit criterion*. In parallel, the managers will be motivated to accomplish whatever *is* made the criterion of their rewards.

The Soviets do not now use profit as the main criterion for rewarding managers. What they *do* use cannot be answered simply, although we have sufficient evidence about the criteria to permit a preliminary discussion of their effect on the performance of enterprises, and of the economy. We can examine the effect of incentives through a problem faced by a manager. Suppose he cannot fulfill his quota from the inputs planned for him. Should he increase his inputs enough to meet the quota, thus raising costs, or should he turn out what he can without raising costs? In this conflict, the manager will be guided by the planners' criteria in granting rewards. If the manager of a neighboring plant gets an award for large output, and the presentation speech ignores his even larger costs, managers will concentrate on quantity without too much regard for costs. A reverse emphasis by the planners would reverse the behavior of managers.

To illustrate further, a factory which turns out ten products, all with different input-output relations, can give rise to the following situations. If the planners emphasize total physical units, the manager will concentrate on those products which are easiest to make, and neglect the harder ones. By this response he may exceed his quota of easy items by 20 per cent at the cost of only a 5 per cent shortage on the hard ones, for a net excess of 15 per cent. If the manager is judged instead by the money value of his output, he will concentrate on items with a high unit value, and let the low value ones slide. If he is judged by the percentage increase in total output over the previous period, he will concentrate on items whose production has in the past been relatively least efficient, even if they are unimportant. If the goal is a reduction in total costs, he will push production of low cost items, and slacken production of high cost ones. If emphasis is on lower cost per unit, he may skimp on quality. If a publicity campaign has been raging over excessive scrap, the manager may (1) encourage loose inspection, (2) increase the amount of labor in relation to materials so as to make the most of every bit of material, or (3) increase the relative output of items with low scrap rates. If labor is scarce and managers are rewarded for reducing labor requirements per unit, they may (1) overproduce items with low labor requirements and underproduce those with high labor requirements, or (2) subcontract the high labor items. If the major goal of the planners is maximum overfulfillment of the plan, the managers will use extra ingenuity to keep their quotas low, so that overfulfillment will be easy.

Nothing in the preceding paragraph is unique to a planned economy. To any alert person who has spent much time in any large organization, these items will strike a responsive chord. As soon as top management emphasizes any one indicator, the subordinates will usually raise that indicator rather promptly, typically to the detriment of some other indicator. The effect on the whole organization may or may not be a net improvement.

The changes in emphasis are not always confined within the enterprise. At the peak of their giantism splurge, the Soviets gave great attention and rewards to reductions in cost per unit. But the "cost" as measured by the planners was only that expended *within* the enterprise. Many huge plants were constructed, to get maximum efficiency *within* the plant. But to keep the huge plant busy, raw materials and finished products had to be transported great distances. The added cost of transportation more than offset the saving in production costs. Transportation then became a bottleneck, whereupon the planners started rewarding managers for keeping transportation costs down, after which the trend was toward smaller, decentralized plants. During the period of giantism, the managers of manufacturing plants reduced *their* costs by shifting part of their costs to the railroads.

All of this reveals the main question. Any *one* success indicator reflects only a single dimension, and sometimes a relatively small one, of the whole productive process. We have defined rational decision making as the process of choosing that alternative whose values exceed its cost, and the measure of successful decision making is the accumulation of an excess of values over costs. In an organization which deals with a multitude of different kinds of values and costs, the measure of the most successful manager is not the best Value/Cost ratio in one or two aspects, but the best ratio for the net effect of *all* facets of the organization.

We have seen that in a market system a manager buys his materials and sells his output in the same markets as his competitors. If so, then the profit of his firm provides a single-dimensional, quantifiable measure of the net effect of all decisions made by the manager. Now it is not out of the question that the Soviets might conclude that for them, too, profit may be the best single indicator of the overall performance of a manager. However, within the context of the Soviet system, that measure would currently suffer several distinct limitations. One is that managers are not currently charged for capital or land, and the value of both their inputs and their outputs is determined by the planners, not the market. Even within these limitations it is nevertheless possible that the Russians will find some measure of profit to be the best single, overall measure of economic performance. The potentialities and shortcomings of such a move cannot be visualized until after some other dynamic aspects of a planned economy have been examined, which will be done in the next chapter, at which point we will observe some actual, though limited, use of both the profit criterion and the profit motive.

Chapter 39

PLANNED ECONOMIES: DYNAMICS AND INNOVATION

THE PREVIOUS chapter outlined some aspects of planning under the general assumption that the planners had complete knowledge of all available factors, desires, and techniques. Once the plan was made, nothing remained but to fulfill it. A relaxation of these assumptions was allowed in the latter part of the chapter to observe that the managers might fill or overfill some parts of the plan at the expense of others, and that their emphasis would be directed toward raising those indicators of production which are currently being rewarded by the planners. Now this is a rational but clumsy technique of managing an economy. It is a "bottleneck" technique, which shifts the attention of managers from one factor to another as one bottleneck is cleared up and another appears. It is rational, since "bottleneck" is another term for scarce factors, and it is economically rational to give more concentrated attention to scarce items. It is clumsy in that it has an all-or-none quality that tends toward pendulum swings (intensive aspect), and it tends to be applied across a wider area of the economy than properly needs to respond in order to correct the condition (extensive aspect).

With more experience the planners may learn to be more sophisticated about these matters, and to tailor the intensity and "extensity" of their bottlenecks to the needs of the case. If and when they do so, however, their efforts will closely approximate those of a price system, and it is an open question whether they will not find a price system (even if a managed one) the simplest technique of control. It is to this kind of problem that the present chapter is addressed.

This approach will make two explicit assumptions: (1) that the planned system has prospered to the point where it can meet all urgent needs of its people, and at least a modest quota of amenities, with or without a military establishment, and (2) we will admit uncertainty and change into the decision system, including accidents, environmental changes, wrong information, and information not worth its cost. The second assumption means that adjustments must be made between the plan and its accomplishment, and the ability of a planned system to make these adjustments has much to do with the feasibility of central planning. A related problem is how well the system can make permanent changes in product or methods, which is the problem of innovation.

SHORT-RUN QUANTITATIVE ADJUSTMENTS

Nature of the Problem

The most obvious way to handle possible bottlenecks is to allow some leeway in the plan itself, as by specifically allocating (say) only 90 per cent of capacity, while leaving the other 10 per cent for contingencies. An accumulated inventory of storable input and output goods can also provide a cushion. Whether imbalances arise from stupidity, national emergency, or unexpectedly easy production, they will take the form of shortages or surpluses of some items. (Conditions requiring change in quality will be discussed in the next section.) How can such situations be handled?

The first problem is informational. If a cement plant is completed ahead of schedule, and turns out 10 per cent more cement than was planned, who should be informed so that the appropriate adjustment can be made? We will assume that a report is made to the central planning agency, where it will be examined in light of the total supply of and uses for cement. If some other plant has reported a shortage, the discrepancy can be taken care of by transshipment. If no other cement plant shows a shortage, and no users are in short supply, several alternatives face the planners. They can, of course, instruct the new plant, or some other plant less well-located, to curtail production. But this wastes productive capacity.

Economically minded planners might canvass various industries to find which might use more cement, either to increase output or, by substituting cement, to decrease the input of some other material. Such activity by central planners parallels the marketing function in market economies, normally performed by sales departments or brokers.

If any user of cement is to increase his consumption, other costs must be increased, since additional labor or other inputs must be increased along with the cement. Let us now make some computations.

Suppose it is September when the first plant reports a surplus. Its full average cost of cement is $5.00 per barrel, which covers fixed and variable costs. Being used for construction, the use of cement is seasonal. Being ruined by moisture, even from the air around it, cement is expensive to store. Being made in large and expensive mills from inexpensive materials (mainly clay and limestone), cement has low variable costs. Let us say that it would cost the new mill $2.00 per barrel to store the cement until the following season, as against $2.50 of variable costs the following summer to make new cement to replace it. The plant and the planners now face the following situation. Computing costs and values from the point of decision forward, cement equal to the amount of the current surplus can be made available the following summer at a yet-to-be-expended cost of $2.00 if the existing surplus is stored, whereas it will cost $2.50 of yet-to-be-expended costs if the existing surplus is scrapped. Hence, if the surplus is not sold this summer its net value to the mill and the planners is only 50 cents per barrel.

Other enterprises can now be informed not merely that cement is in excess, but also that the value to the economy of the excess cement is low. By itself this information may or may not bring some reaction. To shift from information to motives, suppose the planners add: "If you can use any of this cement over and above your planned consumption, you may continue to receive the previous price for your output, but we will charge you only 50 cents per barrel for the *extra* cement, instead of $5.00. The difference may be used at your discretion for contingencies, bonuses to your subordinates, or profit." The many complications need not be pursued to observe the central point.

First, the rationale of this cost calculation is the same whether the system is capitalist and unplanned or socialist and planned. In either case, the cement has a value of only 50 cents to the producing mill, and the mill will be better off to sell it at any price in excess of 50 cents than to keep it until the following year. In either case the logic of pricing it so low is valid only if the surplus is sold *in addition to*, not *instead of*, other cement. Hence, either the capitalist seller or the socialist planner will avoid cutting the price unless he simultaneously assures himself that the cut-priced goods will not replace regular-priced goods. (In both cases, some intermediate position may be optimum.) Once it is understood, in either the capitalist or the socialist economy, a price cut provides both the information that a surplus exists and the motivation to use it.

Market systems during peacetime use prices to allocate resources, while planned systems and market systems during war typically use priorities. Except for degree of refinement, the two are essentially the same thing. A priority system can be thought of as a crude price system, and a price system as a highly refined priority system. The relation can be seen if the cement problem, described above in the language of prices, is redescribed in the language of priorities. Prior to completion of the new mill cement was in short supply, and carried a high priority. A high priority is an instruction to producers to turn out more and to consumers to use less. When the new mill is completed cement moves from shortage to surplus, and its priority rating is reduced. The low priority reverses the previous instructions: producers may now slack off and customers may use it more freely.

But producers are not to stop entirely, nor are users now to waste cement. The question is how *much* less effort shall be put into production, and how *much* more plentifully shall cement be used? As to priorities, how high is high, and how low is low? A price can express the priority much more precisely. To the users of cement a price of 50 cents is a low priority which says: "Use cement in any application where its value in use equals or exceeds 50 cents." To the producers it says: "Do not increase your output of cement at this time unless the marginal cost of so doing is no greater than 50 cents."

In the opposite direction, if cement is scarce it can be given a high priority. But again the priority is more precise if stated as a price, such as $7.00 per barrel. This priority-by-price then states: "If producers can turn out additional cement at a cost of not more than $7.00, they shall do so, while users should not apply cement to any use that does not justify a cost of $7.00." If the planners should actually set the price at $7.00, the managers will be motivated as well as instructed to follow the suggestion.

There is some evidence that Soviet planners do give attention to marginal costs in deciding among alternatives. They are cited, for example, as figuring the marginal, not average, cost of transportation when deciding whether to ship certain materials or to produce them closer to their destination.[1] Such computations bring a more economical location of plants. But unless prices are more flexible than the industry-wide average cost now used by the Soviets, prices cannot provide the information and motives to plant managers which the many shortage and surplus situations require. There does not seem to be too much likelihood that all these decisions could be made well at the top, nor is the motivation as strong at that level.[2]

The price mechanism appears as a technique of efficient allocation in another way. Suppose that some enterprise faces a critical shortage of one raw material, which shortage will cost $50,000 in lost output. If the price of these materials is set by the plan at $10,000, the question now arises whether the manager will be allowed to bid a higher price, say $20,000, to divert these materials from their planned use. If the materials are worth only $10,000 in their alternate uses, to do so would benefit both the plant and the whole economy. The planners might make this

---

[1] See Robert Campbell's "Discussion" in *American Economic Review* (May, 1959), p. 79.

[2] The price of cement in the United States remains almost permanently at essentially an industry-wide-average cost plus profit, with few and slight deviations to reflect changing marginal conditions. The widespread practice of American firms of using administered prices, which do not fluctuate with short-run changes in supply and demand, presumably prevents the American economy, too, from achieving the most efficient short-run allocation.

This discussion is only an introduction to the problem, the whole of which is far more complex. In the United States the fixed costs of producing cement are high, and the demand is inelastic and highly fluctuating. This combination of circumstances could produce ruinously cut-throat competition if the industry were to follow short-run marginal pricing policies. If it is set at competitive, not monopoly levels, a price which is administered at average rather than marginal costs may be more efficient on the whole over the long run.

decision themselves, but to make it intelligently requires that the various ingredients in the decision be given a money value—i.e., a precise priority.

LONGER RUN, QUALITATIVE ADJUSTMENTS

The quantities specified in a plan are predicated on the existing methods of production, or perhaps on improvements expected during the planning period. In the long run a nation must make continuous changes in products and methods if it is not to stagnate. A backward nation making a leap can find enough improvements to keep it busy merely by copying from advanced nations, and much of the tremendous industrial progress of the Russians has resulted from imitating products and methods of the West.

We have already seen that a totally planned system faces difficulties in pricing, and there remains the question whether such a system can create a rational price structure of its own. A parallel question is whether a totally planned system is capable of significant innovation in products and methods. Without necessarily answering the question, we will nevertheless inquire into its nature.

Forms of Innovation

Innovation takes various forms. It may be an improvement[3] in the product itself, such as a more efficient motor, greater durability of roofing material, faster dyes, and so on. It may be improvement in shape and design, in materials, or versatility in use. These improvements may apply to either consumer goods, providing greater satisfaction, or to producer goods, providing greater productivity. These are qualitative changes, in contrast to the quantitative changes discussed in the early part of this chapter, and in the preceding one.

Improvements may also be made in the methods of production, "methods" in the broadest sense including such items as plant layout and the structure of industrial organization as well as the narrower improvements in machines and materials. An improvement in product and method may come together, as when an improvement in a loom may bring better cloth as well as faster production.

Information About Innovation

Innovation faces problems not present in most other decisions. The normal noninnovative decision involves a list of available alternatives, and the values and costs of each.

Viewed as a decision, the unique problem of innovation is that it is concerned mainly with items which are not *in* the list of alternatives—items not initially perceived by the decision maker to be among his op-

---

[3] Some changes which are introduced as improvements are actually less satisfactory than the original. We will recognize this fact, but discuss the problem in terms of changes that *are* improvements.

portunities. Viewed as a control system, innovation is not the sort of deviation from programmed activity which can be detected and fed back for correction. To achieve innovation means to change the program itself along lines not previously thought of: i.e., to experiment. For this reason, innovation cannot be programmed in the usual sense.

This does not mean that all innovation must be left to chance. A program developed for one use can be deliberately applied to another. For example, if automobile engines have been manufactured by automatic methods, the authorities can instruct the managers to apply similar methods to the manufacture of tractor engines. This is one variety of innovation, often referred to as an "adaptive" improvement. Or they can also say, "Here is $5 million. See if you can design an airplane that will fly at 80,000 feet and stay aloft for 40 hours." As contrasted to the applied scientific goals above, pure science can also be provided for. For example, "Find out what you can about the changes in metals when treated at extremely high or low temperatures." Or simply, "With the following budget, see what you can do to expand our knowledge of metallurgy." The Soviets have done things of this sort, and have achieved important innovations in such fields as rocketry, geology, medicine, and others. It still remains true, however, that these innovations are not "programmed" in the usual sense. The planners (or factory managers) allocate people and funds for research, and establish conditions favorable for innovation. But whether innovation comes forth depends much on the knowledge, imagination, and motivation of the people. In this respect, planned and unplanned systems operate in the same essential way. There does not appear to be any inherent quality of either system which either facilitates or inhibits the establishment of conditions under which research, pure or applied, can go forward. There do, however, seem to be some conditions which affect the likelihood that innovation will be stimulated, and the directions toward which it will be applied.

With respect to innovation in public goods, the planned and unplanned systems show some basic similarities. First, the decision whether to try to innovate is a public decision. With respect to rockets, atomic explosions, and the related engineering, the decisions in both the United States and the Soviet Union are public, and the research is financed out of public funds. Certain subdecisions are also parallel in general nature. Should the research be carried out by existing enterprises, or should new ones be created for the purpose? In either case, should the research be carried out by an enterprise which also has manufacturing facilities, such as an aircraft or a chemical producer? Or should it be carried out by an enterprise which conducts research alone, such as a university? In either Russia or the United States, questions of this sort must be answered mainly with reference to the kinds of people available, both for research and for management purposes, and the kinds of related facilities and interests. In both countries the cost of the research is borne largely by the public treasury, and in both there are long negotiations as to how much money the government should provide, and what it can expect in return. In both countries there will also be negotiations over how much discretion the research group may exercise in deciding which experiments to pursue and which to drop, and on the basis of what criteria. There is, of course, an important difference between the countries in who controls the government. In the United States the industrialists or scientists with whom the government negotiates are themselves part of the sponsor group. Because of their possible interest in their taxes, balanced budgets, or other items, they may encourage or restrain government expenditures for these things.

Nevertheless both countries must also make another fundamental decision. Shall all research toward a particular goal be done under a single agency or enterprise? Or, if there are two or more conflicting recommendations among the scientists or enterprise managers, should the government pursue two or more sets simultaneously? If so, shall the two sets of researchers cooperate, or shall each try to outdo the other?

In democracies it is sometimes thought that a dictatorship, having the power to enthrone one approach and bury the other, does not face these problems, or somehow gets greater efficiency from its centralized control. The reverse belief is also sometimes held that the dictatorship, because it is centralized, cannot get the benefit of diversity. To illustrate, in both countries, some experts may believe that guided missiles are superior to ballistic ones, or that liquid fuels are superior to solid, while others hold the reverse beliefs. In deciding such a question in either country, there is no escaping the risk that to ignore either approach may be a grave error, which may leave the enemy far ahead. Since the top decision maker cannot know more on the subject than the scientists, and the scientists disagree, he has little choice but to authorize both approaches to some degree. Although the problem is here stated for *crucial* decisions, its implications are also significant for less crucial ones.

Innovation, and Producing versus Selling

In a completely planned economy the enterprise carries on production functions only. Those activities which in market economies fall under the heading of marketing or sales are carried on by the planners. The enterprise manager thus has no concern whether his product is sold, and he is rewarded for his efficiency in producing.

In a mature market economy, on the other hand, the manager's problem of production is often not so crucial as that of selling. This does not mean that he faces no production problems, or that he can be careless about them, but that he is more likely to be driven out of business from inability to sell than from inability to produce.

The main criterion of sales is a product which economically equals or excels that of other sellers, because of better quality, lower price, or both. The economically inferior product will not sell as well, and its producer will lose sales and perhaps be forced out of business. This effect may be modified by advertising, but will still prevail in areas where advertising is not a determining factor (as in industrial machines and materials), or where it is approximately equal among competitors. The firm which sells more will also be rewarded by higher profit. Enterprise managers are thus motivated to make innovations that will take business away from competitors, who are then forced to match or surpass the original innovations.

Electric motors can illustrate this problem. They are producer goods, widely used in virtually all factories, and they can be produced in an almost endless variety of sizes and technical characteristics. Now if the manufacturers of electric motors are told by the planners to produce certain quantities to certain performance specifications for shipment to other factories, it is easy enough to find whether the managers have met their production quotas. But suppose that the customers think that the motors from plant A are better in design or workmanship than those from plant B. What happens at this stage is crucial to the ability of a planned system to hold its managers to quality standards, and to motivate innovation.

If the customers merely complain to the planners about plant B, the result will be undependable. The planners are simultaneously trying to hold the managers to several different goals, and if quality is made primary, quantity and cost may suffer. On the other hand, if quality is *not* given priority, the manager of plant B will have a less strong motive to improve quality than to keep quantity up and cost down. In any event, quantity is more objective and compelling criterion than quality. Under planning, the manager who turns out poor quality may not suffer a loss of sales, but merely shift the cost of the poor quality to the manager of the consuming plant.

A dramatic change takes place, however, if the users are allowed to specify whether they want motors from A or B. It does not much matter whether they order direct from A and B, or through the planning agency, so long as the users, not the planners, make the decision. For now A's orders and production will rise while B's will shrink dramatically, assuming that the planners allocate the necessary factors to A. Even if quantity remains the criterion of economic performance, the quality dimension is now reflected in it, since the difference in quality has now been recoded as a difference in quantity. Assuming equal fixed costs, A will now show a large profit and B a large loss. Whether he is evaluated by volume of production or of profit, A will be judged the better manager.

Allowing the consuming industry to specify its source not only permits a better evaluation of the supplying managers, but also of the consuming ones. For if the manager has no control over the source and quality of his inputs, he can blame his difficulties on their quality—perhaps legitimately. But if he selects his own source and specifications, he has less legitimate complaint if other managers excel him.

With respect to consumer goods, the Soviets have assured more or less total sale of everything by the simple device of paying the population more than enough to buy everything turned out. Having control of prices, the government can control the inflation which would otherwise result. This does not mean that consumer goods are *never* unsold. Some have been of such poor quality that the people have preferred to keep their money rather than buy, and occasional shipments have gone to wrong places, and been otherwise mishandled.

The ability of buyers to choose their sources is a crucial item in a system. Whether factory managers or consumers, the buyers are better qualified than anyone else to know what they want, and why. But as soon as buyers are given discretion, much of the control of the planners is destroyed. Buyers, not planners, will determine which factory's goods will be used and which not, and thereby determine which factory and industry will expand or contract. If they accept buyer choice, the planners will have to allow resources to flow to the factories which sell their product. Uncertainties and unpredictable fluctuations will also appear, along with some idle resources. An expanding plant may be acquiring additional machines while similar machines stand idle in the declining plant, and one plant may lay workers off while a distant competitor is short of help.

This same problem can be described in another way. If managers are rewarded mainly by the quantity they produce from given inputs, then they will concentrate on quantity and efficiency. In Russia this preoccupation with short run production goals has been so intense that the authorities have virtually "bribed" managers, by raising the price index of their products, to get them to undertake new products or processes.[4] Under such circumstances, they will attend to quality only enough to get their products past normal inspections. They will want innovations in productive techniques which raise output or reduce cost. Whether they will want to make large investments in experimentation will depend on the length of the evaluative period the planners allow. For example, will the planners permit an enterprise to show low output and/or high cost for three to five years in the hope that its position will improve markedly thereafter? If so, the enterprise achieves much freedom to arrange its own input-output ratios. If not, the enterprise can engage in methods research only if it is approved by the planners, in which case decisions about methods research are centralized at the top. This returns us to the earlier problem about research in public goods: if competing approaches are suggested, a strong risk is incurred when one is approved and the other is not.

---

[4] Gregory Grossman, "Soviet Economic Planning: Industrial Prices in the USSR," *American Economic Review* (May, 1959), p. 60.

This point is most important. Under the tight, centrally planned system, if research for a proposed innovation is turned down by the planners, it is *through*. No one can work on it, since the necessary resources will not be appropriated. The normal tendency of central bureaus is to stick to ventures which are relatively sure, but not too spectacular if successful, while saying no to the apparently crackpot idea which might lead to a really brilliant discovery. Defense expenditures may not follow this pattern, since the risk of *not* trying all possible ventures is too great, and great waste will be accepted if occasional great gains are made.

The Russians have made much successful use of glorified suggestion systems, just as have some American firms, and have rewarded some of the ideas rather handsomely. Though useful, these tend to deal with relatively small details, and do not circumvent the necessity of getting approval of the planners if large developmental costs are required. The Russian manager also does not have the protection of patents to give his enterprise a longer term advantage from innovation.

By contrast to tight central planning, under the market system, or under planning loose enough to allow managers great discretion, an idea turned down in one place may be experimented with elsewhere, and no one authority has veto power over new ideas.

In short, it is difficult either to motivate or to evaluate important innovation except through the reward and punishment of rising or falling sales, with the decision to experiment in the hands of the enterprise manager. But such conditions greatly dilute the power and some of the advantages of central planning. The Russians have thus far shown only slight hints that they contemplate allowing some reinvestment of earnings by an enterprise at the discretion of its manager, and this in agriculture.[5]

After noting that most technological progress in Russia has come from copying the West, Campbell concludes that "it would be imprudent to assume that the Russians cannot make technological progress on their own. . . ."[6] But his statement is the precautionary one that avoids saying that something *cannot* be done, and the experience to date does not lead him to expect significant innovation under the Russian system of planning. A possible advantage of tight central controls can occur if the central planners learn of and approve some important technical improvement. Their authority can force all enterprises to adopt it over the objections of the "practical" production managers, who are usually sure they know more about production methods than the "theoretical experimenters." For example, although it was discovered in the United States, the

---

[5] Lazar Volin, "Soviet Agriculture Under Khrushchev," *American Economic Review* (May, 1959), pp. 20–21, 26.

[6] Robert Campbell, *Soviet Economic Power* (New York: Houghton Mifflin Co., 1960, paper), p. 186. The present discussion supplements rather than parallels Campbell's, and the interested reader should consult his Chapters 7 and 8 on "Control over Resources" and "Technical Progress."

highly superior technique of using tonnage oxygen in steel plants had become almost universal practice in Russia, by central order, while many American steel companies were still debating its value. This is only an "adaptive" improvement, however, and gives no clue to true innovation, by which we mean the making of the initial discovery. The military aspects are again excepted. In short, and to combine this with the earlier discussion, the centrally planned system shows no ability or prospect of establishing its own price system (and hence of allocating resources efficiently), of producing significant, widespread, independent innovation, or of responding to consumer wants—unless it adopts a substantial amount of the market technique. We will return to this problem after an excursion into some types of organization other than pure capitalism and pure socialist planning.

THE BROADER PERSPECTIVE

As in other areas of human knowledge, the extreme, pure cases are useful for making sharp distinctions. But life in total is more complex, and this is true in economic organization as elsewhere. We will now look at some of the intermediate states between pure and complete socialist planning and pure capitalist nonplanning.

Capitalist Planning

Although the development of the American economy from the Industrial Revolution to the beginning of the twentieth century can well be thought of as unplanned, much private planning now goes on in the United States. The great bulk of production and employment takes place in a relatively few large corporations. When steel or electric utility companies make new installations or consider abandoning old ones, they think of the probable growth and distribution of the economy and the population for the next 20 to 50 years, and some other industries also think in rather long terms. These plans are not made in isolation. Through trade and professional journals, conferences, and interlocking directorships the plans of these industries are tied with each other, or at least are made with awareness of the thinking of others. This does not mean that planning is comprehensive in the Soviet sense, but that it is by no means haphazard. Further, when these companies make guesses about future development and build their plants accordingly, they do much to mold the actual future developments. Though perhaps on a less grandiose scale, many well-run small firms also do significant long-term planning.

It is true, of course, that the plans of these firms are guided toward "profit" rather than "the public good." But it is not clear what difference this makes. With respect to geographic location, for example, the most desired location is the one which produces the least cost combination with respect to material, labor, market, and transportation, and these calculations are the same for a private as for a public planner. With respect to the planning of capacity, it is sometimes said that private enterprisers "plan for scarcity" rather than for abundance. This also has little meaning when made explicit. Each company has competitors, and each attempts to estimate the future market and the percentage it can sell to. If some company "plans for scarcity"—that is, deliberately builds less capacity than might be used—in the hope of keeping the supply down and the price up, other companies will be encouraged to make up this deficit by greater expansion. Any company that plans for scarcity is inviting its competitors to take a larger share of the market. If capitalist planners actually err on this score, it is probably on the side of over- rather than undercapacity.

In recent years a type of "capitalist planning" has developed in Western Europe. It has the enthusiastic support of capitalists, little from socialists, and is a joint business-government venture which is basically a type of forecasting rather than planning. A joint board of government and business representatives attempts to predict the rate of growth of the economy for the immediate future, perhaps for five to eight years, as well as probable changes in its general structure, such as the arrival of new industries and products. In line with the broad prediction, the board computes the quantities of each of the detailed components that would be required for a balanced economy at the anticipated rate of growth. At first several alternative rates of growth may be sketched, such as 3, 4.5, and 6 per cent, from among which the most reasonable one is selected.

No business firm is directed what to do. But each has a guide as to whether growth or decline can be expected in its own industry, and it can make its plans accordingly. Anyone who believes the plan is wrong can ignore what it suggests. The nearest thing to coercion is that firms seeking loans to make expansions indicated by the plan may find borrowing easy, while those going contrary to the plan may have more difficulty. But anyone with his own money can do what he likes. Even without controls, the plan tends to be self-effectuating, because the motives to conform are stronger than those to deviate. This technique is planning by information rather than by direction and controls. France has been the chief instigator, followed by the British, while some American corporations with foreign subsidiaries are highly interested. India has worked out a technique of comprehensive economic planning which is compatible with democracy on the political front and predominantly private ownership on the economic.[7]

In the other direction, Yugoslavia, whose economy was once centrally planned, has moved far toward decentralization. For practical purposes it has abandoned central planning, though without giving up government ownership of major industries. Two or more enterprises compete in each

---

[7] This description of European planning is condensed from "Europe Charts Its Business Future," *Business Week* (April 7, 1962), pp. 80 ff. Planning in India is described in William N. Loucks, *Comparative Economic Systems* (New York: Harper & Bros., 6th ed., 1961), chap. 31.

major field, on the basis of their own techniques, sources of factors, and estimates of what they can sell. In a different nation the Polish economy more nearly resembles the Soviet arrangement for its industry, but has collectivized only about a quarter of its farms.[8]

Britain and Scandinavia have socialized a few industries, under the sponsorship of a socialist-oriented labor movement. But these are mostly industries having a large element of public interest and regulation in any event, such as transportation, banking, and utilities, or which have done spectacularly badly under private ownership, as in the case of coal mining. Neither area engages in centralized planning or shows signs of moving toward it, unless, perhaps, toward the capitalist variety described above. Meanwhile, most of the advantages that labor movements have traditionally expected of socialism have been achieved under predominantly capitalist systems, notably decent and rising wages and comprehensive cradle-to-grave security. The long-term supporters of socialism in Western Europe are now not enthusiastic for further socialization, which seems unlikely to proceed much further. By contrast, a contrary tendency has arisen in Western Europe for government to assist private enterprise through loans, but without controlling management or moving toward the socialist version of central planning. Such governmental assistance has been particularly large in Germany.

It has been customary to associate socialization with centralization and capitalism with decentralization. In light of the variety of arrangements now in use, this distinction no longer seems useful. Russia represents a highly centralized socialist system, while Yugoslavia is a rather thoroughly decentralized socialist system. The United States is a quite decentralized capitalist nation, though with substantial centralization of private control in a number of highly dominated industries. At the same time Japan is a highly centralized capitalist nation, in which a few people control each major industry, often with cross-industry ties. All four of these nations allow their small and essentially local industries, such as building construction, repair services, and handicrafts, to be decentralized.

Because of the way three terms have been used in the United States in recent years, a brief comment on usage seems in order. In the present framework the term "socialism" refers solely to the public production of private goods, and the usage has logical basis in the distinction between capitalist and socialist beliefs. As to the first of the three terms, certain pressure groups in the United States refer to the production of public goods by government as itself "socialistic," and argue that any growth of government is a "move toward socialism." Regardless of whether the growth of government is desirable, or whether the United States is in fact moving toward socialism, it seems proper for both analytical and policy-making purposes to distinguish between the public production of

---

[8] Alexander Erlich, "The Polish Economy After October, 1956: Background and Outlook," *American Economic Review* (May, 1959), p. 94.

public goods (which is simple government activity) and the public production of *private* goods (which is socialism).

Second, government has intervened to help prevent excessive booms and depressions. This is obviously government intervention in economic affairs. But if this is done solely through monetary and fiscal policy, it is not "socialistic," since the government does not thereby produce private goods. On the other hand, if the government should attempt to stimulate the economy by itself entering into the production of saleable goods, such as electric power, its actions would constitute partial socialization. As noted in Chapter 31, economic stability and rates of growth, although the outcome of private decisions, are essentially public goods. Although these are the indirect outcome of private decisions, they are not "decided" upon, in the normal sense of decision, by the market process.

Third, social security is a technique by which government attempts to stabilize individual incomes and increase individual power. It is essentially a means of redistributing income over time and among persons, using a variety of techniques which in part incorporate the principles of insurance, forced saving, and the graduated income tax. Even under complete, or nearly complete, cradle-to-grave security, as in England, Scandinavia, and Germany, the government does not make such basic decisions about private goods as what to produce, in what quantities, with what factors, or at what prices to sell. Under social security the government does not operate any industries, and the recipients of payments buy all their goods in the market according to their personal preferences. Social security is "socialism" to the extent that the unemployment insurance and pension "industries" are government operated, but only to that extent. As to health, if the government would hire all doctors and provide free medical care to all, then medical care would be socialized. Under actual proposals for national health insurance in the United States, medical *insurance* would be socialized, but not the practice of medicine. By contrast, the public schools are completely socialized; the government owns all facilities, hires all employees, and determines all major policies.

In summary, under the language here used, it is possible for a nation to have large government, firm governmental control of business cycles through monetary and fiscal policy, and full scale social security, while its economy remains completely (except for the reservations in connection with social security) outside the realm of socialist public production of private goods. This discussion is intended solely to clarify terminology, and has no implications about the desirability or undesirability of any such activities.

To the previous paragraph we must add a precautionary note. In actual, historical language the term "socialist" has been used widely and loosely, with a tremendous variety of meanings. Many persons, groups, and political parties throughout the world have called themselves socialists who did not advocate the public production of private goods in the sense described above. At the same time others *have* advocated the public production of private goods in whole or part, but do not call themselves socialists. Here, as elsewhere throughout this volume, when actual usage is loose or not analytically useful, I have chosen a single meaning which is capable of sharp definition. Where usage is as varied as with the term "socialism" it seems more sensible to classify groups or nations by what they do or advocate, not by what they call themselves.

THE LEAP AND BEYOND

We are now open for some fascinating speculation. There is now no reasonable doubt that central controls are capable of achieving notable performance from an economy when one central goal is dominant. Despite seemingly incredible waste motion, democratic nations have performed spectacular feats of production under central planning and control during war. The Russians have made tremendous strides in basic industrialization, largely because through central planning they have directed some 25 per cent of their Gross National Product into investment in plants and machinery. By contrast, the United States rarely invests more than 18 to 20 per cent, and often less.[9]

The Russians have been preoccupied thus far with basic industrialization and with military goods. They now seem to be approaching the stage at which there seems little point in plowing industrial output back indefinitely to create still more industrial equipment, and beyond which substantial conversions could be made to consumer goods. The logic of the position will become successively stronger as industrialization advances, perhaps at a geometric rather than an arithmetic ratio.

Whether the planners like it or not, if and when consumer goods become relatively plentiful, consumers are going to be the real directors of consumer goods production. So long as people are paid in money they can buy some things and not buy others, as they see fit. Except for private goods which might have political significance, and the number would seem negligible, there is little point for even a totalitarian dictatorship to continue to produce more and more indefinitely of things people do not buy, and simultaneously to refuse to produce what they snatch from the shelves the moment it appears. It will then become evident that the ability of an enterprise or industry to sense and produce what the public wants has high economic value, not merely in pleasing the public, but in avoiding the waste of unsold output. Campbell notes that "Russian planners have failed to grasp the notion that economic power is only a means to an end, and that the objective should be the maximum satisfaction of the wants of the population."[10] It would seem that an abundance of consumer goods will some day bring this point inescapably to their attention.

[9] Campbell, *op. cit.,* p. 153.
[10] *Ibid.,* p. 188.

This does not mean that the idea will get through easily. Russia now has a substantial class of planners, with affluence and prestige. Perhaps they *have* already grasped the notion that economic power is primarily a means of satisfying people's wants, but refuse to respond because the thought threatens their privileged position. If so, this aspect of the Russian class structure creates a bias in favor of industrial and military goods, which can be totally planned, and against consumer goods, which cannot.

This returns us to the problem of innovation, and whether the Soviets will allow enterprise managers discretion to vary the design or quality of their products in the hope of increasing their sales, either to the public or to other enterprises. Once the pressure to complete the leap of basic industrialization is past, it seems difficult to imagine that they can do otherwise. But if so, much of the power and decision making will shift inescapably from the central-planning bureau to the enterprise level, as has already occurred in Yugoslavia. This move, too, will presumably be resisted by the bureaucracy of planners.

We have already seen that among the multiple and shifting criteria of successful managers, only that of profit seems to be a single-dimensional, quantitative measure, and that this observation applies equally to the socialist or capitalist enterprise, since it measures the difference between values of inputs and values of outputs. If the planned economy should shift from volume of output to volume of sales, or to profit which is closely related to volume of sales, as the criterion for judging its managers, the managers will then face the same urge as do those in market economies. That is, they will want to increase the desire for their output relative to the desire for that of their competitors, which means a desire to engage in competitive selling, possibly including advertising.

As of the present, Soviet enterprises do show profits, in part planned by the central authorities, and in part the unplanned result of efficiency beyond that anticipated in the plan. Some 20 to 50 per cent of the unplanned profits flow into the enterprise's "director's fund," which the manager can use for bonuses, housing, or other benefits to the managers and workers in the enterprise. This fund provides a definite stimulus to efficiency.[11] This profit is thus far geared only to efficiency in the technical sense of improving the ratio of output to input. Herein, however, is a mechanism already available with which to evaluate and motivate the managers to make their product more saleable and their production techniques more flexible if the system should ever decide to give the enterprise managers more autonomy in procurement and sales.

It is not now possible to guess whether the Russians will engage in such activity in the foreseeable future. As possible indications of a slight move in the direction of enterprise autonomy, the Russian collective farms have been given freedom to buy their farm machinery where they

---

[11] Loucks, *op. cit.,* p. 513.

like,[12] and the construction industry has always been guided to a considerable extent by price mechanisms.[13] We have already noted that collective farms have been allowed some freedom to reinvest their own earnings. We have also seen that the Russian planning and production structure resembles that of a single, large corporation with many subsidiaries. It is perhaps not without significance that some of the largest corporations in the United States maintain multiple subsidiaries which compete with each other as well as with other corporations. This "within-company" competition, accompanied by considerable autonomy of the subsidiary, is thought to be the best available technique for evaluating the managers of the subsidiaries. Khrushchev's main interest has been in agriculture, and the lesson of competition was not lost on him when he visited American farms. In June of 1962 he made a speech to a conference at the Kremlin on the ailing Soviet agricultural output, pointing out the much higher output of American farms and attributing the difference to the stiff competition facing American farmers in costs and efficiency.[14] In short, perhaps the oligopoly capitalism of America's large industries is the model for administering a complex socialist state.

A hundred years after Marx a pattern seems to emerge. The centrally planned socialist economy has not turned out to be the stage which follows a fully industrialized capitalist market system, upon collapse of the latter. Instead it seems to be the technique by which the underdeveloped economy can move rapidly, through conscious controls and sacrifice, to the level of full industrialization. Thereafter the controls and planning may be relaxed, because they no longer function well in the affluent, peaceful society.

If so, this conclusion is tremendously important. In the latter part of this century a large fraction of the world's population may undertake social leaps. If it should turn out that the centralized planning deemed essential to the leap will eventually give way to decentralization and enterprise autonomy, the whole process must be reviewed in a new light. First, for pure efficiency it may be that the leap can be made by centralizing far fewer things than would seem reasonable if the action were seen as a one-way transition to a permanently centralized economy. Such lesser centralization could tap the greater motivations that typically accompany the decentralized, profit-oriented organization. Barring nuclear war, the Russians may well look back a century hence at the first 50 years of their revolution with consternation at the incredible waste and misery expended in centralizing, for the sake of dogma, huge sectors of their economy which they later, for reasons of efficiency, decentralized. Agriculture would seem a notable case. Another is clothing manufacture. The

---

[12] Volin, *op. cit.*, p. 21.

[13] Gregory Grossman, "Industrial Prices in the USSR," *American Economic Review* (May, 1959), p. 61.

[14] *The Cincinnati Enquirer*, July 1, 1962.

Russians are already showing signs of style consciousness. Considering the traditional fragmentation of production and decision making in capitalist clothing industries, it will be fascinating to observe what happens when the Russian planners run head-on into the problem of mass style consciousness.

If the centrally planned leap is expected to be followed by important decentralization, much of the heat might disappear from the ideological conflict—except to the (possibly large) extent that dictators may maintain the conflict for their own internal political survival. That is, the ∗ advocates of central planning may be essentially right for the quick transitions, while the opponents are correct for the long pull. Under this kind of rationale, it might be possible to make more sensible decisions on these questions than at present. Many persons oppose measures "on principle" which they accept as desirable in fact, the principle being that the measure is a move in the wrong direction. We thus find the Soviets refusing eminently sensible amendments to their system on the ground that they reflect "capitalist deviation" or "bourgeois decadence," while Americans do the same on the ground of "creeping socialism." In both cases the label is presumed to make the measure obviously bad. The result is a weakening of the ability of each nation to reach that particular point on the centralization-decentralization scale which is most appropriate to its size, stage of development, and the stability and legitimacy of its government. As indicated in earlier chapters, however, in case of doubt it seems safer to err on the side of decentralization.

These things do not mean that centralized planning is inescapable for the social leap, though a substantial amount seems indicated. Nor, as observed in a previous chapter, does it necessarily imply dictatorship. An unplanned transition may be aggravatingly slow. But planning has its own aggravations. As Campbell observes:

> The Soviet system moves forward on the technological front with a very inelegant and lurching gait. The examples we have considered certainly convey a strong impression of imbalance, lags followed by crash programs, and long delays in getting even simple improvements into operation.[15]

The market system's defense against lags, incidentally, is that bottleneck items will be highly profitable to fill, and attract productive resources.

The Problem of Free Goods

In 1961 the Communist Party in Russia announced its plans and prospects for the coming years. Among other things, it held forth the promise of free public transportation and free housing, along with the continuation of free medicine. The possibility of free goods raises some interesting problems.

In the first place, aside from the air we breathe, sunshine, and a limited list of other things, there are no such things as costless goods, and the

---

[15] *Op. cit.*, p. 185.

word "free" in this connection means "distributed without specific charge." The thought of free goods is enticing. But it is subject to the observation that "free" housing in Russia, like "free" television in the United States, severely limits the consumer's freedom of choice. The amount of limitation varies from one good to another. We will examine several in order to see the nature of the problem, under the assumption that the "free" goods do have production costs. Where relevant, we will assume that the "free" goods are provided by the government.

Something like medical care probably shows the least deprivation of consumer choice, and the least waste, of any goods that might be distributed free. (The present discussion is confined to only one part of the economics of free goods, and does not encompass such things as the doctor-patient relation, or the optimum method of financing or administering medical care.) Those who need medical care avail themselves of it, while the healthy do not. As a result, no cost is incurred in producing this service for those who do not want it. (We will also by-pass the possible distinction between the "desire" for medical service and the "need" for it, and speak here only of the need.) Further, the cost of medical care on the average is a relatively small part of the budget, running to about 4 per cent of income in the United States.

Free education also behaves somewhat like free medical care. Anyone who wants it can receive it. But anyone who does not want it does not take it, and saves the state the cost of producing it for him.[16]

Free local transportation may also be relatively feasible. In a non-subsistence society few people are deterred from using local transportation by its money cost, and after an initial splurge of free riding few people (possibly excepting children) will travel on trolleys, buses, and subways just because they are free. Hence, free local transportation seems unlikely to create much waste of resources for unwanted services.[17] Neither medical care nor transportation can be hoarded by consumers for possible later sale or converted to other use—two important points with reference to services in contrast to material goods, as will be seen below.

Free rent in government-owned housing, however, raises important questions of consumer choice. First, housing is expensive, and amounts to about a tenth of the average family's budget in the United States, not

---

[16] Whether education should be compulsory is a different matter. If so, persons are required to accept it whether they want it or not, and the state often pays for education for persons who do not want it, and who profit little from it. Whether it should be compulsory is a separable question from whether it is wasteful if free and voluntary—the present question.

[17] It is not without significance that some American cities think it cheaper to subsidize public transportation than to build huge expressways to the downtown areas, and it is conceivable that some cities would be better off to provide free public transportation. The computation of such relative costs is complicated by the fact that state and national governments subsidize highway construction in cities, but not mass transportation, and we have seen some of the complications of decision making about municipal transportation in Chapter 31.

counting costs of operation. However, some people prefer to spend much more than the average amount on housing, so as to have more space or more elegant housing, while cutting down on other expenditures. Others prefer to live less graciously, and to devote more money to travel, books, furnishing, gifts, or hobbies. If housing is "free," however, consumers lose this choice. Since they pay nothing, they cannot have more of other goods by accepting less housing than the standard quota. Nor can they get more or better housing in return for less of other things. They are in the same position as the American television viewer who cannot get better programs by paying more, and who can save nothing by taking poorer ones, or by not watching. This arrangement is also wasteful, since it produces more housing than some people would want if given their own choice.

It is possible, of course, to offer housing of varying quality. Families choosing lower grades could be allowed greater amounts of other goods, and the reverse. Whatever it may be called, this is not "free" housing, however, for the better grades require the consumer to sacrifice more in other goods, which is the same as a higher price. To operate such a system for the propaganda value of the "free" label can only make clumsy what could otherwise be a relatively simple method of allocating housing.

As to readily transferable material goods, the case against giving them away free is almost overwhelming. Almost any good has multiple uses, and will be wasted unless a price is charged. If anything would qualify for free distribution, it would seem to be something like pencils and paper. Everyone wants these things. They are relatively cheap to produce, and the wants for them seem limited. Suppose we deal with the ordinary five-cent variety of wood pencil. If they are free for the asking, some persons will shortly use them for marking seed rows in the garden, and others will use them for kindling. Children can use them by the hundreds for toys, and so on. Similar things will happen if paper is free. I have found, for instance, that bundles of old newspapers make excellent landfill when covered with only about an inch of soil. Grass will grow on top almost immediately, and in a few years shrubs will grow in this fill, even before the paper is fully disintegrated. Eventually one has an almost completely organic fill of topsoil, with absolutely no stones. Reams of paper would be even better, since they stack more neatly, and require less cover dirt. The Soviets have already had experiences of this sort. Some years ago they sold breadstuffs in retail stores at subsidized prices. They shortly discovered that town dwellers were buying large quantities for cattle, with the result that expensive human food was taking the place of inexpensive cattle feed. After rejecting several alternative proposals, the Soviets finally made it illegal to keep cattle in the towns.[18]

It is obviously possible to set quotas on "free" goods. But this requires a whole series of controls, such as registration, ration books, and special

---

[18] Volin, *op. cit.*, p. 18.

provision for persons who legitimately want more than the quota. In short, "free" implies controls, at least so far as material goods are concerned. It is much simpler to charge a price representing the cost of production, and then to allow everyone to buy as much as he likes, and use it as he likes. With consumer goods as with producer goods, a price system is the most sophisticated technique of priorities and rationing yet devised or apparently possible.

Chapter 40

THE INFORMATION NEEDS
OF A COMPLEX SOCIETY

PARABLE OF THE INFORMATION MACHINE

I need to know every color that passes beneath my window. So I have set up this machine, which will detect all the colors and make a record of them for me. But green makes me very angry, so I will smash the machine if it reports green. And tomorrow I may not like red, in which case I will smash it if it reports red. But inaccurate information also makes me angry, so I will smash the machine if it reports wrongly, or if it fails to report.

A DICTATOR is in a peculiar situation with respect to information. He needs it, in large quantities, promptly, and accurately. It must come from his subordinates. But much of the information he needs for himself may weaken his controls over his subordinates if they too know it. Absence of the information may weaken his control even more. In a relatively simple society, or during a crisis when allegiance can easily be held, the situation can be muddled through. In a complex society for the long pull the problem must be squarely met. The thesis of this chapter is that a complex society will necessarily allow much freedom in its internal flows of information if it wants to keep up with nations which have such freedom. These conclusions do not necessarily apply to information about foreign relations, where the same logic does not seem to prevail. And the dictator may, of course, curtail flows of information in order to secure his control, even at the cost of reduced efficiency. That he makes a compromise does not, however, eliminate the basic conflict between information freedoms and efficiency of operation. It is pointless to speak of the Hitler and Mussolini dictatorships in this connection, since they were crisis affairs, not geared for long run problems.

We have seen in Chapter 25 that flows of information through an organization affect both its performance (production) and its internal bargains. In the present context, production information is that information needed for the decision making of the government officials. This definition is independent of whether the government is a dictatorship or a democracy. The gist of the present point is that when a totalitarian dictatorship exists for a limited-crisis period, it may be possible to keep production and bargaining information flows substantially isolated, and hold the dictatorship in tight control. But when the dictatorship continues for decades, these two sets of information spill over into and affect each other.

For adaptive behavior, the dictatorship needs information for the first step—identifying the stimulus. It also needs feedback information at the fourth step to evaluate its actions. In the long run, the general nature of the information is the same at both stages, which can be joined for the present discussion.

Whatever outsiders may believe, information about the operation of a complex dictatorship does not come to the central office by carrier pigeon, or by whispers between canapes at state dinners. It can be gathered only by a staff of thousands, whose top members possess sound statistical training, and are guided by statistical, not ideological, criteria. (The dictator cannot smash the machine for giving him information he does not like, and also for giving him distorted information.) Since the government must make decisions with them, its statistics must give an accurate picture of such varied things as (1) the rise or fall of output by product, industry, and region, (2) the changes in price levels and amount of money in circulation, (3) the numbers of persons in each industry and occupation, and some idea of their quality, (4) the number of persons who have received a given level and type of education, (5) the per capita production and consumption of various kinds of food, (6) the ton miles of freight carried each year by water, rail, and air, (7) the ratio of managers rewarded or punished, (8) the crime rate, (9) the incidence of various diseases, (10) the number of men of military age fit for armed service—and a host of others.

There are, of course, many ways in which statistics can be made to give a rosy or dismal view. But there are several factors which militate against operating the whole of a statistical service as a propaganda mill, which factors are basically the reasons why honesty is a more powerful instrument than misrepresentation in long continuing relationships. First is the matter of internal statistical consistency. Statistics on various things are interrelated in scores of ways, and falsification of one item will produce inconsistencies at other points. Second is the matter of policy consistency. If the data are falsified to make one propaganda point, this same falsification may prove embarrassing for some other propaganda effect.

More importantly, when the government settles down from the crude transition stage to the task of running a stable and productive permanent system, it requires many thousands of informed persons to make the sets and subsets of decisions that keep the system going. It requires not only a bureaucracy of thousands in Moscow, but more thousands in the central offices of the regions, and the industry offices into which the regional offices are divided, and so on. The questions are endless. How much more can you managers produce next year than last? To answer, the managers must know what was done last year, and what new resources are available. Why didn't you fill last year's quota? The answer reveals that the supplying industry failed to meet *its* quota. If the enterprise manager says he can increase his output 10 per cent if the planners will give him 10 per cent more steel, and the planners then ask the manager if he can't substitute some other material for steel, the manager and his staff know that the much-publicized increase in steel output is only a fiction. This particular kind of check for consistency of information reveals the conditions under which the manager can operate best— namely, if he has available at his fingertips accurate information about various parts of the economy, so that he can promptly and easily confirm or reject hypotheses about how to solve his own production problems. Even if the final decision in these things is reserved for the top, the man on the site is the only one who can competently and efficiently explore various alternatives. No matter how centralized the apparent final decision, the preliminary explorations of the problem and the narrowing of the range of alternatives must be done at the lower levels. In a large industrial nation this can be done efficiently only if thousands of persons have ready access to accurate and reasonably detailed information.

In this connection it is notable that in the post-Stalin era, Russian statisticians and economists have been vocal in their criticism of some of the earlier statistical methods. Their grounds are not ideological, but simply that distorted statistics produce bad decisions. The bargain being driven between managers and the government in recent years is of the sort: if you want us to make sound decisions, you must give us sound information.

Untold numbers of contacts between enterprises and industries are inescapable in the normal course of production, and each contact conveys information. The central office may boast of the great efficiency of transportation. But if the factory must wait an average of two weeks for a shipment from 500 miles away, the manager and all the men in the plant know better. Factory managers must talk to transportation managers to coordinate their activities (both for supplying the railroads with equipment and for using them for transportation), and each learns the real problems and situations of the other. When operating men get together they talk operating problems, not party propaganda, or they cannot function.

Managing an economy also requires training. Workers must learn to become foremen, foremen to become superintendents, and so on through the regional and national planners. To do these things well requires not only personal experience, but wide exposure to the experiences of others. In the United States thousands of trade and professional bulletins and magazines have tremendous educative value in building leadership, managerial, and technical abilities. They report new products and processes so that managers and foremen can contemplate their possible usefulness.

They contain countless stories of "My Problem and How I Solved It." A manager describes how he reorganized his plant layout and raised output from 10,000 to 15,000 units with a lower cost per unit. A foundry superintendent describes how he removes flashing from castings faster by tumbling instead of grinding. The manager of a super-giant soda fountain reports how he cut five seconds from the average time required to prepare a banana split, and was able to eliminate two fountain clerks—etc., etc., etc. The same people get together in conventions and tell each other many other incidents.

We have little information at this distance as to how much of this kind of thing goes on in Russia. But it seems inescapable that if they are to develop competent managers, similar exchanges of information must already exist or will develop there. If and when they do, larger and larger numbers of people will have access to discussions which directly or indirectly reveal the real state of affairs, and in tremendous detail. Dictatorship or not, if the Russians want a competent bureaucracy they must accept the necessity of widely circulated, accurate information.

SCIENCE AND EDUCATION

Since the Revolution, the Soviets have distinguished between "bourgeois" science and "Marxian" science. The latter follows the lines of dialectical materialism, which insists (to oversimplify somewhat) that only matter is real, and that all other phenomena can be explained in terms of the existence and behavior of matter. Although the Communist doctrine made little difference to such natural sciences as geology and chemistry, it has had an impact on biology, psychology, some aspects of theoretical physics, and, of course, the social sciences.

As to the natural sciences, the Soviets and the Communist Party have gone through a cyclical relation with the scientists. Starting most conspicuously with the "great break" of about 1929–32, the Party has tried to bring the scientists into line with the party doctrine. The result has been the rise of some scientists who apparently accept the Marxist approach, and who ardently defend it in meetings and writings of the scientific societies and their members. But there has continued uninterruptedly a substantial number of the "old specialists." Regarding the intellectual autonomy of the latter:

> In principle they had lost it altogether; to use a favorite expression of the day, they had "disarmed themselves" . . . before the Party's Central Committee. In practice they still enjoyed an almost unimpaired autonomy in their subject matter, and an immeasurable autonomy in ideology—immeasurable because of the mask of silence and possible hypocrisy that covered it.[1]

On the surface, however, the Party functionaries vacillated between requiring the scientists verbally to toe the Party line and insisting that the Party must allow scientists and trainees to be selected solely on the

[1] David Joravsky, "Soviet Scientists and the Great Break," *Daedalus* (Summer, 1960), p. 576.

basis of competence in the field.[2] Some controversies within the fields of quantum physics and relativity have undergone shifting fortunes through the years, and suggest that the Party can be subverted by the scientists as well as the reverse.[3]

Perhaps the outstanding controversy has been that over biological inheritance. The biologist Lysenko has followed Michurin in insisting that acquired traits can be inherited, in direct contradiction of the position of many Soviet biologists and most elsewhere in the world. With the backing of several supporting experiments and the distorted reporting of others, along with the congeniality of his thesis to the Marxist doctrine about the permanent moldability of human behavior, Lysenko had his position adopted as official doctrine in Russia. Following a meeting of the Lenin Academy of Agricultural Sciences in 1948 the opposing school was branded as "reactionary" and "idealistic" and was silenced. Flaws have been found in the Lysenko position, however, the literal following of which inhibits certain work in the field of biochemistry. The Soviets have also been impressed by American developments in breeding new strain of corn by Mendelian, not Lysenkian, procedures. After Stalin's death the opposition to Lysenko became so strong that in 1956 he resigned as president of the Academy.[4] Although the Party seems determined to keep the scientists under its control, the Party is itself by no means monolithic, and both sides of the controversy "possess powerful patrons within the Party."[5]

When or whether natural scientists will be able to pursue their paths without having to report their findings in Marxian verbiage (which is the only kind of conformity that has been seriously enforced in many areas of science) cannot be known at this point. In such fields as medicine, geology, metallurgy, and other pure and applied sciences there is now much interchange of information between Soviet and noncommunist scientists, through meetings and mutual translations of publications. In many parts of natural science the information needs of the society have largely routed or disregarded the ideological ones, at least among the scientists themselves.

Even in the holy-of-holies of Marxist doctrine—economics—the dogma of the ideology is giving way to the needs of accurate analysis. Although they still speak in circumspect language, Soviet economists have denied the innermost sanctum of Marxist doctrine, the labor theory of value. It is only necessary to read a modest group of articles published by Soviet

[2] *Ibid.*, p. 578.

[3] Gustav Wetter, S.J., "Ideology and Science in the Soviet Union: Recent Developments," *Daedalus* (Summer, 1960), pp. 583–90, 601–2.

[4] *Ibid.*, p. 592. As an illustration of the zig-zag course of progress along these lines, Lysenko reportedly again occupied some post as of the time this book went to print, in mid-1963. It seems highly unlikely, however, that his version of heredity will again be pushed, in either biological circles or agricultural experimentation.

[5] *Ibid.*, p. 602.

economists in Russian journals of economics to observe that these economists accept much of capitalist economic analysis, however much the
articles are interlarded with footnote references to Marx, Engels, Lenin,
and Stalin. As to practice, in contrast to writings, we have already seen
that Khrushchev himself now accepts the use of the payoff period in
allocating capital, which is a forthright acknowledgment in all but name
that capital contributes to value, and that its costs must be considered.
When and whether they will similarly compute the opportunity costs of
land, thereby acknowledging in action the gross inadequacy of the Marxian theory of value, cannot be predicted. It can only be noted that if
they want efficient use of their resources they will do so, and they *are*
interested in efficiency.

New discoveries and conclusions in the field of science must move
from the pure through the applied state before they can be translated
into actual use. This can happen effectively only if the managers know
what the scientists are discovering, and the scientists know the problems
of managers. This fact further spreads the scope which must be covered
by accurate information if the system is to function well—on a purely
technical-managerial basis.

A series of related problems arises in connection with education. Because they lasted only about a decade, the meteoric dictatorships of Hitler and Mussolini did not face the full-scale problem of training a whole
new generation of scientists from the ground up, though they did have
to train some to meet various scientific, developmental, and technological
objectives. Dictatorships of earlier centuries also did not face the problem
since, however ruthless, they were not totalitarian in the modern sense,
and science was not sufficiently developed to make much difference to
national welfare. If nothing else, a competent scientist must be thoroughly disciplined in the scientific method. This means not only technical
training in scientific procedures and apparatus, but also a rugged resistance to allowing judgments to be influenced by considerations other than
those which are logically relevant.

Now the capacity of the brain to form logic-tight compartments
sometimes seems incredibly high. Nevertheless the scientific intelligentsia
are not likely to be impressed by the propaganda line of the ruling
regime, which normally has enough internal contradictions to merit the
scorn of intelligent, perceptive persons. Such persons also develop a
backlog of valid criticisms of the ideology and operations of the regime.
We will postpone that aspect of the problem for a moment, however, to
pursue another.

Perhaps even more than the managers, the scientists will have to keep
in constant touch with each other, to report their experiments, their
methods, their conclusions, and their doubts about previous conclusions.
This requires pamphlets, journals, letters, conferences, lectures, and
books. It also requires libraries to house them. The logistics of the devel-

opment of scientific knowledge requires that scientists have much freedom to communicate among themselves, and to report their findings without fear of punishment. With respect to the natural sciences, the Russian scientists have argued for, and are being accorded, increasing amounts of this freedom—excepting classified information of military value, which is also restricted (though with narrower definitions) in the democratic nations. The Russian rulers have no real choice but to grant such freedom or lose out in the international race which now seems to hinge so largely on the physical sciences. The information needs of the scientific community have more power than the desires of a dictatorship to make science conform to their will. In bargaining power terms, the dictatorship needs the scientists more than they need it, and the scientists are increasingly getting their way.

In both Russia and [Nazi] Germany the *instrumental uses of theoretical science* were recognized by the political leadership, and a relatively high degree of autonomy was and is considered functional for the pursuits of totalitarian goals.[6]

The same general situation prevails through teaching. To train a competent physical scientist requires an early solid foundation on which to build. It is not feasible to teach an ideologically approved science to a person for sixteen years, and then suddenly to take him aside in a graduate seminar and teach him the facts of scientific life. Even if it were, some of the graduate students would steal into the undergraduate quarters to give a sneak preview of the real lowdown, and also teach it to their own children. If they are to teach effectively, scientists must teach science as *they* find it.

This problem is often dealt with under the heading of "academic freedom." It is described in terms of the "right" or "freedom" of the teacher to express what he believes. Without in any way deprecating that approach, the relation can also be examined in terms of information flows, and the society's need for such flows. Let us turn first to the rulers themselves. Suppose they want to know whether Polaris missiles launched from American submarines could hit the Kremlin. Even though the scientist's answer may be only an informed guess, it *is* the best information available, and it is imperative to the government that the answer be as accurate and unbiased as the scientist can make it. In giving his answer, the scientist must try to judge whether he will be better off to give his best scientific opinion, even if it contradicts government pronouncements, or to give an answer that supports the government's propaganda. Since men do not rise to the top of dictatorial governments through tactical stupidity, the government officials understand the scientist's position.

The government faces the situation with which the chapter opened. It

---

[6] Walter Hirsch, "The Autonomy of Science in Totalitarian Societies," *Social Forces* (October, 1961), p. 20.

cannot smash the information machine *both* for giving incorrect answers *and* for giving displeasing answers. Though the reverse may be true for some short-run situations, in the long run the government will find it of more value to get accurate answers than patriotic ones. Further, if the scientist spends enough time studying current politics to be sure what the currently patriotic answer is, he will not know enough about his specialty to *know* the correct answer. The information needs of the dictatorship are in this respect identical with those of the democracy. If the authorities want honest answers they must judge and reward the information processors by the competence of their information, not by its pleasing quality. Academic freedom is not only the valued possession of a free society, but also the technique for "protecting" a crucial source of society's information.

Somewhat the same thing can be said of the student-teacher relation. The learning task is long and difficult, and the student needs much guidance. When the student asks questions he must be sure the reply represents the most accurate information the instructor can provide, not what the instructor believes to be patriotic or pleasing to the university administrators or benefactors. Unless the society wishes to complicate greatly the difficult task of learning, it must hold its teachers to standards of competence only, not political conformity. This is not a matter of personal protection of the teacher, as such (though it behaves like one in fact), but a guarantee that students can gain access to the teacher's knowledge.

Freedom of research follows the logic of innovation in addition to the logic of protecting information sources. Where new ideas will come from, and which ideas will eventually turn out to be valuable, cannot be predicted in advance. The specialists in any field are in a far better position than anyone else to know what is known, and what constitutes potentially useful research. For example, if a question arises about the possibility of converting petroleum into synthetic paper, only chemists can judge whether this seems a useful project for research. The authorities, however, can refuse to finance the project, which means that freedom to conduct research involving costs is more circumscribed than freedom to teach and publish. The same is true in democratic societies.

WILL INFORMATION FREEDOMS DESTROY DICTATORSHIP?

A modern society cannot remain operable and make progress without an intelligentsia, be the society democratic or dictatorial. An intelligentsia cannot operate without a rather high level of freedom. If so, will the intelligentsia turn its critical faculties and freedom on a dictatorship and attempt to destroy it? This is the question raised earlier in the chapter, to which we now return.

The discussion thus far has been confined largely to natural sciences, not to social or psychological science, or the humanities. There does not seem to be any compelling reason why the most complete discussion and publication of the findings of natural scientists should challenge the control of a government, so long as the government has enough sense not to tie key ideologies to untenable science—such as Lysenkoism. The regime can utilize the scientific findings of the intellectuals, who in turn can live well and in a sense of freedom provided by the regime. Nor is there any particular reason why the scientists should try to overthrow the regime. It is not uncommon for scientists even in democracies to look with disdain on the rituals, patriotic rites, and manipulations of the mass media which constitute the pragmatic techniques of holding power. Whether in democracy or dictatorship, in enterprises, governments, or other organizations, those who participate in important decisions affecting the public recognize the general prevalence of two stages of decision: first the reasons why the executive committee or the caucus decided as it did, and second the rationalizations they state for public consumption. What the public relations division of a corporation, the press secretary for the White House, or the propaganda ministry of the dictatorship tells the public may or may not coincide with the real reasons for actions, depending on the desired effect.

For such reasons the scientist often feels that the process of actually running a nation is a complex and messy business, and that there is little he can do about it. He finds science fascinating, rewarding, and socially useful, and probably feels that in the long run the scientists will do more good for humanity than the politicians. The relationship in one sense is self-stabilizing. If the political regime is insecure it will not allow much freedom among scientists, and if it is secure the intellectuals' possible attacks on government will not have a chance of succeeding. In any event, the freedom to teach and publish in one's field of specialty does not in itself include freedom to attack the government, at least in those areas of science which have neither direct nor indirect implications for government policy. This is a matter of political freedom, not academic freedom.

Academic and political freedom are closely joined, however, in the social sciences and the humanities. A government legitimizes itself to its people through a variety of myths and rationalizations, along with some *pseudo* or *bona fide* scientific explanations of the cause and effect relations of its actions. An honest historian, political scientist, novelist, sociologist, or economist can do nasty things to the regime if he points out publicly that the government's alleged facts are lies, or its alleged reasons nonsense. The teacher can have a destabilizing effect on the regime if he teaches such things to his classes. The dictatorship therefore scrutinizes the study and teaching done along these lines by individual teachers, and tries to make sure that all who occupy these posts are politically safe. We have nevertheless seen the unorthodox thoughts which Soviet economists clothe in orthodox language. These are mainly for communication among specialists, and the sense of their ideas does not get through to the average citizen in the schools or the press. Presumably the controls are greatest in the fields of political science and political history.

To a lesser but significant degree, the situation in the social sciences also applies to psychology. But the psychologists, too, have conformed partly in fact but more largely in their verbalizations.

The principles of materialism and determinism may have lost their initial importance in Leninism-Marxism. Today they retain mainly their symbolic value as signs of Marxist orthodoxy. By and large, they serve mainly as a test of the ingenuity of scholars in reconciling their work to the principles of philosophical materialism.[7]

Over the long pull the dictatorship also needs information on social and psychological problems. The physical scale of Soviet industry is less efficient than it might be, because the Soviets have apparently never made a single scientific study of the relationship between plant size and efficiency. Here is an area in which it is possible to have economists make studies that will produce useful information for the regime, without in any important way challenging its control. Particularly since the death of Stalin, the government has not only accepted but actively stimulated public criticism of organizational arrangements. For while the Soviets claim to have the key to the perfect society, they acknowledge (at least to themselves) that they still have some things to learn, since the blueprints inherited from Marx are remarkably lacking in detail. Hence, this criticism is handled in the same spirit as scientific inquiry in the natural sciences—it is a search for information which will enable them to make the society operate better. Managers are criticized, performance under the plan is criticized, as are shortages, bumblings, and delays. Complaints about the poor quality and scant quantity of consumer goods appear frequently in the press. The planners are also criticized, and occasionally even the party structure.

It is true (and important) that all such criticism is "authorized." Nothing gets into the press which is not approved by the Party hierarchy. Even though a particular criticism may make no affirmative suggestions, it is "positive" in the sense that it is oriented toward diagnosing a problem with a view toward improving it. It is nevertheless also true (and important) that allowable criticism seems to show a steady widening in scope and influence. The large reorganization of the structure of industry in 1956 was preceded by several years of widespread criticism of the previous structure, along with a variety of exploratory suggestions for remedying it. There were also numerous arguments publicly set forth in favor of greater autonomy for enterprise managers. This part of the change was not accepted in the actual reorganization,

---

[7] Raymond A. Bauer, *The New Man in Soviet Psychology* (Cambridge. Harvard University Press, 1952), p. 185.

and the suggestions for greater autonomy have reportedly subsided for the present.

There is no way of telling how far this extension of criticism will move, and up to now it seems directed mainly at techniques of managing the system and improving production and distribution. It does seem predictable, however, that an increasing variety of human problems will come under systematic scrutiny as the regime gets the problems of broad social contours under control. Just as in market economies, it may be expected that managers will want to know what kinds of motivation systems work best in the factory. How does one select and evaluate employees? What is the effect of primary group attachment on the cohesiveness and productivity of employees? What are the psychological factors determining the span of control of executives; what are the merits of "junior managements" as decision and as training techniques? What are the effects of emotional stresses in the home on a worker's productivity; do men work better under a supervisor who is interested mainly in production or in the worker as a man? Officials responsible for crime prevention will want to know what causes crime and how to reduce it. Managers and officials of cities will want to know the consequences of mixing persons of different cultural and racial background in the same factory or apartment house. The top planners will want to know what motivates managers and lower planners. The number of questions that need answers in order to improve the operation of a complex society is almost endless. As more consumer goods are produced and the variety of production rises, planning controls expressed in physical units will become more and more cumbersome, and the planners will want to know the extent to which price or profit controls and evaluations can be used instead.

Whatever the Russians may call them, all these questions are essentially problems in social science and psychology. They too may come to be investigated, written up in the trade and professional journals, become generally available throughout the nation, and be taught in the universities. It seems safe to predict that the amount of freedom to explore and report on matters of this sort will vary directly with the degree of acceptance of the government.

Certainly an independent political science, along with an independent history of politics, is the last social science a dictatorship can countenance. It would seem, in fact, that freedom to study and publish in this area could not be allowed until and unless the dictatorship is prepared to run the risk of losing its control in some kind of transition to democracy. A great difficulty in this area is that a little freedom may lead to a demand for much more than the government is prepared to allow. The demand may frighten the government into clamping down once more, and make it even more reticent than before to grant any significant freedom of basic political discussion.

Russia may evolve into a "managerial society," and may already have moved far in that direction. By this is meant a nation in which all the important decisions are made by the professional managers, for the simple reason that they are the only persons with sufficient know-how to make the decisions. As a group they would have much freedom to acquire and exchange information among themselves. They would have to work very closely with the scientists and technical people, but the managers would be boss, because it is they who make the decisions which coordinate the work of the scientists and technicians with their own. The general rank and file citizen would have little access to the information used by the managers, both because its circulation might be restricted and because the "commoners" do not know how to use it or care to bother with it. In the United States the rank and file worker is free to read any of the technical, professional, or management journals, which might give him tremendous insight as to how the nation is run. But he does not read these things, and remains largely ignorant, because he lacks the interest or the ability.

The point of the chapter is that to operate a complex society requires a large amount of information, widely dispersed, particularly among the professional and managerial levels. Without such freedom of information, the society's actions can neither progress nor be satisfactorily coordinated. This dispersion of information will severely limit the absolute power of the totalitarian dictator. For he will be dependent on the cooperation of a large number of people who know too much to be seriously misled, and who are too valuable to be jailed, shot, or even seriously offended. It seems unlikely that the days will return to Russia when science can be changed at the convenience of the rulers, or managers can be shipped to the salt mines for underproducing. It also seems probable that positive incentives for workers will predominate, and the general harshness of the first decades of the Soviet government are permanently gone. Like the technological changes, movements in this direction will probably be at a lurching gait, however, and reports in early 1962 indicate the return of punishments for negligent handling of farm equipment.[8]

The dictatorship seems to be widely accepted within Russia (the satellites being a different problem), and the rulers are not actively concerned about internal uprising. In short, the government has recognized or is recognizing the indispensability of information. Meanwhile, the major bargain of the government's control has been accepted, and the government is legitimate in the minds of most Russians.

The above logic applies only to the internal communications of the nation, however. Although the Russians need tremendous amounts of information to coordinate their own efforts with each other, nothing indicates that they need information about international politics to accom-

---

[8] *Cincinnati Post and Times-Star,* January 3, 1962.

plish internal efficiency. The government therefore faces no necessity of relaxing its controls of information about the outside world, international relations, and the nation's foreign policy. It therefore remains in the position to report, and if necessary create, an international crisis that would justify tightening the controls on internal information. The knowledge that it can reverse the trend at any time may be vital to its willingness to loosen the flows of internal information, and to rely increasingly on positive motivations.

Meanwhile, the advantages in international negotiations of dictatorship at home seem so great that the government will hardly subject itself to the possibility of losing this advantage by having to face an election at some strategic point in negotiations. While it is conceivable that a dictatorship might negotiate itself into a democracy if it faced only internal problems, foreign problems seem to provide both the ability and the desire to keep the controls. Information needs might therefore lead us to expect increasing internal freedom within Russia, at least among the intellectual and managerial classes.

Although people in the sciences and arts travel widely to foreign meetings and receive translations of foreign technical journals, these people already occupy a favored status in Russia, in both income and freedom of expression. So they probably feel less dissatisfaction with their position relative to citizens of other nations than do their less fortunate fellows. When they return home, they may communicate among their own group, but any impressions they receive that are unfavorable to Russia will not be made available to the Russian masses. As to those who do communicate, in the spring of 1963 a highly vocal group of insurgent poets, playwrights, and dramatists publicly "acknowledged the error" of their previous objections to the stifling effect of the regime on the human spirit. How far the general progress toward greater freedom of communication will be set back by this new restriction cannot now be discerned.

When or whether the Soviet regime will feel secure enough to allow its people to travel freely abroad, to allow foreign literature into the nation without prior selection or censorship, or to remove government controls over the mass media of communication cannot now be predicted. But the evidence that such developments will take place within the foreseeable future is thin indeed. At least one writer suspects that more vigorous dissent has already developed inside Russia than the regime is prepared to tolerate, and that a return to the rigid dictatorial controls of Stalinism might not be far off.[9] In any event, with respect to the kinds of information that will permit Soviet citizens to evaluate their system as a whole in comparison with those of other nations, the Soviet government apparently intends to operate like the "information

---

[9] Philip Ben, "Pressure on Khrushchev," *The New Republic* (March 9, 1963), pp. 7 f.

group" described in Chapter 33. That is, it will maintain the government's control through information, rather than through violence and terror. For the moment it seems that a level of internal information high enough for reasonably efficient functioning can be achieved without opening up the system for information which might undermine the government's control. There also seems to be not the slightest hint that the government will allow an independent opposition political party, without which a meaningful degree of democracy seems impossible in the complex modern state. In short, the Party will probably find large amounts of information indispensable to running the country as it sees fit; but the Party and its goals—not the people—will remain the arbiter of what information is to be released.

EPILOGUE

WE WILL close with a reminder that this book is an experiment. It is a rather wide ranging experiment to explore whether a meaningful analysis of society can be carried out with far fewer concepts than before. It consists for the most part of the definitions and explanations of a set of interrelated concepts, partly new, partly old, along with a restatement in this partly new language of a broad selection of existing knowledge about human beings and their relationships.

In the spirit of the "scientific" philosophy and the seeming implications of much recent study in psychology and linguistics, the question is not whether the present approach gives a more accurate picture of the social *reality*—of how things really *are*. For reasons outlined in Chapter 3, the question is rather whether this set of concepts has a higher information potential than do others. I believe it has. We may note transactions, especially, which are at the core of the social analysis in this volume. Not only does the present approach to the transaction seem to provide increased understanding of particular relationships. But in addition such diverse and relatively elusive things as bargaining power, freedom, property, social pressures, and slavery, along with authority, responsibility, legitimacy, leadership, and other aspects of organization, can all be precisely defined and meaningfully diagnosed as phases of transactions. This latter fact seems to suggest that the present formulation is an unusually powerful tool of social analysis.

The maximum eventual unity of knowledge will depend on finding a set of analytical concepts for interpersonal relationships which is consistent with those used in psychology, communications, and decision making. Although the social analysis proposed herein does not stand or fall on the materials which precede it, the social analysis has been couched in concepts which are consistent with those used for the preceding materials. Human behavior is seen as the output of a controlled, not an uncontrolled system—a proposition which seems hardly disputable. The effector stage is not explicity discussed, since it lies mainly in the realm of biology, chemistry, and physics, not in the social arena. Our main concern is therefore with the detector and selector stages. These are seen as identical, respectively, with the concept and motive aspects of psychology (perception being attached to the concepts), with the opportunity and preference functions in decision making, with the information and motivation aspects of communications, and with the broader notions of scientific and value judgments generally. When the idea of transformations is added as a means of enlarging opportunities, this same dichotomy is also directly related to the effective and the preference aspects, respectively, of Effective Preference. Effective Preference, in turn, is at the heart of the analysis of transactions, and hence of interpersonal relationships.

The present volume is thus a broad and somewhat hazardous experiment to test whether this particular set of concepts will perform the unifying function so ardently desired by those who fret at having to learn so many different terms and concepts—partly parallel, partly overlapping, and partly contradictory—in order to understand the social behavior of human beings. It simultaneously is a partial test whether such broad-gauged concepts are feasible at all. To note specifically the hazards, this volume implicitly asserts that *all* interpersonal relationships can be expressed and diagnosed as aspects of communications, transactions, organizations, and of that particular total set of self-stabilizing interactions referred to herein as the system of culture. I am sure some readers will protest this proposition, and the list of basic concepts may have to be enlarged—though at the moment I hope and believe that the present set is defensible.

Had I wished to spend another several years before going to print I could have sharpened the interrelations of the parts and improved the style in spots. I might also have dealt more specifically with several other areas, such as the goals of society, systems of states, education, macroeconomics, and social deviation. The basic system itself, however, seems sufficiently gelled, and (I hope) sufficiently clear to the reader that it would appear to be more efficient to open the volume to critical comment at this stage than to spend additional time on refining and polishing concepts which may subsequently have to be scrapped or basically modified.

In his attempts to evaluate the book and its weaknesses, I hope the reader will keep in mind both its experimental nature and the magnitude of its task. At the least, however, it should give him some feel for the language of models, systems analysis, and communications, which language seems to be the probable vehicle in which much of our new information about the behavioral sciences will be expressed for the next decade or so.

INDEXES

INDEX OF NAMES

INDEX OF SUBJECTS

Motives (*Cont.*)
  as cybernetic governor, 260
  and income, 587
  for innovation, 756–60
  in leadership, 498
  in organizational decisions, 475–76
  positive versus negative, 745, 782
  prices as, 201, 583
  primary, Chapter 6
    and secondary as system and subsystem, 101–2
  and profit criterion, 747–49
  and sales volume, 759
  secondary, Chapter 5
    attached to concepts, 133
    about motives, 134
    of Soviet managers, 743–47, 765
  and "urges," 24, 78
Motor concepts, 114–15
Mundugumor, 222, 242
Music
  "all possible combinations," 199
  as communication, 196–98
  syntax in, 198

N

Narcotics
  in England, 445
  as illegal positive goods, 442
Nation, defined, 542
Need(s); *see also* Motives
  "hierarchy of," 100–101
  and income distribution, 733
  versus motive, 93
  reduction, 93
Negative power; *see* Bargaining power in negative goods
Negro
  as caste, 627–28
  vote in Liberia, 624
  voting restrictions, 624–25
Nerves, 16, 21, 60
Neurons, 60
New York Times, 650
Newspapers
  bias in, 645–52
  freedom of press, 643–44
Noise (in communications), 19, 180
Nonviolent resistance, 548
Norms; *see* Consensus, social; Culture, content of
Norris-La Guardia Act, 632
Nuclear family, 244

O

Observations, in science, 31
Obsolescence, 291
  deliberate, 604

Occupation, control of by government, 627
Open-end transactions, 353–54, 534
Operant conditioning, 68
Operational goals, 459
Operations research, 312
Opportunity(ies), 55, 318
  alternative, and bargaining power, 334, 339
  and concepts, 104
  costs, 567
  defined, 263
  defined, 267
  set, 267
Oral
  need, 144
  stage, 148, 239
Order, social, 629
  as power regulation, 619
Organization, Chapters, 21–28
  as amplifier of power, 393
  authority, responsibility and legitimacy in, 465–67
  bargaining power in, 418–29
  communications in, 180, 469, 473, 481–85
  as conflict, 418
  control in residual contribution, 424–25
  as cooperation, 415–18
  decisions in, 468, 473, 481–85
  defined, 269, 413
  diminishing productivity in, 422
  employer and employee views in simple, 417
  evaluation of, Chapter 23
    cooperative, 457–58
    pressure, 459–60
    profit, 452–57
    service, 458–59
  exchange by, 421
  friendship in, 428–29
  goals
    growth as, 517, 518
    of sponsors, 463–64
    of staff, 464–65
  government
    control by, 545
    as formal organization of whole society, 541–44, 618
  joint production aspects, 468–72
  life of its own, 518
  major bargain in, 417
  management
    evaluation of, Chapter 23, 747–49, 757–58, 765
    as hierarchy of bargains, 508–11
  market system as, 583–85
  model of
    complex, Chapter 24–25
    simple, 416

This book has been set on the Linotype in 10 point Janson, leaded 2 points, and 9 point Janson, leaded 1 point. Part titles are in 48 point Civilite; section numbers and titles are in 24 point Egmont Medium; chapter numbers are in 24 point Civilite; chapter titles are in 18 point Egmont Medium. The size of the type page is 27 by 47 picas.